INDEPENDENT AGENCIES IN THE UNITED STATES

Independent Agencies in the United States

LAW, STRUCTURE, AND POLITICS

Marshall J. Breger

Gary J. Edles

OXFORD
UNIVERSITY PRESS

OXFORD
UNIVERSITY PRESS

Oxford University Press is a department of the University of Oxford. It furthers the University's objective of excellence in research, scholarship, and education by publishing worldwide.

Oxford New York
Auckland Cape Town Dar es Salaam Hong Kong Karachi Kuala Lumpur Madrid
Melbourne Mexico City Nairobi New Delhi Shanghai Taipei Toronto

With offices in
Argentina Austria Brazil Chile Czech Republic France Greece Guatemala Hungary
Italy Japan Poland Portugal Singapore South Korea Switzerland Thailand
Turkey Ukraine Vietnam

Published in the United States of America by
Oxford University Press
198 Madison Avenue, New York, NY 10016

Library of Congress Cataloging-in-Publication Data

Breger, Marshall J.
Independent agencies in the United States : law, structure, and politics / Marshall J. Breger, Gary J. Edles.
pages cm
Includes bibliographical references and index.
ISBN 978-0-19-981212-7 ((hardback) : alk. paper)
1. Independent regulatory commissions—United States. 2. Independent regulatory commissions—United States—Rules and practice. 3. Administrative law—United States. I. Edles, Gary J. II. Title.
KF5407.B725 2015
352.2'640973—dc23

2013019924

Note to Readers

This publication is designed to provide accurate and authoritative information in regard to the subject matter covered. It is based upon sources believed to be accurate and reliable and is intended to be current as of the time it was written. It is sold with the understanding that the publisher is not engaged in rendering legal, accounting, or other professional services. If legal advice or other expert assistance is required, the services of a competent professional person should be sought. Also, to confirm that the information has not been affected or changed by recent developments, traditional legal research techniques should be used, including checking primary sources where appropriate.

(Based on the Declaration of Principles jointly adopted by a Committee of the American Bar Association and a Committee of Publishers and Associations.)

To Jennifer Stern Breger
"ne le sue salute abitava la mia beatitudine"
—La Vita Nuova 11:20–22
Marshall Breger
To Nadine Cohen Edles
My partner in Life
and Ernestine Furman
Gary Edles

Contents

Preface

IN 1991, WHEN we served, respectively, as chairman and general counsel of the Administrative Conference of the United States, we undertook a very preliminary survey of the structure and workings of independent agencies. We did so for two reasons. First, to that point, there had been very little comparative information on this topic. Second, we discovered that very few agency officials were aware of how their colleagues at other agencies addressed comparable problems. We then undertook a more extensive, although still introductory, survey into this area that resulted in publication of *Established by Practice: The Theory and Operation of Independent Federal Agencies*, 52 Admin. L. Rev. 1111 (2000). That article recognized that independent agencies were not all alike but differed with respect to a range of structural and operational elements of their independence from the political branches of the government. We also noted the importance of the practical underpinnings for the design and operation of independent agencies. This book builds on those earlier efforts, and we are grateful to the Section of Administrative Law and Regulatory Practice, of the American Bar Association, which publishes the *Administrative Law Review* in conjunction with American University Washington College of Law, for allowing us to use that 2000 article as the starting point for our work here.

We are grateful to numerous students at our respective law schools for excellent research assistance: Joseph Frydman (CUA 2009) for his work on the appendix, Kazi Shama Ahmed (Hull 2013) for her work on the bibliography, and Kimberly Payne (WCL 2012) for her work on Appendix A; Erin DeRiso (CUA 2015), Sarah Leavitt

(CUA 2014), Roger Abbott (CUA 2013), Jamie Bence Rose (CUA 2013), Thomas Bryan (2013), Siobhan Donohue (CUA 2013), John Passmore (CUA 2013), Jessica Gruenberg (CUA 2012), Christina Manfredi McKinley (2009), Joanna Persio (CUA 2010), Sandi Safro (CUA 2008), Linda Bailey (CUA 2007), and Ed Meyers (CUA 2005) for research assistance generally. We hope they found the experience useful. We certainly profited from their work. We most especially want to thank Ed Meyers for his work at the inception and Erin De Riso and John Passmore for their assistance in the "final days."

We thank as well Dean Claudio Grossman of American University, Washington College of Law, and Dean Veryl Miles of the Columbus School of Law, The Catholic University of America (CUA) for their financial support of our research efforts.

We also appreciate the willingness of Professors Patrick Birkinshaw, Chris Bovis, John E. Higgins, Jeff Lubbers, and Heidi Schooner as well as Dr. Mike Varney, Bob Solomon, Solicitor at the FERC, Steve Klitzman at the FCC, and Michael J. Ravnitzky at the Postal Regulatory Commission to read and comment upon portions of the manuscript. We thank Daniel Arbuckle, Emily Bremer, and Chai Feldblum for assistance on particular points. To the extent we failed to follow their good counsel, we take full responsibility.

We note that the manuscript for the book was far along before we became aware of the extraordinary study by David E. Lewis and Jennifer L. Selin, *Sourcebook of the United States Executive Agencies* (ACUS December 2012) (1st ed.), but we have profited greatly from reading it. We also note the value of another ACUS report, Curtis W. Copeland, *Economic Analysis and Independent Regulatory Agencies* (ACUS draft, April 30, 2013), which we came across in the latter stages of our writing, and the insightful work-in-progress of Peter Conti-Brown, which has appeared in various iterations, most recently *The Structure of Federal Reserve Independence*, Rock Center for Corporate Governance (Stanford University), Working Paper Series No. 139 (January 7, 2014), all of which we found most helpful.

Finally, we discovered Anne Joseph O'Connell's essay, *Bureaucracy at the Boundary,* 162 U. Pa. L. Rev. 841 (2014), as we were proofreading the final version of the manuscript. All these works reveal the swiftly moving and evolving scholarship on government structure in general, and the role of independence in particular.

We have special thanks to Julie Kendrick, who was "keeper" of the manuscript and typed the various drafts with good humor and great efficiency. And we thank, as well, Margaret Pooley for additional typing assistance.

1

Introduction

THE INDEPENDENT AGENCIES of the United States government occupy a special, although perhaps ambiguous, constitutional place in the federal establishment. The multimember boards and commissions that are the prototype independent agencies bring together individuals of diverse views, expertise, and backgrounds to tackle legally difficult, technically complex, and often politically sensitive issues.[1] Many multimember agencies have the full range of regulatory authority, that is, they can issue rules, take administrative action to enforce their statutes and regulations, and decide cases through administrative adjudication. Some oversee a specific area of the economy. For example, the Federal Energy Regulatory Commission (FERC) regulates interstate aspects of the electric power, natural gas, oil pipeline, and hydroelectric industries;[2] and the Securities and Exchange Commission (SEC) administers the federal securities law and regulates firms engaged in the purchase or sale of securities, investment companies, and people

---

[1] Earlier book-length studies of the independent agency phenomena include: JAMES E. ANDERSON, THE EMERGENCE OF THE MODERN REGULATORY STATE (1962); MARVER H. BERNSTEIN, REGULATING BUSINESS BY INDEPENDENT COMMISSION (1955); MARVER H. BERNSTEIN, THE GOVERNMENT AS REGULATOR (1972); ROBERT E. CUSHMAN, THE INDEPENDENT REGULATORY COMMISSIONS (1941); WILSON K. DOYLE, INDEPENDENT COMMISSIONS IN THE FEDERAL GOVERNMENT (1939); JAMES O. FREEDMAN, CRISIS AND LEGITIMACY: THE ADMINISTRATIVE PROCESS AND AMERICAN GOVERNMENT 15–96, 125–99 (1978); OMAR V. GARRISON, THE DICTOCRATS: OUR UNELECTED RULERS (1970); LEON I. SALOMON, THE INDEPENDENT FEDERAL REGULATORY AGENCIES (1959); DAVID M. WELBORN, GOVERNANCE OF FEDERAL REGULATORY AGENCIES (1977); PETER WOLL, AMERICAN BUREAUCRACY (1977).

[2] *See* 42 U.S.C. § 7172 (2006). *See also* Energy Policy Act of 2005, Pub. L. No. 109-58, 119 Stat. 594 (codified as amended in scattered sections of 42 U.S.C.).

who provide investment advice.[3] Others have substantive, subject-matter responsibilities that cut across industry lines. For example, the Federal Trade Commission (FTC) enforces a variety of federal antitrust and consumer protection statutes.[4]

In traditional theory, their stock-in-trade is the expert, apolitical resolution of regulatory issues. They are "independent" of the political will exemplified by the executive branch. Because most are also multimember organizations, they tend toward accommodation of diverse or extreme views through the compromise inherent in the process of collegial decision-making.[5]

The Supreme Court conceived of the independent, multimember commission (at least in the 1930s) as follows:

> The commission is to be non-partisan; and it must, from the very nature of its duties, act with entire impartiality. It is charged with the enforcement of no policy except the policy of the law. Its duties are neither political nor executive, but predominantly quasi-judicial and quasi-legislative.... [I]ts members are called upon to exercise the trained judgment of a body of experts appointed by law and informed by experience....
>
> [It is] a body of experts who shall gain experience by length of service—a body which shall be independent of executive authority, except in its selection, and free to exercise its judgment without the leave or hindrance of any other official or any department of the government.[6]

During this same era, the Brownlow Committee viewed independent agencies less charitably, describing them as a "headless 'fourth branch' of the government, a haphazard deposit of irresponsible agencies and uncoordinated powers."[7] Over the years numerous

---

3 15 U.S.C. § 78d (2006).

4 *See, e.g.*, 15 U.S.C. §§ 12, 18a, 45a, 46, 53 (2006).

5 Collegiality has been much discussed on the appellate bench (and sometimes studied). For discussion see Harry T. Edwards, *The Effects of Collegiality on Judicial Decision Making*, 151 U. Pa. L. Rev. 1639, 1648–83 (2003); Harry T. Edwards & Michael A. Livermore, *Pitfalls of Empirical Studies That Attempt to Understand the Factors Affecting Appellate Decision Making*, 58 Duke. L.J. 1895, 1917–64 (2009). For analysis, see Kevin M. Quinn, *The Academic Study of Decision Making on Multimember Courts*, 100 Cal. L. Rev. 1493, 1494–97 (2012); Frank B. Cross & Emerson H. Tiller, *Understanding Collegiality on the Court*, 10 U. Pa. J. Const. L. 257, 257–71 (2008).

6 Humphrey's Ex'r v. United States, 295 U.S. 602, 624, 625–26 (1935) (internal quotation marks and citation omitted) (emphasis omitted).

7 The President's Committee on Administrative Management, Report of the Committee with Studies of Administrative Management in the Federal Government (1937), *reprinted in* Subcomm. on Separation of Powers of the Senate Comm. on the Judiciary, Separation of Powers and the Independent Agencies: Cases and Selected Readings, S. Doc. No. 91-49, at 346 (1969).

articles have surveyed the indicia of independence and the place of independent agencies within a separation-of-powers framework.[8] The Administrative Conference of the United States, the government's expert advisory body on administrative law, published a preliminary comparative survey of the structure and workings of independent agencies in monograph form in 1991. The Conference received numerous requests for copies because it contained comparative information that was immediately useful to agency officials, academic lawyers, and administrative practitioners.[9]

We found it surprising that individuals familiar with a single agency (even those employed at the agency) were relatively unfamiliar with similar issues at other agencies. After Congress abolished the Conference in 1995, later to be revived in 2008,[10] we received telephone inquiries about these subjects from agency members, staff, and private practice lawyers. So, in 2000, we published a new survey of thirty-two independent

[8] *See, e.g., Symposium, The Independence of Independent Agencies*, 1988 DUKE L.J. 215 (1988); *Symposium on Administrative Law: The Uneasy Constitutional Status of the Administrative Agencies*, 36 AM. U. L. REV. 277 (1987); Thomas O. Sargentich, *The Contemporary Debate About Legislative-Executive Separation of Powers*, 72 CORNELL L. REV. 430 (1987); Geoffrey P. Miller, *Independent Agencies*, 1986 SUP. CT. REV. 41 (1986); Peter L. Strauss, *The Place of Agencies in Government: Separation of Powers and the Fourth Branch*, 84 COLUM. L. REV. 573 (1984).

We note as well the growth of quasi-legislative independent, investigative commissions established by Congress and signed by the president, as opposed to commissions appointed wholly by the president. Examples include the National Commission on Terrorist Attacks upon the United States, Intelligence Authorization Act for Fiscal Year 2003, Pub. L. No. 107-306, 116 Stat. 2383 (2002) Title VI, 6 U.S.C. § 101 note (establishing the commission "in the Legislative Branch" *Id.* § 601); Commission on Wartime Contracting in Iraq and Afghanistan, § 841, National Defense Authorization Act for Fiscal Year 2008, Pub. L. No. 110-181, 122 Stat. 3 (establishing a commission with two members appointed by the Senate majority leader, two members appointed by the Speaker of the House, one member appointed by the Senate minority leader, one member appointed by the House minority leader, and two members appointed by the President. *Id.* 841 (b)(1). There is no reference to the branch in which the commission is established); and the Financial Crisis Inquiry Commission (FCIC), Fraud Enforcement and Recovery Act of 2009, Pub. L. No. 111-21, 123 Stat. 1617, § 5 (establishing the FCIC "in the legislative branch" *Id.* § 5(a)). *See* Steven R. Ross, Raphael A. Prober & Gabriel K. Gilbert, *The Rise and Permanence of Quasi-Legislative Independent Commissions*, 27 J.L. & POL. 415 (2012).

[9] For an analysis of the original Administrative Conference of the United States, *see* Marshall J. Breger, *The Administrative Conference of the United States: A Quarter Century Perspective*, 53 U. PITT. L. REV. 813 (1992). *See* Treasury, Postal Service, and General Government Appropriations Act of 1996, Pub. L. No. 104-52, 109 Stat. 480 (1995) (Congress appropriates $600,000 provided that these funds shall only be available for the purposes of the prompt and orderly termination of the Administrative Conference of the United States by February 1, 1996). The Administrative Conference of the United States actually shut down on October 31, 1995. Colman McCarthy, *Mourning an Agency Mugged by Congress*, WASH. POST 1995 WLNR 5931474 (Nov. 7, 1995). Despite the defunding, the Conference's organic statute remained in place. 5 U.S.C. §§ 591–596.

[10] *See* Regulatory Improvement Act of 2007, Pub. L. No. 110-290, 122 Stat. 2914 (2008) (authorizing the Administrative Conference of the United States) and Consolidated Appropriations Act, 2010, Pub. L. No. 111-117, 123 Stat. 3183 (2009) (providing initial appropriation). *See generally* Gary J. Edles, *The Revival of the Administrative Conference of the United States*, 12 TEX. TECH ADMIN. L.J. 281 (2011).

agencies, including two that sit squarely in the executive branch.[11] This book builds on the work contained in that article.

The book reviews the history of independent agencies, their structure and internal operations, notes several similarities and differences among them, and addresses various recurring issues affecting them. We further consider the future of this regulatory form in the twenty-first century. We focus on agencies—whether multimember or not—where at least one individual is appointed by the president to a full-time, fixed-term position with the advice and consent of the Senate and has protection, by statute or custom, against summary removal.

Our definition of "independent" is somewhat arbitrary, but the lack of both doctrinal cohesion and comprehensive information makes the task of definition difficult.[12] For purposes of analysis, we go beyond the traditional independent multimember agencies to take note of some other forms of governmental organization, both domestic and foreign, that embody elements of independence.[13]

We should note that our prime criterion, which is also the courts', for classifying an agency as independent is the extent to which the president is circumscribed in his

---

[11] A summary can be found in the appendix included in Marshall J. Breger & Gary J. Edles, *Established by Practice: The Theory and Operation of Independent Federal Agencies*, 52 ADMIN. L. REV. 1111, 1236–94 (2000).

Some agencies have been deliberately omitted. For example, some boards have members appointed by the president and confirmed by the Senate but the statute provides some mechanism for removal other than presidential removal for cause. *See, e.g.*, 22 U.S.C. § 1622 (2006) (providing that members of Foreign Claims Settlement Commission appointed by president and subject to Senate confirmation do not have a statutory term and may be removed by secretary of state). Others have members appointed by the president but not confirmed by the Senate. *See, e.g.*, 42 U.S.C. § 1975 (2006) (Members of the United States Commission on Civil Rights are appointed by the president, the president pro tempore of the Senate, and the Speaker of the House of Representatives). Numerous boards and other components within agencies are staffed by career civil servants and empowered to undertake certain agency functions affecting the public. The Departmental Grant Appeals Board of the Department of Health and Human Services, for instance, is composed of members appointed by the secretary. *See* 45 C.F.R. § 16.5(a) (1999). The board was originally created by regulation but later given added authority by Congress. *See* Pennsylvania v. U.S. Dep't of Health and Human Services, 80 F.3d 796, 800 (3d Cir. 1996). Although members of employee boards frequently have decisional independence as a matter of agency practice, *see* John H. Frye, III, *Survey of Non-ALJ Hearing Programs in the Federal Government*, 44 ADMIN. L. REV. 261, 343–44 (1992), we do not classify them as "independent" because their members ordinarily can be removed without cause by the appointing official. *See* Kalaris v. Donovan, 697 F.2d 376, 401 (D.C. Cir. 1983). Moreover, we do not include advisory boards that are components of agencies, such as the Social Security Advisory Board, *see* 42 U.S.C. § 903 (2006).

We do not list in appendix A other specialized government institutions, such as government corporations, government sponsored enterprises, or legislative branch agencies, some or all of whose members may be appointed by the president with the advice and consent of the Senate and removable only for cause, although they are discussed in chapter 8. *See e.g.*, 39 U.S.C. § 202 (2006) (describing Postal Service Board of Governors); Mail Order Ass'n of America v. U.S. Postal Serv., 986 F.2d 509, 512–13 (D.C. Cir. 1993) (stating that nine members of Postal Service Board of Governors are appointed by the president with the advice and consent of Senate, and can be removed only for cause).

[12] Certainly the Supreme Court has not provided a definitive definition. We should note, however, the list found in the Paperwork Reduction Act (as amended) 44 U.S.C. § 3502(5).

[13] *See infra* chapters 8 and 10.

removal power. As Kirti Datla and Richard Revesz suggest, other characteristics of independence might include: "removal protection, multimember structure, partisan balance requirements, budget and congressional communication authority, litigation authority, and adjudication authority."[14] Historical understandings may be relevant as well. And recent theorists have developed new perspectives on agency independence, looking at ways in which an agency's reputation among its various "audiences" can boost its legitimacy, which in turn can support its autonomy or independence.[15] The concept of audience draws upon Daniel Carpenter, who suggests that:

> Government agencies live among numerous audiences, and these audiences overlap and blend into one another. Audiences include the political and judicial authorities who endow organizations with power; interest groups and civic associations; organizations of professional and scientific expertise; media syndicates in print and broadcast, and the mass publics who digest the information produced by these syndicates; the companies, corporations, and citizens who are governed by agencies; the clienteles who rely upon agencies for benefits and for order. In political systems like the U.S.—with formal separation of powers among legislative, executive, and judicial branches; with federalist structures that multiply and refract government capacity; and with pluralist political structures that often scatter the forces of business, labor, religion, race and ethnicity—these audiences stand ever more diffuse.[16]

---

14 *See* Kirti Datla & Richard L. Revesz, *Deconstructing Independent Agencies (And Executive Agencies)*, 99 Cornell L. Rev. 769, 772 (2013).

15 The concept of multiple audiences was first developed by the sociological literature by Erving Goffman, The Presentation of Self in Everyday Life 208–37 (1959). The concept of reputation as a source of bureaucratic autonomy is explored in Daniel Carpenter, The Forging of Bureaucratic Autonomy, Reputation, Networks and Policy Innovation in Executive Agencies, 1862–1928 33–35 (2001).

16 Daniel Carpenter, Reputation and Power: Organizational Image and Pharmaceutical Regulation at the FDA 34 (2010). Peter Conti-Brown applies a variant of this perspective to the Federal Reserve Board that he calls the "audience-mechanism framework," noting that

> The audience-mechanism framework defines Fed independence as the separation of the Fed's policy process from other *audiences* by means of *mechanisms*, both legal and environmental. Note the two elements of the definition. First, the Fed is independent, to the extent it is independent, from numerous "audiences," not just from the President. These additional audiences include the President, the Treasury, Congress, private banks, the Reserve Banks, central bankers throughout the world, non-bank market participants, Fed career economists, Fed regulators, other federal agencies, the general public, the courts, and more. The article focuses on three audiences—private banks (through the Reserve Banks), the President (and, somewhat separately, the Treasury), and the Congress—but consideration of the additional audiences named is also essential for a fully developed account of Fed independence.

Thus independence is a function of the relation of the board with different audiences. The issue is "independence from whom, and independence secured how." Peter Conti-Brown, *The Institutions of Federal Reserve Independence* at 3 (Rock Ctr. for Corporate Governance, Working Paper Series No. 139) (June 7, 2013 revision).

We should note that economists and political scientists often use what they call a functional approach, which suggests that "any agency outside the [Executive Office of the President] or Cabinet is an independent agency."[17] As Jacob Gersen notes:

> In the economics and political science literature, however, the idea of independence has a more functional meaning, referring to the degree of actual or effective control exerted over the agency by other political institutions or the agency's location inside or outside the cabinet hierarchy. Unlike the dichotomous legal idea of agency independence, the functional public choice notion is more or less continuous and is marked by a range of institutional features. More functional independence is thought to result when an agency is created outside the existing bureaucratic structure rather than within an existing cabinet department, as was the norm in the early years of the bureaucracy; location within the bureaucratic structure seems to matter.[18]

We do not use this approach, but it is incorporated to some extent in our spectrum analysis taken up below.

Thus, we should make one point explicit. When Congress chooses to use the phrase "independent agency in the executive branch," or other some such, when it creates an agency or commission, that phrase certainly suggests congressional desire that the agency be independent of the president, but it has no legal effect. Such entities are formally as much under the control of the president as any cabinet or executive branch agency (excepting the so-called independent regulatory agencies described throughout this book).[19] Nonetheless, that functional designation may reflect a political or bureaucratic reality. At its inception the administrator of the Environmental Protection Agency (EPA), for political reasons, had significant autonomy.[20] For much of the twentieth century, the FDA was considered "inviolate" against political interference.[21] And as Daniel Carpenter has shown, early in the twentieth century Gifford Pinchot was able to secure the transfer of the management of forest reserves from the Department of the Interior to the Department of Agriculture, notwithstanding the strong opposition of Joe Cannon,

---

17 David E. Lewis & Jennifer L. Selin, The Federal Executive Establishment in the United States 43 (Administrative Conference of the United States, Dec. 2012).

18 Jacob Gersen, *Designing Agencies, in* Daniel Farber and Annie O'Connell Eds., Research Handbook on Public Choice and Public Law 347 (2010) (citations omitted).

19 *See* chapter 3 *infra*.

20 *See* statements of Nixon and the first administrator at *infra* note 35.

21 For the early twentieth century, see Daniel Carpenter, The Forging of Bureaucratic Autonomy 257–75 (2010); for the mid- and late twentieth century, see Daniel Carpenter, Reputation and Power: Organizational Image Pharmaceutical Regulation at the FDA 390–92 and passim (2010).

then Speaker of the House, and most establishment interests.[22] This "bureaucratic autonomy" is reflected in notions of traditions or conventions of independence.[23]

In the appendix we list the fundamental characteristics of over thirty agencies that we believe warrant the title "independent." Most of them are of the traditional, multimember variety, although at least two—the National Indian Gaming Commission and the Board of Veterans' Appeals—consist of a mix of a presidential and various nonpresidential appointees and seem squarely situated within the executive branch departments of government. Others have only a single individual at their heads. Importantly, in our view, not all of these agencies are equally independent.

The concept of a spectrum or continuum is central to our approach.[24] Agencies, we believe, range on a spectrum, with some having a higher degree of independence from political control and oversight than others by virtue of their statutory authority, structure, or culture.[25] Federal Reserve Board members, for example, have the longest statutory term

---

22 *See* the discussion in Daniel Carpenter, THE FORGING OF BUREAUCRATIC AUTONOMY: REGULATION, NETWORKS AND POLICY INNOVATION IN EXECUTIVE AGENCIES, 1862–1928, 1, 275–89 (2001). The classic sociological study of the Forest Service is Herbert Kaufman, THE FOREST RANGER: A STUDY IN ADMINISTRATIVE BEHAVIOR (1962) (a sketch of the service's history and activities of the Forest Service is found at pages 36–47).

23 The term comes from Adrian Vermeule's excellent article of that name, *Conventions of Agency Independence*, 113 COLUM. L. REV. 1163 (2013). A similar term, "institutional autonomy," has been articulated by Douglas North. *See Institutions*, 5 JL. OF ECONOMIC PERSPECTIVES (1991). We view these terms as indistinguishable. We thank Peter Conti-Brown for the latter reference.

24 We use the terms "spectrum" and "continuum" interchangeably. The spectrum/continuum analysis is used by others as well. See, for example, Datla and Revesz, *supra* note 14, at 772–773, 825–827 (arguing that the spectrum/continuum approach should replace the historic dichotomy between independent and executive branch agencies).

25 While not the argument advanced here, some argue the continuum concept can be applied to all entities performing government functions. *See* B. Dan Wood & Richard W. Waterman, *The Dynamics of Political Control of the Bureaucracy*, 85 AMERICAN POLITICAL SCIENCE REVIEW 801, 823 (1991) ("agency responsiveness and stability can roughly be arrayed along a continuum which aligns nicely with certain bureaucratic attributes."); Gersen, *Designing Agencies, supra* note 18 at 347 ("Independence is a legal term of art in public law, referring to agencies headed by officials that the President may not remove without cause. Such agencies are, by definition, independent agencies; all others are not. In the economics and political science literature, however, the idea of independence has a more functional meaning, referring to the degree of actual or effective control exerted over the agency by other political institutions or the agency's location inside or outside the cabinet hierarchy. Unlike the dichotomous legal idea of agency independence, the functional public choice notion is more or less continuous and is marked by a range of institutional features."); Kimberly N. Brown, *Government by Contract and the Structural Constitution*, 87 NOTRE DAME L. REV. 491, 521 (2011) ("If plotted on a constitutional continuum, both private contractors and independent agencies reside somewhere between cabinet-level agencies that function as 'alter egos' of the president and purely private citizens with no ties to government whatsoever."); Datla & Revesz, *supra* note 14, at 769 ("We…reject the binary distinction between independent and executive agencies. Instead all agencies should be regarded as executive and seen as falling on a spectrum from more independent to less independent."). Datla and Revesz also recognize that practical and political factors may influence the degree of independence an agency may have in particular areas. But they argue that, in the final analysis, "[t]he degree of independence from presidential control an agency enjoys should be determined only by looking at the agency's enabling statute." *Id.* at 843.

of individuals at any regulatory agency and are protected against removal by an explicit statutory provision. Moreover, the board possesses what Peter Conti-Brown has described as an independent funding mechanism "without equal in the federal government."[26] Less formally, the board is surrounded by a culture of independence that includes, among other things, a long tradition of bipartisan appointment of its chairs. Equal Employment Opportunity Commission (EEOC) members, in contrast, do not have explicit statutory protection against removal. In the 1970s, the Office of Legal Counsel (OLC) squarely concluded that the commission is an executive, rather than independent, agency.[27] The OLC noted the lack of statutory removal protection and the lack of quasi-judicial or quasi-legislative authority. Although certain bases for the OLC opinion have been undermined somewhat by subsequent events (e.g., the EEOC at the time had entirely executive functions and no quasi-legislative or quasi-judicial functions but now has adjudication and rulemaking authority), the EEOC itself appears to have accepted, at least in some respects, its categorization as an executive agency. For example, it complies with all Office of Management and Budget (OMB) directives applicable to the executive branch, including those relating to Office of Information and Regulatory Affairs (OIRA) review of commission rules. As accurately described by Saikrishna Bangalore Prakash:

> Where a particular independent agency rests on the continuum will change over time given White House aggressiveness, agency assertiveness, congressional vigilance, and the composition of the commission. It also seems fair to say that executive departments and agencies can likewise be placed on a spectrum, with some under more watchful presidential control and others at greater liberty to act at variance with presidential policies.[28]

Of course, Congress calling an agency independent does not, in a functional sense, make it so.[29] Congress has styled and defined certain agencies in a variety of ways; although as Paul Verkuil underscores, there is very little "attempt in the legislative history to explain

---

26 Peter Conti-Brown, *The Institutions of Federal Reserve Independence* at 23 (Rock Center for Corporate Governance, Working Paper Series No. 139, Jan. 2, 2014 revision).

27 *President's Authority to Promulgate a Reorganization Plan Involving the Equal Employment Opportunity Commission*, 1 Op. O.L.C. 248 (1977).

28 Saikrishna Bangalore Prakash, *Imperial and Imperiled: The Curious State of the Executive*, 50 WM. & MARY L. REV. 1021, 1056 (2008).

29 Just as calling an agency private as Congress did with PCAOB does not necessarily make it so. *See* 15 U.S.C. § 7211(a) ("[PCAOB] shall be a body corporate, operate as a nonprofit corporation"); 15 U.S.C. § 7211(b) ("The Board shall not be an agency or establishment of the United States Government, and, except as otherwise provided in this Act, shall be subject to, and have all the powers conferred upon a nonprofit corporation by, the District of Columbia Nonprofit Corporation Act."); Free Enter. Fund v. Pub. Co. Accounting Oversight Bd., 130 S. Ct. 3138, 3148 (2010) ("Despite the provisions specifying that [PCAOB] members are not Government officials for statutory purposes, the parties agree that the board is "part of the Government" for constitutional purposes"). *See also* Lebron v. National R.R. Passenger Corp., 513 U.S. 374, 392–93 (1995) ("it is not for Congress to make the final determination of Amtrak's status as a Government entity").

why Congress ... preferred one organizational format over the other."[30] For example, the National Archives and Records Administration is defined as an "independent establishment in the executive branch,"[31] while the Coordinating Council on Juvenile Justice and Delinquency Prevention is an "independent organization in the executive branch."[32] Meanwhile, entities such as the Election Assistance Commission have been deemed "independent entities"[33] while the Cost Accounting Standards Board is defined as an "independent board."[34]

Consider, as an example, the EPA. At its creation in 1970, President Richard Nixon referred to it as a "strong independent agency."[35] While it can at the times be described

---

30 Paul Verkuil, *The Purposes and Limits of Independent Agencies*, 1988 DUKE L.J. 257, 258 (1988).

31 44 U.S.C. § 2102 (2006). We do not discuss congressional agencies that are considered an area of the legislative branch like the United States Commission on Civil Rights. This commission is considered a legislative agency because the president, the House of Representatives, and the Senate all appoint their own commissioners. Of the eight commissioners, "[four] members of the Commission shall be appointed by the President; [two] members of the Commission shall be appointed by the President pro tempore of the Senate, upon the recommendations of the majority leader and the minority leader, and of the members appointed not more than one shall be appointed from the same political party," and "[two] members of the Commission shall be appointed by the Speaker of the House of Representatives upon the recommendations of the majority leader and the minority leader, and of the members appointed not more than one shall be appointed from the same political party." Civil Rights Commission Amendments Act of 1994, Pub. L. No. 103-419, 108 Stat. 4338 (1994) (codified as amended by 42 U.S.C. § 1975 (2006)). *See* Kenneth L. Marcus, *The Right Frontier for Civil Rights Reform*, 19 GEO. MASON U. C.R. L.J. 77 (2008).

Other "independent establishments in the Executive Branch" include: the National Transportation Safety Board, 49 U.S.C. § 1111 (2006); Defense Nuclear Facilities Board, 42 U.S.C. § 2286 (2006); Office of the Nuclear Waste Negotiator, 42 U.S.C. § 10242 (2006); Armed Forces Retirement Home, 24 U.S.C. § 411 (2006); United States Holocaust Memorial Museum, 36 U.S.C. § 2301 (2006); National Center for Productivity and Quality of Working Life, 15 U.S.C. § 2411 (2006); Office of Personnel Management, 5 U.S.C. § 1101 (2006); and several memorial scholarship and fellowship foundations. *See* 20 U.S.C. §§ 2004, 4502, 4703, 5702 (2006). We note that Congress has defined the term "independent establishment" as used in Title V of the U.S. Code as: "(1) an establishment in the executive branch (other than the United States Postal Service or the Postal Regulatory Commission) which is not an Executive department, military department, Government corporation, or part thereof, or part of an independent establishment; and (2) the Government Accountability Office." 5 U.S.C. § 104. To place the "independent establishment" in context, Congress asserts that for the purposes of Title V the term "Executive agency" includes "an executive department, a Government corporation, and an independent establishment." 5 U.S.C. § 105.

32 42 U.S.C. § 5616 (2006). The functions of the Civil Rights Commission are discussed in Hannah v. Larche, 363 U.S. 420, 440 (1960).

33 42 U.S.C. § 15321 (2006). Other "independent entities of the executive branch" include: the Morris K. Udall Scholarship and Excellence in National Environmental Policy Foundation, 20 U.S.C. § 5603 (2006); Office of Navajo and Hopi Indian Relocation, 25 U.S.C. § 640 (2006); Office of Research Integrity, 42 U.S.C. § 289b (2006).

34 Congress established the Cost Accounting Standards Board as an "independent board" within the Office of Federal Procurement Policy. 41 U.S.C. § 422 (2006).

35 In a Special Message From the President to the Congress About Reorganization Plans to Establish the Environmental Protection Agency and the National Oceanic and Atmospheric Administration, Reorganization Plan No. 3 of 1970 (July 9, 1970). Nixon states: "Because environmental protection cuts across so many jurisdictions, and because arresting environmental deterioration is of great importance to the quality of life in our country and the world, I believe that in this case a strong, independent agency is

as independent or quasi-independent, the president has plenary power to remove its head.[36] Disputes between the EPA and the White House are legion—in both Republican and Democratic administrations. Usually the White House has prevailed. For example, Christine Whitman is thought to have resigned after being pressed by Vice President Cheney to ease pollution controls by allowing older coal-fired power plants to make renovations without installing modern pollution controls under the New Source Review process.[37] And, only recently, the Obama administration ordered the EPA to withdraw its proposed regulation on ozone level standards.[38]

---

needed." He continues: "In proposing that the Environmental Protection Agency be set up as a separate new agency, I am making an exception to one of my own principles: that, as a matter of effective and orderly administration, additional new independent agencies normally should not be created. In this case, however, the arguments against placing environmental protection activities under the jurisdiction of one or another of the existing department and agencies are compelling." *Id.* The first EPA administrator agreed, asserting the agency was an "independent agency." Press Release, William D. Ruckelshaus, Administrator, Envtl. Protection Agency, First Administrator on Establishment of EPA (Dec. 16, 1970) *available at* www2.epa.gov/aboutepa/first-administrator-establishment-epa.

36 *See* Jack Lewis, *The Birth of the EPA*, 11 EPA J. 6 (1985) (noting rationales for EPA independence: "first, the primary mission of each existing department would bias any decisions it made on a government wide basis…; second, the same factors might raise questions about the objectivity of any existing department as a standard setting body for other agencies and departments." *Id.* at 8).

37 Her resignation letter stated that she wanted to spend more time with her family. Letter of Christine Whitman to President George W. Bush, May 20, 2003, http://yosemite.epa.gov/opa/admpress.nsf/e013d28c3c3eb28b85257359003d480b/d4ff1eb843da7ea085256d2d005ef686!OpenDocument. *See also* Katherine Q. Seele, *Often Isolated, Whitman Quits as EPA Chief*, N.Y. Times, May 22, 2003. Whitman later confessed that she felt unable to sign the White House proposal. *See* Christine Whitman, It's My Party Too 185 (2007). For a review of the entire controversy, *see* George A. Krause & Brent M. Dupay, *Coordinated Action and the Limits of Presidential Control over the Bureaucracy: Lessons from the Bush Presidency*, *in* President George W. Bush's Influence over Bureaucracy and Policy 81, 87–94 (Colin Provert & Paul Teske eds., 2009). *See also* Barton Gellman, Angler: The Cheney Vice Presidency 204–08 (2008).

Such conflicts are not a new phenomenon. After a heated argument with the White House over review of one of the EPA's first enforcement actions, Administrator William Ruckelshaus pledged to resign "if environmental decisions are overruled because of political considerations." John Quarles, Cleaning Up America: An Insider's View of the Environmental Protection Agency 68–70 (1976). "Before accepting reappointment in Nixon's second term, Ruckelshaus stipulated the two conditions under which he would continue to serve. One was that his top staff would not be changed. The other was that the system previously established for clearance of EPA regulations by the President's Office of Management and Budget must be clarified so that final authority over regulatory decisions clearly rested within EPA. President Nixon agreed to both of these conditions." *Id.* at 117–18. It is hard to imagine such demands by a presumptive agency executive for decisional independence being taken seriously today.

38 In this case, the Obama administration's Office of Information and Regulatory Affairs (OIRA) sent a "return letter" to the EPA challenging the merits of the ozone regulation submitted and requesting their reconsideration of the rule. Letter from Cass R. Sunstein, Adm'r of OIRA, to Lisa P. Jackson, Adm'r of EPA (Sept. 2, 2011) (regarding National Ambient Air Quality Standards for Ozone, 75 Fed. Reg. 2938) (Jan. 19, 2010) (Proposed Rule), *available at* www.whitehouse.gov/sites/default/files/ozone_national_ambient_air_quality_standards_letter.pdf. *See also* Juliet Eilperin, *Obama Halts Tighter Rules on Ozone Emissions*, Wash. Post, Sept. 3, 2011, at A01; Cass R. Sunstein, *The Office of Information and Regulatory Affairs: Myths and Realities*, 126 Harv. L. Rev. 1838 (2013). *See further* Jennifer Nou, *Agency*

One can go further along the spectrum to include government created entities that were created with some level of political autonomy from traditional government rules and regulations. These include entities that we might style as quasi-government agencies.[39] These are hybrid organizations that have a legal affiliation with the federal government while concurrently having characteristics that are traditionally more associated with the private sector.[40] Such hybrid organizations are not considered agencies of the government due to the overlap of private and public characteristics; nonetheless, they are an integral element used by the "administrative state" for the implementation of governmental functions.[41] In addition, hybrid organizations have become an attractive option following the divergence of governmental management paradigms.[42] Despite the differences between competing schools of thought, hybrid organizations within the quasi government suggest a shift away from hierarchical leadership structures, toward

Self-Insulation under Presidential Review, 126 HARV. L. REV. 1755, 1801 (2013). The rule became a point of contention among political and policy advisors to the President. John Broder, *Obama Administration Abandons Stricter Air Quality Standards*, N.Y. TIMES, Sept. 2, 2011, *available at* http://www.nytimes.com/2011/09/03/science/earth/03air.html?_r=1&hp ("Lisa P. Jackson, the E.P.A. administrator, has pushed hard for a tougher ozone standard, telling associates that it was one of the most important regulatory initiatives she would handle during her tenure. But she found herself on the losing end of a fight with top White House economic and political advisers, who were persuaded by industry arguments that the 2008 ozone rule was due to be reviewed in two years anyway and who were concerned about the impact on state, local and tribal governments that would bear much of the burden of compliance"). Subsequent FOIA requests revealed that top White House officials were consumed with the decision, which was considered in light of powerful interest groups and a looming presidential election. *See Obama Regulations Chief Pressed Attacks on Ozone Standards*, THE HILL, Aug. 8, 2012, *available at* http://thehill.com/blogs/e2-wire/e2-wire/242667-obama-regs-chief-pressed-attacks-on-ozone-standards.

39 KEVIN KOSAR, CONG. RESEARCH SERV., RL30533, THE QUASI GOVERNMENT: HYBRID ORGANIZATIONS WITH BOTH GOVERNMENT AND PRIVATE SECTOR LEGAL CHARACTERISTICS 1 (2011). Kosar, on behalf of the Congressional Research Service, frequently updates the report, which was originally written by Ronald Moe prior to his retirement from the Congressional Research Service. Anne Joseph O'Connell refers to entities that have aspects of both government entities and private sector entities as "bureaucracy at the boundary." Anne Joseph O'Connell, *Bureaucracy at the Boundary*, 162 U. PA. L.REV. 841, 852–861 (2014).

40 KOSAR, *supra* note 39 at 2. Kevin Kosar of the Congressional Research Service has identified five key factors within the political realm that can be attributed to the growing trend of choosing this form of quasi government option:

> (1) The desire to avoid creating another federal "bureaucracy"; (2) the current controls on the federal budget process that encourage agencies to develop new sources of revenues; (3) the desire by advocates of agencies and programs to be exempt from central management laws, especially statutory ceilings on personnel and compensation; (4) the contemporary appeal of generic, economic-focused values as the basis for a "new public management"; and (5) the belief that management flexibility requires entity-specific laws and regulations, even at the cost of less accountability to representative institutions. *Id.* at 1.

41 *Id.* at 1–2.

42 *Id.* at 31–32. The Unified Executive Management structure was challenged in the 1960s with the emergence of the New Public Management school. Based on public choice theory, the premise of New Public Management is that the government and private sectors are subject to "many of the same economically derived behavioral norms" given their fundamental similarities. *Id.*

the increased desire for "change and managerial risk-taking."[43] However classified, these entities have neither the formal nor de facto indicia of independence and are not the primary focus of this book.

Principal among these independent entities within an American context are government corporations.[44] Despite the absence of a general provision of law clearly defining government corporations and their attributes, the government corporation is a practical option when the government is reorganizing or creating a new agency.[45] Historically, the practicality of the government corporation has proved to be a critical tool during national emergencies. For example, the United States Emergency Fleet Corporation was organized a mere ten days after the declaration of World War I, followed by the creation of the War Finance Corporation shortly thereafter.[46] Then, again in the 1930s, government corporations such as the Tennessee Valley Authority (TVA) and the Reconstruction Finance Corporation were established to address the devastation left in the wake of the Great Depression.[47]

Continuing along the continuum one can identify "a number of organizations that fall between the categories of private sector and governmental entities."[48] Structured as "instrumentalit[ies] of government," rather than agencies, these entities are employed to address concerns in policy areas where traditional agencies appear ill-equipped, or unable, to function.[49] Entities such as government sponsored enterprises (GSEs), standard setting organizations (SSOs), and self-regulatory organizations (SROs) function as public-private partnerships, which substantively delegate some part of traditional, core governmental functions to the private sector. As Kimberly Brown suggests: "Contractors exercising governmental functions should... be viewed as anatomically related to government actors within a structure that leads all the way to the president. If a constitutional continuum is accepted as a substitute concept for the public/private divide, new frontiers in the privatization debate might open."[50]

---

43 *Id.*

44 We use the terms "government corporation," "federal government corporation," and "public corporation" interchangeably.

45 Kevin Kosar, Cong. Research Serv., RL 30365, Federal Government Corporations: An Overview 13 (2011) [hereinafter Kosar, Fed. Government Corps.].

46 Harold Archer Van Dorn, Government Owned Corporations 10–11 (1926) (while the provision establishing the corporation occurred a year earlier, it was only after the United States' entry into World War I that the U.S. Emergency Fleet corporation was actually incorporated).

47 Kosar, Fed. Government Corps., *supra* note 45, at 13. Principal among those within a foreign context are British quasi-nongovernmental organizations—or "quangos"—and the British regulatory agencies that have emerged since privatization replaced government ownership of industry during the Thatcher era of the 1980s. It is our belief that the emergence of independent governmental entities in countries with somewhat less of a market tradition than the United States is the result of an evolution of independent government institutions as a pragmatic accommodation to societal needs. *See generally* chapter 10.

48 Kevin R. Kosar, *Government-Sponsored Enterprises (GSEs): An Institutional Overview, in* Quasi Government Organizations 53 (James F. Turbane ed., 2009).

49 *Id.* at 56.

50 Conti-Brown, *supra* note 26, at 507.

Agency procedures, practices, and traditions have evolved differently to facilitate each agency's specific substantive mission. Yet some generalities about agency operations can be gleaned. In this connection, we believe that tradition matters. Lore can be as important as law. On one level, tradition matters because the evolution of agency custom, and its culmination in established practice, manifests a pragmatic adaptation of law to the needs of individualized administration. On another level, it matters because it reflects the integration of accountability and efficiency. Generally speaking, an evolving practice reflects a consensus (or at least an acceptance) among agency members and staffs, the private sector, and the politically accountable branches of government regarding reasonable ways of doing business. Often, agency practice becomes enmeshed with law.

The Federal Reserve Board is a good example. By statute, its members have the longest term of any independent agency—fourteen years[51]—and its chair has a separate statutory four-year term as chair.[52] By tradition, though, the appointment of the chair has been essentially bipartisan. In fact, since the 1950s nearly all board chairs have been reappointed by presidents of the other party. For example, Chairman William McChesney Martin, the longest serving board chair, served five presidents from 1951 to 1970. Likewise, Chair Alan Greenspan served under presidents of both parties from 1987 to 2006. More significantly, the chair of the Federal Reserve Board lacks statutory "for cause" removal protection. While such protection for the chair has been considered at various times, Congress has not granted any such statutory protection.[53] Although it would be possible to argue that implicit "for cause" protection exists, as the Supreme Court has acknowledged in other cases, it appears tradition and expectation play a key role in the reluctance of any president to remove a sitting chair.[54] No president has ever attempted such a removal, but such action has been considered.[55] President Lyndon Johnson reportedly asked his attorney general, Nicholas Katzenbach, about his removal

---

[51] The president's power to designate terms was limited to the first board in 1935. Now, all get fourteen-year terms. 12 U.S.C. § 242 (2012).

[52] *Id.*

[53] Adrian Vermeule, *Conventions of Agency Independence*, 113 COLUM. L. REV. 1163, 1176 n.65 (2013).

[54] *Id.* at 1196 ("I suggest that there is a strong unwritten norm protecting the Fed Chair from removal. Whatever the relevant statutes say, it is currently unimaginable that a President would fire the Fed Chair because of disagreements over macroeconomic policy"). Even some conservative legal theorists support the idea of Fed independence. John O. McGinnis and Michael B. Rappaport, *Reconciling Originalism and Precedent*, 103 NW. UNIV. L. REV. 803, 850 n.173 ("While we believe that the appropriate precedent rules do not protect the decisions that allow the creation of independent agencies from being overruled (assuming as we believe that they conflict with the original meaning), one important exception may exist to this claim. We are inclined to believe that the independence of the Federal Reserve is now so well accepted that it should be regarded as an entrenched precedent.").

[55] Akhil Reed Amar, *The President, the Cabinet, and Independent Agencies*, 5 U. ST. THOMAS J.L. & PUB. POL'Y 36, 59–60 (2010) (discussing that past presidents have not publicly argued that Federal Reserve independence raised constitutional concerns. Robert J. Delahunty, formerly of the Department of Justice OLC, notes, "[w]e thought about it in Bush I, but it came to nothing."). However, at least three Fed chairs have "functionally been removed" during their terms. Conti-Brown, *supra* note 26, at 37.

power regarding Federal Reserve Board chair William McC. Martin. Robert Bremner, Martin's biographer, reports that President Johnson was "[a]dvised that 'termination for cause' did not include disagreement with administration policies, and that in the Fed's fifty-one years of existence no attempt had ever been made to remove a sitting Fed governor, [so] Johnson let the matter drop."[56] At the same time, established practice will have greater or lesser effect depending on political context and public opinion.[57]

We offer our study for two reasons. First, these matters are the grist of the day-to-day operations of federal agencies. Second, these issues do not appear to command quite the same academic attention as doctrinal issues, and comparative data is either unknown or uncollated. We share Cass Sunstein's view that the next generation of administrative law scholarship should shift its focus from its "traditional preoccupation with the judiciary to a focus on congressional and bureaucratic processes[,] ... [which] remain ill-understood despite the fact that they have far more important roles in government regulation."[58]

In the same way we have taken account of the growing interest in comparative administrative law as a way of better understanding the context in which the independent agency developed.[59] In chapter 10 we briefly survey the emergence, growth, and variety of independent agencies in Europe, and beyond. One observer suggests that in Europe "it is unclear what European agencies are supposed to be independent of."[60] What is not unclear, though, is that a need for some form of independence appears to be required as a means of accommodating the tension between autonomy and accountability in democracies other than the United States.

In order to understand the importance of the independent agency, it is imperative to examine how they developed. We begin this study with a review of the creation of the Interstate Commerce Commission (ICC), and focus on how the independent agency form evolved, not from institutional logic but from historical contingency. As one observer has noted: "[T]he independent commission as an organizational form did not emerge full-blown with the passage of the Interstate Commerce Act. Rather, it evolved over the course of several decades, coming to maturity late in the Progressive Era."[61]

---

56 Robert P. Bremner, Chairman of the Fed: William McChesney Martin Jr. and the Creation of the Modern American Financial System 203 (2004). *See generally* chapter 12 *infra*; Vermeule, *supra* note 53 at 1163, 1179 & n. 45.

57 *See id.* at 1179.

58 Cass R. Sunstein, *Administrative Substance*, 1991 Duke L.J. 607, 642 (1991).

59 For just a few examples of a "subdiscipline" that twenty years ago was hardly included in library catalogues, *See* Susan Rose-Ackerman & Peter Lindseth, eds., Comparative Administrative Law (Elgar 2010); John Bell, Comparative Administrative Law: The Oxford Handbook of Comparative Administrative Law (Oxford 2006); George Bermann, Charles H. Koch, Jr., & James T. O'Reilly, Administrative Law of the European Union, 6 vols. (ABA, 2008). There is even a blog devoted to the subject—see Comparative Administrative Law, blogs.law.yale.edu/blogs/compadlaw/.

60 Miroslava Scholten, *"Independent, Hence, Unaccountable"? The Need for a Broader Debate on Accountability of the Executive*, 4 Review of European Administrative Law 5, 9 (2011).

61 Marc Allen Eisner, Regulatory Politics in Transition 48 (1993).

Our review convinces us that the Supreme Court's 1935 characterization of the genus independent agency is overly romanticized or, at least, outdated. Certainly the revealing debate over independent agencies in the Supreme Court's *Fox* opinion suggests a more nuanced view.[62] Since World War II we have seen a trend toward growth in the power of the president—what some have called "presidentialism," that is to say an effort to "interpret the constitutional design as creating a largely autonomous executive branch, in which the president enjoys a robust range of inherent authorities, both foreign and domestic, which are beyond the power of Congress to regulate or the authority of the courts to review."[63] This tendency can be found in both Democratic[64] and Republican[65] administrations and, not surprisingly, has been met by a degree of judicial pushback.[66]

---

62 FCC v. Fox, 556 U.S. 502, 547 (2009) (including the observation of four justices that an independent agency's "comparative freedom from ballot-box control makes it all the more important that courts review its decisionmaking to assure compliance with applicable provisions of the law—including law requiring that major policy decisions be based upon articulable reasons").

63 PETER SHANE, MADISON'S NIGHTMARE: HOW EXECUTIVE POWER THREATENS AMERICAN DEMOCRACY, 27 (2009). Shane contrasts "presidentialism" with "pluralism." "Pluralists," Shane notes, "'interpret' the checks and balances system to emphasize the roles that the Constitution assigns to the multiple institutions of our national government in holding each other to account. In the pluralist view, the scope of permissible presidential initiative depends very much on the actions of Congress and the courts." *Id.* Others have called it the "imperial" presidency. ARTHUR M. SCHLESINGER, JR., THE IMPERIAL PRESIDENCY (1973). *See also* ERIC POSNER & ADRIAN VERMEULE, THE EXECUTIVE UNBOUND: AFTER THE MADISONIAN REPUBLIC (2011).

64 For a discussion of "presidentialism" in the Clinton Administration, *see* Elena Kagan, *Presidential Administration*, 114 HARV. L. REV. 2245, 2281–85 (2005) ("President Clinton treated the sphere of regulation as his own, and in doing so made it his own, in a way no other modern President has done."). For the Obama administration, *see* Charlie Savage, *Shift on Executive Power Lets Obama Bypass Rivals*, N.Y. TIMES, Apr. 23, 2012, at A1. *See also* Charles Krauthammer, *The Imperial Presidency Revisited*, WASH. POST WRITERS GRP., Jul. 5, 2012, 2012 WLNR 20308904. ("During the Bush-43 years, we were repeatedly treated to garment-rending about the imperial presidency, to major hyperventilation about the 'unitary executive.' Yet the current administration's imperiousness has earned little comparable attention.").

65 For the expansion of domestic presidential power in the George W. Bush administration, *see* Harold J. Krent, *From a Unitary to a Unilateral Presidency*, 88 B.U. L. Rev. 523 (2008) ("President Bush's centralization efforts, even in routine administrative matters, have stretched our understanding of the unitary executive almost beyond recognition." *Id.* at 524); Mark J. Rozell & Mitchel A. Sollenberger, *Executive Privilege: The Bush Record and Legacy, in* TESTING THE LIMITS: GEORGE W. BUSH AND THE IMPERIAL PRESIDENCY 199–218 (Mark J. Rozell & Gleaves Whitney eds., 2009); JACK GOLDSMITH, THE TERROR PRESIDENCY: LAW AND JUDGMENT INSIDE THE BUSH ADMINISTRATION (2007) ("...fear [of the terrorism threat] created enormous pressure to stretch the law to its limits in order to give the President the powers he thought necessary to prevent a second 9/11." *Id.* at 11). For the Bush administration in foreign policy, JACK GOLDSMITH, POWER AND CONSTRAINT: THE ACCOUNTABLE PRESIDENCY AFTER 9/11 (2012); and, of course, JOHN YOO, THE POWERS OF WAR AND PEACE: THE CONSTITUTION AND FOREIGN AFFAIRS AFTER 9/11 (2005).

For a critique of the Bush administration's "presidentialist" approach *see* PETER M. SHANE, MADISON'S NIGHTMARE; HOW EXECUTIVE POWER THREATENS AMERICAN DEMOCRACY (2009) "Under George W. Bush, the merger of partisanship and executive ambition finally crystallized into a theory and practice of a unilateral presidency that truly threatened—and, if it persists under his successors will continue to threaten—American democracy." *Id.* at 175. Most of the critiques, however, concerned foreign policy issues.

66 In the foreign affairs arena, *see* Hamdi v. Rumsfeld, 542 U.S. 507 (2004); Boumediene v. Bush, 553 U.S. 723 (2008); Medellin v. Texas, 552 U.S. 491 (2008). And, in the domestic arena, *see* Massachusetts v. E.P.A., 549

For his part, the president has always had power to influence regulatory direction through the appointment process. He can also influence regulatory direction through the oversight of independent agency budget requests and the ability of such agencies to introduce and comment on legislation (both with notable exceptions), and the control of agency litigation (again, with notable exceptions). At the same time, Congress drafts the enabling statutes that confer on agencies their fundamental authority, controls their budgets through the appropriations process, and can sway their substantive decisions through the oversight process. So independent agencies reflect the resolution of a tug-of-war between agency factions and the political branches and allow policy warfare to be waged subtly, away from "center court," where affected interests can jockey for dominance. The actual operations of independent agencies, if not the theory, are in effect, a sort of Queensberry Rules of engagement.

On the other hand, the Brownlow Committee's comments were equally wide of the mark. The administrative process, although according agencies considerable discretion, is not as unprincipled as the committee portrayed it. In our view, structural and organization elements and statutory constraints, along with agency traditions and practices, have evolved together to permit independent agencies to conduct their business fairly and effectively while keeping them somewhat above the political fray. Agency structures, procedures, and practices have grown up pragmatically rather than theoretically to provide a reasonably impartial playing field for the resolution of factual and policy issues in discrete areas of government activity.

Often lost in the examination of these two extremes is a recognition that individual independent agencies differ. They range across a spectrum that blends intersecting elements of independence, autonomy, accountability, and methods of control by one or both of the political branches. The classic indicia of independence that may tilt them in the direction of congressional rather than presidential control, for example, but provide a degree of autonomy from both, are that individuals serve on multimember bodies under a fixed term of years accompanied by statutorily guaranteed protection against removal except for some form of "good cause." This is true of some, but not all, "independent" agencies. The members of a number of agencies, such as the SEC, lack statutorily guaranteed protection against removal.[67] The Supreme Court has never expressly held that individuals on these bodies possess removal protection, but they are nonetheless regarded as having such protection under an "inefficiency, neglect of duty,

U.S. 497 (2007). Arthur Schlesinger, Jr., has suggested that under George W. Bush, the "imperial presidency" was "born again." ARTHUR M. SCHLESINGER, JR., WAR AND THE AMERICAN PRESIDENCY xvi (2004).

67 *See* Peter L. Strauss, *On the Difficulties of Generalization: PCAOB in the Footsteps of Myers, Humphrey's Executor, Morrison, and Freytag*, 32 CARDOZO L. REV. 2255, 2261 (2011) [hereinafter Strauss, *On the Difficulties of Generalization*]. *See* chapter 5, *infra*.

or malfeasance in office" standard taken from the original FTC Act.[68] Justice Stephen Breyer has observed that they are actually protected by "a political environment, reflecting tradition and function that would impose a heavy political cost upon any president who tried to remove a commissioner of the agency without cause."[69] Certain agencies exhibiting elements of independence are, like their cabinet department counterparts, headed by a single individual, thus tending to make them more politically accountable to an appointing president—or so it is thought. Agencies, by legislative design or simply evolution and tradition, differ significantly in their level of autonomy from one or both of the political branches of government regarding their finances, control over litigation, and capacity to submit their own budgets to Congress and respond directly to legislative requests from Congress without presidential interference. The powers of agency chairs differ, thus according a president greater or lesser control over agency decisions.

In short, within the broad kingdom of agencies there exists not only what might be considered a genus of independent agencies having a degree of similarity but also individual species within that genus, each with almost a unique blend of characteristics. The continued existence of the genus seems inevitable, and new species will either be replicated or invented, while the occasional species will become extinct.

As lawyers we plead guilty to a focus on structure, one that looks in detail on the rise of the bureaucratic form we call the independent agency or commission. We recognize the work of Stephen Skowronek[70] and Theda Skocpol,[71] who have focused on capacity-building in the American nation-state, and Daniel Carpenter, who has focused on bureaucratic autonomy as indicia of independence,[72] and adopt at points some of their insights. But as lawyers we focus on legal structure and legal process in our understanding of the independent agency. That, in itself, is a significant task.

---

[68] Free Enter. Fund v. Pub. Co. Accounting Oversight Bd., 130 S. Ct. 3138, 3148–3149 (2010) ("The parties agree that the Commissioners cannot themselves be removed by the President except under the *Humphrey's Executor* standard of 'inefficiency, neglect of duty, or malfeasance in office,' . . . we decide the case with that understanding"). *See* Strauss, *On the Difficulties of Generalization, supra* note 67, at 2277 (critiquing the failure of the Court to address the SEC commissioner's "for cause" protection, Strauss summarizes, ". . . the majority decided by bare assertion a question of law on which their holding that the PCAOB 'for cause' removal provision was unconstitutional utterly depended—relying on party choices of how to argue the case"). *See also* S.E.C. v. Blinder, Robinson & Co., Inc., 855 F.2d 677, 681 (10th Cir. 1988) (". . . for the purposes of this case, we accept appellants' assertions in their brief, that it is commonly understood that the President may remove a commissioner only for 'inefficiency, neglect of duty or malfeasance in office'").

[69] Free Enter. Fund v. Pub. Co. Accounting Oversight Bd., 130 S. Ct. 3138, 3183 (2010) (Breyer, J., dissenting).

[70] Stephen Skowronek, Building a New American State: The Expansion of National Administrative Capabilities, 1877–1920 (1982).

[71] Theda Skocpol, Protecting Soldiers and Mothers: The Political Origin of Social Policy in the United States (1992); Theda Skocpol, State and Party in America's New Deal (1995). For a thoughtful exploration see Bringing the State Back In (Peter Evans, Dietrich Rueschemeyer & Theda Skocpol eds., 1985).

[72] Daniel Carpenter, The Forging of bureaucratic Autonomy: Regulation, Networks, and Policy Innovation in Executive Agencies, 1882–1928 (2001).

2

How the Independent Agency Developed

THE SEARCH FOR EXPERTISE

A. The Interstate Commerce Commission

The emergence of the modern independent regulatory agency at the federal level began in the late nineteenth century when Congress established the ICC to regulate the railroads. As a result, independence became inextricably associated with multimember tribunals. Prior to the establishment of the ICC, several states utilized the regulatory commission structure in their attempts to regulate the railroad industry.[1] As Robert Cushman noted, "Regulatory commissions were . . . the normal outgrowth of a broader state commission movement which dated back to the early nineteenth century."[2]

The concept of federal-level independence, however, did not originate with the ICC. When Congress established the Department of the Treasury in 1789, the department possessed indicia of independence from the executive and indeed was not described as an executive department. For instance, the secretary of the treasury reported directly to Congress.[3] "In the Congress, the secretary of the treasury was seen as an indispensable, direct arm

---

[1] ROBERT CUSHMAN, THE INDEPENDENT REGULATORY COMMISSIONS 26 (1972) ("[I]n 1887, ten states had set up 'strong' commissions . . . possessing actual rate-making powers.").

[2] *Id.* at 19.

[3] *See* Act of Sept. 2, 1789, ch. 12, § 2, 1 Stat. 65, 66. GERHARD CASPER, SEPARATING POWER: ESSAYS ON THE FOUNDING PERIOD 42 (1997). *But see* Steven G. Calabresi & Christopher S. Yoo, *The Unitary Executive During the First Half-Century*, 47 CASE W. RES. L. REV. 1451, 1480–81 (1997) (describing President Washington's "firm control over the Treasury Department during his presidency"). The Calabresi and Yoo history of "unitariness," now collected in book form, provides a reconceptualized understanding of the historical record. STEVEN G. CALABRESI & CHRISTOPHER S. YOO, THE UNITARY

of the House in regard to its responsibilities for revenues and appropriations."[4] This was especially significant because, at the time, the Treasury Department was larger than the rest of the entire federal government.[5] Furthermore, although the president retained power to remove the comptroller of the department, the president did not have "directory control over him," as "the Comptroller was to exercise judgment independent from the President."[6]

Lawrence Lessig and Cass Sunstein explain that early Congresses "vested different degrees of control in the President... undermin[ing] the claim that the founding vision was motivated by a single organizational ideal."[7] Recent commentators, for instance, have noted that district attorneys (now called United States attorneys) initially enjoyed considerable independence from the executive branch.[8] This is because early attorneys general understood the opinions clause of the Judiciary Act of 1789,[9] which established the office of attorney general, to be a limitation on their authority, "rather than [the basis for] a general power to control legal opinions throughout the executive branch."[10] These attorneys general used the limitation as a justification for refusing to advise district attorneys in their prosecutions. The district attorneys thus conducted federal prosecution free from the control and jurisdiction of the attorney general, whose "function was merely to advise the President and the Cabinet."[11] Attorney General William Wirt opined that the president's duty to ensure that laws are faithfully executed does not include power to intervene and review cases without express congressional authorization.[12] In an

---

Executive: Presidential Power from Washington to Bush (2008). Interestingly, under the Articles of Confederation, there was no president or executive branch, and the Treasury was controlled by a series of congressional committees and was accountable exclusively to Congress. In 1784, the Continental Congress even experimented with a three-member Board of Treasury. Mark Walston, The Department of the Treasury 29 (1989).

4 Casper, *supra* note 3, at 44.

5 *See* Ron Chernow, Op-Ed, *Alexander Hamilton's Last Stand*, N.Y. Times, July 11, 2004, sec. 4, at 13.

6 *See* Lawrence Lessig, *Readings by Our Unitary Executive*, 15 Cardozo L. Rev. 175, 183–85 (1993). *See also* 1 Richard J. Pierce, Jr., Administrative Law Treatise § 2.5, at 75 (5th ed. 2010).

7 Lawrence Lessig & Cass R. Sunstein, *The President and the Administration*, 94 Colum. L. Rev. 1, 31–32 (1994). Lessig and Sunstein examine early presidential control over the original Department of the Navy, Department of War, Post Office, and attorney general. *See id.* at 12–38.

8 *See* Albert Langeluttig, The Department of Justice of the United States 2 (1927) (providing a historical account of the Department of Justice and noting that "[t]he Attorney General was given no supervision or control over the district attorneys"); Charles Tiefer, *The Constitutionality of Independent Officers as Checks on Abuses of Executive Power*, 63 B.U. L. Rev. 59, 74–75 (1983).

9 *See* Judiciary Act of 1789, ch. 20, § 35, 1 Stat. 73, 93 (authorizing the attorney general to provide legal opinions and advice to the president and department heads).

10 Lessig, *supra* note 6, at 188 (emphasis omitted). *See also* Keith S. Brown & Adam Candeub, Independent Agencies and the Unitary Executive Debate: An Empirical Critique 10 (Mich. State Univ. College of Law, Legal Studies Research Paper Series, Research Paper No. 06-04), *available at* http://papers.ssrn.com/sol3/papers.cfm?abstract_id=1100125## ("While the Judiciary Act of 1789 did create the office of Attorney General, it did not create a 'department' under him.").

11 Tiefer, *supra* note 8, at 75.

12 1 Op. Att'y Gen. 624, 625–30 (1823).

opinion letter to President Monroe, dated October 20, 1823, Wirt advised the president against intervening in the Treasury Department's financial settlement with Major Joseph Wheaton over various expense claims. Wirt noted "there is no proviso for an appeal to the president."[13] Wirt further stated:

> To interpret [the Take Care] clause of the constitution so as to throw upon the President the duty of a personal interference in every specific case of an alleged or defective execution of the laws, and to call upon him to perform such duties himself, would be not only to require him to perform an impossibility himself, but to take upon himself the responsibility of all the subordinate executive officers of the government—a construction too absurd to be seriously contended for.[14]

Wirt continued:

> The constitution assigns to Congress the power of designating the duties of particular officers: the President is only required to take care that they execute them faithfully. For example: our laws provide that there be established at the seat of government a General Post Office, under the direction of a Postmaster General; and they direct that he (the Postmaster General) "shall establish post offices, and appoint postmasters, at all such places as appear to him expedient on the post roads that are or may be established by law." Suppose that the Postmaster General should fail to appoint a postmaster at some place where an office is established by law: can the President make such appointment? I apprehend not; for there is no law that authorizes it. The power of appointment is given by law exclusively to the Postmaster General; and the constitutional charge to the President to take care that the laws be faithfully executed, goes no farther, in this instance, than to require him to see that the Postmaster General makes the appointment. He is not to perform the duty, but to see that the officer assigned by law performs his duty *faithfully*—that is, *honestly*: not with perfect correctness of judgment, but *honestly*. If the postmaster shall appoint one applicant while the President prefers another, the President cannot interfere with the appointment; because the selection is referred by law to the judgment of the postmaster alone."[15]

However, in *The Jewels of the Princess of Orange*, Attorney General Roger B. Taney determined that the president could order a district attorney to terminate a prosecution.[16] In *Princess of Orange*, a thief stole jewels belonging to the Dutch Princess of Orange while

---

13 *Id.* at 627–28.

14 *Id.* at 625.

15 *Id.* at 626.

16 2 Op. Att'y Gen. 482, 487 (1831).

in Europe and was arrested with them in New York.[17] The district attorney began a forfeiture action on behalf of the United States, but the president wanted to return the jewels to the Netherlands royal family. Taney reasoned that the innocent princess should not face forfeiture of her stolen jewels, and that the president had the power to execute the law by ordering the termination of the action.[18]

While the antebellum administrative state only fitfully recognized the need for executive direction and control, it also found little use for judicial review of administrative action.[19] As Kenneth Culp Davis indicated: "The presumption was one of unreviewability throughout the 19th century."[20] This structure aimed to "maintain a strict separation" between the courts and the executive.[21] In *Decatur v. Paulding*, the Supreme Court observed that "[t]he interference of the Courts with the performance of the ordinary duties of the executive departments of the government, would be productive of nothing but mischief; and we are quite satisfied that such a power was never intended to be given to them."[22]

This modest approach to judicial review of executive power was reconsidered following the Civil War. In the second half of the nineteenth century, the national government was facing the challenge of regulating potential economic monopolies—particularly the

---

[17] *Id.* at 483.

[18] *See id.* at 484–87, 491–92.

> The district attorney might refuse to obey the President's order; and if he did refuse, the prosecution, while he remained in office, would still go on; because the President could give no order to the court or the clerk to make any particular entry. He could only act through his subordinate officer, the district attorney, who is responsible to him, and who holds his office at his pleasure. And if that officer still continued a prosecution which the President was satisfied ought to be discontinued, the removal of the disobedient officer, and the substitution of one more worthy in his place, would enable the President, through him, faithfully to execute the law.

Id. at 489.

[19] Marbury v. Madison, 5 U.S. 137, 150, 165–66 (1803) (asserting the power to review "ministerial" executive acts and to compel the executive by issuing a writ of mandamus, but holding that political or discretionary actions "are only politically examinable"). *See* Frederic P. Lee, *The Origins of Judicial Control of Federal Executive Action*, 36 Geo. L.J. 287, 292–93 (1948) (explaining that the *Marbury* Court "avoided forcing the issue with the executive"). Nonetheless, over the course of the nineteenth century, the Court was extremely reluctant to review executive decisions. As an example—albeit extreme from a modern perspective—the Court refused to compel the secretary of the navy to pay Stephen Decatur's widow her pension, as required by a private act of Congress. Decatur v. Paulding, 39 U.S. 497, 513–14 (1840). Rather than ruling on the merits, the Court held that it lacked jurisdiction because the action fell within the secretary's discretionary power. *Id.* (holding that the secretary's duty to disburse the pensions, "whether imposed by act of Congress or by resolution, are not mere ministerial duties"). *See also* Ann Woolhandler, *Judicial Deference to Administrative Action—A Revisionist History*, 43 Admin. L. Rev. 197, 221 (1991) (discussing *Decatur* and the Court's reluctance to review executive decisions).

[20] 5 Kenneth Culp Davis, Administrative Law Treatise § 28:1, at 254 (2d ed. 1984).

[21] Jerry L. Mashaw, *Rethinking Judicial Review of Administrative Action: A Nineteenth Century Perspective*, 32 Cardozo L. Rev. 2241, 2250 (2011).

[22] *Decatur*, 39 U.S. at 516. *See also* Martin v. Mott, 25 U.S. 19, 31–32 (1827) (holding statutes conferring discretionary power make the recipient the sole judge of the facts on which such discretion should be exercised).

railroads, which were "a central, if not the major, element in the political, economic, and social development of the United States."[23] With the statutory creation of national regulation through the ICC in 1887, courts began to examine the powers of administrative entities. In 1897, the Supreme Court rejected the ICC's conclusion that its statutory power to determine the reasonableness of rates included the power to prescribe rates.[24]

The presumption of unreviewability, however, was not reversed until the Court's 1902 decision in *American School of Magnetic Healing v. McAnnulty*.[25] Judicial reviewability of agency action in the post–Administrative Procedure Act (APA) era was later expressly established in *Abbott Laboratories v. Gardner*.[26] Nonetheless, at least since passage of the Hepburn Act in 1906, courts have recognized the ICC's expertise and accorded considerable decisional deference to the ICC findings of fact and resolution of conflicts in the evidence.[27]

1. REGULATION IN BRITAIN

The ICC itself was a natural derivation of the administrative commissions employed by various states[28] and Britain.[29] Britain created its rail regulatory commission in 1888 after nearly a half century of varying practical efforts to develop a workable regulatory framework. The House of Commons first comprehensively evaluated its railroads as early as 1839, in response to shipper complaints of monopoly practices. It appointed a committee to investigate the veracity of the allegations. The committee became convinced that competition was—and would be—insufficient to protect the public, and that intermittent remedial legislation (such as laws that required rate reductions based on railroad profits) could be easily evaded. Therefore, the select committee proposed that Britain adopt some form of railroad regulation.[30]

Accepting the committee's recommendation, Parliament enacted the Railway Regulation Bill in 1840, which delegated certain powers over railways to a government

---

23 Gabriel Kolko, Railroads and Regulation 1877–1916 1 (1965).

24 Interstate Commerce Comm'n v. Cincinnati, New Orleans & Tex. Pac. Ry. Co., 167 U.S. 479, 500 (1897).

25 187 U.S. 94 (1902).

26 Abbott Labs. v. Gardner, 387 U.S. 136, 140 (1967).

27 *See, e.g.*, Ill. Cent. R.R. Co. v. Interstate Commerce Co., 206 U.S. 441, 454 (1907). *See also* Mashaw, *supra* note 23, at 2245 ("After the Hepburn Act, the Supreme Court beat a hasty retreat from its previously intrusive review of ICC orders. . . .").

28 *See* Cushman, *supra* note 1, at 19 (noting that more than twenty states had already established commissions).

29 In discussing regulation in Britain, we rely on three principal sources: C. D. Foster, Privatization, Public Ownership and the Regulation of Natural Monopoly (1992); Henry Parris, Government and the Railways in Nineteenth-Century Britain (1965); and a 1886 report by the Senate Committee on Interstate Commerce that preceded passage of the Act to Regulate Commerce of 1887, S. Rep. No. 49-46, pt. 1 (1886).

30 *See* Parris, *supra* note 29, at 8–9.

department—the Board of Trade.[31] The bill required that railroads give the Board of Trade notice before opening a new line, but the board lacked power to prevent operation.[32] The board also entertained complaints against railroads but lacked power to pursue them.[33] The bill did require railroads to submit copies of their existing and future bylaws, which the board could disapprove. Perhaps most important, the board received the right to comment on private bills,[34] which was Parliament's principal method of regulation until the latter part of the nineteenth century.[35]

Overall, the board's powers "were neither numerous nor extensive,"[36] and the private bill system "did more to protect private interests than to promote the public interest."[37] The board attempted to establish a regulatory bureaucracy by creating a Railway Department, but given its limited power to make advisory opinions rather than to regulate the industry, the board proved ineffectual.[38] The board's attempt at oversight was also hindered by political compromise, which would exist until deregulation took root in the latter third of the twentieth century. As Foster has noted, until the 1880s, Parliament resisted any attempt to appoint commissioners with significant power and status.[39]

In 1844, when a parliamentary committee again reviewed railroad regulation, it proposed that the government acquire the railroads and recommended a twenty-one-year transition period.[40] The board's powers were substantially reduced and partially superseded by the Railway Department, which was under the direction of the president of the Board of Trade.[41] In 1846, the Whigs came to power and enacted legislation that first established a tribunal independent of the Board of Trade, known as the Commissioners of Railways, to regulate the railways.[42] This Whig reform responded to criticism that the Board of Trade lacked sufficient stature and performed work through its clerks.[43]

---

31 *See id.* at 28, 30.

32 *See id.* at 30, 37.

33 *See id.* at 42.

34 *See id.* at 57–60 (describing the department's participation in the legislative process).

35 *See* FOSTER, *supra* note 29, at 17–18, 20 (describing the use of private bills as regulatory devices). *See also* DONALD SHELL, THE HOUSE OF LORDS 176 (1988) (noting the importance of private bills in the nineteenth century and explaining that they "enable individuals, groups or bodies to do something which the law of the land . . . does not otherwise allow"). These bills, also sometimes deemed "parliamentary contracts," were effectively licenses that conferred operational rights on railways and outlined conditions. FOSTER, *supra* note 29, at 17–18. Viewed as contracts involving private property, they were generally immune from subsequent legislation. *See id.* at 18.

36 PARRIS, *supra* note 29, at 30.

37 *Id.* at 57.

38 *See id.* at 31–35 (describing the early staffing and duties of the department).

39 *See* FOSTER, *supra* note 29, at 21.

40 *See* S. REP., *supra* note 29 at 55.

41 *See* PARRIS, *supra* note 29, at 61–63.

42 *Id.* at 103.

43 *Id.* at 107 ("One of the criticisms had been that the policy of the Board was decided by mere clerks.").

Parliament effectively controlled the commission, which was to have five members—only three of whom would be paid.[44] It was assumed that the commission's president and unpaid members would be members of Parliament.[45] Quorum requirements further reflected parliamentary control, as only two members were necessary to constitute a quorum to conduct business.[46] The 1846 legislation, however, gave the commissioners no new powers and only transferred those previously enjoyed by the Board of Trade.[47] The Commissioners of Railways had become no more effective than the Board of Trade, and when its president was replaced by the former Board of Trade president, even its independence flagged.[48] Parliament subsequently shifted responsibility over the railroads back to the Board of Trade in 1851.[49] In Parris's view, "[t]he transfer of responsibility to the Commissioners was an experiment which failed."[50]

In 1872, Parliament established yet another committee—a Joint Committee on Railways—to undertake a study of the past forty years of government regulation.[51] Like its predecessors, the Joint Committee concluded that competition had been stifled and that legislation had failed to redress the problem.[52] In its view, the chief anticompetitive evils were discriminatory prices between long-haul and short-haul traffic, and unduly high rates—essentially the same factors that influenced U.S. regulation.[53] However, the Joint Committee concluded that a statutory remedy for these perceived abuses was impracticable. Its recommended solution was a new tribunal "to take supervision of the transportation interests of the kingdom . . . with authority to enforce the laws relating to railways and canals, to hear complaints and adjust differences, and to advise Parliament upon questions of railway legislation."[54] The new commission was to be made up of at least three members, including "an eminent lawyer" and another "acquainted with railway management."[55] In response, Parliament transferred the board's powers to a

---

44 *Id.* at 103.

45 *Id.*

46 *Id.*

47 *Id.*

48 *Id.* at 105–06 ("Thus . . . the Commissioners of Railway had become by 1848 in fact, though not in name, a department of the Board of Trade.").

49 *Id.* at 129. The board continued to superintend the railroads until 1873. *See* S. Rep. No. 49-46, pt. 1, at 58 (1886) (stating that a new railway commission was created in 1873).

50 Parris, *supra* note 29, at 112. In 1865, a royal commission recommended against government acquisition. *See* S. Rep., *supra* note 29 at 56. ("[I]t is not expedient for the Government to avail itself of its reserved right to purchase railways.").

51 *Id.* at 59; *see also* Parris, *supra* note 29, at 221.

52 *See* S. Rep., *supra* note 29 at 57.

53 *Id.* at 58.

54 *Id.*

55 Foster, *supra* note 29, at 46.

newly created Railway Commission, which acquired the power to handle the public's complaints.[56]

The commission scheme emerged from several practical considerations by the Joint Committee. The committee reasoned that the courts were too expensive a forum and lacked expertise, although they historically coped reasonably well with resolving issues of rate reasonableness. On the other hand, the Board of Trade had expertise but was insufficiently "judicial." Committees of Parliament were ineffective regulatory mechanisms because of their constantly shifting memberships.[57] Thus, the solution was an expert, relatively permanent body with adjudicative power.[58]

There was little parliamentary discussion about procedures the Railway Commission was to employ, which were to be "as simple and inexpensive as is consistent with giving due notice and hearing questions openly and fairly."[59] When established, the Railway Commission was actually composed of one judge and two nonlawyer assessors.[60] It adopted legal procedures and rules of evidence, and its cases were presented by barristers.[61] The new commission initially received a five-year charter,[62] but in 1886 Parliament introduced legislation that renamed the agency the Railways and Canal Commission, made it permanent, required railroads to submit certain traffic tables and tariffs,[63] and gave it additional power to control rates.[64] The bill passed in 1888—nearly a half century after regulatory efforts began.[65]

2. STATE REGULATION IN THE UNITED STATES

Railroad regulation emerged in the United States nearly simultaneously with British regulation. The intellectual impetus for government oversight, including the form that it should take, was the brainchild of Charles Francis Adams, Jr.—the scion of a distinguished family line that included two U.S. presidents.[66] Between 1866 and 1878, Adams

---

56 *See* S. Rep., *supra* note 29 at 58 (stating that the new commission had "jurisdiction over all matters in relation to the interchange of traffic, and to all contracts between railway companies, as well as complaints of undue preferences and of other violations of railway laws").

57 *See* Foster, *supra* note 29, at 46 (quoting the joint committee as saying that "a committee of the Houses of Parliament would have no permanence").

58 *See id.* at 46.

59 *Id.* at 46 (internal quotation marks omitted).

60 *Id.* at 48.

61 *Id.*

62 *See* S. Rep., *supra* note 29 at 58.

63 *See* Parris, *supra* note 29, at 223–24; Foster, *supra* note 29, at 47–48.

64 *See* Foster, *supra* note 29, at 48 (stating that the new commission "had the authority of a high court").

65 *See* Parris, *supra* note 29, at 223; Foster, *supra* note 29, at 47.

66 Adams's father served as minister to Great Britain during the Civil War. Raymond Seitz, appointed by the first President Bush as the only career diplomat to serve as U.S. ambassador to Britain, considers Adams, Sr., the best U.S. ambassador to Britain in history. "Largely through his own wits, Adams stopped the

wrote several influential articles about the economics of railroad operation. His most famous work, *Chapters of Erie, and Other Essays*, was a muckraking book coauthored with his brother Henry Adams.[67] They argued that the railroads, if unsupervised, would become natural monopolies, but he also believed that government operation or regulation would stifle efficiency and innovation.[68] In his view, the state legislatures were ill-equipped to regulate the industry effectively because they made political decisions to appease constituents, which stifled the market. Further, politicians lacked the requisite market knowledge. By contrast, industry experts who understood the economics of the industry would render efficient regulation. Summarizing Adams's approach, Thomas McCraw wrote:

> The legislative branch could not do the job of intelligent regulation. "Knowledge cannot possibly creep into the legislature, because no one remains in the legislature long enough to learn." In order to close the gap between public and private interests, analytical expertise must somehow be made a permanent part of the government.[69]

Adams proposed creating what he called a "sunshine commission"—an impartial body of experts that would investigate, examine, and report on railroad activities but would not have enforcement power.[70] As Richard Stillman observed:

> Adams understood the importance of the application of long-term expertise to public issues.... Nonetheless, he distrusted giving too much authority to a permanent set of government officials who could, in the long run, abuse their power by operating beyond the boundaries of community control or accountability.[71]

In reaching his conclusions, Adams carefully evaluated Britain's inability—as of the mid-1870s—to create a commission with effective power.[72]

The Massachusetts Board of Railroad Commissioners, established in 1869, reflected Adams's influence. It had three well-paid, nonpartisan members with overlapping terms.[73]

British from recognizing the Southern Confederacy. Had London done so, transatlantic history would have been profoundly and permanently transformed." RAYMOND SEITZ, OVER THERE 61 (1998).

67 CHARLES F. ADAMS, JR., & HENRY ADAMS, CHAPTERS OF ERIE, AND OTHER ESSAYS (1871).

68 *Id.* at 414–17.

69 THOMAS K. MCCRAW, PROPHETS OF REGULATION 15 (1984). For an insightful review of the inadequacy of the Massachusetts legislature to regulate public utilities, including railroads, see Leonard D. White, *The Origin of Utility Commissions in Massachusetts*, 29 J. POL. ECON. 177, 185–89 (1921).

70 *See* MCCRAW, *supra* note 69, at 15.

71 *See* RICHARD J. STILLMAN II, CREATING THE AMERICAN STATE: THE MORAL REFORMERS AND THE MODERN ADMINISTRATIVE WORLD THEY MADE 55 (1998).

72 *See* FOSTER, *supra* note 29, at 227–28.

73 *See* STILLMAN, *supra* note 71, at 57.

Adams, in fact, served as one of the first three Massachusetts commissioners.[74] The commission had the right to investigate high rates and publicize its findings but had no enforcement power.[75] The first commission with actual power to establish reasonable rates, the Illinois Railroad and Warehouse Commission, was established in 1871.[76]

By 1886, state railroad regulation in general—and the commission form of regulation in particular—was widespread. Of the thirty-eight states then in existence, thirty had some form of railroad regulation.[77] Of these, twenty-five states had adopted a commission form.[78] The remaining five relied on legislative intervention.[79] Despite the prevalence of regulation at the state level, the constitutional and geographical limitations on state agencies prevented their regulatory control of large, interstate railroads.[80] The need for a federal approach became evident.

As Cushman noted, "[b]etween 1868 and 1886, more than 150 [railroad regulation] bills were introduced in Congress."[81] Two competing approaches emerged. The House, led by Representative John H. Reagan, a Texas Democrat, viewed the commission structure as a substitute for action rather than an effective remedy and urged legislation that provided for judicial enforcement.[82] In contrast, the Senate legislation, sponsored by Shelby M. Cullom, a Republican from Illinois, provided for the establishment of an administrative oversight commission.[83] Through the early 1880s, Congress was deadlocked between these structural options.[84] Ultimately, on March 17, 1885, Senator

---

[74] *Id.* at 57.

[75] *See* 1 I. L. SHARFMAN, THE INTERSTATE COMMERCE COMMISSION: A STUDY IN ADMINISTRATIVE LAW AND PROCEDURE 15 (1931). New Hampshire had established the first railroad commission in 1844. *See* S. REP. NO. 49-46, pt. 1, at 65 (1886). However, until 1884 it lacked the power to establish rates and, in this respect, was typical of other New England commissions of the era that followed the Adams model. *See id.* at 116.

[76] *See* S. REP., *supra* note 29 at 71–72. The rate fixed was prima facie evidence of reasonableness in court actions for overcharges and the burden of proof was on the railroad to demonstrate that any higher rate was reasonable. *See id.* The Illinois model was followed by several midwestern states. *See id.* at 71; SHARFMAN, *supra* note 75, at 15.

[77] *See* S. REP., *supra* note 29, at 65.

[78] *See id.* at 64.

[79] *See id.* at 65.

[80] *See* Angel Manuel Moreno, *Presidential Coordination of the Independent Regulatory Process*, 8 ADMIN. L.J. AM. U. 461, 463 n.2 (1994) ("The growth of interstate railways transportation promptly surpassed the operational resources and constitutional powers of the states....").

[81] CUSHMAN, *supra* note 1, at 40–41. *See* BUREAU OF STATISTICS, INTERSTATE COMMERCE COMMISSION ACTIVITIES 1887–1937 29–30 (1937).

[82] *See* LEWIS H. HANEY, A CONGRESSIONAL HISTORY OF RAILWAYS IN THE UNITED STATES 288–92 (1910) ("The House bill provided no executive machinery in the shape of a commission, but left enforcement to the courts.").

[83] *Id.* at 290.

[84] *See* 1 THE ECONOMIC REGULATION OF BUSINESS AND INDUSTRY: A LEGISLATIVE HISTORY OF U.S. REGULATORY AGENCIES 18 (Bernard Schwartz ed., 1973) (noting that a bill introduced by Congressman Reagan passed the House in 1878, but failed to make it out of a Senate committee, while Senator Cullom introduced a bill that passed the Senate in 1885 but did not pass in the House).

Cullom effectively wrested congressional leadership from the House,[85] when the Senate adopted a resolution that established a select committee of five senators to investigate and report on the subject of railroad regulation.[86] According to Senator Cullom, a colleague proposed the fact-finding committee due to the lack of detailed information about the railroad industry, which hampered the Senate's consideration of Cullom's legislation.[87]

On January 18, 1886, the Senate Committee on Interstate Commerce, chaired by Senator Cullom, issued a 216-page report covering virtually all issues affecting transportation regulation.[88] The committee examined the British history of regulation and provided a state-by-state summary of state statutes and the work of state commissions.[89] With the release of the committee report, the Senate was now armed with the necessary intellectual firepower to command the debate. In the same year, the Supreme Court decided *Wabash, St. Louis & Pacific Railway Co. v. Illinois*, which held that a state regulatory agency could not regulate the rates of interstate railroads[90] and prompted increased demand for federal legislation.[91] Kolko asserted that, by the time the Court decided *Wabash* in October 1886, Congress had already determined regulation was needed.[92] The Senate had approved a revised version of the Cullom Bill in May 1886, and although there was still debate between the House and Senate over certain provisions, the decision to regulate was foreordained.[93] Cushman, however, surmised that *Wabash* did have some effect upon Congress's efforts to enact the legislation. Cushman wrote that the case's "precise and immediate effect upon Congressional leaders remains

---

85 *See* SHELBY M. CULLOM, FIFTY YEARS OF PUBLIC SERVICE 314 (2d ed. 1911) (describing the introduction of Cullom's resolution providing for the establishment of a Senate committee to study and report on railroad regulation). Shelby Moore Cullom had a lengthy, if not distinguished, political career. He was a Republican from the earliest days of the party's founding, and proudly proclaimed that "at the opening of the Congressional campaign of 1858, I followed [Abraham Lincoln] firmly and without mental reservation into the ranks of the Republican party." *Id.* at 28. He was elected to the first of three terms in the U.S. House of Representatives in 1865, became a member of the Illinois House of Representatives in 1872, was elected Speaker of the House in 1873, and appointed the committee that drafted the legislation creating the Illinois Railroad and Warehouse Commission. *See* 2 APPLETONS' CYCLOPAEDIA OF AMERICAN BIOGRAPHY 27 (James Grant Wilson & John Fiske eds., 1887). That commission was the first in the country to possess effective rate-setting power. *See* S. REP. NO. 49-46, pt. 1, at 71–73 (1886). Cullom also served as governor of Illinois before coming to the U.S. Senate in 1883. APPLETONS' CYCLOPEDIA, *supra*. Following passage of the Act to Regulate Commerce in 1887, the Senate established a permanent Committee on Interstate Commerce. Senator Cullom chaired that committee for many years. *See* CULLOM, *supra*, at 327–28.

86 *See* CULLOM, *supra* note 85, at 314–15.

87 *Id.* at 314.

88 *See* HANEY, *supra* note 82, at 290 (calling the "'Cullom Report'... probably the most influential document in shaping the Act of 1887.").

89 *See* S. REP., *supra* note 29, at 54–137.

90 Wabash, St. Louis & Pac. Ry. v. Illinois, 118 U.S. 557, 577 (1886).

91 *See* KOLKO, *supra* note 23, at 33. CUSHMAN, *supra* note 1, at 38.

92 *See* KOLKO, *supra* note 23, at 33.

93 *See id.*

in doubt; but it made federal regulation clearly imperative, and the Interstate Commerce Act of 1887 was passed within a few months."[94]

Prior to passage of the bill, the railroads registered a complaint that they were not adequately consulted—despite their refusal to participate in the committee's investigation.[95] By then it was too late; establishment of a commission form of federal regulation seemed inevitable. First, as the committee found, individual states faced both constitutional and geographical constraints in their efforts to regulate the railroads.[96] Congress was also familiar with Britain's experiences leading to the establishment of a permanent railway commission pursuant to the Regulation of Railways Act of 1873.[97] Although there was some concern in Congress over conferring direct authority on the president to regulate what was the most significant aspect of the American economy,[98] the members of Congress were mainly concerned with bipartisan control of the commission. The limitation that not more than three of the five members of the commission could be from the same political party evidenced this concern. Cushman stated, "[i]mpartiality, or at least neutrality, was looked upon as more important than expertness."[99] A minority of members in the House also seemed prepared to accept the commission approach because they envisioned any new legislation as experimental.[100]

The railroads' support for, or at least acquiescence in, national regulation by a commission eliminated any remaining obstacle to the bill's passage.[101] Senator Charles Van Wyck of Nebraska argued that corporations sought national commissions as a lawful method of self-protection.[102] Congressman Reagan also stated that "[t]he Senate bill is . . . preferred by the railroad corporations, because under it they see greater chances for trickery and

---

94 CUSHMAN, *supra* note 1, at 38.

95 *See* CULLOM, *supra* note 85, at 319.

96 *See supra* note 89.

97 *See* 17 CONG. REC. 7292 (1886) (statement of Rep. Caldwell) (discussing the British commission). Some members of Congress believed Britain's efforts at railroad regulation had been ineffectual. *See id.* ("England has passed many hundred statutes in the abortive attempt to regulate these matters, and the greatest failure of all the thirty-three hundred has been her commission."). Cushman noted that the British Railway Commission of 1873 influenced the movement toward creation of the ICC but had "a much better American reputation than it deserved." CUSHMAN, *supra* note 1, at 512.

98 *See* RICHARD D. STONE, THE INTERSTATE COMMERCE COMMISSION AND THE RAILROAD INDUSTRY: A HISTORY OF REGULATORY POLICY 23 n.25 (1991) ("[M]embers of Congress were afraid to allow the president to directly influence railroad regulation.").

99 CUSHMAN, *supra* note 1, at 63.

100 *See* 19 CONG. REC. 8576 (1888) (statement of Rep. Crisp) (stating that some members considered the law establishing the ICC to be "largely experimental"). However, the minority of the House committee prepared to accept a commission form of regulation preferred a regulatory entity within an existing cabinet department. *See* 17 CONG. REC. 7285 (1886) (statement of Rep. O'Neill).

101 *See* KOLKO, *supra* note 23, at 3, 41 ("Indeed, the railroads, not the farmers and shippers, were the most important single advocates of federal regulation from 1877 to 1916. Even when they frequently disagreed with the details of specific legislation, they always supported the principle of federal regulation as such.").

102 *See* 17 CONG. REC. 3825 (1886) (statement of Sen. Van Wyck).

evasion; with whatever chances there may be for their controlling... the commission."[103] Kolko adds that the railroads desired regulation to stop the rate wars that had drastically driven rates down over the years and to regulate those companies who refused to enter into, or abide by, pooling agreements.[104] Even Senator Cullom, a longtime advocate of the commission approach, acknowledged: "Every one knows that the railroad companies themselves have finally become reconciled to some national legislation, because they have not been able to protect themselves, one from another."[105]

Ultimately, Congress passed legislation containing provisions from both the Cullom and Reagan bills.[106] During the House-Senate conference, Congressman Reagan was successful in retaining the central element of the House bill, namely the antipooling provision.[107] However, in doing so, he was forced to concede substantially to Senator Cullom's views on other matters.[108]

3. PLACE IN THE EXECUTIVE BRANCH

When Congress established the ICC through the Act to Regulate Commerce in 1887, it left unclear the extent of the ICC's independence.[109] The ICC's members were somewhat insulated from presidential control by the Act's "inefficiency, neglect of duty, or malfeasance in office" removal provision and staggered terms.[110] One scholar also noted that the initial appointments to the ICC came mostly from the public sector rather than the railroad industry, which may have lessened industry control.[111] However, sections 18 and 21 of the original Act to Regulate Commerce accorded the secretary of the interior control over the agency.[112] Staff hires, salaries, and expenditures of the ICC were subject to approval by its secretary, who was also responsible for furnishing the ICC with suitable offices and supplies.[113] The secretary was also to receive the commission's annual

---

103 17 CONG. REC. 7283 (1886) (statement of Rep. Reagan).

104 *See* KOLKO, *supra* note 23, at 34–35.

105 18 CONG. REC. 171 (1886) (statement of Sen. Cullom).

106 *See* KOLKO, *supra* note 23, at 44.

107 *See* CULLOM, *supra* note 85, at 321–22 (noting that Reagan yielded on nearly every provision except the antipooling provision).

108 *Id. See also* KOLKO, *supra* note 23, at 43.

109 Act to Regulate Commerce, ch. 104, §§ 11, 21, 24 Stat. 379, 383 (1887).

110 *Id.*

111 Mark F. Kightlinger, *Nihilism with a Happy Ending?: The Interstate Commerce Commission and the Emergence of the Post-Enlightenment Paradigm*, 113 PENN. ST. L. REV. 113, 135 (2008). *But see* KOLKO, *supra* note 23, at 46–49 (arguing that the original commissioners were plainly sympathetic to the railroads).

112 Act to Regulate Commerce, ch. 104, §§ 18, 21, 24 Stat. 379, 386–87. The nineteenth-century Interior Department has been called "the Department of the Great Miscellany." LEONARD D. WHITE, THE REPUBLICAN ERA: 1869–1901 175 (1958).

113 *See* Act to Regulate Commerce § 18. The office space provision was not unusual; the Act establishing the DOJ required the superintendent of the Treasury building to provide office space for the new department. Act of June 22, 1870, ch. 150, § 13, 16 Stat. 162, 164. That arrangement lasted until construction of

report and transmit it to Congress.[114] Cushman observed that placement of the ICC in the Interior Department was essentially for housekeeping purposes, "a sort of carry-over from earlier proposals and a reflection of the idea that the new agency ought not to be left in a vacuum."[115] He also added that Congress expressed little concern over this arrangement, as "whatever independence the new commission was supposed to have was not incompatible with the location of the commission in the Department of the Interior."[116]

Two years later, however, the secretary's authority over the ICC was eliminated by statute and the ICC became functionally independent of the executive branch.[117] Although the change was supported by both the commission and secretary,[118] several members of the House and Senate were opposed. Senator Teller voiced concern that removing the ICC from the Department of the Interior would bestow some independence upon it:

> I do not think the objection that supervision is an annoyance to the Secretary of the Interior or anything of that kind is sufficient. I do not think a body of this kind should make its report to Congress. I think the report should be made to some Department of the Government, and by it be transmitted to Congress.[119]

Nonetheless, the statute was enacted two days before the inauguration of President Benjamin Harrison, a Republican, by a Democratic Congress. Some commentators have argued that it was passed in part to free the ICC from presidential influence.[120] However,

---

the present Justice Department building. *See* Susan Low Bloch, *The Early Role of the Attorney General in Our Constitutional Scheme: In the Beginning There Was Pragmatism*, 1989 DUKE L.J. 561, 620 n.188. Even today, such arrangements are used. *See, e.g.*, 42 U.S.C. § 7412 (r)(6)(P) (2006) (requiring the EPA administrator to provide "such support and facilities as may be necessary for operation of the [Chemical Safety and Hazard Investigation] Board."). The original ICC initially, and briefly, occupied two rooms in a building also occupied by the Geological Survey. The commission was soon given more substantial quarters in what was then the tallest privately owned building in Washington and one of the first to have an elevator. As its need for space increased, the commission moved again in 1917, and lastly in 1934 to the building it occupied until the agency's demise. *See* FRANK N. WILNER, COMES NOW THE INTERSTATE COMMERCE PRACTITIONER 58–59 (1993).

114 *See* Act to Regulate Commerce, § 21.

115 CUSHMAN, *supra* note 1, at 62.

116 *Id.*

117 Act of Mar. 2, 1889, ch. 382, §§ 7–8, 25 Stat. 855, 861–862. Section 7 of the 1889 Act eliminated the requirement that the secretary approve salaries and expenses, and Section 8 authorized the commission to submit reports directly to Congress. *Id.*

118 *See* 19 CONG. REC. 6001 (1888) (statement of Sen. Cullom) (noting that the secretary and the commission supported the ICC's removal from the Interior Department).

119 19 CONG. REC. 6001 (1888) (statement of Sen. Teller).

120 MARVER H. BERNSTEIN, REGULATING BUSINESS BY INDEPENDENT COMMISSION 23 (1955) ("Mr. Reagan of Texas, the author of the interstate commerce bill, said that since a railroad lawyer named Ben Harrison had been elected President, he did not trust the President any more with this matter, so he invented the... independent commission." (quoting Louis Brownlow) (internal quotation marks omitted)); *see also* Paul R. Verkuil, *The Purposes and Limits of Independent Agencies*, 1988 DUKE L.J. 257, 259

the initiative to separate the ICC from the Interior Department was prompted by both the secretary of the interior and the ICC, of which Republican Thomas Cooley was chair and the most influential member. Moreover, Republican Senator Cullom—a chief architect of both the original statute and the 1889 changes—supported the change. He argued that the interior secretary's oversight was "purely formal" and subjected both the ICC and the secretary to unnecessary administrative burdens without any countervailing benefits.[121] The intent was not to make the ICC independent or vest it with authority to wield power outside the domain of the executive branch.[122]

With little discretionary power, the ICC was rather weak and ineffectual until Congress passed the Hepburn Act at the turn of the century, which empowered the ICC with rate-making authority.[123] This 1906 legislation was influenced by the progressive movement, which valued an entity removed and independent from politics. Progressives' distrust in government, along with the growing number of corporate trusts and conglomerations, prompted Congress to enact legislation that aimed to "eliminate or prevent those forms of industrial organization and corporate behavior which threatened to undermine market mechanisms.... The new regulatory regime was, in essence, market-corrective."[124] Progressives viewed the independent regulatory commission as an important conduit through which market correction was administered. In their view, the independent regulatory agency infused by expertise

---

and n.7 (explaining the argument that Congress created the independent agencies to expand its own influence while diminishing presidential influence) (citing SENATE COMM. ON GOVERNMENTAL AFFAIRS, STUDY ON FEDERAL REGULATION: REGULATORY ORGANIZATION, S. DOC. NO. 95-91, at 31 (1977)).

121 19 CONG. REC. 5150 (1888) (statement of Sen. Cullom). Although the change may have accorded with railroad objectives, it is unlikely to have been prompted by partisan considerations. Such a significant structural change could not have taken place without Senator Cullom's consent or at least acquiescence.

122 Few recent histories of the ICC discuss this structural change—one that to our modern understanding is very significant indeed. Paul R. Verkuil, however, stated that the ICC was originally an executive agency that "became 'independent' in 1889." Paul R. Verkuil, *The Status of Independent Agencies After Bowsher v. Synar*, 1986 DUKE L.J. 779, 708 n.7. Peter Strauss, however, noted that the change reflects "efforts to improve its practical workability after the lessons of experience, not the result of a new theory about the proper ordering of executive (or administrative) government; that came later." Peter L. Strauss, *The Place of Agencies in Government: Separation of Powers and the Fourth Branch*, 84 COLUM. L. REV. 573, 609 n.140 (1984).

123 Hepburn Act, ch. 3591, § 4, 34 Stat. 584, 589 (1906). For a description of the Hepburn Act and its legislative history, see Thomas W. Merrill, *Article III, Agency Adjudication, and the Origins of the Appellate Review Model of Administrative Law*, 111 COLUM. L. REV. 939, 955–59 (2011).

124 MARC ALLEN EISNER, REGULATORY POLITICS IN TRANSITION 27–28 (1993). *See also* WILLIAM E. NELSON, THE ROOTS OF AMERICAN BUREAUCRACY, 1830–1900 82 (1982) ("Reformers in the last third of the nineteenth century turned to science to accomplish their reconstructive task."). Some commentators believe that this distrust in government encompassed the judicial system as well. *See* MORTON J. HORWITZ, THE TRANSFORMATION OF AMERICAN LAW 1870–1960: THE CRISIS OF LEGAL ORTHODOXY 225 (1992) ("As the Progressive disenchantment with the competence of courts to perform social engineering tasks combined with a loss of faith in the sensitivity of judges to questions of social justice, the effort to replace courts with administrative experts became more pronounced.").

was "judged…more democratic than the alternative of bureaucratic socialism."[125] According to Marc Allen Eisner, "[i]t was envisioned as an institution capable of compensating for the shortcomings of the 'political' institutions of American government."[126] As such, it was essential for expert administrators with technical competence in the various areas of regulation to staff independent regulatory commissions. One commentator noted that progressives had "an abiding faith in regulation, expertness, and the capacity of American government to make rational decisions provided experts in the administrative agencies could remain free from partisan political considerations."[127] They "honestly believed in the almost unlimited potential of science and administration,"[128] as democracy was equated with science and regulatory agencies were "envisioned as the political arm of science."[129] For the progressives, then, reliance on experts together with independence from the political melee was thought to safeguard the commissions from partisan politics while enabling the experts to make logical decisions based on empirical data.[130]

---

125 James T. Kloppenberg, Uncertain Victory: Social Democracy and Progressivism in European and American Thought 1870–1920, 361 (1986).

126 Eisner, *supra* note 124, at 44. The use of expertise as a neutral contrast to the "political" was most advanced in municipal politics, as with the Bureau of Municipal Research in New York. *See* Kenneth Finegold, Experts and Politicians: Reform Challenges to Machine Politics in New York, Cleveland, and Chicago 22–24 (1995). Some suggest that the reform movement's focus on expertise reflects the conquest and assertion of social status by collectively self-defined experts. *See* Magali Sarfatti Larson, The Rise of Professionalism: A Sociological Analysis 138–47 (1977). *See also* Magali Sarfatti Larson, *The Production of Expertise and the Constitution of Expert Power, in* The Authority of Experts: Studies in History and Theory 28, 28 (Thomas L. Haskell ed., 1984) ("What has led theorists of different persuasions to speak of experts as a new and perhaps rising class, distinct from either capital or labor, is the autonomy that experts enjoy in advanced capitalist societies." (citation omitted)).

127 Bernstein, *supra* note 120, at 36.

128 Richard L. McCormick, The Party Period and Public Policy: American Politics from the Age of Jackson to the Progressive Era 287 (1986). *See also* Steven J. Diner, A Very Different Age: Americans of the Progressive Era 201 (1998) (asserting that "[t]he activist government envisioned by reformers relied upon scientific experts to staff new, impartial administrative agencies.").

129 Kloppenberg, *supra* note 125, at 361, 384 (positing whether independence would free "regulatory agencies[]…from private power for democratic purposes….").

130 David W. Noble, The Progressive Mind 1890–1917 37 (rev. ed. 1981) (discussing this view as "Harmony through Technological Order"). *Compare* The Issue of Federal Regulation in the Progressive Era 50 (Richard Abrams ed., 1963) (asserting that concern for resource conservation "grew out of the political implications of applied science"). Conservation was considered an issue better left for experts to address rather than politicians. *Id.* "Since resource matters were basically technical in nature, conservationists argued, technicians, rather than legislators, should deal with them….Pressure group action, logrolling in Congress, or partisan debate could not guarantee rational and scientific decisions….Conservationists envisaged…a political system guided by the ideal of efficiency and dominated by the technicians who could best determine how to achieve it." *Id.*

This "political explanation" regarding the ICC's creation, however, "is the subject of much controversy." Stephen G. Breyer, Richard B. Stewart, Cass R. Sunstein, Adrian Vermeule & Michael E. Herz, Administrative Law and Regulatory Policy 17 (7th ed. 2011). As one account noted, reasons surrounding the ICC's creation are uncertain:

> A traditional view is that the ICC was created to protect shippers (especially small shippers) from the exercise of monopoly power and rate discrimination by larger carriers. Another view sees the

In sum, contrary to common belief, the ICC was most likely not devised to be a new independent form of government located outside the tripartite system. Its resultant form arose from political negotiations responding to the need for efficient regulation of the railroad industry. In his authoritative work on independent agencies, Robert Cushman stated:

> In the thinking of those responsible for the Act, independence, if it meant anything, appears to have meant bipartisanship, as a guarantee of impartiality. Independence of executive domination seems not to have been thought of and was certainly not discussed, but independence of one-sided partisan control was a matter of great moment.[131]

Cushman also noted:

> There was virtually no discussion of the commission's relation to Congress. Congress was, of course, creating the commission and assigning its powers, but there is nothing to suggest that the legislative leaders looked upon the commission as having a relation to Congress different from that of any other administrative agency.... It was assumed that the commission would aid Congress directly by giving it expert information on railroad problems, and it was also assumed that the commission would remain under the supervision of Congress in the sense that its status and duties would be subject to legislative revision from time to time.[132]

This said, by the 1920s the ICC emerged "as the signal triumph of the Progressive reconstitution. Here, the old mode of governmental operations was most completely superseded, and the reintegration of the American state with the new industrial society most clearly consummated. The agency...acquired the responsibility for supervising all aspects of the national railway system in accordance with the most advanced precepts of

---

> commission as a response to a "market failure" that produced "destructive competition" and wasteful and duplicative services. On this view, the commission was established not merely to shift income from railroads to shippers, but to advance a more general public interest in an efficient transportation system through planning by expert administrators. This view is reflected in the notion that the ICC was to be "independent" of politics and be composed of commissioners and staff experts in railroading. A revisionist view is that the commission was created and administered to advance the interests of the railroads by protecting them against the rigors of competition. Others have asserted that the ICC was "captured" not by the railroads but by shippers, and that shortsighted and inept regulation fatally weakened the railroads by destroying innovation and denying them needed revenues.

Id. at 17–18.

131 *See* CUSHMAN, *supra* note 1, at 61. This notion, reflected in a cap on the number of members from one political party on most boards and commissions, has endured.

132 *Id.* at 60.

scientific management.... It was all the promises of the new American state rolled into the expansion of national administrative capacities."[133]

In the 1930s, Isaiah L. Sharfman, describing the agency form as manifested in the ICC, noted that "[t]he Commission is no more a part of the national administration—in the sense of being an instrument for furthering the particular political ends of the party in power—than is the Supreme Court, and executive influence is as manifestly out of place in the one case as it would be in the other."[134] An apocryphal yet paradigmatic story is told by Robert Calhoun, who states that

> Warren Harding was supposed to have come to the Commission at a conference while they were discussing a rate case. He was told to leave, that it was improper for the President of the United States to try to influence the Commission, and he hadn't been invited: "You'd better leave." And Herbert Hoover did the same thing—was told the same thing. I mean, he was meddling.[135]

It was not until many years after the establishment of the ICC that the notion of independence developed.[136] However, throughout the Progressive Era and the New Deal, a multitude of new agencies were established using the ICC as their prototype. These include the Federal Reserve Board, 1913; FTC, 1914; Federal Radio Commission, 1927; Federal Power Commission (FPC), 1930; SEC, 1934; Federal Communications Commission (FCC), 1934; National Labor Relations Board (NLRB), 1935; Bituminous Coal Commission, 1935; Federal Maritime Commission, 1936; and the now defunct Civil Aeronautics Board, 1938. As the independent agency form began to flourish, its constitutionality became an issue of considerable debate, and disputes over the issue of separation of powers have continued since that time.

The ICC itself remained a freestanding agency from 1889 until its abolition on December 31, 1995.[137] Coming full circle, Congress returned the ICC's successor agency—the Surface Transportation Board (STB)—to a cabinet department, this time the Department of Transportation (DOT).[138] The new board describes itself as a "bipartisan, decisionally independent, adjudicatory body, organizationally housed within the Department of Transportation."[139]

---

133 Daniel P. Carpenter, The Forging of Bureaucratic Autonomy: Regulations, Networks, and Policy Innovation in Executive Agencies, 1862–1928 8 (Princeton 2001).

134 Sharfman, *supra* note 75, pt. 2, at 454.

135 Robert L. Calhoun, The Interstate Commerce Commission, 1912–1937, 16 Trans. L. Rev. 59, 66 (1987–88). Whether true or not, this anecdote reflects the commission's self-image at the time.

136 Eisner, *supra* note 124, at 48.

137 *See Stroke of Clinton's Pen Fells ICC, Oldest Regulatory Agency*, L.A. Times, Dec. 31, 1995, at A13; David S. Broder, *Rebels Without a Pause,* Wash. Post Mag., Dec. 31, 1995, at 13.

138 *See* Interstate Commerce Commission Termination Act of 1995, Pub. L. No. 104-88, 109 Stat. 803 (1995).

139 Surface Transp. Bd., 1996/1997 Annual Report 1 (1998).

B. The Federal Trade Commission

As the number of commissions grew, indicia of independence were defined by replication. Apolitical expertise, which provided the justification for independence, was embodied in the establishment of the FTC. The FTC emerged as the need for an antitrust commission became evident. The American industrial sectors and transactional commerce grew throughout the late 1800s and early 1900s, which resulted in a spate of mergers and consolidations by big businesses of smaller and similar entities.[140] Despite passage of early legislation intended to prohibit monopolies, mergers continued unabated.[141] With little or no competitive market in many larger industries, prices were often fixed or inflated by the monopolies that controlled them, which caused public frustration.[142] In an attempt to fix the growing problem, Congress passed the Sherman Antitrust Act, which bans "[e]very contract, combination in the form of trust or otherwise, or conspiracy, in restraint of trade or commerce among the several States, or with foreign nations."[143] However, problems implementing and enforcing the Act were immediately apparent due to its ambiguous and possibly overexpansive language.

In *Standard Oil Co. of New Jersey v. United States,* the Supreme Court concluded that "restraint of trade" determinations were to be made by a judge, based on a fact-specific inquiry, and only when a contract unreasonably burdened commerce.[144] This left courts to decide cases on an "ad hoc" basis—judges had no "rational, consistent, and comprehensive doctrine" on which to make decisions.[145] This led to public concern that judges could decide cases based on their experiences rather than the

---

140 *See* W. Stull Holt, The Federal Trade Commission: Its History, Activities and Organization 2 (1922).

141 In one four-year period during the later nineteenth century more than a thousand firms disappeared as a result of mergers. Marc Winerman, *The Origins of the FTC: Concentration, Cooperation, Control, and Competition*, 71 Antitrust L.J. 1, 6 (2003).

142 *See* Charles S. Devas, *Monopolies and Fair Dealing*, 12 Int'l J. Ethics 59, 59–68 (1901) (expressing disappointment and frustration of Americans endeavoring to individually maintain businesses as the "sanctuary of free trade has been submerged; and free competition ... is visibly failing"). Noting that the government is ill-suited to administer and regulate monopolies, as "[l]aw courts and legislatures have been corrupted; stock exchanges manipulated; the working classes confronted with arbitrary dominion; inventors compelled to sell their patents to the monopolist at his own price; [and] individuals who incur his enmity exposed to ruin by discrimination in prices," Devas proposed that it was up to "modern economists, to establish law and order ... in the vast regions that their predecessors had abandoned to anarchy." *Id.* at 61–64.

143 Sherman Antitrust Act, 15 U.S.C. § 1 (2006).

144 221 U.S. 1, 65 (1911).

145 Gary R. Roberts, *The Evolving Confusion of Professional Sports Antitrust, the Rule of Reason, and the Doctrine of Ancillary Restraints*, 61 S. Cal. L. Rev. 943, 1000 (1988). *See* Gilbert H. Montague, *Antitrust Laws and the Federal Trade Commission, 1914–1927*, 27 Colum. L. Rev. 650, 652 (1927).

tenets of business and industry.[146] Thus, the need grew for a specialized agency that would utilize experts capable of explicating and adjudicating fact-specific inquiries in their respective fields.

Prior to creation of the FTC, the Senate Committee on Interstate Commerce enumerated the tasks it believed an antitrust commission would conduct.[147] Cushman explained that "[t]he duties that such a commission would perform were outlined by the committee: first, extensive activities in the field of investigation; second, the administration of some system of licensing corporations engaged in interstate commerce; and third, the rendering of expert aid to the courts and to the Department of Justice in the dissolution of trusts and other unlawful combinations."[148] These duties were adopted and expanded by the Federal Trade Commission Act. Proponents believed that the commission should be "quasi-judicial" in character and focused on this concept as the basis for creating the new independent agency.[149] Senator Francis Newlands, a strong supporter of the independent agency concept, stated, "we want a body of administrative law built up. This can not [sic] be well done by the single occupant of an office.... Such work must be done by a board or commission of dignity, permanence, and ability, independent of executive authority."[150] It was also believed that the commission needed independence in order to correct "the partisan and pressure-controlled administration of the antitrust laws by the Department of Justice."[151]

When the FTC was finally created in 1914, it was tasked with determining and preventing "unfair methods of competition."[152] The FTC, modeled after the ICC for "its independent power and authority,"[153] also had authority to issue cease-and-desist orders against offenders—duties that afforded the new agency far more power than the 1887 ICC.[154] To achieve effective business regulation, the trade commission was to be completely removed from the political fray. Senator Morgan stressed this point repeatedly, stating that "[w]hatever we do in regulating business should be removed as far as possible from political influence."[155]

---

146 *See* Montague, *supra* note 145, at 652.

147 *See* Cushman, *supra* note 1, at 183.

148 *Id.*

149 *See id.* at 190–91.

150 51 Cong. Rec. 11,092 (1914) (statement of Sen. Newlands).

151 Cushman, *supra* note 1, at 189.

152 Federal Trade Commission Act, ch. 311, § 5, 38 Stat. 717, 719 (1914) (codified as amended at 15 U.S.C. § 41-58 (2006)). The phrase "unfair methods of competition" proved ambiguous, and the commission's authority to define it was challenged repeatedly in the courts. The enabling statute allowed the courts to fetter the commission for several years. *See* Thomas C. Blaisdell, Jr., The Federal Trade Commission: An Experiment in the Control of Business 17–36 (1932).

153 *See* Cushman, *supra* note 1, at 189 (citing 51 Cong. Rec. 8842 (1914) (statement of Rep. Covington)).

154 Federal Trade Commission Act § 5.

155 Cushman, *supra* note 1, at 190 (quoting 51 Cong. Rec. 8857 (1914) (statement of Sen. Morgan)).

The commission's independence also depended on securing "a body of experts" capable of resolving problems of a highly complicated and technical nature.[156] Congressional supporters believed that the FTC, with its independent qualities of expertise and nonpartisanship, would instill public confidence in its work.[157] Senator Newlands, for instance, foresaw a focused agency of expertise, whose suggestions and recommendations would be acceptable both politically and by the private sector. He recommended that the commission be composed of "very high-class men, very able men," skilled in their fields, to enable effective oversight.[158] This goal is reflected in the original Federal Trade Commission Act, which included unambiguous provisions providing specific and compensated roles for "attorneys, special experts, [and] examiners... as it may from time to time find necessary for the proper performance of its duties."[159]

A new type of administrative expert emerged to perform such duties—the scientific expert. As noted above, scientific analysis was a cornerstone of progressive ideology, and the scientific expert was seen as one removed from partisan politics. Commentators of the time described the scientific expert as the man who "knows how and why."[160] New Deal

---

[156] *Id.* at 191.

[157] *Id.* at 192 ("This confidence, particularly upon the part of the business world, was felt to be of vital importance. Sound policy with respect to business regulation could hardly emerge in an atmosphere of suspicion and distrust.").

[158] 51 CONG. REC. 11,528, 11,596 (1914) (statement of Sen. Newlands). On another occasion Newlands noted that the Bureau of Corporations, an agency made up of experts, should be used as a precedential mechanism for employing experts as the bureau "has done much good work of investigation, and which has trained a band of experts whose experience and efficiency should, of course, be availed of." 51 CONG. REC. 11,081, 11,082 (1914) (statement of Sen. Newlands).

[159] Federal Trade Commission Act, ch. 311, § 2, 38 Stat. 717, 718 (1914) (codified as amended at 15 U.S.C. § 41-58 (2006)). In practice, however, only a limited number of experts were employed during the early years of the commission, and those who were employed were compensated at a level considerably below that of FTC attorneys. FED. TRADE COMM'N, ANNUAL REPORT OF THE FEDERAL TRADE COMMISSION (1916), ***available at*** www.ftc.gov/os/annualreports/ar1916.pdf.

[160] *See* SAMUEL HABER, EFFICIENCY AND UPLIFT: SCIENTIFIC MANAGEMENT IN THE PROGRESSIVE ERA 1890–1920 105 (1964) (internal quotation marks and citation omitted) (emphasis omitted). Haber claims that the "scientific expert became the prototype of all administrators." *Id.* at 104. This notion was pioneered by such men as Frank J. Goodnow, who wrote several influential books around the turn of the century espousing the importance of separating politics from administration.

> The fact is, then, that there is a large part of administration which is unconnected with politics, which should therefore be relieved very largely, if not altogether, from the control of political bodies. It is unconnected with politics because it embraces fields of semi-scientific, *quasi*-judicial and *quasi*-business or commercial activity—work which has little if any influence on the expression of the true state will. For the most advantageous discharge of this branch function of administration there should be organized a force of governmental agents absolutely free from the influence of politics. Such a force should be free from the influence of politics because of the fact that their mission is the exercise of foresight and discretion, the pursuit of truth, the gathering of information, the maintenance of a strictly impartial attitude toward the individuals with whom they have dealings, and the provision of the most efficient possible administrative organization.

FRANK J. GOODNOW, POLITICS AND ADMINISTRATION 85 (1900). *See also* FRANK GOODNOW, THE PRINCIPLES OF THE ADMINISTRATIVE LAW OF THE UNITED STATES 33–42 (1905).

theorist James M. Landis has asserted that "[w]ith the rise of regulation, the need for expertness became dominant."[161] Thus, there began an increased focus on credentials.[162]

Progressives heralded the skills of efficiency experts who could apply scientific evaluation and analysis to maximize utility and reduce waste and inconsistency that plagued the government and administrative state.[163] Haber has observed that progressives aimed to create "an honored and important profession of administrators having special skills and a special ethic."[164] Influential scholars and politicians, such as Louis D. Brandeis[165] and Woodrow Wilson,[166] also advanced the cause of scientific management. Curiously,

---

161 JAMES M. LANDIS, THE ADMINISTRATIVE PROCESS 23 (1938). Landis articulated the advantages to be gained by reliance on a specialized group with the skill, experience, and time to dedicate to the resolution of regulatory issues. *Id.* at 23–26. For a background on *The Administrative Process*, see DONALD A. RITCHIE, JAMES M. LANDIS: DEAN OF THE REGULATORS 84–87 (1980).

162 *See* BURTON J. BLEDSTEIN, THE CULTURE OF PROFESSIONALISM: THE MIDDLE CLASS AND THE DEVELOPMENT OF HIGHER EDUCATION IN AMERICA 38, 126–28 (1976) (discussing the expanded use of titles such as "doctor" or "engineer," and the increased emphasis on higher education). Gerald Frug contends that experts fulfill a critical role in American bureaucracy, and that within this structure the role of the executive is imperative. *See* Gerald E. Frug, *The Ideology of Bureaucracy in American Law*, 97 HARV. L. REV. 1277, 1318–26 (1984). The executive's "function is 'leadership,' and his qualifications derive from his expert knowledge of how to exercise leadership." *Id.* at 1319 (citation omitted).

163 *See* HABER, *supra* note 160, at 107–08 (describing Frederick W. Taylor's proposal in the early 1900s to place efficiency experts in high government posts to direct the introduction of efficiency measures throughout government departments). This concept was actually adopted at one point for the navy yards and army arsenals.

164 *Id.* at 103.

165 *See* MCCRAW, *supra* note 69, at 92 (noting Brandeis's support for "scientific management" techniques to improve efficiency). Brandeis used scientific management as a tool with which to club monopolies. In 1910, he represented shippers' interests before the ICC in the Advance Rate Case. The railroads sought an across-the-board rate increase for freight hauls, which was vehemently opposed by the shipping industry. Brandeis successfully argued that the solution for the railroad companies was efficiency rather than a rate increase. The rate increase was denied. As one commentator concluded, "[t]he Brandeis view of scientific management allowed a politically insecure and institutionally limited ICC to take refuge in a strong disciplinary posture in administrative regulation." STEPHEN SKOWRONEK, BUILDING A NEW AMERICAN STATE: THE EXPANSION OF NATIONAL ADMINISTRATIVE CAPACITIES, 1877–1920 269–70 (1982).

166 *See* Woodrow Wilson, *Democracy and Efficiency*, 87 ATLANTIC MONTHLY 289, 299 (1901) (expressing support for "a trained and thoroughly organized administrative service instead of administration by men privately nominated and blindly elected"). As an academic, Wilson had written approvingly of the independent expert agency. *See* Woodrow Wilson, *The Study of Administration*, 2 POL. SCI. Q. 197, 217 (1887) (explaining the relationship between public opinion and administration, and expressing the ideal of "a civil service cultured and self-sufficient enough to act with sense and vigor," but one "intimately connected with the popular thought"); *see also* Marshall J. Breger, *Thoughts on Accountability and the Administrative Process*, 39 ADMIN L. REV. 399, 399–402 (1987) (discussing Wilson's views on the separation of politics from administration). It should be noted, however, that when Wilson campaigned for the presidency, he adopted a more skeptical view of expertise. During a Labor Day campaign speech in New York, he exhorted:

> What I fear, therefore, is a government of experts. God forbid that in a democratic country we should resign the task and give the government over to experts. What are we for if we are to be [scientifically] taken care of by a small number of gentlemen who are the only men who understand the job? Because if we don't understand the job, then we are not a free people. We ought to resign our free institutions and go to school to... find out what it is we are about.

however, neither the Federal Trade Commission Act nor the ICC statute that served as its model had any express statutory requirements for professional expertise.[167]

C. The Federal Power Commission

With the creation of the FPC in 1920 came a noteworthy departure from the ICC model. Concerns over the nation's power supply following World War I coupled with fragmented federal responsibility for hydroelectric power led Congress to examine the need for comprehensive control of hydroelectric power generation.[168] This led to the Federal Water Power Act of 1920.[169] As the Supreme Court observed:

> The central purpose of the Federal Water Power Act was to provide for the comprehensive control over those uses of the Nation's water resources in which the Federal Government had a legitimate interest; these uses included navigation, irrigation, flood control, and, very prominently, hydroelectric power—uses which, while unregulated, might well be contradictory rather than harmonious.[170]

A CROSSROADS OF FREEDOM: THE 1912 CAMPAIGN SPEECHES OF WOODROW WILSON 83 (John Wells Davidson ed., 1956).

167 *See* Federal Trade Commission Act, ch. 311, § 5, 38 Stat. 717, 719 (1914) (codified as amended at 15 U.S.C. § 41-58 (2006)); Act to Regulate Commerce, ch. 104, §§ 11, 21, 24 Stat. 379, 383 (1887).

168 *See* Beth C. Bryant, Comment, *FERC's Dam Decommissioning Authority Under the Federal Power Act*, 74 WASH. L. REV. 95, 101 (1999) (indicating that early regulatory efforts by the federal government involved a "piecemeal, restrictive approach"); Jason Pinney, Note, *The Federal Energy Regulatory Commission and Environmental Justice: Do the National Environmental Policy Act and the Clean Air Act Offer a Better Way?*, 30 B.C. ENVTL. AFF. L. REV. 353, 365 (2003) (noting that creation of the original FPC resulted, in part, from "fear that the United States' involvement in World War I had depleted coal and oil reserves to dangerously low levels, and that waterpower provided an effective alternative energy source").

169 Federal Water Power Act of 1920, Pub. L. No. 66-280, 41 Stat. 1063.

170 Fed. Power Comm'n v. Union Electric Co., 381 U.S. 90, 98 (1965) (footnote omitted).

> The Federal Water Power Act...was the result of efforts to bring about a comprehensive water power development scheme to replace the piecemeal, restrictive approach of previously enacted federal laws. It was the culmination of a lengthy battle between conservationists, led by President Theodore Roosevelt and Gifford Pinchot, and a coalition of private hydropower developers and states' rights advocates. Both sides sought to bring about private development of waterpower, but on vastly different terms. Conservationists wanted strong federal control over waterpower development to protect the public interest, while developers sought to minimize federal control. Both groups brought tremendous pressure to bear on Congress, and the struggle for water power legislation lasted for fifteen years.

Bryant, *supra* note 168, at 100–01 (footnotes omitted). It might be noted that, in the same year that Congress enacted the Federal Water Power Act, the Transportation Act of 1920 amended the original Interstate Commerce Act to give the ICC the job of rationalizing the nation's rail network along with its historic responsibility for preventing unjust or discriminatory pricing. Transportation Act of 1920, Pub. L. No. 66-152, 41 Stat. 456.

To supervise the oversight of water power development, Congress chose the multimember commission model and created the FPC.[171]

The original FPC deviated from the ICC model in certain important respects concerning independence. First, the commission was composed of the secretaries of war, interior, and agriculture, who each had some responsibility over the waterways. The original FPC had only a single permanent employee, an executive director, and was staffed by personnel on loan from other agencies. This employment scheme was logical, given the focus of the Federal Water Power Act of 1920 on comprehensive development, rather than regulation, of hydroelectric power. Indeed, one student commentator has noted that the 1920 FPC "was not meant to regulate private sector power, but instead to coordinate federal hydroelectric projects."[172] Second, due to cabinet secretary involvement, security of tenure as FPC members was a nonissue.

At the urging of the three cabinet secretaries, whose day-to-day workloads prevented their serious attention to the FPC, Congress reorganized the FPC in 1930 as a more traditional multimember agency with five members selected solely to serve the commission.[173] Despite this change, Congress chose not to include the prototypic "for cause" removal provision that had been included in the ICC statute. According to scholars, the removal provision clause was deleted from the original bill because the bill's sponsor believed that the Supreme Court had in the Myers case in 1928 established the president's plenary removal power over regulatory commissioners.[174]

---

171 Federal Water Power Act of 1920 § 1. Because it focused on water power development, the 1920 Act did not give the FPC power to regulate electric utility rates. However, states also lacked power to regulate such rates. In Public Utilities Commission of Rhode Island v. Attleboro Steam & Electric Co., 273 U.S. 83 (1927), the Supreme Court held that state authority over a rate increase involving interstate electric transmission imposed a burden on interstate commerce. Because both the FPC and states lacked authority, the so-called Attleboro Gap emerged. *See* Jim Rossi, *The Electric Deregulation Fiasco: Looking to Regulatory Federalism to Promote a Balance Between Markets and the Provision of Public Goods*, 100 MICH. L. REV. 1768, 1782 (2002). Congress filled the gap with the Federal Power Act of 1935, which gave the FPC the power to regulate electric utility companies engaged in interstate commerce. Federal Power Act of 1935, ch. 687, 49 Stat. 838, 839 (codified at 16 U.S.C. § 791a (2006)). Congress's response to the *Attleboro* decision parallels its response to railroad regulation. *See supra* notes 90–94 and accompanying text.

172 Michael Coyn Mateer, Casenote, *When the Lights Go Out: The Impact of House Bill 6 on Regional Transmission Organizations and the Reliability of the Power Grid*, 12 GEO. MASON L. REV. 775, 780 (2004) (footnote omitted).

173 Act to Reorganize the Federal Power Commission, Pub. L. No. 71-412, 46 Stat. 797 (1930). The Supreme Court indicated that the 1930 Act reorganized the commission "so as to improve its administrative capacity." *See* First Iowa Hydro-Electric Coop. v. Fed. Power Comm'n, 328 U.S. 152, 172 n.17 (1946).

174 Christopher S. Yoo, Steven G. Calabresi & Laurence D. Nee, *The Unitary Executive During the Third Half-Century*, 1889–1945, 80 NOTRE DAME L. REV. 1, 73 (2004). *See* Myers v. United States, 272 U.S. 52 (1928) (holding executive officers must be subject to removal by the president). *See also* Free Enter. Fund & Beckstead and Watts, LLP v. Pub. Co. Accounting Oversight Bd., 130 S. Ct. 3138, 3183 (S. Ct. 2010) (Breyer, J., dissenting) (noting that the FPC was one of at least three agencies created between the *Myers* and *Humphrey's Executor* decisions when Congress may have believed it would be unconstitutional to include a "for cause removal" provision).

Congressional attitudes shifted in the wake of the Supreme Court's 1935 *Humphrey's Executor* decision, in which the Court held that Congress could place restrictions on the president's power to remove members of multimember regulatory agencies who exercise responsibilities "as a legislative or as a judicial aid."[175] Although Congress did not immediately amend the statutory provisions governing the FPC, its members subsequently clarified the FPC's purpose. Senator Burton Wheeler, chairman of the Senate Committee on Interstate Commerce, explained that Congress had deliberately "made the [Federal Power] Commission an independent agency, not a part of any executive department. Thus Congress eliminated outside executive control."[176] Similarly, Chairman Clarence Lea of the House Committee on Interstate and Foreign Commerce stated that in administering its statutory responsibilities, the FPC "is acting merely as an arm of the Congress in performing duties of a detailed and specialized character which the Congress, busy with many public affairs, could not hope to cope with directly."[177] In 1977, when Congress replaced the FPC with the FERC, it engrained FERC's independent status into the statute itself. The Department of Energy Organization Act of 1977 describes FERC as "an independent regulatory commission" within the Department of Energy (DOE), and explicitly replicated the 1887 ICC statutory provision that members may only be removed from office for "inefficiency, neglect of duty, or malfeasance in office."[178]

D. The National Labor Relations Board

During the early to mid-twentieth century, Congress reverted to the ICC model as a template for a multitude of new independent regulatory commissions, including the NLRB.[179] By the close of the Progressive Era, the association between expertness and independence had strengthened, and many members of Congress favored industry experts as key decision-makers within independent agencies.

The NLRB has roots in the National Industrial Recovery Act (NIRA), a key part of President Franklin D. Roosevelt's New Deal.[180] In order to execute NIRA reforms related

175 Humphrey's Ex'r v. United States, 295 U.S. 602, 628 (1935).

176 Burton K. Wheeler, *The Federal Power Commission as an Agency of Congress*, 14 Geo. Wash. L. Rev. 1, 4 (1945).

177 Clarence F. Lea, *The Federal Power Commission as an Agency of Congress*, 14 Geo. Wash. L. Rev. 5, 7 (1945).

178 Department of Energy Organization Act, Pub. L. No. 95-91, 91 Stat. 565, 582 (1977). The House-Senate Conference Committee expressly noted its adoption of the "independent regulatory commission" language. *See* H.R. Rep. No. 95-539 (1977) (Conf. Rep.), *reprinted in* 1977 U.S.C.C.A.N. 925, 942.

179 Cushman, *supra* note 1, at 188 ("A controlling force moving legislative leaders to create the independent Federal Trade Commission was the model of the Interstate Commerce Commission.").

180 National Industrial Recovery Act, Pub. L. No. 73-90, 48 Stat. 195 (1933). The NLRB, like the ICC, also has some roots in the regulation of railroads. The Railway Labor Act governs labor disputes in the railway

to labor, Executive Orders established the National Labor Board (NLB) in 1933.[181] The NLB was initially composed of five representatives of labor and five representatives of industry, "all very well known in their respective fields," who received no compensation for their service.[182] The industry representatives included the presidents of General Electric, Standard Oil, and the chemical manufacturing company E. L. du Point de Nemours. The labor representatives included mainly American Federation of Labor officials. Senator Robert Wagner, who later drafted the National Labor Relations Act, served as the NLB's impartial chairman.[183] The NLB was designed to mediate industrial disputes related to union representation elections and NIRA violations.[184] It was also intended to improve employer compliance with Section 7(a) of NIRA, which provided that employees had "the right to organize and bargain collectively through representatives of their own choosing."[185] However, the NLB lacked any real power to enforce Section 7(a), and the Supreme Court eventually declared NIRA unconstitutional.[186]

Following the demise of the NLB, Congress created the first NLRB in 1934 by joint resolution.[187] The NLRB enjoyed more independence than the NLB; it was empowered to exercise jurisdiction in an 7(a) dispute and make unreviewable findings of fact.[188] Further, whereas the NLB members had been voluntary, part-time, partisan representatives, the first (sometimes called the "old") NLRB was composed of three paid, full-time, and impartial presidential appointees further removed from the political and corporate fray.[189] President Roosevelt appointed the initial three members: Lloyd Garrison, dean of the University of Wisconsin Law School; Harry Millis, a labor economist from the University of Chicago; and Edwin S. Smith, a former labor and industries commissioner for the state of Massachusetts.[190] However, like the NLB, the first NLRB lacked power to enforce its orders.[191]

---

industry. Arbitration and mediation of these disputes are overseen by the Railway Labor Board. Legislative history related to the NLRB reveals congressional desire to model the new labor board after the Railway Labor Board, which was viewed as a successful model for that industry. *See* 78 CONG. REC. 3443 (Mar. 1, 1934) (statement of Sen. Wagner), *in* NAT'L LABOR RELATIONS BD., LEGISLATIVE HISTORY OF THE NATIONAL LABOR RELATIONS ACT 1935, 17 (vol. 1 1985).

181 Exec. Order No. 6763 (1934). See, Joan Flynn, *A Quiet Revolution at the Labor Board: The Transformation of the NLRB, 1935–2000*, 61 OHIO ST. L.J. 1361 (2000).

182 *To Create a National Labor Relations Board: Hearings Before the S. Comm. on Educ. and Labor*, 73d Cong. 12–13 (1934) (statement of Sen. Wagner) (explaining that the NLB was a "body of citizens appointed by the President, really not holding any public office at all"... tak[ing] no oath nor... receiv[ing] compensation").

183 *Id.* (statement of Sen. Wagner).

184 NAT'L LABOR RELATIONS BD., NLB AND "THE OLD NLRB," www.nlrb.gov/who-we-are/our-history/nlb-and-old-nlrb (last visited May 18, 2014). During its existence the NLB settled over one thousand strikes and eighteen hundred other labor disputes. *Id.*

185 National Industrial Recovery Act, Pub. L. No. 73-90, § 7(a), 48 Stat. 195, 198 (1933).

186 A. L. A. Schechter Poultry Corp. v. United States, 295 U.S. 495 (1935).

187 H.R.J. Res. 375, 74th Cong. (1934).

188 *See id.*

189 *See* NAT'L LABOR RELATIONS BD., *supra* note 184.

190 *Id.*

191 *Id.*

Motivated to fix the failures of the NLB and the first NLRB, Senator Wagner introduced the National Labor Relations Act, which was signed into law on July 5, 1935.[192] Commonly called the Wagner Act, it provided for a new NLRB with a permanent board empowered to enforce its investigative responsibilities rather than merely mediate labor disputes.[193] The Act authorized the new NLRB to issue "cease and desist [orders] from such unfair labor practice, and to take such affirmative action, including reinstatement of employees with or without back pay, as will effectuate the policies of this Act."[194] A steel producer challenged the Act's constitutionality, but the 1937 Supreme Court found that "collective bargaining is often an essential condition of industrial peace" and upheld the National Labor Relations Act under the commerce clause.[195]

The National Labor Relations Act authorizes the president to appoint board members, but the extent of formalized executive influence over NLRB members ends there.[196] Congress included an explicit "for cause" removal provision in the new statute. As Justice Breyer explained:

> [D]uring the 9-year period *after* this Court decided *Myers,* and thereby cast serious doubt on the constitutionality of all "for cause" removal provisions, but *before* it decided *Humphrey's Executor,* which removed any doubt in respect to the constitutionality of making commissioners of independent agencies removable only for cause.... Congress created at least three major federal agencies without making *any* of their officers removable for cause.... [O]nly *one month* after *Humphrey's Executor* was decided, Congress returned to its pre-*Myers* practice of including such provisions in statutes creating independent commissions.[197]

As revealed by the Act's legislative history, the president's power over the composition of the NLRB was a matter of debate. Senator Robert La Follette, a member of the Senate Committee on Education and Labor, pushed to extend NLRB terms for longer than five years to keep the board "independent of immediate reversal of political fortune."[198]

---

192 National Labor Relations Act, Pub. L. No. 74-198, 49 Stat. 449 (1935).

193 *Id.* § 3, 49 Stat. at 451.

194 *Id.* § 10(c), 49 Stat. at 454.

195 NLRB v. Jones & Laughlin Steel Corp., 301 U.S. 1, 37, 42 (1937) ("Although activities may be intrastate in character when separately considered, if they have such a close and substantial relation to interstate commerce that their control is essential or appropriate to protect that commerce from burdens and obstructions, Congress cannot be denied the power to exercise that control.").

196 Precision Castings Co. v. Boland, 13 F. Supp. 877, 884 (W.D.N.Y. 1936) ("Like the Federal Trade Commission, the National Labor Relations Board is an independent agency largely free from executive control except in the matter of appointment.").

197 Free Enter. Fund v. Pub. Co. Accounting Oversight Bd., 130 S. Ct. 3138, 3183 (2010) (Breyer, J., dissenting) (citations omitted) (noting that the three agencies were the SEC, FCC, and FPC). The NLRB was the agency that received "for cause" protection a month after *Humphrey's Executor.*

198 *National Labor Relations Board: Hearings Before the S. Comm. on Educ. and Labor,* 74th Cong. 64 (1935) (statement of Sen. La Follette), *in* Nat'l Labor Relations Bd., *supra* note 180, at 1440–41.

Other committee members suggested that presidential appointments be based on recommendations made by a "fair nominating commission of... 20 men, representatives of all interests in the country."[199]

Although some members of the Senate Committee on Education and Labor favored a board composed only of representatives of industry and labor, others preferred impartial members separated from corporate pressures, who did not solely represent the industries.[200] Senator J. Hamilton Lewis, for instance, argued that even if the board included disinterested members, "the responsibility of these decisions should primarily be placed upon the representatives of industry and representatives of labor."[201] Senator Green, however, argued that the board should be headed by an impartial chairman to balance the competing interests of industry and labor and to "create a better state of mind among the working people and the employers of the Nation."[202] The committee also debated the length of time each board member should serve. Senator Perkins, then secretary of the committee, argued that lengthy terms would "give the board continuity,... disinterestedness, and... the services of persons who gradually acquire from a long period of service a certain expertness in those particular problems."[203] Despite such contention over the specific makeup of the board, committee members realized that experts in labor and industry were necessary to "keep the board in touch with current activities and current thought in the industrial field on both sides, and to keep it from being a purely remote judicial tribunal that [had] no real and vivid relationship to the industrial needs of the moment."[204]

The committee eventually agreed to create a three-member board, although the number was later increased to five.[205] The members were not expected to represent industry or labor, as the board "was established with the understanding that its members would be nonpartisan and neutral."[206] The board remained primarily neutral for eighteen years, with members hailing from academia or government.[207] In 1952, however, President

199 *Id.* at 534–35.

200 *See To Create a National Labor Relations Board: Hearings Before the S. Comm. on Educ. and Labor*, 73d Cong. 111, 155–56 (1934).

201 *Id.* at 155–56 (statement of Sen. Lewis).

202 *Id.* at 111 (statement of Sen. Green).

203 *Id.* at 23 (statement of Sen. Perkins).

204 *Id.* (statement of Sen. Perkins).

205 National Labor Relations Act of 1935, Pub. L. No. 74-198, 49 Stat. 449 (codified as amended at 29 U.S.C. § 151); Labor Management Relations (Taft-Hartley) Act, ch. 120 § 3(a), 61 Stat. 136, 139 (1947) (codified as amended at 29 U.S.C. § 153 (2006)). *See also* James J. Brudney, *Isolated and Politicized: The NLRB's Uncertain Future*, 26 Comp. Lab. L. & Pol'y J. 221, 243 (2005) (explaining that Congress modified the board's structure in 1947, when it increased the number of members). Brudney explains that Congress intended the five-member board to remain "nonpartisan and impartial." *Id.* at 244.

206 *Id.* at 243.

207 Ronald Turner, *Ideological Voting on the National Labor Relations Board*, 8 U. Pa. J. Lab. & Emp. L. 707, 716 (2006).

Dwight Eisenhower—the first Republican elected since the National Labor Relations Act's enactment—appointed management-oriented members to the board.[208] Although later Democratic presidents continued to appoint neutral members, the board has consisted largely of management or union-side members since President Richard Nixon appointed members in 1970.[209] Charles J. Morris argued that this "flawed appointment process" has made the board, as well as the National Labor Relations Act, less effective.[210]

Due to such appointments, the NLRB in recent years has been considered the most partisan independent agency.[211] As Joan Flynn noted, partisan appointments are "near-lethal to the prospects that a Board member will vote for any rule or policy that would materially disadvantage his or her side of origin."[212] Thus, several regulations have been voted in by one board and quickly voted out by another. In its 1962 *Hollywood Ceramics Co.* decision, the NLRB held that an election would be set aside when there had been a material misrepresentation of fact prior to the election.[213] Following criticism on several grounds—including free speech, delays, and increased litigation—a later board abandoned this standard in 1977.[214] Rather, the board held in *Shopping Kart Food Market, Inc.* that elections would be set aside for coercive behavior only, which required less board intervention.[215] The following year, the NLRB reinvoked the *Hollywood Ceramics* approach in *General Knit.*[216] It explained that *Shopping Kart* prevented the board from ensuring fairness in elections.[217] Then, in 1982, the board returned to the "sound rule" expressed in *Shopping Kart* in its *Midland National Life Insurance Co.*

---

208 *Id.* (noting that Eisenhower appointee Guy Farmer was a former management attorney, and appointee Albert Beeson had worked as a director for the industrial sector).

209 *Id. See also* Charles J. Morris, *How the National Labor Relations Act Was Stolen and How it Can Be Recovered: Taft-Hartley Revisionism and the National Labor Relation Board's Appointment Process*, 33 BERKELEY J. EMP. & LAB. L. 1, 6 (2012) (explaining that "every Republican administration from Dwight D. Eisenhower to George W. Bush" has appointed board members opposed to the Act's policy).

210 *Id.* at 7. Morris explains that "just as the Equal Employment Opportunities Commission was never intended to be balanced between pro-employment-discrimination and anti-employment-discrimination" the "NLRA was never intended to be an agency between pro-collective-bargaining adherents and anti-collective-bargaining... adherents." *Id.* at 9. Rather, he argues that NLRB appointees should enforce the Act's central purpose—protecting unionization rights of workers. *Id.*

211 Brudney, *supra* note 205, at 254.

212 *See* Flynn, *supra* note 181, at 1401.

213 Hollywood Ceramics Co., 140 N.L.R.B. 221 (1962), *overruled by* Midland Nat'l Life Ins. Co., 263 N.L.R.B. 127 (1982).

214 Thomas J. O'Dowd, Comment, *The* Hollywood Ceramics–Shopping Kart *Merry-Go-Round: Where Will It Stop?* 166–67, SANTA CLARA L. REV. 157, 166–68 (1980) (explaining that the *Hollywood Ceramics* decision resulted in "the Board's extensive analysis of campaign propaganda, restrictions on free speech, varying applications of the rule by the Board and the courts, increased litigation and reduced election finality." (footnote omitted)).

215 Shopping Kart Food Market, Inc., 228 N.L.R.B. 1311 (1977). *See also* O'Dowd, *supra* note 214, at 168.

216 General Knit, 239 N.L.R.B. 619 (1978), *overruled by* Midland Nat'l Life Ins. Co., 263 N.L.R.B. 127 (1982).

217 *Id.* at 620.

decision.[218] These divergent decisions, according to Leonard Bierman, are a "recurrent problem" with the NLRB and "usually occur when the political composition of the Board changes."[219] Nonetheless, the NLRB is still regarded as both an independent and "expert" agency.[220]

Independence, however, is a concept distinct from expertise. For example, an expert in agricultural science employed by a chemical company who engaged in agency decision-making would not be considered independent.[221] Alternatively, a completely independent, relatively untutored layperson may be fairly ignorant of the matter at hand. This, of course, is the storied role of the juror[222] or the proverbial "man on the Clapham omnibus."[223]

---

218 Midland Nat'l Life Ins. Co., 263 N.L.R.B. 127, 129 (1982).

219 Leonard Bierman, *Judge Posner and the NLRB: Implications for Labor Law Reform*, 69 MINN. L. REV. 881, 884 n.18 (1985).

220 *See* NLRB v. Link-Belt Co., 311 U.S. 584, 597 (1941) (holding courts cannot substitute their own judgment for that of the NLRB because the board is an "expert" agency dealing with a "specialized" field); C. J. Krehbiel Co. v. NLRB, 844 F.2d 880, 885 (D.C. Cir. 1988) ("Congress has charged the Board, a special and expert body, with the duty of judging the tendency of electoral flaws to distort 'the employees' ability to make a free choice.'" (quoting Amalgamated Clothing & Textile Workers v. NLRB, 736 F.2d 1559,1563–64 (D.C. Cir. 1984))). *See also* Jeffrey M. Hirsch, *Law of Termination: Doing More with Less*, 68 MD. L. REV. 89, 145 (2008) (noting that though the NLRB was created to provided "expert enforcement" of National Labor Relations Act policies, its enforcement has been the subject of much criticism throughout the years).

221 In 2004 the Office of Management and Budget issued an information quality bulletin for peer review that requires administrative agencies to conduct peer review of "scientific information disseminations that contain findings or conclusions that represent the official position of one or more agencies of the federal government." OFFICE OF MGMT. & BUDGET, EXEC. OFFICE OF THE PRESIDENT, FINAL INFORMATION QUALITY BULLETIN FOR PEER REVIEW 8 (2004), *available at* www.whitehouse.gov/sites/default/files/omb/assets/omb/memoranda/fy2005/m05-03.pdf. Peer review evaluations are theoretically conducted by "experts in the relevant field who are independent of the agency and have no . . . conflict of interest with respect to the outcome of the agency's decision." J. B. Ruhl & James Salzman, 84 WASH. U. L. REV. 1, 24 n.93 (2006). However, peer reviewer independence is not always assured. *See* Rick E. Melberth & Gary D. Bass, *In Defense of Regulatory Peer Review*, 38 ENVTL. L. REP. NEWS & ANALYSIS 10561, 10562 (2008) (noting that "the pool of experts to conduct peer reviews is often very limited—and those most skilled and represented in peer review panels too often have ties to regulated interests").

222 The independent, unbiased nature of the juror is central to American tradition. *See* HARRY KALVEN, JR., & HANS ZEISEL, THE AMERICAN JURY 8 (1966) (noting that although the judge "as a result of training, discipline, recurrent experience, and superior intelligence, will better be able to understand the law and analyze the facts than laymen," the jury's "very inexperience is an asset because it secures a fresh perception of each trial, avoiding the stereotypes said to infect the judicial eye").

223 The proverbial "man on the Clapham omnibus" idiom describes a reasonable man—the average person against whom the conduct of a defendant might be judged. *See* McGuire v. W. Morning News Co. (1903) 2 K.B. 100, 109; Frederick Schauer, *On the Supposed Jury-Dependence of Evidence Law*, 155 U. PA L. REV. 165, 188 (2006).

E. Federal Reserve Board: Independence as Needed

Notwithstanding structures designed to cosset expertise, agencies may yield, sometimes voluntarily, to political will. One example is the Federal Reserve Board, which has often been considered the paradigm "independent" agency, even though, as discussed in chapter 1, it lacks any explicit "for cause" removal protection.[224]

Although the Federal Reserve was created to separate politics from monetary policy, "two political appointees—the Secretary of the Treasury and the Comptroller of the Currency—served as ex officio members of its board, with the Secretary as board chairman."[225] The 1935 Banking Act later removed the secretary and comptroller from the board,[226] but political forces constantly challenged the Fed's autonomy during the first four decades after its inception.

Despite structurally freeing the Federal Reserve from political influence, the Banking Act did not ameliorate political pressures exerted on the Fed by the administration and Congress. From 1933 to 1941, under pressure from President Roosevelt, the Federal Reserve took a backseat to Congress, the Treasury, and the Roosevelt administration.[227] In fact, the Federal Reserve Board had "little influence on the decisions and was often uninformed about Treasury actions and plans."[228] Congress and the Roosevelt administration intervened in the country's monetary policy in a variety of ways. They took

---

[224] *See supra* chapter 1, notes 51–57 and accompanying text.

[225] *See* ALLAN H. MELTZER, A HISTORY OF THE FEDERAL RESERVE, VOL. I, 1913–1951 4, 65–67 (2003) ("the 1912 election shifted control of Congress to the Democrats. Many Democrats were willing to accept a central bank only if it was under political control.") The sponsors of the legislation claimed the political members would help the agency serve "the general public interest" and not "special interests." H.R. REP. NO. 74-742, at 1, 6 (1935). Michael Taylor, however, argues that it is political ties that permit the Federal Reserve to be independent. Michael Taylor, *Central Bank Independence: The Policy Background, in* BLACKSTONE'S GUIDE TO THE BANK OF ENGLAND ACT 1998 14–15 (1998).

[226] MELTZER, *supra* note 225, at 4. concise description of the legislative maneuvering that led to this result can be found in SIDNEY HYMAN, MARRINER ECCLES: PRIVATE ENTREPRENEUR AND PUBLIC SERVANT 187 (1976). The politics of the 1935 Act is discussed in *id.* at 168–70. *See* Banking Act of 1935, Pub. L. No. 74-305, 49 Stat. 684 (1935).

[227] MELTZER, *supra* note 225, at 415; *see also* DONALD R. WELLS, THE FEDERAL RESERVE SYSTEM: A HISTORY 61 (2004) ("When Roosevelt took office on March 4, 1933... FDR, using powers left over from World War I, declared a nationwide closing of all banks until Congress, which had been called into a special session, could enact emergency legislation."). Eugene Meyer, chair of the board, resigned in 1933, which gave President Roosevelt the opportunity to install Eugene Black. After Eugene Black's resignation a year later, Roosevelt replaced him with Marriner Eccles, a favorite among the administration due to his firm commitment to Keynesian economics. *Id.* at 61, 67. *See also* EDWIN WALTER KEMMERER & DONALD L. KEMMERER, THE ABC OF THE FEDERAL RESERVE SYSTEM 146 (12th ed. 1950) ("[Eccles's] ideas... resembled the well-worked-out theories of the English economist John Maynard Keynes. It is not surprising, therefore, to find that an administration that appointed Eccles to a key post because they liked his thinking should shortly find the persuasive writings of Keynes even more to their liking.").

[228] MELTZER, *supra* note 225, at 415.

the United States off the gold standard,[229] congressionally mandated the "Fed [to] issue 'reserve notes' not backed by gold,"[230] and directed the Fed "to impose selective credit controls and strict lending standards on its member banks, including interest rate ceilings and prohibitions on checking and savings deposits, and margin requirements on private borrowing for purchases of corporate securities, housing, automobiles, and other consumer durables."[231] Most notably, between 1941 and 1951, the Fed pegged low interest rates at the Treasury Department's direction.[232]

Board chair Marriner Eccles described his position as a "routine administrative job," because the Federal Reserve "merely executed Treasury decisions."[233] This was particularly true during World War II, when the Fed stated "[i]n time of war the duty of the

---

229 ANN-MARIE MEULENDYKE, U.S. MONETARY POLICY & FINANCIAL MARKETS 31 (1998); *see also* Stephen Slivinski, *The Evolution of Fed Independence*, REGION FOCUS, Fall 2009, at 5. The Roosevelt administration initially issued an Executive Order on April 5, 1933, that criminalized the possession of monetary gold. *See* MELTZER *supra* note 225, at 426–28. On January 30, 1934, Congress responded by passing the Gold Reserve Act, which required the Federal Reserve to surrender all of its gold and gold certificates to the Treasury Department. Gold Reserve Act of 1934, ch. 6, § 2, 48 Stat. 337.

230 Slivinski, *supra* note 229, at 5.

231 Timothy A. Canova, *Black Swans and Black Elephants in Plain Sight: An Empirical Review of Central Bank Independence*, 14 CHAP. L. REV. 237, 250 (2011).

232 Timothy A. Canova, *Democracy's Disappearing Duties: The Washington Consensus and the Limits of Citizen Participation*, in DEMOCRATIC CITIZENSHIP AND WAR 203 (Yoav Peled et al. eds., 2011). ("Throughout this 'pegged period,' the Federal Reserve's subservient position was enforced not by statute, but by political convention and necessity." (citation omitted)). The interest rates were initially pegged to help the Treasury Department pay for World War II. *Id.* at 204 ("It was only after those policy decisions had been made by the politically accountable branches of government that it would become 'the duty of the Federal Reserve to see to it that the banking system is in a position to absorb any public debt essential for war expenses that is not purchased by investors other than banks'"). During the "pegged period," the administration implemented wage and price controls, high taxes, and bond sales to prevent inflation and keep consumer prices stable. Timothy A. Canova, *American Wartime Values in Historical Perspective: Full-Employment Mobilization or Business as Usual*, 13 ILSA J. INT'L & COMP. L. 1, 15 (2006). For a discussion of the relationship between the Department of the Treasury and the Federal Reserve, *see* DONALD F. KETTL, LEADERSHIP AT THE FED 45–81 (1986).

233 MARRINER S. ECCLES, BECKONING FRONTIERS: PUBLIC AND PERSONAL RECOLLECTIONS 382 (1951). Regarding the World War II era, Eccles states, "[T]he Board of Governors had come to have few or no responsibilities beyond the discharge of mechanical duties." *Id.* at 384. However, Eccles did recognize the importance of Federal Reserve independence. In 1951, Eccles released a confidential memorandum relaying the substance of a meeting between the Open Market Committee and the president in 1951 in order to contradict the impressions of the meeting released by the White House. *See* SIDNEY HYMAN, MARRINER S. ECCLES 343–51 (1976). By way of justification of his actions, Eccles explained, "We should publicly inform the President, the Treasury, and the Congress of what we propose to do, and then do it. Otherwise the public will get the impression that we have capitulated and lack the courage to discharge our responsibilities. If Congress objects to our actions it can change the law; but until it does that, we have a clear responsibility to check inflation—in so far as we can do this within the framework of our authority...." MARRINER S. ECCLES, BECKONING FRONTIERS: PUBLIC AND PERSONAL RECOLLECTIONS 497–98 (1951).

Federal Reserve, as of everyone, is to support the country's war effort."[234] It further noted that the "prevention of inflation had to become secondary" to the demands of the war.[235]

The subservient role of the Federal Reserve continued until the Treasury-Fed Accord of March 1951 freed the Federal Reserve from its obligation to the Treasury Department to keep interest rates pegged.[236] The "divorce" document was short, if not, to some, opaque:

> The Treasury and the Federal Reserve System have reached full accord with respect to debt-management and monetary policies to be pursued in furthering their common purpose to assure the successful financing of the Government's requirements and, at the same time, to minimize monetization of the public debt.[237]

Since then, the Fed—as with other postwar control boards in the West—has trumpeted its independence from political considerations.[238]

The 1970s saw the first efforts of congressional pushback, in which Congress attempted to increase its oversight capacity over the Federal Reserve by enacting legislation changing board membership and prescribing policy objectives. These efforts did not significantly impact the Fed's "independence paradigm."

More recently, pressure on the Federal Reserve to increase its transparency and accountability has markedly increased. Although critics warned this would inhibit

---

[234] Board of Governors, Fed. Reserve Sys., The Federal Reserve System: Its Purposes and Functions 105 (2d ed. 1947); *see also* Canova, Democracy's Disappearing Duties, *supra* note 232, at 203; Kemmerer & Kemmerer, *supra* note 227, at 179 ("Most of the time [the Fed] took their orders from the Treasury without much protest, like good soldiers."). The Federal Reserve acted with similar deference to the executive during World War I. Regarding this period, Meltzer explains, "Independence was sacrificed to maintain interest rates that lowered the Treasury's cost of debt finance. The [Federal Reserve] System became subservient to the Treasury's perceived needs." Meltzer *supra* note 225, at 85.

[235] Board of Governors, *supra* note 234, at 107; *see also* Canova, Democracy's Disappearing Duties, *supra* note 232, at 204.

[236] Robert L. Hetzel & Ralph F. Leach, *The Treasury-Fed Accord: A New Narrative Account*, 87 Fed. Res. Bank Richmond Econ. Q. 33, 51 (2001).

[237] *See* Press Release, Treasury Dep't, Joint Announcement by the Secretary of the Treasury and the Chairman of the Board of Governors, and of the Federal Open Market Committee, of the Federal Reserve System (Mar. 4, 1951), *available at* www.richmondfed.org/publications/research/special_reports/treasury_fed_accord/historical_documents/pdf/treasury_statement_03_04_1951.pdf, 38 Bd. of Governors of the Fed. Res. Sys. Ann. Rep. 99 (1951). The "opaque" comment is the judgment of Peter Conti-Brown, *The Structure of the Federal Reserve System*, 48, Working Paper Series No. 139, Rock Center for Corporate Governance (Jan. 2, 2014 revision).

[238] Although it enjoys independence in implementing monetary policy, the Federal Reserve remains subject to judicial review for enforcement actions as a bank supervisor. Heidi Mandanis Schooner, *The Role of Central Banks in Bank Supervision in the United States and the United Kingdom*, 28 Brook. J. Int'l L. 411, 435 n.72 (2003).

Fed political independence,[239] the 2008 global financial meltdown provided the political momentum needed to pressure the Fed into becoming more transparent. On July 15, 2010, Congress passed the Dodd-Frank Wall Street Reform and Consumer Protection Act (Dodd-Frank), which required the U.S. Government Accountability Office (GAO) to perform "a one-time audit of all loans and other financial assistance provided [by the Federal Reserve] during the period beginning on December 1, 2007 and ending on the date of enactment of this Act" (which was July 21, 2010).[240]

---

239 Editorial, *Transparently Destructive: The House's Financial Reform Bill Includes an Assault on the Fed's Independence*, WASH. POST, Dec. 19, 2009, at A16. The Federal Reserve claimed that transparency regarding its lending operation would lead "to a loss of public confidence in the [borrowing] institution, a sudden outflow of deposits (a 'run'), a loss of confidence by market analysts, a drop in the institution's stock price, a withdrawal of market sources of funding, acceleration of existing loans to the institution, and, in extreme cases, closure of the institution." Memorandum of Points and Authorities in Support of Defendant's Motion for Summary Judgment at 21, Bloomberg, L.P. v. Bd. of Governors of the Fed. Reserve Sys., 649 F. Supp. 2d 262 (S.D.N.Y. 2009).

240 Dodd-Frank Wall Street Reform and Consumer Protection Act, Pub. L. No. 111-203, § 1109, 124 Stat. 1376 (2010); *see* Brady Dennis, *Lawmakers Agree to Expand Audit of Federal Reserve*, WASH. POST, June 17, 2010, at A15. The audit revealed that from 2007 to 2010, the Federal Reserve loaned $16 trillion to U.S. and international banks. Matthew Cardinale, *First Federal Reserve Audit Reveals Trillions in Secret Bailouts*, INTER PRESS SERVICE (Aug. 28, 2011), http://ipsnews.net/news.asp?idnews=104913. A GAO report concluded that "[t]he scale and nature of this assistance amounted to an unprecedented expansion of the Federal Reserve System's traditional role as lender-of-last-resort to depository institutions." U.S. GOV'T ACCOUNTABILITY OFFICE, FEDERAL RESERVE SYSTEM: OPPORTUNITIES EXIST TO STRENGTHEN POLICIES AND PROCESSES FOR MANAGING EMERGENCY ASSISTANCE 1 (2011).

However, this was not the first time the Fed had been subjected to congressionally mandated audits; the first time was in 1978. The Federal Banking Agency Audit Act required the comptroller general to perform audits of "the Federal Reserve Board, all Federal Reserve Banks, and their branches and facilities" and report the findings to Congress "as frequently as may be practicable." Pub. L. No. 95-320, 92 Stat. 391 (1978). *See also supra* note 238. The purpose of the audits was to address the "inadequate or no authority in the past for regular audits" of the Federal Deposit Insurance Corporation, the Federal Reserve System, and the Office of the Comptroller of the Currency, the responsibilities of which went "to the core of national economic wellbeing." 95 CONG. REC. H6196–97 (daily ed. Jun. 29, 1978) (statement of Rep. Benjamin Rosenthal). Unlike the audit required by the Dodd-Frank Act, the 1978 statute explicitly "preclude[d] the GAO from auditing Federal Reserve Board monetary policy deliberation, decision or implementation." *Id.* The Dodd-Frank audits focused on specific operation policies "between December 1, 2007 and the July 21, 2010 enactment of [the Dodd-Frank Act]," Pub. L. No. 111-203, 124 Stat. 1376 (2010).

In January 2014, Rep. Scott Garrett introduced the Federal Reserve Accountability and Transparency Act of 2014, which would require the Federal Reserve to "submit to the Committee on Financial Services of the House of Representatives and the Committee on Banking, Housing, and Urban Affairs of the Senate unredacted copies of the Board of Governors' Review of Regulatory Supervisory Audit" as well as other board performance reviews; H.R. 3928, 113th Cong. (2nd Sess. 2014). The Act would also require the Fed to perform "stress test" rulemaking by issuing regulations, after providing for public notice and comment, that provide for at least three different sets of conditions under which the evaluation required by this subsection shall be conducted, including baseline, adverse, and severely adverse, and methodologies including models used to estimate losses on certain assets, and "[w]henever the Board adopts or amends a regulation designated as a 'major rule'" it shall include in the release an assessment plan which "shall consider the costs, benefits, and intended and unintended consequences of the regulation." *Id.* The bill also includes stringent ethnics requirements and detailed language concerning Board of Governors testimony and responses to congressional inquiries. *Id.*

The courts have also helped increase the Fed's transparency. In 2008, Bloomberg, L.P. and Fox News Network submitted Freedom of Information Act (FOIA) requests to the Federal Reserve demanding the release of details "about loans that the twelve Federal Reserve Banks made to private banks in April and May 2008 at the Discount Window and pursuant to *ad hoc* emergency lending programs."[241] The Fed denied these FOIA requests, and the news companies sued. On March 19, 2010, the courts agreed with Fox and Bloomberg and ordered the Fed to release the records.[242]

Despite the increased transparency, some critics—such as Congressman Ron Paul—have advocated abolishing the Fed completely.[243] Paul credits the nation's current economic problems to the Federal Reserve's monetary policy.[244] In his opinion, "[t]he Federal Reserve should be abolished because it is immoral, unconstitutional, impractical, promotes bad economics, and undermines liberty."[245]

The Fed, however, has remained a practical amalgam of the independence and cooperation that is required for the regulation of a modern economy. Its seven members have fourteen-year terms—the longest of any independent agency. Only one of these lengthy terms expires in every two-year period; therefore, assuming every board member serves a full term, a president may only appoint two members during his first term.[246] In addition, in contrast to any other independent agency, the board's chair is statutorily protected

---

241 Bloomberg, L.P. v. Bd. of Governors of the Fed. Reserve Sys., 601 F.3d 143, 145 (2d Cir. 2010); *see* Fox News Network, LLC v. Bd. of Governors of the Fed. Reserve Sys., 601 F.3d 158, 159 (2d Cir. 2010).

242 Bloomberg, L.P., 601 F.3d at 150; *see also* Fox News Network, 601 F.3d at 159 ("[T]he information unambiguously at issue in the Fox News requests—the identity of the borrowing bank, the dollar amount of the loans, the collateral securing the loans, and the loan origination and maturity dates—is not protected from disclosure by Exemption 4. The Board is therefore required to disclose responsive records it had previously deemed except…"). The Clearing House Association, a party to the Bloomberg suit, filed a petition with the U.S. Supreme Court to hear the case. The Supreme Court denied the writ, which resulted in the Federal Reserve fully complying with the decision of the appeals court and releasing the information requested by Bloomberg and Fox News. This was the first time in history "a court has forced the Fed to reveal the names of banks that borrowed from its oldest lending program, the 98-year-old discount window." Greg Stohr & Bob Ivry, *Fed Will Release Bank Loan Data as Top Court Rejects Appeal*, BLOOMBERG (Mar. 21, 2011), www.bloomberg.com/news/2011-03-21/fed-must-release-bank-loan-data-as-high-court-rejects-appeal.html. The issues are well laid out in Kara Karlson, Note, *Checks and Balances: Using the Freedom of Information Act to Evaluate the Federal Reserve Banks*, 60 AM. U. L. REV. 213 (2010

243 *See* RON PAUL, END THE FED 141 (2009). Congressman Paul urges Congress to get rid of the central bank and get the country back on the gold standard. *Id.* at 144, 204 ("The gold standard with no Fed would impose discipline.…Just as in our household budgets in hard times, lawmakers would realize that they can't do all things.").

244 *Id.* at 141. Paul argues against what he considers the Fed's inflationary policies and pegging of interest rates at artificially low levels. *Id.* at 123–40 ("The Fed, short of being abolished, should have been prohibited from creating money and credit out of thin air and exerting monopoly control of the system with authority to set interest rates.").

245 *Id.* at 141.

246 *See* 12 U.S.C. § 242 (2006 & Supp. IV 2011).

against removal for a four-year period. The chair is also traditionally reappointed, irrespective of the president's party affiliation. These factors bestow significant decisional independence on the board and its chair in areas within their exclusive jurisdiction.

In areas of concurrent jurisdiction, however, the Federal Reserve interacts closely with the political branches of government. In its manual, *The Federal Reserve System, Purposes and Functions*, the board acknowledges:

> Members of the Board of Governors are in continual contact with other policy makers in government. They frequently testify before congressional committees.... The Board has regular contact with members of the President's Council of Economic Advisors and other key economic officials. The Chairman also meets from time to time with the President of the United States and has regular meetings with the Secretary of the Treasury.[247]

The Federal Reserve System also contains elements of a public-private partnership. Although the Federal Reserve Board itself is headquartered in Washington, D.C., it oversees twelve separate Federal Reserve Districts, each with its own Federal Reserve Bank. The Banks submit an annual budget to the board for approval,[248] and are involved with the board's regulation of the flow of credit and monetary policy. They also have direct authority over depository institutions.[249] The Federal Reserve Banks are considered the "operating arms" of the banking network, and "combine both public and private elements in their makeup and organization."[250] Each Federal Reserve Bank generates its own income but returns earnings in excess of its normal operating costs to the Treasury annually.[251] They can also sue and be sued in their own capacity.[252] Although each Federal Reserve Bank is under the general authority of the Federal Reserve Board, each has a nine-member board of directors overseeing operations. Each regional bank's board contains three classes of directors, Class A, Class B, and Class C.[253] Class A and B directors are elected by commercial banks of the regional district, with Class B directors representing public interests, and Class C directors are appointed by the Board of Governors.[254]

247 The Federal Reserve System, Purposes and Functions 5 (9th ed. 2005).

248 *Id.* at 10.

249 *Id.*

250 *Id.*

251 The Fed "retains the amount it needs to finance its own operation." Edwin Rubin, *Hyperdepoliticization*, 47 Wake Forest L. Rev. 631, 668 (2012). In 2013, that amount was $1.8 billion. Press Release, Bd. Of Governors of the Fed. Reserve Sys., Preliminary unaudited results of payments for 2013 (Jan. 10, 2014).

252 12 U.S.C. § 341 (2006).

253 The Federal Reserve System, *supra* note 247, at 10.

254 *Id.*; Canova, *supra* note 231, at 304.

The Federal Reserve Banks are considered both "fiscal agents of the United States"[255] and corporations, due to governance by individual boards that are elected by private banking institutions.[256] For purposes of tort liability under the Federal Tort Claims Act, the Federal Reserve Banks are not considered government agencies.[257] However, the Federal Reserve Banks are deemed government instrumentalities for purposes of the Service Contract Act.[258] The distinction comes from differing tests applied by courts. The United States District Court for the District of Columbia determined that Federal Reserve Banks are federal agencies under the Service Contract Act in *Brink's, Inc. v. Board of Governors of the Federal Reserve System*.[259] The Court noted that the Federal Reserve Banks themselves had "resorted to the courts to assert their governmental character when it has been in their interest to do so" and that the purpose of the Service Contract Act supported a finding of their governmental nature.[260] In *Lewis v. United States*, however, the United States Court of Appeals for the Ninth Circuit determined that a Federal Reserve Bank was not a federal agency subject to Federal Trade Commission Act liability due to the government's limited control over daily banking operations.[261] The court also noted that the Federal Reserve Banks were privately owned entities rather than federal instrumentalities.[262]

In *Scott v. Federal Reserve Bank of Kansas City*, the United States Court of Appeals for the Eighth Circuit followed the Ninth Circuit's determination, and ruled that the Federal Reserve Bank of Kansas City was not a federal agency for purposes of a race discrimination suit under Title VII.[263] In making its determination, the Eighth Circuit utilized six factors expounded by the Ninth Circuit's *In Re Hoag Ranches* decision: (1) the extent to which the entity performs a governmental function; (2) the scope of the government's involvement; (3) whether the entity's operations are government financed; (4) whether persons other than the government have a proprietary interest in the entity; (5) whether the entity is referred to as an agency in statutes; and (6) whether the entity is treated as a branch of the government for purposes of other statutes.[264]

In declining to determine whether Federal Reserve Banks are federal instrumentalities, the United States Court of Appeals for the Third Circuit recognized that "[i]nstrumentality jurisprudence has never been characterized by particular clarity," and noted that "strong arguments have been made in favor of such status."[265]

---

255 12 U.S.C. § 391 (2006).

256 THE FEDERAL RESERVE SYSTEM, *supra* note 247, at 10.

257 Lewis v. United States, 680 F.2d 1239, 1243 (9th Cir. 1982).

258 Brink's, Inc. v. Bd. of Governors of the Fed. Reserve Sys., 466 F. Supp. 116, 117 (D. D.C.1979).

259 *Id.*

260 *Id.* at 119.

261 *Lewis*, 680 F.2d at 1241.

262 *Id.*

263 Scott v. Fed. Reserve Bk. of Kansas City, 406 F.3d 532, 538 (8th Cir. 2005).

264 *Id.* at 536–37; *In re* Hoag Ranches, 846 F.2d 1225, 1227–28 (9th Cir. 1988).

265 Fasano v. Fed. Reserve Bk. of New York, 457 F.3d 274, 281–82 (3d Cir. 2006).

F. Observations

The creation of independent agencies reveals a considerable degree of pragmatic evolution and development. Independence was not an essential element in their creation. Rather, the multimember structure of the ICC emerged as a default model following experimentation in both Britain and the United States, and due to political compromise in the nineteenth century. Yet the ICC served as the model for other independent agencies as the relationship between expertise and independence took hold. Building upon this model, agencies developed unique structures and operations due to their differing missions. For example, political realities shifted the NLRB from a technocratic to a more politically accountable body when Republicans first came to power following the enactment of the NLRA. The Federal Reserve Board has also balanced the need for independence with a requirement of political cooperation as required by its own needs. Therefore, despite such common elements, each independent agency is distinctive and adapts to the realities of its mission.

Whether intended or not, the historic ideology buttressing the independent regulatory agency has been the theory of expertise. As this chapter indicates, expertise was the mantra of the Progressive Era, and public administration was seen as a "science."[266] So strong was this belief in the power of expertise that James Landis, doyen of administrative law before becoming dean at Harvard, noted that all or most regulatory bodies (not just the independent regulatory agencies) developed expertise in their task, which resulted in practical independence from executive direction.[267]

The mantra of expertise faced considerable pushback toward the end of the New Deal with the passage of the APA,[268] which combined the discretion of experts and heightened judicial review of agency action.[269] Still, it was not until the early 1960s that scholars

---

266 Woodrow Wilson, *The Study of Administration*, 2 POL. SCI. Q. 197, 197 (1887). After publishing this article, Wilson adopted a more skeptical view of expertise as a presidential candidate. *See* A CROSSROADS OF FREEDOM, *supra* note 166.

267 LANDIS, *supra* note 161, at 23–24.

268 Administrative Procedure Act, Pub. L. No. 79-404, 60 Stat. 237 (1946). For the context in which the APA developed, see Daniel R. Ernst, *The Politics of Administrative Law: New York's Anti-bureaucracy Clause and the O'Brian-Wagner Campaign of 1938 in the Late New Deal*, 27 L. & HIST. REV., no. 2, 2009, at 1, *available at* http://scholarship.law.georgetown.edu/cgi/viewcontent.cgi?article=1580&context=facpub. *See also,* JOANNA L. GRISINGER, THE UNWIELDY AMERICAN STATE: ADMINISTRATIVE POLITICS SINCE THE NEW DEAL, 59–108 (Cambridge, 2012). For the ideological disputes and legislative compromises leading to the passage of the APA, see George B. Shepherd, *Fierce Compromise: The Administrative Procedure Act Emerges from New Deal Politics*, 90 NW. U. L. REV. 1557 (1996). For the role of the Attorney General's Committee on Administrative Procedure on the drafting of the APA, *see* Joanne Grisinger, *Law in Action: The Attorney General's Committee on Administrative Procedure*, 20 JL. OF POLICY HISTORY 379 (2008).

269 In interpreting the APA, the Supreme Court noted that Congress had expressed a "mood" deserving more aggressive review. Universal Camera Corp. v. NLRB, 340 U.S. 474, 487 (1951). *See also* Alfred S. Neely,

recognized that the "theoretical underpinnings of administrative expertise had been largely undermined."[270] Part of this was due to the increasing focus by economists on public choice theory, which holds that government agencies, like bureaucrats generally, seek to maximize their power and position.[271] In that regard, groups such as "Nader's Raiders" increased recognition of the consequences of "agency capture,"[272] which undercut belief in an autonomous public-regarding bureaucracy.

A second reason was the growth after World War II of "interest group pluralism" as a theory of democracy[273] and its reflection in administrative law.[274] Through the increased acceptance of interest group pluralism as a theoretical prism by which to view the political process, the administrative process became understood as less a forum for ascertaining the public interest than a vehicle for interest representation.[275] Indeed, as Mark Tushnet incisively notes, "Interest-group bargaining—a form of politics—was relocated into administrative agencies, and the Progressive claim that administrative agencies pursued science rather than politics became difficult to sustain."[276]

Still, neither Congress nor the courts is prepared to dispose of the notion of bureaucratic expertise completely—and the independent agency meets this need. As we hope this book makes clear, there is still a place for expertise in the administrative state.

Justice Frankfurter, Universal Camera and a Jurisprudence of Judicial Review of Administrative Action, 25 U. Tol. L. Rev. 1 (1994) (analyzing the *Universal Camera* decision).

270 Daniel J. Gifford, *The New Deal Regulatory Model: A History of Criticisms and Refinements*, 68 Minn. L. Rev. 299, 316 (1983).

271 *See* David B. Spence & Frank Cross, *A Public Choice Case for the Administrative State*, 89 Geo. L.J. 97, 121 (2000). *See generally*, Glen O. Robinson, American Bureaucracy: Public Choice and Public Law (1991); William A. Niskanen, Jr., Bureaucracy and Representative Government (1971); Jerry L. Mashaw, Greed, Chaos, and Governance: Using Public Choice to Improve Public Law (1997); William A Niskanen, Jr., Bureaucracy and Representative Government (1971); Glen O. Robinson, American Bureaucracy: Public Choice and Public Law (1991). For an insightful review of the issues raised by public choice for administrative law, *see* Jerry Louis Mashaw, *Public Law and Public Choice: Critique and Rapprochement, in* Research Handbook on Law and Public Choice and Public Law 19 (Daniel A. Farber & Anne Joseph O'Connell eds., 2010) (2009).

272 *See* Spence & Cross, *supra note* 271, at 121 ("[A]gency capture...maintains that agencies become servants of the entities that they are supposed to regulate.").

273 The classic texts are Robert Dahl, A Preface to Democratic Theory 63–89 (1956); David Truman, The Governmental Process (1951); Earl Latham, Group Basis of Politics (1952).

274 Daphne Barak-Erez, *The Administrative Process as a Domain of Conflicting Interests*, 6 Theoretical Inquiries L. 193, 200 (2005). Barak-Erez suggests that "the decision-making process of the administrative agency in actuality entails a fundamental balancing of conflicting interests, similar to that conducted by the legislature." *Id.* at 196.

275 *See* Richard B. Stewart, *The Reformation of American Administrative Law*, 88 Harv. L. Rev. 1667, 1802–05 (1975) (criticizing the interest representation structure for agency actions).

276 Mark Tushnet, *Administrative Law in the 1930s: The Supreme Court's Accommodation of Progressive Legal Theory*, 60 Duke L.J. 1565, 1567 (2011).

3

Theories of Agency Independence

A. Theory of the Unitary Executive

The constitutionality of the independent agency was not an issue of considerable debate until many decades after the establishment of the ICC in 1887.[1] The Progressive and New Deal eras saw the proliferation of many new independent agencies that wielded considerable power. This induced many scholars to speculate on the constitutionality of agencies seemingly located outside the reach of the executive branch. Over the past few decades, there has been a resurgence of efforts to centralize the executive functions.[2] As a result, debates concerning issues of separation of powers and its consequent impact on independent agencies have once again proliferated.

---

1 Interstate Commerce Act, 24 Stat. 379, 379–388 (1887) (repealed 1995).

2 President Obama issued several Executive Orders encouraging independent agencies to respond to the administration's regulatory review initiatives. *See* Exec. Order No. 13,579, 76 Fed. Reg. 41587 (July 14, 2011) (further encouraging independent regulatory agencies to cooperate voluntarily with the regulatory review process); Exec. Order No. 13,563, 76 Fed. Reg. 3821 (Jan. 18, 2011) (encouraging independent agencies to take part in the regulatory review process). Under President George W. Bush, OMB director John Graham sought to entice independent agencies to cooperate with Office of Information and Regulatory Affairs initiatives through the use of "prompt letters." *See infra* chapter 6, pt. D, notes 118–119 and accompanying text. *See also* Exec. Order No. 12,866, 3 C.F.R. 638 (1993) (President Clinton) (improving the efficiency and public accessibility of federal regulatory process); Exec. Order No. 12,498, 3 C.F.R. 323 (1985) (President Reagan) (creating regulatory planning process and reducing regulatory burdens and duplication); Exec. Order No. 12,291, 46 Fed. Reg. 13,193 (1981) (President Reagan) (reducing regulatory burdens imposed by federal agencies); Exec. Order No. 12,044, 3 C.F.R. 152 (1978) (President Carter) (streamlining the agency rulemaking process); Exec. Order No. 11,821, 39 Fed. Reg. 41,501 (1974) (President Ford) (requiring agencies, under direction of OMB director, to perform inflation impact statements for all legislative proposals and rules).

Some commentators view the independent agency as analytically unconstitutional. The rejection of the notion of agency independence flows naturally from the "theory of the unitary executive" sketched out first in Alexander Hamilton's classic discussion of executive power, *The Federalist* No. 70, in which he wrote that "[t]he ingredients which constitute energy in the Executive are first, unity; secondly, duration; thirdly, an adequate provision for its support; [and] fourthly, competent powers."[3] The unitary theory is derived from the "vesting" and "take care" clauses of Article II of the Constitution. Unitary theorists understand the vesting clause, which provides that "[t]he executive Power shall be vested in a President,"[4] to mean that executive power is vested *only* in the president, so Congress is precluded from placing agencies outside the executive branch. Furthermore, these theorists believe that the president himself and only the president must undertake those enumerated powers explicitly granted by the Constitution, and in general "take Care that the Laws be faithfully executed."[5] The argument suggests that this duty can be discharged only if those federal agencies that perform traditionally executive functions are understood to be agents of the president and responsible to him. Any other structure, the argument runs, would undermine accountability and thus collapse the notion that "the buck stops here."

The precise meaning of the vesting clause has been much debated and is central to arguments over the theory of the unitary executive. On the one hand, scholars like Edwin Corwin argue that it was intended "simply to settle the question of whether the executive branch should be plural or single and to give the executive a title."[6] Still, others have suggested that the clause's grant of "executive power" is plenary—in some way creating a "reservoir of power comparable to that of an eighteenth-century British king."[7]

Those subscribing to the "completion power" theory suggest that the vesting clause, when considered with the take care clause, provides for a broad base of executive plenary authority akin to a royal prerogative—at least in some contexts.[8] As Jack Goldsmith and John Manning explain it, the completion power is "the President's authority to prescribe incidental details needed to carry into execution a legislative scheme, even in the

---

[3] THE FEDERALIST NO. 70, at 199 (Alexander Hamilton) (Roy P. Fairfield ed., 2d ed. 1981) ("This unity may be destroyed in two ways: either by vesting the power in two or more magistrates of equal dignity and authority; or by vesting it ostensibly in one man, subject, in whole or in part, to the control and co-operation of others, in the capacity of counsellors to him.").

[4] U.S. CONST. art. II, § 1, cl. 1.

[5] *Id.* § 3.

[6] Edwin S. Corwin, Comment, *The Steel Seizure Cases: A Judicial Brick Without Straw*, 53 COLUMBIA L. REV. 53 (1953). *See also* Bruce Ledewitz, *The Uncertain Power of the President to Execute the Law*, 46 TENN. L. REV. 757 (1984).

[7] Robert G. Natelson, *The Original Meaning of the Constitution's "Executive Vesting Clause": Evidence from Eighteenth Century Drafting Practice*, 31 WHITTIER L. REV. 1, 4 (2009) (citing Steven G. Calabresi & Saikrishna Prakash, *The President's Power to Execute the Laws*, 104 YALE L.J. 541, 578–79 (1994), and discussing the eighteenth century grants of power from which the framers likely drew in drafting the vesting clause).

[8] Robert J. Reinstein, *The Limits of Executive Power*, 59 AM. U. L. REV. 259, 264 (2009).

absence of any congressional authorization to complete that scheme."[9] The completion power theory has thus been dubbed the "modern equivalent of the royal prerogative."[10] But, this extreme view of the vesting clause is certainly not without critics—even among those who support the vesting clause as a plenary grant of presidential powers. As Steven Calabresi has noted, the clause "confers on the President a grant of 'executive power' not a grant of 'regal power,'" and to assert that the president's executive power includes something akin to a "royal prerogative" would be "preposterous."[11]

Proponents of a unitary executive view the federal bureaucracy as a pyramid, with the president as the accountable official at the top. But there appear to be as many theories and answers as there are commentators. According to Akhil Reed Amar, unitary executive theorists "come in many flavors and sizes."[12] At one end of the spectrum, David Rivkin contends that both constitutional and policy considerations support a unitary, elected, visible executive.[13] Calabresi and Rhodes argue that the constitutional text supports the theory of unitary executive, but acknowledge that there are "several versions" of theory.[14] Judge Frank Easterbrook appears to endorse the theory of a unitary executive on policy grounds but accepts the lack of constitutional precision about the actual operation

---

9 Jack Goldsmith & John Manning, *The President's Completion Power*, 115 YALE L.J. 2280, 2282 (2006) ("Congress can limit it, for example, by denying the President the authority to complete a statute through certain means or by specifying the manner in which a statute must be implemented. But in the absence of such affirmative legislative limitation or specification, courts and Presidents have recognized an Article II power of some uncertain scope to complete a legislative scheme"). *Compare* Harold Hongju Koh, *Setting the World Right*, 115 YALE L.J. 2350, 2368–70 (2006) (noting that "upon examination, their completion power is just another term for an implied Necessary and Proper Clause for the President, a power that—unfortunately for these authors—the Framers chose to give to Congress, not the President.... The recent constitutional debate over presidential signing statements has raged precisely because the President has claimed an unenumerated Article II power to interpret a statutory scheme faithfully not to Congress's intent, but rather to his own reading of what that scheme's goals might be"). *See also* Reinstein, *supra* note 8, at 309; Glen Staszewski, *Textualism and the Executive Branch*, 2009 MICH. ST. L. REV. 143, 171–74 (2009) (noting that because "statutes are inherently ambiguous"..., "[p]ublic officials who are responsible for implementing the law will therefore necessarily have substantial discretion, which should be exercised in a manner that leads to the 'successful execution' of 'legislative programs' under the relevant circumstances").

10 Reinstein, *supra* note 8, at 264.

11 Steven G. Calabresi, *The Vesting Clause as Power Grant*, 88 NW. U. L. REV. 1377, 1392–93 (1994). As Ryan Alford makes abundantly clear, the 18th Century conflicts between King and Parliament ended the "practical subordination of the King to Parliament." Ryan Patrick Alford, Not Even Wrong: The Use of British Constitutional History to Defend the Vesting Clause Thesis 19 (Oct. 27, 2012) (unpublished manuscript), *available at* http://papers.ssrn.com/sol3/papers.cfm?abstract_id=2167760. Thus the royal prerogative was "reduced to the status of a legal fiction, as it could only be exercised on the advice of a cabinet minister responsible to the Parliament." *Id.*

12 Akhil Reed Amar, *The President, the Cabinet, and Independent Agencies*, 5 U. ST. THOMAS J.L. & PUB. POL'Y 36, 49 (2010).

13 David B. Rivkin, Jr., *The Unitary Executive and Presidential Control of Executive Branch Rulemaking*, 7 ADMIN. L. J. AM. U. 309, 309–10 (1993).

14 *See, e.g.*, Steven G. Calabresi & Kevin H. Rhodes, *The Structural Constitution: Unitary Executive, Plural Judiciary*, 105 HARV. L. REV. 1153, 1158 & n.10 (1992).

of the executive in practice.[15] Similarly, Charles Fried, the Reagan solicitor general who argued many of the "unitary executive" cases, confessed that:

> The vision I offer is not literally required by the words of the Constitution. Nor did the framers' intent compel this view. No, that vision must be discerned from the structure of the document as a whole.... Most of all, it is a vision based on the best and most compelling extrapolation from what was written in that text, what was said about it, and what was dreamed of by those who inspired it. These are arguments unlikely to impress the literal-minded temper of the present Court.[16]

For his part, Colin Diver suggests that "the history of the administrative state is an unending contest between Congress and the President for control of the bureaucracy,"[17] while Geoffrey Miller claims that presidential control of agencies goes from weak to strong along a continuum that depends on functions and role of particular agencies.[18]

Based on historical examination, the theory presented by Lessig and Sunstein suggests that although the modern conception of the unitary executive is inconsistent with the framers' practices, the inconsistencies are not necessarily fatal to the modern unitary position.[19] Rather, the pair hypothesize that the deviation between the framers' actual practice and the practices that would be expected under the modern unitary theory are due to the fact that "the national government has changed dramatically since the founding, and so too has the national presidency."[20] In fact, the authors suggest that it took the young republic some years to understand the necessity of a unitary executive for the structure of the Constitution.

Proponents of the unitary executive tend to hinge their arguments on formalist conceptions of the Constitution. As Justice Scalia noted in his dissent to the *Morrison* decision, "'The executive Power shall be vested in a President of the United States'.... this does not mean *some of* the executive power, but *all* of the executive power."[21] Most of the approaches to the unitary theory employ a formalistic approach to constitutional interpretation, which strictly enforces the allocation of executive power in the executive and

---

[15] Frank H. Easterbrook, *Unitary Executive Interpretation: A Comment*, 15 Cardozo L. Rev. 313, 316, 321 (1993).

[16] Charles Fried, Order and Law: Arguing the Reagan Revolution 170–71 (Simon & Schuster 1991).

[17] Colin S. Diver, *Presidential Powers*, 36 Am. U. L. Rev 519, 519 (1987).

[18] Geoffrey Miller, *The Unitary Executive in a Unified Theory of Constitutional Law: The Problem of Interpretation*, 15 Cardozo L. Rev. 201, 202 (1993).

[19] Lawrence Lessig & Cass R. Sunstein, *The President and the Administration*, 94 Colum. L. Rev. 1, 2–4, 85–87 (1994).

[20] *Id.* at 85.

[21] Morrison v. Olson, 487 U.S. 654, 705 (1988) (Scalia, J., dissenting).

legislative power in Congress.[22] Both formalism and functionalism are often intertwined by supporters of the unitary executive, such as Lessig and Sunstein,[23] who contend that a unitary executive is crucial to carrying out the founder's desire for accountability.

Although unitary theorists differ in varying degrees over the extent of the president's executive power,[24] there is a consensus that the power to remove subordinates who do not follow the president's directives, or in whom he no longer has confidence, is vital to his supervisory ability and authorized by the Constitution.[25] Under the rubric of the unitary executive theory, courts, as in *Wiener v. United States*, have tended to exempt only those agencies possessed of some semblance of adjudicatory function from "at will" removal.[26] Indeed, as one earlier commentator suggested, "[w]here, in addition to their other functions, these commissions have been entrusted with judicial power, there has been a noticeable tendency to justify their independent position in terms of that power alone."[27]

A more extreme view of the unitary executive—a sort of "unitary executive maximus" theory—emerged during the presidency of George W. Bush. No longer concerned only with the notion of executive control over the federal bureaucracy, this theory also involves a notion of inherent presidential authority.[28] As Justice Thomas's dissent

---

22 This understanding is clearly expressed in *INS v. Chadha*: "The Constitution sought to divide the delegated powers of the new federal government into three defined categories, legislative, executive and judicial, to assure, as nearly as possible, that each Branch of government would confine itself to its assigned responsibility. The hydraulic pressure inherent within each of the separate Branches to exceed the outer limits of its power, even to accomplish desirable objectives, must be resisted." 462 U.S. 919, 951 (1983). In contrast, proponents of "functionalism" argue that the Constitution does not create an absolute separation of powers, but allows for the blending of powers in order to promote accountability among the coordinate branches. *See* Morrison v. Olson, 487 U.S. 654, 694–95 (1988). Functionalists, for instance, allow Congress to vest "quasi-legislative" and "quasi-judicial" power in independent agencies which are not directly accountable to the president. *Id.* at 687–91. For a more detailed discussion of the distinctions between formalism and functionalism, see Thomas W. Merrill, *The Constitutional Principle of Separation of Powers*, 1991 SUP. CT. REV. 225, 229–35.

23 Lessig & Sunstein, *supra* note 19, at 1, 2–3, 5.

24 *See, e.g.*, Calabresi & Rhodes, *supra* note 14, at 1165–68 (discussing varying unitary theory models).

25 *See, e.g.*, Morton Rosenberg, *Congress's Prerogative over Agencies and Agency Decision Makers: The Rise and Demise of the Reagan Administration's Theory of the Unitary Executive*, 57 GEO. WASH. L. REV. 627, 634 (1989) (arguing that Congress has "virtually plenary power to create the administrative bureaucracy and to shape the powers, duties, and tenure of the offices and officers of that infrastructure in a manner best suited to accomplish legislative ends"); Peter L. Strauss, *Formal and Functional Approaches to Separation-of-Powers Questions—A Foolish Inconsistency?*, 72 CORNELL L. REV. 488, 494–95 (1987) (describing the "strong executive" model).

26 357 U.S. 349, 352 (1958).

27 WILSON K. DOYLE, INDEPENDENT COMMISSIONS IN THE FEDERAL GOVERNMENT 41 (1939).

28 *See* Cynthia Farina, *False Comfort and Impossible Promises: Uncertainty, Information Overload, and the Unitary Executive*, 12 U. PA. J. CONST. L. 357, 376–78 (2010) ("This account permits the simultaneous insistence that the President is entitled to virtually complete autonomy *and* is uniquely motivated to govern in the national interest. No one can direct presidential judgment because the Constitution gives the executive power to the duly elected President alone.").

in *Hamdi v. Rumsfeld* notes, "Congress... has a substantial and essential role in both foreign affairs and national security. But it is crucial to recognize that judicial interference in these domains destroys the purpose of vesting primary responsibility in a unitary executive.... Congress cannot anticipate and legislate with regard to every possible action the President may find it necessary to take [and] the President may very well have inherent authority to detain those arrayed against our troops."[29]

While this view is certainly controversial, Steven Calabresi has suggested that there is at least some originalist basis for it. In a 2008 interview, he noted that "[t]he executive power was understood as being quite broad in 1787.... Moreover, the Constitution says Congress can act only when both houses concur and the courts can act only when there is a case or controversy. Anything the government does that does not involve bicameralism and presentment or adjudication... is executive and is in the president's domain."[30] However, as Julian Ku notes, Calabresi, in conjunction with Christopher Yoo, sought to distance the unitary executive theory from the broad notions of presidential power embraced by the Bush administration in their 2008 book *The Unitary Executive*.[31] According to Calabresi and Yoo's work, "[a]ccepting the theory of the unitary executive does not necessarily require accepting the claims of inherent executive power advanced by the Bush administration... aside from the power to remove and direct, the theory of the unitary executive is ultimately agnostic about the question of the scope of executive power."[32]

For a period of time, it appeared that the theory of the "unitary executive" would place the constitutionality of the independent agencies at serious risk.[33] In *Buckley v. Valeo*,[34] the Supreme Court invalidated a portion of the Federal Election Campaign Act because

---

29 Hamdi v. Rumsfeld, 542 U.S. 507, 582–88 (2004) (Thomas, J., dissenting).

30 Cited in Farina, *supra* note 28, 377 n.88.

31 *See* Julian Ku, *Unitary Executive Theory and Exclusive Presidential Powers*, 12 U. PA. J. CONST. L. 615 (2010).

32 STEVEN G. CALABRESI & CHRISTOPHER YOO, THE UNITARY EXECUTIVE: PRESIDENTIAL POWER FROM WASHINGTON TO BUSH 429 (2008).

33 *See, e.g.*, Hospital Corp. of Am. v. FTC, 807 F.2d 1381, 1392 (7th Cir. 1986) (noting that the petitioner's argument, if accepted, would result in every independent agency being declared unconstitutional); Ticor Title Ins. Co. v. FTC, 625 F. Supp. 747, 751 (D.D.C. 1986) (stating that the plaintiff's challenge to the constitutionality of the FTC as an independent agency raised "a serious and substantial issue of considerable public importance" that "has never been fully adjudicated"). *But see* FTC v. American Nat'l Cellular, Inc., 810 F.2d 1511, 1517 (9th Cir. 1987) (Tang, J., concurring) (upholding the enforcement power of the independent agency).

One curious case placed a shadow over the independent status of these agencies even while affirming their enforcement powers. In *SEC v. Bilzerian*, 750 F. Supp. 14 (D.D.C. 1990), the District Court for the District of Columbia rejected a separation-of-powers challenge to the vesting of civil enforcement authority in the SEC. Noting that "Congress has no power or control over the enforcement activities of the SEC," the court concluded that "it is clear that the SEC is within the executive branch." *Id.* at 17. For a general discussion of challenge to the constitutionality of independent agencies, see Survey, *Constitutional Challenges to Independent Agency Enforcement Action*, 2 ADMIN. L.J. 423 (1988).

34 424 U.S. 1 (1976).

it violated the doctrine of separation of powers.[35] The legislation contained a provision that provided for congressional appointment of several members to the FEC. The court deemed this bequest of authority unconstitutional for violating the powers assigned to the president in Article II of the Constitution.[36] In September 1985, Attorney General Ed Meese suggested, in a speech to the Federal Bar Association, that "[t]he real law-making power in Washington is wielded neither by Congress nor the President, but by relatively anonymous members of the federal agencies."[37] These officials, he argued, are accountable to neither the president nor Congress. "It should be up to the President to enforce the law," he declared.[38] "Federal agencies performing executive functions are themselves properly agents of the executive. They are not 'quasi' this or 'independent' that. In the tripartite scheme of government, a body with enforcement powers is part of the executive branch of government."[39] Meese urged that "[w]e should abandon the idea that there are such things as 'quasi-legislative' or 'quasi-judicial' functions that can be properly delegated to independent agencies."[40]

During the following year, in *Bowsher v. Synar*, the U.S. Supreme Court overturned a provision of the Gramm-Rudman-Hollings Act that gave the comptroller general, who was removable only by Congress, the authority to review certain actions of the executive branch.[41] The Court categorized the comptroller general as an agent of Congress[42] and concluded that the delegation was an unconstitutional retention of executive power by Congress.[43] During oral argument, the solicitor general told the justices that the proponents of the constitutionality of the challenged Gramm-Rudman-Hollings Act were trying to "scare" them with the argument that upholding the lower court on the constitutional issue would endanger the independent agencies, such as the FTC and the Federal Reserve Board.[44] At this, Justice O'Connor interposed: "They scared me with it."[45]

---

35 *See id.* at 140–41.

36 *See* U.S. CONST. art. II, § 2, cl. 2. The president may, with the advice and consent of the Senate, appoint and commission "Officers of the United States." *See also Buckley*, 424 U.S. at 140–41.

37 Address by Edwin Meese, III, Federal Bar Association Annual Banquet (Sept. 13, 1985) at 5, U.S. Dept. of Justice Main Library, *available at* http://www.justice.gov/ag/aghistory/meese/1985/09-13-1985.pdf [hereinafter Meese Address]. *See also* Howard Kurtz, *Agencies' Authority Challenged: Justice Dept. Seems to Side with Conservatives on Regulatory Power*, WASH. POST, Jan. 3, 1986, at A17.

38 Meese Address, *supra* note 37.

39 *Id.*

40 *Id.*

41 *See* Bowsher v. Synar, 478 U.S. 714 (1986).

42 *See id.* at 731.

43 *See id.* at 726.

44 *See Arguments Before the Court: Gramm-Rudman-Hollings Act—Separation of Powers*, 54 U.S.L.W. 3709, 3709–10 (1986).

45 *Id.* Finally, it is worth remembering that Chief Justice Burger's draft opinion in *Bowsher* was far stronger and specifically, so his colleagues believed, imperiled the independence of administrative agencies. Bernard Schwartz, *An Administrative Law "Might Have Been"—Chief Justice Burger's* Bowsher v. Synar *Draft*, 42 ADMIN. L. REV. 221, 233–49 (1990).

While there is no doubt that *Morrison* creates a theory limiting the unitary executive, it remains to be seen whether its legacy is the demise of formalist thinking regarding the executive power and independent agencies.[46] Certainly, later courts have sustained the *Morrison* principle of resistance to legislative encroachment on traditional executive functions, culminating in *Free Enterprise Fund*, which underscored that the notion of a removal power twice removed shows insufficient respect for presidential authority.[47]

But one must be careful not to read too far into *Morrison*'s independence principle. *Morrison* concerns a highly unusual fact pattern—a case in which the executive is being asked to investigate itself.[48] Notwithstanding the untrammeled freedom of the independent counsel to undertake the prosecution function (one traditionally executive), the counsel's decision whether or not to prosecute by its very nature encompasses an adjudicative function as well.[49] It must decide that there is enough evidence to warrant going forward. Thus, *Morrison* may be understood as a narrow holding with exceedingly broad language—language upon which those who seek to expand the penumbra of independence rely inordinately at times. Indeed, Davis and Pierce believe that the door may not be closed entirely. In *Freytag v. Commissioner*, they point out, four justices criticized the U.S. Supreme Court's *Humphrey's Executor* decision.[50] Davis and Pierce observe that "*Freytag* illustrates the surprising extent to which the entire

---

[46] There is certainly a clear line of post-*Morrison* cases on which "formalists" can continue to rely. *See* Free Enter. Fund v. Pub. Co. Accounting Oversight Bd., 130 S. Ct. 3138, 3152 (2010); Metropolitan Wash. Airports Auth. v. Citizens for the Abatement of Aircraft Noise, Inc., 501 U.S. 252 (1991); Hechinger v. Metropolitan Wash. Airports Auth., 36 F.3d 97 (D.C. Cir. 1994); FEC v. NRA Political Victory Fund, 6 F.3d 821, 824 (D.C. Cir. 1993); Schisler v. State, 907 A.2d 175, 201 (Md. 2006). *See also* Lindh v. Murphy, 96 F.3d 856, 890 (7th Cir. 1996), *rev'd on other grounds*, 521 U.S. 320 (1997).

[47] Free Enter. Fund v. Pub. Co. Accounting Oversight Bd., 130 S. Ct. 3138, 3153–55 (2010).

[48] Indeed, then solicitor general Charles Fried confessed that he expected the government's argument to lose, as the law in question

> had too strong an appeal to the public's common sense.... And the spectacle of the administration launching this rather arcane argument of principle in order to ward off investigations of the President's close friends was just too unattractive. As I feared and should have predicted, not only the particular attack but the whole enterprise ran aground and was smashed to pieces.

FRIED, *supra* note 16, at 160.

[49] This adjudicative function is highlighted if one examines a comparative decision not to prosecute—the decision of Israeli attorney general Elyakim Rubenstein not to indict former prime minister Benjamin Netanyahu because he lacked sufficient evidence. *See* Deborah Sontag, *No Prosecution for Netanyahu in Graft Inquiry*, N.Y. TIMES, Sept. 28, 2000, at A1. It should be noted that in Israel "prosecutorial discretion is susceptible to judicial review, as is any other type of administrative discretion." Yoav Dotan & Menachem Hofnung, *Interest Groups in the Israeli High Court of Justice: Measuring Success in Litigation and Out-of-Court Settlements*, 23 LAW & POLICY, 1, 9 (Nov. 1, 2001); *see also* Yoav Dotan, *Should Prosecutorial Discretion Enjoy Special Treatment in Judicial Review: A Comparative Analysis of the Law in England and Israel*, 1997 PUB. LAW 513, 523–31 (Spring 1997).

[50] 501 U.S. 868, 920–21 (1991) (Scalia, J., O'Connor, J., Kennedy, J., and Souter, J., concurring in part and in the judgment).

modern structure of government rests on an uncertain and controversial constitutional foundation."[51]

Many scholars oppose the premise of the unitary executive and instead embrace a notion of broad congressional power that justifies divesting the president of unqualified executive power.[52] They maintain that the necessary and proper clause[53] grants to Congress the power to structure the executive department and insulate subordinate officers from unfettered removal power of the president.[54] Thus, Charles N. Steele and Jeffrey H. Bowman argue that the necessary and proper clause, read in conjunction with the appointments clause, authorizes Congress to enforce federal legislation by creating independent agencies, such as the FEC.[55]

B. Other Efforts to Centralize Executive Power

The impulse to centralize executive power goes beyond reining in the independent agencies and extends into the administration's policy-making process. Continuing this notion of centralizing authority in the White House itself and not just the executive branch, recent presidents have exponentially expanded their White House staff, often blurring the distinction between the president's authority to receive advice and the

---

51 *See* 1 KENNETH CULP DAVIS & RICHARD J. PIERCE, JR., ADMINISTRATIVE LAW TREATISE § 2.5, at 64 (3d ed. 1995). For a view that the debate over the president's removal power is really a "symbol of the struggle between Congress and the President for control over policy-making" with only "limited real-world significance," see Jonathan L. Entin, *Synecdoche and the Presidency: The Removal Power as Symbol*, 47 CASE W. RES. L. REV. 1595, 1595, 1601 (1997).

52 *See, e.g.*, Robert V. Percival, *Presidential Management of the Administrative State: The Not-So-Unitary Executive*, 51 DUKE L.J. 963, 1006–12 (2001) (arguing that presidential control of agency decision-making "confronts not only legal difficulties, but also substantial policy concerns" due to White House inclination to pursue "short-term political gains" rather than promote the objectives of congressional regulatory schemes); Cynthia R. Farina, *Undoing the New Deal Through New Presidentialism*, 22 HARV. J.L. & PUB. POL'Y 227, 236–37 (1998) (taking the position that the voices of a "diverse citizenry" will not be protected effectively under the unitary executive approach); Michael A. Fitts, *The Paradox of Power in the Modern State: Why a Unitary, Centralized Presidency May Not Exhibit Effective or Legitimate Leadership*, 144 U. PA. L. REV. 827, 856–76 (1996) (contending that the centralization of the modern executive reduces opportunities for cooperation and conflict mediation, and encouraging the public to evaluate the executive as an individual rather than an institution).

53 U.S. CONST. art. II, § 8, cl. 18.

54 *See, e.g.*, Saikrishna Prakash, *Removal and Tenure in Office*, 92 VA. L. REV. 1779, 1792–93 (2006) (asserting that "[j]ust as the Necessary and Proper Clause authorizes the creation of offices and the specification of their functions, so too does the Clause authorize... [several de facto]... forms of congressional removals").

55 Charles N. Steele & Jeffrey H. Bowman, *The Constitutionality of Independent Regulatory Agencies Under the Necessary and Proper Clause: The Case of the Federal Election Commission*, 4 YALE J. ON REG. 363, 368–69, 378–380 (1987) (contending that the necessary and proper clause, read in conjunction with appointments clause, authorizes Congress to create independent agencies such as the FEC to enforce federal legislation).

executive authority of principal officers (which requires of course the advise and consent function of the Senate).[56]

One modern effort to increase presidential control of the bureaucracy generally has been the creation of the White House "czar" system. While these czars have only tangentially impacted independent agencies, they are worth considering for their effect on the power of the presidency more generally. Certainly, the president has a right to a corps of advisors. The question is whether and to what extent they will go beyond advice-giving to the kind of discretion and operational role normally associated with "officers" of the United States, whom of course require the Senate's "advice and consent."[57] Presidents since Franklin Roosevelt have made use of an institutionalized White House staff to assist in expanding presidential control of policy.[58] President Roosevelt established a multitude of new agencies that reported directly to him and impinged upon the traditional jurisdiction of the cabinet departments.[59] With the creation of the new Executive Office of the President in 1939, Roosevelt began to see his primary task as being "chief manager of the executive branch."[60]

President Nixon's attempt to centralize policy-making power from administrative agencies to the White House staff expanded this proposition when he proposed to create four new "super-departments."[61] One Nixon aide described Nixon's efforts as an attempt to create a "full-scale, parallel-regulatory apparatus within the White House."[62] Nixon also attempted to create a "supersecretary" in Henry Kissinger, who for two years played a dual roll as both secretary of state and presidential advisor for national security. However, Kissinger himself later reflected that this duality was not effective and placed him at a disadvantage within the administration.[63]

Presidents Nixon, Reagan, Carter, George H. W. Bush, and Clinton all utilized policy-specific, non-Senate-confirmed advisors;[64] however, statistics indicate that the

---

56 *See* Stephen Hess & James P. Pfiffner, Organizing the Presidency 1 (3d ed. 2002).

57 U.S. Const. art. II, § 2, cl. 2.

58 Hess & Pfiffner, *supra* note 56.

59 *Id.* at 2.

60 *Id.; see also* John P. Burke, The Institutional Presidency 8 (2d ed. 2000).

61 Bradley H. Patterson, Jr., The White House Staff: Inside the West Wing and Beyond 26 (2000).

62 Richard Nathan, The Administrative Presidency 34–43 (1983).

63 Henry Kissinger, Years of Upheaval 435 (1982).

64 President Reagan, a former governor who had been campaigning since 1968, had spent two decades promoting his policy ideas and was more concerned with policy implementation than policy development. Hess & Pfiffner, *supra* note 56, at 134. Presidents George H. W. Bush and Bill Clinton each appointed skilled and competent cabinet secretaries and developed a good working relationship between the president, the cabinet and the White House staff; nevertheless, Hess explains that the continued "expanding role of government and the need for policy integration and central control led to the growth of the White House at the expense of the cabinet" under their administrations. *Id.* at 148. Attempting to centralize policy in the White House, Clinton nearly doubled the size of his cabinet, posting an additional eleven top officials at cabinet level rank: chief of staff, CIA director, OMB director, Council of Economic Advisers chair, EPA director, U.S. trade representative, "drug czar," FEMA director, Small Business Administration

George W. Bush and Obama administrations have most vastly expanded the number of "czars" used by the executive branch.[65] Some estimates account for thirty-six czar positions in total that existed under the George W. Bush administration.[66] However, Obama White House officials and others have disputed the scope of the expansion, noting that the Senate confirmed several officials, such as the "regulatory czar" and "technology czar."[67]

The Obama administration has made extensive use of White House advisors, suggesting such officials do not have to be an "advise and consent" officer of the United States to drive policy.[68] Some critics point out that Congress has fewer tools to hold presidential advisors accountable, and the White House stoutly resents congressional attempts to do so. Thus while Congress has held the chief of staff in contempt at various times for failing to testify or disclose subpoenaed documents, these citations have been of little consequence.[69] The White House has claimed that "immediate presidential advisers are constitutionally immune from compelled congressional testimony about matters that arise during their tenure as presidential aides and relate to their official duties."[70]

---

director, UN representative, and counselor to the president. HESS & PFIFFNER, *supra* note 56, at 152 (citing UNITED STATES GOVERNMENT MANUAL 1996–97 89 (Government Printing Office 1997)).

65 Jonathan D. Puvak, Note, *Executive Branch Czars, Who Are They? Are They Needed? Can Congress Do Anything About Them?*, 19 WM. & MARY BILL RTS. J. 1091, 1097–98 (2011).

66 *See* Michael Fletcher & Brady Dennis, *Obama's Many Policy "Czars" Draw Ire From Conservatives*, WASH. POST, Sept. 16, 2009, at A6.

67 Kara Rowland, *Policy Czars Remain on Job as Objections Simmer*, WASH. TIMES, July 22, 2011, at A1.

68 Aaron J. Saiger, *Obama's "Czars" for Domestic Policy and the Law of the White House Staff*, 79 FORDHAM L. REV. 2577, 2599 (2011). *See also* Stephen Dinan, *Czar War Escalates Between Congress, White House*, WASH. TIMES, Oct. 23, 2009, at A1, A3.

69 For instance, in July 2007, former White House counsel Harriet E. Miers (who had resigned as White House counsel in Jan. 2007) and White House chief of staff Joshua B. Bolten refused to testify before the House Judiciary Committee about the controversial firing of nine U.S. attorneys, citing executive privilege. On February 14, 2008, the House as a whole voted to hold both Miers and Bolten in contempt of Congress for failing to provide subpoenaed documents. Two weeks later, House Speaker Nancy Pelosi called on Attorney General Michael B. Mukasey to file criminal contempt charges against Miers and Bolten. Mukasey refused on the ground that "non-compliance...did not constitute a crime" because both had properly invoked executive privilege. Letter from Attorney General Michael B. Mukasey to Representative Nancy Pelosi, Speaker of the House 2 (Feb. 29, 2008), *available at* http://gulcfac.typepad.com/georgetown_university_law/files/mukasey.pelosi.0228.pdf (last visited Aug. 7, 2012). For a detailed account of this clash between Congress and the Executive, see Josh Chafetz, *Executive Branch Contempt of Congress*, 76 U. CHI. L. REV. 1083, 1086–93 (2009). In his historical study of the contempt power, Chafetz concludes that Congress has little power in these clashes, because it has largely ceded enforcement of contempt to the judiciary since the 1970s. *Id.* at 1155–56.

70 *See* Letter of White House Counsel to Fred F. Fielding (Aug. 1, 2007), *available at* http://www.fas.org/sgp/bush/olc080107.pdf. Attorney General Janet Reno adopted similar reasoning in her letter to President Clinton advising that he assert executive privilege in response to congressional subpoena seeking testimony by the White House counsel regarding Clinton's decision to offer clemency to sixteen individuals, including his brother. "[I]n many respects, a senior advisor to the President functions as the President's alter ego, assisting him on a daily basis in the formulation of executive policy and resolution of matters affecting the military, foreign affairs, and national security and other aspects of his discharge of his constitutional

Theoretically, this raises the issue of whether the individual czar is merely advising the president as a White House staff member, or whether he or she is carrying out executive policy, which would make that individual a principal officer, necessarily appointed with the advice and consent of the Senate, and accountable for the purpose of testifying before committees.[71]

In February 2009, Democratic Senator Robert Byrd issued a letter to President Obama challenging the naming of several White House policy czars, who were not appointed with the advice and consent of the Senate, and who appeared to be largely accountable to only the President,[72] on the grounds that the czars have taken "direction and control of programmatic areas that are the statutory responsibility of Senate-confirmed officials."[73] These objections have not, however, applied equally to all the czar positions. As Senator Russ Feingold described the situation, the various czar positions fall into three categories. The first, and least problematic, is those czars whose positions were created by statute and who are appointed by the president with advice and consent of the Senate.[74] Feingold remarked, "I have no concerns about [this group] and frankly, no one else should either."[75] The second group, also not problematic to Feingold, are those czars whose positions report directly to a Senate-confirmed officer.[76] The third and most

---

responsibilities. Subjecting a senior presidential advisor to the congressional subpoena power would be akin to requiring the President himself to appear before Congress on matters relating to the performance of his constitutionally assigned executive functions.... [C]ompelling one of the President's immediate advisers to testify on a matter of executive decision-making would also raise serious constitutional problems, no matter what the assertion of congressional need." Janet Reno, Assertion of Executive Privilege with Respect to Clemency Decision (Sept. 16, 1999), *available at* http://www.justice.gov/olc/falnpotus.htm (last visited Aug. 7, 2012).

71 Elizabeth Warren's dual role as advisor to the president on financial activity and a special assistant in the Treasury Department brought this issue into focus. *See* Sewell Chan, *Consumer Advocate to Lead New Watchdog Agency as Assistant to Obama*, N.Y. TIMES, Sept. 16, 2010, at B3. *See also* Brady Dennis, *Warren Expected to be Adviser*, WASH. POST, Sept. 16, 2010, at A18. Republicans quickly pointed out the potential constitutional issues with Warren's positioning. *See* Brady Dennis, *Capitol Hill Divided on Obama Plan to Bypass Approval for Elizabeth Warren*, WASH. POST, Sept. 17, 2010, at A14. The story of Elizabeth Warren and the new consumer watchdog agency is recounted in chapter 7, section D, subsection 3.

72 *See* Margaret Talev, *Byrd Challenges Obama on Naming of Policy Czars*, PITTSBURGH POST-GAZETTE, Feb. 28, 2009, at A9.

73 Paul Light, *Nominate and Wait*, N.Y. TIMES, Mar. 24, 2009, at A27.

74 The complaints were not limited to Republicans. Both Senators Robert Byrd and Russell Feingold inveighed, on constitutional grounds, against the promiscuous use of czars. *See, e.g.*, Manu Raju, *Democrats Join GOP Czar War*, POLITICO, Sept. 17, 2009. *See also Examining the History and Legality of Executive Branch "Czars," Before the Subcomm. on the Constitution of the Sen. Comm. on the Judiciary*, 111th Cong. (2009) (statement of Sen. Russ Feingold).

75 *Id.*

76 *Id.* ("All of these positions are housed outside of the White House and all of these officials' responsibilities are determined by a superior who Congress has given the power to prescribe duties for underlings.").

problematic category are those positions housed within the White House itself, not subject to FOIA requests or to congressional requests for testimony.[77]

The extent of the czars' influence remains unknown, but their prevalent place within the Obama administration at least raises a question as to what role they will play in the regulatory process, including in policy areas governed by independent agencies.[78] Opposition to the Obama czars has been severe.[79] After Congress inserted a rider to the 2010 budget that prohibited funding for the salaries of various White House czars including the assistant to the president for energy and climate change, the health care "czar" and the energy "czar,"[80] the president rejected this prohibition in his signing statement.[81]

C. The Functionalist Response to the Unitary Executive Theory

Morton Rosenberg, who studied separation-of-powers questions from his perch at the Congressional Research Service, argues that the unitary executive lacks substantial constitutional basis and "subverts our delicately balanced scheme of separated but shared powers."[82] Similarly, Peter Strauss, rejecting any notion of a "neat division" of government functions, argued: "congressional judgments about appropriate structure would serve so long as they observed the two prescriptive judgments embodied in the Constitution: that the work of law-administration be under the supervision of a unitary,

---

[77] *Id.*

[78] Jim Tozzi, a former OIRA deputy administrator, has called for required disclosure of all communications between the policy czars and agencies proposing regulations. Environmental Protection Agency, *Regulatory Critics Seeks Broad Disclosure for White House "Czars,"* INSIDE EPA, Mar. 6, 2009. Exec. Order No. 12,866 currently requires public disclosure of all OIRA written communications with agencies during the regulatory process, but the new policy czars, though insiders capable of influencing the regulatory process, will not fall within OIRA. *Id.* Regardless, some commentators are not as skeptical about the czars' role, rather noting that proliferation in the use of czars is a direct result of the "glacial pace" of Senate confirmations, forcing Presidents to expand White House staff. Light, *supra* note 73, at A27.

[79] For a full review of the history, see Kevin Sholette, *The American Czars*, 20 CORNELL J.L. & PUB. POLICY 219, 222–27 (2010). *See also* Saiger, *supra* note 68, at 2578.

[80] The actual language reads:

Sec. 2262. None of the funds made available by this division may be used to pay the salaries and expenses for the following positions:

(1) Director, White House Office of Health Reform.
(2) Assistant to the President for Energy and Climate Change.
(3) Senior Advisor to the Secretary of the Treasury assigned to the Presidential Task Force on the Auto Industry and Senior Counselor for Manufacturing Policy.
(4) White House Director of Urban Affairs.

Department of Defense and Full-Year Continuing Appropriations Act, H.R. 1473, 112th Cong. § 2262 (2011) (enacted) (defunding czars' offices for health, climate, the automobile industry, and urban affairs).

[81] White House, Office of the Press Secretary, Statement by the President on H.R. 1473 (Apr. 15, 2011), *available at* http://www.whitehouse.gov/the-press-office/2011/04/15/statement-president-hr-1473.

[82] Rosenberg, *supra* note 25, at 634.

politically accountable chief executive; and that the structures chosen permit, even encourage, the continuation of rivalries and tensions among the three named heads of government, in order that no one body become irreversibly dominant."[83] As Calabresi and Rhodes observe, "the non-unitarians offer various functionalist theories of executive power that they believe better comport with the historical data, the Supreme Court's case law, and the relevant structural concerns."[84]

Functionalism then advocates an alternative model that allows for permeability between the branches. This "functionalist" approach argues that Congress may, by statute, adjust or alter the tripartite division of federal power so long as it does not undermine a core function or responsibility of one of the branches.[85] For the "functionalist," two questions predominate: first, does the act in question prevent a branch from performing a "core" function, and second, will such action "alter the balance of authority" between the branches?[86] Thus, for example, in *United States v. Nixon*, the Supreme Court adopted a functionalist approach when it examined on the one hand the nature of the disputed activity—the general privilege of confidentiality of presidential communications—and the administration of the criminal justice system on the other, and held that allowing the assertion of executive privilege "to withhold evidence that is demonstrably relevant in a criminal trial would... gravely impair the basic function of the court."[87]

---

83 Peter L. Strauss, *The Place of Agencies in Government: Separation of Powers and the Fourth Branch*, 84 Colum. L. Rev. 573, 667 (1984).

84 Calabresi & Rhodes, *supra* note 14, at 1170. *See also* Martin S. Flaherty, *Relearning Founding Lessons: The Removal Power and Joint Accountability*, 47 Case W. Res. L. Rev. 1563, 1566 (1997) (arguing that historical record does not evince consensus at time of founding in support of presidential removal power, and that evidence tends more toward opposition to such power).

85 *See, e.g.*, Youngstown Sheet & Tube Co. v. Sawyer, 343 U.S. 579, 634–55 (1952) (Jackson, J., concurring); Humphrey's Ex'r v. United States, 295 U.S. 602, 629 (1935) (recognizing need for quasi-legislative or quasi-judicial agencies, which have officers independent of executive control). *See generally* James M. Landis, The Administrative Process 15 (1938) (explaining administrative process needs to be more than "simply an extension of executive power" in order for agency to carry out its duties); Strauss, *The Place of Agencies in Government: Separation of Powers and the Fourth Branch*, *supra* note 83, at 578, 616–21 (advocating use of "checks and balances approach" language rather than "functional approach" language); Strauss, *Formal and Functional Approaches to Separation-of-Powers Questions—A Foolish Inconsistency?*, *supra* note 25 (arguing that while formalism has its advantages, U.S. government can clearly be described as functional); Harold Bruff, *Presidential Power and Administrative Rulemaking*, 88 Yale L.J. 451, 498 (1979) (stating "presidential supervision of officers should vary with the function involved"); Harold Bruff, *Presidential Management of Agency Rulemaking*, 57 Geo. Wash. L. Rev. 533, 537 (1989) (explaining that "functional analysis favors complex arrangements blending the powers of the branches; formalism tends to condemn them"). *See also* Harold J. Krent, *Fragmenting the Unitary Executive: Congressional Delegations of Administrative Authority Outside the Federal Government*, 85 Nw. U. L. Rev. 62, 64 (1990) (examining "constitutional delegations outside the federal government").

86 Bowsher v. Synar, 478 U.S. 714, 776 (1986) (White, J., dissenting). In the *Morrison* iteration of this standard, the action cannot "involve an attempt by Congress to increase its own powers at the expense of the Executive Branch." Morrison v. Olson, 487 U.S. 654, 694 (1988).

87 United States v. Nixon, 418 U.S. 683, 711–12 (1974).

Although not styled as such, the first articulation of the "functionalist" approach was in *Humphrey's Executor v. United States*,[88] which limited the expansive reach of *Myers* by holding that the framers intended to limit the removal power to "purely executive officers."[89] In contrast to *Myers*, the *Humphrey's Executor* Court dealt with a strange beast: an FTC commissioner, whom it viewed, as it did all independent agency commissioners, to be in certain respects "quasi-legislative" and in others "quasi-judicial," but in any event, "wholly disconnected from the executive."[90] Consequently, the Court held that Congress could set limits on the president's removal power vis-à-vis these officials.

Some functionalists, however, argue that a unitary system does not actually enhance accountability, but in fact undermines it. Heidi Kitrosser, for instance, points to examples such as the firing of the U.S. attorneys during the George W. Bush administration, in which the president avoided public revelation of his policy decision while maintaining control behind the scenes. She notes that a "unitarian system enhances the ability of the president... to influence agency actions away from the public eye.... 'the very opposite of accountability.'"[91]

Another example Kitrosser provides is the interaction between the White House and EPA in late 2007. The EPA compiled an extensive report on climate change, including recommendations for the regulation of greenhouse gases. The report was forwarded to the White House, who refused to open it, and when Congress sought to have the report disclosed, the White House refused, claiming executive privilege.[92] According to Kitrosser, because of the "structural and historical tools at the President's disposal to keep secrets, he and his proxies are well equipped to misrepresent his influence on the administrative process."[93] Other critics endorsing the view that the unitary executive does not function to foster accountability include Martin Flaherty, who argues that the separation of powers embodied in the Constitution serves to "ensur[e] that the branches of government would remain balanced, extending accountability throughout the government and making government more efficient than it had been."[94] And, this was often accomplished "at the expense of accomplishing a clean division of powers."[95]

---

[88] *See* Humphrey's Ex'r v. United States, 295 U.S. 602 (1935).

[89] *Id.* at 629–32. Note that Strauss suggests that *Humphrey's Executor* proposes a "radical" approach to separation of powers, emphasizing the "need to place agencies *in* one or another branch, maximally free from intrusion by the others." Strauss, *supra* note 83, at 611. He muses that the Court's formalism here might have been the result "of growing executive totalitarianism in Europe—in which resistance to broad executive authority was only to be expected." *Id.* at 612 n.154.

[90] *Humphrey's Ex'r*, 295 U.S. at 628–30.

[91] Heidi Kitrosser, *The Accountable Executive*, 93 Minn. L. Rev. 1741, 1764–65 (2009) (quoting Peter M. Shane, *Political Accountability in a System of Checks and Balances: The Case of Presidential Review of Rulemaking*, 48 Ark. L. Rev. 161, 173 (1995)).

[92] *Id.* at 1767–68.

[93] *Id.* at 1769.

[94] Martin Flaherty, *The Most Dangerous Branch*, 105 Yale L.J. 1725, 1783–85 (1996).

[95] *Id.*

Some functionalists point to the underdevelopment of the separation of powers in practice notwithstanding the constitutional text. Although the modern unitary theory would suggest presidential control over those responsible for prosecution of federal laws, the framers established no general or centralized body for federal prosecution, nor were those prosecuting federal law answerable to the president.[96] The Judiciary Act of 1789 created the Office of the Attorney General, but the attorney general did not actually oversee or direct the prosecution of federal law violations in federal courts by the district attorneys.[97] In fact, the main responsibility of early attorneys general was to represent the United States in the Supreme Court. They worked part-time and maintained their own private practices.[98]

The existence of early *qui tam* actions further withdrew the power of federal prosecutions from the president's control by placing the power to prosecution violations in the hands of private citizens.[99] The Supreme Court has noted that *qui tam* actions "have been in existence for hundreds of years in England, and in this country ever since the foundation of our government."[100] As Peter Shane has remarked, it is "extremely unlikely" that "the founding generation conceptualized criminal prosecution as an inherently executive function," given that in England criminal prosecution was not vested with the Crown and in many colonies and states early criminal prosecutions were handled by judicially appointed prosecutors.[101] In fact, the first Congress employed *qui tam* actions

---

96 Lessig & Sunstein, *supra* note 19, at 15–17.

97 *Id.* at 16–17. In fact, an earlier version of the Act would have allowed the Supreme Court to appoint the attorney general, and the lower courts to appoint district attorneys. Susan Low Bloch, *The Early Role of the Attorney General in our Constitutional Scheme: In the Beginning There Was Pragmatism*, 1989 DUKE L.J. 561, 567 (1989).

98 Jerry L. Mashaw & Avi Perri, *Administrative Statutory Interpretation in the Antebellum Republic*, 2009 MICH. ST. L. REV. 7, 19 (2009); *see also* Charles Gardner Geyh & Emily Field Van Tassel, *The Independence of the Judicial Branch in the New Republic*, 74 CHI.-KENT L. REV. 31, 74 n.169 (1998) ("Attorneys General were part-time officials in the early years of the country, and were paid relatively low salaries with the expectation that they would earn their primary living through private practice.") (citing Bloch, *supra* note 97, 591). The position of attorney general was a low-paying job with few prerequisites and was "a part-time position until the mid-nineteenth century." Bloch, *supra* note 97, at 567, 599 n.121.

99 Lessig & Sunstein, *supra* note 19, at 19–20 ("Both through citizens access to federal grand juries, and through civil *qui tam* actions...citizens retained the power to decide whether and in what manner to prosecute for violations of federal law. Here too the decision whom to prosecute and what crime to charge was placed in a person not subject to presidential direction or removal."). The *qui tam* actions of the past have been incorporated into the whistle-blower statutes of today. *See, e.g.*, Civil False Claims Act, 31 U.S.C. §§ 3730(b), 3730(d) (2004) (permitting private citizens to sue on the government's behalf those who bring a false claim for payment, such as healthcare fraud, to the government); 25 U.S.C. §§ 81, 201 (2000) (Indians and Indian tribes whistle-blower statute); 35 U.S.C. § 292 (2000) (allowing *qui tam* action for false marking of patents); 46 U.S.C. § 80103 (permitting *qui tam* action against those who steal property from a shipwreck). *See generally* Christina Orsini Broderick, Note, *Qui Tam Provisions and the Public Interest: An Empirical Analysis*, 107 COLUM. L. REV. 949 (2007); Michael Rich, *Prosecutorial Indiscretion: Encouraging the Department of Justice to Rein in Out-of-Control Qui Tam Litigation Under the Civil False Claims Act*, 76 U. CIN. L. REV. 1233, 1235 (2008).

100 Martin v. Trout, 199 U.S. 212, 225 (1905).

101 Peter Shane, *The Separation of Powers and the Rule of Law: The Virtues of "Seeing the Trees,"* 30 WM. & MARY L. REV. 375, 379 (1989).

in a variety of contexts, including in the enforcement of liquor import duties, the prevention of unlicensed trade with Indian tribes, and copyright infringement.[102]

The unitary theory also deviates from historical practice in the organization of executive departments. Although unitariness should call for "all departments . . . to be arranged hierarchically, all subordinate to the president and all answerable to him in the exercise of all discretionary functions," such was not the case.[103] For example, while the president originally had plenary control over the Department of Foreign Affairs and could remove the secretary of that department, the framers did not provide him such control over the Department of the Treasury.[104] However, Lessig and Sunstein conclude that, despite these historical discrepancies, rejection of the unitary theory is not required, asserting that "a strongly unitary executive is the best way of keeping faith with the most fundamental goals of the original scheme," including coordination, accountability, and efficiency.[105]

D. Political Will and Independence

Recently, commentators have begun to understand independence through the lens of political science and public choice theory. These approaches do not limit themselves to legal criteria but look to a wider set of criteria in assessing the independence of agencies.

---

102 Evan Caminker, *The Constitutionality of Qui Tam Actions*, 99 YALE L.J. 341, 342 n.3 (1989). The modern version of the "*Qui Tam*" is, of course, the "whistle-blower action," where a private person can bring an action under a statute against another private party for violating the law, and receive a portion of the penalty paid to the government if the suit is successful. For instance, under the False Claims Act, a private person who is aware that another private party made a false or fraudulent claim may "bring a civil action . . . for the person and for the United States Government . . . in the name of the Government." 31 U.S.C. § 3730(b); 31 U.S.C. § 3729. Although modern *qui tam* actions typically have been implemented to enforce public health or safety laws, Sarbanes-Oxley broke new ground by providing whistle-blower protection for private persons "who raise concerns about financial matters that implicate violations of federal securities laws." Daniel P. Westman, *The Significance of Sarbanes-Oxley Whistleblower Provisions*, 21 THE LAB. LAW. 141, 142 (2005), *available at* http://www.mofo.com/files/Publication/58a50224-9d8d-4d9c-9ab3-0d66054f5a7e/Presentation/PublicationAttachment/de62f0fd-63c0-42cb-b7bd-f5db1cb81f63/05FallLaborLawyer.pdf; Sarbanes-Oxley Act, 18 U.S.C. § 1514(A) (2002). *See* Vermont Agency of Natural Res. v. United States *ex rel.* Stevens, 529 U.S. 765, 780–88 (2000) (holding that private individuals may not bring an action under the False Claims Act in federal court on behalf of the United States against a state or state agency).

103 Lessig & Sunstein, *supra* note 19, at 22.

104 *Id.* at 26–29. The authors note that in enacting the Department of the Treasury, Congress shielded the comptroller from presidential direction.

105 *Id.* at 85–86, 94. It is interesting to note that a 1996 opinion from the OLC, outlining general separation-of-powers issues, gave weight to the "scholarly consensus," including the work of Lessig and Sunstein, that the principle of separation of powers was "originally understood to be flexible, open-ended, and consistent with a variety of actual institutional relationship among the three branches [and that] early *practice* under the Constitution reflected a loose rather than strict understanding of the required separation." The Constitutional Separation of Powers Between the President and Congress, 20 Op. O.L.C. 124, 134 n.33 (1996).

Among these approaches is an assessment of the will to assert political control or what we will call political will. Some commentators believe that in order to understand how independent agencies operate, variables that impact agencies other than their structural organization and indicia of independence must be analyzed. Neal Devins believes that "the focus of agency analysis should encompass interbranch power and expectations as well as agency structure."[106] In his article "Political Will and the Unitary Executive: What Makes an Independent Agency Independent?," Devins claims that the political will exerted by the president, Congress, and independent agencies invariably affects the outcome of power struggles, notwithstanding the independent structure of the agency. Devins discusses executive litigation over litigation control and compares the effect of political will in several recent controversies concerning litigation authority.[107] His study demonstrates that a president who adheres to a strong paradigm of the unitary executive and strategically exerts political will in an altercation can be victorious, notwithstanding a structurally independent agency.[108] While his is a sociological observation about how agency–executive dynamics work in practice (rather than a normative point alone), it would be foolish to ignore his empirical analysis.[109]

There is a theoretical debate among commentators over whose interests the Department of Justice (DOJ) should represent when it controls litigation. There are several models that serve to justify the respective views. Under the bureaucratic theory of representation—the most common model—the agency is the policy-making client and the DOJ acts as the agency's advocate.[110] Opponents of this model promote the theory of the unitary executive and maintain that the DOJ represents the policies of the president to secure a unified executive branch through policy coordination and centralization.[111] Devins argues that while structural factors such as litigation and removal authority often influence the choice of models, political will is the principal factor that determines which of these models will prevail.[112] When the DOJ wields litigation authority, for example, the president can successfully implement his policies and coordinate the executive branch if he strategically exerts his will.

---

106 Neal Devins, *Political Will and the Unitary Executive: What Makes an Independent Agency Independent?*, 15 CARDOZO L. REV. 273, 274 (1993).

107 We address litigation control in more detail in chapter 6, section B.

108 *But see* Harold J. Krent, *The Sometimes Unitary Executive: Presidential Practice Throughout History*, 25 CONST. COMMENT. 489, 510 (2009) (reviewing STEVEN G. CALABRESI & CHRISTOPHER S. YOO, THE UNITARY EXECUTIVE: PRESIDENTIAL POWER FROM WASHINGTON TO BUSH (2008)). Krent argues that where presidential administrations have encouraged one agency to sue another the unitary executive model is undercut because under his conception of the unitary executive "each official's decision [to pursue the litigation] represents that of the president." *Id.* In other words, "[i]n many litigations the executive branch itself has not treated the federal government as one indivisible entity." *Id.*

109 *See* Devins, *supra* note 106, at 311–12.

110 *See id.* at 279.

111 *See id.*

112 *See id.*

Devins illustrates this point by comparing the different approaches adopted by the Carter and Reagan administrations. During the Carter administration, Attorney General Griffin Bell believed that the DOJ should advocate the position of the agency and took pains to shield the solicitor general's office from the political will of the White House.[113] In sharp contrast, both presidents Ronald Reagan and George H. W. Bush forcefully exerted their will to centralize the executive branch, and during their administrations, the DOJ proved to be an effective conduit through which policy was implemented and advanced.[114]

During the Reagan administration, a power struggle reflecting these conflicting philosophies arose between the EEOC and the DOJ.[115] In 1983, the DOJ discovered that the EEOC was preparing to file an amicus brief in *Williams v. City of New Orleans*[116] in support of affirmative action, which contradicted a brief previously filed by the DOJ.[117] Although the multimember commission has authority to litigate certain employment discrimination issues involving private parties before lower federal courts, the DOJ has exclusive authority to litigate matters concerning state and local governments.[118] The DOJ viewed the EEOC's amicus brief as an attempt to thwart its exclusive authority.[119] The situation was further complicated by the fact that the EEOC had been instrumental in ensuring that federal agencies implemented affirmative action plans under the Carter administration and that during the Carter administration, the solicitor general had allowed the EEOC to file briefs conflicting with the DOJ's briefs.[120]

---

113 *See id.* at 281 (quoting Bell saying that DOJ lawyers "must take care not to interfere with the policy prerogatives of our agency clients") (internal quotation marks and citation omitted). *See also* Griffin B. Bell, *The Attorney General: The Federal Government's Chief Lawyer and Chief Litigator, or One Among Many?*, 46 FORDHAM L. REV. 1049, 1061 (1978). *Compare* Elliott Karr, *Independent Litigation Authority and Calls for the Views of the Solicitor General*, 77 GEO. WASH. L. REV. 1080, 1081 (2009). Indeed, during that period Senator Ervin introduced a bill to make the DOJ an independent agency. *See* S. 2803, 93rd Cong. 2d Sess. (1978). Hearings on the legislation revealed serious constitutional concerns regarding the executive's authority to enforce and carry out the laws. *See Removing Politics From the Administration of Justice: Hearings on S. 2803 and S. 2978 Before the Subcomm. on Separation of Powers of the Senate Comm. on the Judiciary*, 93d Cong., 2d Sess. 2 (1974).

114 *See* Devins, *supra* note 106, at 280-81.

115 *See id.* at 285–92 (describing the conflict between the EEOC and DOJ). *See also* Margaret H. Lemos, *The Other Delegate: Judicially Administered Statutes and the Nondelegation Doctrine*, 81 S. CAL. L. REV. 405, 448–49 (2008) (discussing various means of political control of agencies); *see also* Margaret H. Lemos, *The Consequences of Congress's Choice of Delegate: Judicial and Agency Interpretations of Title VII*, 63 VAND. L. REV. 363, 388 (2010).

116 Williams v. City of New Orleans, 729 F.2d 1554 (5th Cir. 1984).

117 *See* Devins, *supra* note 106, at 286–87.

118 *See* 42 U.S.C. § 2000e-5(f)(1) (1994).

119 *See* Devins, *supra* note 106, at 287 (noting the DOJ's view that executive branch should speak with one voice in civil rights cases involving state and local governments, and that the DOJ was the appropriate entity for expressing government's uniform position).

120 *See id.* at 290. By Exec. Order No. 12,067, President Carter gave the EEOC authority to develop standards and guidelines that federal agencies should follow in complying with equal opportunity laws. Exec. Order No. 12,067, 3 C.F.R. 206 (1979), *reprinted in* 42 U.S.C. § 2000e at 542 (1994).

In contrast, the Reagan administration wanted the executive to speak in a unitary voice in matters it considered of major importance, such as affirmative action. Faced with a DOJ opinion asserting sole litigating authority, the EEOC surrendered.[121] Devins attributes the surrender of the EEOC to pressure exerted at a meeting among the EEOC chair, Clarence Thomas, the EEOC general counsel, David Slate, the White House counsel, Ed Meese, Attorney General William French Smith, and DOJ Civil Rights Division chief William Bradford Reynolds.[122]

An independent agency's efforts to exert its political will may be bolstered by several tools that the agency may have at its disposal. Its organizational structure and enabling statute provide the agency with a measure of independent authority. The greater the authority allocated to the agency by Congress, the greater its freedom from the executive branch. Often, though, the measure of an independent agency's political will is dependent upon the actions of Congress or the president, or their failure to intercede. Devins suggests that "agency independence is necessarily qualified. Independence from the executive may mean dependence upon the Congress. Furthermore, independence from the executive[] may be temporal—depending on shifting White House attitudes towards unitariness or competing policy demands that yield disunitariness in interpretation."[123] A vigilant president will make it more difficult for an agency to effectuate its own policies. Likewise, if Congress chooses to, it can closely regulate an agency through legislation and oversight. Although Congress defines the parameters of the agency's powers through legislation, it would be inefficient and perhaps even contrary to congressional self-interest to regulate agencies' daily activities in this manner.

Further, in 1992, the U.S. Postal Service was successful in thwarting the will of President George H. W. Bush by strategically exerting its own political will. A dispute arose between the Postal Service and the Postal Rate Commission concerning rate-making authority.[124] The DOJ challenged the independence of the service and tried to position itself as arbiter between the entities to centralize the dispute.[125] However, the Postal Service is endowed with much more independence than the Postal Rate Commission, a fact that was instrumental in the service's ultimate victory. President Bush attempted to directly compel the service's Board of Governors to acquiesce, and when that tactic failed, even though he had recently lost the 1992 election, he threatened to remove the board members, who refused to comply with his directive.[126] Those board

---

[121] *See* Devins, *supra* note 106, at 288.

[122] *See id.*

[123] *Id. at* 312.

[124] *See id.* at 308.

[125] *See id.*

[126] *See id.* at 308 & n.171 (citing Letter from President George Bush to Bert Mackie, Governor, U.S. Postal Service (Jan. 4, 1993)).

members sought an injunction against the president to prevent their removal, which was granted.[127]

In this matter, the president failed in his attempts to unify the executive branch and stymie viewpoints contradictory to those of the DOJ and himself. Not only did he ignore the independent structure of the Postal Service, but he tried to "strong-arm" the board members after he lost the 1992 election. With his departure imminent, President Bush's power was emasculated, a point the board members used to their advantage. The decision to exert his authority when his political power was at its weakest was a grave tactical error. As a result, the executive branch's constitutional authority was unable to overcome the structural barriers of the Postal Service.[128] Those structural barriers included limits on presidential removal power, the absence of a presidential role in selecting two of the board members, and a statutory grant of independent litigation authority.[129]

Michael Herz suggests that *United States v. Interstate Commerce Commission*[130] provides another example of agency independence stifling attempted executive control over litigation.[131] In that case, the Supreme Court found justiciable a suit brought by the United States against the ICC due to the ICC's refusal to order certain railroads to refund allegedly unlawful fees paid to them by the U.S. Army. Herz argues that as an alternative to the Court's actual rationale for justiciability,[132] the judiciary could properly resolve such a case because the initial proceeding before the ICC was an adjudication over which Congress had removed the president's authority to dictate the outcome.[133]

Interagency litigation may, however, be of actual benefit to the president's political objectives by allowing him to advance conflicting interests, or at least avoid advancing one set of interests over the other. The president might restrain his influence and allow courts to resolve intrabranch or interagency disputes rather than risk his own political

---

127 *See* Devins, *supra* note 106, at 310.

128 *See id.* at 310–11. In 1981, the DOJ's OLC declined to bring the Postal Service within the reach of an Executive Order that gave the attorney general authority to coordinate the enforcement of various anti-discrimination laws. *See* Status of the United States Postal Service as an "Executive Agency" Under Exec. Order No. 12,250, 5 Op. O.L.C. 239, 240–41 (1981) (concluding that Postal Service was not an "executive agency" under Executive Order in part because "Congress intended to grant the Service at least some measure of insulation from control by the President and to place the Service in a separate category from the conventional executive departments").

129 *See* Devins, *supra* note 106, at 210–11.

130 337 U.S. 426 (1949).

131 Michael Herz, *United States v. United States: When Can the Federal Government Sue Itself?*, 32 Wm. & Mary L. Rev. 893, 918 (1991).

132 The Court actually reasoned that although it is well-established that a plaintiff may not sue himself, "courts must look behind names that symbolize the parties to determine whether a justiciable case or controversy is presented." 337 U.S. at 430. And here, there was a traditionally justiciable controversies as to whether the railroads where barred from extracted the fees from the United States. *Id.*

133 Herz, *supra* note 131, at 918 ("Because Congress had already removed the ICC's decision from presidential influence, however, permitting judicial review constituted no further intrusion on executive authority.").

capital. For instance, in *Metro Broadcasting v. Federal Communications Commission*,[134] a case involving FCC preferences for minority broadcasters, the second Bush administration allowed for dual filings by the FCC and the solicitor general both to appease social conservatives and to still allow Bush's FCC nominees to convince Congress of their support for affirmative action programs.[135]

Finally, as we discuss in chapter 9, the internal operation of agencies can also bear on the relative strength of a president to control agency behaviors. By and large, Presidents pay more attention to the appointment of the chair of a multimember agency than they do to the selection of other members. Agency chairs are usually more in touch with presidential objectives than their colleagues. So the relationship between a chair and his or her colleagues, which is a function of structure, practice, and personality, will have an effect on presidential control of the agency.

E. Presidential Directive Authority

There is one more issue it is necessary to raise related to the political will theory—the theory of presidential directive authority, sometimes called presidential directory authority or the presidential control model.[136] This approach contrasts with the traditional view of presidential power over executive branch agencies by stressing that Congress "possesses broad…power to structure the relationship between the president and the administration."[137] And further, "by virtue of this power, Congress can insulate discretionary decisions of even removable (that is, executive branch) officials from presidential dictation."[138] Thus, Congress can vest the agency chair with virtually unlimited authority to exercise his or her discretion in specific areas.[139] This has been called the "'not-so-unitary executive' or 'dis-unitary executive'" approach.[140] Such congressional

134 497 U.S. 547 (1990).

135 Neal Devins & Michael Herz, *The Uneasy Case for Department of Justice Control of Federal Litigation*, 5 U. Pa. J. Const. L. 558, 579 (2003).

136 The iconic statement of this position can be found in Elena Kagan's article *Presidential Administration*, which notes "Congress possesses broad, although not unlimited, power to structure the relationship between the President and the administration, even to the extent of creating independent agencies, whose heads have substantial protection from presidential removal." Elena Kagan, *Presidential Administration*, 114 Harv. L. Rev. 2245, 2250 (2001). *See also* Lisa Schultz Bressman & Michael P. Vandenbergh, *Inside the Administrative State: A Critical Look at the Practice of Presidential Control*, 105 Mich. L. Rev. 47, 47 (2006) (noting the "broad scholarly endorsement" and the "bipartisan political support" for the presidential control model, but criticizing the validity of that model).

137 Kagan, *supra* note 136, at 2250.

138 *Id.*

139 *Id.*

140 Robert V. Percival, *Who's in Charge? Does the President Have Directive Authority over Agency Regulatory Decisions?* 79 Fordham L. Rev. 2487, 2488 (2011). Percival has earlier argued for this approach in *Presidential Management of the Administrative State: The Not So Unitary Executive*, 51 Duke L.J. 963 (2001).

authorizations often include specific grants of authority to the agency or administration to act. The Occupational Safety and Health Administration (OSHA) statute, for instance, states that the administrator of OSHA should make rules to effectuate the Occupational Safety and Health Act.[141] Under the traditional view, "[t]he president cannot simply say to agency heads, 'Regulate in this lawful way because I direct you to do so,' and assume that the direction will be controlling itself, so long as an agency head has the relevant regulatory authority under a statute."[142]

The presidential directory model would allow the president to order agencies to engage in specific activities.[143] There are two variations on the "presidential directive authority doctrine." The first argues that presidential directive authority is constitutionally required. This, of course, is a simple application of the theory of the unitary executive to a member of the executive branch.[144]

A second approach, explored by Elena Kagan, suggests that when statutes provide that substantive regulatory decisions are to be made by heads of the agencies, these statutes should be interpreted to grant the president directive authority *unless* the statute expressly forbids it.[145]

Kagan[146] powerfully argues that when a statute does not specifically exclude presidential directive authority it should be allowed.[147] Her view is based on the extensive use of

---

141 Occupational Safety and Health Act, 29 U.S.C. § 655(a) (2006) ("the Secretary shall... by rule promulgate as an occupational safety or health standard any national consensus standard, and any established Federal standard, unless he determines that the promulgation of such a standard would not result in improved safety or health for specifically designated employees.").

142 Thomas O. Sargentich, *The Emphasis on the Presidency in U.S. Public Law: An Essay Critiquing Presidential Administration*, 59 ADMIN. L. REV. 1, 7–8 (2007).

143 *Id.* at 7–11.

144 This viewpoint has been well argued by CALABRESI & YOO, *supra* note 32 (*passim*).

145 Kagan, *supra* note 136, at 2330–31. In contrast with either approach to the Presidential Directive Authority, most countries explicitly vest the chief executive with the authority to direct official action. For instance, the French Constitution grants the prime minister the power to "direct the actions of the Government" and the "power to make regulations." 1958 Const. art. 21 (Fr.), translated by French Nat'l Assembly, http://www.assemblee-nationale.fr/english/8ab.asp (last visited Oct. 9, 2011). Nevertheless, the French political system does not fit easily into American notions of the unitary executive. While the French president appoints the prime minister, *id.* at art. 8, Article 21 designates the prime minister as the one who "directs the operation of the government," *id.* at art. 21, and the president presides over the Council of Ministers, *id.* at art. 9, and must sign "the ordinances and decrees deliberated on in the Council of Ministers." *Id.* at art. 13.

146 Kagan was dean of Harvard Law School and was deputy director of the Domestic Policy Council under President Bill Clinton. She served as the solicitor general for the United States. Robert Barnes, *Harvard Dean, Chosen as Solicitor General, Goes Before Senators,* WASH. POST, Feb. 10, 2009, A4. She now serves as a justice on the Supreme Court.

147 Kagan, *supra* note 136, at 2251. But see Kevin M. Stack, *The Statutory President*, 90 IOWA L. REV. 539 (2005), who argues that for presidential statutory action there should be "a fundamental requirement that statutory authorization be traceable to an identifiable statutory source." *Id.* at 581. Stack concedes that the source can be implied in the statute, but says that the implication can not go further than the intent of Congress. *Id.* at 571–72. Stack's suggestion is that the president should be viewed like every other federal agency. *Id.* at 542.

directive authority by President Bill Clinton during his presidency.[148] This approach is part of a broader acceptance of what Kagan calls "presidential administration." In her view, "presidential administration" consists of review by OIRA, presidential directives, and a president's appropriation of agency determination as his own. She argues that "[b]y the close of the Clinton Presidency, a distinctive form of administration ... 'presidential administration'—had emerged, at the least augmenting, and in significant respects subordinating, other modes of bureaucratic governance."[149]

Kagan's approach finds some support in recent empirical evidence. Lisa Bressman and Michael Vandenbergh, for instance, studied the validity of presidential directive authority from the agency perspective—surveying top political officials at the EPA from both the George H. W. Bush and Clinton administrations.[150] While not finding a wholesale validation of the model, Bressman and Vandenbergh did conclude the model is legitimate, though "more complex and less positive" then previous scholarly endorsements.[151] They found, for instance, that "many respondents reported that the White House was heavily involved in a small number of big rules ... but [had] hardly any [involvement] in plenty of other rulemakings."[152] Bressman and Vandenbergh also found that the White House did play some role in energizing agency action, with 50 percent of respondents stating that White House involvement "sometimes energized the agency and induced it to be more active."[153] Sally Katzen, former administrator of OIRA during the Clinton administration, is critical, however, of Bressman and Vandenbergh's decision to focus their study on the EPA.[154] Katzen argues that the EPA is atypical as an independent agency because a number of its senior officials "had previously been environmental activists or state or local environmental officials ... who had forcefully advocated the importance of protection—indeed, improving—the environment."[155] Such prior experience, she speculates, may have caused President Clinton to issue fewer directives to induce the EPA to take action than he otherwise would have, and thus the practice of presidential directive authority may be more prevalent within other agencies.[156]

---

148 Clinton was the first president to impose formal regulatory oversight over independent agencies by requiring that before agency rules were finalized, they were to be submitted for review to the Office of Management and Budget. *See* Exec. Order No. 12,866, 58 Fed. Reg. 51,735 (1993).

149 Kagan, *supra* note 136, at 2250.

150 *See* Bressman & Vandenbergh, *supra* note 136, at 47.

151 *Id.*

152 *Id.* at 67.

153 *Id.* at 76. Twenty-nine percent of respondents said it "often did." *Id.* at 76–77.

154 *See* Sally Katzen, *A Reality Check on an Empirical Study: Comments on "Inside the Administrative State,"* 105 MICH. L. REV. 1497, 1499 (2007).

155 *Id.*

156 *Id.* Bressman and Vandenbergh found that only 28 percent of respondents were involved in a regulatory matter that was the subject of a presidential directive issued in the form of a public memorandum to the EPA administrator. Bressman & Vandenbergh, *supra* note 136, at 82–83.

There are also historical examples of "presidential administration," but these examples suggest that presidential directive authority was not considered the default position in the face of congressional silence. The embargo of 1807–1809 provides an example. Faced with continual threats from French and British ships on American commerce, Congress enacted the embargo in 1807.[157] In structuring the embargo Congress gave significant authority to the president, allowing him to "decide specific cases, to direct the activities of lower-level enforcement personnel, and to suspend the operation of the embargo (with such exceptions as he deemed prudent)."[158] As Jerry Mashaw notes, while granting such unlimited authority to the president represents what we think of today as "presidential administration," the embargo legislation "instead of presuming presidential authority... explicitly conferred enforcement or directive authority on the President."[159]

Regardless, Kagan's view no doubt reflects the robust role of the executive in using the White House as a "bully pulpit" in setting the domestic agenda.[160] It may also reflect political reality in that most agency heads would be delighted to defer to their president and allow him to set and take credit for setting an agency agenda.[161] For his part, Cary Coglianese incisively noted:

> the supposed constitutional rule limiting presidents to mere oversight of agencies is incapable of neutrally circumscribing either presidential or administrative behavior.

---

[157] An Act Laying an Embargo on All Ships and Vessels in the Ports and harbors of the United States, ch. 5, 2 Stat. 451 (1807). Congress subsequently enacted several other laws related to the embargo in order to provide necessary and effective enforcement mechanisms. Jerry L. Mashaw, *Governmental Practice and Presidential Direction: Lessons from the Antebellum Republic?*, 45 WILLAMETTE L. REV. 659, 674–76 (2009).

[158] Jerry L. Mashaw, *Reluctant Nationalists: Federal Administration and Administrative Law in the Republican Era, 1801–1829*, 116 YALE L.J. 1636, 1657 (2007).

[159] Mashaw, *supra* note 157, at 677. Mashaw also points out that President Jefferson did not rely solely on the legislation directing his authority; rather, he went back to Congress a number of times to seek further authority when the enforcement mechanisms he was initially provided with failed to be adequate. *Id.*

[160] During his presidency, George W. Bush expanded regulatory review to require officers within certain agencies to report not to the agency head, but rather to the president. *See* Exec. Order No. 13,422, 72 Fed. Reg. 2763 (Jan. 18 2007) (revoked by Exec. Order No. 13,497, 74 Fed. Reg. 6113 (Jan. 30, 2009)).

[161] Bressman & Vandenbergh, *supra* note 136, at 54. Bressman and Vandenbergh argue that the presidential control model, though empirically weak, theoretically increases the accountability of agencies, legitimizing their actions. *Id.* ("With the president at the helm, agencies were no longer 'headless.' Indeed, they had the best leader possible. Because the president is the one official elected by the entire nation, he is more responsive to and representative of the people than Congress."). However, they further point out that political accountability stemming from presidential control depends on the extent to which such control is transparent to the public. *Id.* at 78. Bressman and Vandenbergh's survey of EPA employees found that 97 percent of respondents felt that White House involvement in EPA policy was either "not visible to the public or only somewhat visible to the public." *Id.*

> The purported legal rule at issue distinguishes between presidential influence (or oversight) and presidential control (or decision), the former being permissible and the latter not....
>
> Unfortunately, any theoretical difference between influence and control, or between oversight and decision, will not be observed in practice.[162]

Or at least is unlikely to be observed in practice. Nevertheless, as Thomas Sargentich has pointed out, energetic presidentialism is not without its risks. Centralization of executive oversight at the expense of Congress could undermine the system's checks and balances, which are "central to a deliberative democracy in which the peoples' different viewpoints are shared and deliberated to arrive at outcomes with broad appeal."[163]

Of course, this problem in the past did not have an impact on the independent agencies as they were considered formally "independent." Nonetheless, increased use of presidential directive authority cannot help but bleed into the autonomy of the independent agency, in expectations at least, if not in formal law. As David Barron and Peter Strauss have pointed out, "[i]n the real world... agency officials may be primed to jump when merely asked (but not directed) to do so, given 'the tendencies both of some leaders to appoint yes men, and of other appointees (those not meeting this description) to feel the impulses of political loyalty to a respected superior,'"[164] and independent agencies can hardly be immune from such influence. According to Barron, what ultimately matters "is whether agencies are functioning in practice as autonomous—not simply whether, as a formal matter the White House or the agency issues a given regulatory decision."[165]

F. Observations

There are a wide variety of hypotheses about agency independence. But practical rather than theoretical considerations motivated creation of the first independent agency, the ICC, in 1887. And constitutional and statutory texts, which are often ambiguous or

---

[162] Cary Coglianese, *Presidential Control of Administrative Agencies: A Debate over Law or Politics?*, 12 U. PA. J. CONST. L. 637, 645–46 (2010).

[163] Sargentich, *supra* note 142, at 5–6.

[164] David J. Barron, *From Takeover to Merger: Reforming Administrative Law in an Age of Agency Politicization*, 76 GEO. WASH. L. REV. 1095, 1121 (2008) (citing Peter L. Strauss, *Overseer, or "The Decider"? The President in Administrative Law*, 75 GEO. WASH. L. REV. 696, 714 (2007)).

[165] Barron, *supra* note 164, at 1121 (explaining that independent agency actors are clearly not immune from White House influence, Barron notes that "there is a real difference between a Federal Communications Commission run by Reed Hundt and one run by Michael Powell. That neither served at the pleasure of the President did not preclude the nation's Chief Executive Officer from shaping the direction of federal communications regulatory policy." *Id.* at 1101. Commissioner Hundt served as chair of the FCC under President Clinton, while Commissioner Powell served as chair under President George W. Bush.

imprecise, can be read either literally or in context in light of history. There is intellectual heft in various theories but no inevitable truth for all situations. Supreme Court decisions have not consistently applied a particular approach or theory. Rather, they apply a literal or functional approach depending on circumstances. Presidents ordinarily press vigorously for acceptance of some form of unitary executive theory and will continue to do so, although they must concede limitations to that approach. Congress will push back, although they may be frustrated at times in their lack of ability to enforce their model. As Devins contends, political will can influence the outcome of interbranch power struggles over independent agencies in individual cases. There may be reasons why, in a particular situation, either the president or Congress will choose to yield. In the circumstances, it is unlikely that any one theory of agency independence will carry the day in all cases. Certainly absolutist theories—whether a unitary executive or concluding that Congress has plenary power to create an administrative bureaucracy—are unlikely to triumph. That is because the administrative state is, at its heart, designed pragmatically to solve problems, with constitutional constraints nonetheless protecting the central functions of each political branch by placing boundaries on efforts by Congress or the president to push their authority beyond limits tolerable in a meaningful separation-of-powers system. So all three branches of government will continue to operate in the practical model that produced the ICC.

4

The Modern Agency

STRUCTURE AND APPOINTMENTS

A. Historical Characteristics of Independence

Section 11 of the Act to Regulate Commerce of 1887 created both the ICC and the basic organizational model for the modern multimember independent agency.[1] The ICC's statute provided for:

> [F]ive Commissioners, who shall be appointed by the President, by and with the advice and consent of the Senate. The Commissioners... shall be appointed for terms of six years, except that any person chosen to fill a vacancy shall be appointed only for the unexpired term of the Commissioner whom he shall succeed. Any Commissioner may be removed by the President for inefficiency, neglect of duty, or malfeasance in office. Not more than three of the Commissioners shall be appointed from the same political party. No person in the employ of or holding any official relation to any common carrier subject to the provisions of [the statute], or owning stock or bonds thereof, or who is in any manner pecuniarily interested therein, shall enter upon the duties of or hold such office. Said Commissioners shall not engage in any other business, vocation, or employment. No vacancy in the Commission shall impair the right of the remaining Commissioners to exercise all the powers of the Commission.[2]

[1] Act to Regulate Commerce, ch. 104, § 11, 24 Stat. 379, 383 (1887).

[2] *Id.*

A majority of these commissioners was needed to constitute a quorum for business transactions.[3] Further, as the statute was silent regarding the selection of a chairman, the commission itself—rather than the president—exercised the authority to choose its own chairman.[4]

The ICC served as the prototype for agencies such as the Federal Reserve Board (created in 1913), the FTC (created in 1914), the U.S. Shipping Board (created in 1916), the Federal Radio Commission (created in 1927), and the Federal Power Commission (created in 1930).[5] Indeed, "one measure of the success that the ICC was perceived as having in its first fifty years was its imitation in the creation of later agencies."[6]

As part of the Paperwork Reduction Act, Congress articulated a list of nineteen independent agencies, all of which are multimember:

> the Board of Governors of the Federal Reserve System, the Commodity Futures Trading Commission, the Consumer Product Safety Commission, the Federal Communications Commission, the Federal Deposit Insurance Corporation, the Federal Energy Regulatory Commission, the Federal Housing Finance Agency, the Federal Maritime Commission, the Federal Trade Commission, the Interstate Commerce Commission, the Mine Enforcement Safety and Health Review Commission, the National Labor Relations Board, the Nuclear Regulatory Commission, the Occupational Safety and Health Review Commission, the Postal Regulatory Commission, the Securities and Exchange Commission, the Bureau of Consumer Financial Protection, the Office of Financial Research, [and the] Office of the Comptroller of the Currency.[7]

Although Congress expanded the list to include "any other similar agency designated by statute as a Federal independent regulatory agency or commission," it declined to delineate the characteristics of such agencies.[8]

I. MODERN DEFINITIONS OF INDEPENDENCE

No general, all-purpose statutory or judicial definition of "independent agency" exists. Bernard Schwartz noted that "[t]he key to independence is security of tenure."[9] Thus,

---

3 *Id.* § 17.

4 Distinguished jurist and academic Thomas Cooley was selected by his colleagues as the ICC's first chairman. *See* Heather J. Gradison, *Welcome, The Interstate Commerce Commission Centennial Proceedings*, 16 TRANSP. L.J. 37, 37–38 (1987).

5 Morton Rosenberg, *Congress's Prerogative over Agencies and Agency Decisionmakers: The Rise and Demise of the Reagan Administration's Theory of the Unitary Executive*, 57 GEO. WASH. L. REV. 627, 657 (1989).

6 THOMAS K. MCCRAW, PROPHETS OF REGULATION 62 (1984) ("Most of the later federal commissions were patterned on the Interstate Commerce Commission, in appointment and tenure of members and in relationships with the existing branches of government—legislative, executive, and judicial.").

7 44 U.S.C. § 3502(5) (2006). *See also* Exec. Order No. 12,866, 3 C.F.R. 638 (1993), *reprinted in* 5 U.S.C. § 601 (1994) (adopting the Paperwork Reduction Act definition for purposes of OIRA regulatory planning and review).

8 44 U.S.C. § 3502 (5).

9 BERNARD SCHWARTZ, ADMINISTRATIVE LAW § 1.10, at 20 (3d ed. 1991).

it is not surprising that Kenneth Culp Davis and Richard Pierce define independent agencies as those that are "insulated from presidential control in one or more ways."[10] This notion of "tenure-plus" has led some to suggest that independence means bipartisanship,[11] nonpartisanship,[12] rule by experts,[13] or freedom from congressional[14] or executive influence.[15] An even more extreme view believes independent agencies should be completely independent of both the legislative and executive branches. In a dispute with Congress over striker replacement legislation, former chairman of the NLRB William Gould wrote that "it is vital that independent administrative agencies remain free of interference from both the legislative and executive branches of government."[16]

However, notions of agency independence often coincide with notions of congressional control. For example, Democratic Speaker of the House Sam Rayburn once told President Kennedy's FCC chairman Newton Minow: "Your agency is an arm of the Congress [and] you belong to us."[17] Republican Senator Robert Packwood also touted this view when he reminded Reagan's FCC chairman Mark Fowler: "[Y]ou are a creature of Congress and you are to attempt to administer…laws in accordance with what you think Congress has intended."[18] In a letter to President Carter on December 17, 1977, six congressional chairmen and eight ranking members proclaimed that "Congress, and not the executive, controls the

---

[10] 1 Kenneth Culp Davis & Richard Pierce, Administrative Law Treatise (1994) § 2.5, at 46.

[11] *See id.* (noting that most independent agencies have "statutory limits on the number of members that can be of the same political party").

[12] *See, e.g.*, Robert Cushman, The Independent Regulatory Commissions 189–90 (1972) (submitting that the Interstate Commerce Commission and the Federal Trade Commission were created to promote technocratic, nonpartisan administration); Steven J. Diner, A Very Different Age: Americans of the Progressive Era 201 (1998) (suggesting that the Progressives established independent agencies in order to avoid partisan regulation).

[13] *See* James M. Landis, The Administrative Process 23–24 (1938) (arguing that the need for experts corresponds with the increase in regulation because "the art of regulating an industry requires knowledge of the details of its operation, [and the] ability to shift requirements as the condition of the industry may dictate").

[14] For instance, the 2010 Dodd-Frank Act insulated the newly minted Consumer Financial Protection Bureau from the congressional appropriations process in order to preserve the independence of the bureau. Dodd-Frank Wall Street Reform and Consumer Protection Act, Pub. L. No. 111-203, § 1017, 124 Stat. 1976 (2010). For a discussion of independent funding authority, see chapter 6, section C.

[15] *See* 1 I. L. Sharfman, The Interstate Commerce Commission: A Study in Administrative Law and Procedure, pt. 2, at 454 (1931); for a discussion of agency independence from centralized executive branch regulatory review, see chapter 6, section D.

[16] Joan Flynn, *"Expertness for What?": The Gould Years at the NLRB and the Irrepressible Myth of the "Independent" Agency*, 52 Admin. L. Rev. 465, 512 n.193 (2000) (quoting Letter by NLRB Chairman Gould to Republican Members of House Economic and Educational Opportunities Committee April 19, 1995, Daily Labor Report, Apr. 20, 1995, at *E-1, *E-2 (emphasis omitted)). *But see* James A. Gross, The Reshaping of the National Labor Relations Board: National Labor Policy in Transition 1937–1947, 261 (1981) ("[The board] is in many ways…a creature of Congress and the executive.").

[17] *See* Neal Devins, *Congress, the FCC, and the Search for the Public Trustee*, 56 Law & Contemp. Probs. 145, 148–49 (1993) (quoting Speaker Rayburn) (citation omitted).

[18] *Universal Telephone Service Preservation Act of 1983: Joint Hearings on S. 1660 and H.R. 3621 Before the S. Comm. on Commerce, Science, and Transportation and H. Comm. on Energy and Commerce*, 98th Cong. 67 (1983) (remarks of Sen. Packwood, Chairman, S. Comm. on Commerce, Science, and Transportation).

guidelines for independent regulatory agencies. Congress created these agencies. Congress provided for their organization. Congress adopted their statutory mandates. Congress controls their budgets and oversees their performance. Congress specifies agency Procedures."[19] Independent agency chair Reed Hundt recognized the "omnipresence of congressional influence on the commission's work" and conceded that "[a]s a matter of law, the White House could not tell the FCC Chairman or the commissioners how to vote."[20] Nevertheless, he noted that he, "and any agency head, preferred the White House to approve of [his] agenda."[21]

Congress has utilized a variety of techniques to exercise "control" over the executive branch and independent agencies: the advice and consent function,[22] the Congressional Review Act,[23] oversight hearings,[24] and particularly appropriations hearings.[25] Using the appropriations process, Congress has sought to cut an agency's budget after it issued a rule of which Congress disapproved.[26] It has also sought congressional hearings on cases

---

19 *See* Letter from Senator Abe Ribicoff et al. to President Carter, Dec. 16, 1977, *reprinted in* 124 CONG. REC. S4863–4864 (1978).

20 *See* REED E. HUNDT, YOU SAY YOU WANT A REVOLUTION: A STORY OF INFORMATION AGE POLITICS 19 (2000).

21 *Id.* at 13. For a discussion of the "analytical" difficulty of distinguishing between independent and executive agencies, see Jonathan L. Entin, *The Removal Power and the Federal Deficit*, 75 KY. L.J. 699, 768 (1987).

22 There are two ways in which the advice and consent power becomes a tool of supervision. The first is the very direct fact that the Senate has a say in personnel and can refuse to approve appointments if it expects that a nominee will not execute something in the manner favored by the Senate. This power is often used to "convince" the president to nominate an individual in line with that senator's wishes. The second, less direct consequence of the Senate's power is that approval of appointments can be used as leverage over related and even completely unrelated areas in which the Senate has an interest in the execution of laws. Jack Beermann, *Congressional Administrations*, 43 SAN DIEGO L. REV. 61, 110–11 (2006).

23 5 U.S.C. §§ 801–808 (2006). *See* MORTON ROSENBERG, CONG. RESEARCH SERV., RL 30116, CONGRESSIONAL REVIEW OF AGENCY RULEMAKING: UPDATE AND ASSESSMENT OF THE CONGRESSIONAL REVIEW ACT AFTER A DECADE 6–7 (2008) (noting that the only rule to be nullified by the Congressional Review Act was OSHA's ergonomic standard in 2001.) *See generally* Note, *The Mysteries of the Congressional Review Act*, 122 HARV. L. REV. 2162, 2164 (2009). For a historical discussion, see Daniel Cohen & Peter L. Strauss, *Congressional Review of Agency Rulemaking*, 49 ADMIN. L. REV. 95 (1996).

24 A classic discussion can be found in Seymour Scher, *The Congressional Committee Members as Independent Agency Overseers*, 34 AM. POL. SC. REV. 911, 917 (1960). *See also* Matthew D. McCabbins & Thomas Schwartz, *Police Patrols v. Fire Alarms*, 28 AM. JL. OF POL. SCI. 165 (1984); Arthur Lupie & Matthew McCabbins, *Learning From Oversight: Fire Alarms and Police Patrols Reconstructed*, 10 J.L. ECON. & ORG. 96 (1994).

25 H.R. RES. 1023, 112th Cong. (2011). *See also* Katie Sheppard, *House Votes to Block EPA Climate Regs*, MOTHER JONES (Feb. 18, 2011, 7:28 p.m.), http://motherjones.com/blue-marble/2011/02/house-votes-block-epa-climate-regs (noting that the House of Representatives passed a continuing resolution that "include[d] a massive cut to the EPA's budget" in connection with barring the EPA from regulating greenhouse gas emissions).

26 *See, e.g.*, James B. Stewart, *As a Watchdog Starves, Wall St. Is Tossed a Bone*, N.Y. TIMES, July 16, 2011, at A1 (reporting that the "the Republican-controlled appropriations committee cut the Securities and S.E.C.'s responsibilities were vastly expanded under the Dodd-Frank Wall Street Reform and Consumer Protection Act"); Edward Wyatt & Ben Protess, *Foes Revise Plan to Curb New Agency*, N.Y. TIMES, May 5, 2011, at B1 ("Legislators also have called for the [Consumer Financial Protection Bureau] to be subject to the Congressional appropriations process. As established, its budget is set as a percentage of the Federal Reserve's budget and is not subject to approval by Congress."); David Rogers, *GOP Steps Up Efforts to Cut Funding for U.S. Agencies Opposed by Its Allies*, WALL ST. J., July 13, 1995, at A12 ("House Republicans are accelerating their efforts to use spending bills to restrict federal agencies that have angered the GOP's

pending in administrative courts so as to influence those proceedings,[27] and passed appropriations riders forbidding an agency from spending money to implement rules of which it disapproves.[28] Further, Congress has used the appropriations process to "hobble" those agencies it failed to prevent coming into being.[29]

---

business and conservative allies. The National Labor Relations Board, the Environmental Protection Agency, and the Occupational Safety and Health Administration are the most prominent targets.").

27 *See* Editorial, *Overreach on Oversight*, WASH. POST, Aug. 22, 2011, at A14 (commenting on the Boeing NLRB imbroglio, the editorial stated that "Mr. Issa and his committee have gone beyond questioning the NLRB's policy to threatening to interfere with a legitimate—even if misguided—legal proceeding. This month, the panel issued a subpoena demanding a slew of documents involving the NLRB action against Boeing. The committee wants to know how the NLRB's Office of General Counsel decided to target Boeing and whether it did so in cahoots with the White House or a union. The agency has resisted turning over certain documents it says could jeopardize its ability to pursue its case. Lafe Solomon, the NLRB's acting general counsel, testified before the committee this summer; the board has also turned over more than 1,500 pages related to the Boeing matter.").

28 One well-known example is the rider preventing the DOJ from advocating in oral argument the per se rule in resale price maintenance antitrust cases even though it had made that argument previously in an amicus brief. *See* Departments of Commerce, Justice and State, the Judiciary, and Related Agencies Appropriations Act of 1984, Pub. L. No. 98-166, 97 Stat. 1071, 1102 (1983) (cited in J. Gregory Sidak, *The Recommendation Clause*, 77 GEO. L.J. 2079, 2080 n.6 (1989)); *see also* Act of Sept. 30, 1988, Pub. L. No. 100-202, § 605, 101 Stat. 1329-1, 1329-38 (discussed in Peter J. Hammer, *Antitrust Beyond Competition: Market Failures, Total Welfare, and the Challenge of Intramarket Second-Best Tradeoffs*, 98 MICH. L. REV. 849, 915 n.176 (2000)); Act of Oct. 18, 1986, Pub. L. No. 99-500, § 605, 100 Stat. 1783, 1783-73. Another iconic example is the rider forbidding the expenditure of funds on all new Endangered Species Act listings and designation by the Fish and Wildlife Service, which was attached to an emergency supplemental appropriations bill. *See* Pub. L. No. 104-134, 110 Stat. 1321-159 to 1321-160 (1996); Emergency Supplemental Appropriations and Recessions for the Department of Defense to Preserve and Enhance Military Readiness Act of 1995, Pub. L. No. 104-6, ch. 4, 109 Stat. 73, 86 (appropriating funds to the Department of the Interior and related agencies).

Of the funds made available under this heading in Public Law 103-332—

(1) $1,500,000 are rescinded from the amounts available for making determinations whether a species is a threatened or endangered species and whether habitat is critical habitat under the Endangered Species Act of 1973 (16 U.S.C. 1531 et seq.); and

(2) none of the remaining funds appropriated under that heading may be made available for making a final determination that a species is threatened or endangered or that habitat constitutes critical habitat (except a final determination that a species previously determined to be endangered is no longer endangered but continues to be threatened.)

To the extent that the Endangered Species Act of 1973 has been interpreted or applied in any court order (including an order approving a settlement between the parties to a civil action) to require the making of a determination respecting any number of species or habitats by a date certain, that Act shall not be applied to require that the determination be made by that date if the making of the determination is made impracticable by the rescission made by the preceding sentence.

The entire saga is told in Jaron M. Patlis, *Riders on the Storm, or Navigating the Crosswinds of Appropriations and Administration of the Endangered Species Act: A Play in Five Acts*, 16 TUL. ENVTL. L.J. 257 (2003), who describes the rider as "infamous." *Id.*

29 Jessica Holser, *House Panel Targets Consumer Bureau, SEC Budgets*, WALL ST. J., June 23, 2011, http://online.wsj.com/news/articles/SB10001424052702303339904576404102094921400 (noting that Rep. Jo Ann Emerson "acknowledged that some Republicans want[ed] to hobble the agency created by the Dodd-Frank financial law by depriving it of funds"). The Consumer Financial Protection Bureau is a recent example. *See* Peter Schroeder, *GOP Targets Funding of Consumer Bureau*, THE HILL (June 15, 2011,

Despite Congress's control function (or perhaps because of it), Congress generally supports agencies' independence from executive branch interference. Thus, former SEC Chairman Harold Williams "acted like [a] traditional independent agency head[]" by not talking to the White House during a 1978 dispute.[30] The White House also has an incentive to refrain from interference. For example, on at least three separate occasions between 1953 and 1956, President Eisenhower's assistant Sherman Adams intervened in three separate federal agency investigations on behalf of his good friend Bernard Goldfine. These contacts included inquiries both to the FTC about mislabeling of garments and fabrics manufactured at Goldfine's Northfield Mills[31] and to the SEC regarding its investigation into Goldfine's real estate companies.[32] Although Adams claimed he never interfered with their administrative investigations, his intervention resulted in a "pass" for Goldfine at least once.[33] This, coupled with gifts he received from Goldfine—including an "infamous" vicuña coat[34]—led to Adams's resignation in 1958.[35]

2:03 p.m.), http://thehill.com/blogs/on-the-money/appropriations/166531-gop-sets-sights-on-consumer-bureau-in-latest-approps-bill.

30 *See* Lisa Schultz Bressman & Robert B. Thompson, *The Future of Agency Independence*, 63 VAND. L. REV. 599, 646 n.244 (2010).

31 After Northfield Mills received the letter requesting information about the misrepresentation and mislabeling of its fabrics, Mr. Goldfine reached out to Mr. Adams to see "what had prompted [the letter]." H.R. REP. NO. 85-2711, at 47 (1959) (quoting Letter from Sherman Adams, Assistant to the President, to Rep. Oren Harris, Chairman, Special Subcommittee on Legislative Oversight (June 12, 1958)). This induced Mr. Adams to reach out to the chairman of the FTC, Edward F. Howrey, to inquire about the investigation. William M. Blair, *Inquiry Indicates That Goldfine Got Agencies' Favors*, N.Y. TIMES, July 12, 1958, at 1; H.R. REP. NO. 85-2711, at 47 (1959). Subsequently, Chairman Howrey prepared a memorandum for Mr. Adams detailing the reason for the letter and identifying the company who initially filed the complaint against Mr. Goldfine's company. *The Administration: Man in the Storm*, TIME, June 30, 1958, *available at* http://www.time.com/time/magazine/article/0,9171,891889,00.html; *see* H.R. REP. NO. 85-2711, at 48 (1959). The letter also stated that "if Northfield will give adequate assurances that all their labeling will be corrected, the case can be closed on what we call a voluntary cooperative basis." H.R. REP. NO. 85-2711, at 49 (1959). Mr. Adams forwarded this memorandum to Mr. Goldfine, which was later determined a violation of the FTC's rule against disclosing complainants' names. *See* William M. Blair, *Goldfine Case Toppled Adams*, N.Y. TIMES, Sept. 23, 1958, at 19.

32 In 1956, Mr. Adams reached out to the SEC after hearing complaints from Mr. Goldfine about its investigation into his real estate companies. Instead of personally contacting the SEC, Mr. Adams requested that the special counsel to the president call the SEC to acquire more information about this case. William M. Blair, *Adams Concedes Calling Agencies; Denies Pressure*, N.Y. TIMES, June 13, 1958, at 1.

33 Again, in 1956, Mr. Goldfine's companies were under investigation for the mislabeling of their garments and fabrics. This time, Sherman Adams arranged a meeting between Chairman Howrey and Mr. Goldfine. William M. Blair, *Adams Concedes Calling Agencies; Denies Pressure*, N.Y. TIMES, June 13, 1958, at 1. This led to the Chief of the Division of Wool, Fur, and Flammable Fabrics' decision not to pursue criminal prosecution but rather issue a consent order. *See* H.R. REP. NO. 85-2711, at 45 (1959).

34 *See* H.R. REP. NO. 85-2711, at 48 (1959) ("Before the House Special Subcommittee on Legislative Oversight came new charges that Adams received a vicuna coat and an Oriental rug from Goldfine, and also that Goldfine had paid Adams' hotel bills at the Waldorf-Astoria in Manhattan as well as others in Boston."); *see also The Administration: Man in the Storm*, TIME, June 30, 1958, *available at* http://www.time.com/time/magazine/article/0,9171,891889,00.html.

35 *See* William M. Blair, *Goldfine Case Toppled Adams*, N.Y. TIMES, Sept. 23, 1958, at 19.

2. ORGANIZATIONAL STRUCTURE

The organization of modern multimember agencies follows the commission form established in the 1887 ICC statute, which has become synonymous with independence.[36] Agencies typically employ an odd number of members, with no more than a bare majority from the same political party. Members serve fixed, staggered terms that are often for an odd number of years extending beyond the four-year presidential term. This organizational structure is intended to dilute the effect that transitory political events may have on agency policy and maintain the agency's political independence.

These term requirements, however, do not alone guarantee independence. In *Parsons v. United States*, a nineteenth-century case, the Supreme Court concluded that the president could remove a U.S. attorney by appointing a new attorney—despite the existence of a four-year term.[37] More recently, the United States Court of Appeals for the Third Circuit similarly concluded that the president could remove a U.S. marshal who is appointed to a four-year term.[38] Thus, in order to preserve independence, agency removal must be protected against removal except "for cause." The protection against summary removal originally received constitutional approval in *Humphrey's Executor v. United*

---

36 Interstate Commerce Act, Pub. L. No. 49-41, 24 Stat. 379, 379–388 (1887) (repealed 1995).

37 167 U.S. 324, 343 (1897). Use of this power by former Attorney General Alberto Gonzales in firing nine U.S. attorneys led to a political scandal within the Bush administration, as the firings were largely seen as based on political loyalty and not job performance. *See* Editorial, *A Scandal That Keeps Growing*, N.Y. TIMES, May 6, 2007, at 13. Media reports speculated that the U.S. attorneys were fired based on their choices to investigate certain public corruption cases as well as their failure to investigate certain voter fraud complaints. *See* DEP'T OF JUSTICE, INVESTIGATION INTO THE REMOVAL OF NINE U.S. ATTORNEYS IN 2006 53 (2008). Though Gonzales claimed the removals were not for inappropriate reasons, the scandal may historically be seen as the reason for his resignation. *See* Alberto R. Gonzales, *They Lost My Confidence*, USA TODAY, Mar. 7, 2007 (stating that the removals were based on "reasons related to policy, priorities and management—what have been referred to broadly as 'performance-related' reasons" and that "[w]e have never asked a U.S. attorney to resign in an effort to retaliate against him or her or to inappropriately interfere with a public corruption case."); Eric Lichtblau & Scott Shane, *Attorney General Held Firm on War Policies*, N.Y. TIMES, Aug. 28, 2007, at A1 (describing the reasons for the attorney general's resignation). In September 2008 the Office of the Inspector General for the DOJ released the report of its investigation into the resignation of the nine U.S. attorneys. The report found that Gonzales had delegated evaluation of U.S. attorneys to Kyle Sampson, the DOJ chief of staff, later failing to "carefully [evaluate] the basis for each U.S. Attorney's removal or [attempt] to ensure that there were no improper political reasons for the removals." DEP'T OF JUSTICE, INVESTIGATION INTO THE REMOVAL OF NINE U.S. ATTORNEYS IN 2006 328 (2008).

38 Chabal v. Reagan, 841 F.2d 1216, 1219, 1222–23 (3d Cir. 1988). The Third Circuit rested its decision in part on the marshal's status as a "purely executive" officer, a ground subsequently undermined by the Supreme Court's 1988 decision. *Id.* at 1218–19. *See* Morrison v. Olson, 487 U.S. 654, 689 (1988) ("our present considered view is that the determination of whether the Constitution allow Congress to impose a 'good cause'-type restriction on the President's power to remove an official cannot be made to turn on whether or not that official is classified as 'purely executive.'"). However, it found, alternatively, that the statute does not manifest a congressional intent to confer "for cause" removal protection, a consideration that remains relevant. *See Chabal*, 841 F.2d at 1222–23 (contrasting the statute with that at issue in *Humphrey's Ex'r*).

States,[39] and continues to be the critical criterion by which scholars distinguish between "independent" and executive branch agencies.[40]

Surprisingly, the members of several independent agencies—including those at the FCC, the Federal Election Commission (FEC), the International Trade Commission (ITC), and the SEC—lack statutory removal protection. However, the Supreme Court has accepted the independence of SEC members,[41] and lower courts have assumed for cause removal for National Credit Union Association (NCUA) appointees,[42] and have suggested that the president's removal power over members of the FEC may be limited to good cause.[43]

Finally, like their executive branch counterparts, multimember independent agencies typically possess a combination of rulemaking, enforcement, and adjudication powers and functions.[44] When regulatory powers are conferred on cabinet departments, however, Congress has occasionally permitted separate multimember boards to adjudicate cases in what is known as a "split enforcement" model. For example, OSHA is part of the Department of Labor,[45] but Congress placed its adjudication responsibilities in the hands of the Occupational Safety and Health Review Commission, which is not affiliated with the Department of Labor.[46] Congress similarly divided mine safety

---

39 295 U.S. 602 (1935). *See generally* William E. Leuchtenburg, *The Case of the Contentious Commissioner: Humphrey's Ex'r v. U.S.*, *in* FREEDOM AND REFORM: ESSAYS IN HONOR OF HENRY STEELE COMMAGER 276, 278–312 (Harold M. Hyman & Leonard W. Levy eds., 1967) (providing history of and analysis of *Humphrey's Ex'r*).

40 *See, e.g.*, DAVIS & PIERCE, *supra* note 10, § 2.5, at 46. ("The characteristic that most sharply distinguishes independent agencies is the existence of a statutory limit on the president's power to remove the head (or members) of an agency."); PETER L. STRAUSS, AN INTRODUCTION TO ADMINISTRATIVE JUSTICE IN THE UNITED STATES 15 (1989) ("Because [independent commission] members are appointed for fixed terms from which they cannot be dismissed without formal cause, they are more remote from presidential influence and control than the more usual 'executive' agency.").

41 Free Enter. Fund v. Pub. Co. Accounting Oversight Bd., 537 F.3d 667, 669 (D.C. Cir. 2008), *aff'd in part, rev'd in part and remanded*, 130 S. Ct. 3138 (2010). *See also* SEC v. Blinder, Robinson & Co., 855 F.2d 677, 681 (10th Cir. 1988).

42 Swan v. Clinton, 100 F.3d 973, 983 (D.C. Cir. 1996).

43 Fed. Election Comm'n v. NRA Political Victory Fund, 6 F.3d 821, 826 (D.C. Cir. 1993) ("Appellants would distinguish Morrison on the grounds that the Act explicitly empowered the Attorney General (hence the President) to remove an independent counsel for 'good cause.' Here the statute is silent as to the President's removal authority, and therefore appellants argue that he has none. However, statutory silence could imply that the President actually enjoys an unrestricted power of removal.... The Commission suggests that the President can remove the commissioners only for good cause, which limitation is implied by the Commission's structure and mission as well as the commissioners' terms. We think the Commission is likely correct, but, in any event, we can safely assume that the President would at minimum have authority to discharge a commissioner for good cause—if for no other").

44 *See generally* STRAUSS, *supra* note 40, 15–16 (discussing the rulemaking, enforcement, and adjudicatory authorities of independent agencies).

45 29 U.S.C. §§ 651–678 (2007).

46 *See* Benjamin W. Mintz, *Administrative Separation of Functions: OSHA and the NLRB*, 47 CATH. U. L. REV. 877, 877–908 (1998); George Robert Johnson, Jr., *The Split-Enforcement Model: Some Conclusions from the OSHA and MSHA Experiences*, 39 ADMIN. L. REV. 315, 315 (1987).

responsibility by mandating that the Mine Safety and Health Administration develop mining safety standards, while granting the Federal Mine Safety and Health Review Commission adjudicatory powers to resolve challenges to those standards.[47]

Congress separated these functions in response to fear that concentrating rulemaking, enforcement, and adjudicative power in one body, would compromise due process and credibility. As Senator Javits noted, an "independent Panel approach would...preserve due process more easily, and thereby instill much more confidence in the whole program in workers and businessmen alike."[48]

B. Appointments

The president, with the advice and consent of the Senate, generally appoints members of multimember independent agencies;[49] however, there is a model of mixed presidential and nonpresidential appointment. For example, the president appoints the chairman of the National Indian Gaming Commission with the advice and consent of the Senate, but the secretary of the interior appoints the other two members.[50] All members serve three-year terms and can only be removed for good cause.[51] At the Board of Veterans' Appeals, the chairman is appointed by the president with the advice and consent of the Senate to a six-year term, while other members are appointed by the secretary of veterans affairs, with mere approval by the president and recommendation by the board's chairman.[52]

Appointments to regulatory boards and commissions reflect a variety of considerations. Geography is one concern; for example, no more than one member of the Federal Reserve Board may be appointed from any one Federal Reserve District.[53] More notably,

---

47 *See generally* Johnson, *supra* note 46, at 315. Split enforcement has also been suggested for other areas such as in the administration of social security disability. Paul R. Verkuil & Jeffrey S. Lubbers, *Alternative Approaches to Judicial Review of Social Security Disability Cases*, 55 ADMIN. L. REV. 730, 773 (2003).

48 SUBCOMM. ON LABOR, S. COMM. ON LABOR & PUBLIC WELFARE, LEGISLATIVE HISTORY OF THE OCCUPATIONAL SAFETY AND HEALTH ACT OF 1970, at 195 (1970).

49 *See, e.g.*, 12 U.S.C. § 241 (1994) (Federal Reserve Board); 47 U.S.C. § 154(a) (1994) (Federal Communications Commission). It is worth noting that some commentators have observed that appointments to independent agencies may require "greater and longer scrutiny" during the senate approval process than appointments to other executive agencies because once appointed they cannot be fired at will and are not traditionally subject to close presidential supervision. Brett Kavanaugh, *Separation of Powers During the Forty-Fourth Presidency and Beyond*, 93 MINN. L. REV. 1454, 1465 (2009).

50 *See* 25 U.S.C. § 2704(b)(1) (1994). Those appointed by the secretary of the interior are known as "associate members." *Id.* § 2704(b)(1)(B).

51 *See id.* §§ 2704(b)(4)(A), 2704(b)(6).

52 *See* 38 U.S.C. §§ 7101(b)(1), 7101A(a) (1994 & Supp. 1998). There is no constitutional prohibition on presidential appointees serving on decisional bodies with members whom they can appoint and remove. *See* Silver v. U.S. Postal Serv., 951 F.2d 1033, 1040–41 (9th Cir. 1991).

53 *See* 12 U.S.C. § 241 (1994).

agency statutes generally require political balance by prohibiting more than a bare majority of members from the same political party. Some exceptions exist—statutes governing the NLRB, Occupational Safety and Health Review Commission, and Federal Mine Safety and Health Review Commission, contain no requirements pertaining to political balance.[54] But as a practical matter, tradition may dictate appointment criteria, as illustrated by the NLRB.[55] Congress created the NLRB in 1935 as a tribunal of theoretically impartial government referees, but President Eisenhower, the first Republican president since passage of the 1935 statute, broke with tradition and appointed individuals with overt management backgrounds. Recent presidents have typically appointed two management-oriented members (generally Republicans), two labor-oriented members (generally Democrats), and a chair from an ostensibly neutral background (such as government or academia), who is seen as the swing vote.[56]

Some scholars have argued that statutory political party restrictions violate the president's power under the appointments clause.[57] The statutory requirement that no more than three of six FEC commissioners come from the same political party has been criticized as "no mere technicality but a continuing assault on the political liberty whose preservation is the principal object of the Constitution's separation of governmental powers."[58] Presidents Jimmy Carter and George H. W. Bush also expressed reservations with political party restrictions on presidential appointments. When President Bush signed the National Community Service Act of 1990, he indicated that provisions limiting his appointment power to the board administering the Act's programs were "without legal force or effect."[59] Carter, in signing the appropriations bill

---

[54] *See* 29 U.S.C. § 153(a) (1994) (NLRB); 29 U.S.C. § 661(a) (1994) (OSHRC); 30 U.S.C. § 823(a) (1994) (FMSHRC). *See generally* Kevin S. Brown, *Partisans & Partisan Commissions*, 17 Geo. Mason L. Rev. 789, 794 (2010) (discussing partisan independent agencies and the constitutional and administrative law debates concerning the constitutionality and/or desirability of requiring the president to appoint agency heads belonging to the opposing party and, more generally, permitting agencies to be independent of direct executive control).

[55] *See* chapter 2, section D.

[56] For a thorough history of the appointments at the NLRB, see Joan Flynn, *A Quiet Revolution at the Labor Board: The Transformation of the NLRB 1935–2000*, 61 Ohio S. L.J. 1361 (2000). *See also* Catherine L. Fisk, *The Role of the Judiciary When the Agency Confirmation Process Stalls: Thoughts on the Two-Member NLRB and the Questions the Supreme Court Should Have, But Didn't, Address in* New Process Steel, L.P. v. NLRB, 5 FIU L. Rev. 593 (2010).

[57] *See* Joshua Kershner, *Political Party Restrictions and the Appointments Clause: The Federal Election Commission's Appointments Process Is Constitutional*, 32 Cardozo L. Rev. 615, 619 (2010) ("Existing scholarly opinion concludes that political party restrictions on appointments to the FEC violate the Appointments Clause"). No court that we know of has adopted this perspective.

[58] Jamie B. Raskin, *"A Complicated and Indirect Encroachment": Is the Federal Election Commission Unconstitutionally Composed?*, 52 Admin L. Rev. 609, 610 (2000).

[59] George H. W. Bush, *Presidential Statement on Signing the National and Community Service Act of 1990*, 2 Pub. Papers 1613 (Nov. 16, 1990), *available at* Gerhard Peters & John T. Woolley, *The American Presidency Project*, http://www.presidency.ucsb.edu/ws/index.php?pid=19052 (balking at the provision that the

for the ITC, similarly objected to a provision requiring the incoming chairman to be from a different political party from the outgoing chairman.[60] Some statutes contain precatory language without genuinely circumscribing the president's choices in any significant way. For example, Postal Regulatory Commissioners are "solely chosen" on the basis of their technical and professional qualifications,[61] and members of the Federal Reserve Board must be selected with "due regard to a fair representation of the financial, agricultural, industrial, and commercial interests, and geographical divisions of the country."[62]

This said, it is clear that the political party qualification can be easily circumvented. Take, as example, the United States Commission on Civil Rights (USCCR), admittedly a legislative agency. One member, Abigail Thernstrom, switched her registration from Republican to Independent so as to be appointed vice chair of the commission in 2001 and switched back to the GOP in 2007 to be reappointed by President Bush.[63]

Most contemporary statutes do not require professional qualifications for agency membership. However, some statutes do establish specific qualifications. The statute establishing the STB as the successor to the ICC requires that two of the three members have a professional background in transportation, while at least one member must have

---

board must be "balanced according to the race, ethnicity, age and gender of its members," and must include no more than eleven members of the same political party).

60 *See* Kershner, *supra* note 57, at 24; Jimmy Carter, *Presidential Statement on Signing the U.S. International Trade Commission Appropriations Bill*, 2 PUB. PAPERS 1479 (Aug. 18, 1977), *available at* Gerhard Peters & John T. Woolley, *The American Presidency Project*, http://www.presidency.ucsb.edu/ws/index.php?pid=7972 (objecting that the selection restrictions "may unduly limit the President's ability to select the best available leadership for the Commission").

61 39 U.S.C. § 502.

62 12 U.S.C. § 241 (2006).

63 In 2001, President Bush appointed Abigail Thernstrom as a Republican member of the commission. *See* Bob Drogin, *Rights Panel Backs Florida Voting Report Amid Dissent*, L.A. TIMES, June 9, 2001, *available at* http://articles.latimes.com/2001/jun/09/news/mn-8314 (noting that, in 2001, "four democrats, three independents, and one Republican sit on the Commission," and that "Abigail Thernstrom [was] the lone Republican"). In 2004, two members left the commission—one Democratic and one Independent. *See Two Set for Civil Rights Panel*, WASH. TIMES, Dec. 6, 2004, *available at* http://www.washingtontimes.com/news/2004/dec/6/20041206-124320-6048r/. President George W. Bush appointed two replacement members, Gerold Reynolds and Ashley Taylor. *See id.* He also appointed Abigail Thernstrom as the commission's new vice chairman. *See id.* Although Thernstrom had originally been appointed to the commission as a Republican, she changed her registration to Independent, thus allowing Bush to appoint more than the four Republican members allowed by the commission's regulations. *See* 45 C.F.R. § 701.10; *see also Two Set for Civil Rights Panel*, WASH. TIMES, Dec. 6, 2004, *available at* http://www.washingtontimes.com/news/2004/dec/6/20041206-124320-6048r/ (describing Thernstrom as "a Republican appointee who is registered independent"); Darryl Fears, *Civil Rights Commission Prepares for a New Era: Conservative Bush Appointees Replace Liberals*, WASH. POST, Dec. 9, 2004, at A31. (noting that Thernstrom is "an independent who is conservative"). However, the current biography for Abigail Thernstrom listed on the commission's website states that her political affiliation is Republican, implying that Thernstrom has returned to the Republican Party. *See Abigail Thernstrom, Vice Chair*, U.S. CIVIL RIGHTS COMM'N, http://www.usccr.gov/cos/bio/thernstr.htm (last visited May 16, 2014) ("Political Affiliation: Republican").

professional or business experience in the private sector.[64] At least two of the three members of the National Indian Gaming Commission must be enrolled in an Indian tribe.[65] Like members of the STB,[66] members of the Defense Nuclear Facilities Board[67] have professional qualification requirements as well.

Of course, all this specificity can go too far in cabining the president.[68] In 1884, Congress passed the Act for the Relief of Fitz John Porter, which called for his appointment to the position of army colonel.[69] President Chester A. Arthur vetoed the bill because it was "either unnecessary and ineffective or it involves an encroachment by the legislative branch of the Government upon the authority of the executive."[70] The Hay Army Bill of 1916 contained restrictive requirements that would have allowed only one person, Judge Henry M. Carson of Representative Hay's district, to fill the position of judge advocate general.[71]

Some multimember agencies traditionally have had their members selected from the ranks of the agency staff. According to a major study of regulatory agencies by the Senate Government Operations Committee in 1977, four of the nineteen appointments to the SEC between 1961 and 1977 were career staff employees.[72] Not surprisingly, many regulatory commission appointments are made from individuals closely associated with the regulated industry. Indeed, leading representatives of the regulated sector are often consulted on agency appointments.[73] Moreover, many agency appointees have the support of a key member of Congress. The Senate Government Operations Committee found that no less than a third of the appointments to the FTC and the FCC almost

---

64 *See* 49 U.S.C. § 701(b)(2).

65 *See* 25 U.S.C. § 2704(b)(3).

66 For the members of the STB, "[a]t least 2 members of the board shall be individuals with a professional standing and a demonstrated knowledge in the fields of transportation or transportation regulation, and at least one member shall be an individual with professional or business experience (including agriculture) in the private sector." 49 U.S.C. § 701(b)(2).

67 For the Defense Nuclear Facilities Safety Board, members must be "appointed from civilian life" who are "United States citizens who are respected experts in the field of nuclear safety with a demonstrated competence and knowledge relevant to the independent investigative and oversight functions of the board." 42 U.S.C. § 2286(b)(1). Interestingly, members of the Nuclear Regulatory Commission do not have such requirements. *See* 42 U.S.C. § 5841(a)–(b).

68 *See generally supra* notes 57–60 and accompanying text.

69 James D. Richardson, A Compilation of the Messages and Papers of the Presidents: 1789–1897, Vol. VII, at 221 (1898). *See* Act for the Relief of Fitz-John Porter, H.R. 1016, 48th Cong. (1884).

70 *See* Chester A. Arthur, *Veto Message* (July 2, 1884), *available at* Gerhard Peters & John T. Woolley, *The American Presidency Project*, http://www.presidency.ucsb.edu/ws/index.php?pid=68971#axzz1jYV3Lb70.

71 H.R. Rep. No. 64-695, at 5 (1916) (Conf. Rep.); *see also Army Bill Passes; Vote is 349 to 25—Hay Admits Carson Joker*, N.Y. Times, May 21, 1916 (reporting that the House adopted the Army Reorganization bill conference report commanding the Judge Advocate General position to be filled by someone who was "not less than 45 nor more than 50 years of age, who shall have been for ten years a judge of the Supreme Court of the Philippine Islands, shall have served for two years as a captain in the regular or volunteer army and shall be proficient in the Spanish language and laws."). *See* Kershner, *supra* note 57, at 25 n.191.

72 *See* Senate Comm. on Gov't Operations, Study on Federal Regulation, S. Doc. No. 95-25, at 129 (1977).

73 *See id.* at 127.

entirely resulted from congressional sponsorship.[74] The committee also found that in a much larger number of cases, support from Congress was one of several major factors involved in the appointment decision,[75] which is evidence that partisan considerations can override issues of expertise, experience, or even regulatory philosophy. Indeed, the Senate Commerce Committee observed that the extent to which partisan political considerations dominated the commission appointment process was "alarming" given that "other factors—such as competence, experience, and even, on occasion, regulatory philosophy—are only secondary considerations."[76]

Federal patronage historically benefits congressmen in two ways. David E. Lewis explains: "First, these positions permit members of Congress with a means by which to influence policy directly—provided, that is, that members have influence over who is selected."[77] Securing an appointment based on patronage may also be politically beneficial to a party's or a member's individual election prospects.[78] Lewis continues: "Members of Congress, particularly those from the president's party, are actively involved in recommending persons for appointed positions. To the extent they are successful, this can provide electoral benefits for the member. Appreciative constituents or groups express their gratitude through electoral support."[79] Following criticism that politicization of the appointment process has diminished government performance, proposals have emerged urging reduction of the number of political appointees or more stringent qualifications for key executive branch jobs.[80]

Political scientists have criticized this relationship between Congress, the administrative agencies, and private interest groups as being an "iron triangle."

> In its classic form, [the "iron triangle"] theory involves three actors: an agency, the congressional committee that oversees that agency, and a powerful interest group. In order to secure favorable regulations, the interest group (so the story goes) will aggressively lobby committee members and provide support, financial or otherwise, for the members' reelection efforts. Those committee members will then pressure the agencies to enact favorable regulations. Because the rest of Congress will be largely oblivious to the activities of that committee and the agency, this

---

74 *See id.* at 154.

75 *See id.*

76 *See, e.g.*, SENATE COMM. ON COMMERCE, 94TH CONG., APPOINTMENTS TO THE REGULATORY AGENCIES: THE FEDERAL COMMUNICATIONS COMMISSION AND THE FEDERAL TRADE COMMISSION (1949–1974) 391 (Comm. Print 1976). *See also* Floyd Norris, *Independent Agencies, Sometimes in Name Only*, N.Y. TIMES, Aug. 8, 2013, at B1 (suggesting that, apart from agency chairmen, senior senators of both parties may have the de facto power in choosing agency members, with the president adopting an influential senator's choice).

77 DAVID E. LEWIS, THE POLITICS OF PRESIDENTIAL APPOINTMENTS 64 (2008).

78 *Id.* at 65.

79 *Id.*

80 *Id.* at 212–18.

"iron triangle" will inevitably cater to the interest group's narrow desires to the detriment of the public interest.[81]

The iron triangle theory centers the administrative decision-making process around industries in order to explain bureaucratic behavior.[82] Mancur Olson's well-known book *The Logic of Collective Action* provided early support for the iron triangle theory by hypothesizing that small, closely knit groups of individuals—who have an organizational advantage over large unorganized groups—will act collectively to acquire private goods for their groups at the expense of the larger public.[83] This argument follows earlier critiques that argue agencies unduly favor organized interests—particularly regulated industries—at the expense of "comparatively unorganized interests such as consumers, environmentalists, and the poor."[84]

1. PRINCIPAL AND INFERIOR OFFICERS OF THE UNITED STATES

In discussing appointments, it is both necessary and challenging to define "officer." The Supreme Court has defined "officer" as "any appointee exercising significant authority pursuant to the laws of the United States."[85] The position must also be for "a public station, or employment conferred by the appointment of government... embrac[ing] the ideas of tenure, duration, emolument, and duties,"[86] whereas nonofficers are employees engaged in "lesser functionaries subordinate to officers of the United States."[87] Of the government's millions of employees, only a few have an officer status.[88]

---

81 Nicholas Bagley & Richard L. Revesz, *Centralized Oversight of the Regulatory State*, 106 Colum. L. Rev. 1260, 1284 (2006).

82 *Id.*

83 Mancur Olson, The Logic of Collective Action 3 (2d prtg. 1971) ("In the sharing of the costs of efforts to achieve a common goal in small groups, there is however a surprising tendency for the 'exploitation' of the great by the small."). Bagley and Revesz note that Olson's book as well as George Stigler's application of it to the legislative and regulatory process stamped the iron triangle theory with a seal of economics approval. Bagley & Revesz, *supra* note 81, at 1284–85. *See* George J. Stigler, *The Theory of Economic Regulation*, 2 Bell. J. Econ. & Mgmt. Sci. 3 (1971).

84 Richard B. Stewart, *The Reformation of American Administrative Law*, 88 Harv. L. Rev. 1669, 1684–85 (1975). *See also* Louis L. Jaffe, *The Effective Limits of the Administrative Process: A Reevaluation*, 67 Harv. L. Rev. 1105, 1107–14 (1954). For a discussion of the iron triangle concept, see Gordon Adams et al., The Iron Triangle: The Politics of Defense Contracting 24–26 (1981). *See also* Frederick V. Malek, Washington's Hidden Tragedy: The Failure to Make Government Work 173–74 (1978). The relationship has also been dubbed by some commentators as a system of "subgovernments." *See, e.g.*, Steven K. Bailey, Congress in the Seventies 61–62 (2d ed. 1970).

85 Buckley v. Valeo, 424 U.S. 1, 126 (1976) (per curium).

86 United States v. Hartwell, 73 U.S. 385, 393 (1868) (Full-time clerk in the office of U.S. treasurer is an inferior officer).

87 *Buckley*, 424 U.S. at 126 n.162 (citing Auffmordt v. Hedden, 137 U.S. 310, 327 (1890)).

88 *See* H. Comm. on Oversight & Gov't Reform, 112th Cong., United States Government Policy and Supporting Positions 197–200 (Comm. Print 2012) (over eight thousand executive

Tenure and duration are highly relevant to determining whether one is an officer, as the term does not include those working on government contracts as they are "necessarily limited in [their] duration and specific in [their] objects."[89] Examples of those workers on limited contracts include those engaged in a civil surgeon's duties[90] or appraisers working for the government on an as needed basis.[91]

Appointing a federal officer largely depends on whether the officer is an inferior or principal officer. The appointments clause states:

> [The President] shall nominate, and by and with the Advice and Consent of the Senate, shall appoint Ambassadors, other public Ministers and Consuls, Judges of the supreme Court, and all other Officers of the United States, whose Appointments are not herein otherwise provided for, and which shall be established by Law: but the Congress may by Law vest the Appointment of such inferior Officers, as they think proper, in the President alone, in the Courts of Law, or in the Heads of Departments.[92]

Although the clause explicitly sets forth two distinct procedures for appointing federal officers,[93] it does not indicate how to distinguish between the two types of officers. The Supreme Court has refused to set a bright line rule, which has resulted in doctrinal instability.[94]

In *Morrison v. Olson*, the Court utilized a number of nonexclusive factors to determine whether an independent counsel was a principal or inferior officer.[95] These factors included the attorney general's ability to remove the officer "for good cause,"[96] limitations on the term of office,[97] limitations on the jurisdiction of the counsel,[98] and the

---

branch positions are "subject to noncompetitive appointment," and only approximately twelve hundred of those appointments require Senate approval).

In 2012, the president signed into law an Act ending the Senate confirmation requirement for roughly two hundred appointed positions. *See* Presidential Appointment Efficiency and Streamlining Act of 2011, Pub. L. No. 112-166, 126 Stat. 1283 (2012) (generally striking "by and with advice and consent of the Senate" from statutes establishing appointed positions).

89 *Hartwell*, 73 U.S. at 393.

90 United States v. Germaine, 99 U.S. 508, 512 (1879).

91 Auffmordt v. Hedden, 137 U.S. 310, 326–28 (1890) (appraiser hired for a specific tax dispute not an officer); *see also* United States v. Eaton, 169 U.S. 331, 343 (1898) (vice consul who assumes a consul's duties under "special and temporary conditions . . . is not thereby transformed into the superior and permanent officer").

92 U.S. Const. art. II, § 2, cl. 2.

93 *Germaine*, 99 U.S. at 509–10.

94 *See infra* notes 101–48 and accompanying text.

95 Morrison v. Olson, 487 U.S. 654, 671–72 (1988).

96 *Id.* at 663.

97 *Id.* at 672.

98 *Id.*

amount of authority given to the officer.[99] One lower court summarized the *Morrison* approach as follows:

> Under *Morrison*, we examine several factors to determine whether an officer is a principal or an inferior officer. First, we inquire whether the officer is subject to removal by a higher Executive Branch official. Second, we look at whether the officer is empowered to perform only certain, limited duties. Finally, we look at whether an officer's duties are limited in jurisdiction. Generally, if an officer is limited in "tenure, duration, [and] . . . duties," those findings lead to the conclusion that she is an inferior officer. Stanley was the United States Trustee for Region 17 of the United States (including the Northern and Eastern Districts of California and the District of Nevada), and she was initially appointed to a five-year term. Her position was limited geographically, temporally, and topically. If she was an officer at all, she was most certainly an inferior officer. It is well established that Congress may vest the appointment of inferior officers in the Department of Justice.[100]

Nearly ten years after deciding *Morrison*, the Court heard *Edmond v. United States*, an appointments clause challenge to the Coast Guard Court of Criminal Appeals.[101] In *Edmond*, the Court noted that the distinction between inferior and principal officers lies in the existence of a superior officer who supervises the inferior officer's work,[102] and not simply in application of the *Morrison* factors.[103] Noting that the purpose of the appointments clause was to "preserve political accountability relative to important Government assignments,"[104] the Court set forth its new approach to inferior–principal status: "'inferior Officers' are officers whose work is directed and supervised at some level by others who were appointed by Presidential nomination with the advice and consent of the Senate."[105] Although the Court did not overrule *Morrison*, the *Edmond* decision did reformulate the inferior office test to focus on subordinance rather than an officer's range of duties.[106]

---

99 *Id.* at 671–72.

100 Stanley v. Gonzales, 476 F.3d 653, 659 (D.C. Cir. 2007) (citations omitted). In this case, the D.C. Circuit found that a bankruptcy trustee was an inferior officer who could be dismissed at will.

101 Edmond v. United States, 520 U.S. 651, 653 (1997).

102 *Id.* at 662–63.

103 *Id.* at 661. ("Petitioners are quite correct that [the conclusions of *Morrison*] do not hold with regard to the officer of the military judge . . . It is not 'limited in tenure.' . . . Nor are military judges 'limited in jurisdiction. . . .") (quoting *Morrison*, 487 U.S. at 672).

104 *Edmond*, 520 U.S. at 663.

105 *Id.*

106 *See* Jay Bybee & Tuan Samahon, *William Rehnquist, the Separation of Powers, and the Riddle of the Sphinx*, 58 STAN. L. REV. 1735, 1758 (2006) ("*Edmond* does not purport to overrule *Morrison*. Instead, it characterizes *Morrison* as not purporting to 'set forth a definitive test' for what counts as an inferior officer.").

Interestingly, the *Edmond* opinion was authored by Justice Scalia, the sole dissenter in *Morrison*, where he wrote that "the independent counsel is not an inferior officer because she is not subordinate to any officer in the Executive Branch." Scalia also noted that "[d]ictionaries in use at the time of the Constitutional Convention gave the word 'inferiour' two meanings which it still bears today: (1) 'lower in place, . . . station, . . . rank of life, . . . value or excellencey,' and (2) 'subordinate.'"[107] The original intent approach is further supported by historical evidence of the early congressional handling of appointments, which often expressly denominated as "inferior offices" those positions subordinate to positions designated as "principal offices."[108] The organic statutes for the Department of Foreign Affairs,[109] the Department of War,[110] and the Department of the Treasury[111] all authorized principal officers, to whom inferior officers answered as subordinates.

Ultimately, the Court in *Edmond* found that oversight by the judge advocate general and review by the Court of Appeals for the Armed Forces was sufficient to find the judges to be inferior officers.[112] This inferior–principal distinction, however, based solely on the question of supervision, is inherently unstable.[113] For example, the undersecretary of defense for policy is a principal officer who has "responsibility for supervising and directing activities of the Department of Defense relating to export controls" and has "overall control and supervision . . . for the activities of the Department of Defense for combating terrorism."[114] At the same time he or she "is subordinate to the Secretary

---

[107] *Morrison*, 487 U.S. at 719. Justice Blackmun's conference notes from Morrison show that both Justices Rehnquist and O'Connor rejected the application of a bright-line subordination rule to determine in inferior officer status, though this rejection is not explicitly presented in the Court's opinion. *See* Bybee & Samahon, *supra* note 106, at 1757–58.

[108] *See* Tuan Samahon, *Are Bankruptcy Judges Unconstitutional? An Appointments Clause Challenge*, 60 Hastings L.J. 233, 254–55 (2008).

[109] Act for Establishing an Executive Department, To Be Denominated the Department of Foreign Affairs, ch. 4, § 1, 1 Stat. 28, 29 (1789).

[110] Act to Establish an Executive Department, To Be Denominated the Department of War, ch. 7, §§ 1–2, 1 Stat. 49, 49–50 (1789).

[111] Act to Establish the Treasury Department, ch. 12, § 1, 1 Stat. 65 (1789).

[112] *Edmond*, 520 U.S. at 664–66.

[113] Justice Souter's concurrence in *Edmond* foreshadows the difficulty in application of the supervision test for determining inferior principal status. Unlike the majority, Souter was unwilling to say that the "mere existence of a 'superior' officer" is dispositive. *Edmond*, 520 U.S. at 668 (Souter, J., concurring). Souter argues that supervision and control is necessary to establishing inferior officer status, but it is not alone sufficient. *Id.* at 667. He argues that there is no single condition sufficient to establishing inferior officer status; instead, courts must take a "detailed look at the powers and duties of [officers] to see whether reasons favoring their inferior officer statues within the constitutional scheme weigh more heavily than those to the contrary." *Id.* at 668. If review of the powers leaves uncertainty for the court then, according to Souter, deference should be given to legislative judgment. *Id.* at 668–69.

[114] 10 U.S.C. § 134. *See Morrison*, 487 U.S. at 722 (Scalia, J., dissenting) ("To be sure, it is not a sufficient condition for 'inferior' officer status that one be subordinate to a principal officer. Even an officer who is subordinate to a department head can be a principal officer.").

of Defense."[115] And the deputy secretary of defense, a principal officer, who is "Chief Management Officer" of the department, is still required to "perform such duties and exercise such powers as the Secretary of Defense may prescribe."[116]

Thus it is not surprising that efforts have been made to circumvent *Edmond* and treat government officials with significant discretion as principal officers under the appointments clause. As Samahon notes, "*Morrison* and *Edmond*'s uneasy coexistence has not gone unnoticed by the lower courts and commentators."[117] In fact, Samahon has uncovered several judicial attempts to reconcile the cases.[118] One approach distinguishes *Edmond* and *Morrison* on the basis that *Edmond* governs intrabranch appointments, while *Morrison* governs interbranch appointments.[119] This approach finds support in *Freytag v. Commissioner*, an appointments case heard three years after *Morrison* and several years before *Edmond*, in which the Court declined to use *Morrison*'s four-factor test to determine whether special trial judges in the Tax Court were inferior officers because the "case [did] not involve an 'interbranch appointment.'"[120]

In *United States v. Gantt*, the Ninth Circuit attempted to reconcile the cases by distinguishing between conditions *necessary* to establish inferior officer status and conditions *sufficient* to establishing such status.[121] This third approach to reconciling *Morrison* and *Edmond* appears to be the most widely accepted interpretation of the two cases.[122] In determining whether an interim U.S. attorney was an inferior officer, the Ninth Circuit in *Gantt* rejected subordination as a necessary condition for such status. It accounted for *Morrison* by noting that an officer without a superior could be inferior where the discretionary balancing of the *Morrison* factors justified such determination.[123] Thus, satisfaction of the *Morrison* factors could be sufficient to show inferior officer status. *Edmond* was not, however, ignored by the court, which reasoned that the interim U.S. attorneys were "subject to closer supervision by a superior than the judges of the Coast Guard Court" in *Edmond*.[124]

---

115 10 U.S.C. § 134.

116 10 U.S.C. § 132(b). Interestingly, the deputy secretary shall be "appointed from among persons most highly qualified for the position by reason of background and experience, including persons with appropriate management experience. A person may not be appointed as Deputy Secretary of Defense within seven years after relief from active duty as a commissioned officer of a regular component of an armed force." *Id.* § 132(a).

117 Samahon, *supra* note 108, at 258.

118 *Id.* at 258–67.

119 *Id.* at 261–64.

120 Freytag v. Comm'r, 501 U.S. 868, 881 (1991).

121 *See* 194 F.3d 987, 998 (9th Cir. 1999).

122 *See* Samahon, *supra* note 108, at 260 n.231 (noting adoption of this approach by the First and Ninth Circuits, as well as in the District of Columbia and the Eastern District of Arkansas).

123 *Gantt*, 194 F.3d at 999 n.6.

124 *Id.* at 999.

The United States District Court for the District of Columbia followed the *Gantt* approach in the politically charged case against I. Lewis "Scooter" Libby. In 2006, lawyers for Libby sought a dismissal of his indictment on the grounds that the special counsel was a principal officer whose appointment violated the requirement of the Senate's advice and consent.[125] Libby's lawyers argued that *Edmond* established the bright line rule that the court had previously refused to set. In the Libby case, the acting attorney general created the position of special counsel and vested it with the power of the attorney general, "independent of the supervision or control of any officer of the Department [of Justice]."[126] According to Libby, the delegation to the special counsel abdicated all oversight by the attorney general.[127] In order to establish that the special counsel was a principal officer, Libby had to distinguish it from the independent counsel, which the Supreme Court had determined to be an inferior officer in *Morrison v. Olson*.[128] Libby contended that "if a principal officer were permitted to grant plenary authority to another person subject to no direction or supervision at all, the Appointments Clause would be a dead letter."[129] Further, the special counsel is free to determine the jurisdiction of his investigation, and can unilaterally expand the matters that he investigates.[130] In contrast, under the Ethics in Government Act, the independent counsel's jurisdiction was determined by a three-judge panel, and any request to expand that jurisdiction could be unilaterally rejected by the attorney general, a decision that was not subject to any review. Further, there was an annual review of each independent counsel's investigation to determine whether it had continued too long. In Libby's case, there was no such

---

125 In a July 14, 2003, a *Washington Post* column, written in response to allegations by Robert Wilson that the Bush administration had misled the public prior to the 2003 invasion of Iraq, Robert Novak mentioned that Wilson's own wife, Valerie Plame, had been sent to Niger by the CIA to investigate the suspected Iraqi purchase of uranium yellowcake. Robert D. Novak, *Mission to Niger*, WASH. POST, July 14, 2003, at A31. The column led to charges that the "two senior administration officials" had illegally "outed" Plame in retaliation for Wilson's criticism of the administration. *See Key Players in the CIA Leak Investigation*, WASH. POST, July 3, 2007, http://www.washingtonpost.com/wp-srv/politics/special/plame/Plame_KeyPlayers.html. On Oct. 31, 2003, Special Prosecutor Patrick Fitzgerald indicted I. "Scooter" Libby, assistant to the vice president for national security affairs, chief of staff to the vice president, and assistant to the president from 2001 to 2005, who was eventually convicted on charges of obstruction of justice, perjury, and making false statements. *See* Press Release, Dep't of Justice, White House Official I. Lewis Libby Indicted on Obstruction of Justice, False Statement and Perjury Charges Relating to Leak of Classified Information Revealing CIA Officer's Identity (Oct. 28, 2005), *available at* http://www.justice.gov/archive/osc/documents/libby_pr_28102005.pdf; Neil A. Lewis, *Libby Guilty of Lying in C.I.A. Leak Case*, N.Y. TIMES, Mar. 7, 2007. However, on July 2, 2007, President Bush commuted his thirty-month sentence. George W. Bush, Grant of Executive Clemency, A Proclamation by the President of the United States of America (Jul. 2, 2007), *available at* http://georgewbush-whitehouse.archives.gov/news/releases/2007/07/20070702-4.html.

126 United States v. Libby, 429 F. Supp. 2d 27, 42 (D.D.C. 2006).

127 United States v. Libby, 498 F. Supp. 2d 1, 19 (D.D.C. 2007).

128 *Morrison*, 487 U.S. at 672.

129 Mot. of Libby to Dismiss at 7, United States v. Libby, 2006 WL 3890266 (No. 05-394).

130 *Id.* at 18.

oversight from any person. Relying on *Morrison*, Libby contended that this broad discretion makes the special counsel a principal officer, requiring presidential nomination and the advice and consent of the Senate.[131]

The district court rejected Libby's arguments and denied the motion.[132] In its opinion, the court determined that the special counsel was not a principal officer because there was sufficient oversight by the attorney general, and *Morrison* dictated that the special prosecutor was an inferior officer. In addition, the court stated "because the *Morrison* factors did not appropriately fit the facts of [*Edmond*], the Supreme Court in *Edmond* predicated its conclusion that the Coast Guard Court of Criminal Appeals judges were constitutionally inferior officers on *alternative* grounds."[133] According to the district court, each of the *Morrison* factors applied equally to Libby's case, and therefore the special prosecutor was an inferior officer whose appointment did not violate the appointments clause.[134] Such attempts to reconcile *Morrison* and *Edmond* as consistent precedents still fail to set an exclusive test for distinguishing between principal and inferior officers.[135]

The distinction between an inferior officer and a "mere employee" is also an important consideration for appointments clause purposes, as the clause does not govern appointment of a mere employee. As stated in *Buckley v. Valeo*, employees are "lesser functionaries subordinate to officers of the United States."[136] Indeed, "[o]ne 'may be an agent or employee working for the government and paid by it, as nine-tenths of the persons rendering service to the government undoubtedly are, without thereby becoming its office[r].'"[137]

And adding to our catalogue of examples of "employees," the D.C. Circuit in *Tucker v. Commissioner* recently found that certain employees of the Internal Revenue Service's office of appeals (specifically "team managers," "settlement officers," and "appeal officers") are employees, not "inferior officers."[138] The Court found that the three "appeals employees" "do not exercise significant authority within the meaning of the Appointments Clause cases."[139]

---

131 *Id.* at 18–21.

132 *Id.*

133 *Id.* at 15.

134 *Id.* at 14.

135 *Id.* at 16.

136 424 U.S. 1, 126 (1976) (per curiam). In contrast, the Freytag court found that officers "perform more than ministerial tasks." *Freytag*, 501 U.S. at 881.

137 Free Enter. Fund v. Pub. Co. Accounting Oversight Bd., 130 S. Ct. 3138, 3160 n.9 (2010); United States v. Germaine, 99 U.S. 508, 509 (1879).

138 *See* Tucker v. Comm'r, 676 F.3d 1129, 1137 (D.C. Cir. 2012). During oral arguments before the D.C. Circuit judges, appellant Larry Tucker limited his challenge to "team managers." *Id.* at 1132. However, the D.C. Circuit found its analysis applied equally to team managers, settlement officers, and appeals officers. *Id.*

139 *Id.* at 1133.

The Circuit Court noted that "the main criteria for drawing the line between inferior Officers and employees not covered by the clause are (1) the significance of the matters resolved by the officials, (2) the discretion they exercise in reaching their decisions, and (3) the finality of those decisions."[140]

And the court further determined that in this case the "lack of discretion is determinative, offsetting the effective finality of Appeals employees' decisions within the executive branch."[141] Thus the court concluded that, as a result, "Office of Appeals team managers, settlement officers, and appeals officers are not inferior Officers who must be appointed in conformity with the Appointments Clause."[142]

In *Freytag*, the Supreme Court explained that unlike mere employees, inferior officers undertake more than ministerial duties—rather they carry out "important functions" and exercise "significant discretion" in carrying out their job duties. The Court concluded that special trial judges of the Tax Court who "perform[ed] more than ministerial tasks," including taking testimony, conducting testimony, ruling on admissibility of evidence, and enforcing discovery orders, were inferior officers whose appointment must conform with the appointments clause.[143]

And in *Landry* the D.C. Circuit determined that administrative law judges (ALJs) within the Federal Deposit Insurance Corporation (FDIC) were employees because they could not make final finding decisions but only recommendations to the head of the FDIC.[144] As a result, the ALJs presumably do not exercise significant authority.[145]

Of course, other ALJs, as for example, Social Security Administration (SSA) ALJs have more extensive statutory powers and would be viewed by some as more than mere employees. At least five active Supreme Court justices take this view.[146]

---

140 *Id.*

141 *Id.* at 1134.

142 *Id.* at 1137.

143 *Freytag*, 501 U.S. at 881–82. Compare Kuretski v. Comm'r, No. 13-1090 (D.C. Cir. June 20, 2014), which concluded that the Tax Court, despite being described by statute as a "Court of Law," exercised "Executive authority as part of the Executive Branch." *Id.* at 2. So Tax Court judges may be removed by the president without violating separation-of-powers principles, although the statute requires that they can only be removed after "notice and opportunity for public hearing, for inefficiency, neglect of duty, or malfeasance in office...." *See infra* note 223 for a fuller discussion of *Freytag*.

144 Landry v. FDIC, 204 F.3d 1125, 1133–34 (D.C. Cir. 2000).

145 *See* Free Enter. Fund, 130 S. Ct. at 3213-14 (Breyer, J., dissenting); Kevin M. Stack, *Agency Independence After PCAOB*, 32 CARDOZO L. REV. 2391, 2408 n.101 (2011); Peter L. Strauss, *On the Difficulties of Generalization in the Footsteps of* Myers, Humphrey's Executor, Morrison, *and* Freytag, 32 CARDOZO L. REV. 2255, 2279–80 & n.69 (2011).

146 *See Free Enter. Fund*, 130 S. Ct. at 3180–81 (Breyer, J., dissenting, joined by Stevens, Ginsburg, & Sotomayor, JJ.) (asking whether the majority's holding that dual for cause insulation is unconstitutional would affect ALJs who might be considered "Officers"); *Freytag*, 501 U.S. at 910 (Scalia, J., concurring in part and concurring in the judgment, joined by O'Connor, Kennedy & Souter, JJ.) ("[ALJs] are all executive officers." (emphasis omitted)).

Thus even where members of independent agencies may not be considered officers of the United States, those who carry out "important functions" and exercise discretion can likely only be appointed in conformity with the Constitution's requirements for appointment of inferior officers. This had led to the interesting question, now resolved, of who counts as a "head of department" for the purposes of appointing inferior officers.[147]

2. CHANGING CHARACTER OF AN APPOINTMENT

An interesting issue arises when Congress fails to update the appointment process for an office that has evolved substantially. For instance, bankruptcy judges originally handled ministerial tasks such as receiving property, administering oaths, and taking proof of debts.[148] Now, bankruptcy judges have accumulated significant discretion and authority over the years, as well as substantial protections against removal.[149] The process of appointing these judges, however, has remained very similar. Although the president appointed bankruptcy judges for a brief period in the late twentieth century, Congress has since returned to its original appointment scheme, which allows for appointment by the courts of law.[150] The evolution of the bankruptcy judges' position, however, suggests that at least under *Morrison*, they may be considered principal officers. This raises the possibility that the current appointment scheme is unconstitutional.[151]

A related inquiry concerns whether it should matter constitutionally if the job duties of an officer appointment in conformance with the appointments clause change during his or her term. Some shifting in duties is likely no concern,[152] but there must be some limit.[153] This can be seen from a heuristic hypothetical posed by scholars. David Aras and Ryan Scott propose such a hypothetical: "Suppose Congress amended the duties of the Ambassador to Switzerland by requiring that the Ambassador make at least one annual visit to Washington to consult with the President concerning Swiss politics. In addition, Congress also gave the Ambassador the option to sit as a Justice of the Supreme Court during the visit."[154]

---

147 *See infra* notes 216–25 and accompanying text.

148 *See* Samahon, *supra* note 108, at 239.

149 *Id.* at 239–41.

150 Bankruptcy Amendments and Federal Judgeship Act, Pub. L. No. 98-353, 98 Stat. 333 (1984).

151 *See* Samahon, *supra* note 108, at 295–96.

152 Gary Lawson notes that initial appointments have "always been understood, quite sensibly, to include the authority to implement new and changed statutory authorizations"—as Congress frequently modifies the laws under which an appointee was confirmed. Gary Lawson, *Burying the Constitution Under a TARP*, 33 HARV. J.L. & PUB. POL'Y 55, 67–68 (2010).

153 *See* Weiss v. United States, 510 U.S. 163, 163–64 (1994) (suggesting that in some situations the position may be so different from the position to which the officer was initially appointed that a new confirmation would be required for the officer to constitutionally hold that office).

154 David R. Aras & Ryan W. Scott, *Are Senior Judges Unconstitutional?*, 92 CORNELL L. REV. 453, 501 (2007).

Very little scholarly analysis exists on this subject, and further, the Supreme Court has handled the issue only once—and even then, only in the context of military officers serving as military judges.[155] Recent events, however, have brought the issue into view. Gary Lawson raised concerns that the treasury secretary's administration of the Troubled Asset Relief Program (TARP)—a $750 billion expenditure providing for the government's purchase of troubled assets—violates the appointments clause because the TARP administration was not "germane" to the secretary's responsibilities at the time he was appointed and the sheer scope of TARP might require a new appointment.[156] While it is far from clear that TARP violates the Constitution on this ground, it does foreshadow the potential for an appointments clause challenge to future congressional attempts to legislate creatively within the administrative structure already in place.[157]

3. *FREE ENTERPRISE FUND* IN THE LOWER COURTS

The most recent broaching of independence and accountability issues—including those related to the appointment power,[158] the removal power,[159] and the meaning of a board or commission, the terms "inferior" and "principal" officer,[160] and the proper interpretation of the term "heads of departments"[161]—have been raised during litigation surrounding

---

155 *Weiss*, 510 U.S. at 165 (1994). The Court held that the officers assuming the role of military judges was not unconstitutional because the role of military judge was "germane" to the position to which they were initially appointed. *Id.* at 173–74.

156 Lawson, *supra* note 152, at 69 ("The sheer scope of the program may be enough to require a new appointment for anyone who is going to administer it. Even if scope alone does not make the appointment unconstitutional, the federal government's purchases of ownership stakes in private financial institutions may be sufficiently novel to go beyond the functions of the Treasury Secretary contemplated by a reasonable President or Senate in 2006.").

157 Potential for a similar issue can also be seen in the context of individuals appointed as inferior officers, whose duties may broaden to point that the officer should properly be considered a principal officer. *See id.* at 69 n.68.

158 *See Free Enter. Fund*, 130 S. Ct. at 3162–64 (finding that PCAOB members are inferior officers, that the commission's powers are "vested in the Commissioners jointly"); Free Enter. Fund v. Pub. Co. Accounting Oversight Bd., 537 F.3d 667, 672–75 (D.C. Cir. 2008) (holding that the PCAOB did not violate appointment power because board members are accountable to the commission).

159 *See Free Enter. Fund*, 130 S. Ct. at 3151–61 (holding that the second layer of for cause protection violates that appointment clause); *id.* at 3165–71 (Breyer, J., dissenting) (arguing for a functionalist understanding, and that the president has other means beside removal of controlling executive officers); *Free Enter. Fund*, 537 F.3d at 675 (finding that other checks aside from removal are available). Kavanaugh argues that the removal power is "critical to the President's power to control the Executive Branch." *Free Enter. Fund*, 537 F.3d at 686–87 (Kavanaugh, J., dissenting) (contending that the double for cause removal provision is inconsistent with *Morrison*).

160 *See Free Enter. Fund*, 130 S. Ct. at 3162–63 (finding that the commission "constitutes a 'Department'"). The majority and the dissent in the D.C. Circuit opinions debate on the structure of the board vis-à-vis the commission, and whether the board members are principal or inferior officers. *Free Enter. Fund*, 537 F.3d at 675–78.

161 U.S. CONST. art. II, § 1.

the Public Company Accounting Oversight Board (PCAOB) in *Free Enterprise Fund v. Public Co. Accounting Oversight Board.*[162]

The case has been dubbed "the most important separation-of-powers case regarding the President's appointment and removal powers... in the last 20 years."[163] Indeed, Richard Pildes named it the "latest battlefront over the 'unitary executive branch' theory of the Constitution."[164] The academic conversation regarding PCAOB has been unusually extensive; it began at the Court of Appeal level,[165] continued after the oral argument,[166] and extended beyond the Supreme Court's decision.[167] Although issues surrounding the appointments clause and the unified theory of the executive were contested, the Supreme Court focused only on the question of "double" for cause removal, thus minimizing the impact of the decision on the concept of the independent agency.

The Sarbanes-Oxley Act of 2002 created the PCAOB "to oversee the audit of public companies that are subject to the securities laws... to protect the interests of investors and further the public interest in the preparation of informative, accurate, and independent audit reports."[168] The board (or independent commission) is charged with establishing, amending, and modifying rules for auditing, attestation, quality control, and ethics standards to be used by registered public accounting firms in the preparation of audit reports.[169] To isolate the board from political pressure, the Act states that it shall be a "nonprofit corporation" and not an agency or establishment of the United States.[170] In

---

162 Free Enter. Fund v. Pub. Co. Accounting Oversight Bd., 130 S. Ct. 3138, 3155 (2010).

163 *Free Enter. Fund*, 537 F.3d at 685 (Kavanaugh, J., dissenting).

164 Richard H. Pildes, *Separation of Powers, Independent Agencies, and Financial Regulation: The Case of the Sarbanes-Oxley Act*, 5 N.Y.U. J.L. & Bus. 485, 86 (2009).

165 *See, e.g.*, Recent Case, *Free Enterprise Fund v. Public Co. Accounting Oversight Board, 537 F.3d 667 (D.C. Cir. 2008), cert. granted, 77 U.S.L.W. 3431 (U.S. May 18, 2009) (No. 08-861)*, 122 Harv. L. Rev. 2267, 2270 (2009); Julian Helisk, Essay, *The Fault, PCAOB, Lies Not in the Appointments Clause, but in the Removal Power, That You Are Unconstitutional*, 77 Geo. Wash. L. Rev. 1063 (2009); Whitney Innes, *The Unaccountability of the Accounting Regulators: Analyzing the Constitutionality of the Public Company Accounting Oversight Board*, 42 J. Marshall L. Rev. 1019 (2009).

166 For commentary after the oral argument, see, e.g., Donna Nagy, *Is the PCAOB a "Heavily Controlled Component" of the SEC? An Essential Question in the Constitutional Controversy*, 27 U. Pitt. L. Rev. 361 (2010) (commenting on the significance of the upcoming Supreme Court decision, and arguing that the board violates the appointments clause).

167 For postdecision analyses, see Richard Pildes, *Free Enterprise Fund, Boundary-Enforcing Decisions, and the Unitary Executive Branch Theory of Government Administration*, 6 Duke J. Const. L. & Pub. Pol'y 1 (2010) (characterizing the Court's opinion as an expansive but idiosyncratic application of the theory of the unitary executive that would be limited in its impact); Hans Bader, *Free Enterprise Fund v. PCAOB: Narrow Separation-of-Powers Ruling Illustrates That the Supreme Court Is Not "Pro-Business,"* 2009–2010 Cato Sup. Ct. Rev. 269 (criticizing the decision of the Court to sever the for cause provision rather than striking down the board, despite centrality of the PCAOB to Sarbanes-Oxley); Kent H. Barnett, *Avoiding Independent Agency Armageddon*, 87 Notre Dame L. Rev. 1349 (2013).

168 15 U.S.C. § 7211(a) (2000 & Supp.).

169 15 U.S.C. § 7213 (a)(1) (2006).

170 15 U.S.C. § 7211(b). This can be inferred from the legislative history. Sen. Phil Graham's explanation for the "strange" structure of the PCAOB was that the legislature "want[ed] it to be private, but [the

addition, Congress has insulated the board from political influence by stating that the SEC can only remove board members for "good cause shown."[171] At the same time, the power to appoint the members of the board is vested solely in the SEC.[172] Only two of its five members are to be certified public accountants.[173] This configuration prompted a lawsuit challenging the board's constitutionality. Not surprisingly, the *Free Enterprise Fund* plaintiffs argued that the members of the PCAOB were principal officers and, therefore, vesting their appointment in the SEC violates the appointments clause.

Notwithstanding the statute's explicit language that the board "shall not be an agency or establishment of the United States Government,"[174] both petitioners and the Justice Department treated Congress's designation as irrelevant, given that board members exercised "significant authority pursuant to the laws of the United States" within the meaning of *Buckley v. Valeo*.[175] Because of the broad regulatory and enforcement powers exercised by the board, plaintiffs argued that its members are officers of the United States and therefore their appointment must be by presidential nomination with the advice and consent of the Senate.[176] Applying *Edmond*, the D.C. Circuit concluded that board members are, in fact, inferior officers.

The majority found that under *Edmond*, the key to supervision is whether the officer has any "power to render a final decision on behalf of the United States unless permitted to do so by other Executive officers."[177] Thus, because the board's exercise of its wide-ranging policy-making and enforcement duties were subject to significant checks

legislature] want[ed] it to have governmental powers." 148 CONG. REC. 12,122 (2002) (statement of Sen. Graham). *See* Public Company Accounting Reform and Investor Protection Act of 2002, 148 CONG. REC. S6327-06, S6330, 2002 WL 1460831, 9–10 (quoting former Fed chair Paul Volcker and former SEC chair Arthur Levitt) (Sen. Oxley on the need for a "truly independent oversight body"); S. REP. NO. 107-205, at 9 (2002) (on the need for an "independent body of inspectors"). *See also* Donna M. Nagy, *Playing Peekaboo with Constitutional Law: The PCAOB and Its Public/Private Status*, 80 NOTRE DAME L. REV. 975, 980 (2005) (The PCAOB's legislative history is replete with references to the benefits gained from the board's "strength" and "independence."). For a detailed discussion of the legislative history, see *id.* at 997–1007.

171 15 U.S.C. § 7211(e)(6); *see also Free Enter. Fund*, 130 S. Ct. at 3174 ("the justification for insulating the 'technical experts' on the Board from fear of losing their jobs due to political influence is particularly strong. Congress deliberately sought to provide that kind of protection."). As a result, the board is protected by an additional level of tenure protection that is unprecedented. *Id.* at 3147 ("Here the President cannot remove an officer who enjoys more than one level of good-cause protection, even if the President determines that the officer is neglecting his duties or discharging them improperly. That judgment is instead committed to another officer, who may or may not agree with the President's determination, and whom the President cannot remove simply because that officer disagrees with him.").

172 15 U.S.C. § 7211(e)(4).

173 *Id.* § 7211(e)(2).

174 *Id.* § 7211(b).

175 *Buckley*, 424 U.S. at 126.

176 *Free Enter. Fund*, 537 F.3d at 672.

177 *Id.* (quoting *Edmond*, 520 U.S. at 665).

by the SEC, the members were inferior officers.[178] Judge Kavanaugh's strong dissent, however, highlighted the instability of using supervision as the basis for determining inferior–principal status.[179] He argued that under *Edmond* the key to supervision was removal-at-will.[180] If an officer is removable only for cause, according to Kavanaugh, he or she will ordinarily not be "directed and supervised" unless a statute provides that for cause removal may be based on failure to follow a supervisor's directions, or the statute provides that a superior officer may affirmatively manage the officer's ongoing conduct and exercise of their executive authority.[181] Unlike the majority, Kavanaugh was not satisfied that Sarbanes-Oxley provisions granting SEC commissioners authority to amend board rules or enforcement actions effectively supervised the board.[182] To Kavanaugh, this was after-the-fact supervision that failed to satisfy *Edmond*.[183]

4. *FREE ENTERPRISE FUND* IN THE SUPREME COURT

On appeal to the Supreme Court, the issue was again debated during oral arguments. While counsel for the Free Enterprise Fund stressed the board's double for cause removal as fatal to its constitutionality,[184] Solicitor General Elena Kagan argued that "removal is just a tool…not the ultimate constitutional question. The ultimate constitutional

---

[178] *Free Enter. Fund*, 537 F.3d at 672. The court noted the requirement that the SEC approve all PCAOB rules as well as the SEC's authority to review PCAOB inspections and the SEC's power to remove PCAOB members for good cause. *Id.* at 673–75. As for the requirement that the SEC approve all PCAOB rules, the court rejected the Free Enterprise Fund's argument that Sarbanes-Oxley created a Chevron like standard of deference for PCAOB determinations. Rather, the court reasoned that 15 U.S.C. § 7217(b)(3) "reflects an intent to require the Commission itself to determine whether Board rules are consistent with the statutes *and* the public interest." *Id.* at 673. Based on these mechanisms, the court concluded that the PCAOB's work is "directed and supervised at some level" by the SEC commissioners, establishing the inferior officer status of PCAOB members. *Id.* at 672.

[179] Free Enter. Fund v. Public Co. Accounting Oversight Bd., 537 F.3d 667, 686 (D.C. Cir. 2008) (Kavanaugh, J., dissenting).

[180] *Id.* at 707 ("*Edmond* and the basic principles underlying Article II teach that they key initial question in determining whether an executive officer is inferior is whether the officer is removable at will.").

[181] *Id.* at 709.

[182] *Id.* at 709–11.

[183] *See id.* at 710–11 ("[T]he Board contends that after-the-fact review of Board sanctions by the SEC suffices to show that the SEC directs and supervises the Board.… That makes little sense. One would not say, for example, that a U.S. Attorney is directed and supervised by a federal district court in his or her investigative decisions just because the court ultimately would have an opportunity to review any indictment or subpoena challenge.").

[184] Free Enterprise Fund argued that "[the board members] are principal officers for three reasons under Edmond: They run their own shop; the commission has no control over the officers on the board, since it can only remove them in these extraordinarily narrow situations and…can only review part of its work product.… The removal provision is particularly important here. The board can pursue policies that the SEC absolutely abhors." Transcript of Oral Argument at 28–29, Free Enter. Fund v. Public Co. Accounting Oversight Bd., 130 S. Ct. 3138 (2010) (No. 08-861). Chief Justice Roberts dubbed the double for cause removal as "for cause squared." *Id.* at 44.

question is the level of presidential control, and the presidential control [over the board's activities] is exactly the same as it is with respect to the SEC staff's activities."[185] During oral argument, the justices appeared split on the issue. Justice Ginsburg, for instance, dubbed PCAOB pursuance of a policy disagreed with by the SEC a "highly unlikely scenario."[186] In contrast, Justice Scalia argued that "the president has adequate control over the SEC only because he can dismiss the chairman... the activity here is not governed by the chairman of the SEC... the governance of this board is by the members of the SEC... [the] syllogism breaks down at that point."[187]

In a five-to-four decision the Supreme Court found the removal process of the PCAOB unconstitutional.[188] It severed the offending clause, substituting, on its own authority, removal-at-will by the SEC board.[189] However, the Court also found this limitation severable from the Sarbanes-Oxley Act, and held that the SEC's appointment power did not violate the appointments clause.[190] By offering up a constitutional "work-around" the Court allowed the PCAOB to continue operating within the bosom of the SEC. Thus, the concept of the independent agency dodged the bullet.[191] As Jack Beermann suggested, "the PCAOB decision came in like a lion but went out like a lamb."[192]

Specifically, the Court ignored *Edmond* and the most compelling claim brought by the petitioners—that designation as an inferior officer should be determined by the breadth of the "inferior's" discretionary authority.[193] The Court unanimously rejected the argument that *Edmond*'s focus on an employee's responsibility and ambit of discretion made PCAOB members principal officers.[194] *Freytag* notwithstanding, the Court found that the SEC was a stand-alone department that could appoint inferior officers.[195]

For the Court, the constitutional flaw in the PCAOB's structure was that the member could only be removed for cause, and that the removal was to be made by SEC

185 *Id.* at 43–44.

186 *Id.* at 29.

187 *Id.* at 31.

188 Free Enter. Fund v. Public Co. Accounting Oversight Bd., 130 S. Ct. 3138, 3151 (2010).

189 *Id.*; *see* Sarbanes-Oxley Act of 2002, Pub. L. No. 107-204, § 101(e)(6), 116 Stat. 745, 752.

190 *Free Enter. Fund*, 130 S. Ct. at 3160.

191 *See, e.g.*, Bader, *supra* note 167, at 269. (lamenting the extremely narrow "minimalism" of the Court's decision); Jack M. Beermann, Essay, An Inductive Understanding of Separation of Powers or Why the PCAOB decision Doesn't Change Anything Yet 1 (Boston U. Sch. of Law, BU Working Paper, No. 10-24), *available at* http://www.bu.edu/law/faculty/scholarship/workingpapers/2010.html (concluding that "[t]he PCAOB decision came in like a lion but went out like a lamb").

192 *Id.* at 1. In a later iteration of the article Beermann notes that "the Court in PCAOB did not deliver on the opinion's promise of a major reform to the law of separation of powers." Jack M. Beermann, *An Inductive Understanding of the Separation of Powers*, 63 ADMIN. L. REV. 467, 470 (2011).

193 Pildes, *supra* note 167, at 6.

194 *Free Enter. Fund*, 130 S. Ct. at 3162–64.

195 *Id.* at 3162.

commissioners, who themselves were removable only for cause. The Court found this double level of for cause removal to be an unacceptable dilution of the president's executive authority[196] and that such "dual for cause limitations on the removal of board members contravenes the constitution's separation of powers."[197] But the Court cured this defect by reading an *at will* standard of removal into the PCAOB statute.[198] At the end, as Peter Strauss points out, the Court resolved "every element of the PCAOB's authority save the formal tenure protection of its members."[199]

In his forceful dissent, Justice Breyer urged a functionalist approach to recognizing innovative government structures that meet the complexity of the administrative state.[200] "Administrative Units," he suggested, "come in many different shapes and sizes" and make use of "a host of different organizational structures."[201] The PCAOB's removal and appointment mechanism, he argued, were designed to insulate "experts" from "political influence"[202] and assist efforts to "regulate through impartial adjudication."[203] Breyer suggested that Roberts's opinion would create bureaucratic mayhem. Even if the

196 *Id.* at 3147 ("The President cannot 'take Care that the Laws be faithfully executed' if he cannot oversee the faithfulness of the officers who execute them.") (quoting U.S. CONST. art. II, § 1, cl. 1). The Court has noted that the president is very limited in ability to remove the SEC commissioners "except under the Humphrey's Executor standard of 'inefficiency, neglect of duty, or malfeasance in office.'" *Id.* at 3148 (quoting Humphrey's Ex'r v. United States, 295 U.S. 602, 620 (1935)). *But see* Free Enter. Fund v. Public Co. Accounting Oversight Bd., 537 F.3d 667, 679–80 & 680 n.8 (D.C. Cir. 2008) (remarkably notes that the president's removal power of the SEC commissioners "'for inefficiency, neglect of duty, or malfeasance in office' are 'very broad and ... could sustain removal ... for any number of actual or perceived transgressions'" (quoting Bowsher v. Synar, 478 U.S. 714, 729 (1986))). This expansive approach cuts back on the notion of "for cause" independence.

197 *Free Enter. Fund*, 130 S. Ct. at 3151.

198 *Id.* at 3161.

199 Strauss, *supra* note 145, at 2283.

200 *Free Enter. Fund*, 130 S. Ct. at 3169.

201 *Id.* The statutes are varied. "Sometimes they delegate administrative authority to the president directly, e.g., 10 U.S.C. § 203(a)(1); 42 U.S.C. § 5192(c); sometimes they place authority in a long-established Cabinet department, e.g., 7 U.S.C. § 1637b(c)(1); 12 U.S.C. § 5221(b)(2) (2006 ed., Supp. II); sometimes they delegate authority to an independent commission or board, e.g., 15 U.S.C. § 4404(b); 28 U.S.C. § 994; sometimes they place authority directly in the hands of a single senior administrator, e.g., 15 U.S.C. § 657d(c)(4); 42 U.S.C. § 421; sometimes they place it in a sub-cabinet bureau, office, division or other agency, e.g., 18 U.S.C. § 4048; sometimes they vest it in multimember or multiagency task groups, e.g., 5 U.S.C. §§ 593–594; 50 U.S.C. § 402 (2006 ed. and Supp. II); sometimes they vest it in commissions or advisory committees made up of members of more than one branch, e.g., 20 U.S.C. § 42(a); 28 U.S.C. § 991(a) (2006 ed., Supp. II); 42 U.S.C. § 1975; sometimes they divide it among groups of departments, commissions, bureaus, divisions, and administrators, e.g., 5 U.S.C. § 9902(a) (2006 ed., Supp. II); 7 U.S.C. § 136i–l(g); and sometimes they permit state or local governments to participate as well, e.g., 7 U.S.C. § 2009aa–l(a). Statutes similarly grant administrators a wide variety of powers—for example, the power to make rules, develop informal practices, investigate, adjudicate, impose sanctions, grant licenses, and provide goods, services, advice, and so forth." *See generally* 5 U.S.C. § 500 et seq.

202 *Free Enter. Fund*, 130 S. Ct. at 3170, 3174 (Breyer, J., dissenting).

203 *Id.* at 3169.

Court's criteria were applied "as stringently as possible," he argued, "hundreds, perhaps not thousands, of high level government officials would be swept within the scope of the Court's ruling,"[204] including "virtually all of the leadership of the Chemical Safety Board, the Federal Mine Safety and Health Review Commission, and the National Mediation Board."[205] He listed 573 high-ranking officials removable only "for cause,"[206] and noted that over 1,584 ALJs[207] and 210,000 active duty commissioned military officers would be swept within the Court's ruling[208]

However, both the majority and the minority of the Court assumed—while explicitly declining to decide—that members of the SEC had "for cause" removal protection although the statute failed to confer it.[209] Whether the PCAOB is ultimately judged as a transformative opinion for our understanding of the unitary executive or a "boundary-enforcing" decision of limited import may "not be knowable until the Court chooses to speak on these issues again."[210] Though still relatively recent, the decision has had a limited impact in lower courts.[211] Nonetheless, as numerous commentators have pointed out, the logic of the opinion could extend to single for cause removal as well as double for cause removal.[212]

---

204 *Id.* at 3179.

205 *Id.*

206 *Id.* at 3180.

207 *Id.* at 3213–14 (Appendix C). After discussing Senior Executive Service appointees, the majority declined to "address" the matter in this case. *Id.* at 3161 (majority opinion). Richard Pierce has argued that the removal process for the SSA's ALJs is unconstitutional because they are insulated from the president by three layers of restrictions. As a result, theses judges are not subordinate and thus principal officers. Richard J. Pierce, Jr., *What Should We Do about Administrative Law Judge Disability Decisionmaking?* 26 (George Washington U. Law Sch. Public Law & Legal Theory Paper, Paper No. 573, 2011), *available at* http://ssrn.com/abstract=1890770 ("The Court has used two criteria to decide whether an officer is an inferior to a principal officer—the extent of the principal officer's ability to overrule the officer's decisions and the extent of the principal officer's ability to remove the officer.") (citing Edmond v. United States, 520 U.S. 651, 662–66 (1997)).

208 *Free Enter. Fund*, 130 S. Ct. at 3181 (Breyer, J., dissenting). But the majority rejects this point, noting that "we see little analogy between our Nation's armed services and the Public Company Accounting Oversight Board." *Id.* at 3160 (majority opinion).

209 *Id.* at 3138 (majority opinion); 3170–71 (Breyer, J., dissenting).

210 Pildes, *supra* note 167, at 1.

211 *See, e.g.*, Intercollegiate Broad. Sys. v. Copyright Royalty Bd., 684 F.3d 1332, 1335 (D.C. Cir. 2012) (finding the Copyright Royalty Board was unconstitutional because the librarian of Congress would have "substantive input" over the decisions of administrative judges, who are appointed by the president). *See also* Tucker v. Comm'r, 676 F.3d 1129 (D.C. Cir. 2012). *Compare* Aziz Z. Huq, *Removal as a Political Question*, 65 STAN. L. REV. 1, 3 (2013) ("But big things often have small beginnings. The *Free Enterprise Fund* principle cannot easily be limited to 'dual for-cause' regimes. Rather, the decision's fundamental logic 'calls into question the constitutionality of hundreds of other governmental positions' buffered from presidential control. . . .").

212 Neomi Rao, *A Modest Proposal: Abolishing Agency Independence in* Free Enterprise Fund v. PCAOB, 79 FORDHAM L. REV. 2541, 2560 (2011) ("This formulation is at best ambiguous about the constitutionality of the SEC's single layer of independence from the President's control. . . . The logic of the opinion,

Although the point was not addressed during the Supreme Court oral arguments, the plaintiffs in *Free Enterprise Fund* had argued in the lower courts that even if the members of the board were inferior officers, the appointments would still be unconstitutional,[213] because the Constitution instructs that the appointment of inferior officers be vested "in the President alone, in the Courts of Law, or in the Heads of Departments."[214] The plaintiffs argued that because the SEC is an "independent" agency, it is therefore not a department of the federal government as required by the Constitution.[215] Further, in the event that the SEC is a "department," the appointment by the SEC as a whole, rather than by the chairman, arguably violates the plain language of Article II, which entrusts the delegation to the "Heads of Departments."[216] These arguments, however, were rejected by the D.C. Circuit.[217] According to the majority, SEC commissioners constitute "Heads of Departments" because the SEC is a "Cabinet-like" body that exercises executive authority over a major aspect of government policy, and because the commissioners are appointed by the president with advice and consent of the Senate.[218] These arguments were given short shrift by the Supreme Court as well, finally tamping down the question specifically left open in *Freytag* whether a "principal agenc[y], such as . . . the Security and Exchange Commission, is a Departmen[t]"[219] under the appointments clause even though it is a "free-standing, self-contained entity in the Executive Branch."[220] The Court found that:

> Because the Commission is a freestanding component of the Executive Branch, not subordinate to or contained within any other such component, it constitutes a "Departmen[t]" for the purposes of the Appointments Clause."[221]

however, strongly suggests that control over independent agencies such as the SEC is not sufficient, precisely because separation of powers requires the President to have full oversight and control over executive branch officials").

213 Brief of Plaintiff-Appellants at 36–37, Free Enter. Fund v. Public Co. Accounting Oversight Bd., 537 F.3d 667 (D.C. Cir. 2008) (No. 07-5127), 2007 WL 4973854.

214 U.S. Const. art. II, § 2.

215 Brief of Plaintiff-Appellants at 36–37, Free Enter. Fund v. Public Co. Accounting Oversight Bd., 537 F.3d 667 (D.C. Cir. 2008) (No. 07-5127), 2007 WL 4973854.

216 *Id.*

217 *Free Enter. Fund*, 537 F.3d at 677.

218 *Id.* at 676–77 ("As used in the Appointments Clause, the phrase 'Heads of Departments' suggests that the Departments referred to are themselves in the Executive Branch or at least have some connection with that branch. . . . The Supreme Court has explained that Departments refers to the subdivisions of power of the Executive into departments for the more convenient exercise of that power.") (citations omitted). The Supreme Court has described departments as being "like the Cabinet-level departments . . . which are limited in number and easily identified." *Id.* at 676.

219 *Freytag*, 501 U.S. at 887 n.4.

220 *Id.* at 915.

221 *Free Enter. Fund*, 130 S. Ct. at 21.

In an opaque comment, the Court left open the bedrock question of the status of the SEC in other contexts. "We express no view on whether the Commission is thus an 'executive Departmen[t]' under the Opinions Clause, Art II, § 2, cl. 1 or under Section 4 of the Twenty-First Amendment." *Id.* at 21 n.11.

Not giving up, the petitioners further argued that only the chair of the commission is the commission's "Head." Rejecting this effort as well, the Court noted that:

> The Commission's powers, however, are generally vested in the Commissioners jointly, not the Chairman alone.... As a constitutional matter, we see no reason why a multimember body may not be "Hea[d]" of a "Departmen[t]" that it governs. The Appointments Clause necessarily contemplates collective appointments by the "Courts of Law," Art. II, § 2, cl. 2, and each House of Congress, too, appoints its officers collectively, see Art. I, § 2, cl. 5; *id.*, § 3, cl. 5.[222]

Freytag, again, guided the lower courts' interpretation of what is meant by "heads of departments" for appointments clause purposes—where the majority explained that heads of departments includes only "executive divisions like the Cabinet-level departments...limited in number and easily identified. Their heads are subject to the exercise of political oversight and share the President's accountability to the people."[223] In *United States v. Mouat,* the Court also indicated that an appointment could be considered to have been made by the "head of department" if, by statute, the appointment was subject to the approval of the head of department.[224] Outside the independent agency context, appointment of certain government actors by other government actors who are not clearly "heads of departments" has raised academic and legal concern that appointments are being carried out in violation of the appointments clause.[225]

---

222 *Free Enter. Fund*, 130 S. Ct. at 3163.

223 Freytag v. Comm'r, 501 U.S. 868, 886 (1991). *Freytag* was a unanimous result. Justice Blackmun found for the five-member majority that the Tax Court was a "Court [ ] of Law" for appointments clause purposes. *Id.* at 890–92. In a four-member concurrence, Justice Scalia rejected this reasoning finding that the Court was a department in the sense of a freestanding, self-contained entity in the executive branch. *Id.* at 914–22.

224 124 U.S. 303, 307–08 (1888) ("[I]t is alleged that [the claimant's] appointment as pay-master's clerk...although made by a pay-master in the United States navy, has indorsed on it the approval of D. B. Harmony, acting secretary of the navy. If there were any statute which authorized the head of the navy department to appoint a pay-master's clerk, the technical argument, that the appointment in this case, although actually made by Paymaster White-house, and only approved by Harmony as acting secretary in a formal way...might still be considered sufficient to call this an appointment by the head of that department. But there is no statute authorizing the secretary of the navy to appoint a pay-master's clerk, nor is there any act requiring his approval of such an appointment....").

225 *See* Petition for Writ of Certiorari, Transologic Tech. v. Dudas, 555 U.S. 813 (2008) (No. 07-1303). For a discussion of the appointment of administrative patent judges by the director of the Patent and Trademark Office, see John F. Duffy, *Are Administrative Patent Judges Unconstitutional?*, 77 Geo. Wash. L. Rev. 904, 909 (2009) (concluding that the appointments are "almost certainly unconstitutional" because the director of the Patent and Trademark Office is subordinate to the secretary of commerce and therefore cannot qualify as a cabinet level department head). The issue was brought to the Supreme Court's attention in a recent writ for certiorari. *See* Petition for Writ of Certiorari, Transologic Tech. v. Dudas, 555 U.S. 813 (No. 07-1303) (denied). Congress passed a legislative "fix," see Act of August 12, 2009, Pub. L. No. 110-313, § 1(a), 122 Stat. 3014, 3014 (amending 35 U.S.C. § 6(d) (2006)).

A similar claim was made regarding the Copyright Royalty Board, a three-member board appointed by the librarian of Congress and responsible for setting rates and determining distributions of statutory license royalties.[226] In *Intercollegiate Broadcasting System, Inc.*, the board was challenged on two grounds.[227] First, its members, who can only be removed for "misconduct or neglect of duty," were, in light of their responsibilities and the lack of direct control by a principal officer, arguably themselves principal officers who had to be appointed by the president with Senate approval. Second, even if they were considered to be inferior officers, the librarian of Congress was not the head of a department who could appoint inferior officers. The D.C. Circuit agreed that they were principal officers. However, the D.C. Circuit solved the constitutional appointment problem by following the Supreme Court's lead in *Free Enterprise Fund*, simply eliminating the statutory removal protection so that the board members were subject to unconditional removal by the librarian of Congress.[228] That transformed them into inferior officers. The court then concluded that the Library of Congress, although having both legislative and executive functions, was a "component of the executive branch" and thus a "department," and the librarian of Congress was the head of a department capable of appointing inferior officers.[229]

At times courts choose consciously to efface an appointments clause problem. Consider the Federal Open Market Committee, which is composed of twelve members. These include the seven members of the Board of Governors of the Federal Reserve System and the president of the Federal Reserve Bank of New York. The four remaining members come from the eleven board Bank presidents. These four members serve year-long terms, after which they rotate.[230] The five bank presidents are not appointed pursuant to the procedures ordained by the appointments clause. Unlike their seven colleagues, who are nominated by the president and confirmed by the Senate, these five members are selected by the boards of directors of the several Federal Reserve Banks.[231] Senator Donald Riegle of Michigan sued, claiming that it was his right as a senator to vote under the appointments clause on the nomination of the five members chosen by the boards of the Banks.[232] The D.C. Circuit used the doctrine of equitable jurisdiction "to dismiss the case on the ground that judicial action would improperly interfere with the legislative process."[233] Other circuits have similarly bypassed the issue.

---

226 *See* 17 U.S.C. § 801(a).

227 Intercollegiate Broadcasting Sys., Inc. v. Copyright Royalty Bd., 684 F.3d 1332, 1336 (D.C. Cir. 2012), *cert. denied*, 133 S. Ct. 2735 (2013).

228 *Id.* at 1343.

229 *Id.* at 1342–43.

230 *See* Federal Reserve System, Board of Government of the Federal Reserve System, Federal Open Market Committee, http://www.federalreserve.gov/monetarypolicy/fomc.htm.

231 Melcher v. Fed. Open Mkt. Comm., 836 F.2d 561, 562 (D.C. Cir. 1987). *See* 12 U.S.C. § 263(a) (1982).

232 Riegle v. Fed. Open Mkt. Comm., 656 F.2d, 873 (D.C. Cir. 1981).

233 *Riegle*, 656 F.2d at 882.

5. RECESS APPOINTMENTS

Nomination by the president and confirmation by the Senate is the primary constitutional method of appointing the principal officers of the government.[234] However, the Constitution's recess appointments clause (Const. art. II, § 2, cl. 3) provides that "[t]he President shall have Power to fill up all Vacancies that may happen during the Recess of the Senate, by granting Commissions which shall expire at the End of their next Session."

Recess appointees have the same powers while in office that they would have if appointed with Senate confirmation.[235] The president may use his recess appointment power to fill vacant positions or replace agency members who are continuing to serve beyond their ordinary statutory term (called "holdover" members), although the power to replace holders may depend on the terms of the agency's statute.[236] The president may also use the recess appointment power to reappoint an incumbent whose term as a Senate-confirmed member expired during a recess.[237]

Recess appointments can ruffle senatorial feathers—even if the president's party controls the Senate—by compromising senatorial confirmation prerogatives and, thus, dampening senators' political influence. In addition, individuals of recognized stature can be difficult to recruit for such an uncertain post.

President Clinton faced this problem when William Gould, a highly regarded Stanford law professor, left after what turned out to be an unexpectedly contentious tenure as chair of the NLRB, which has traditionally had two management-oriented members (generally Republican) sitting alongside two labor-oriented members (generally Democrats), plus a chair from an ostensibly neutral background, such as government or academia. President Clinton plucked from retirement John Truesdale, a seventy-seven-year-old career NLRB employee, to fill Gould's seat on the multimember board.[238]

---

[234] NLRB v. Noel Canning, 134 S. Ct. 2550, 2558-59 (2014).

[235] Evans v. Stephens, 387 F.3d 1220, 1223–24 (11th Cir. 2004) (en banc). *See generally* The Constitutional Separation of Powers Between the President and Congress, 1996 OLC LEXIS 6, at *122 (May 7, 1996). *See also* Jeff VanDam, Note, *The Kill Switch: The New Battle over Presidential Recess Appointments*, 107 Nw. U. L. Rev. 361 (2012) (discussing recent developments in the Bush and Obama administrations related to recess appointments).

[236] *See* Swan v. Clinton, 100 F.3d 973, 985–88 (D.C. Cir. 1996) (upholding a recess appointment to replace holdover member of National Credit Union); Staebler v. Carter, 464 F. Supp. 585 (D.D.C. 1979) (upholding, in case of first impression, the president's power to replace a holdover member of the FEC with recess appointee). *But see* Wilkinson v. Legal Servs. Corp., 80 F.3d 535, 537 (D.C. Cir. 1996) (noting the division among district courts over whether it is permissible under the recess appointments clause to replace holdover appointees with recess appointments).

[237] President's Authority to Make a Recess Appointment to the National Labor Relations Board, 2001 OLC LEXIS 27 (2001). *See generally* Shannon Cain, *The Case for Judicial Review of President Obama's January 4 Recess Appointments*, 64 Admin. L. Rev. 993 (2012) (suggesting possible bases on which a reviewing court could uphold the appointments and clarify existing presidential authority).

[238] There is no statutory "holdover" provision for NLRB members. *See* 29 U.S.C. § 153(a) (2010).

At the time Chairman Gould left, the management, that is, "Republican," seats were filled, and a Republican Senate during the last two years of the Clinton administration was reluctant to approve a Democratic nominee to a full five-year term. However, in the absence of a fifth member, the NLRB would likely have deadlocked on key issues. Truesdale agreed to come out of retirement, and as a highly respected career bureaucrat who had already served on the NLRB on several occasions over a decades-long career, he was politically tolerable. The Senate later confirmed Truesdale to a full term, but he had to agree, as a condition of confirmation, to resign upon the election of a new president. Overall, the compromise provided a quality appointment for a two-year period, avoided a regulatory stalemate, and preserved important presidential and senatorial prerogatives.[239]

Until the Supreme Court's 2014 decision in the *Noel Canning* case,[240] the contours of the power of the president to fill vacancies remained unclear, and several areas of controversy had emerged: (1) what counts as a recess, (2) what is meant by the phrase "Vacancies that may happen during the Recess" and (3) what, if anything, can Congress do to restrict the president's constitutional powers.[241] While the Court's decision has not quieted the controversy, it has, at least, resolved the issues.

a. What Counts as a Recess?

The founding fathers provided for recess appointments as a limited alternative to the primary appointment and confirmation process so that a president could fill vacancies and keep government operating when the normal appointment and confirmation process was unavailable, or, in the Court's words, "to permit the Executive Branch to function smoothly when Congress is unavailable."[242]

There has never been any doubt that the recess appointment power can be used in between designated sessions of Congress, that is, during an intersession recess.[243] Perhaps the most unusual example of intersession recess appointments occurred in 1903, when President

---

239 This story is related in CINDY SKRZYCKI, THE REGULATORS: ANONYMOUS POWER BROKERS IN AMERICAN POLITICS 63–65 (2003). For an excellent history of the transformation of the appointment process at the NLRB, on which we have drawn, see Flynn, *supra* note 56, at 1361 (noting that the board "has come 180 degrees from its origins in the New Deal era"). *See also* Fisk, *supra* note 56.

240 Noel Canning, 134 S. Ct. 2550.

241 For a general discussion of these (and other) questions, see Blake Denton, *While the Senate Sleeps: Do Contemporary Events Warrant a New Interpretation of the Recess Appointments Clause?*, 58 CATH. U. L. REV. 751 (2009).

242 Noel Canning, 134 S. Ct. at 2566.

243 *See, e.g.*, Henry B. Hogue, *The Law: Recess Appointments to Article III Courts*, 34 PRESIDENTIAL STUD. Q. 656, 660–61 (2004) (detailing instances in which Supreme Court justices have been appointed during a recess). *See also* Thomas A. Curtis, Note, *Recess Appointments to Article III Courts: The Use of Historical Practice in Constitutional Interpretation*, 84 COLUM. L. REV. 1758, 1770–72 (1984).

Theodore Roosevelt made over one hundred recess appointments in the "instant" between the Senate adjourning a special session and beginning a new one.[244] The *New York Times* characterized Roosevelt's appointments as follows:

> The fact that Secretary Root has advised the President that he may make the nominations of Gen. Wood and the rest of the army officers in the inappreciable space of time assumed to exist between the end of the extra session and the beginning of the regular session, disposes one to await the reasoning by which such advice is sustained before condemning it. But on the face of the provisions of the Constitution it appears preposterous.[245]

The Senate was equally displeased, holding hearings on the matter in the Judiciary Committee in 1905:

> It can not by any possibility be deemed within the intent of the Constitution that when the Senate is in a position to receive a nomination by the President, and,

---

244 *See Special Session Is Merged into Regular*, N.Y. TIMES, Dec. 8, 1903, at 1. The bulk of the nominations were among officers, but about twenty-five were civilian appointments, including that of William D. Crum to be customs collector of the Port of Charleston. *See* S. RPT. 58-4389 at 1 (1905); *see also* JAY WEXLER, THE ODD CLAUSES: UNDERSTANDING THE CONSTITUTION THROUGH TEN OF ITS MOST CURIOUS PROVISIONS (2011) (indicating that Teddy Roosevelt appointed 160 officers in what he described as "'constructive' split-second recess that must have existed between the two sessions").

The political backstory to this unusual initiative is of interest. Crum was African American, and his appointment in 1902 as customs collector was strenuously opposed by "Pitchfork" Ben Tillman, an arch-segregationist senator from South Carolina. *See* EDMUND MORRIS, THEODORE REX 198–99 (2001). In response, Roosevelt announced that he would appoint Crum to the position. *Id.* at 304; *see also* Willard B. Gatewood, *William D. Crum: A Negro in Politics*, 53 J. NEGRO HIST. 301, 311 (1968). Although the Republican Party begrudgingly supported Crum's nomination, South Carolina Democrats vehemently opposed Roosevelt's action, stating that it was a "reckless and irresponsible course." *Id.* Due to Tillman's influence, the Senate refused to consider the nomination. *See id.* at 312; *see also Crum Nominated Again*, WASH. POST, Apr. 29, 1904, at 4. Roosevelt responded by placing Crum in the position despite the Senate's inaction. *See* Gatewood, *supra*, at 313. However, because the Senate had not confirmed Crum's appointment, Crum could not receive any salary for his work. *Id.* Two years later, during which time Crum acted as postmaster of Charleston without pay, Roosevelt finally convinced the Senate to take up the nomination, and the Senate confirmed him on January 7, 1905. *See Crum Nominated Again*, WASH. POST, Apr. 29, 1904, at 4.

Although some media sources at the time maintained that Crum's race did not play a major role in this controversy, others noted that racism was in fact a chief concern for those opposing Crum's nomination. *See W. D. Crum Confirmed*, N.Y. TIMES, Jan. 7, 1905, at 5 (noting that "[t]he race issue played only an insignificant part in the discussion, which related chiefly to the subject of constructive recesses"); *but see Crum Case Goes Over*, WASH. POST, Apr. 28, 1904, at 4 (discussing the heated argument between Senators Spooner and Daniel over the subject of Crum's racial background); MORRIS, *supra* at 198–99 (discussing Senator Tillman's vehement opposition to Crum's nomination on account of Crum's race); Seth M. Scheiner, *President Theodore Roosevelt and the Negro, 1901–1908*, 47 J. NEGRO HIST. 169, 175 (1962) (noting that "[m]any southerners considered it a disgrace for a Negro to serve in such a high official post in the 'Cradle of the Confederacy'").

245 Editorial, *The Infinitesimal Recess*, N.Y. TIMES, Dec. 8, 1903, *available at* http://query.nytimes.com/gst/abstract.html?res=F40911FD3E5B11738DDDA10894DA415B838CF1D3.

therefore, to exercise its function of advice and consent, the President can issue, without its advice and consent, commissions which will be lawful warrant for the assumption of duties for a federal office.[246]

The Senate also noted that there was no appreciable time during which the Senate would have been unable to receive and consider nominations by the president.[247] Indeed, the Senate report suggested that "[t]he theory of 'constructive recess' constitutes a heavy draft upon the imagination."[248] Nonetheless, the recess appointments stood.

Whether intrasession breaks constitute a "recess" for constitutional purposes is a more difficult question. The OLC has argued that the term "recess" must be given a practical construction, that it may include intrasession breaks, and that the president is entitled to make a good faith determination of whether a given recess is sufficient to trigger his recess appointment authority.[249] The comptroller general has likewise agreed that an intrasession break of sufficient length can constitute a recess for purposes of the recess appointment clause.[250] The Supreme Court has now fully addressed the issue. In a five to four split on this point, the majority concluded that the term "recess" includes "an intra-session recess of substantial length,"[251] but that "a recess of more than 3 days but less than 10 days in presumptively too short to fall within the Clause."[252]

A trilogy of Court of Appeals decisions in 2013 had sparked the Supreme Court's first examination of the recess clause in U.S. history. *Noel Canning* involved three recess appointments to the NLRB during a period when the Senate was conducting "pro forma" sessions twice a week in an effort to stifle the president's recess appointment authority. In *Noel Canning v. NLRB*,[253] a panel of the D.C. Circuit found appointments made during a three-day period between pro forma sessions to be unconstitutional. Thereafter, a

---

246 39 Cong. Rec. 3824 (daily ed. Mar. 2, 1905) (report of the Senate Judiciary Committee).

247 *Id.*

248 S. Rep. No. 58-438 at 3 (1905).

249 *See* Lawfulness of Recess Appointments During a Recess of the Senate Notwithstanding Periodic Pro Forma Sessions, 36 Op. O.L.C. 2 (2012) [hereinafter OLC Pro Forma Sessions Opinion].

250 Opinion of Comptroller General Warren to Director, Administrative Office of the United States Courts, Appointments—Recess Appointments, 28 Comp. Gen. 30, 34 (July 16, 1948).

251 Noel Canning, 134 S. Ct. at 2561.

252 *Id.* at 2567. The view that an intrasession recess is covered by the recess clause had some support in earlier case law. *See* Evans v. Stephens, 387 F.3d 1220 (11th Cir. 2004) (en banc). Starting from a presumption that the president is acting constitutionally when exercising one of his express powers, the court looked at the text of the Constitution and the prior instances of recess appointments and found that an intrasession recess qualified under the clause. *Id.* at 1224–26. Important to the court was the fact that twelve presidents have appointed over 285 "Officers of the United States" during intrasession recesses. *Id.* at 1226. Judge Barkett dissented. In her view, '[h]ad the Framers intended to include intra-session as well as inter-session recesses, they could very easily have used the phrase 'during a recess of the Senate.' They chose instead to adopt a singular construction: 'the Recess of the Senate.'" *Id.* at 1228, n. 2.

253 705 F.3d 490 (D.C. Cir. 2013).

panel of the Third Circuit, in a two-to-one decision, followed suit in *NLRB v. New Vista Nursing and Rehabilitation*,[254] and a panel of the Fourth Circuit, also in a two-to-one decision, agreed in *NLRB v. Enterprise Leasing Co., Southeast, LLC*.[255]

The Supreme Court granted certiorari in the *Noel Canning* case.[256] The two principal questions were novel and obviously of considerable constitutional importance, and there was a substantial split in the circuits. Moreover, the D.C. Circuit's opinion was wide-reaching. The Supreme Court also included for review the question of whether pro forma sessions effectively keep the Senate in session so as to prevent a recess.[257]

As noted, the Supreme Court then resolved all questions. Both Justice Breyer, writing for five members of the court, and Justice Scalia, writing for the other four, closely examined the text, structure, purpose, and history of the recess clause—agreeing on the ultimate result that President Obama's appointments were unconstitutional, but strongly disagreeing on the reasons. Justice Breyer's opinion concluded that the constitutional text bearing on intrasession recesses was ambiguous but could be read to permit intrasession appointments. He placed heavy reliance on historical practice over two hundred years as he saw it to support his result. He also observed that "restricting the Clause to inter-session recesses would frustrate its purpose."[258] A more difficult question, he pointed out, was deciding how long a recess must be to come within the clause. Acknowledging that the clause itself sets no limit, he determined, based on the practice of recess appointments over the years, that a recess of under ten days is presumptively too short.

As to whether the pro forma session had their intended effect of preventing the president from making recess appointments, the majority concluded that they had. The majority held that "for purposes of the recess appointments clause, the Senate is in session when it says it is, provided that, under its own rules, it retains the capacity to transact Senate business"[259]—a condition the majority found satisfied in this case. Justice Scalia disagreed with the majority's primary conclusion that the clause should embrace intrasession recesses. Harking back to the founding era, he argued that the term "recess" had a well-understood meaning and that "[t]he period *between* two sessions was known as 'the recess.'"[260] Justice Scalia also rejected the majority's reading of historical practice.[261] In his view, intrasession recess appointments were not made during the most

254 719 F.3d 203 (3d Cir. 2013).

255 722 F.3d 609 (4th Cir. 2013).

256 NLRB v. Noel Canning, 705 F.3d 490 (D.C. Cir. 2013), *cert. granted*, 133 S. Ct. 2861 (June 24, 2013) (No. 12-1281).

257 The solicitor general had urged the Court not to address this issue because it had not been addressed by the lower courts. See Reply Brief for Appellant Petitioner, at 5–7, NLRB v. Noel Canning, 134 S. Ct. 2550 (2014).

258 Noel Canning, 134 S. Ct. at 2564.

259 *Id.* at 2574.

260 *Id.* at 2596.

261 *Id.* at 2600-05.

relevant first 130 years of the country's history and were not used to any considerable degree until the period following World War II.[262]

b. What Counts as a Vacancy?

The president's recess appointment power extends to filling "Vacancies that may happen during the Recess of the Senate."[263] What counts as such a vacancy is a controversial issue. One view is that the Constitution only authorizes the president to fill vacancies that actually arise while the Senate is in recess. The D.C. Circuit, in *Noel Canning*, endorsed this reading.[264] The opposing view is, of course, that the timing of the vacancy's occurrence is irrelevant—the president may fill a vacancy that exists during a recess, regardless of whether it occurred before or during the recess.[265] In *Evans v. Stephens*,[266] the Eleventh Circuit accepted this reading of the Constitution.

The Supreme Court has now resolved the question. In the majority's view, "[i]n light of some linguistic ambiguity, the basic purpose of the Clause, and the historical practice... the phrase 'all vacancies' includes vacancies that come into existence while the Senate is in session.[267] Justice Breyer acknowledged that his construction of the clause was not "the most natural meaning of 'happens' as applied to a 'vacancy' (at least to a modern ear)."[268] Nonetheless, harking back to comments by Thomas Jefferson, he observed that the clause is susceptible to two constructions[269] and found that the purpose of the clause, that is, to permit the president to have a full complement of subordinates when the Senate is unavailable to confirm them, and the historic practice under it, warrants the broader meaning the majority gives it.[270]

Justice Scalia, writing for four justices, disagreed. He argued that at the time the Constitution was drafted "a vacancy that *happened* during the Recess was most reasonably understood as one that *arose* during the recess."[271] Any alternate reading would have permitted appointments under the recess appointment clause to subsume the primary method of appointment.[272] Moreover, Justice Scalia's reading of history was broadly inconsistent with the majority's analysis.[273]

---

262 *Id.* at 2603-04.

263 U.S. CONST. art. II, § 2, cl. 2.

264 705 F.3d at 507–11.

265 *See, e.g.*, Michael Herz, *Abandoning Recess Appointments? A Comment on Hartnett (and Others)*, 26 CARDOZO L. REV. 443, 445 (2005).

266 Evans v. Stephens, 387 F.3d 1220 (11th Cir. 2004) (en banc).

267 Noel Canning, 134 S. Ct. at 2573.

268 *Id.* at 2567.

269 *Id.* at 2567–68.

270 *Id.* at 2568–73.

271 *Id.* at 2606–07.

272 *Id.* at 2607.

273 *Id.* at 2610–18.

The case, of course, poses significant underlying issues for constitutional doctrine and government administration. Which political branch of government needs greater judicial protection from the other? Justice Scalia stands with the Congress in opposition to what he perceives as a continual presidential aggrandizement of power. He describes the majority's analysis as an "adverse-possession theory of executive authority: Presidents have long claimed the powers in question, and the Senate has not disputed those claims with sufficient vigor, so the Court should not 'upset the compromises and working arrangements that the elected branches of Government themselves have reached.'"[274] Adrian Vermeule has likewise observed that the decision of the Court of Appeals striking down the president's recess appointments in *Noel Canning* (and, presumably, Justice Scalia's approach, although Vermeule wrote before the Supreme Court's decision was issued) serves as "a precaution against the risk of executive aggrandizement, or even presidential despotism."[275] On the other hand Judge Greenaway's dissenting opinion in *NLRB v. New Vista Nursing and Rehabilitation* reflected his concern that "the President must be formidable enough to countermand Congress and prevent the Senate from eviscerating his appointments prerogative through its use of advise and consent."[276] How does that dilemma get resolved? Cass Sunstein refers, in this regard, to "political Burkeans," that is, those who take into account long-standing accommodations and practices between the elected branches of government. The minority's approach would have severely curtailed, if not eliminated altogether as a practical matter, the president's recess authority. Justice Scalia believes that such a result is compelled by the text, structure, and history of the recess appointment clause and that the Court's duty is to pronounce it. But it is probably not a practical problem in any event. In Justice Scalia's view, the recess appointment clause "is, or rather, should be, an anachronism—essentially an historic relic, something whose original purpose has disappeared."[277]

The majority's approach still accords nearly unlimited power on the Senate. But its narrow reading of the recess clause avoids the significant constitutional questions regarding the definition of a recess, does not upset to quite the same degree the historic, although uncomfortable, balance between the elected branches in the appointment process, and leaves appointments generally, and recess appointments in particular, largely to practical, political accommodation. In November 2013, the Senate changed its rules to permit the president's executive branch nominations (and judicial nominations below the Supreme Court level) to move forward to confirmation by a simple majority vote in the Senate.[278] So the issue of recess appointments is no longer likely to be as pressing as before.

---

274 *Id.* at 2592.

275 Adrian Vermeule, *Reaction Recess Appointments and Precautionary Constitutionalism*, 126 Harv. L. Rev. F. 122 (2013).

276 719 F.3d at 255 (Greenaway, J., dissenting).

277 Noel Canning, 134 S. Ct. at 2598.

278 Paul Kane, *Reid, Democrats Trigger "Nuclear" Option; Eliminate Most Filibusters on Nominees*, Wash. Post, Nov. 22, 2013, at A1.

c. Legislative Efforts to Restrict the President's Recess Appointment Power

As a practical matter, Congress has used various techniques to confine the president's recess appointment powers. Section 5503 of Title V of the U.S. Code prohibits payment to recess appointees except in three circumstances: if (1) the vacancy occurred within thirty days of the end of a congressional session; (2) a nomination was pending when the Senate recessed; or (3) a nomination was rejected within thirty days before a recess and another individual receives the recess appointment.[279] Therefore, there may be some situations where the president has the constitutional power to make a recess appointment but cannot fill a vacancy because the appointee must be willing to work without receiving monetary compensation.[280]

Without question a highly controversial element of the constitutional clash over the use of recess appointments is the Senate's refusal to vote on some of President Obama's appointments and its strategy to block recess appointments by remaining in session indefinitely through the use of "pro forma" sessions. The technique of failing to recess formally has been used since 2007.[281] In 2011, for example, as earlier discussed, the Senate agreed to "adjourn and convene for pro forma sessions only, with no business conducted" twice a week between December 17, 2011, and January 23, 2012.[282] The Senate seemingly believes that such pro forma sessions have the effect of rendering any break too short to qualify as a "recess" for constitutional purposes,[283] and has subsequently pointed out that even during these short breaks important business is conducted.[284] President Obama, relying on a detailed legal opinion by the OLC, nonetheless made recess appointments during this period in order to allow two government agencies to function.[285] Perhaps more controversial was his appointment of Richard Cordray to head the Consumer Financial Protection Bureau (CFPB). He also filled three vacancies on the NLRB, thus

---

279 5 U.S.C. § 5503(a)(1)–(3). *See* U.S. Gov't Accountability Office, B-150847, Memorandum to the Chairman of the Interstate Commerce Commission, 52 Comp. Gen. 556, 556–58 (1973) (informing the ICC that commissioner appointed by recess appointment should not receive payment under 5 U.S.C. § 5503). For discussion of the statutory history of this provision, see Steven M. Pyser, *Recess Appointments to the Federal Judiciary: An Unconstitutional Transformation of Senate Advice and Consent*, 8 U. Pa. J. Const. L. 61, 78–79 (2006).

280 If pay is prohibited under 5 U.S.C. § 5503, some have argued that appointees accepting positions without pay violate the Anti-Deficiency Act, which does not allow the federal government to accept "voluntary services." 31 U.S.C. § 1342. However, the GAO has found that if pay is not mandated by statute, the prohibition on voluntary services can be waived and accepted as "gratuitous" services. Vivian S. Chu, Cong. Research Serv., RL 33009, Recess Appointments: A Legal Overview 17–18 (2011).

281 *See* OLC Pro Forma Sessions Opinion, *supra* note 249, at 2.

282 157 Cong. Rec. S8783 (daily ed. Dec. 17, 2011). *See also supra* notes 241 and 259 and accompanying text.

283 OLC Pro Forma Sessions Opinion, *supra* note 249, at 2.

284 *See, e.g.*, 157 Cong. Rec. S8789 (daily ed. Dec. 23, 2011) (extending the payroll tax cut).

285 *See generally* OLC Pro Forma Sessions Opinion, *supra* note 249. *See also* 158 Cong. Rec. S24 (daily ed. Jan. 23, 2012) (remarks of Senator Grassley, railing against the OLC Opinion that defended recess appointments).

bringing that board to full strength.[286] In both cases, appointments were needed to keep the agencies operating. As discussed earlier, these appointments have generated substantial litigation regarding their constitutionality.[287]

There is a further constitutional twist to the use of "pro forma" sessions. This practice was originally introduced by the Senate acting alone.[288] During the 112th Congress, however, the House of Representatives decided not to join in any concurrent resolution of adjournment, thus requiring the Senate to use pro forma recesses to avoid a recess of more than three days.[289] As a result, the House is now indirectly involved in the appointment process heretofore thought to belong exclusively to the president and the Senate.

As noted earlier, the immediate problem, although not the constitutional issue, seems to have been solved through political compromise. In mid-July 2013, facing a threat by the Senate majority leader to launch an effort to amend the Senate's filibuster rules, a small group of Republican senators, led by John McCain, joined by their Democratic colleagues, reached a compromise that brings the recess crisis to at least a temporary end. In exchange for Senator Harry Reid dropping his proposal to change the filibuster rules, the group of senators agreed to confirm Richard Cordray to head the CFPB. President Obama withdrew two controversial nominations to the NLRB in return for a promise that the Senate would confirm new nominees.[290] This resolution is obviously preferable

---

[286] On January 13, 2012, the National Association of Manufacturers and several other industry groups challenged the constitutionality of the newly appointed NLRB board members, introducing the issue into an ongoing suit. *See* Motion for Leave to Supplement Complaint and Objection to Substitution of Defendants, Nat'l Ass'n of Mfg. v. NLRB, No. 1:11-cv-01629-ABJ (2012), *available at* http://sblog.s3.amazonaws.com/wp-content/uploads/2012/01/Motion.pdf. *See also* Peter Schroeder, *Republican Lawmakers Begin Pushback Against Obama Recess Appointments*, THE HILL (Jan. 30, 2012, 12:16 a.m.), http://thehill.com/policy/finance/207277-republican-lawmakers-begin-pushback-against-obama-recess-appointments-.

[287] For further discussion of the oral argument in the D.C. Circuit Court of Appeals, see Peter T. Tschanz, *NLRB Hears Oral Argument in* Noel Canning v. NLRB, LEXOLOGY, Dec. 7, 2012, http://www.lexology.com/library/detail.aspx?g=a590e532-c355-45d8-8c7e-fce2cc20405f (pointing out that the Justice Department argued it had "100 years" of precedent supporting such appointments, but also indicating that at least one judge seemed resistant to this approach). *See also* Mark Theodore, *Oral Arguments Heard over Validity of Recess Appointments of NLRB Members*, JD SUPRA LAW NEWS Dec. 7, 2012, http://www.jdsupra.com/legalnews/oral-arguments-heard-over-validity-of-re-72105/ (noting that at least one judge on the panel indicated it would be most appropriate for the Senate to better define the terms of its recess and pro forma sessions). The Seventh Circuit dismissed a similar suit on technical grounds. *See* Richards v. NLRB, 702 F.3d 1010 (7th Cir. 2012).

[288] HENRY B. HOGUE, CONG. RESEARCH SERV., RS 21308, RECESS APPOINTMENTS: FREQUENTLY ASKED QUESTIONS 11–12 (2013).

[289] *Id.* at 12. The Constitution prohibits either house from adjourning for more than three days without the consent of the other. U.S. CONST. art. 1, § 5, para. 4.

[290] *See generally* Jonathan Weisman & Jennifer Steinhauer, *Senate Strikes Filibuster Deal, Ends Logjam on Nominees*, N.Y. TIMES, July 17, 2013, at A1, A14; Paul Kane & Ed O'Keefe, *Senate Reaches Tentative Deal on Filibuster Rules*, WASH. POST, Jul. 17, 2013, at A1.

to any sweeping constitutional ruling that would effectively restrict, if not deprive, the president of his recess appointment power.

6. CONCERNS OVER LENGTH OF APPOINTMENT OF UNITED STATES ATTORNEYS

The Patriot Act Reauthorization Bill of 2005, signed into law in March 2006, contained another controversial clause that allowed the president to appoint U.S. attorneys to vacant seats, for a potentially indefinite term, without the advice and consent of the Senate.[291] Previously, the Senate was required to confirm the president's appointment of U.S. attorneys to fill vacancies within 120 days.[292] The provision quickly became the subject of significant criticism for overpoliticizing the role of U.S. attorneys who, by the nature of their job, must at some level make determinations as to which cases to investigate and which defendants to prosecute.[293] Critics suggested that the interim appointment provision, in conjunction with the executive removal authority over U.S. attorneys, created "an opportunity for the President to remove a U.S. Attorney midterm to disrupt an ongoing investigation or prosecution or to fill the vacant position with a political crony who can help the President pursue his or her own agenda."[294] Due to allegations that the Bush administration had purposefully utilized the interim appointment provisions to fill the seats of the U.S. attorneys controversially removed by in 2006, the Preserving United States Attorney Independence Act was passed in 2007.[295] The Act restored the provision requiring Senate confirmation of an interim U.S. attorney within 120 days.[296]

---

291 USA PATRIOT Improvement and Reauthorization Act of 2005, Pub. L. No. 109-177, § 502, 120 Stat. 192, 246 (2006) (repealed by Preserving United States Attorney Independence Act of 2007, Pub. L. No. 110-34, 121 Stat. 224). The reauthorization bill deleted 28 U.S.C. § 546 (c)–(d) (2000), effectively extinguishing the 120-day limit on the appointment of interim U.S. attorneys. USA PATRIOT Improvement and Reauthorization Act of 2005 § 502, 120 Stat. at 246.

292 Prior to the enactment of the 2005 statute, provisions related to the length of the interim appointment required that:

> (c) A person appointed as United States attorney under this section may serve until the earlier of—
> (1) the qualification of a United States attorney for such district appointed by the President under section 541 of this title; or
> (2) the expiration of 120 days after appointment by the Attorney General under this section.

28 U.S.C. § 546 (2000). Adam Liptak, *For Federal Prosecutors, Politics Is Ever-Present*, N.Y. TIMES 43, Mar. 18, 2007, http://query.nytimes.com/gst/fullpage.html?res=990CE5D71F31F93BA25750C0A9619C8B63&pagewanted=all.

293 *See* David C. Weiss, *Nothing Improper?: Examining Constitutional Limits, Congressional Action, Partisan Motivation, and Pretextual Justification in the U.S. Attorney Removals*, 107 MICH. L. REV. 317, 318–19 (2008) ("'Law enforcement is not automatic. It isn't blind.... If the prosecutor is obliged to choose his case, it follows that he can choose his defendants. Therein is the dangerous power of the prosecutor.'" (quoting Morrison v. Olson, 487 U.S. 654, 727–28 (1988) (Scalia, J., dissenting)).

294 Laurie L. Levenson, *Live and Learn: Depoliticizing the Interim Appointments of U.S. Attorneys*, 31 SEATTLE U. L. REV. 297, 315–16 (2008).

295 Preserving United States Attorney Independence Act of 2007, Pub. L. No. 110-34, 121 Stat. 224.

296 *Id.*

7. "PACKAGING" APPOINTMENTS

The requirement of Senate confirmation makes it fairly common for a president to "package" or "pair" nominees to multimember agencies to accommodate individual senators or interest groups. During the Reagan administration, Senator Paul Laxalt sought a Washington appointment for his former law partner Reese Taylor, who had also served as chairman of the Nevada Public Service Commission when Senator Laxalt was governor.[297] Taylor was tapped to be chairman of the ICC. Importantly, Taylor was not seen as especially sympathetic to the deregulatory initiatives then taking place at the ICC.[298] So his appointment was "paired" with Democrat Andrew Strenio to maintain a deregulatory majority on the commission. Chairman Taylor was thereafter simply a dissenting vote in deregulatory decisions.[299] In fact, Taylor's frustration over the commission's role led to public statements advocating the abolition of the ICC.[300] When Congress reduced the number of ICC commissioners from seven to five, effective December 31, 1985, it eliminated the seats held by Taylor and Strenio.

The practice is well established at the NLRB. It was apparently used in 1947 when the board was expanded from three to five members and a Republican and a Democrat were simultaneously appointed.[301] But, until recent times, it was more likely that a president would simply appoint a member of the opposite party who was amenable to his policies.[302] In her thoroughgoing analysis of the appointment and voting patterns at the NLRB, Joan Flynn concludes:

> Under the new regime [Reagan administration and thereafter] . . . and in particular during the Clinton years, the President has receded into the background, and a "you pick two, we pick two" mentality has taken over; instead of all concerned

---

[297] Betty Jo Christian, *The Impact of Antitrust on the Transportation Industry—Has Deregulation Gone Too Far, Too Fast?*, 54 ANTITRUST L.J. 465 (1985) (biographical introduction of Chairman Taylor).

[298] *See generally* Jill E. Fisch, *How Do Corporations Play Politics?: The FedEx Story*, 58 VAND. L. REV. 1495, 1523 n.191 (2005) (quoting a report by the Joint Economic Committee, and Paul Stephen Dempsey, *Congressional Intent and Agency Discretion—Never the Twain Shall Meet: The Motor Carrier Act of 1980*, 58 CHI.-KENT L. REV. 1, 56 n.231 (1981)).

[299] *See, e.g.*, Haslerig Trucking Co., Inc. Extension—General Commodities Contract Services, 1985 MCC LEXIS 422 (ICC, May 14, 1985) 15–16 (trucking); Pine Hill-Kingston Bus Corp. Extension—New York and New Jersey Regular Routes etc., 1984 MCC LEXIS 564 (ICC, June 11, 1984 (buses); Exemption from Regulation-Boxcar Traffic, 367 ICC 425, 463 (1983), *aff'd in part, vacated in part*, Brae Corp. v. United States, 740 F.2d 1023 (D.C. Cir. 1984), *cert. denied*, 471 U.S. 1069 (1985) (rail).

[300] *See* Paul Stephen Dempsey, *Transportation Deregulation—On a Collision Course?*, 13 TRANSP. L.J. 329, 378 n.199 (1984) (quoting Taylor's comments to a Senate committee, and James C. Miller III, *Keynote Address to ICC Centennial Celebration*, April 3, 1987, 16 TRANSP. L.J. 40, 44–45 (1987)).

[301] *See* William B. Gould, IV, *The NLRB at Age 70: Some Reflections on the Clinton Board and the Bush II Aftermath*, 26 BERKELEY J. EMP. & LAB. L. 309, 311–12 (2005) (noting the appointments of Republican J. Copeland and Democrat Abe Murdock).

[302] *Id.* at 309, 312.

> agreeing upon—or at a minimum acquiescing in—the appointment of a particular individual, the rival camps have simply divided up the pie between them: the President and/or key Senate Democrats pick one or more nominees, and key Senate Republicans pick one or more others.[303]

James Brudney likewise observes:

> Board appointments now tend to come in the form of packaged deals: the White House, interested groups, and a small number of Senators on each side agree on a group of union-sided and management-sided individuals who can then be recess-appointed without objection or confirmed without senatorial notice.[304]

Michael Stein refers to this practice at the NLRB as "batching" and notes that the NLRB under Chairman Gould "frequently operated at less than full strength, since Democratic senators preferred voting against disagreeable pairings."[305]

The practice of appointing FEC members in pairs is now commonplace,[306] although not surprising at an agency deliberately designed to have an equal number of Republican and Democratic members.

The appointment of individuals from the opposite party who shared the president's perspective retained for the president a considerable degree of policy control. Pairing or packaging, on the other hand, diminishes his appointment prerogatives and enhances the influence of individual senators.[307]

---

303 Flynn, *supra* note 56, at 1445.

304 James J. Brudney, *Isolated and Politicized: The NLRB's Uncertain Future*, 26 Comp. Lab. L. & Pol'y 221, 252 (2005). Brudney points out, in this connection, that for about two decades after 1985 only one hearing was held on 29 NLRB appointments. *Id.* at 252 n.147.

305 Michael Ashley Stein, Book Review, *Hardball, Politics and the NLRB*, 22 Berkeley J. Emp. & Lab. L. 507, 509–10 (2001).

306 Amanda S. LaForge, *The Toothless Tiger—Structural, Political and Legal Barriers to Effective FEC Enforcement: An Overview and Recommendations*, 10 Admin. L. Rev. Am. U. 351, 374 (1996).

307 *See generally* Dennis P. Walsh, *Procedural Barriers That Prevent the NLRB from Resolving Major Workers Rights Issues*, 15 Empl. Rts. & Emp. Pol'y J. 545, 546–48 (2011); Brudney, *supra* note 304 at 252. Paul Kane, *Deal at Hand on Nominees*, Roll Call, June 20, 2002; *Adelstein Confirmed*, Electronic Media, Nov. 18, 2002, at 1 (reporting Jonathan Adelstein's nomination for a seat on the FCC received Senate confirmation as part of a package deal that included dozens of nominees for various federal appointments); Doug Halonen, *FCC's Ness, Furchtgott-Roth to Exit*, Electronic Media, Feb. 5, 2001, at 2 (reporting a package deal was reached between Democrats and Republicans leading to an agreement to fill FCC positions); Doug Halonen, *Ness Closer to Confirmation; FCC Commissioner's Campaign Nears End*, Electronic Media, Mar. 27, 2000, at 4 (explaining an FCC nominee's "best hope for confirmation" is a bipartisan package deal with another federal nominee who has strong GOP support); *Furchtgott-Roth Said to Lead Candidates for FCC Post*, Tel. Rep., Feb. 10, 1997 ("For months congressional sources have maintained that since two Commission seats are open—one Republican and one Democrat—any potential nominee likely would be part of a 'package deal' with the White House.").

C. Observations

The president's authority as chief executive to appoint members of independent regulatory agencies is his most significant power to control an agency's regulatory agenda or at least try to assure some compatibility with his policies. As a consequence, Congress has often pushed back against this authority. The typical restrictions on that authority that require, for example, bipartisan balance on most multimember agencies and membership terms that ordinarily do not allow a president to replace all agency members during his four-year term of office have been criticized on constitutional grounds. But they are accepted limitations on the president's appointment authority. Moreover, the need for political accommodation with Congress often means that, as a practical matter, members of Congress have significant influence over a president's choices. That is even true—or perhaps more true—with regard to minority members of multimember agencies who are often sponsored by senators or others in Congress who are not of the president's party. The requirement of Senate confirmation makes it fairly common for a president to need to "package" or "pair" nominees to multimember agencies to accommodate individual senators or interest groups. Congress has likewise used its appropriations power and its internal procedures, such as holding "pro forma" sessions, to frustrate recess appointments.

In a handful of situations, Congress has used idiosyncratic appointment regimes that may move certain multimember agencies down the spectrum of diminished independence. For example, we have included the Board of Veterans' Appeals and the National Indian Gaming Commission among agencies we consider independent because their chairs are appointed by the president, must be confirmed by the Senate, and can only be removed for cause. But members of these boards other than their chairs are appointed by cabinet secretaries (the appointment of Board of Veterans' Appeals members is approved by the president). Importantly, they all serve only three-year (albeit renewable) terms. To be sure, the two associate members of the National Indian Gaming Commission have good cause removal protection and the members of the Board of Veterans' Appeals are typically career civil servants. Nonetheless, many members of the National Indian Gaming Commission have, in fact, served only a single three-year term.[308] Congress has by statute expressly placed the Board of Veterans' Appeals "under the administrative control and supervision of a chair directly responsible to the Secretary [of Veterans Affairs]."[309] The board's own website describes it as "a part of the VA" and designates its members as "Law Judges"[310] who are paid at the same level as

---

308 *See* Nat'l Indian Gaming Comm'n, www.nigc.gov/About_Us/Commission.aspx (last accessed Jan. 2, 2014).

309 38 U.S.C. § 7101(a).

310 *See* U.S. Dep't of Veterans Affairs, Bd. of Veterans' Appeals, www.bva.va.gov (last accessed Jan. 2, 2014).

ALJs.[311] Members of the board, apart from the chair, must be "recertified" at least once every three years under performance standards developed by the chair with the approval of the secretary. So the nonchair members have significant similarities to other federal employees, and the secretary retains at least some degree of practical oversight. In short, the appointment process is far from simple and reflects major elements of political compromise despite its constitutional underpinnings.

From a legal perspective, we should note that the lack of clarity in the Supreme Court's understanding of the contours of the appointed choice nurtures seeds of much future litigation. The term "inferior officer," for one, includes tensions that may contain elements of instability. The *Morrison* decision lays out a multifactored approach to defining "inferior officer" with some preference to the range of an officer's discretion.[312] The *Edmond* definition of inferior as someone who has a relationship with some higher ranking officer or officers[313] fits uneasily with the broader *Morrison* analysis. Indeed some have suggested that *Edmond* overruled *Morrison sub silentio*, at least with respect to the definition of "inferior officers."[314] All this is in aid of the argument that certain government workers should be classified as inferior officers rather than employees and, if so, such inferior officers must be appointed by the president or head of a department.

Originalists and adherents of a maximal "theory of the unitary executive" have pressed hard on the appointments clause, deploying it to claim that a wide swath of government officials were appointed by flawed constitutional means. In that regard some have argued for a limiting definition of "head of department."[315] Yet appointments reflecting idiosyncratic criteria persist.

---

311 5 U.S.C. § 5372.

312 *Morrison*, 487 U.S. at 671–72.

313 *Edmond*, 520 U.S. at 662–63.

314 Samahon, *supra* note 108, at 264.

315 James Pfander argues that the Constitutional authorization for Congress to vest the appointment of an inferior officer in the "courts of law" would make the tradition of the Chief Justice appointing Article III judges to specialty courts unconstitutional. James E. Pfander, *The Chief Justice, the Appointment of Inferior Officers and the "Court of Law" Requirement*, 107 Nw. U. L. Rev. 1125 (2013). Such courts include Judicial Panel on Multidistrict Litigation, 28 U.S.C. § 1407(d) (2006), the Alien Terrorist Removal Center, 8 U.S.C. § 1532(a) (2006) ("The Chief Justice . . . shall publicly designate 5 district court judges from 5 of the United States judicial circuits."), as well as the two courts identified in the Foreign Intelligence Surveillance Act, the Foreign Intelligence Surveillance Act Court and the Foreign Intelligence Surveillance Act Court of Review, 50 U.S.C. § 1803(a)–(b) (2006).

5

The Modern Agency

REMOVAL PROTECTION AS AN INDICATOR OF INDEPENDENCE

A. Introduction

The English Crown, and its colonial governors, had express powers to appoint subordinates but lacked the express authority to remove them. Instead, the removal issue was determined by the text of the commission granted to the individual. The Crown could grant a commission "to an individual and his heirs; for the officer's life; during good behaviour . . . ; or during the Crown's Pleasure."[1] Parliament later restricted the removal power of some officers, but the absence of such a restriction left the Crown's power unfettered.[2] A similar power was found in colonial governors, and subsequently in the state governments.[3]

Under the Articles of Confederation, Congress was given the power to make appointments,[4] and while the Articles were in effect Congress was responsible for removals as well.[5] At the Constitutional Convention the powers of the Congress

---

[1] Saikrishna Prakash, *Removal and Tenure in Office*, 92 VA. L. REV. 1779, 1820 (2006).

[2] *Id.*

[3] *Id.*

[4] ARTICLES OF CONFEDERATION of 1781 art. 9, § 5.

[5] Under the Articles of Confederation, the executive had no textually conferred removal powers, although there was a provision for recall by state legislature of delegates to the Congress of the Confederation. *Id.* at art. 5. An example of the removal power of the Continental Congress can be found in the removal of Thomas Paine, noted political activist and author, from his position as the secretary of the Congressional Committee on Foreign Affairs, for his writings about the French Revolution. *See* 13 JOURNALS OF THE CONTINENTAL CONGRESS 32–33 (Jan. 7, 1779), *available at* Library of Congress, American Memory, at http://memory.loc.

under the Articles of Confederation were given to the president.[6] While the Constitution specifically provides that the President "shall nominate, and by and with the Advise and Consent of the Senate, shall appoint Ambassadors, other public Ministers and Consuls, Judges of the supreme Court, and all other Officers of the United States, whose Appointments are not herein otherwise provided for,"[7] there is no constitutional provision regarding removal.[8] The subject of removals was not mentioned during the Constitutional Convention,[9] and no explanation was left as to why.[10]

It was not until the First Congress sought to establish the Department of Foreign Affairs that the question of who had the removal power was debated. Congress could not come to an agreement regarding the means of removing the new secretary. The House of Representatives broke into four factions each seeking a different rule. One opinion held that impeachment was the sole means of removal because it was the only method provided by the Constitution.[11] A second possibility was that Congress alone had the power to determine who would make removal, at least in the case of inferior officers, because Congress had the power to determine who would appoint them.[12] A third option, championed by Alexander Hamilton, was that the President could remove only with the advice and consent of the Senate, mirroring the appointment process.[13] Hamilton believed this would prevent a complete change of officers with every presidential election and discourage a spoils system.[14] The final option was that the President alone exercised the removal power.[15] James Madison, as first leader of the House, argued that the vesting clause[16] gave the President complete executive

gov/ammem/amlaw/lwjc.html. For a thorough accounting of Paine's life, see JACK FRUCHTMAN, THOMAS PAINE: APOSTLE OF FREEDOM (1996).

6 Myers v. United States, 272 U.S. 52, 110 (1926).

7 U.S. CONST. art. II, § 2.

8 The exception is for removal by impeachment. U.S. CONST. art. I, § 2, cl. 5.

9 *Myers*, 272 U.S. at 110.

10 Theodore Y. Blumoff, *Illusions of Constitutional Decisionmaking: Politics and the Tenure Powers in the Court*, 73 IOWA L. REV. 1079, 1095 (1988).

11 For the position of Congressman Smith from South Carolina, see James Madison's Speech in Congress on Presidential Removal Power, June 16–17, 1789, *in* JAMES MADISON WRITINGS 453, 458 (Jack N. Rakove ed., 1999).

12 *See id.* (explaining the position of Congressman Sherman of Connecticut).

13 *See The Federalist* No. 77 (Alexander Hamilton) ("Those who can best estimate the value of a steady administration will be most disposed to prize a provision, which connects the official existence of public men with the approbation or disapprobation of that body, which from the greater permanency of its own composition, will in all probability be less subject to inconstancy, than any other member of the government.").

14 *See id.*; *see also* 1 JOURNAL OF THE SENATE OF THE UNITED STATES OF AMERICA 441 (Washington, Gales & Seaton 1820) (reporting a Senate order that required Secretary Hamilton to provide information to Congress).

15 Blumoff, *supra* note 10, at 1096.

16 U.S. CONST. art. II, § 1.

powers in the absence of a specific exemption.[17] Because the Constitution did not give the removal power to another branch, it rested with the president alone.[18] Madison argued that this interpretation was further supported by the take care clause,[19] which requires the president to "take care that the laws be faithfully executed."[20] After debate, the House, under the leadership of Madison, and the Senate, with a tie broken by Vice President Adams, passed the Decision of 1789, giving the sole power of removal to the president.[21]

The Decision of 1789 is the name given to the bill passed by Congress to form the Foreign Affairs Department (today's State Department), which included a provision allowing the President to remove the secretary of the department. The provision sparked debate in the Congress with arguments over the intent of Congress and the power of removal, but eventually was passed. The Decision of 1789 is often cited as congressional consent to presidential power of removal. For many years after the Decision of 1789 even those who disagreed accepted this position as irrefutable, if not by correct interpretation, at least by consistent practice.[22]

B. Early Congressional and Judicial Attacks on Removal by the President

The seemingly unqualified power of the president to remove officers adopted in the Decision of 1789 came under attack from both the courts and the Congress itself. In *Marbury v. Madison*,[23] Chief Justice Marshall questioned the exclusive right of executive removal. The law creating Marbury's position allowed him to hold the office for five years independent of the president. Therefore, Marshall argued, President Jefferson was powerless to remove President Adams's appointment, stating that "if the officer is by law not removable at the will of the President; the rights he has acquired are protected by the law, and are not resumable by the President. They cannot be extinguished by executive authority, and he has the privilege of asserting them in like manner as if they had been derived from any other source."[24] This was all dicta, of course, as the Court did not have

---

17 Lance Banning, The Sacred Fire of Liberty: James Madison and the Founding of the Federal Republic 276 (1995).

18 *Id.* at 277.

19 U.S. Const. art. II, § 3.

20 Banning, *supra* note 17, at 277.

21 Act of July 27, 1789 ch. 4; 1 Stat. 28, 29.

22 Steven G. Calabresi & Christopher S. Yoo, *The Unitary Executive During the First Half-Century*, 47 Case W. L. Rev. 1451, 1560 (1997).

23 5 U.S. (I Cranch) 137 (1803).

24 *Id.* at 167.

jurisdiction over the case.[25] The implication, however, was that Congress could legislate to limit the president's removal power.[26]

Although Congress applied the same model in creating the War Department,[27] any notion that this model was to govern all removals was quickly ended. Later in 1789, Congress debated the establishment of the Treasury Department. Unlike the other two departments Congress had already created, there was strong support in Congress to treat the Treasury Department officers differently.[28] Indeed, the statutes creating the departments expressly designated the Departments of War and Foreign Affairs as executive departments while the Department of Treasury lacked this designation.[29] Madison, who had just championed the Decision of 1789, argued that "there may be strong reasons why an officer of this kind should not hold his office at the pleasure of the executive

---

25 *Id.* at 138. Chief Justice Marshall reasoned that the Court lacked original jurisdiction over the mandamus action because the Constitution does not provide such original jurisdiction and Congress, through the Judiciary Act of 1789, did not have the power to give the Court original jurisdiction over cases not provided for in the Constitution, and that the Supreme Court was the ultimate arbiter of the Constitution's meaning. *Id.* William Van Alstyne, in his well-known article, points out that Marshall treated the jurisdictional question as if it had only two parts: "(1) is section 13 of the 1789 Judiciary Act which purports to grant such power unconstitutional in that it attempts to enlarge the original jurisdiction of the Supreme Court in violation of Article III, and (2) is the Court free to make its own determination of this question in deciding whether it should proceed with the case?" William W. Van Alstyne, *A Critical Guide to* Marbury v. Madison, [1969] DUKE L.J. 1, 14. Van Alstyne argues that Marshall failed to adequately address a preliminary question of statutory interpretation: "Did the Judiciary Act authorize [the mandamus] action to original in the Supreme Court?" *Id.* at 14–16 (acknowledging that an argument could have been made that the Judiciary Act did not attempt to grant original jurisdiction in Marbury's case).

26 Jonathan L. Entin, *The Removal Power and the Federal Deficit: Form, Substance, and Administrative Independence*, 75 KY. L.J. 699, 720 (1987).

27 Act to establish an Executive Department, To Be Denominated the Department of War, ch. 7, 1 Stat. 49 (1789); *See* Gerhard Casper, *An Essay in Separation of Powers: Some Early Versions and Practices*, 30 WM. & MARY L. REV. 211, 227 (1989).

28 On a basic level, the difference is apparent in the explicit creation of the offices themselves. When creating the Departments of Foreign Affairs and War, Congress explicitly created only the offices of the secretary and clerk. Act to Establish an Executive Department, To Be Denominated the Department of War § 2, 1 Stat. 49–50 (1789); Act for Establishing an Executive Department, to be Denominated the Department of Foreign Affairs § 2, 1 Stat. 28-–29 (1789). When it came to the Department of the Treasury, however, Congress enumerated six officers, including the secretary, comptroller, auditor, treasurer, register, and an assistant secretary. Act to Establish the Treasury Department § 1, 1 Stat. 65–67 (1789). Further, while the secretaries of war and foreign affairs received tasks from the president, the officers at Treasury had duties to Congress. *See* Act to Establish an Executive Department, To Be Denominated the Department of War § 1, 1 Stat. 49–50 (1789) *and* Act for Establishing an Executive Department, To Be Denominated the Department of Foreign Affairs § 1, 1 Stat. 28–29 (1789).

29 *Compare* Act for Establishing an Executive Department, To Be Denominated the Department of Foreign Affairs § 1, 1 Stat. 28–29 (1789) *and* Act for Establishing an Executive Department, To Be Denominated the Department of War § 1, 1 Stat. 49–50, 67 (1789). In the Act to establish the Treasury department, Congress charged the secretary with fulfilling several tasks. The Acts creating the departments of War and Foreign Affairs, however, generally instructed the respective secretaries to carry out instructions from the president. Jerry L. Mashaw, *Governmental Practice and Presidential Direction: Lessons from the Antebellum Republic?*, 45 WILLAMETTE L. REV. 659, 665–67 (2009).

branch."[30] Many in Congress did not see the comptroller's role as an executive function; rather it was seen as an essential support to the House in originating revenue laws under Article I.[31] Madison sought a solution that would maintain a role for the President, Senate, and House overseeing the Comptroller's performance, who would serve for a term of years.[32] Ultimately, the Secretary remained removable by the President.[33] Although the statute created significant congressional control over the Secretary's functions, it remained silent regarding presidential control.[34]

George Washington clearly believed that he had the authority to remove officers. During his presidency, he removed almost two dozen officers for whom there was no statute granting him the power to do so.[35] The only explanation is that President Washington believed that he had the constitutional authority to remove these officers.[36] Washington apparently also believed in hedging his bets. Many of the commissions he granted expressly reserved the power of removal for the President, at his pleasure.[37] An exception existed in the commissions for Article III judges, which were indefinite and during "good behaviour."[38]

In response, Congress made efforts to cabin the removal power, proposing a variety of tenure acts. As early as 1814 Congress attempted to limit the removal power of the President by requiring him to announce vacancies and provide an explanation for removals.[39] The bill failed because the Senate concluded "that it did not have the right

---

30 1 ANNALS OF CONG. at 635–36.

31 Casper, *supra* note 27, at 227 (quoting 1 ANNALS OF CONG. 607 (statement of Rep. Sherman)). According to the Statute:

> "That it shall be the duty of the Comptroller to superintend the adjustment and preservation of the public accounts; to examine all accounts settled by the Auditor, and certify the balances arising thereon to the Register; to countersign all warrants drawn by the Secretary of the Treasury, which shall be warranted by law; to report to the Secretary the official forms of all papers to be issued in the different offices for collecting the public revenue, and the and the manner an form of keeping and stating the accounts of several persons employed therein. He shall moreover provide for the regular and punctual payment of all monies which may be collected, and shall direct prosecutions for all delinquencies of officers of the revenue, and for debts that are, or shall be due to the United States."

1 Stat. 68 (1789). Colonial and state precedent may also have been partly the source of the notion that the Treasury Department functioned within the legislative branch. Colonial and state models tended to leave financial administration to legislative committees. *See* Mashaw, *supra* note 29, at 5.

32 Casper, *supra* note 27, at 238 (citing 12 THE PAPERS OF JAMES MADISON, at 265–66).

33 An Act To Establish the Treasury Department § 7, 1 Stat. 65,67 (1789).

34 Under Madison's plan, the president remained authorized to remove as before. Because of the term of years, the Senate could retain some control through its advice and consent function. The House would be able to retain its control through its power to impeach and adjust salaries. Casper, *supra* note 27, at 240.

35 Saikrishna Prakash, *Removal and Tenure in Office, supra* note 1 at 1827. The officers removed included "ministers, consul, tax collectors, surveyors, and various military officers." *Id.*

36 *Id.*

37 *Id.* at 1827–28.

38 *Id.* at 1819.

39 *See* Charles Warren, *Presidential Declarations of Independence*, 10 B.U. L. REV. 1, 5 (1930).

to make such an inquiry."[40] In 1820 Congress succeeded in passing a law that set the tenure for certain appointed officials, but the law was without bite because it allowed for removal "at pleasure."[41] Despite the fact that the law placed no formal limits on the president's removal power, it was widely denounced as an impermissible encroachment on presidential powers.[42] In 1826 Congress again attempted to pass a bill requiring the President to report and explain removals to the Senate, but the bill again failed.[43] Similar resolutions were considered in 1830 and 1833 during Jackson's administration.[44] After Jackson removed Treasury Secretary William J. Duane for failure to follow his orders,[45] Congress became more determined to limit the president's removal powers.[46] Despite the fact that he was censured for his actions,[47] Jackson continued to defend his power of removal, stating that:

> The whole executive power being vested in the President, who is responsible for its exercise, it is a necessary consequence that he should have a right to employ agents of his own choice to aid him in the perforemance [*sic*] of his duties, and to discharge them when he is no longer willing to be responsible for their acts.[48]

In the end, Congress was unable to pass the bill that would have required Senate consent for removals[49] and the power of the president to remove was implicitly

---

40 Calabresi & Yoo, *supra* note 22, at 1508.

41 Tenure of Office Act, ch. 102, § 1, 3 Stat. 582, 582 (1820).

42 Calabresi & Yoo, *supra* note 22, at 1516–19.

43 Report from the Select Committee on Reducing Executive Patronage, S. Doc. No. 88, 19th Cong., 1st Sess. 1–15 (1826). The Senate adjourned without acting on the bills proposed by the committee. *See* Calabresi & Yoo, *supra* note 22, at 1525.

44 *See* S. Doc. No. 103, 21st Cong., 1st Sess. (1830); S. Doc. No. 41, 22nd Cong., 1st Sess. (1832).

45 *See* Leonard D. White, The Jacksonians, 34–37 (1954). President Jackson wanted to remove government funds from the United States bank, a power vested in the treasury secretary. Jackson did not challenge this authority, nor the authority of the secretary to make an independent judgment, but believed he could remove the secretary for *exercising* that judgment when it contradicted his own. *Id.* In a cabinet meeting Jackson explained: "[u]pon [the president] has been devolved... the duty of superintending the operation of the Executive Departments of the Government and seeing that the laws are faithfully executed. In the performance of this high trust it is his undoubted right to express to those whom the laws and his own choice have made his associates in the administration of the Government his opinion of their duties under circumstances as they arise. It is this right which he now exercises." 3 A Compilation of the Messages and Papers of the Presidents 1237–38 (James D. Richardson ed., 1897) Duane refused to remove the deposits or to resign.

46 3 Robert V. Remini, Andrew Jackson and the Course of American Democracy 1883–1845 149 (1984). President Jackson was the first to directly remove a cabinet officer because he was unable to force a resignation. *Id.* at 101.

47 *Id.* at 151. This remains the only censure of a president by Congress resulting from the removal of an officer of the United States. Prakash, *supra* note 1, at 1 & n.6.

48 3 A Compilation of the Messages and Papers of the Presidents 1298–99 (James D. Richardson ed., 1897) (Pres. Jackson protesting his censure before the Senate of the United States on April 15, 1834).

49 The Senate passed the bill by a vote of thirty-one to sixteen, but it never made it out of committee in the House. S. Doc. No. 109, 23d Cong., 2d Sess. (1835). *See also* White, *supra* note 45, at 41–42.

conceded.[50] Indeed, during the 1835 debates over the president's removal power, Daniel Webster was of the view that, as an original proposition, he would not have accorded the president that power. Nevertheless, based on the first forty-five years of the country's history, he conceded that the President had such power. The Decision of 1789, in his view, "has been established by practice, and recognized by subsequent laws, as the settled construction of the Constitution."[51]

Congress finally succeeded in creating a role for itself in the removal process in 1863. President Lincoln, without argument,[52] signed into law a bill that required the advice and consent of the Senate for the removal of the comptroller of currency.[53] Then, during the presidency of Andrew Johnson, the Reconstruction Congress passed the Tenure in Office Act of 1867, requiring Senate approval for the removal of all commissioned civil officers; specifically the Act stated that officers "shall hold their offices respectively for and during the term of the president by whom they may have been appointed . . . subject to removal by and with the advice of the Senate."[54] It was President Johnson's firing of Secretary of War Edwin Stanton that led to his impeachment, which failed in the Senate.[55] The House, in bringing the articles of impeachment against Johnson, charged that his high crimes included violating the Tenure in Office Act by unilaterally removing Stanton and appointing General Lorenzo Thomas in his place, to a position that the House alleged was not vacant because of the unlawful removal.[56] Johnson's lawyers noted the ambiguity of the Act's language in reference to its application to appointees who, like Stanton, were held over from Lincoln's presidency and not ever officially appointed by Johnson himself.[57] At least some of the defecting Republican senators who voted to acquit Johnson likely accepted that the Act was ambiguous.[58]

However, within two years of its enactment, the Tenure in Office Act was partially repealed,[59] allowing the President to suspend officers during a Senate recess without

---

50 Calabresi & Yoo, *supra* note 22, at 1559.

51 *Myers*, 272 U.S. at 151.

52 Steven G. Calabresi & Christopher S. Yoo, *The Unitary Executive During the Second Half Century*, 26 HARV. J.L. & PUB. POL'Y 667, 735 (2003) (suggesting that Lincoln's failure to respond to the incursion on his power was a political decision in order to maintain wartime unity).

53 Act of Feb. 25, 1863, ch. 58, 12 Stat. 665. This act was amended the next year to allow for removal of the comptroller after the president explained his reasons to the Senate, but not requiring Senate advice and consent. Act of June 3, 1864, ch. 106, § 1, 13 Stat. 99. *See also* Entin, *supra* note 26, at 721.

54 An Act Regulating the Tenure of Certain Civil Offices, Mar. 2, 1867, ch. 154, § 1, 14 Stat. 430.

55 MICHAEL LES BENEDICT, THE IMPEACHMENT AND TRIAL OF ANDREW JOHNSON 95–99, 181 (1973).

56 *See* DAVID O. STEWART, IMPEACHED: THE TRIAL OF PRESIDENT ANDREW JOHNSON AND THE FIGHT FOR LINCOLN'S LEGACY 157–59 (2009).

57 *Id.* at 207–08.

58 A statement released by Senator Trumbull of Illinois, explaining his reasons for voting to acquit Johnson, read: "[i]f the question was, is Andrew Johnson a fit person for President? I should answer, *no*," but, noted Trumbull, removal of the president could not be sought for "misconstruing a doubtful statute." *Id.* at 281.

59 Act of Apr. 5, 1869, ch. 10, § 2, 16 Stat. 6, 7.

providing a reason, as long as he informed the Senate of such action.[60] The suspension became permanent when the Senate confirmed a new nominee to the position. In effect this allowed the president to make a removal by nominating a new person and getting Senate approval.[61] A few years later Congress enacted separate legislation that required Senate consent for the removal of some postal officers.[62] While the Tenure in Office Act was completely repealed in 1887,[63] the statute regarding postal officers remained until it was declared unconstitutional in 1926.[64]

At the same time the Pendleton Act altered the civil service, and restricted the spoils system, as positions were filled increasingly based on candidates' merits and policy positions.[65] The Pendleton Act required civil service appointments to be made to those with the highest scores on civil service exams,[66] although it contained no provision on removals. In theory, "politicians would not press for removals if they could not secure the appointment of their favorites. Make it impossible for them to secure appointment, and the pressure would instantly disappear and arbitrary removal cease."[67] In fact, three years after the Act was passed the removal rate for employees covered by the Act was 6.2 percent while the removal rate for employees not covered varied between 25 percent and 71 percent depending on their department.[68]

C. The Historic Removal Trilogy: *Myers*, *Humphrey's Executor*, and *Wiener*

The Constitution does not address, in express terms, the respective roles of the President and Congress with respect to the removal of federal officers.[69] As discussed earlier,

---

60 *Id.*

61 *Id.*

62 Act of June 8, 1872, ch. 355, § 2, 17 Stat. 283, 284. It was this act that was declared unconstitutional by the Supreme Court in *Myers*.

63 Act of Mar. 3, 1887, ch. 353, 24 Stat. 500.

64 *Myers*, 272 U.S. at 163–64.

65 The Pendleton Act of Jan. 16, 1883, ch. 27, 22 Stat. 403. Entin, *supra* note 26, at 723 noting that with the passage of the Pendleton Act the Tenure in Office Act was no longer necessary to protect against a spoils system. *See also* Ari Hoogenboom, *The Pendleton Act and the Civil Service*, 64 AM. HIST. REV. 301, 315–16 (1959).

66 Section 2, 22 Stat. 403.

67 LEONARD D. WHITE, THE REPUBLICAN ERA, 340 (1958) (quoting George William Curtis).

68 *Id.* at 841 (citing Report of the Special Committee of the National Civil-Service Reform League, March 16, 1887).

69 *But see* Jonathan L. Entin, *Synecdoche and the Presidency: The Removal Powers as Symbol*, 47 CASE W. RES. L. REV. 1595, 1599 (1997) (reasoning that "[t]he Constitution's explicit limitation on the President's appointment power suggests that we should be reluctant to embrace the unitarian view of the removal power. If the chief executive cannot unilaterally select the team that will implement his policies, why infer—in the face of textual silence—that he must have unfettered discretion to fire?").

whether Congress may, by legislative enactment, limit or restrict the President's removal power grew to be the subject of great debate and the source of the conflict that led to the impeachment trial of President Andrew Johnson.

Several early cases upheld the authority of the President to remove subordinates. The Supreme Court in *Parsons v. United States* determined that the President could remove a district attorney for the good of the country, although he was appointed to a four-year term.[70] According to the Court, the four-year term acted as a term limitation rather than a positive grant of tenure.[71] In *Shurtleff v. United States*, the Court upheld the validity of the President's removal of a member of a board of appraisers that was established by Congress.[72] Congress had provided for removal only for inefficiency, neglect of duty, or malfeasance in office, but the Court reasoned that the President's general power of appointment provided justification for removal of the officer.[73] These cases forecasted the Court's later decision in *Myers v. United States*,[74] the first case in a trilogy of well-known twentieth-century Supreme Court removal power decisions.

In *Myers v. United States*, the Court concluded that the President's power to appoint carries with it the power to remove.[75] Chief Justice Taft's opinion for the majority, and the dissenting opinions, extensively reviewed the history of the issue. Chief Justice Taft employed a formalistic approach to the determination of the president's ability to remove a postmaster of the United States. The power to remove superior officers, according to the Court, was "incident to the power of appointment" and therefore resided exclusively with the President.[76] The Court also noted that inferior officers, the appointment of whom the Constitution allows Congress to vest in department heads,[77] could have tenure protection. Because Congress could decide who appointed these officers, it could also impose limitations on when those officers could remove them.[78] In determining whether an officer was "superior" or "inferior," the Court deferred to Congress. If the appointment required the advice and consent of the Senate, the appointee was a superior officer

---

70 Parsons v. United States, 167 U.S. 324, 343 (1897); *see also* Bruce Y. Curry, Note, *President's Power of Removal—Consent of United States Senate:* Myers v. United States, 6 OR. L. REV. 165, 166–67 (1926–1927) (citing *Parsons* in a note analyzing the recently decided case of *Myers*).

71 Steven Breker-Cooper, *The Appointments Clause and the Removal Power: Theory and Séance*, 60 TENN. L. REV. 841, 858 (1995).

72 Shurtleff v. United States, 189 U.S. 311, 318–19 (1903) (holding that president had power to remove official on grounds other than those specifically mentioned in Customs Administrative Act).

73 *See id.*

74 *See* Curry, *supra* note 70, at 166.

75 *Myers*, 272 U.S. at 176 (holding invalid a statute that prevented the president from removing executive officers who had been appointed by him).

76 *Id.* at 161.

77 U.S. CONST. art. II, § 2.

78 *Myers*, 272 U.S. at 161. If, however, Congress was silent regarding limiting removal or limiting removal to the party that appointed, the removal power remained with the president at his will. *Id.*

removable by the President at will.[79] If the appointment was vested in a department head, Congress could limit the removal power.[80]

Several years later, in *Humphrey's Executor v. United States*, the Court limited the broad scope of the *Myers* decision by concluding that the President's removal power constitutionally could be conditioned by Congress in certain circumstances. *Humphrey's Executor* upheld a statutory "for cause" limitation on the President's removal power over a commissioner of the FTC.[81] The Court, employing a functional analysis, distinguished between an "administrative body" that performed "quasi-legislative" and "quasi-judicial" functions, where such limitation was found permissible, and agencies that were "an arm or an eye of the executive," where such limitation was not permissible.[82] It concluded that an official who performed "purely executive" duties was subject to the President's unqualified removal power, but an official whose duties were commingled between the branches enjoyed a measure of independence that was provided by restricting the President's removal power.[83] The Court, however, did not explain whether a position was "purely executive" because of its placement within the executive branch or because of the nature of the position.

Finally, in *Wiener v. United States*, the court invalidated President Eisenhower's removal of a member of the War Claims Commission on the ground that there existed a "for cause" limitation on the President's removal power, despite the lack of an explicit statutory condition.[84] The Court determined that Congress had intended the commission to perform adjudicative functions, not "purely executive" functions, and that therefore the President was precluded from exercising unfettered removal power.[85] Numerous lower court decisions have inferred a prohibition on the President's summary removal power. See, for example, *Swan v. Clinton* (relying on *Wiener*[86] for the proposition that a court may be able to infer congressional intent regarding presidential removal power from the nature of the function vested in the agency by Congress);[87] *FEC v. NRA Political Victory Fund* (agreeing that a good cause limitation may be implied by agency's structure and mission and presence of statutory term of office);[88] *SEC v. Blinder, Robinson & Co.* (concluding that Congress can limit the grounds for presidential removal of a member of a multimember regulatory agency to inefficiency, neglect of duty, or malfeasance in

---

79 *Id.*

80 *Id.*

81 Humphrey's Ex'r v. United States, 295 U.S. 602, 629 (1935).

82 *Id.* at 628–29.

83 *Id.* at 627–29. The Court emphasized that the FTC was a "non-partisan," "impartial[]" and "quasi-judicial and quasi-legislative" agency and was not by nature an executive agency. *Id.* at 624. As such, restricting the president's ability to remove the commissioner did not interfere with any executive right.

84 357 U.S. 349, 356 (1958).

85 *See id.* at 352, 354–55.

86 357 U.S. at 353.

87 100 F.3d 973, 983 (D.C. Cir. 1996).

88 6 F.3d 821, 826 (D.C. Cir. 1993).

office);[89] and *SEC v. Bilzerian* (noting that "[w]hile the Act does not expressly give the President the power to remove a commissioner, it is generally accepted that the President may remove a commissioner for inefficiency, neglect of duty, or malfeasance in office").[90] A Congressional Research Service official suggests that there are at least thirteen "independent" agencies without a removal provision in their statutes.[91]

D. The *Morrison* "Twist"

The decision in *Morrison v. Olson*,[92] involving the for cause removal provision of the independent counsel statute, has modified the *Humphrey's Executor* and *Myers* analysis. The Court reexamined the underpinnings of *Myers* and *Humphrey's Executor* and made it clear that neither the organizational structure and placement of the agency nor the duties of an agency official per se affect Congress's ability to confer some measure of independence by restricting removal power functions.[93] Rather, the issue is whether "the removal restrictions are of such a nature that they impede the President's ability to perform his constitutional duty" to see that the laws are faithfully executed.[94] By sustaining the "for cause" removal provision with respect to the independent counsel, the Court seems to have ended, at least for now, any serious challenge to the applicability of a "for cause" removal provision to members of multimember agencies. It may even have created a predicate for application of such provisions to some executive branch agencies as well. The critical question now seems to be whether there has been an aggrandizement or encroachment that interferes with the execution of the President's duties; the fact that a presidential appointee performs executive functions no longer automatically immunizes that official from congressional efforts to restrict the President's removal power. As Justice White indicated in his dissent in *Bowsher v. Synar*, the FTC, even at the time of the *Humphrey's Executor* case, performed what would now be considered executive functions.[95] *Morrison* nevertheless left for statute-by-statute resolution the question whether Congress intended to confer some form of statutory protection on government officials. In *Morrison*, the congressional intent clearly was to do so.

Nor is it critical after *Morrison* that such appointee serve on a multimember board "outside" the executive branch—which is logical because the first "independent" official

---

89 855 F.2d 677, 681–82 (10th Cir. 1988).

90 750 F. Supp. 14, 16 (D.D.C. 1990) (citation omitted).

91 *See Reviewing the Performance of the Social Security Administration as an Independent Agency: Hearing Before the Subcomm. on Social Security of the House Comm. on Ways and Means*, 104th Cong. 12 & n.19 (1996) [hereinafter *SSA Hearing*] (testimony of Rogelio Garcia, Congressional Research Service).

92 487 U.S. 654 (1988).

93 *See id.* at 690–93.

94 *Id.* at 691.

95 478 U.S. 714, 761 n.3. (1986) (White, J., dissenting).

of government, after all, was the Comptroller of the Treasury Department.[96] Although *Morrison* dealt with an "inferior" officer, that is, one not appointed by the President with the advice and consent of the Senate, both *Humphrey's Executor* and *Wiener* dealt with the President's removal power over officers appointed by the President and confirmed by the Senate. Thus, there are issues that will be argued in the future, but for now, the legitimacy of the independent agency has been validated.

E. Grounds for Removal

The President may plainly remove certain officials, such as Cabinet secretaries, and other "officers of the United States" for no reason and without explanation.[97] In contrast, the Act to Regulate Commerce of 1887 contained the prototype removal provision that has been used, with occasional linguistic variations, in most agency enabling statutes. It provides that agency members can only be removed by the President for "inefficiency, neglect of duty, or malfeasance in office."[98] There is no accepted definition of these statutory terms.[99] Nonetheless, it now seems clear that the Interstate Commerce Commission Act, and those successor statutes that used it as a model, constrain to some degree the President's power to remove officials without either reason or explanation.

In determining the degree of independence to grant independent agencies, Congress has implemented a number of different approaches to limiting the President's power to remove a government official.[100] In making this determination, Congress must balance between granting too much independence, leading to an unaccountable agency, and too little independence, which is likely to result in unwanted outside control.[101] One way in which Congress mandates the amount of independence of an agency is to impose varying restrictions on the President's ability to remove agency officials.

---

96 *See* 1 Kenneth Culp Davis & Richard Pierce, Administrative Law Treatise (1994), § 2.5.

97 Myers v. United States, 272 U.S. 52, 134 (1926).

98 Act of Feb. 4, 1887, ch. 104, § 11, 24 Stat. 379, 383.

99 *See* Lawrence Lessig & Cass R. Sunstein, *The President and the Administration*, 94 Colum. L. Rev. 1, 110 (1994) (noting that the Supreme Court has failed to define "inefficiency, neglect of duty, or malfeasance in office").

100 *See Health Care Financing Administration's Role and Readiness in Medicare Reform: Hearing Before the S. Comm. on Fin.*, 106th Cong. 25–27 (2000) (statement of Rogelio Garcia, Specialist in American National Government and Finance Division, Congressional Research Service).

101 For cause removal restrictions can lead to frustration when seeking to assign blame and accountability. This problem was highlighted during the 2008 presidential campaign, when Senator John McCain called for the firing of the Christopher Cox, the SEC chairman, who was widely alleged to have ineffectively overseen stock market manipulation leading up to the 2008 recession. *See* Carrie Johnson, *Crises Poses Big Test for Markets' Regulator*, Wash. Post, Sept. 19, 2008, at D1. The immediate response from many was that the president had no power to remove Cox on that basis. *See* Brett Kavanaugh, *Separation of Powers During the Forty-Fourth Presidency and Beyond*, 93 Minn. L. Rev. 1454, 1473 (2009).

A number of statutes limit the President's authority to remove officials to specific grounds that are specified in the statute creating the position, some of which are specific to the office being filled. For example, judges on the United States Court of Appeals for Veterans Claims are appointed[102] to a fixed term of fifteen years.[103] During their term, the President may only remove judges "on the grounds of misconduct, neglect of duty, or engaging in the practice of law."[104] Before the removal takes effect, however, the judge must be presented with "full specification of the reasons for removal" as well as a chance to be heard.[105]

If membership on an independent board requires the members to meet certain qualifications, failure to maintain those qualifications could be grounds for dismissal under certain statutes. An example of this is membership on the National Mediation Board, for which any person with certain financial interests would not be eligible for appointment.[106] Under the statute, members may only be removed from office for "inefficiency, neglect of duty, malfeasance in office, or ineligibility."[107] Another example of this would be a position that requires the individual to maintain a security clearance from the government. In the event that the individual loses the clearance, courts have found that the removal of the official was proper.[108] In addition, there are other statutes that create independent agencies that do not have an eligibility requirement that retain the same language.

While the notion of firing for cause is in some sense a sign of having an independent federal agency status, it is the clearest example of what are the consequences of being "independent." Thus, many commentators have taken the position that "for cause" dismissal is not merely a consequence of being independent but, in fact, a—or perhaps the—necessary condition or criterion of being independent. Put this way it is in fact part of the very definition of independence rather than a consequence that is often—or always—associated with "independence."

The problem with that approach is that there are a number of statutes creating executive branch agencies that have limited the president's power to dismiss employees in ways that apparently limit the President's "at will" power. They encompass a number of categories.

---

102 The judges are appointed by the president with the advice and consent of the Senate. 38 U.S.C. § 7253(b).

103 38 U.S.C. § 7253(c).

104 38 U.S.C. § 7253(f)(1).

105 38 U.S.C. § 7253(f)(2).

106 45 U.S.C. § 154 (First).

107 *Id.* Although the Court of Veterans Affairs statute requires that every judge be a member in good standing of a state bar or of a federal court in order to be appointed to the court, 38 U.S.C. § 7253(b), there is not a corresponding ground for removal in that statute. *See* 38 U.S.C. § 7253(f). This, taken literally, would prohibit the removal of a judge who let his membership of a bar lapse. This anomalous result would likely be avoided by finding that the judge had neglected a duty in failing to maintain bar membership, or if disbarred the action that led to disbarment would likely also qualify as malfeasance in office.

108 *See, e.g.*, Carlucci v. Doe, 488 U.S. 93 (1988).

In some instances Congress has given "officers of the United States" a term of years with no "for cause" or reporting requirement. An example would be U.S. attorneys.[109] Other examples include officers of the FBI,[110] who are conventionally viewed as executive branch officials. This has been interpreted to mean that the term cannot be longer than the stated number of years, but could be shorter.[111]

In a second case, Congress provides employees with a term of years but requires that the President notify Congress when he summarily removes some of these people. The statute governing the undersecretary for health of the Veterans Department, for example, has both a four-year term and a reporting requirement.[112]

In a third case, the appointment includes that there is no term of years but, there is a reporting requirement. This is the case with most presidentially appointed inspector generals.[113] In the inspector general example, the reporting requirement requires not

---

[109] 28 U.S.C. § 541. An example of the lack of protection for U.S. attorneys can be found in the events immediately after President Clinton took office. President Clinton sought the resignation of seventy-seven U.S. attorneys who were appointed by Presidents Reagan and Bush. Aaron Epstein, *Controversy Seethes as Prosecutor Leaves*, HOUS. CHRON., Apr. 3, 1993, at A8. Although presidents had previously removed U.S. attorneys, this was controversial because one of the attorneys removed was involved in a continuing investigation of Representative Rostenkowski. *Id.* Because of the political aspects of this removal, some called it the "March massacre." *Id.* President Reagan summarily fired all the inspector generals when he first took office. CARMEN R. APAZA, INTEGRITY AND ACCOUNTABILITY IN GOVERNMENT: HOMELAND SECURITY AND THE INSPECTOR GENERAL 5 (2011) 5 (noting that President Reagan removed all of the serving inspector generals without informing them "until the following day when they received letters from a presidential assistant advising them that they had been fired"); PAUL CHARLES LIGHT, MONITORING GOVERNMENT: INSPECTORS GENERAL AND THE SEARCH FOR ACCOUNTABILITY 103–05 (1993) (noting that Reagan eventually rehired five of the fired Carter inspector generals).

[110] In 1993, President Clinton removed William Sessions as director of the FBI after he had served less than six years of a ten-year term. *See Changes at the Top for the F.B.I.*, N.Y. TIMES, Jul. 21, 1993, at A16.

[111] However, President Obama did succeed in securing an extension for Robert Mueller, whose ten-year term was set to expire on Aug. 2, 2011. On July 27, 2011, the Senate voted unanimously to extend Mueller's term through September 2013. Ray Gustini, *Senate Votes Unanimously to Keep Robert Mueller as FBI Director*, NAT'L J., Jul. 27, 2011, http://www.nationaljournal.com/dailyfray/senate-votes-unanimously-to-keep-robert-mueller-as-fbi-director-20110727. Sen. Rand Paul, who cited constitutional concerns over the extension process, initially held up the Senate vote. Charlie Savage, *Republicans Hold Up Vote on Extension of F.B.I. Term*, N.Y. TIMES, July 16, 2011, at A13.

[112] Where there is a reporting requirement, obviously Congress does not intend to infringe on the president's removal power. Earlier commentary took a more nuanced view, suggesting "[w]here the officer performs executive functions it is responsible to interpret such a statute as giving the President the power to remove at will." William J. Donovan & Ralstone R. Irvine, *The President's Power to Remove Members of Administrative Agencies*, 21 CORNELL L. REV. 215, 234 (1936). In a nineteenth-century case for salary for a territorial judge appointed for a four-year term but dismissed earlier on technical grounds, Justice McClean urged: "as the president is bound to see the laws faithfully executed, the power to remove unfaithful or incompetent officers is necessary. This may be admitted to be a legitimate argument, as commonly applied to executive officers.... But however strongly this may refer to the political officers of the Government, how can it apply to judicial office?" U.S. ex. rel. Goodrich v. Guthrie, 58 U.S. 284, 310 (1854). *See also* Parsons v. United States, 167 U.S. 324 (1897) (district attorney); Military Power of the President to Dismiss from Serv., 4 Op. Atty. Gen. 1 (1842) (navy officer).

[113] Inspector General Act of 1978, 5 U.S.C. App. 3 § 3(b).

only notice but the reasons for removal as well.[114] There has been recent interest in revising the statute to provide some term or for cause protection for the inspector generals.[115] Speaking for the inspector generals, Gaston L. Gianni—vice chair of the President's Council on Integrity and Efficiency—testified that the inspector general community supported the addition of protections in the statute.[116]

In the fourth case, Congress restricts the President's power to dismiss officers for "cause." No statute has set out an exhaustive list of what constitutes "for cause." For instance, 5 U.S.C.A. § 7521 simply states that "[a]n action may be taken against an administrative law judge appointed" for "good cause," without providing any further details as to what "good cause" entails.[117] We have no clear judicial understanding of the meaning of "cause" or "good cause" for an executive branch "officer."

As a result, precise contours of the President's power in this regard are less than clear. In *Humphrey's Executor*, the President had expressly requested Humphrey's resignation because the commissioner's views did not coincide with those of the President on "either the policies or the administering of the Federal Trade Commission."[118] In that case, President Roosevelt told an FTC commissioner whom he wanted to remove that "I do not feel that your mind and my mind go along together on either the policies or the administering of the Federal Trade Commission, and . . . I think it best for the people of this country that I should have a full confidence."[119] The court at least impliedly concluded that such ground was not embraced within a "for cause" standard.

In its *Wiener* decision, the Court suggested that removal for cause had to involve "the rectitude" of the government official.[120] However, in *Bowsher v. Synar*, the Supreme Court noted that the terms are "very broad."[121] Plainly, the nature of an official's duties affect whether a President may remove him summarily. Thus in *Wiener*, the Court ruled that the adjudicatory purpose of the War Claims Commission precluded the President's removal of a commissioner at will.[122]

Professors Lessig and Sunstein suggest that, contrary to conventional wisdom, the "for cause" provisions can be interpreted to allow a President to remove an independent

---

114 *Id.*

115 *See Legislative Proposals and Issues Relevant to the Operations of the Inspectors General: Hearing Before the S. Comm. on Governmental Affairs*, 106th Cong. 7–10 (2000) (statement of Gaston L. Gianni, Jr., Inspector General, Federal Deposit Insurance Corporation).

116 *Id.*

117 Under 5 U.S.C. § 7521, administrative law judges are entitled to a hearing before being removed for "good cause."

118 *Humphrey's Ex'r*, 295 U.S. at 619 (internal quotations omitted).

119 *See Id.*

120 *Wiener*, 357 U.S. at 356.

121 The *Bowsher* Court continued: ". . . as interpreted by Congress, [the statutory terms] could sustain removal . . . for any number of actual or perceived transgressions." 478 U.S. 714, 729 (1986).

122 357 U.S. at 354–56.

agency member under a broad array of circumstances, including a commissioner's frequent or important failure to follow the President's wishes with respect to what is required by sound policy.[123] Professor Peter Strauss argues that the President's request for Humphrey's resignation was "founded in failure of trust, not breach of discipline," so the case does not fully answer the question of what consequences might follow from a commissioner's failure to honor specific presidential policy directives.[124] Strauss appears prepared to concede that Congress may "forbid unilateral presidential removal for 'no reason at all'" if the official is "principally an adjudicator."[125] But he suggests that a court might sustain removal of an independent agency member for a refusal to follow certain presidential directives, such as a directive to perform a requested economic analysis of a proposed regulation.[126] Professor Laurence Tribe observes that:

> Statutes that permit removal of agency officers for such "causes" as "neglect of duty" might... be construed to "sustain removal... for any number of actual or perceived transgressions of the [removing authority's] will," ... thereby avoiding the question whether Congress could constitutionally insulate such officers from all political accountability by making them removable only for such politically "neutral" causes as dishonesty.[127]

In contrast, Peter Shane has argued that the President can only remove officers for failing to comply with a legal mandate.[128] Moreover, a President's inability to remove

---

[123] *See* Lessig & Sunstein, *supra* note 99, at 110–11.

[124] Peter L. Strauss, An Introduction to Administrative Justice in the United States 615 (1989). *Compare* Power of the President to Remove Presidential Appointees from the National Capital Planning Commission, 6 Op. O.L.C. 191, 196 (1982) (stating that the nature of functions, coupled with statutory silence on the subject of removal, permits the president to remove officials summarily).

[125] Strauss, *supra* note 124, at 615–16.

[126] *See* Strauss, *supra* note 124, at 667 n.402. The Administrative Conference of the United States endorsed the notion of presidential review of rulemaking initiatives of independent agencies. *See* Recommendation 88-9, Presidential Review of Agency Rulemaking, 54 Fed. Reg. 5207 (1989). *See also* Oral Argument at 47:18–22, Free Enterprise Fund v. Public Company Accounting Oversight Board, 130 S. Ct. 533 (2010) (No. 08-861), *available at* http://www.supremecourt.gov/oral_arguments/argument_transcripts/08-861.pdf. Chief Justice Roberts asked "Can the President pick up the phone and fire the SEC commissioners?" to which then solicitor general Elena Kagan replied, "The President can pick up the phone and fire the SEC commissioners for cause, however 'cause' has been defined." The chief justice followed up by asking whether the SEC commissioners could be removed by the president, which the solicitor general said was uncontested, and added: "And we are not contesting the question that the SEC commissioners, themselves, are removed by the President for cause under, I would say, a very broad for cause provision, in the way that *Bowsher* suggested, not something that's niggling and technical." *Id.* at 53:18–21.

[127] Laurence H. Tribe, American Constitutional Law § 4-10, at 254 n.45 (2d ed. 1988) (quoting *Bowsher*, 478 U.S. at 728).

[128] Peter M. Shane, *Independent Policymaking and Presidential Power: A Constitutional Analysis*, 57 Geo. Wash. L. Rev. 596, 609 (1989).

a member of an independent agency need not imply, as Strauss points out, that "total removal of the FTC as a policymaking organ of government from presidential oversight or control would be within [Congress's] power."[129] Following Presidents Reagan and Bush, President Clinton, for example, made independent agencies subject to the regulatory planning aspect of his Executive Order on review of agency rules.[130]

Occasionally, Congress departs from using the archetypal removal clause and uses slightly different formulations without any apparent intent to alter the fundamental criteria for removal. For example, the statute governing the National Indian Gaming Commission employs the language "neglect of duty, or malfeasance in office, or for *other* good cause shown"[131]—a hint, at least, that Congress sees neglect of duty and malfeasance in office as illustrations of a generic "good cause" ground for removal. Some agency statutes are silent with regard to the President's power to remove agency members from office.[132] But since the Court in *Wiener* read into statutory silence a limitation on the President's removal power because of the agency's intrinsic adjudicatory character,[133] it can be fairly assumed that the absence of "for cause" removal language does not automatically preclude the imposition of such a limitation. Indeed, in its most recent look at "for cause" removal protection, the Court assumed, although it explicitly declined to decide, that members of the SEC had "for cause" removal protection although the statute failed to confer it.[134]

Congress's decision to cloak individuals with "for cause" protection is eclectic. Three positions in the military have such protection. For example, the chief of the Army Reserve is appointed by the President and confirmed by the Senate and has a four-year term, but the statute authorizes his earlier removal "for cause."[135] The same is true of the chief of the Air Force Reserve.[136] Oddly, the chief of the Naval Reserve is appointed to a term "determined by the Chief of Naval Operations" that is "normally" four years ("normally" is statutory language). But he, too, can be removed earlier "for cause."[137] An example from the civilian sector is the statute governing the chief actuary of the SSA,

---

129 STRAUSS, *supra* note 124, at 616.

130 Exec. Order No. 12, 866, 58 Fed. Reg. 51735 (Oct. 4, 1993). *See generally* Christopher S. Yoo, Steven G. Calabresi, & Anthony J. Conangelo, *The Unitary Executive in the Modern Era, 1945–2000*, 90 IOWA L. REV. 601, 713–15 (2005).

131 25 U.S.C. § 2704(b)(6) (1994) (emphasis added).

132 *See, e.g.*, 7 U.S.C. § 4a (1994) (Commodity Futures Trading Commission); 12 U.S.C. § 1752a (1994) (NCUA); 47 U.S.C. § 154 (1994 & Supp. IV 1998) (FCC).

133 *See Wiener*, 357 U.S. at 354–56.

134 Free Enter. Fund v. Public Co. Accounting Oversight Bd., 130 S. Ct. 3138 (2010).

135 10 U.S.C. § 3038 (a), (c).

136 10 U.S.C. § 8038 (a), (c).

137 The "for cause" protection was inserted into one of the statutes, then simply carried over into the others with a notation that it was following the earlier pattern.

whose position description was changed in 1997 to include "for cause protection."[138] Another illustration is the now-expired independent counsel statute which gave the attorney general authority to remove an independent counsel for "good cause."

> An independent counsel appointed under this chapter may be removed from office, other than by impeachment and conviction, only be the personal action of the Attorney General and only for good cause, physical disability, mental incapacity, or any other condition that substantially impairs the performance of such independent counsel's duties.[139]

Certain senior officers of the United States, including those with "for cause" removal protections, customarily give an incoming president a letter of resignation to allow the new President to decide whether he or she wishes to retain him. For instance, on December 1, 2008, President George W. Bush's chief of staff sent a letter instructing Cabinet secretaries and heads of departments to gather letters of resignation from political appointees, with the exception of federal inspector generals and appointees with fixed terms of office.[140] For his part, President Kennedy asked for and received resignation letters from all the chairmen of federal regulatory agencies except for the chairman of the Federal Reserve Board.[141]

Congress's use of "for cause" removal protection is as much a policy as a legal issue. Should, for example, "the job of the director of Central intelligence be considered a political one that turned over each time the White House changed hands? Or should the job be kept separate from politics?"[142] Thus while Bill Clinton removed George H. W.

---

138 *See* Balanced Budget Act of 1997, Pub. L. No. 105-33, § 4643, 111 Stat. 251, 487–88 (codified as amended at 42 U.S.C. § 1317 (2006)), which states:

> "The Chief Actuary shall be appointed by, and in direct line of authority to, the Administrator of such Administration. The Chief Actuary shall be appointed from among individuals who have demonstrated, by their education and experience, superior expertise in the actuarial sciences. The Chief Actuary shall exercise such duties as are appropriate for the office of the Chief Actuary and in accordance with professional standards of actuarial independence. The Chief Actuary may be removed only for cause." *Id.* at 488. The controversy over the actuary erupted in the spring of 2003, when Richard Foster, the then actuary, was threatened with dismissal if he gave information on the cost of the Medicare Reform Act directly to Congress. *See* Sheryl Gay Stolberg & Robert Pear, *Mysterious Fax Adds to Intrigue over Drug Bill*, N.Y. TIMES, Mar. 18, 2004. The then administrator of Medicare, Tom Scully, argued: "Rick felt he was an independent operator," said Mr. Scully, who resigned in December to join a law firm. "My view was that the actuary is part of the executive branch. We had to have some ability to know what he was doing." N.Y. TIMES, Mar. 18, 2004.

Id. at A24.

139 28 U.S.C. § 596 (1994) (lapsed June 30, 1999); *see* Ethics in Government Act of 1978, Pub. L. No. 95-521, § 598, 92 Stat. 1824 (codified as amended at 28 U.S.C. §§ 591–99 (1994), lapsed June 30, 1999).

140 *See* Alexis Simendinger & Shane Harris, *Please Resign, Bush Tells Political Appointees*, NAT'L J., Dec. 8, 2008.

141 Yoo, Calabresi, & Colangelo, *supra* note 130, at 644.

142 JAMES MANN, THE RISE OF THE VULCANS: THE HISTORY OF BUSH'S WAR CABINET 267 (2004).

Bush's appointee from his position as director of central intelligence shortly after assuming office, former President Bush urged his son not to follow suit.[143] "Automatically replacing the director in each new administration would tend to politicize what essentially is a career service that is supposed to be beyond politics."[144]

F. Procedures for Removal

Most agency statutes are silent on what procedures (if any) the President must follow before removing an agency member from office for good cause.[145] However, as early as the turn of the twentieth century, the Supreme Court indicated that "for cause" appointees were entitled to notice and hearing before they could be removed from office. In its 1901 decision in *Reagan v. United States*,[146] the Court stated that where causes of removal are specified by Constitution or statute, "notice and hearing are essential." It elaborated on this requirement two years later. In *Shurtleff v. United States*,[147] the Court reiterated that where removal is sought pursuant to statute for "inefficiency, neglect of duty, or malfeasance in office ... the officer is entitled to notice and a hearing." The Court also determined that inclusion of explicit causes for removal did not, in the context of that statute at least, prevent the President from removing the individual for other reasons. However, the Court hinged that aspect of its decision on the lack of any fixed term of office. A different construction of the statute, Justice Peckham observed, would "give an ... [official] the right to hold that office during his life or until he shall be found guilty of some act specified in the statute. If this be true, a complete revolution in the general tenure of office is effected."[148] That is no longer an issue under modern statutes. Members of independent agencies all serve for a fixed term.

The Supreme Court's due process jurisprudence of the 1970s did nothing to undermine this conclusion. An agency member's constitutional claim depends on having a property right in continuing employment, as the contrasting iconic opinions in *Board of Regents of State Colleges v. Roth*[149] and *Perry v. Sindermann*[150] underscore. Furthermore, in *Cleveland Board of Education v. Loudermill*,[151] the Court ruled that persons classified

---

143 *Id.* at 268.

144 George Bush and Brent Scowcroft, A World Transformed 21 (1998).

145 *See, e.g.*, 42 U.S.C. § 5841(e) (1994) (NRC).

146 182 U.S. 419, 425 (1901).

147 Shurtleff v. United States, 189 U.S. 311, 313–14 (1903).

148 *Id.* at 316.

149 Bd. of Regents of State Colleges v. Roth, 408 U.S. 564, 576–77 (1972) (holding that a person only obtains a property interest in a benefit if they have a legitimate claim of entitlement, not merely an abstract need or desire).

150 Perry v. Sindermann, 403 U.S. 593, 601–03 (1972) (finding absence of explicit contractual provisions does not foreclose the possibility of property interest in continued employment).

151 470 U.S. 532, 538–39 (1985).

as civil servants under state law who could only be terminated for cause possessed a property right in job security. The *Shurtleff* decision, of course, had been largely to the same effect. It had determined that an individual appointed by the President with the advice and consent of the Senate who may only be removed for "inefficiency, neglect of duty, or malfeasance in office" qualifies for due process protections.[152] Thus, if the member has a statutory right to continued employment, he or she cannot be deprived of the job without due process.[153]

However, that jurisprudence also teaches that due process requires only "such procedural protections as the particular situation demands."[154] Generally, something less than a full APA-style evidentiary hearing is sufficient to satisfy constitutional requirements.[155] In *Arnett v. Kennedy*,[156] the Court upheld a federal employee's dismissal under a statute that set out procedures short of full APA procedures when federal employees could be removed "for such cause as will promote the efficiency of the service." Endorsing the so-called bitter with the sweet argument, three justices upheld the statute that provided for notice of the charges preferred against the employee, an opportunity to respond in writing, and a prompt written decision by the agency.[157] Justices Powell and Blackmun were unprepared to endorse the notion that Congress could designate the procedures to be followed when it creates a statutory right to federal employment, but upheld the dismissal because they believed that the statute provided a reasonable set of procedural protections consistent with due process.[158] The Court later expressly rejected the "bitter with the sweet" argument in *Cleveland Board of Education v. Loudermill*.[159] It acknowledged that the question in each case was "what process is due," and concluded that one cannot be deprived of constitutionally protected substantive rights except through procedures that fully satisfy due process.[160] That question is now decided under the familiar test set out in *Mathews v. Eldridge*, which determined that due process requires a balancing of three factors: (1) the private interest that will be affected by the official action; (2) the risk of erroneous deprivation of such interest through the procedures used, and the probable value, if any, of additional or substitute procedural safeguards; and (3) the

152 *Shurtleff*, 189 U.S. at 314.

153 *See also* Goss v. Lopez, 419 U.S. 565, 573 (1975) (citations omitted) ("[A] state employee who under state law... has a legitimate claim of entitlement to continued employment absent sufficient cause for discharge may demand the procedural protections of due process.").

154 Morrissey v. Brewer, 408 U.S. 471, 481 (1972).

155 *See* Marcello v. Immigration & Naturalization Serv., 349 U.S. 302, 311 (1955) (upholding the constitutionality of deportation proceeding that did not fully comply with APA hearing procedures).

156 416 U.S. 134 (1974).

157 *Id.* at 163–64.

158 *Id.* at 164–71 (pretermination hearing not required for federal civil servant where there is provision for full, posttermination evidentiary hearing).

159 470 U.S. 532, 540-41 (1985).

160 *Id.* at 541.

government's interest, including the administrative and financial burdens to the government of additional or substitute procedures.[161]

In contrast with most statutes, the National Labor Relations Act, and the Federal Labor Relations Act which was modeled after it, expressly provide that agency members of the NLRB and Federal Labor Relations Act may be removed only "upon notice and hearing."[162] The statute governing the Board of Veterans' Appeals is also an anomaly. It creates different procedural requirements depending on which member is sought to be removed. The chairman may only be removed by the President for specified cause, while other members of the board may be removed by the Secretary of Veterans Affairs for poor performance or other causes. The chairman may be removed only "after notice and opportunity for hearing,"[163] while other board members may be removed either following a specific set of statutorily delineated procedures, if removal is based on performance, or after an APA hearing, if removal is based on other causes.[164]

Neither the "notice and hearing" requirement contained in the NLRB, Federal Labor Relations Act, and Board of Veterans' Appeals statutes (with the exception noted above) nor due process considerations require the President to follow the strictures contained within the APA. The APA is applicable only when an adjudication is "required by statute to be determined on the record after opportunity for an agency hearing."[165] None of the agency statutes that provide for "notice and hearing" uses the talismanic "on the record" formulation, and the Supreme Court attaches some significance to it.[166] Although the lack of the "on the record" language is not dispositive,[167] the omission of the phrase may be construed as evidence that Congress intended for something other than an APA hearing.[168] In fact, in the Board of Veterans' Appeals statute, Congress uses the term

161 Matthews v. Eldridge, 424 U.S. 319, 335 (1976).

162 29 U.S.C. § 153(a) (1994) (NLRB); 5 U.S.C. § 7104(b) (1994) (Federal Labor Relations Authority).

163 38 U.S.C. § 7101(b)(2) (1994).

164 *See id.* § 7101A(e).

165 5 U.S.C. § 554(a) (1994). *See generally* Gary J. Edles, *An APA-Default Presumption for Administrative Hearings: Some Thoughts on "Ossifying" the Adjudication Process*, 55 ADMIN. L. REV. 787, 796 (2003).

166 *See* United States v. Allegheny-Ludlum Steel Corp., 406 U.S. 742, 757 (1972) (observing in a case involving a rulemaking proceeding that APA hearing requirements apply "only where the agency statute, in addition to providing a hearing, prescribes explicitly that it be on the record") (internal quotation marks and citations omitted).

167 *See* Steadman v. SEC, 450 U.S. 91, 96 n.13 (1981) (requiring APA hearing despite lack of "on the record" language); United States v. Florida East Coast Ry. Co., 410 U.S. 224, 238 (1973) (stating that lack of the magic words is not determinative if the statute contains "other... language having the same meaning").

168 *See* Railroad Comm'n of Tex. v. United States, 765 F.2d 221, 227 (D.C. Cir. 1985) ("Formal proceedings do not attach to a requirement of a 'hearing'; such proceedings would obtain only on the requirement of a 'hearing on the record.'"); *see also* City of W. Chicago v. Nuclear Reg. Comm'n, 701 F.2d 632, 641 (7th Cir. 1983) (stating that "in the absence of these magic words... Congress must clearly indicate its intent to trigger the formal, on-the-record hearing provisions of the APA") (citations omitted); Independent U.S. Tanker Owners Comm. v. Lewis, 690 F.2d 908, 922 n.63 (D.C. Cir. 1982) (ruling that adjudication was informal because there was no requirement of hearing "on the record" in statute and such requirement

"notice and opportunity for hearing" with respect to the board's chairman, but specifically provides for an "APA hearing" for other board members in certain circumstances.[169]

To be sure, at least one court has interpreted "opportunity for" language to require an APA hearing.[170] But the more recent trend is to examine the type of hearing right Congress intended to create in each situation, according *Chevron* deference to a reasonable agency construction of the statute.[171] Given the circumstances, especially the statutory distinction between the method of removal of the chairman and other board members, it seems almost certain that Congress intended to accord the board chairman hearing rights akin to those provided other independent agency officials across the government.[172]

Finally, it now seems clear, after years of debate over the issue, that there is no longer any presumption that even a statutory hearing requirement mandates an APA hearing. Rather, any statutory ambiguity is to be resolved by the agency responsible for administration of the statute.[173] Where, as is the case in the typical statute governing members of independent agencies, there is no express hearing requirement at all, it would seem that the President has the authority to shape the nature of any hearing that might be required by considerations of due process.

Perhaps as important in light of constitutional considerations, the Supreme Court has determined that, absent some express statement by Congress, the President is not

could not be reasonably inferred from legislative history); *see generally* Keith Werhan, *Delegalizing Administrative Law*, 1996 U. ILL. L. REV. 423, 445–47 (noting unwillingness of courts to infer formal hearing requirement absent "on the record" language).

169 *See* 38 U.S.C. §§ 7101(b)(2), 7101A(e)(2) (1994).

170 *See* Seacoast Anti-Pollution League v. Costle, 572 F.2d 872, 876 (1st Cir. 1978), *cert. denied*, 439 U.S. 824 (1978).

171 Dominion Energy Brayton Point, LLC v. Johnson, 443 F.3d 12, 15–16 (1st Cir. 2006) (court's conclusion in *Seacoast Anti-Pollution League* that a statutory "public hearing" requirement compels an APA hearing must now yield to a reasonable agency construction of an ambiguous hearing requirement); Chemical Waste Mgmt., Inc. v. EPA, 873 F.2d 1477, 1482 (D.C. Cir. 1989) (in light of Supreme Court's *Chevron* decision, court no longer applies a preference for an APA hearing but, instead, leaves to the agency the responsibility for construing an ambiguous statutory hearing requirement); *see also* William Funk, *Close Enough for Government Work?—Using Informal Procedures for Imposing Administrative Penalties*, 24 SETON HALL L. REV. 1, 20–21 (1993) (stating that statutory "notice and opportunity for hearing" language need not necessarily trigger a formal hearing before an ALJ). *See generally* Patricia M. Wald, *Judicial Review in Midpassage: The Uneasy Partnership Between Court and Agencies Plays On*, 32 TULSA L.J. 221, 232 n.70 (1996) ("[T]he occasions where an evidentiary hearing is required seem to be steadily diminishing.").

172 *Compare* Duquesne Light Co. v. EPA, 698 F.2d 456, 481–82 (D.C. Cir. 1983) (determining that use of term "public hearing" in one place in statute and hearing "on the record" in another evinces a congressional intent that less formal procedures suffice under public hearing requirement).

173 *Compare* Dominion Energy Brayton Point, LLC v. Johnson, *supra* note 171 (relying on the Supreme Court's decision in National Cable & Telecommunications Ass'n v. Brand X Internet Services, 545 U.S. 967 (2005), the First Circuit abandons its earlier-held presumption that a statutory hearing requirement mandates an APA hearing.) Henceforth, the agency (here, the president) may shape any hearing requirements in light of the three *Matthews v. Eldridge* factors. *See* Matthews v. Eldridge, 424 U.S. 319, 334–35 (1976).

to be considered an "agency" for purposes of the APA, so APA procedures are presumptively inapplicable. In *Franklin v. Massachusetts*, the Supreme Court noted that "[a]s the APA does not expressly allow review of the President's actions, we must presume that his actions are not subject to its requirements."[174]

Few examples of appropriate procedures are available, in large part because regulatory commissioners generally acquiesce in a President's request that they resign, fail to challenge their removal, or negotiate some face-saving exit. As Professor Paul R. Verkuil has observed, the threat of removal is an effective method of obtaining resignations from commissioners. He speculates that Presidents have in the past and might in the future require commissioners to provide signed resignation in advance of appointment as means of circumventing for cause removal restrictions.[175] President Nixon removed Raymond Lapin from his post on the Federal National Mortgage Association (Fannie Mae) at a time when Fannie Mae was part of the Treasury Department and the President could only remove directors for cause. Lapin briefly challenged his ouster in court but dropped the suit two months later.[176]

President Franklin Roosevelt actually met personally with the members of the Tennessee Valley Authority (TVA) before removing one of its members. Members of the TVA were appointed by the President to a fixed term, with the advice and consent of the Senate, but did not have "for cause" protection and were removable by the President summarily.[177]

Former Civil Aeronautics Board chairman Robert Timm was advised that the White House Counsel's Office was planning to hold a "hearing" on his activities while in office for the purpose of determining whether he should be removed from office for cause. The hearing was characterized as an "evidence-gathering inquiry" to be presided over by the counsel to the President. Timm thereafter resigned.[178]

The procedures proposed in the *Timm* case satisfy due process prerequisites. "The core of due process," the Supreme Court has often observed, "is the right to notice and a meaningful opportunity to be heard."[179] In *Cleveland Board of Education v. Loudermill*,[180] due process was satisfied where a dismissed public employee received

---

[174] 505 U.S. 788, 800–01 (1992). *Compare* Public Citizen v. United States Dep't of Justice, 491 U.S. 440, 465–67 (1989) (applying Federal Advisory Committee Act to committee that advises president in connection with his constitutional appointment powers would raise serious separation-of-powers questions).

[175] Paul R. Verkuil, *Jawboning Administrative Agencies: Ex Parte Contacts by the White House*, 80 COLUM. L. REV. 943, 955 & n.74 (1980).

[176] *See* Eric Pace, *Raymond H. Lapin, 67, Dead; Fought Nixon at Fannie Mae*, N.Y. TIMES, Apr. 6, 1986, at A38.

[177] *See* Morgan v. TVA, 115 F.2d 990, 991, 992–94 (6th Cir. 1940).

[178] *See In re* Robert D. Timm, 223 Ct. Cl. 639, 639 (1980); *see also Timm Resigns, Hits White House Staff*, AVIATION WK. & SPACE TECH., Dec. 15, 1975, at 28.

[179] Lachance v. Erickson, 522 U.S. 262, 266 (1998).

[180] *See* 470 U.S. 532 (1985).

notice of the charges against him, an explanation of the supporting evidence, and a chance to present his side of the story.[181] The fact that a senior subordinate official—here the counsel to the President—actually hears the evidence, does not violate due process.[182]

A final and intriguing question is what remedy exists if an independent agency member is removed improperly. Can he or she sue the President for reinstatement? In *Franklin v. Massachusetts*, the Supreme Court held that the President is not ordinarily considered an "agency" for purposes of the APA so that statute does not serve to waive general principles of sovereign immunity.[183] However, there may be other statutory avenues. The D.C. Circuit in *National Treasury Employees Union v. Nixon* concluded that, pursuant to 28 U.S.C. § 1361, it could exercise mandamus jurisdiction over the President "to compel an officer or employee of the United States or any agency thereof to perform a duty owed to the plaintiff."[184] However, in that case the D.C. Circuit declined to exercise its mandamus power over the president, finding that when President Nixon failed to comply with his obligation to implement a federal employee pay adjustment under the Federal Pay Comparability Act, the more appropriate remedy was a declaratory decree.[185] The court's holding was, however, limited to finding that mandamus could lie for ministerial and obligatory acts of the president and other cabinet level officials.[186]

---

181 *See id.* at 546; *cf.* Duke Power Co. v. Nuclear Regulatory Comm'n, 770 F.2d 386, 389 (4th Cir. 1985) (stating that for informal agency adjudication, commission did not have to hold formal hearing with trial-type procedures but could rely on informal hearing in which written factual and legal materials were submitted); Indep. U.S. Tanker Owners Comm. v. Lewis, 690 F.2d 908, 922–23 (D.C. Cir. 1982) (requiring agencies in informal adjudications to provide "some opportunity for interested parties to be informed of and comment upon the relevant evidence before the agency"); Goss v. Lopez, 419 U.S. 565, 582 (1975) (holding in case involving student's ten-day suspension from school that student had to be "given an opportunity to explain his version of the facts" after being told "what he is accused of doing and what the basis of the accusation is").

182 *See* Morgan v. United States, 298 U.S. 468, 481–82 (1936) (stating that evidence need not be taken by deciding official but may be received and analyzed by "competent subordinates," provided that deciding official considers that evidence in making final decision); *cf.* Duke Power Co., 770 F.2d at 390 (approving informal presentation to staff that makes recommendation to decisional official).

183 *See* 505 U.S. 788, 800–01 (1992).

184 *See* 492 F.2d 587, 592 n.4, 616 (D.C. Cir. 1974); *see also* Jonathan R. Siegel, *Suing the President: Nonstatutory Review Revisited*, 97 COLUM. L. REV. 1612, 1614–15 (1997). "Nonstatutory review" as used by Siegel refers to cases in which a plaintiff sues a government official in his or her individual capacity to avoid the doctrine of sovereign immunity. *See id.* Siegel argues that the approach has its antecedents in Marbury v. Madison, 5 U.S. (1 Cranch) 137 (1803). *See* Siegel, *supra*, at 1614. *See generally* Laura Krugman Ray, *From Prerogative to Accountability: The Amenability of the President to Suit*, 80 KY. L.J. 739 (1991–1992) (examining precedent allowing suits against the president and the rationale, or lack thereof, for such suits).

185 *Nat'l Treasury Employees Union v. Nixon, supra* note 184, at 616.

186 *Id.* at 603–04.

G. End of Service

Members of multimember agencies serve a fixed term of years ranging between three[187] and fourteen years,[188] with five- or seven-year terms being fairly common.[189] Although statutes differ, it is not uncommon for a statute to allow an agency member to remain in his or her post as a "holdover" member until a successor is appointed and confirmed.[190] Some statutes allow continuation in office for a limited period beyond the expiration of a member's term. Members of the STB, for example, may serve "until a successor is appointed and qualified, but for a period not to exceed one year."[191] Members of the SEC may not serve "beyond the expiration of the next session of Congress subsequent to the said fixed term of office."[192] The term of a member of the Nuclear Regulatory Commission (NRC), in contrast, is five years specifically commencing on July 1, with no provision for continuation following expiration of the term.[193]

Resignation of members before the ends of their terms is commonplace, especially when a new president takes office.[194] At times, an agency member will tender a resignation subject to the appointment and confirmation of a successor. The OLC has concluded that this practice is perfectly permissible.[195]

Individuals whose terms have expired and are serving as "holdovers" may not claim the protection of the "for cause" removal provision. In *Swan v. Clinton*, the D.C. Circuit determined that a holdover member of the NCUA board was not entitled to removal protection, even if such protection were available to Board members during their appointed terms.[196] Although the statute was silent regarding the removal, the circuit court made clear that fact was not dispositive. Under the statute, the members were to

---

187 *See, e.g.*, 25 U.S.C. § 2701(National Indian Gaming Commission); 45 U.S.C. § 154 (National Mediation Board).

188 *See* 12 U.S.C. § 241 (Federal Reserve Board).

189 *See*15 U.S.C. § 78d(a) (establishing the SEC with five-year terms); 47 U.S.C. § 154(c) (establishing the FCC with five-year terms); 15 U.S.C. § 2053 (governing the Consumer Product Safety Commission); 15 U.S.C. § 41 (establishing seven-year terms for the FTC).

190 *See, e.g.*, 49 U.S.C. § 1111(c) (statute governing the National Transportation Safety Board permits such "holdover" members).

191 49 U.S.C. § 701(b)(3).

192 15 U.S.C. § 78d.

193 42 U.S.C. § 5841(c).

194 In early 2009, U.S. attorneys Mary Beth Buchanan and Alice Martin, both appointed by President George W. Bush, caused controversy when they released statements indicating their intent to continue in their positions after Bush's term ran out. Martin eventually resigned her post in June 2009. Mary Beth Buchanan finally resigned on Nov. 6, 2009, to run for Congress in Pennsylvania's Fourth Congressional District. *See* Robert Gordon & Mary Orndorff, *Martin to Resign Post on Friday*, BIRMINGHAM NEWS, Jun. 17, 2009, at 1.

195 Presidential Appointees—Resignation Subject to the Appointment and Qualification of a Successor, 3 Op. O.L.C. 152 (1979).

196 100 F.3d 973, 988 (D.C. Cir. 1996).

step down at the end of their appointed terms unless they were to remain as holdovers under specific provisions of the statute designed to ensure continuity[197] The court found that the President could remove a holdover member without providing cause because the removal protection was not necessary to promote the continuity of the agency.[198] Further, the court feared that if it allowed the removal protection to protect holdovers, the Senate may be able to control the terms of executive officers by refusing to act on presidential appointments, which would violate the separation of powers.[199]

The OLC, when asked to address the issue of removing holdover officials who do not have "express tenure protection," determined that there should not be protection during a holdover period.[200] The OLC found that there should not be an inferred protection during the regular term, much less the holdover period.[201] In analyzing *Swan* and other cases dealing with holdovers, the OLC noted that courts are likely to ask two questions—first, whether there should be tenure protection for the actual term, and second, if so, whether that protection should extend into the holdover period.[202] The first question is to determine whether Congress has demonstrated a need for independence in an agency to allow the proper completion of the assigned functions.[203]

H. An International Twist on the Removal Issue

The issue of whether the President can remove the head of a bilateral treaty-based organization recently arose in the context of the International Boundary Commission, the body chartered to physically maintain the United States–Canada border. This commission is a treaty-based binational commission "whose sole concern is the... [5,525-mile]

197 *Id.* at 985. Further, under the terms of the statute, members could not be appointed to successive terms. *Id.*

198 *Id.* at 986.

199 *Id.*

200 Memorandum Opinion for the Counsel to the President, Removal of Holdover Officials Serving on the Federal Housing Board and the Railroad Retirement Board, 21 Op. O.L.C. 135 (1997). In a separate opinion, regarding appointments to the Holocaust Memorial Council, the OLC also found that appointments are not complete until there has been an "open, *unequivocal* act" by the president—typically the signing of an appointee's commission—demonstrating the completion of the appointment. President Clinton indicated his intent to appoint an individual to a seat on the council toward the end of his term, requesting a background check on that individual and also signaling his approval of the candidate in a letter to the director of presidential personnel. However, no formal commission was ever signed. The OLC determined that the commission had never been completed and as such the individual was never appointed to the council, but also noted that even if she had been appointed, President Bush's subsequent appointment of a third party to the vacant council seat was a removal of President Clinton's intended appointee. Memorandum Opinion for the Counsel to the President, Appointment of a Member of the Holocaust Memorial Council, 2003 OLC Lexis 14 (2003).

201 *Id.*

202 *Id.* at 2.

203 *Id.*

physical border between the United States and Canada."[204] Originally created under the Treaty of 1908 for the purpose of defining the boundary, the commission was permanently established in 1925 upon realization that maintenance would have to be continuous.[205] Since 1908, the commission has maintained the boundary, which is shown on 256 official boundary maps, with the assistance of over one thousand survey control sites, and the regular inspection of over eight thousand monuments and reference points.[206] In addition, the commission also controls a "twenty foot wide clear vista along the land boundary line," which covers 1,349 miles of land, and requires constant clearing of forest and brush to clearly demarcate the boundary.[207] The commission "is made up of two Commissioners; one appointed in the United States and one in Canada," with the President being responsible for appointing the U.S. commissioner, who reports to the secretary of state.[208] Both the 1908 and 1925 treaties describe how appointments of commissioners are made, with the 1925 treaty stating that Commissioners serve until "death, resignation, or other disability."[209]

In 2007, a federal district court analyzed the legality of an appointed officer's removal, an issue of first impression. In *Leu v. International Boundary Commission*,[210] the court concluded that President Bush had the authority to remove and replace Commissioner Schornack, even though the IBC operates "independently from the Canadian and American governments," leaving uncertainty as to whether the U.S. commissioner is an officer of the United States.[211] While the court acknowledged that the plain language

---

204 David C. Weiss, *The International Boundary Commission, Treaty Interpretation, and the President's Removal Power*, 41 Loy. U. Chi. L.J. 39, 47 (2009).

205 Int'l Boundary Comm'n, http://www.internationalboundarycommission.org/boundary.html (last visited Jan. 28, 2014).

206 *Id.*

207 *Id.*

208 *About Us*, Int'l Boundary Comm'n, http://www.internationalboundarycommission.org/about.html (last visited Jan. 28, 2014).

209 Leu v. Int'l Boundary Comm'n, 523 F. Supp. 2d 1199, 1206 (W.D. Wash. 2007), *vacated on other grounds*, 605 F.3d 693 (9th Cir. 2010). *See generally* Jason Buhi & Lin Feng, *The International Joint Commission's Role in the United States–Canada Transboundary Air Pollution Control Regime: A Century of Experience to Guide the Future*, 11 Vt. J. Envtl. L. 107, 131 (2009).

210 *Leu*, 523 F. Supp. 2d at 1207.

211 Weiss, *supra* note 204, at 59. Seth Barrett Tillman has directed us to close analysis of the constitutional language in the appointments clause ("Officer of the United States," art. II, § 2, cl. 2), the impeachment clause ("The President, Vice President and all civil officers of the United States," art. II, § 2), the incompatibility clause ("office ... under the United States," art. I, § 6, cl. 4), the commissions clause ("The President ... shall commission all officers of the United States," art. II, § 3), and the foreign emoluments clause ("No Title of Nobility shall be granted by the United States: And no person holding any Office of Profit or Trust under them," art. I, § 9, cl. 8). As Tillman points out, each textual variant of the term the "office" or "officer" has a different meaning in our constitutional framework. In particular, Tillman argues that the president neither holds an "office" of the United States nor is an "officer" of the United States. Among other views, Tillman notes that for incompatibility clause purposes, the president is not part of the executive branch. For the incompatibility clause, see Seth Barrett Tillman, *Why Our Next President May Keep His or Her*

of the 1908 and 1925 treaties support an argument that Commissioners have lifetime tenure, the court rejected that reading.[212]

The court relied on the commission of appointment signed by President Bush, which stated that Commissioner Schornack's appointment is "during the pleasure of the President of the United States for the time being."[213] Because there was no evidence that Commissioner Schornack ever objected to the terms in the commissioning document, the court held that he was "estopped from arguing that he is not terminable at will."[214]

The court made several other observations in determining the legality of Schornack's removal. The court noted the nearly absolute absence of life tenure among political appointees, with the exception of federal judges. Also, the language of Schornack's commission states his appointment was "during the pleasure of the President of the United States for the time being." And precedent requires any objection to a commission's terms be made prior to the end of the term—something Schornack failed to do. These factors, in addition to the tradition of deference to the President's power over foreign affairs, led the court to hold that Schornack's removal was legal.

In addition to the aforementioned reasoning, the court stated its reluctance to "intrude on the President's powers in matters of foreign affairs," and openly expressed that this was a case that might fall within the political question doctrine.[215] Furthermore, the court stated that "Treaties and other international agreements generally do not create judicially enforceable individual rights,"[216] and a reading of the 1908 and 1925 treaties do not suggest that IBC Commissioners have a rights to their post, or a right to a "certain process for removal."[217]

I. Observations

The key to agency independence remains the restriction on the President's power to remove individuals from office only for "cause." In the Supreme Court's definitive

Senate Seat: A Conjecture on the Constitution's Incompatibility Clause, 4 DUKE J. CONST. L. & PUB. POL'Y 107 (2009). For the foreign emoluments clause, see Seth Barrett Tillman, *Citizens United and the Scope of Professor Teachout's Anti-Corruption Principle*, 107 NW. U. L. REV 319, 405–09 (2012). *Accord,* Application of Emoluments Clause to Part-Time Consultant for the Nuclear Regulatory Commission, 10 Op. O.L.C. 96, 98 (1986) ("Prior opinions of this Office have assumed without discussion that the persons covered by the Emoluments Clause were 'officers of the United States' in the sense used in the Appointments Clause, U.S. Const. art. II, § 2, cl. 2."). Akhil Reed Amar takes a different view of the president and the emoluments clause. AKHIL REED AMAR, AMERICA'S CONSTITUTION: A BIOGRAPHY 182 (2005).

212 *Leu*, 523 F. Supp. 2d at 1207.

213 *Id.* at 1208 (citing United States v. Wilson, 290 F. 3d 347, 359 n.2 (D.C. Cir. 2002), which suggested in dicta that a commissioner is bound by the terms stated in the commissioning document).

214 *Id.*

215 *Id.*

216 *Id.* at 1209.

217 *Id.* at 1211.

decision in *Humphrey's Executor* in 1935,[218] such restriction when contained in an agency's organic statute withstood constitutional challenge. What is now far more controversial is whether agency members who do not have statutory removal protection may nonetheless be insulated from summary presidential removal.

A reasonable argument can certainly be made that individuals at agencies whose statutes do not confer removal protection may be removed by the president for any reason.[219] However, agencies whose statutes lack formal removal protection have been considered independent by both Congress and Presidents on much the same basis as those with formal statutory restriction. The FCC and SEC are perhaps the best known, but not the only, examples. Over the years, the courts have, from time to time, endorsed this understanding by concluding, suggesting, or accepting that some combination of factors or agency organization or responsibilities may serve to accord members such removal protection despite the lack of explicit legislative language. In an evolutionary fashion, the practice of treating these agencies as independent may well have morphed into constitutional doctrine.[220]

It certainly has become what Adrian Vermeule calls a "convention" of the administrative state.[221]

This can be seen as well in this approach of commentators on the independent agency form. In the 1950s (let alone earlier) it was believed that "only through nomination for appointment and the power to remove Commissioners for malfeasance is the President granted any control over independent agencies."[222] That is to say, other than appointment and removal, the independent agencies are free from presidential influence. By the 1980s, discussion revolved around whether the "just cause" exception includes a refusal to follow presidential orders.[223] This reflects a modern shift to "presidentialism" in constitutional theory and "formalism" in constitutional interpretation.[224]

---

[218] *Humphrey's Ex'r*, 295 U.S. 602, 631–32 (1935).

[219] See, for example, Note, *The SEC Is Not An Independent Agency*, 126 Harv. L. Rev. 781 (2013).

[220] That the Supreme Court may some day nonetheless upset this evolutionary result cannot be entirely dismissed. *See* Immigration & Naturalization Serv. v. Chadha, 462 U.S. 919 (1983) (overturning the legislative veto despite its historic acceptance by Congress and the president).

[221] *See* Adrian Vermeule, *Conventions of Agency Independence*, 113 Colum. L. Rev 1163, 1178 (2013); *see also* Akhil Reed Amar, *The President, the Cabinet, and Independent Agencies*, 5 U. St. Thomas J.L. & Pub. Pol'y 36, 37 (2010).

[222] Anthony F. Arpaia, *The Independent Agency—A Necessary Instrument of Democratic Government*, 69 Harv. L. Rev. 483, 487 (1956).

[223] *See, e.g.*, Geoffrey P. Miller, *Independent Agencies*, 1986 Sup. Ct. Rev. 41, 44 ("The thesis of this article is that Congress may not constitutionally deny the President the power to remove a policy-making official who has refused an order of the President to take an action within the officer's statutory authority.").

[224] *See supra* chapter 1, text at notes 66–69.

6

The Modern Agency

OTHER INDICIA OF INDEPENDENCE

THE PRESIDENT'S POWER to appoint government officials, subject to Senate approval, and his coordinate power to remove them, are a central element underpinning his authority and responsibility to control and manage the executive branch. As a consequence, as discussed in earlier chapters, the ability of Congress to influence the appointment process and constrain the president's removal authority by statute has become a defining element of agency independence, at least from the president. But other aspects of agency structure and operation also contribute to agency independence. We discuss some of these in this chapter.

A. Control of Agency Submissions to Congress

Since the 1920s, the executive branch, through the Bureau of the Budget (which was succeeded by the OMB) has asserted the authority to review legislation proposed by agencies, testimony and comments to be offered by agencies regarding pending legislation, and agencies' budgetary proposals.[1] The clearance process, although lacking a direct statutory basis, has evolved, in the words of Richard Neustadt, as "a long series of 'accidental,' unforeseen accretions."[2] Neustadt reviews the historical development of

---

[1] Richard E. Neustadt, *Presidency and Legislation: The Growth of Central Clearance*, 48 AM. POL. SCI. REV. 641, 642–50 (1954). For a general history, see SHELLEY LYNNE TOMKIN, INSIDE OMB: POLITICS AND PROCESS IN THE PRESIDENT'S BUDGET OFFICE (1998).

[2] Neustadt, *supra* note 1, at 668.

the clearance process in his article "Presidency and Legislation: The Growth of Central Clearance."[3]

The Budget and Accounting Act of 1921 created the Bureau of the Budget and directed executive branch agencies to transmit their budget estimates to the president for inclusion in an overall federal budget request.[4] Prior to passage of the Act, all agencies, including the ICC, submitted their budgets directly to Congress.[5] Immediately following passage of the Budget and Accounting Act, the Budget Bureau required agencies to submit for clearance proposals for legislation or expressions of views on pending legislation that had budget or appropriations implications.[6] During the Roosevelt administration, the Budget Bureau issued Budget Circular 336, which affirmatively required "by direction of the President" that "*all* agency proposals for legislation and all reports on pending legislation be cleared through the Budget Bureau."[7] Legislative proposals and testimony had to contain a statement, still used to this day, indicating "whether the proposal was or was not in accord with the President's program."[8]

Despite passage of the Budget and Accounting Act, independent agencies resisted the executive's attempts to review their proposals. Robert L. Calhoun, former legislative counsel to the ICC, notes that during the 1930s, President Roosevelt wrote to ICC chairman Joe Eastman, requesting that "proposed legislation be taken up with the Executive Branch." The ICC demurred and ultimately agreed to give the OMB any proposed legislation five minutes after it was submitted to Congress.[9] Independent agencies continued to submit their budget requests directly to Congress until statutory amendments enacted in 1939 made it clear that independent agencies were included within the purview of the Act.[10] Nonetheless, despite the absence of any express statutory authority, some independent agencies continued to assert a right to transmit their views on non-budget matters without Bureau of the Budget approval.

By the 1970s, Congress, presumably desirous of giving independent agencies additional statutory bases for their resistance, changed its strategy. Thereafter, provisions were placed in specific acts that allowed selected agencies to submit their legislative proposals, views on legislation, and even budget requests, directly to Congress without OMB clearance.[11] This authority prevents the OMB from demanding changes in

3 *Id.* at 642–50. James Blumstein provides an updated overview of regulatory review by the Executive Office of the President. *See* James F. Blumstein, *Regulatory Review by the Executive Office of the President: An Overview and Policy Analysis of Current Issues*, 51 DUKE L.J. 851 (2001).

4 Act of June 10, 1921, ch. 18, §§ 207, 213, 42 Stat. 20, 22–23 (codified as amended at 31 U.S.C. § 1108 (1994)).

5 *See* Neustadt, *supra* note 1, at 643.

6 *See id.* at 644.

7 *Id.* at 649–50 (emphasis added).

8 *Id.* at 650.

9 *See* Robert L. Calhoun, *The Interstate Commerce Commission, 1912–1937*, 16 TRANSP. L.J. 59, 67 (1987–1988).

10 *See* Reorganization Act of 1939, Pub. L. No. 76-19, § 201, 53 Stat. 565.

11 *See, e.g.*, Trade Act of 1974, Pub. L. No. 93-618, ch. 36, §§175 (a)(1), 88 Sat. 1978, 2011(1975) (codified as amended at 19 U.S.C. § 2232) (requiring the president to submit the budget request of the ITC to Congress

the agency's proposals, but allows the administration to comment subsequently on the agency's presentation. Other statutes require that an agency's legislative proposals be transmitted simultaneously to Congress and the President.[12] The concurrent submission provision does not, on its face, prohibit the OMB from suggesting (or even requiring) changes, but ensures that Congress will be apprised of the agency's original position. Some statutes have a mix of these procedures.[13]

Altogether, forty-four agencies make use of some form of legislative or budgetary authority allowing them to bypass various OMB approval requirements.[14] This includes agencies with both formal statutory bypass authority as well as agencies that, despite the lack of statutory authority, bypass the OMB by custom. Predictably, the OMB has noted that such authority "erode[s] Presidential control over Executive branch policies and operations."[15]

Agencies with legislative bypass authority provided by statute include the Farm Credit Administration,[16] the FERC,[17] and the Small Business Administration.[18] The National Transportation Safety Board,[19] the STB,[20] and the Commodity Futures Trading Commission,[21] among others, enjoy both budgetary and legislative bypass.

Several agencies—including the Federal Maritime Commission, FTC, FCC, NRC, and U.S. ITC—although lacking express statutory authority, send communications to Congress without submitting them first to the OMB.[22] They appear to assert their historic status as independent regulatory agencies as justification for this action.[23] The

---

without revision); Pub. L. No. 93-495, § 111, 88 Stat. 1500, 1506 (codified as amended at 12 U.S.C. § 250 (1994)) (exempting the SEC and various agencies regulating financial institutions from the requirement of clearance for their legislative proposals, testimony, and comments).

12 *See, e.g.*, Department of Energy Organization Act, Pub. L. No. 95-91, 96 Stat. 582 (1977) (establishing the FERC).

13 *See, e.g.*, Commodity Futures Trading Commission Act of 1974, Pub. L. No. 93-463, 88 Stat. 1389 (1974) (establishing the Commodity Futures Trading Commission).

14 Memorandum from Jim Dukes, Assistant Director for Legislative Reference, Office of Management and Budget, to OMB Policy Officers (Feb. 20, 2001) [hereinafter Memorandum from Jim Dukes]. This document, which contains a detailed list, can be found at https://www.citizen.org/documents/OMBDocument1.pdf.

15 *Id.* at 1.

16 Farm Credit Act of 1971, Pub. L. No. 92-181, § 5.18(3), 85 Stat. 583, 622.

17 Department of Energy Organization Act, Pub. L. No. 95-91, § 401(j), 91 Stat. 565, 583 (1977).

18 Small Business Act and Small Business Investment Act of 1958, Amendments, Pub. L. No. 94-305, § 206, 90 Stat. 663, 670 (1976).

19 Independent Safety Board Act of 1974, Pub. L. No. 93-633, § 304(b)(7), 88 Stat. 2166, 2170 (1975).

20 ICC Termination Act of 1995, Pub. L. No. 104-88, § 201, 109 Stat. 803, 934 (1995).

21 Commodity Futures Trading Commission Act of 1974, Pub. L. No. 93-463, § 101(a)(3), 88 Stat. 1389, 1390.

22 Memorandum from Jim Dukes, *supra* note 14, at 8. Other agencies that "informally" bypass the OMB include: the Commission on Civil Rights, Corporation for Public Broadcasting, Court of Appeals for Veterans Claims, Legal Services Corporation, Marine Mammal Commission, Amtrak, TVA, United States Institute for Peace, and United States Postal Service. *Id.*

23 *See Reviewing the Performance of the Social Security Administration as an Independent Agency: Hearing before the Subcomm. on Social Security of the H. Comm. on Ways and Means*, 104th Cong. 14 (1996)

OMB has notably acknowledged and seemingly acquiesced to this "informal" or "customary" bypass.[24] However, in a recent FOIA litigation brought by Public Citizen, the OMB opposed disclosure of those agencies whose customary bypass it accepts, arguing that its policy of not requiring compliance with review was not a final agency action subject to FOIA requirements.[25]

The D.C. Circuit rejected the argument, and the documents were released.[26] Most revealing was the OMB's acknowledgment of its long-standing acquiescence in the refusal of many independent agencies to comply with the requirements for prior submission and approval of legislative proposals. Its comments on the FTC were typical:

> The FTC has no statutory legislative bypass but acts as if it does: it does not ordinarily submit legislation or reports or testimony on legislation to OMB for clearance. OMB has made no effort in recent memory to subject the FTC to the requirements of Circular A-19.[27]

As for the NRC, the OMB observes that that commission "does not acknowledge OMB's central clearance authority."[28]

From time to time, the OMB nonetheless seeks the views of independent agencies on pending legislation. As a general rule, a referral is not made to any so-called bypass agency "unless the agency agrees to refrain from forwarding to Congress OMB-referred materials or its response to an OMB referral."[29] As far as the FTC is concerned, the OMB states:

> OMB does refer legislative materials to the FTC on a case-by-case basis, however, particularly with respect to matters likely to have a direct impact on that agency (e.g., concerning revisions of the laws governing unfair trade practices).[30]

[hereinafter *Social Security Administration as an Independent Agency*] (statement of Rogelio Garcia, Specialist in American National Government, Congressional Research Service) (listing the five agencies as the Federal Maritime Commission, FTC, NRC, STB, and ITC); *see also* appendix A, *infra*. The SSA submits its budget to the OMB, which is in turn included unrevised with the president's budget to Congress. *See Social Security Administration as an Independent Agency, supra,* at 8; 42 U.S.C. § 904(b) (2006) (providing statutory authority); *see generally* 31 U.S.C. § 1108 (2006) (outlining process for submission of budget to the president for independent agencies). *See also* Note, *Independence, Congressional Weakness, and the Importance of Appointment: The Impact of Combining Budgetary Autonomy with Removal Protection*, 125 HARV. L. REV. 1822, 1824 (2012).

24 Memorandum from Jim Dukes, *supra* note 14, at 5 (noting that although the reporting requirements do cover these agencies "the agencies generally do not comply... [and] [i]n some cases, these *de facto* bypasses have been in effect for many years.").

25 *See* Public Citizen, Inc. v. OMB, 569 F.3d 434, 442–44 (D.C. Cir. 2009).

26 *Id.*

27 Memorandum from Jim Dukes, *supra* note 14, at 19.

28 *Id.* at 20.

29 *Id.* at 1.

30 *Id.* at 19.

B. Control of Litigation

Except as otherwise authorized by statute, the conduct of the federal government's litigation rests with the DOJ.[31] Still, there is much evidence that this department is far from monolithic in the way in which it employs its attorneys for representation.[32] Indeed, Neal Devins has correctly observed that "[t]he reach of Department of Justice control in general and Solicitor General control in particular is ill-suited to generalization."[33] Congress has authorized various independent agencies to represent themselves in court in certain situations, often in response to perceived failures by the DOJ to adequately represent the agencies.[34] Litigating authority is more frequently granted to independent agencies than to executive agencies.[35]

Control over litigation was a much-debated issue when the ICC was created.[36] The original Act to Regulate Commerce placed the enforcement of ICC orders in the hands of the federal district attorneys, under the direction of the attorney general.[37] The

---

[31] *See* 28 U.S.C. §§ 516–19 (1994).

[32] James R. Harvey III, Note, *Loyalty in Government Action Litigation: Department of Justice Representation of Agency Clients*, 37 WM. & MARY L. REV. 1569, 1575 (1996).

[33] Neal Devins, *Unitariness and Independence: Solicitor General Control over Independent Agency Litigation*, 82 CAL. L. REV. 255, 278 (1994).

[34] For example, the FTC received statutory litigation authority in 1975. For certain types of cases, authority was granted only if, after notice, the attorney general failed to act within 45 days. *See* Magnuson-Moss Warranty—Federal Trade Commission Improvement Act, Pub. L. No. 93-637, § 204, 88 Stat. 2183, 2199 (1975) (codified as amended at 15 U.S.C. § 56). *See also* Michael Herz & Neal Devins, *The Consequences of DOJ Control of Litigation on Agencies' Programs*, 52 ADMIN. L. REV. 1345, 1348 (2000). Herz and Devins also point to some similar examples in the history of the EPA. For instance, the EPA may represent itself in court to enforce several environmental statutes only in situations where the administrator has determined that "the Attorney General will not act, or will not act soon enough." *Id.* at 1350–51. *See also* Federal Water Pollution Control Act Amendments of 1972, Pub. L. No. 92-500, § 2, 86 Stat. 816, 889 (codified as amended at 33 U.S.C. § 1366); Safe Drinking Water Act, Pub. L. No. 93-523, § 2, 88 Stat. 1660, 1691 (1974) (codified as amended at 42 U.S.C. § 300j-9(f)).

[35] Neal Devins & Michael Herz, *The Battle That Never Was: Congress, The White House, and Agency Litigation Authority*, 61 LAW & CONTEMP. PROBS. 205, 208 (1998). However, congressional vesting of independent litigating authority is by no means limited to independent agencies. To date Congress has vested such authority in a range of other government entities, including government corporations like the FDIC and executive agencies such as the Office of the Comptroller of the Currency and the Department of Labor. Neal Devins & Michael Herz, *The Uneasy Case for Department of Justice Control of Federal Litigation*, 5 U. PA. J. CONST. L. 558, 561 & n.11 (2005).

[36] *See* Angel Manuel Moreno, *Presidential Coordination of the Independent Regulatory Process*, 8 ADMIN. L.J. AM. U. 461, 502–03 (1994) ("In the early stages of regulation, IRCs were authorized to handle their own legal matters without the intervention of the attorney general. Indeed, until the passage of the Judges Act of 1925, the ICC and the FTC prepared their own requests for writs of certiorari and argued their own cases before the Supreme Court. As a general rule, the attorney general, through the Office of the Solicitor General, both of whom are political officials and not 'expert regulators,' litigates for the government, but some IRCs enjoy limited enforcement and appeal power").

[37] *See* Act of Feb. 4, 1887, ch. 104, § 16, 24 Stat. 379, 384.

1889 amendments left the ICC's litigation relationship with the Justice Department unchanged.[38] Statutory changes in 1906 divided litigation responsibility between the agency and the executive branch. The Justice Department retained responsibility for ICC orders involving the payment of money, while the commission obtained authority "in its own name" to seek enforcement of all other orders.[39] Changes to the statute governing the courts in 1911 created some ambiguity over the ICC's overall litigation authority. The changes enacted clearly gave the attorney general litigation authority over cases in the Commerce Court (which then included enforcement of all ICC orders other than those for the payment of money), but gave the ICC the right to appear as a party through its own lawyers in all cases involving the validity of ICC orders and to represent itself in the Supreme Court when the solicitor general declined to do so.[40]

As originally passed, the Hobbs Act mandated that cases involving the ICC could not be discontinued without the commission's consent.[41] Under the current version of the Act, the ICC's successor agency—the STB—may intervene in any court proceeding in which one of its orders may be enjoined, set aside, or suspended, including cases in the Supreme Court, without regard to the action of the attorney general.[42] The Act granted authority for the FCC, the Federal Maritime Commission, and the Department of Agriculture to appear directly in certain court cases.[43] The FTC has similar authority,[44] as does the FEC.[45]

In addition to the STB, the Hobbs Act also provides that as parties whose interests may be affected if one of their orders is or is not enjoined, set aside, or suspended, the FCC, NRC, and FMC may also intervene in any proceeding to review such an order, including cases in the Supreme Court, without regard to the action of the attorney general.[46] The SEC, EEOC, and FERC have authority to litigate in the courts of appeals,

---

38 *See* Act of Mar. 2, 1889, ch. 382, §§ 3, 5, 25 Stat. 855, 858–860 (amending §§ 12 and 16 of the 1887 Act, respectively, but maintaining role of federal district attorneys in the enforcement of commission actions).

39 *See* Act of June 29, 1906, ch. 3591, § 5, 34 Stat. 584, 591 (amending § 16 of the 1887 Act). *See also* Todd Lochner, Note, *The Relationship Between the Office of Solicitor General and the Independent Agencies: A Reevaluation*, 79 Va. L. Rev. 549, 550–51 (1993) (arguing for greater agency independence in Supreme Court litigation).

40 Act of Mar. 3, 1911, ch. 231, § 212, 36 Stat. 1087, 1150–1151.

41 *See* Act of Mar. 3, 1911, ch. 231 § 212, 36 Stat. 1150, 1150–1151.

42 *See* Administrative Orders Review Act, 28 U.S.C. § 2323 (2006) (also known as the "Hobbs Act").

43 *See* Act of December 29, 1950, ch. 1189, 64 Stat. 1129.

44 15 U.S.C. § 56 (2006); *see, e.g.*, United States v. Restland Funeral Home, Inc., 51 F.3d 56 (5th Cir. 1995).

45 For a discussion of FEC litigation through the mid-1990s, see George F. Fraley, III, Note, *Is the Fox Watching the Henhouse? The Administration's Control of FEC Litigation Through the Solicitor General*, 9 Admin. L.J. Am. U. 1215 (1996). *But see* ICC v. Southern Ry. Co., 543 F.2d 534, 539 (5th Cir. 1976) (concluding that the 1911 legislation, and subsequent statutes, did not confer authority on the ICC to litigate in its own name).

46 *See* 28 U.S.C. § 2348 (1994).

and the Consumer Product Safety Commission has authority to litigate in the district court.[47]

Because the DOJ has broad authority to conduct the government's litigation in the absence of an express statutory directive to the contrary, or as a matter of convenience or convention, even at those agencies that have some form of independent litigation authority, the DOJ frequently conducts litigation in those cases that involve issues unrelated to the agency's substantive mission but common to all departments and agencies, such as FOIA cases, damage actions against agency officials, and suits involving personnel matters.[48]

These arrangements reflect a highly practical approach. First, the DOJ controls topics that have implications for all agencies across government. Second, the DOJ retains litigation responsibility in areas in which it has developed far more experience and expertise than individual independent agencies that would otherwise litigate the issues only occasionally.

Devins aptly describes the current situation as follows: "[T]here are several agencies whose arrangements are so complex that they defy description.[49] [The] patchwork nature of independent agency litigating authority is rooted in historical and organizational bases."[50] Devins has also noted that under recent presidential administrations, there is a "near absence of litigation conflicts between independent agencies and the Solicitor General's office," as opposed to instances of such conflict during the Nixon, Carter, and Reagan administrations.[51] According to Devins, during the Nixon and Carter administrations, independent agencies often filed competing briefs, or made oral arguments, that conflicted with the positions of the solicitor general.[52] This forced courts to choose between deferring to the solicitor's interpretation of a statute and deferring to

---

47 *See* Devins, *supra* note 33, at 278–79 & nn.122–29 (summarizing the litigating authority of various independent agencies).

48 *See infra* appendix A (e.g., Commodity Futures Trading Commission, FERC).

49 Devins, *supra* note 33, at 279. For example, in FEC v. NRA Political Victory Fund, 513 U.S. 88, 98–99 (1994), the court dismissed the FEC's petition for certiorari and denied the agency the right to represent itself before the Supreme Court. The court determined that the FEC's enabling statute did not provide the agency with independent litigation authority. As a result, the DOJ now wields complete power to prosecute campaign finance abuses and enforce federal election laws. Absent an express delegation of independent litigation authority contained within an agency's enabling statute, other independent agencies may find that the litigation authority they previously enjoyed has been eliminated. *See generally* Alane Tempchin, Note, *Fall from Grace:* Federal Election Commission v. NRA Political Victory Fund *and the Demise of the FEC's Independent Litigating Authority*, 10 Admin. L.J. Am. U. 385, 398–99 (1996).

50 Devins, *supra* note 33, at 279.

51 Neal Devins & David Lewis, *Not-So Independent Agencies: Party Polarization and the Limits of Institutional Design*, 88 B.U. L. Rev. 459, 494 (2008). Local 28, Sheet Metal Workers' International Association v. EEOC, 478 U.S. 421 (1986), provides an example of such conflict. In *Sheet Metal Workers,* the solicitor general unilaterally reversed the EEOC's position in an affirmative action case in which it was a named party. The EEOC was "flatly told that it was a part of the Executive Branch and would have to swallow Department of Justice opposition to affirmative action." Devins, *supra* note 33, at 299.

52 Devins & Lewis, *supra* note 51, at 494.

the agency's own interpretation of the law. Since the Reagan administration, however, a "precipitous decline in the filing of competing briefs" may be indicative of the rise of the unitary executive and the emphasis on executive branch cohesion.[53]

In the wake of *Chevron*, Courts have been left to resolve procedural and structural distinctions between independent agencies and executive branch agencies. In his recent work, Randolph May argues that independent agencies should not receive *Chevron* deference, because this would be inconsistent with our constitutional values that promote political accountability and public participation in the democratic process.[54] May argues that courts should treat executive and independent agencies with different levels of deference despite the absence of differentiation between executive and independent agencies in the APA. May asserts that *Chevron* merely meant to tip the scales in the agencies' direction, not to create a substantial barrier between executive and independent agencies.[55] Therefore, courts should not use *Chevron* to diminish the constitutional preference for political accountability, which is best served by giving less deference to independent agencies.[56]

Joan Solanes Mullor rejects this position on the basis that post-*Chevron* Supreme Court cases have emphasized procedural safeguards and the role of agency expertise, rather than political accountability, in justifying deference to agencies' interpretations.[57] In addition, Mullor proposes that independent agencies fit particularly well with these values, as their enabling statutes require a greater transparency and administrative process than many other agencies.[58] While *Chevron* may have left some ambiguity or suggestion that independent agencies should not receive the same level of deference as their more politically responsive counterparts, Mullor concludes that subsequent cases have resolved this potential conflict.[59] In the recent Dodd-Frank Act, Congress took the unusual step of directing that interagency conflicts over statutory interpretation be resolved in favor of the interpretation contained in regulations by the new CFPB, thus validating *Chevron* in approach if not in terms.[60]

---

53 *Id.* at 495. Devins notes, for instance, that both the Clinton and George W. Bush administrations prevented the FEC and SEC from filing competing briefs with the Supreme Court. *Id.*

54 Randolph J. May, *Defining Deference Down, Again: Independent Agencies,* Chevron *Deference, and* Fox, 62 ADMIN. L. REV. 433, 440 (2010).

55 *Id.* at 442.

56 *Id.* at 446. In contrast, Margaret Lemos argues that "considerations of [agency] expertise suggest that the Solicitor General should refrain from substituting his judgment for that of the specialist agent for precisely the same reasons that judges do." Margaret H. Lemos, *The Solicitor General as Mediator Between Court and Agency*, 2009 MICH. ST. L. REV. 185, 210 (2009).

57 Joan Solanes Mullor, *Why Independent Agencies Deserve Chevron Deference* 42–43 (InDret, Vol. 4, 2010, working paper), *available at* http://ssrn.com/abstract=1738187.

58 *Id.* at 15.

59 *Id.* at 35.

60 12 U.S.C. § 5512(b)(4)(B). For a general discussion of congressional efforts under the Dodd-Frank Act to resolve interagency conflicts, including directions given by Congress with regard to the application of

Interagency conflicts raise the question of whether litigation is at all possible between government entities if conflicts mature. This question is far from settled. Most courts find that one agency of the government cannot sue another (based on the black letter view that a party cannot sue itself)[61] and have found exceptions only where in the court's view the "real [party] in interest" is not a government agency.[62]

But the situation may change when one or both parties are independent agencies. The OLC has mostly opposed independent agency litigation on the grounds that "intra-executive branch litigation would likely contravene Articles II and III of the Constitution."[63]

In *SEC v. FLRA*, the Federal Labor Relations Agency claimed the SEC committed unfair labor practices by unilaterally implementing a new salary payment plan after negotiations between the National Treasury Employees Union and the SEC came to an impasse.[64]

Chevron, see Jacob E. Gersen, *Administrative Law Goes to Wall Street: The New Administrative Process*, 65 ADMIN. L. REV. 689, 716–25 (2013).

61 United States v. ICC, 337 U.S. 426, 430–32 (1949) (noting "[t]here is much argument with citation of many cases to establish the long-recognized general principle that no person may sue himself.").

62 As one scholar notes, "[t]he talismanic 'a person cannot sue herself' collapses, however, when the 'person' is the United States government." Michael Herz, *United States v. United States: When Can the Federal Government Sue Itself?*, 32 WM. & MARY L. REV. 893, 895 (1991). This was found to be the case in *United States v. ICC*, where the DOD challenged a commission order as a participant in interstate commerce, using the rail system. 337 U.S. 426, 432 (1949) (finding "[t]he Interstate Commerce Act contains adequate provisions for protection of Commission orders by the Commission and by the railroads when, as here, they are the real parties in interest."). Furthermore, "the presence of legal adversity depends upon whether some source of law has removed from one of the parties, or from the President of the United States, the power conclusively to resolve the dispute." William K. Kelley, *The Constitutional Dilemma of Litigation Under the Independent Counsel System*, 83 MINN. L. REV. 1197, 1213 (1999).

While lower courts have been willing to entertain interagency litigation, the Supreme Court has only "twice expressly permitted such litigation to proceed," in *United States v. ICC*, and *United States ex rel. Chapman v. Federal Power Commission*, 345 U.S. 153 (1953). Joseph W. Mead, *Interagency Litigation and Article III*, 47 GA. L. REV. 1217, 1238–40 (2013). As discussed, the *United States v. ICC* court permitted the DOD's litigation against the ICC because of the presence of railroads as a party. 337 U.S. 426, 430–32 (1949). In *Chapman*, the Court determined that petitioners had standing where "the Secretary of the Interior and an association of nonprofit rural electric cooperatives... challenged the authority of the Federal Power Commission to grant to the respondent power company, VEPCO, a license to construct a hydroelectric generating station...." United States ex rel. Chapman v. Fed. Power Comm'n, 345 U.S. 153, 154 (1953).

In fact, "independent agencies are, as a practical matter, more likely to be involved in interagency litigation, and many (although not all) of the cases where agencies have been adverse involved an independent agency." Mead, *supra*, at 1251.

63 Enforcement Jurisdiction of the Special Counsel for Immigration Related Unfair Employment Practices, 16 Op. O.L.C. 121, 128–31 (1992). The OLC has often found that "litigation between two executive agencies would not appear to involve the requisite adversity of interests to constitute a 'Case[]' in 'Controvers[y]' within the meaning of Article III" and thus there the Executive branch is the only real party in interest. *Id.* at 129. *See also* Admin. Assessment of Civil Penalties Against Fed. Agencies Under the Clean Air Act, 21 Op. O.L.C. 109 (1997); Constitutionality of Nuclear Regulatory Comm'n's Imposition of Civil Penalties on the Air Force, 13 Op. O.L.C. 131, 138–39 (1989); Proposed Tax Assessment Against the USPS, 1 Op. O.L.C. 79, 80–82 (1977).

64 SEC v. FLRA, 568 F.3d 990, 990–93 (D.C. Cir. 2009).

The D.C. Circuit found this to be a "constitutional oddity"[65] justiciable in that an "independent agency can be sufficiently adverse to a traditional executive agency to create a justiciable cause,"[66] relying of course on *Humphrey's Executor v. United States*.[67]

C. Independent Funding Authority

A significant indicator of agency autonomy is possession of an independent funding source separate from the appropriations process. As one commentator has suggested, "[f]unding is key to independence."[68] For example, the Federal Reserve Board,[69] the Office of the Comptroller of the Currency,[70] the PCAOB,[71] the NCUA,[72] the Pension

65 SEC v. FLRA, 568 F.3d 990, 996–97 (2009). (Kavanaugh, J., concurring) (acknowledging the "anomaly" created by the litigation because "[b]oth the SEC and the FLRA are agencies in the Executive Branch, yet one is suing the other in an Article III court."). This was not the first time that the FLRA had brought suit against another executive agency for alleged unfair labor practices. *See* NLRB v. FLRA, 2 F.3d 1190,1192 (D.C. Cir. 1993) (reviewing "a decision and order of [FLRA] requiring that the NLRB bargain over a proposal advanced by the National Labor Relations Board Union...find[ing] that the proposal is not sufficiently tailored to redress the harms suffered by the particular employees who are in fact adversely affected"); Dep't of Treasury, IRS, v. FLRA, 494 U.S. 922, 924 (1990) (reviewing the "determination of the [FLRA] that, under Title VII of the Civil Service Reform Act of 1978 (Act), [the IRS] must bargain with the National Treasury Employees Union (NTEU or Union) over a proposed contract provision subjecting to grievance and arbitration procedures claims that the IRS failed to comply" with OMB laws).

66 SEC v. FRLA, 568 F.3d 990, 997 (2009) (Kavanaugh, J., concurring).

67 295 U.S. 602 (1935) (holding that presidents lack complete control over independent agencies, which allows for justiciable causes to exist between an independent and an executive agency). *See* chapter 5, sections C and D (regarding removal protection); *See also* United States v. Nixon, 418 U.S. 683, 693 (1974) (rejecting the president's claim that the issue was not within the jurisdiction of the court because "the mere assertion of a claim of an 'intra-branch dispute,' without more, has never operated to defeat federal jurisdiction; justiciability does not depend on such a surface inquiry."); United States v. FMC, 694 F.2d 793, 796 (D.C. Cir. 1982) (concluding that the DOJ had standing to challenge rates assigned by the Federal Maritime Commission).

68 Steven A. Ramirez, *Depoliticizing Financial Regulation*, 41 WM. & MARY L. REV. 503, 589 (2000).

69 12 U.S.C. § 243 (2006).

70 12 U.S.C. § 16. Rather than receiving appropriations from Congress, the Office of the Comptroller of the Currency funds its operations "primarily by assessments on national banks and federal savings associations," as well as revenue from investments. *See id. See also* OFFICE OF THE COMPTROLLER OF THE CURRENCY, ABOUT THE OCC, http://www.occ.gov/about/what-we-do/mission/index-about.html (last visited May 26, 2014) (explaining the process by which the Office of the Comptroller of the Currency provides its own funding). The Office of Thrift Supervision operated similarly. However, its authorities were transferred to the Office of the Comptroller of the Currency under the Dodd-Frank Act of 2010. 12 U.S.C. § 1833b (2010). For the establishment of the Office of Thrift Supervision, see Robert Cooper, *The Office of Thrift Supervision*, 59 FORDHAM L. REV. S363, S366–67 (1991); for the transfer of its functions, see Dodd-Frank Wall Street Reform and Consumer Protection Act, Pub. L. No. 111-203, § 312, 124 Stat. 1376, 1521–1522 (2010).

71 15 U.S.C. § 7211(f)(5) (2006). The PCAOB funds its operations by collecting fees from companies whose financial statements they review. *See id.* The SEC reviews and approves the PCAOB's budget each year. 15 U.S.C. § 7211(c)(7) (2006).

72 12 U.S.C. § 1755 (2006). *See also* Note, *Independence, Congressional Weakness, and the Importance of Appointment: The Impact of Combining Budgetary Autonomy with Removal Protection*, *supra* note 23, at

Benefit Guarantee Corporation,[73] the Farm Credit Administration,[74] and the FDIC[75] are all authorized to levy assessments against their "clients."[76]

Congress has also authorized some agencies to self-fund up to the amount provided for in annual appropriations bills.[77] An example is the FCC, which is authorized to "assess and collect regulatory fees to cover the costs" of FCC expenditures, but only up to the limit set in the appropriations bill.[78] Congress has not given the FCC complete freedom in this respect, resulting in the FCC having limited ability to self-fund to cover the amount of its appropriations.[79] Many do not consider this as true self-funding, as the agencies are limited by the annual appropriations process.[80] Other agencies have been authorized to self-fund through collecting fines that they may keep rather than transfer to the Treasury.[81]

Two agencies—the Federal Reserve Board and the CFPB—appear to have the most sweeping ability to finance independently. As noted above, the Federal Reserve has authority to levy assessments against the banks it regulates. But, much of its budget comes from "interest earnings from the portfolio of U.S. government securities and federal agency mortgage-backed securities in the System Open Market Account."[82] As Peter Conti-Brown has detailed, the board's statutory exemption from the annual

---

1823 & n.12. The NCUA funds its operations by collecting an annual operating fee from each federal credit union. 12 U.S.C. § 1755(a). Any leftover funds from these fees are invested by the secretary of the treasury, and the NCUA is authorized to use any revenue from these investments. 12 U.S.C. § 1755(e)(1)–(3).

73 The Pension Benefit Guarantee Corporation funds its operations by collecting insurance premiums from private companies. *See* PENSION BENEFIT GUARANTEE CORP., WHO WE ARE, http://www.pbgc.gov/about/who-we-are.html (last visited May 26, 2014); *see also* 29 U.S.C. § 1001A(c)(4) (2006) (stating that the Pension Benefit Guarantee Corporation will be "a financially self-sufficient program").

74 *See* 12 U.S.C. §§ 2245, 2250 (2006). The Farm Credit Administration funds its operations and the salaries of its employees and board members through assessment fees and revenue from investments. *Id.*

75 *See* U.S. GOV'T ACCOUNTABILITY OFFICE, GAO-13-291, FINANCIAL AUDIT: FEDERAL DEPOSIT INSURANCE CORPORATION FUNDS' 2012 AND 2011 FINANCIAL STATEMENTS (2013).

76 Other self-funded agencies include the Farm Credit System Insurance Corporation, 12 U.S.C. § 2277a-9 (2012) (creating the Farm Credit Insurance Corporation Insurance Fund); Federal Prison Industries, Inc., 18 U.S.C. § 4126 (2012) (directing the establishment and uses of the Prison Industries Fund); and the Bureau of Engraving and Printing, 31 U.S.C. § 5142 (2006) (describing the Bureau of Printing and Engraving Fund). *See* Survey of Self-Funded Agencies (May 2011) (unpublished survey) (on file with authors). *See also* Charles Kruly, *Self-Funding and Agency Independence*, 81 GEO. WASH. L. REV. 1733 (2013).

77 *See* Kruly, *supra* note 76, at 1735 n.6.

78 47 U.S.C. § 159(a)(1)–(2) (2006).

79 *See* 47 U.S.C. § 159(a)(1) (2006); *see also* Kruly, *supra* note 76, at 1735 n.6.

80 For distinctions drawn among self-funding variations, see U.S. GOV'T ACCOUNTABILITY OFFICE, GAO-02-864, SEC OPERATIONS, IMPLICATIONS OF ALTERNATIVE FUNDING STRUCTURES 2 (2002).

81 We do not consider this to be self-funding.

82 BD. OF GOVERNORS OF THE FED. RESERVE SYS., ANNUAL REPORT: BUDGET REVIEW (2010), *available at* http://www.federalreserve.gov/boarddocs/rptcongress/budgetrev10/ar_br10.pdf (quoted in Peter Conti-Brown, *The Structure of Federal Reserve Independence* 22, Rock Ctr. for Corporate Governance, Working Paper Series No. 139 (Jan. 2, 2014 version), *available at* http://www.law.stanford.edu/sites/default/files/publication/431459/doc/slspublic/SSRN-id2275759.pdf).

appropriations process, and its assessment authority, have been augmented informally to create what he describes as an independent funding mechanism "without equal in the federal government."[83]

The CFPB is funded by the Board of the Directors of the Federal Reserve "in the amount determined by the Director [of the CFPB] to be reasonably necessary to carry out the authorities of the CFPB under Federal consumer financial law." As part of the Republican "pushback" against the present structure of the CFPB, some in Congress have recently proposed that the CFPB obtain funding through ordinary appropriations procedures.[84]

While the SEC is currently funded by congressional appropriations, it collects more in fines each year than its annual appropriation.[85] However, all fines must be turned over to the Treasury.[86] In the past, proposals were made to consider a self-funding mechanism for the SEC. In the 1990s, Chair Arthur Levitt urged a change in the agency's funding.[87] In 2010, Chair Schapiro urged Congress to authorize self-funding for the agency in the wake of the fallout from the financial crisis.[88] Most recently, Brooksley Born, former chair of the Commodity Futures Trading Commission, urged self-funding for both the SEC and the Commodity Futures Trading Commission as a mechanism to ensure that the agencies would have adequate funds to perform their "enormous new responsibilities

---

83 Conti-Brown, *supra* note 82, *at* 23. *See generally id.* at 23–32. The nuanced summary is likely more accurate than Steven Ramirez's claim that "the Fed is the only regulatory agency that is totally self-funded." Ramirez, *supra* note 68, at 525.

84 They would argue this approach serves to increase accountability. For discussion of the CFPB, see chapter 7, section D, subsection 3.

85 The commission's budget will increase by nearly a billion dollars by 2015 under the Dodd-Frank Act. *See* Dodd-Frank, § 991(c), amending 15 U.S.C. § 78kk.

86 In 2010, the SEC collected $2.8 billion in penalties and disgorgement. *See* Securities and Exchange Commission, FY 2010 Performance and Accountability Report, at 11, *available at* http://www.sec.gov/about/secpar/secpar2010.pdf. The Dodd-Frank Act permits the commission to retain a small reserve in the Treasury of funds collected from registrants, to use as needed, but not to exceed $50 million per year or $100 million total. *See* Dodd-Frank, § 991(d), amending 15 U.S.C. § 78d. *See also Top Securities Lawyers Call for Self-Funded SEC*, N.Y. TIMES DEALBOOK, June 11, 2010, http://dealbook.nytimes.com/2010/06/11/top-securities-lawyers-call-for-self-funded-s-e-c/.

87 *See Oversight Hearing on the Mutual Fund Industry: Hearing Before the Subcomm. on Securities of the S. Comm. on Banking, Housing, and Urban Affairs*, 103rd Cong. 62 (1993) (statement of Arthur Levitt, SEC chair). *See also* Joel Seligman, *Godwin Seminar, Self-Funding for the Securities and Exchange Commission*, 28 NOVA. L. REV. 233, 240 (2004); Luis Aguilar, *Creating Reform That Is Sustainable for Investors*, 10 J. INT'L BUS. & L. 115, 121–22 (2011).

88 *See* Mary L. Schapiro, Chair, Sec. & Exchange Comm'n, Statement Concerning Agency Self-Funding (Apr. 15, 2010), *available at* http://www.sec.gov/news/speech/2010/spch041510mls.htm. Schapiro urged the Senate to take up legislation reforming this process. *See* Letter from Mary L. Schapiro, Chairman, Sec. & Exchange Comm'n, to Harry Reid, Senator, Majority Leader (Apr. 15, 2010), *available at* http://www.sec.gov/news/speech/2010/spch041510mls-reid-letter.pdf; Letter from Mary L. Schapiro, Chairman, Sec. & Exchange Comm'n, to Mitch McConnell, Senator, Minority Leader (Apr. 15, 2010) *available at* http://www.sec.gov/news/speech/2010/spch041510mls-mcconnell-letter.pdf.

under the Dodd-Frank Act."[89] Born stressed the importance of providing the agencies with a funding stream not controlled by Congress that would allow them to deal with systemic risk.[90] Although an early Senate version of the Dodd-Frank Act did include some self-funding,[91] the final version of the bill did not.[92]

On occasion Congress provides agencies with self-funding authority but with the restriction that it can only collect funds up to a sum authorized by Congress. In this way Congress retains control over the agency's budget even though that budget is funded by "user fees" and other fees or fines it may collect. A good example is the FCC.[93]

It is, perhaps, ironic that self-funding, presumably by the regulated community, is seen as a way to ensure agency independence presumably from Congress—rather than an exercise of "regulatory capture" by clients who would presumably be the agency's funders.

One perhaps inadvertent benefit of self-funding is that agencies like the Federal Housing Finance Agency (FHFA) are unaffected by budget sequesters as they are self-funded. For another example, Robert Broadsky explains:

> The Patent and Trademark Office, as part of the Commerce Department, derives its funding from fees paid by users of the patent and trademark system. But the agency actually asks for appropriations from Congress matching what they expect to collect in patent fees in a given fiscal year.... For the fiscal 2012 budget, the office requested $2.71 billion, the same amount it anticipated in patent and trademark fees next year.[94]

Even as self-funding distances agencies from congressional control, it ineluctably increases the power of presidential appointment and of Senate confirmation.[95] At the same time it "leaves the President with more relative control, through his power to control the agency head."[96] Thus, "[a]ll other things being equal, the agency will likely have moved along the continuum from 'independent agency' to an entity that bears a closer resemblance to a traditional executive agency."[97] Thus the unintended consequence of self-funding may be less agency autonomy, not more.

---

89 *See* Brooksley Born, *Self-Funding of Regulators Would Help Fiscal Mess*, POLITICO (Mar. 10, 2013, 9:03 p.m.), http://www.politico.com/story/2013/03/self-funding-of-regulators-would-help-fiscal-mess-88666.html (arguing that self-funding insulates regulators from political pressures and ultimately keeps them from becoming accountable to the entities they were created to regulate).

90 *Id.*

91 *See* Restoring American Financial Stability Act of 2010, S. 3217, § 991, 111th Cong. (2010).

92 *See* Dodd-Frank Act, Pub. L. No. 111-203, 124 Stat. 1376 (2010).

93 47 U.S.C. § 159 (a)(1) (2006).

94 Robert Broadsky, *Shutdown? What Shutdown*, GOV'T EXEC., Feb. 25, 2011, *available at* http://www.govexec.com/oversight/2011/02/shutdown-what-shutdown/33403/.

95 Kruly, *supra* note 76, at 1741.

96 *Id.*

97 *Id.* at 1742; *see also* Note, *Independence, Congressional Weakness, and the Importance of Appointment: The Impact of Combining Budgetary Autonomy with Removal Protection, supra* note 23, at 1824 ("when the

D. Freedom from Centralized Office of Information and Regulatory Affairs Review

1. THE EVOLUTION OF CENTRALIZED REVIEW

In contrast with centralized control of budget and legislative matters discussed earlier, centralized review of executive agency regulation goes back only to the administration of Richard Nixon, who created a "quality of life review," under which the OMB required a rudimentary cost-benefit analysis of various EPA proposals.[98] For his part, President Ford increased executive control over agency rules when he created the inflation-fighting "Council on Wage and Price Stability" to coordinate the war against inflation.[99]

Building on these nascent efforts, President Carter issued Executive Order 12,044 in 1979, which created a regulatory analysis review group to perform basic cost-benefit analysis on major regulations.[100] He also signed the Paperwork Reduction Act of 1980,[101] which established OIRA within the OMB to serve as a formal entity through which the President could exercise centralized review.[102]

These early efforts aside, President Reagan's 1981 promulgation of Executive Order 12,291[103] must be considered a "sea change"[104] in White House regulatory policy. This order institutionalized regulatory review by requiring executive branch agencies to submit proposed rulemakings, along with a cost-benefit analysis, to OIRA for review.[105]

---

traditional independent agency model is combined with self-funding... control is substantially diminished, especially because of reduced Congressional power. Thus, appointment becomes the primary means of control").

98 See discussion in BARRY FRIEDMAN, REGULATION IN THE REAGAN-BUSH ERA: THE ERUPTION OF PRESIDENTIAL INFLUENCE 27–28 (1995) ("quality of life review" was instituted in response to "the rapid flow of ambitious regulations being promulgated at the EPA."). *See also* Memorandum from George P. Shultz, Dir., Office of Mgmt. & Budget, for the Heads of Departments and Agencies: Agency Regulations, Standards, and Guidelines Pertaining to Environmental Quality, Consumer Protection, and Occupational and Public Health and Safety (Oct. 5, 1971), *available at* Center for Regulatory Effectiveness, http://www.thecre.com/ombpapers/QualityofLife1.htm. The Nixon experience is detailed in Jim Tozzi, *OIRA's Formative Years: The Historical Record of Centralizing Regulatory Review Preceding OIRA's Founding*, 63 ADMIN. L. REV. 37, 43–50 (2011). Tozzi actually traces the idea of centralized regulatory review back to Lyndon Johnson. *Id.* at 40–43.

99 Inflation Impact Statements, Exec. Order No. 11,821, 39 Fed. Reg. 41,501 (Nov. 27, 1974).

100 Exec. Order No. 12,044, 3 C.F.R. § 152 (Mar. 23, 1978).

101 Pub. L. No. 96-511, 94 Stat. 2812 (1980) (codified as amended at 44 U.S.C. §§ 3501–3521 (2006)). This was the last bill signed by Carter during his presidency. The statute was amended in 1995. The 1980 Act and its legislative history are well discussed in William F. Funk, *The Paperwork Reduction Act: Paperwork Reduction Meets Administrative Laws*, 24 HARV. J. ON LEGIS. 1, 26–35 (1987).

102 Pub. L. No. 96-511, 94 Stat. 2812 (1980) (codified at 44 U.S.C. § 3503 (2006)).

103 Exec. Order No. 12,291, 46 Fed. Reg. 13,193, 13,194 (1981).

104 Helen G. Boutrous, *Regulatory Review in the Obama Administration: Cost-Benefit Analysis for Everyone*, 62 ADMIN. L. REV. 243, 247 (2010).

105 The early years of the Reagan OIRA are reviewed in James C. Miller III, *The Early Days of Reagan Regulatory Relief and Suggestions for OIRA's Future*, 63 ADMIN. L. REV. 93, 96–99 (2011).

In 1985, Reagan issued Executive Order 12,498,[106] which required all agencies to submit an annual regulatory agenda for OIRA review.[107] It required each agency, on an annual basis, to submit a regulatory plan to OIRA that discusses and prioritizes the significant regulations it intends to issue that year.[108]

While the Reagan review process was controversial at its inception[109] (on both constitutional and policy grounds),[110] it has, for better or worse, "become a permanent part of the institutional design of American government."[111] By now, "the legality of the program appears to be beyond serious question."[112] President George H. W. Bush continued the regulatory review procedures put in place by the Reagan administration, with minor changes,[113] although he did create a new "Council on Competitiveness" chaired by Vice President Dan Quayle, which was "modeled after President Reagan's Regulatory Relief Task Force."[114] The council was authorized to resolve disputes between the OMB and the agencies.

---

106 Exec. Order No. 12,498, Regulatory Planning Process (Jan. 4, 1985) 3 C.F.R. § 323 (1986) (revoked by Exec. Order No. 12,866, 3 C.F.R. § 638 (1993), reprinted in 5 U.S.C. § 601 (2006)).

107 That order required agencies to compile a regulatory plan of all substantial regulations the agencies planned to propose, and a cost-benefit analysis of such proposed regulations for OIRA review. Exec. Order No. 12,498 at §§ (1)–(2).

108 Exec. Order No. 12,866, 58 Fed. Reg. 51735 (Oct. 4, 1993).

109 The controversy is laid out in Richard H. Pildes & Cass R. Sunstein, *Reinventing the Regulatory State*, 62 U. Chi. L. Rev. 1, 3–6 (1995).

110 For a critique on policy grounds, see Alan B. Morrison, *OMB Interference with Agency Rulemaking: The Wrong Way to Write a Regulation*, 99 Harv. L. Rev. 1059, 1062–64 (1986). For a critique on constitutional grounds, see Morton Rosenberg, *Presidential Control of Agency Rulemaking, an Analysis of Constitutional Issues That May Be Raised by Executive Order 12,291*, 23 Ariz. L. Rev. 1199, 1199–1202 (1981). For a defense on policy grounds, see Christopher C. Demuth & Douglas H. Ginsberg, *White House Review of Agency Rulemaking*, 99 Harv. L. Rev. 1075 (1986). *See also* Peter M. Shane, *Presidential Regulatory Oversight and the Separation of Power: The Constitutionality of Executive Order No. 12,291*, 23 Ariz. L. Rev. 1235 (1981).

111 Robert V. Percival, *Who's in Charge? Does the President Have Directive Authority over Agency Regulatory Decisions?*, 79 Fordham L. Rev. 2487, 2505 (2011). This view was confirmed ten years later when two scholars opined that "centralized review of agency rulemaking has arguably become the most important institutional feature of the regulatory state." Nicholas Bagley & Richard Revesz, *Centralized Oversight of the Regulatory State*, 106 Colum. L. Rev. 1260, 1260 (2006).

Lisa Bressman and Robert Thompson note that regulatory review processes have become "permanent fixtures of the regulatory state because they simultaneously speak to political, managerial, and normative values" that are essential to agency functions. *See* Lisa Schultz Bressman & Robert B. Thompson, *The Future of Agency Independence*, 63 Vand. L. Rev. 599, 621 (2010).

112 Harold H. Bruff, *Presidential Power Meets Bureaucratic Expertise*, 12 U. Pa. J. Const. L. 461, 485 (2010).

113 Office of Mgmt. & Budget, Regulatory Program of the United States Government, April 1, 1990–March 31, 1991 5 (1990). The Bush administration also encountered criticism when refusing to approve the reauthorization of the Paperwork Reduction Act in 1989 with the addition of increased OMB public disclosure requirements. Congress, in retaliation, refused to confirm the new OIRA administrator until a compromise was reached.

114 John D. Graham et al., *Managing the Regulatory State: The Experience of the Bush Administration*, 33 Fordham Urb. L.J. 953, 963 n.52 (2006). *See also* Percival, *supra* note 111, at 2511.

On September 30, 1993, President Clinton promulgated Executive Order 12,866, the most substantive changes to OIRA review since the Reagan administration.[115] Under E.O. 12,866 regulatory review was much more transparent;[116] it made use of more precise cost-benefit criteria including non-quantitative criteria such as equitable, distributive considerations. Its focus on "significant regulatory actions, however, was not much different than E.O. 12, 291."[117]

Upping the ante, OMB director John Graham (during the George W. Bush administration) added an innovation known as the "prompt letter" to OIRA's regulatory oversight arsenal. Rather than simply react to the rulemaking proposals that were being submitted, OIRA would issue a prompt letter to suggest an issue that the OMB believed was worth agency priority.[118] Prompt letters typically went to executive branch agencies recommending that a specific action be taken.[119] The OMB also issues "review letters," a relatively new phenomenon by which the OMB will review regulations in progress and advise the agency to consider certain factors before finalizing the rule.[120] The letters might also advise the agency to consider promulgating further rules after one set of rules

---

115 Exec. Order No. 12,866, 3 C.F.R. § 638 (1993), *reprinted in* 5 U.S.C. § 601 (2006). *See infra* notes 123–31 and accompanying text (regarding revisions to Exec. Order No. 12,866 by Presidents George W. Bush and Obama); Robert W. Hahn & Cass R. Sunstein, *A New Executive Order for Improving Federal Regulation? Deeper and Wider Cost-Benefit Analysis*, 150 U. PA. L. REV. 1489, 1490 (2002) (despite President Reagan and President Clinton's partisan differences, both were fundamentally committed to cost-benefit balancing). *See also* Bressman & Thompson, *supra* note 111, at 620–21; see also colloquium discussion in Charles J. Cooper, Robert D. Dinerstein et al., *The Fifth Annual Robert C. Byrd Conference on the Administrative Process: The First Year of Clinton/Gore Reinventing Government or Refining Reagan/Bush Initiatives?*, 8 ADMIN. L.J. AM. U. 23 (1994); Mark Seidenfeld, *A Big Picture Approach to Presidential Influence on Agency Policy-Making*, 80 IOWA L. REV. 1, 41–47 (1994) (discussing the new procedural and substantive constraints on OIRA discretion introduced by Exec. Order No. 12,866).

116 Curtis W. Copeland, *The Role of the Office of Information and Regulatory Affairs in Federal Rulemaking*, 33 FORDHAM URB. L.J. 1257, 1270–73 (2006).

117 Both referred to regulations with an estimated cost of over $100 million a year. Exec. Order No. 12,866 at 3(L).

118 John D. Graham, *Saving Lives Through Administrative Law and Economics*, 157 U. PA. L. REV. 395, 460–63 (2008). *See also* Memorandum from John D. Graham for the President's Management Council, Sept. 20, 2001, at 5 (declaring that "[t]he purpose of a prompt letter is to suggest an issue that OMB believes is worthy of agency priority").

119 Graham, *Saving Lives Through Administrative Law and Economics, supra* note 118, at 461. According to Graham, an OIRA prompt letter, unlike a (nondiscretionary) presidential directive, is "a public request by OIRA, to a regulator, that a rulemaking be initiated or completed, that information relevant to a regulatory program be disclosed to the public, or that a piece of research or analysis relevant to rulemaking be conducted." *Id.*

120 *See, e.g.*, Letter from Susan E. Dudley, Adm'r, Office of Information and Regulatory Affairs, to Gus Coldebella, Gen. Counsel & Regulatory Policy Officer, Dep't of Homeland Security (Dec. 7, 2007), *available at* Office of Info. & Regulatory Affairs, http://www.reginfo.gov/public/postreview/Coldebella.pdf (providing comments regarding the "Secure Flight Program" proposed rule).

has already been finalized.[121] Whether such letters are an effective tool for shaping agency policy as an instrument of presidential control remains unclear.[122]

Late in his presidency, George W. Bush issued Executive Order 13,422,[123] which had potential to significantly increase centralized control of regulations.[124] The Executive Order required that each agency "designate one of the Agency's Presidential appointees to serve as the agency's regulatory policy officer" and sign off on all regulations, thus placing a political appointee on the top of the agency regulatory development process.[125] Further, it added regulatory review of "guidance documents"[126] and made a number of other significant changes.[127]

For his part, President Obama reversed the Bush administration's efforts to further centralize regulatory review by eliminating the prompt letter and "regulatory policy officer."[128] Instead, Obama augmented President Clinton's Executive Order 12,866 by way of Executive Orders 13,563 and 13,579.[129] Those Executive Orders only marginally

---

121 *See, e.g.*, Letter from Cass R. Sunstein, Adm'r, Office of Information and Regulatory Affairs, to David Strickland, Adm'r, Nat'l Highway Traffic Safety Admin. (Mar. 19, 2010), *available at* Office of Info. & Regulatory Affairs, http://www.reginfo.gov/public/postreview/Tire_Fuel_Efficiency_Consumer_Information_Final_Rule.pdf (proposing the agency refine labelling regulations established in the "Tire Fuel Efficiency Consumer Information Program" final rule).

122 After leaving office, Dr. Graham defended the use of prompt letters and urged codification of the process. Graham, *Saving Lives Through Administrative Law and Economics, supra* note 118, at 532–34. Although not entirely unsympathetic to this proactive approach to regulatory analysis, some observers have been dismissive of the prompt letter as a significant device, in one case even describing it as a "sideshow." Bagley & Revesz, *supra* note 111, at 1280 (arguing that while the prompt letter is a sideshow, the main event is the review of regulations to avoid disproportionate regulatory costs). Bagley and Revesz further argue that a newly overhauled executive order combined with additional resources was necessary to "fully institutionalize an innovation like the prompt letter." *Id. See also* Cass R. Sunstein, *The Office of Information and Regulatory Affairs: Myths and Realities*, 126 HARV. L. REV. 1838, 1849 (2013) (noting that the "prompt letter" has been replaced by less formal means of contact between OIRA and the agencies).

123 Exec. Order No. 13,422, 72 Fed. Reg. 2763 (Jan. 18, 2007) (revoked by Exec. Order No. 13,497, 74 Fed. Reg. 6113 (Jan. 30, 2009)). For a powerful critique of Exec. Order No. 12,866, see *Amending Executive Order 12,866: Good Governance or Regulatory Usurpation? Part I and Part II: Hearing Before the House Comm. On Science and Technology*, 110 Cong. 23 (2007) (statement of David C. Vladek, Director, Institute for Public Representation).

124 Specifically, we refer to the clause requiring agencies to "identify in writing the specific market failure . . . it intends to address," and specifying that "agency head[s] shall designate one of the agency's Presidential Appointees to be its Regulatory Policy Officer," and "no rulemaking shall commence nor be included on the Plan without the approval of the agency's Regulatory Policy Office." Exec. Order No. 13,422 §§ 1(a)(1), 4(b), 5(b), 3 C.F.R. 191, 191–93 (2008) (revoked by Exec. Order No. 13,497, 74 Fed. Reg. 6113 (Jan. 30, 2009)).

125 Exec. Order No. 13,422, 3 C.F.R. 191, 193 § 5(b).

126 *Id.* at 3 C.F.R. 191, 192 § 4(b).

127 *Id.* at 193 C.F.R. 191, 193 § 7.

128 *See* Exec. Order No. 13,497, 3 C.F.R. 218 (2010) (revoking Exec. Orders Nos. 13,258 and 13,422).

129 Exec. Order No. 13,579, 76 Fed. Reg. 41,587 (July 11, 2011). In a Wall Street Journal op-ed, President Obama announced that he was ordering "a government-wide review of the rules already on the books to remove outdated regulations that stifle job creation and make our economy less competitive." President Obama, *Toward a 21st-Century Regulatory System*, WALL ST. J., Jan. 18, 2011, at A17. According to President

changed the substance of the Clinton requirements, adding the need to account for values that are difficult or impossible to quantify, including "equity, human dignity, fairness, and distributive impacts."[130] The Clinton order, in contrast, spoke only of the need to consider "distributive impacts" and "equity."[131]

2. THE APPLICATION OF CENTRALIZED REGULATORY REVIEW AUTHORITY TO THE INDEPENDENT AGENCIES

While the growth of centralized OIRA review has had a significant impact on the executive branch agencies, the impact on the independent regulatory agencies has been measured at best. No matter how robust its rhetoric, the executive branch has been generally loath to require independent agencies to follow OIRA oversight procedures.[132] The Kennedy administration did sweep independent agencies within its ethics standards.[133] Mostly, however, the executive branch either has claimed constitutional infirmity—that regulatory oversight would interfere with an agency's independence[134]—or that it has the power but has chosen not to use it, presumably for political reasons.[135]

Obama, his administration was "seeking more affordable, less intrusive means to achieve the same ends—giving careful consideration to benefits and costs." *Id.*

130 Exec. Order No. 13,563, 76 Fed. Reg. 3821 (Jan. 21, 2011).

131 Exec. Order No. 12,866, 3 C.F.R. § 638 (1993), *reprinted in* 5 U.S.C. § 601 (2006).

132 *See Regulatory Accountability Act of 2011: Hearing on H.R. 3010 Before the H. Comm. on the Judiciary*, 112th Cong. 40 (statement of C. Boyden Gray) (advising the House to pass legislation requiring independent agencies to submit to regulatory oversight).

133 Exec. Order No. 10,939, *To Provide a Guide on Ethical Standards to Government Officials*, May 5, 1961. *See* Christopher S. Yoo et al., *The Unitary Executive in the Modern Era*, 1945–2004, 90 Iowa L. Rev. 601, 643–45 (2005).

134 For further discussion, see *infra* notes 137–63 and accompanying text.

135 *Id.; see generally APA at 65: Is Reform Needed to Create Jobs, Promote Economic Growth, and Reduce Costs?: Hearing before the Subcomm. on Courts, Commercial and Administrative Law of the H. Comm. on the Judiciary*, 112th Cong. 41–42 (2011) (testimony of Peter Strauss, Betts Professor of Law, Columbia Law School) (noting "[S]houldn't Congress also bring the independent regulatory commissions under these mandates? Presidents haven't done that, as I understand it, only because they fear the political costs to their relationship with you, with the Congress. Given the extraordinary range of rulemaking Dodd-Frank requires of independent commissions, Congress ought to welcome this change"). *Compare* Rena Steinzor, *The Independent Agency Regulatory Analysis Act, as Critiqued by Co-Sponsor Susan Collins and Me*, CPR Blog (Nov. 1, 2012), http://www.progressivereform.org/CPRBlog.cfm?idBlog=E42958C4-B61A-8FDA-62ACBF689F7D0313 (arguing that Congress created independent agencies to resist "presidential political meddling" and that subjecting these agencies to executive orders would undercut this purpose); Letter from former OIRA administrators to Senator Lieberman, Chairman, S. Comm. on Homeland Security & Governmental Affairs (Sept. 13, 2012), *available at* http://www.portman.senate.gov/public/index.cfm/files/serve?File_id=563c60e4-3770-4329-b1aa-ff51752cd750 (asserting that independent agencies should be held to the same "good government" standards as their executive counterparts, without compromising independence by permitting judicial review of independent agencies' compliance with OIRA processes). This position parallels a recommendation of the Administrative Conference of the United States. *See* Admin. Conference of the United States, *Recommendation 88-9: Presidential Review of Agency Rulemaking* (1988), http://www.acus.gov/sites/default/files/documents/88-9.pdf.

The Carter administration was the first to address these questions in the context of regulatory review, noting that regulatory review can

> be extended by the President to the independent regulatory agencies. The purpose of the proposals is to improve procedure, set up work schedules and plans for the more efficient discharge of the agencies' duties, and improve the proficiency of personnel by appropriate training programs directed to the drafting of regulations. In the light of the President's overall fiscal responsibilities it also appears appropriate for him to require that the agencies take into account the economic impact of their decisions.[136]

Notwithstanding this conclusion, the Carter administration's contribution to regulatory reform, Executive Order 12,044,[137] did not cover independent agencies. Many commentators, including the American Bar Association, criticized this presidential "minimalism."[138]

---

136 Memorandum from John M. Harmon, Assistant Attorney General, Office of Legal Counsel, to Simon Lazarus, Associate Director, Domestic Council, *President's Authority to Impose Procedural Reforms on the Independent Regulatory Agencies* (July 22, 1977), *available at* Center for Regulatory Effectiveness, http://www.thecre.com/pdf/Carter_DOJOpinion072277.pdf. For more discussion, see Memorandum from Simon Lazarus to Wayne Granquist, *Applicability of Executive Order to Implement Agencies* (Dec. 9, 1977), stating:

> "[T]he President would appear to be empowered to issue an order applicable to such agencies, first by virtue of his constitutional responsibility to "take care that the Laws be faithfully executed." Art. III, section 3. Even though the agencies may be independent, their failure to perform their duties under law is said to be a legitimate part of the President's concern. *See Landis, Report on Regulatory Agencies to the President-Elect 32–33 (1960);* Redford, *The President and the Regulatory Commissions*, 44 TEX. L. REV. 238, 307–08 (1965); CARY, POLITICS AND THE REGULATORY AGENCIES 18–23 (1967).

While the White House memorandum cited two prior executive orders that extended application to independent agencies, they were orders regarding standards of conduct of government employees generally. *See also* Richard J. Pierce, Jr., *Saving the Unitary Executive Theory from Those Who Would Distort and Abuse It: A Review of* The Unitary Executive *by Steven G. Calabresi and Christopher S. Yoo*, 12 U. PA. J. CONST. L. 593, 607 (2010).

137 Exec. Order No. 12,044, 43 Fed. Reg. 12,661 (Mar. 23, 1978). *See* Paul R. Verkuil, *Jawboning Administrative Agencies: Ex Parte Contacts by the White House*, 80 COLUM. L. REV. 943, 947–49 (1980) (describing President Carter's attempts to improve agency coordination and accountability). OMB director, Jim McIntyre, noted at the time: "The Department of Justice is of the opinion that the President has the constitutional and statutory authority to require independent agencies to comply with the procedural reforms in this Executive Order. That view is strongly contested by all but one of the independent agencies that commented (the Nuclear Regulatory Commission made no objection), and by many Senators and Congressmen." Memorandum for the President from James McIntyre, March 1978, *available at* Center for Regulatory Effectiveness, http://www.thecre.com/pdf/Carter_OMBMemoMarch1978.PDF.

138 AM. BAR ASS'N, COMM'N ON LAW AND THE ECON., FEDERAL REGULATION: ROADS TO REFORM 85 (1979) ("The final [Carter] order... leaves the 'independent' agencies untouched because many of them objected on legal and policy grounds. A majority of the commission regrets this omission."). However, Victor Rosenblum contemporaneously noted that

> You may recall that, in the early draft of that Executive Order [12,044] the independent regulatory commissions were included. But when objections were raised to the language of that draft as posing

However, this was not the case for the Paperwork Reduction Act, which contained an unusual provision dealing with independent regulatory agencies.[139] While independent agencies are required to submit information collection requests for OIRA approval, an independent agency may override the OMB's veto by a majority vote of its members.[140] When an information collection requirement is contained in a proposed rulemaking and the OMB director disapproves that requirement, the same independent agency override applies.[141] This override power has rarely been exercised.[142]

The pattern was set. In one way or another, later presidents suggested with greater or lesser certainty that they had the power to regulate independent agencies, but did not do so for "political" reasons, choosing instead to draft various memoranda to the independent agencies urging them (with greater or lesser fervor) to comply voluntarily.

Thus we can consider the various presidents since Carter. In a February 12, 1981, OLC draft memorandum on independent regulatory agencies, written in the run-up to Executive Order 12,291, the Reagan administration DOJ offered an argument that regulatory review should be extended to independent agencies. Specifically, the draft memorandum stated:

> We believe that the foregoing constitutional and statutory analysis supports the application to the independent agencies of those portions of the Order that would be extended to them. The principal requirement is that independent agencies prepare RIA's [regulatory impact analyses]. These analyses would have only an indirect effect on substantive discretion, since the identification of costs and benefits and the particular balance struck would be for the agency to make. It should also

---

> some severe constitutional problems, the text of the draft was changed and the final draft did not apply Executive Order 12,044 as a matter of law to the independent regulatory commissions.

Victor Rosenblum in Lloyd N. Cutler, Moderator, *Managing the Regulatory Process*, 32 ADMIN L. REV. 239, 261 (1980).

139 *See* discussion in CURTIS W. COPELAND, ECONOMIC ANALYSIS AND INDEPENDENT REGULATORY AGENCIES 34–36 (Apr. 30, 2013), *available at* http://www.acus.gov/sites/default/files/documents/Copeland%20Final%20BCA%20Report%204-30-13.pdf.

140 44 U.S.C. § 3507(c)(1982). *See also* 44 U.S.C. § 3507(f)(1) ("An independent regulatory agency which is administered by 2 or more members of a commission, board, or similar body, may by majority vote void ... an exercise of authority under subsection (d) of section 3507 concerning that agency [regarding information collections that are part of a proposed rule]").

141 *See* 44 U.S.C. § 3507(f)(1)(B).

142 We know of only four instances of independent agencies overruling the OMB. The Civil Aeronautics Board, the NCUA, and the FCC overrides are discussed in William F. Funk, *The Paperwork Reduction Act: Paperwork Reduction Meets Administrative Law*, 24 HARV. J. ON LEGIS. 1, 34–35 n.201 (1987). The fourth, a 1992 NRC override, is described in Quality Management Program and Misadministration: NRC Override of OMB Disapproval of NRC Information Collection Request, 57 Fed. Reg. 41376 (Sept. 10, 1992). Donald Arbuckle, former deputy director of OIRA, has noted, "I do not recall any OIRA disapproval or independent agency override during my tenure as Deputy from 1996 to 2006." Email from Donald Arbuckle to Marshall Breger (May 18, 2014). There does not appear to be any OIRA listing or collection of such overrides.

> be possible for OMB to prescribe criteria for independent agencies to follow in preparing their RIA's, to consult with them in the process, and to disagree with an independent agency's analysis on the administrative record. None of these actions would directly displace the agencies' ultimate discretion to decide what rule best fulfills their statutory responsibilities.[143]

The draft memo continued:

> If the dicta of *Humphrey's Executor* are taken at face value, the President's constitutional power to supervise the independent agencies is limited to his power of appointment, and none of the proposed Order's requirements may legally be applied to independent agencies. We believe, however, that there are several reasons to conclude that the Supreme Court would today retreat from these dicta.[144]

While this February 12 memorandum was signed, it was never released. The Executive Order that was released the following day, Executive Order 12,291, tracked the February 12 memo except that it deleted the section pertaining to independent agencies.[145] Some say the language on independent agencies was removed because the DOJ did not want to overload the OMB.[146] Others, such as Sally Katzen, suggest that the legal advisors to the drafters concluded that the president had authority to review independent agency rulemakings but that the decision not to do so was "essentially for political reasons—namely, deference to Congress, which traditionally views the IRCs [independent regulatory commissions] as 'its agencies, not the President's.'"[147] Some have further argued that the expansive language was not used for fear "that Congress would seek to countermand such a reach."[148] Instead, Executive Order 12,291 *recommended*

---

[143] Memorandum from Larry L. Simms, Acting Ass't Atty. Gen., Office of Legal Counsel to the Hon. David Stockman, Dir., Office of Mgmt. & Budget 7 (Feb. 12, 1981), *reprinted in Role of OMB in Regulation: Hearing Before the Subcomm. on Oversight and Investigations of the H. Comm. on Energy and Commerce*, 97th Cong. 152 (1981) [hereinafter Feb. 12 Memo]. We are grateful to Curtis Copeland of the Library of Congress for this reference. A "bootleg" version of the Feb. 12 memo was published in the *Legal Times* of July 27, 1981, at 24.

[144] Feb. 12 Memo, *supra* note 143, at 24.

[145] *See generally* Exec. Order No. 12,291, 46 Fed. Reg. 13,193 (1981).

[146] *See* Kim Masters, *Legal Support for Strategy on "Independents" Revealed*, LEGAL TIMES, July 20, 1981, at 1. The draft memorandum was dated Feb. 12, 1981, the final redacted opinion was signed by Larry Simms on Feb. 13, and the actual Executive Order was issued on Feb. 17. *Id.* at 9.

[147] Sally Katzen, *OIRA at Thirty: Reflections and Recommendations*, 63 ADMIN. L. REV. 103, 109 (2011).

[148] Bressman & Thompson, *supra* note 111, at 620. A close reading of the February 12 memo suggests that its conclusion is less definitive than some have suggested. For instance, the memo notes, "it is clear that the president's exercise of supervisory powers must conform to the legislation enacted by Congress." It further states that "[in] issuing directives to govern the Executive Branch, the President may not . . . require or permit agencies to transgress boundaries set by Congress." *See* Feb. 12 Memo, *supra* note 143, at 154.

that independent agencies voluntarily adopt the requirements that applied to executive branch agencies.[149]

Vice President Bush followed up with a letter dated March 25, requesting voluntary compliance.[150] But not many independent agencies complied. For example, the FTC split four-to-four on a vote over whether it could legally comply with all of the Executive Order and thus it refrained from doing so.[151] In an accompanying statement, Commissioner Michael Pertschuk articulated that:

> Presidential oversight of FTC rulemaking is neither contemplated by nor consistent with the system for Congressional review of Commission rules. Indeed, if OMB were given special access to the Commission's final notices of rulemaking and final regulatory analyses prior to their publication, it would have an opportunity for advance review that Congress did not even confer upon itself. For these reasons, I would consider any initiative by the Commission, without authorization from Congress, to provide preferential status to the executive branch in our rulemakings to be a violation of the principle of independence reaffirmed by Congress in the FTC Improvements Act.[152]

In a report to Congress, the OMB reported that seven agencies "agreed to abide by the spirit and principles of the Executive Order."[153]

By the time of the George H. W. Bush administration, when James Blumstein was nominated to be OIRA administrator, it was clear that in Blumstein's view (presumably tracking administration policy), the president did not have the power to extend OIRA review to independent agencies:

> I think there is a bright-line distinction that I would draw regarding congressional delegation of authority to an agency. In the context of an "independent regulatory body such as the... Federal Communications Commission, the president" (through OIRA) cannot hold up an agency action because of a disagreement "on policy grounds," [and the] "Executive Orders do not purport to establish a regulatory review process that controls those independent regulatory agencies."

Jim Blumstein, *Regulatory Review by the Executive Office of the President: An Overview and Policy Analysis of Current Issues*, 51 DUKE L.J. 851, 876 (2001).

149 *See* Exec. Order No. 12,291 § 6(b), 46 Fed. Reg. 13,193, 13,196 (1981).

150 "To the extent you can comply with the spirit of the order, this will help demonstrate to the American people the willingness of all components of the federal government to respond to their concerns about unnecessary intrusion of government into their daily lives." Specimen of Letter Sent to Independent Agencies, Executive Office of the President, Materials on President Reagan's Program of Regulatory Relief 94–95 (June 12, 1981). *See* Merrill Brown, *Agencies Reject Pleas for OMB Review*, WASH. POST, July 9, 1981, at D9.

151 *See* Letter of David A. Clanton, Chairman, Federal Trade Commission, to Vice President George Bush (June 25, 1981) (reprinted in *Role of OMB in Regulation: Hearing Before the Subcomm. on Oversight and Investigations of the H. Comm. on Energy and Commerce*, 97th Cong. 187–91 (1981)).

152 Separate Statement of Commissioner Michael Pertschuk (reprinted in *Role of OMB in Regulation: Hearing Before the Subcomm. on Oversight and Investigations of the H. Comm. on Energy and Commerce*, 97th Cong. (1981)). *See* Merrill Brown, *Agencies Reject Pleas for OMB Review*, WASH. POST, July 9, 1981, at D9.

153 EXECUTIVE OFFICE OF THE PRESIDENT, MATERIALS ON PRESIDENT REAGAN'S PROGRAM OF REGULATORY RELIEF 12 (June 12, 1981).

Thus when it comes to the provision of information about the regulatory agenda, Executive Order 12,498 extended the coordination of the regulatory planning process to the independent agencies. But when it came to the substance of regulations, OIRA did not require regulatory review of independent agency rules, although it did so when it came to regulatory coordination.

This pattern continued under the Clinton administration. While Sally Katzen, Clinton OIRA administrator, has argued that the Clinton administration had legal authority to bring independent agencies under its regulatory review process, she suggests it chose not to do so for political reasons.[154] Nonetheless, there was significant debate during the Clinton years about extending the OIRA process to independent agencies, a change favored by conservative think tanks like the Center for Regulatory Effectiveness,[155] as well as liberal thinkers like Cass Sunstein.[156]

During the George W. Bush administration, OMB director John Graham tried to entice the independent agencies to respond to the Bush administration's OIRA initiatives. In 2003, OIRA sent a prompt letter to six independent agencies regarding forty-nine rules and two guidance documents that were "nominated" by affected interests for modification or rescission; OIRA requested that the agencies "consider these public nominations and, for those they consider to be possible candidates for reform, place their evaluations

---

154 *See* Katzen, *supra* note 147. In April 2011, Katzen confirmed that

> President Reagan's advisers and President Clinton's advisers both declined to include IRCs [independent regulatory commissions] in their executive orders—not because they did not have the authority to do so, but rather for political reasons. In both cases, it was clear that the executive orders were taking a very big step—President Reagan in establishing decisional criteria based on economic analysis and for President Clinton in retaining a centralized review process that had been strongly criticized by Democrats in Congress and opposed by significant parts of his base. In both cases, it was enough to take these steps without further antagonizing those on the Hill who saw the "independence" of IRCs as insulating or protecting them from edicts of the president.

Sally Katzen, Remarks at Resources for the Future Conference, *Can Greater Use of Economic Analysis Improve Regulatory Policy at Independent Regulatory Commissions?* 3 (Apr. 7, 2011), *available at* www.rff.org/Documents/Events/Workshops%20and%20Conferences/110407_Regulation_KatzenRemarks.pdf.

Interestingly, in fulfilling its responsibilities under Executive Order 13,272, the Small Business Administration did attempt to secure reports from the independent agencies, with mixed results. Small Business Administration, AGENCY COMPLIANCE WITH EXECUTIVE ORDER 13272, A REPORT TO THE OFFICE OF MANAGEMENT AND BUDGET, September 2003, at 9–10. Still, when it comes to information-gathering standards—as with the Data Quality Act, 33 U.S.C. § 3516, which required the OMB to develop procedures by which federal agencies would improve the "quality, objectivity, utility, and integrity of information (including statistical information) disseminated by Federal agencies...," independent agencies had to respond to OMB guidelines and OIRA oversight. *OMB Guidelines for Ensuring and Maximizing the Quality, Objectivity, Utility, and Integrity of Information Disseminated by Federal Agencies* (OMB Data Quality Guidelines), 67 Fed. Reg. 369, 376 (Jan. 3, 2002).

155 *See* CENTER FOR REGULATORY EFFECTIVENESS, A BLUEPRINT FOR OMB REVIEW OF INDEPENDENT REGULATION (2002), *available at* http://www.thecre.com/pdf/blueprint.pdf.

156 *See* Hahn & Sunstein, *supra* note 115, at 1490–98.

on their websites."[157] Notwithstanding these requests for voluntary compliance with the president's regulatory review initiative, a series of OIRA "Annual Reports to Congress on the Costs and Benefits of Federal Regulations" indicates that such compliance was minimal. For instance, the 2005 Report indicates that the rules submitted by the four cooperating independent agencies provided "relatively little quantitative information on the benefits" of the rules, and that only one of four of the economically significant rules finalized by independent agencies reported monetized benefits.[158]

In an incisive review of Obama as a "presidentialist" president, Cary Coglianese pointed out that:

> On his very first day in office, President Obama issued a presidential memorandum on transparency and open government that proved distinctive in the way that it asserted authority over independent agencies. President Obama wrote that "[t]he independent agencies should comply with the Open Government Directive," using the same verb—"should"—that the memo used for executive branch agencies.[159]

---

157 Memorandum from John D. Graham to Heads of Selected Independent Agencies, *Independent Agency Response to Public Regulatory Reform Nominations* (Jan. 22, 2003). *See* Percival, *supra* note 111, at 2514–15.

158 OFFICE OF MGMT. & BUDGET, OFFICE OF INFO. & REGULATORY AFFAIRS, VALIDATING REGULATORY ANALYSIS: 2005 REPORT TO CONGRESS ON THE COSTS AND BENEFITS OF FEDERAL REGULATIONS AND UNFUNDED MANDATES ON STATE, LOCAL, AND TRIBAL ENTITIES 18 (2005), *available at* http://www.whitehouse.gov/sites/default/files/omb/inforeg/2005_cb/final_2005_cb_report.pdf. Similar results were reported in the 2006, 2007, 2008, 2009, 2010, and 2011 Reports. 2006 Report at 12–13; 2007 Report at 13–15; 2008 Report at 17–18; 2009 Report at 22–24; 2010 Report at 27–29; 2011 Report at 30–32. These OMB Reports are available at http://www.whitehouse.gov/omb/inforeg_regpol_reports_congress/. *See also* COPELAND, *supra* note 139, at 115 (recommending that the agencies voluntarily adopt the economic principles set out in OMB Circular A-4, including "(1) a statement of need for the regulatory action, including a description of the problem that the agency seeks to address, any statutory or judicial directives, and the extent of agency discretion permitted; (2) an examination of plausible alternative regulatory approaches (e.g., no regulation, State or local regulation, differing levels of stringency, informational measures, and the use of performance objectives instead of detailed regulatory directives); and (3) an estimate of the benefits and costs—both quantitative and qualitative—of the proposed regulatory action and its main alternatives").

159 Cary Coglianese, *Presidential Control of Administrative Agencies: A Debate over Law or Politics?*, 12 U. PA. J. CONST. L. 637, 639 (2010); *see* Memorandum on Transparency and Open Government, 74 Fed. Reg. 4685 (Jan. 21, 2009). "Presidentialism" is defined as the attempted assertion of presidential power over the policy of executive agencies. Coglianese, *supra*, at 637–38. While one can make too much of this, President George W. Bush, in contrast, only "requested" independent agencies to comply with his governmental reform memorandum, and President Clinton merely "asked," "encouraged," and "requested" independent agencies to comply with his directives. For George W. Bush, see Memorandum on Implementing Government Reform, 37 WEEKLY COMP. PRES. DOC. 1028 (July 11, 2001) ("Independent agencies are requested to comply with this memorandum."). For Clinton, see Exec. Order No. 13,132, 64 Fed. Reg. 43,255 (Aug. 4, 1999) ("Independent regulatory agencies are encouraged to comply with the provisions of this order."); Executive Memorandum on Plain Language in Government Writing, 63 Fed. Reg. 31,885 (June 1, 1998) ("I ask the independent agencies to comply with these directives."); Memorandum on Implementing Management Reform in the Executive Branch, 58 Fed. Reg. 52,393 (Oct. 1, 1993) ("Independent agencies are requested to adhere to this directive."). I am indebted to Cary Coglianese for this insight.

Then, in an apparent retreat, Obama in his January 22, 2011, Executive Order noted above specifically chose not to explicitly extend the Executive Order's reach beyond the Clinton parameters.[160] Still, in a less formal guidance memorandum dated February 2, 2011,[161] Cass Sunstein, the administrator of OIRA, pointed out that:

> Executive Order 13563 does not apply to independent agencies, but such agencies are encouraged to give consideration to all of its provisions, consistent with their legal authority. In particular, such agencies are *encouraged* to consider undertaking, on a voluntary basis, retrospective analysis of existing rules.[162]

Numerous congressional hearings were conducted in the months following the promulgation of Executive Order 13,563 to assess the success of this OMB "request." When it became apparent that independent agencies, including the Consumer Product Safety Commission, FCC, and FERC, did not adhere to the recommendation, they were summoned to Congress to explain their lack of compliance. After a request from Republicans on the House Energy and Commerce Committee, the FCC agreed to conduct its own "independent" retrospective review.[163]

Soon it became clear that independent agencies were neither voluntarily conducting retrospective review nor undertaking serious cost-benefit analysis on their own.[164] In fact, the OMB reports indicate that the level of voluntary compliance under the Obama administration was similar to that under the George W. Bush administration. Thus in 2012, the OMB found that in FY 2011, "[t]he independent regulatory agencies, whose regulations are not subject to OMB review under EO 12,866, issued 17 major final rules."[165] Of these seventeen rules, eleven offered at least some rudimentary form of cost-benefit analysis.[166] Only three of these rules considered monetized costs, and none

---

160 Exec. Order No. 13,563, 76 Fed. Reg. 3821 (Jan. 18, 2011). Specifically Exec. Order No. 13,563 adopted the definition of agency used in Exec. Order No. 12,291, which excluded independent agencies. *See* Exec. Order No. 13,563 at § 1(b).

161 Cass Sunstein, Memorandum for the Heads of Executive Departments and Agencies and of Independent Regulatory Agencies (Feb. 2, 2011).

162 *Id.* at 6 (emphasis added).

163 Exec. Order No. 13,563, Improving Regulation and Regulatory Review, 76 Fed. Reg. 3821 (2011).

164 *See The Views of the Administration on Regulatory Reform: An Update: Hearing Before the Subcomm. on Oversight and Investigations of the H. Comm. on Energy and Commerce*, 112th Cong. 12–50 (June 3, 2011) (testimony of Cass R. Sunstein, OIRA administrator, OMB). In an exchange with Rep. Steve Scalise (R-Louisiana), Sunstein conceded that only one independent agency—the NLRB—had responded to the OMB "request" following the promulgation of Exec. Order No. 13,563. *Id.* at 19–21.

165 Office of Mgmt. & Budget, 2012 Report to Congress on the Benefits and Costs of Federal Regulations and Unfunded Mandates on State, Local, and Tribal Entities 4 (2012), *available at* http://www.whitehouse.gov/sites/default/files/omb/inforeg/2012_cb/2012_cost_benefit_report.pdf.

166 *Id.* at Table 1-8, 35–37.

considered monetized benefits.[167] In its draft 2013 report on the benefits and costs of federal regulations in FY 2012, the OMB noted that the independent agencies not subject to OIRA review issued twenty-one major final rules in the fiscal year.. (Ten were promulgated by the Commodity Futures Trading Commission alone, and the majority were promulgated jointly with the SEC.)[168] Of the twenty-one rules, sixteen provided some information on the benefits and costs,[169] but only six monetized costs, and none monetized benefits.[170] Not surprisingly, the OMB argues that "it would be highly desirable to obtain better information on the benefits and costs of the rules issued by independent regulatory agencies. The absence of such information is a continued obstacle to transparency, and it might also have adverse effects on public policy."[171]

Empirical surveys, albeit "quick and limited," suggest that "the analysis conducted by the IRC's [independent regulatory commissions] [are] generally the minimum required by statute."[172] Indeed, one commentator has suggested (with a straight face) that future empirical studies of the use of cost-benefit analysis by federal agencies could "use the independent regulatory agencies as a control group, given that they are not subject to the formal presidential review process."[173] Thus, it was no surprise that in a follow-up to his 2011 Executive Order, President Obama stated that regulatory decisions by independent regulatory commissions "should be made only after consideration of their costs and benefits (both quantitative and qualitative),"[174] suggesting, by implication, "that the economic analyses prepared by independent regulatory commissions do not measure up to those of the executive branch agencies."[175]

In sum, when it comes to peripheral areas of control such as information requests and data quality, the executive is far more prepared to exercise authority over independent agencies. But whether for reasons legal or political, it is not yet ready to do so regarding substantive decisions.

We should further note that some cross-cutting reporting statutes do, in fact, impact on independent agencies. We have already noted the Paperwork Reduction Act (PRA), under which independent agencies are required to secure OIRA approval for

---

167 *Id.*

168 Office of Mgmt. & Budget, 2013 Draft Report to Congress on the Benefits and Costs of Federal Regulations and Unfunded Mandates on State, Local, and Tribal Entities 30 (2013), *available at* http://www.whitehouse.gov/sites/default/files/omb/inforeg/2013_cb/draft_2013_cost_benefit_report.pdf.

169 *Id.*

170 OMB reports are discussed in Copeland, *supra* note 139, at 61–86. There was a significant change from the 2012 OMB Report discussed therein.

171 Office of Mgmt. & Budget, *supra* note 168, at 30.

172 Arthur Fraas & Randall Lutter, *On the Economic Analysis of Regulations at Independent Regulatory Commissions*, 63 Admin. L. Rev. (Special Ed.) 213, 216 (2011).

173 Jennifer Nou, *Agency Self-Insulation Under Presidential Review*, 126 Harv. L. Rev. 1755, 1804 (2013).

174 Exec. Order No. 13,579, 76 Fed. Reg. 41587 (July 14, 2011).

175 Fraas & Lutter, *supra* note 172, at 236.

paperwork requests subject to an agency override.[176] Other cross-cutting statutes that are seemingly applicable to independence agencies include the Regulatory Flexibility Act (RFA), the National Environmental Policy Act (NEPA), the Congressional Review Act (CRA), and the Unfunded Mandates Reform Act.[177] But, as Copeland points out, their impact on independent agencies is not significant.[178] We note as well that numerous agency-specific statutes either explicitly or by judicial construction require specific independent agencies to undertake some version of accounting for costs and benefits.[179] For example, the Consumer Product Safety Commission is required by statute to engage in formal regulatory analysis and provide a statement explaining the projected costs and benefits before promulgating a rule.[180] Likewise, the D.C. Circuit required the SEC to engage in some form of cost-benefit analysis in *Business Roundtable v. SEC*.[181]

In an accompanying memorandum dated July 22, 2011,[182] Cass Sunstein reiterated that independent regulatory agencies should follow 13,579 and provides a template for independent agencies to use in preparing retrospective analysis of their rules.[183] That follow-up memo specifically "asks" each independent regulatory agency to "produce plans for retrospective analysis of existing rules so as to determine whether any such

---

176 *See supra* note 101 and accompanying text.

177 *See* Copeland, *supra* note 139, at 31–36. Copeland notes, "[m]ost independent regulatory agencies, however, are not explicitly required to prepare cost-benefit analyses before issuing their rules." *Id.* at 31. For more recent examples, see Independent Agency Regulatory Analysis Act of 2013, S. 1173, 113th Cong. (2013) and Independent Agency Regulatory Analysis Act of 2012, S. 3468, 112th Cong. (2012).

178 *See* Copeland, *supra* note 139, at 37.

179 See discussion in Copeland, *supra* note 139, at 38–55. Some agency-specific statutes include 15 U.S.C. § 2058(f)(2), which requires the Consumer Product Safety Commission to engage in certain costs analysis before issuing new rules, the Energy Policy and Conservation Act (42 U.S.C. § 6295(o)), which requires that the DOE assess the benefits of energy efficiency regulations, and Section 1102(b) of the Social Security Act (42 U.S.C. § 1302(b)), which "requires the Department of Health and Human Services to prepare an initial regulatory impact analysis if a proposed rule issued under certain statutory authorities may have a significant impact on the operations of a substantial number of small rural hospitals." Copeland, *supra* note 139, at 28–29. The newly created CFPB is subject to "standards of rulemaking" under Section 1022(b)(2)(A) of the Dodd-Frank Act. *See* 12 U.S.C. § 5512; *see generally* Copeland, *supra* note 139, at 48–49. In addition, Copeland notes that several agencies are not even covered by these less stringent requirements. *See* Copeland, *supra* note 139, at 55.

180 15 U.S.C. § 2058(f).

181 Bus. Roundtable v. SEC, 647 F.3d 1144, 1152 (D.C. Cir. 2011) ("By ducking serious evaluation of the costs that could be imposed upon companies from use of the rule by shareholders representing special interests, particularly union and government pension funds, we think the Commission acted arbitrarily."). *See* the discussion in Jill E. Fisch, *The Long Road Back: Business Roundtable and the Future of SEC Rulemaking*, 36 Seattle U. L. Rev. 695 (2013).

182 Memorandum from Cass Sunstein, Administrator, Office of Info. & Regulatory Affairs to the Heads of the Independent Regulatory Agencies, *Executive Order 13579, "Regulation and Independent Regulatory Agencies"* (Jul. 22, 2011), *available at* http://www.whitehouse.gov/sites/default/files/omb/memoranda/2011/m11-28.pdf.

183 *Id.*

regulations should be modified, streamlined, expanded, or repealed" to either increase the effectiveness or decrease the burdens necessary for achieving the agencies regulatory goals.[184] The Sunstein memo then takes "one step back" so to speak, pointing out that "it is understood that this guidance is issued with full respect for the independence of the agencies to which it is addressed, and hence nothing said here is meant to be binding." The dispute over the reach of the executive branch into the independent agencies continues undiminished. In August 2012, Senators Rob Portman (R-Ohio), Mark Warner (D-Virginia), and Susan Collins (R-Maine) introduced the Independent Agency Regulatory Analysis Act of 2012, which would affirm the president's power to issue an Executive Order requiring independent agencies to submit cost-benefit analyses to OIRA for regulatory review.[185]

The legislation would set up an innovative approach to hold agencies accountable, by means of transparency and public scrutiny. The SEC and other independent agencies would submit significant proposed and final rules, along with supporting analysis, for review by OIRA.[186] Although OIRA would not have the power to reject a rule, it would evaluate the quality of the agencies' cost-benefit analysis and place its assessment in the public record.[187] If OIRA found that an agency failed to comply with the new requirements, the agency would be obligated to respond to OIRA's assessment and justify its position and underlying analysis. Judicial review of the agency's compliance would not

---

[184] *Id.; see also Enhanced Oversight after the Financial Crisis: The Wall Street Reform Act at One Year: Hearing Before the S. Comm. on Banking, Housing, and Urban Affairs*, 112th Cong. 11 (2011) (statement of Neal S. Wolin, Deputy Secretary, U.S. Dep't of the Treasury).

[185] Independent Agency Regulatory Analysis Act of 2012, S. 3468, 112th Cong. (2012). Although the Senate Committee on Homeland Security and Governmental Affairs was planning a vote on the bill in November 2012, committee chair Joseph Lieberman delayed the vote. *See* Mark Gongloff, *Senate Delays Vote on Bill That Would Banish Financial Regulation to Cost-Benefit Analysis Hell*, HUFFINGTON POST, Nov. 14, 2012, http://www.huffingtonpost.com/2012/11/14/senate-bill-financial-regulation-cost-benefit-analysis_n_2123460.htm; Theresa Tritch, *Making Independent Agencies Less Independent*, N.Y. TIMES TAKING NOTE (Nov. 6, 2012, 5:44 p.m.), http://takingnote.blogs.nytimes.com/2012/11/06/making-independent-agencies-less-independent/; Barbara S. Mishkin, *Agency Review Bill Opposed by CFPB, Federal Banking Regulators and Consumer Groups*, CFPB MONITOR (Nov. 1, 2012), http://www.cfpbmonitor.com/2012/11/01/agency-review-bill-opposed-by-cfpb-federal-banking-regulators-and-consumer-groups/. Similarly, the Republican-supported Clearing Unnecessary Regulatory Burdens Act called for including independent agencies in the regulatory review requirements of the Act. This Act adopts the definition of agency used in 44 U.S.C. § 3502(1) (2006), which includes independent agencies as well as regulatory agencies. The Act, which was introduced on March 16, 2011, has not seen further action. *See* Clearing Unnecessary Regulatory Burdens Act, S. 602, 112th Cong. (2011).

[186] The bill authorizes the president, by Executive Order, to require independent agencies to submit an analysis of the costs and benefits of "economically significant rules," list feasible alternatives, and explain "why the planned regulatory action is preferable...." Independent Agency Regulatory Analysis Act of 2012, S. 3468, 113th Cong. § 3(b) (2012).

[187] The bill would authorize the administrator of OIRA to "submit for inclusion in the rulemaking record" a nonbinding assessment of the independent agency's cost-benefit analysis. *Id.* § 3(c).

be permitted, but the exchange between OIRA and the agency would be included in the rulemaking's administrative record.[188]

The six financial services independent agencies have publicly opposed the bill, writing that it "would give any President unprecedented authority to influence the policy and rulemaking functions of independent regulatory agencies and would constitute a fundamental change in the role of independent regulatory agencies."[189]

For their part, a bipartisan group of OIRA administrators wrote to assert that "this bipartisan bill would improve the quality of rulemaking by independent regulatory agencies by affirming the president's authority to extend to independent agencies the same principles of regulation that have long governed executive agencies."[190]

E. Selection of Agency Vice Chairs

When the ICC was created as the first of the modern independent multimember agencies, Congress allowed it to choose its own chair. Over the years, in a series of reorganization plans and statutory adjustments, the power to select an agency's chair has, by and large, passed to the president. Nonetheless, at a handful of multimember agencies, the statute allows the agency members themselves to select a vice chair who serves essentially in the role of chair in the absence of a presidentially appointed chair.[191] In the absence of a chair, the vice chair, although not chosen for that post by the president, can exercise considerable day-to-day authority over the operation of the agency, at least for a limited period until the president appoints a new chair. Practical constraints nonetheless exist. A vice chair still requires agency approval for major policy initiatives, and an individual seeking reappointment as an agency member may operate in a manner that does not unnecessarily upset the incumbent administration.

Whether an agency has inherent authority to select an "acting chair" in the absence of a presidentially appointed chair is not entirely clear. The OLC has consistently held that

---

188 The agency may choose not to comply, but must submit an explanation of its decision in the rulemaking record. *Id.* Moreover, "[t]he compliance or noncompliance of an independent regulatory agency with the requirements of an Executive order issued under this Act shall not be subject to judicial review." *Id.* § 4(a).

189 *Top Regulators Warn on Expanding President's Powers*, REUTERS, Oct. 28, 2012, http://www.reuters.com/article/2012/10/28/us-financial-regulation-senate-idUSBRE89R0BZ20121028.

190 Press Release, Sen. Rob Portman, Clinton, Reagan, Bush Administration Regulatory Chiefs Endorse Portman-Warner Reform Bill (Sept. 14, 2012), *available at* http://portman.senate.gov/public/index.cfm/press-releases?ID=e7963af9-94c4-48cd-9178-ad5a00242cc2. A copy of the letter by the seven former OIRA administrators across three presidential administrations was included in the press release, and is also available at: http://portman.senate.gov/public/index.cfm/files/serve?File_id=563c60e4-3770-4329-b1aa-ff51752cd750.

191 *See, e.g.*, 15 U.S.C. § 2053(d) (Consumer Product Safety Commission); 39 U.S.C. § 502(e) (Postal Regulatory Commission).

statutory silence prevents an agency from explicitly designating an individual as "acting chairperson" when the chair's position is vacant.[192]

F. Observations

As discussed in chapters 2 and 5, the core of "independence" is often seen as insulation from summary presidential removal, either through statutory protection or accepted customary practice. However, as Kenneth Culp Davis and Richard Pierce indicate, it may involve something more. Agencies may be considered "independent" if they are "insulated from presidential control in one or more ways."[193] This key notion of "tenure-plus" has led some to suggest that independence means bipartisanship, nonpartisanship, deference to experts, or freedom from other elements of executive, and at times even congressional, control or influence.

Not all independent agencies possess these additional elements of independence to the same degree. As a consequence, not all independent agencies are equally independent. The recent contretemps over the CFPB has far less to do with the director's five-year term or statutory removal protection than it does with these other elements of independence. This bureau may bypass the president with regard to legislative recommendations, it has significant independent litigation authority—it may even represent itself in the Supreme Court if the attorney general declines to do so[194]—and it lacks multimember status that would otherwise give minority members of Congress some influence over appointment and encourage some element of decisional compromise. But perhaps most important, it has near-total financial autonomy from both the president and Congress.

The question of financial autonomy has become increasingly important in assessing agency independence. While funding was formerly a low visibility criterion, of late, it has become important to the "independence" analysis of commentators[195] and of Congress.[196] As scholars hone in on concrete and empirical issues of legislative control, the issue of funding is seen as increasingly important.

---

192 Authority of the Chemical Safety and Hazard Investigation Board to Delegate Power, 2002 OLC LEXIS 5 (Apr. 19, 2002).

193 1 Kenneth Culp Davis & Richard Pierce, Administrative Law Treatise § 2.5 (1994).

194 12 U.S.C. § 5564(e).

195 *See* John H. Cushman, Jr., *Senate Stops Consumer Nominee*, N.Y. Times, Dec. 9, 2011, at B1 (describing Senator McConnell's objection to the CFPB's single member head and self-funded structure); Robert G. Kaiser, *How a Crusade to Protect Consumers Lost Its Steam*, Wash. Post, Jan. 31, 2010, at G1 (noting that Senator Dodd "want[ed] consumer protection to have a dedicated source of funding to better insulate it from budget pressures").

196 *See generally supra* text accompanying notes 68–97. *See also* Letter from Mitch McConnell & Richard Shelby, U.S. Senators, to Barack Obama, President of the United States (May 2, 2011) (on file with author); *see also* Letter from Rob Portman, Senator, to Richard Cordray, Dir., Consumer Financial Protection Bureau (Feb. 1, 2013), *available at* http://www.portman.senate.gov/public/index.cfm/files/

A clearly controversial criterion of independence is the extent to which independent agencies are exempt from the various aspects of OMB review, particularly OIRA review. As discussed earlier in this chapter, the first efforts to centralize agency activity invoked strong criticism on constitutional grounds.[197] Today, however, the consensus of scholars supports some form of centralized OIRA review as acceptable, if not desirable.[198] Many urge the review be extended by Congress to independent agencies.[199] Still, in this age of hyperpartisanship one may wonder if there is some value in maintaining a modicum of autonomy for the independent agencies. This is particularly true in the case of rulemaking as agencies have a clear alternative of setting policy through adjudication.

In a unitary executive paradigm, the space for independence is limited. But, as a practical matter, independence from presidential and even congressional control continues to flourish.

serve?File_id=19ea1aeb-0d57-4cc9-8610-07a8f22fc4f2 (asking Cordray, who had recently been nominated as CFPB director, to remain committed to accountability reforms).

197 *See supra* section D, subsection 1.

198 *See supra* note 112. While the Administrative Conference has not recommended that agencies adopt centralized review, it has suggested that "[t]he Administrative Conference believes that it is in the interest of the independent regulatory agencies, the executive branch, Congress, the courts, and the public that independent regulatory agencies' current practices relating to the benefit-cost analysis be documented." Admin. Conference of the United States, *Recommendation 2013-2: Benefit-Cost Analysis at Independent Regulatory Agencies* 4 (Jun. 13, 2013), *available at* http://acus.gov/sites/default/files/documents/Recommendation%202013-2%20%28Benefit-Cost%20Analysis%29_0.pdf. Sally Katzen has also commented on the codification of cost-benefit analysis. *See The Office of Information and Regulatory Affairs: Federal Regulations and Regulatory Reform: Hearing Before the Subcomm. on Regulatory Reform, Commercial and Antitrust Law of the H. Comm. on the Judiciary*, 113th Cong. (Sept. 30, 2013) (statement of Amb. C. Boyden Gray, Boyden Gray & Associates, PLLC), *available at* http://judiciary.house.gov/index.cfm/2013/9/the-office-of-information-and-regulatory-affairs-federal-regulations-and-regulatory-reform. Although she originally disagreed with the practice, she later changed her mind after leaving OIRA. *Id.* (agreeing with Katzen that "extending cost-benefit analysis to independent agencies is 'a no-brainer'").

199 *See supra* text accompanying notes 185–90.

7

Institutional Design

THE TENSION BETWEEN AUTONOMY AND ACCOUNTABILITY

A. Introduction

Only recently have scholars begun to focus on the issue of institutional design. Generally, they have addressed the relationship of agency design to agency performance. For example, scholars have long argued that a multimember agency with staggered terms creates conditions of less partisanship and fewer policy swings than an agency chaired by a single head.[1] When the head is an "at will" officer of the president rather than an individual with a statutory term of office, the likelihood of policy swings as administrations change becomes even greater.[2] The argument has been that one can "hardwire" an institutional

[1] Rachel E. Barkow, *Insulating Agencies: Avoiding Capture Through Institutional Design*, 89 TEX. L. REV. 15, 19–21 (2010). *See also* Neal Devins & David E. Lewis, *Not-So Independent Agencies: Party Polarization and the Limits of Institutional Design*, 88 B.U. L. REV. 459, 463–65 (2008) ("long commissioner tenure, staggered terms, and political insulation are intended to facilitate a non-political environment where regulatory experts can apply their knowledge to complex policy problems"); Lisa Schultz Bressman & Robert B. Thompson, *The Future of Agency Independence*, 63 VAND. L. REV. 599, 613 (2010) (suggesting that Congress often commits issues to independent agencies, such as the Federal Reserve Board and the Financial Accounting Standards Board, to promote continuity); Janice A. Beecher, *The Prudent Regulator: Politics, Independence, Ethics, and the Public Interest*, 29 ENERGY L.J. 577, 581 (2008) ("Requirements for party diversity, staggered terms, and the more limited use of selection criteria, intend to mitigate partisan influence and policy swings, along with associated instability, inconsistency, and uncertainty").

[2] *See supra* note 1. The Progressives institutionalized the independent agency to promote expert, nonpartisan decision-making. *See* discussion in Barkow, *supra* note 1, at 19–21.

structure to make autonomy more or less likely by adopting a particular institutional design.[3]

However, as the examples laid out in this book make clear, when all is said and done the institutional design of individual agencies is not necessarily a controlling predictor of agency independence. One must also look at how multiple agencies interact, the relative powers of Congress and the executive branch, political culture, and, of course, the individual characteristics and idiosyncrasies of individual commissioners.[4]

This chapter will consider a number of agencies that attempted to shift from multi-member to single-member, some of which successfully did so and some which failed in the effort, including the NRC, FERC, SSA, and FHFA. The chapter will conclude with the strange and complex journey of the CFPB through its difficult "birth" process to still contested fate.

B. The Staying Power of Independent Regulatory Agencies

The independent agency has developed deep roots in the American administrative state. Agency evolution reflects a political calculation of a specific time and place drawn first from the nineteenth-century British and state experience in railroad regulation, followed by the Progressive movement's elevation of experts and "the science of administration," the crisis of the Great Depression and the response of the New Deal, and the growth of the "administrative state."[5]

The conventional view is that government agencies in the United States never die; that once established "[their] resources favour [their] own survival and the longer agencies survive, the more likely they are to continue to survive."[6] But this myth of agency immortality is not proven by historical experience. Herbert Kaufman found that of 421 agencies in existence between 1923 and 1947 only 27 were terminated by

---

3 Barkow, *supra* note 1, at 61. For example, Barkow suggests requiring appointees "to have policy making experience in the subject matter." *Id.*

4 *See, e.g.*, Keith Bradley, *The Design of Agency Interactions*, 111 COLUM. L. REV. 745 (2011). According to Bradley,

> The administrative state is an interlocking web of relationships between agencies, in which the influence that agencies have on each other may be as important as their direction by the executive and legislative branches.... Far from operating independently subject to political command, administrative agencies respond to checks and influences from their sibling agencies to such a degree that the most effective way for a President to steer the administrative state may often be to manipulate the system of checks.

Id. at 746–47. *See also* Neal Kaytal, *Internal Separation of Powers: Checking Today's Most Dangerous Branch from Within*, 115 YALE L.J. 2314, 2324–27 (2006) (arguing that agency overlap is a positive feature of the modern administrative state and is consistent with principle of Separation of Powers).

5 *See generally supra* chapter 2.

6 THEODORE J. LOWI, THE END OF LIBERALISM 309 (1979).

1973.[7] But David Lewis reports that more than half of the agencies created after 1946 were terminated by 1997.[8]

Independent agencies are no different. Some agencies were created to address temporary problems, and were eventually terminated because they completed their work. For example, the National Bituminous Coal Commission was established in 1935 as a temporary multimember agency within the Department of the Interior.[9] Cushman observes that there was no discussion in Congress of the commission's status within the Interior Department, although the interior secretary later testified that he in fact exercised no control over the National Bituminous Coal Commission's activities.[10] Key features of the commission's enabling statute were declared unconstitutional in 1936 in *Carter v. Carter Coal Co.*[11] Although the agency was later resuscitated by the Bituminous Coal Act of 1937,[12] it was again eliminated as part of a presidential reorganization plan in 1939,[13] and its functions were transferred directly to the Interior Department. Cushman observes that the commission "passed out of the picture, apparently unlamented."[14]

More recently, in 1994, Congress created the Assassination Records Review Board as a temporary agency to identify, collect, examine, and disseminate materials relating to the assassination of President John F. Kennedy.[15] The board was composed of five members, appointed by the president with Senate confirmation, with a statutory requirement that they come from among individuals with distinguished professional reputations and without regard for political affiliation, and include one lawyer and one professional historian.[16] Its members could only be removed for cause.[17] In an unusual statutory provision, members were expressly authorized to challenge their removal in court, and the court was expressly authorized to order reinstatement.[18] The board had an explicit three-year term, but its original authorization was extended for an additional

---

[7] Herbert Kaufman, Are Government Agencies Immortal? 29–63 (1976).

[8] David Lewis, *The Politics of Agency Termination: Confronting the Myth of Agency Immortality*, 64 J. Pol. 89 (2002).

[9] *See* Bituminous Coal Conservation Act of 1935, Pub. L. No. 74-402, 49 Stat. 991, 992–993 (1935).

[10] *See* Robert E. Cushman, The Independent Regulatory Commissions 379–80 (1972).

[11] 298 U.S. 238 (1936).

[12] Pub. L. No. 75-48, chap. 127, 50 Stat. 72.

[13] Reorganization Plan No. 2 of 1939. *See* Sunshine Anthracite Coal Co. v. Adkins, 310 U.S. 381, 388 n.2 (1940).

[14] Cushman, *supra* note 10, at 388–89.

[15] President John F. Kennedy Assassination Records Collection Act of 1992, Pub. L. No. 102-526, § 7, 106 Stat. 3443, 3449.

[16] *Id.* § 7(b)(1), (5).

[17] *Id.* § 7(g)(1) (members may only be removed due to impeachment and conviction or by action of the president for "inefficiency, neglect of duty, malfeasance in office, physical disability, mental incapacity, or any other condition that substantially impairs the performance of the member's duties").

[18] *See id.* § 7(g)(3)(A).

year.[19] The board completed its mission, submitted its final report, and went out of business on September 30, 1998.[20]

The number of independent agencies has not grown significantly since the Great Society. At times, individual multimember agencies disappeared because they transmogrified into more modern versions. For example, in 1975, Congress created the ITC[21] as the successor agency to replace the United States Tariff Commission, originally established in 1916.[22] In 1977, the FERC replaced the FPC and, as explained more fully in chapter 2, commission members for the first time received explicit, statutory "for cause" removal protection. The STB in 1995 emerged, phoenix-like, from the ashes of the ICC, but smaller and with more limited powers.[23] Still, while individual agencies come and go, the genus remains.

Newer multimember agencies at times play more a supervisory than a regulatory role—different from their earlier counterparts.[24] Some newer agencies were previously components of larger units. But few multimember agencies have actually been abolished in recent years. The most important agency to be abolished was the Civil Aeronautics Board, although some scholars have portrayed the replacement of the ICC[25] by the STB as a highly symbolic "abolition."[26]

While the government has done little to "retire" independent regulatory agencies, recent administrations have actively sought to increase control over executive branch agencies and in some ways extend such control to independent agencies as well. This approach was in accord with the views of the American Bar Association, which in 1979 issued a landmark report on regulatory reform suggesting that White House regulatory

---

19 *See* Pub. L. No. 105-25, 111 Stat. 240 (1997).

20 *See* Pub. L. No. 102-526, § 7(o), 106 Stat. 3443, 3452 (1992); *see also* H.R. Rep. No. 105-138 (1997) (amending the President John F. Kennedy Assassination Records Collection Act of 1992); H.R. Rep. No. 103-587 (1994) (discussing need for further legislation for release of Kennedy Assassination Records).

21 *See* Pub. L. No. 93-618, § 171, 88 Stat. 2009 (1975) (codified at 19 U.S.C. § 1330 (1994)).

22 Revenue Act of 1916, Ch. 463, § 700, 39 Stat. 795.

23 The ICC was abolished under Title I of the ICC Termination Act of 1995. Pub. L. No. 104-88, 109 Stat. 803, 804 (1995). The Surface Transportation Board was created under Title II of the Act. *Id.* at 932–43. *See* William G. Mahoney, *The Interstate Commerce Commission/Surface Transportation Board as Regulator of Labor's Rights and Deregulator of Railroads' Obligations: The Contrived Collision of the Interstate Commerce Act with the Railway Labor Act*, 24 Transp. L.J. 241, 260–61 (1997).

24 *See infra* section F.

25 Theodore J. Lowi, *President v. Congress: What the Two-Party Duopoly Has Done to the American Separation of Powers*, 47 Case W. Res. L. Rev. 1219, 1227 (1997).

26 *See* Jim Chen, Book Note, *The Nature of the Public Utility: Infrastructure, the Market, and the Law*, 98 Nw. U. L. Rev. 1617, 1638 (2004) (referring to the ICC's abolition as "a symbolic gesture" in light of the deregulatory reach of earlier statutes).

review encompass independent agencies.[27] It reflects, as well, increasing acceptance of a "presidential control" model of administrative law.[28]

C. Unsuccessful Shift to the Single Member Option

Occasionally, multimember boards have been replaced by single administrators. But most congressional efforts to restructure multimember bodies to centralize control have resulted in legislative paralysis. This is due principally to division among relevant interest groups and executive branch opposition to any desiderata of agency independence for the new entities.

1. NUCLEAR REGULATORY COMMISSION

In the wake of the Three Mile Island nuclear accident, a "maze of reform proposals" were introduced for the NRC in Congress.[29] The President's Commission on the Accident at Three Mile Island argued for "a total restructuring of the NRC, proposing that it become "an independent agency within the executive branch, headed by a single administrator, who is in every sense chief executive officer, to be chosen from outside NRC."[30] The

---

27 American Bar Ass'n, Commission on Law & the Economy, Federal Regulation: Roads to Reform 68–91 (1979) [hereinafter ABA Report]. The ABA Report recommended that independent agencies be subject to executive branch review, along the lines of the original Carter Report. It stated:

> Many of the independent agencies have been entrusted with primary missions that may conflict with other statutory goals, and they ought to be subjected to the same balancing discipline as other regulatory agencies. Exceptions should be made only for those agencies and functions (e.g., the money market functions of the Federal Reserve Board...) as to which a broad consensus exists that they should remain free of presidential influence.

Id. at 85. *See* Lloyd N. Cutler, Moderator, *Managing the Regulatory Process*, 32 Admin L. Rev. 239, 242–43 (1980). To prevent agencies from narrowly focusing on their own interests at the expense of broader executive goals, Cutler suggests that the president should have the power to review actions by independent agencies, to require them to submit cost-benefit analyses of proposed rules, and to direct agencies to reconsider particular actions. *Id.* at 242–43.

28 Kirti Datla & Richard L. Revesz, *Deconstructing Independent Agencies (and Executive Agencies)*, 98 Cornell L. Rev. 769, 824–42 (2013) (developing the notion of the "presidential" control model).

29 *Nuclear Regulatory Commission Reorganization Legislation: Hearings on H.R. 2126, H.R. 3049, H.R. 3124, H.R. 3285, H.R. 4134, H.R. 4140 Before the Subcomm. on Energy and the Env't of the House Comm. on Interior and Insular Affairs*, 100th Cong. 1 (1988) [hereinafter *NRC Hearings*] (statement of Rep. Morris Udall, Chairman, Subcomm. on Energy and the Env't).

We note that the NRC came into existence only five years earlier with the demise of its predecessor agency, the Atomic Energy Commission, in 1974. The classic discussion of the rise and fall of this commission is Frank Baumgartner and Bryan D. Jones, *Agenda Dynamics and Agency Subsystems*, 53 J. of Politics 1044 (No. 4, 1991).

30 *See generally* The President's Commission on the Accident at Three Mile Island Report, The Need for Change: The Legacy of TMI 22 (Oct. 1979), *available at* ThreeMileIsland.org, Dickinson College, http://threemileisland.org/downloads//188.pdf. [hereinafter TMI Comm'n Report].

report commented that "[i]t is not clear to us what the precise role of the five NRC commissioners is, and we have evidence that they themselves are not clear on what their role should be."[31] Members of the commission noted that they were "skeptical" whether the NRC commissioners were "a suitable body for the management of an emergency, and of the agency itself."[32]

The commission's recommendations culminated in congressional proposals to merge the NRC into the DOE, creating a governance structure that relied heavily on an administrator and dissolving the commission approach that had characterized the agency to date.[33] These proposals turned on a desire to remove core functions from the commission and create positions with greater accountability. Representative Frank Horton pointed out that the single administrator approach would have a "great appeal from an economic and efficiency viewpoint."[34] This approach reemerged later in the decade, as the chair of the Subcommittee on Energy and the Environment and others urged placing the commission's core safety responsibilities in an executive agency under presidential control.[35] The single administrator approach was also explored, both in the context of the agency as an independent regulatory body and within the executive branch.[36] Six separate bills were introduced in the House of Representatives, covering the waterfront of administrative reorganization and issues and affirming conflicting approaches to reorganization. In particular, two bills, H.R. 3285 and H.R. 4134, would have replaced the Commission with a single administrator.[37] H.R. 3285 would also have established a statutorily independent inspector general and a brand new multimember independent Nuclear Safety Board responsible for investigating events at both NRC-regulated and DOE-owned facilities, combining the single administrator approach without doing away with the commission structure completely.[38]

---

31 *Id.* at 21.

32 *Id.*

33 *See* Reorganization Plan No. 1 of 1980 (Nuclear Regulatory Commission), § 2. Prior to congressional efforts, President Carter voiced opposition to the push for reform "[b]ecause public concerns about the safety of nuclear power are serious." President's Energy Regulatory Message to Congress, 35 Cong. Q. 404 (1977).

34 *Reorganization Plan No. 1 of 1980 (Nuclear Regulatory Commission): Hearing before a Subcomm. of the H. Comm. on Government Operations*, 96th Cong. 17 (1980) (statement of Representative Frank Horton). The President's Commission Report noted that the administrator "should have substantial discretionary authority over the internal organization and management of the new agency, and over personnel transfers from the existing NRC. Unlike the present NRC arrangement, the administrator and major staff components should be located in the same building or group of buildings." *See* TMI Comm'n Report, *supra* note 30, at 61.

35 *See NRC Hearings*, *supra* note 29, at 1 (statement of Rep. Morris Udall, Chairman, Subcomm. on Energy and the Env't).

36 The President's Report noted that the Nuclear Regulatory Commission "should be restructured as a new independent agency in the executive branch." *See* TMI Comm'n Report, *supra* note 30, at 61.

37 *See NRC Hearings*, *supra* note 29, at 1 (statement of Rep. Morris Udall, Chairman, Subcomm. on Energy and the Env't); *id.* at 237, 239 (statement of Lando W. Zech, Jr., Chairman, NRC).

38 *See id.* at 237 (statement of Lando W. Zech, Jr., Chairman, NRC).

One 1988 legislative proposal focused on the need for independence in agency investigations. The proposal would create a three-person Nuclear Safety Investigation Board. While the board is housed within the NRC, its chair is nominated by the president with Senate confirmation required. Two members are approved by the administrator of the Nuclear Safety Agency.[39] The three members serve fixed terms and can only be removed for cause.[40] Several bills reflected these concerns by internal restructuring, in an effort to quell the internal squabble between the NRC's executive director for operations and the director of its Office of Investigations.[41] H.R. 3285 and H.R. 4134, for example, would also have eliminated the position of executive director for operations, while H.R. 3124 would have elevated the position to a presidential appointee, confirmed by the Senate.[42] H.R. 4140 would have established the Office of Investigations as a statutory office, and it would have required the office to report to the commission.[43] H.R. 2126 addressed the issue of the inspector general and the Office of Investigations, but injected a separate issue by proposing new protections for whistle-blowers.[44] Finally, H.R. 3049 addressed conflicts of interest by precluding the appointment to the commission of any individual who had a significant financial relationship with a regulated entity in the two years prior to the appointment.[45]

A bare majority of the commission supported the single administrator concept,[46] but only if the new administrator were to be entirely free of traditional OMB regulatory

---

[39] *See id.* at 94–96. The Nuclear Safety Agency, which was proposed by this legislation but never established, was meant to replace the NRC. *Id.* The proposed new agency would be an independent regulatory agency that would carry out all of the functions of the NRC. *Id.*

[40] We take this example from Peter Strauss, *The Purposes and Limits of Independent Agencies*, 1988 DUKE L.J. 257, 274–75 (1988). For the text of the legislative proposal, see S. 2443, 100th Cong. (2d. Sess. 1988). (Nuclear Regulation Reorganization and Reform Act of 1988), *introduced*, 134 CONG. REC. S6843 (daily ed. May 26, 1988); S. REP. NO. 364, 100th Cong. (2d Sess. 1988).

[41] The President's Commission noted that the internal structure of the NRC was not conducive to a proactive regulatory system. *See* TMI COMM'N REPORT, *supra* note 30, at 61–62.

[42] *See* 134 CONG. REC. S6843 (statement of Rep. Gejdenson) (referring to the undermining by NRC staff of Office of Investigations examinations of licensee wrongdoing and noting House Subcommittee Chairman Udall's letter to the NRC urging it not to place the Office of Investigations under the executive director for operations); Matthew L. Wald, *Report Contradicts Reason Given by Nuclear Officials for an Inquiry*, N.Y. TIMES, Dec. 9, 1989, at A12 (noting conflicts between the NRC's chief of staff and senior staff of the Office of Investigations). *See also NRC Hearings, supra* note 29, at 239 (statement of Lando W. Zech, Jr., Chairman, NRC).

[43] *See NRC Hearings, supra* note 29, at 242.

[44] *See id.* at 240.

[45] *See id.* at 243; *see also* Ben A. Franklin, *Nuclear Officials Assailed as Biased*, N.Y. TIMES, Apr. 22, 1987, at A1 (concerning allegations that top management at NRC improperly assisted regulated companies and noting congressional claims that a "distinctly cozy relationship" existed between commission's top manager and a regulated company).

[46] *See NRC Hearings, supra* note 29, at 147 (statement of Lando W. Zech, Jr., Chairman, NRC) (stating that "the Commission majority on this issue is very marginal").

oversight.[47] A fourth commissioner thought that things were fine as they were and that the Sunshine Act was at the heart of the commission's institutional problems because it impeded collegiality.[48] The fifth commissioner, who would later become chair, supported retention of the multimember NRC but wanted enhanced administrative powers for the chair.[49]

Congressional efforts to ensure independence from presidential oversight for the new agency was virtually a kiss of death for any legislation. The DOJ strongly opposed the creation of any independent board as part of the new agency regime on constitutional grounds.[50] The OMB opposed giving the new agency authority to bypass the OMB on legislative, budgetary, and regulatory matters.[51] In due course, the reform effort simply collapsed, and the Senate indefinitely postponed legislation to reorganize the functions of the NRC in 1988.[52]

2. FEDERAL ENERGY REGULATORY COMMISSION

The short-lived effort to replace the FERC with a single administrator was a surprise element of the Bush administration's 1991 National Energy Strategy. Introduction of the National Energy Strategy itself "followed 10 years of work by lobbyists, academics, true-believer congressional staff members, think-tank scholars, policy specialists and a handful of aggressive industry leaders."[53] However, the George H. W. Bush administration's effort to abolish the FERC was "an eleventh hour recommendation" by Vice President Quayle's Competitiveness Council.[54] As Energy Secretary James Watkins observed: "This proposal was developed independently of the National Energy Strategy by the Vice President's Council on Competitiveness. It is included here because it

---

[47] *See id.* at 232 (statement of Lando W. Zech, Jr., Chairman, NRC) (explaining that majority of NRC believed it should not be subject to OMB regulatory oversight).

[48] *See id.* at 213 (statement of Frederick M. Bernthal, Commissioner, NRC) (arguing that Sunshine Act undermined concept of collegial decision-making). The effect of the Sunshine Act on agency collegiality across government is discussed in chapter 9, section B(2), *infra*.

[49] *See NRC Hearings*, *supra* note 29, at 223 (statement of Kenneth C. Rogers, Commissioner, NRC) (urging that chair be made responsible for management of all operational matters).

[50] The department said that it would recommend a presidential veto of any bill that contained a new, independent-style board. *See* Letter of Thomas M. Boyd, Acting Assistant Attorney General, to Sen. Quentin N. Burdick, Chairman, S. Comm. on Env't and Public Works (Mar. 21, 1988), *reprinted in* 134 CONG. REC. 20,792 (1988).

[51] The OMB, too, was prepared to recommend that the president veto the bill. *See* Letter of James C. Miller, Director, OMB, to John Glenn, Chairman, Senate Comm. on Gov't Affairs (July 26, 1988), *reprinted in* 134 CONG. REC. 20,794 (1988).

[52] *See* 134 CONG. REC. 20,870 (1988) (request of Sen. Byrd).

[53] Thomas W. Lippman, *Utility Industry Overhaul: Surprisingly Static-Free*, WASH. POST, June 11, 1992, at A25.

[54] *Johnston Urges Spinoff of FERC Plan to Speed Senate Action on NES*, PLATT'S OILGRAM NEWS, Mar. 8, 1991, at 6.

complements the reform and streamlining of the regulatory infrastructure for the natural gas and hydroelectric power industries contained in the National Energy Strategy."[55]

The proposed abolition of the FERC appears to have been a sweeping response to the chronic delays that were seemingly endemic in the agency's proceedings.[56] But such significant structural change not only threatened prevailing arrangements but lacked both the sense of urgency and the consensus of "elite opinion" that Martha Derthick and Paul Quirk believe is essential to reform.[57] There had also been little, if any, political preparation. As a result, Congressman John Dingell, the chairman of the House Energy and Commerce Committee, urged the administration to separate it from the overall energy initiative,[58] while Senator Bennett Johnston, the Senate Energy Committee chairman, opposed the initiative from the outset.[59] Elements of the regulated sector opposed the measure as well.[60]

The FERC itself seems to have been taken a bit by surprise. Its chair, Martin Allday,[61] was a Texas lawyer and personal friend of President Bush who had been involved in Republican activities but had served on the commission for only about a year.[62] Vice President Quayle was careful not to link the FERC abolition proposal to any administration dissatisfaction with Allday's chairmanship.[63] At the same time, Chair Allday was publicly noncommittal about the proposal. In March 1991, he defended his agency's performance but offered no specific comment on the reorganization.[64] Three months later, when pressed by a House committee for FERC's views on the pending legislation, Chair Allday chose to submit only a staff analysis of the legislation that included the following, somewhat Delphic, observation:

> To the best of our knowledge, neither the Chairman nor the Commission recommended a legislative proposal regarding the transfer of its functions. It is our

---

55 *See* Letter of Secretary James D. Watkins, Dep't of Energy, to Dan Quayle, President of the Senate (Mar. 4, 1991), *reprinted in* 137 CONG. REC. S2795 (daily ed. Mar. 6, 1991).

56 *See* James H. McGrew, *Let's Streamline, Not Abolish FERC*, PUB. UTIL. FORT., June 15, 1992, at 12 (rejecting abolition of the FERC as a way to streamline it).

57 *See* MARTHA DERTHICK & PAUL J. QUIRK, THE POLITICS OF DEREGULATION 238–39 (1985).

58 *See* Lori M. Rodgers, *NES: A Mixed Bag Receives Mixed Reactions*, PUB. UTIL. FORT, Apr. 1, 1991, at 36 (stating that proposal faced uncertain future in Congress because of Rep. Dingell's opposition).

59 *See NES Package Sees Replacing FERC with Gas, Electricity Commission*, PLATT'S OILGRAM NEWS, Mar. 1, 1991, at 4 (citing Senate Energy Committee Chairman Johnson at an Interstate Natural Gas Ass'n of America meeting).

60 *See* McGrew, *supra* note 56, at 12.

61 *See* 1989 PUB. PAPERS 1345, 1345 (Oct. 16, 1989) (announcing President Bush's intent to nominate Allday as chair of the FERC).

62 *See Allday Tells President April 12 Is His Last Day at FERC*, ENERGY DAILY, Mar. 2, 1993, at 4.

63 *See FERC Restructuring Plan Is Unveiled: Johnston, Dingell Unimpressed*, INSIDE F.E.R.C., Mar. 4, 1991, at 1 (praising Allday's performance and promoting the FERC's accomplishments).

64 *See id.*

understanding that Chairman Allday was consulted prior to the proposal being submitted to the Congress.[65]

In a surprisingly noncommittal fashion for an agency under existential attack, the staff noted that "there are both advantages and disadvantages in the independent commission and single administrator structures, which have been the focus of much debate throughout the years."[66] The staff paper nonetheless defended the FERC's operations, explaining:

> The independence of the Commission does not stand in the way of a coordinated national energy policy.... [W]e do not understand the basis of the Council's claim that the Commission's current structure hampers Congress in the performance of its oversight and legislative roles.... [Although] [t]he multiple membership of the Commission sometimes adds to the length of its decisionmaking process ... we know of no studies that have compared the extra time it takes to obtain a majority vote of a collegial body to the time expended in getting approval for an important regulatory action through the various layers of an executive department and, in the case of regulations, through the OMB review process.[67]

The staff argued that "the independence and fixed terms of Commissioners enhance the continuity and stability of administrative decisionmaking by enabling Commissioners to serve long enough to develop expertise and by minimizing, or providing a transition phase for, policy shifts that otherwise might occur after a change in the Administration."[68]

As a practical matter, the FERC may well have recognized that, by the time it submitted its response in June 1991, the reorganization proposal was a dead letter.[69] The overall energy legislation passed with virtually no opposition.[70] But the attempt to abolish the FERC failed, and the FERC remains resilient.[71]

---

65 Staff Report and Analysis in Response to Chairman Dingell's May 11, 1991 Letter of Chairman Martin Allday, Chairman, FERC 3 (June 14, 1991), *reprinted in National Energy Strategy (Part 6), Hearing Before the H. Subcomm. on Energy and Power of the Comm. on Energy and Commerce*, 102d Cong. (1991).

66 *Id.* at 4.

67 *Id.* at 5–7.

68 *Id.* at 8.

69 *FERC Restructuring Takes Back Seat as Senate Energy Markup Begins*, INSIDE F.E.R.C., Apr. 22, 1991, at 1.

70 *See* Lippman, *supra* note 53, at A25 (reporting that bill passed with a vote of 381 to 37 in the House and 94 to 4 in the Senate).

71 *See, e.g.*, S1678, 104th Cong. (1996) (proposing abolition of the DOE); 142 CONG. REC. S3404 (daily ed. Apr. 16, 1996) (statement of Sen. Grams introducing S.1678, a bill to abolish the Energy Department, leaving the FERC as a fully independent agency).

D. A Preference for the Single Member Option

1. SOCIAL SECURITY ADMINISTRATION

Changes in the structure of the SSA runs somewhat counter to this trend. The Depression-era SSA has had an interesting institutional history.[72] In 1935, President Roosevelt sent Congress legislation to establish a Social Insurance Board as part of the Department of Labor. After receiving the legislation, the House and Senate divided on the institutional placement of the new entity. The Senate backed the Roosevelt approach, and the House favored the creation of an independent agency.[73] In the end, the House view prevailed. The Social Security Act of 1935 established a three-member agency known as the Social Security Board[74] to administer the old age and survivors insurance, unemployment compensation, and public assistance programs. Board members were appointed by the president with the advice and consent of the Senate, serving six-year terms, no more than two of whom could be from the same political party. The board had many of the characteristics of an independent multimember agency except, as was common during this period, it did not have an explicit statutory provision governing removal of members.[75]

A mere four years after its creation, the board lost its independent status. In Reorganization Plan 1 of 1939, President Roosevelt created the Federal Security Agency, a subcabinet level entity, to administer a range of programs, including the U.S. Public Health Service, the Civilian Conservation Corps, and the Office of Education.[76] The reorganization plan retained the Social Security Board, but it was placed under the jurisdiction of the Federal Security Agency. The agency's administrator permitted the Social Security Board to continue its program in an independent manner.[77] The board's functions were thereafter to be administered "as a part of the Federal Security Agency under the direction and supervision of the Federal Security Administrator." The board's Office of General Counsel was consolidated with the Office of General Counsel of the Federal Security Agency.

---

[72] Except as noted, the material in this section is adapted from the SSA Organizational History contained on the SSA's website. *See* Social Security Admin., *Social Security Administration History*, http://www.ssa.gov/history/orghist.html (last modified Aug 1, 2011).

[73] *See* Wilbur J. Cohen, *The Development of the Social Security Act of 1935: Reflections Some Fifty Years Later*, 68 MINN. L. REV. 379, 397 nn.123–27 (1983). One author indicates that the opposition to the Labor Department rested on its seeming friendliness to labor factions, although gender animus toward Labor Secretary Frances Perkins may have played a role. *See* Kathleen M. Keller, *Federalizing Social Welfare in a World of Gender Difference: A History of Women's Work in New Deal Policy*, 8 S. CAL. REV. L. & WOMEN'S STUD. 145, 169 (1999).

[74] *See* Social Security Act of 1935, ch. 531, 74-271, § 701, 49 Stat. 635 (1935).

[75] *See id.*

[76] Reorganization Plan No. 1 of 1939, 3 C.F.R. 1290 (1938–1943), *reprinted in* 5 U.S.C. app. at 1429 (1994).

[77] Social Security Admin., *supra* note 72.

In 1946, the board lost its multimember status. Reorganization Plan 2 of 1946 abolished the Social Security Board and transferred its functions directly to the Federal Security Agency. The agency delegated most of its powers to the commissioner of social security, although the agency administrator retained authority over the Appeals Council.[78] President Truman said that the Federal Security Agency had, in Reorganization Plan 1, taken the first step in establishing lines of responsibility for social security functions within the agency. The abolition of the Social Security Board was but a further delineation of those responsibilities that made it more aligned with the way internal organizations were managed in federal departments.[79] In the 1993 congressional hearings that discussed the viability of establishing the SSA as an independent agency, Elmer B. Staats, former comptroller general, commented that: "The history of the Social Security Board in the 1930's reflects great confusion in the roles of the Board and the Executive Director ... it is inevitable that when you have a board or commission trying to administer a huge program of this type, there are going to be differences of opinion. Those become public. Those add to the uncertainty of the public as to what is going on and how the program is carried out."[80] In addition, the president explained that reorganization was necessary to "reduce the number of agencies by consolidating those having similar functions and to abolish such agencies or functions thereof as may not be necessary for the efficient conduct of the Government."[81] The Federal Security Agency administrator created the position of SSA commissioner and named the board's chair as the first commissioner of social security.

In 1953, the Federal Security Agency was abolished, and its functions, including those of the SSA, were transferred to the newly established Department of Health, Education, and Welfare.[82] Later, the SSA became a central part of the Department of Health and Human Services when that department was established in 1980.[83] There was, however, continued disquiet surrounding the institutional status of the SSA.

The issue came to the fore when a growing agency backlog of disability cases coupled with an effort to create a peer review system among ALJs that would ensure greater adjudicative quality control led to fears of an erosion of ALJ decisional independence.[84]

---

78 Charles H. Koch, Jr., & David A. Koplow, *The Fourth Bite at the Apple: A Study of the Operation and Utility of the Social Security Administration's Appeals Council*, 17 FLA. ST. U. L. REV. 199, 235 (1990).

79 Reorganization Plan No. 2 of 1946, Message of the President, 3 C.F.R. 10 (1943–1948), *reprinted in* 5 U.S.C. app. at 1448 (1994).

80 *Establishing the Social Security Administration as an Independent Agency: Before the S. Comm. on Finance*, 103d Cong. 14–15 (1993) [hereinafter *Social Sec. Admin. as Independent Agency Hearing*] (statement of Hon. Elmer B. Staats, Comptroller Gen. of the United States (1966–1981)). General Staats was a graduate student in the 1930s and associated with the Social Security Board.

81 Reorganization Plan No. 2 of 1946, Message of the President, *supra* note 79.

82 *See* Reorganization Plan No. 1 of 1953, 3 C.F.R. 1022 (1949–1953), *reprinted in* 5 U.S.C. app. at 1488 (1994).

83 *See* Department of Education Organization Act, Pub. L. No. 96-88, § 509, 93 Stat. 668 (1980).

84 The issue is controversial. *See* Ass'n of Admin. Law Judges v. Heckler, 594 F. Supp. 1132, 1133–35 (D.D.C. 1984) (finding that Department of Health and Human Services so-called Bellman Review Program may violate decisional independence of ALJs but that changes in program preclude need for prospective

A report issued by the Federal Courts Study Committee in 1988 noted that: "The Social Security Administration has made controversial efforts to limit the number and amount of claims granted by the administrative law judges, leading to widespread fears that the judges' proper independence has been compromised."[85]

Because ALJs are employees of the very agencies whose cases they decide, the integrity of the SSA ALJs as an institution has at times been called into question. An erosion of ALJ decisional independence is therefore a reasonable corollary to the lack of institutional independence of the SSA. As a result, the committee recommended that the ALJs should be cloaked with "sufficient institutional independence to avoid the reality or appearance" of political control by the SSA. It further urged Congress to create an independent agency within the executive branch that would employ all ALJs, not just SSA ALJs.[86]

In 1981, the National Commission on Social Security Reform (informally known as the Greenspan Commission after its chairman, Alan Greenspan) was appointed by Congress and the president to study and make recommendations regarding the problems that Social Security faced at that time.[87] One of the issues addressed was the status of the SSA as an independent agency. The majority, led by Senator Daniel Patrick Moynihan, recommended that the SSA be a separate independent agency, headed by a bipartisan board.[88] However, the members of the commission were unable to reach a consensus, and Congress established the Congressional Panel on Social Security Organization to conduct a further study on the issues involved in making the SSA an independent agency.[89]

That study was conducted by a three-member panel of experts and headed by Elmer Staats, former comptroller general. Witnesses on the panel argued that a program of such significant size and complexity should be headed by a single administrator, and a presidential appointee who would be advised by a bipartisan board.[90] The panel

---

relief). *See also* Nash v. Califano, 613 F.2d 10, 15 (2d Cir. 1980) (ALJs have a statutory right to decisional independence).

85 Fed. Courts Study Comm., Report of the Federal Courts Study Committee 55 (Apr. 2, 1990). The Federal Courts Study Committee was established by the 100th Congress to "examine problems and issues" currently confronting the nation's courts, and to "Develop a long-range plan for the future of the federal judiciary." Pub. L. No. 100-702, § 102, 102 Stat. 4644 (1988) (codified at 28 U.S.C. § 1331 (West Supp. 1992)). It consisted of fifteen members appointed by Chief Justice William H. Rehnquist according to Congress's statutory instruction, *viz.*, that they be "representative of the various interests, needs and concerns which may be affected by the jurisdiction of the Federal courts." Pub. L. No. 100-702, § 103(b) (1988).

86 Fed. Courts Study Comm., *supra* note 85, at 56.

87 Nat'l Comm'n on Social Security Reform (Greenspan Commission), Social Security Reform (1983), *available at* http://www.ssa.gov/history/reports/gspan.html.

88 *Id.*

89 *Social Sec. Admin. as an Independent Agency Hearing, supra* note 80.

90 Rita L. DiSimone, *Social Security Administration Created as an Independent Agency: Public Law 103-296*, Social Sec. Bulletin, Vol. 58 No. 1, at 57 (1995).

concluded that a single administrator—which when coupled with an advisory board would provide a balance between the need for a strong administrator responsible to the president—and a board that would provide advice, assistance, and protection for the integrity of the Social Security Program.[91] The panel's report was submitted to Congress on June 12, 1984.

Congressional pressure for an independent agency intensified in 1986 when the House passed H.R. 5050, calling for an independent SSA to be governed by a three-member board appointed by the president and confirmed by the Senate. Although the Senate acted on other Social Security provisions contained in this legislation, it did not take up the independent agency measure, which died at the close of the 99th Congress.[92] A similar bill was introduced in the 101st Congress,[93] but no action was taken. In the 103rd Congress, the Clinton administration initially opposed making SSA independent, but later backed away from that position somewhat as the president did not want to antagonize Senator Moynihan because the latter's support was needed to pass health care reform legislation.[94] On March 2, 1994, by voice vote the Senate passed its version (S. 1560). The House passed its version, H.R. 4277, on May 17, 1994, by a recorded vote of 413 to 0. House-Senate conferees met to resolve their differences on H.R. 4277, and on August 11, on a recorded vote of 431 to 0, the House passed H.R. 4277. On August 15, 1994, the president signed the bill into law.[95] The *New York Times* commented that this was done "ostensibly to protect the agency's trove of money from the 'political mischief' of free-spending bureaucrats."[96]

The SSA was to exist as an "independent agency in the executive branch," separate from the Department of Health and Human Services.[97] The SSA would be headed by a commissioner appointed for a six-year term whose independence would be protected by a similar statutory provision stating that "he may be removed from office only following a presidential finding of malfeasance."[98] The new agency would be advised by a Social Security Advisory Board, composed of three members appointed by the president, by and with the advice and consent of the Senate. A member of the board may be removed only pursuant to a finding by the president of malfeasance or neglect of duty.[99]

---

[91] *Id.*

[92] *Id.*

[93] H.R. 3299, 101st Cong. (1990).

[94] Spencer Rich, *Independent Agency for Social Security Approved by Senate*, WASH. POST, Mar. 3, 1994, at A6.

[95] Social Security Independence and Program Improvements Act of 1994, Pub. L. No. 103-296, 108 Stat. 1464.

[96] Michael Wines, *House Backs Independence For Social Security Agency*, N.Y. TIMES (May 18, 1994), http://www.nytimes.com/1994/05/18/us/house-backs-independence-for-social-security-agency.html.

[97] 42 U.S.C. § 901.

[98] *See* 42 U.S.C. § 902(a)(3) (1994).

[99] *Id.*

The impetus behind an independent SSA emanated primarily from a desire to separate Social Security policy-making from economic and budgetary decisions affecting the rest of the federal government. Considering Social Security unique among federal social programs because of its self-financing nature and "implied compact" with the nation's workers to pay "earned" retirement, survivor, and disability benefits, proponents of the SSA's independence wanted to insulate it from everyday political, fiscal, and operational decisions of the government.[100] Senator Moynihan said making the agency an independent agency would give it "more visibility, more accountability, insulate it from politics and ensure that the agency would always have an appointed commissioner with full authority."[101]

2. FEDERAL HOUSING FINANCE AGENCY

The financial crisis of 2008 caused turmoil and uncertainty in virtually every area of the American financial system.[102] Two institutions greatly affected were the GSEs Fannie Mae and Freddie Mac.[103] The Federal National Mortgage Association (Fannie Mae) was created by Congress in 1938.[104] The original purpose of Fannie Mae was to purchase, hold, or sell FHA insured mortgages.[105] In its initial form, Fannie Mae was a federal agency.[106] The 1968 Charter Act split Fannie Mae into two parts—Fannie Mae and the Government National Mortgage Association (Ginnie Mae). The Act made Fannie Mae a "government sponsored private corporation," which would be shareholder owned but under government regulation through the Department of Housing and Urban Development.[107] Ginnie Mae would remain a government agency and retain control of special assistance programs.[108] The last of Fannie Mae's government stock was retired in September 1968.[109]

The Federal Home Loan Mortgage Corporation (Freddie Mac) was created in 1970 through the Emergency Home Finance Act to stimulate the secondary mortgage

---

100 *See supra* text accompanying note 88.

101 Rich, *supra* note 94.

102 A good introduction to these events can be found in ROGER LOWENSTEIN, THE END OF WALL STREET (2010).

103 Thomas Combs, *A Proposal for Regulation of the Government Sponsored Entities*, 84 St. John's L. Rev. 759, 759 n.1 (2010) (noting that a GSE is a "corporate entity...that has a federal charter, is privately owned, is under the direction of a board of directors, a majority of which is elected by private owners....").

104 National Housing Act Amendments of 1938, 52 Stat. 8 (as codified at 12 U.S.C § 1701a (2006)).

105 Combs, *supra* note 103, at 762.

106 Fannie Mae, *About Fannie Mae*, http://www.fanniemae.com/kb/index?page=home&c=aboutus (last visited Sept. 10, 2011).

107 12 U.S.C. § 1716b (2006).

108 *Id.*

109 Fannie Mae, *About Fannie Mae—Our Charter*, http://www.fanniemae.com/resources/file/aboutus/pdf/fm-amended-charter.pdf (last visited July 20, 2014).

market.[110] Freddie Mac was created as a "body corporate under the direction of a Board of Directors."[111] At this time Freddie Mac was governed by the Federal Home Loan Bank Board, limiting ownership of stock to certain financial institutions, mostly savings and loans.[112] It became a shareholder-owned entity in 1989, after its board voted to allow stock to be publicly traded for the first time.[113] Both Fannie and Freddie have had the ability to issue low-interest mortgage loans because their congressional charters afford them the implicit (although not explicit) financial backing of the government.[114] Both entities have their headquarters in Washington, D.C., and are exempt from federal, state, and local taxes.[115] At the time of the 2008 housing crisis these two entities held about $5.4 trillion worth of mortgage debt, about half of the entire mortgage debt in the country.[116] The subprime mortgage crisis put the stability of both Fannie and Freddie in dire straits.

Because of the large amount of debt held by Fannie and Freddie, and their importance to the financial system as a whole, Congress was forced to take action. The Housing and Economic Recovery Act of 2008 gave the Treasury the authority to aid in salvaging Fannie and Freddie.[117] The Act created the FHFA, an agency that placed Fannie and Freddie in a conservatorship.[118] In a statement released September 7, 2008, FHFA director James Lockhart described the conservatorship as "a statutory process designed to stabilize a troubled institution with the objective of returning the entities to normal business operations. FHFA will operate as the conservator to operate the entities until they are stabilized."[119] The conservatorship entitled the government to take temporary control of the entities, with changes including shake-ups of top management at both GSEs and the Treasury working to inject capital and stabilize interest rates.[120] President Bush called the plan to place Fannie and Freddie under temporary government control "critical to returning the economy to stronger sustained growth in the future."[121] Treasury

---

110 Emergency Home Finance Act of 1970, Pub. L. No. 91-351, § 303, 84 Stat. 450, 452 (codified as amended at 12 U.S.C. § 1452).

111 *Id.*

112 Nathaniel C. Nash, *Freddie Mac Clears Stock Sale*, N.Y. TIMES, July 14, 1988, http://www.nytimes.com/1988/07/14/business/freddie-mac-clears-stock-sale.html.

113 *Id.* (Freddie Mac sale of shares to public permitted as of January 1, 1989).

114 Cynthia M. Hajost, *From Oversight to Conservatorship: What Does the Housing and Economic Recovery Act of 2008 Hold for GSE's Fannie Mae and Freddie Mac?*, 18 J. AFFORDABLE HOUSING & CMTY. DEV. L. 3, 4 (2008).

115 12 U.S.C. § 1452(e) (2006).

116 David Ellis, *U.S. Seizes Fannie and Freddie*, CNN MONEY (Sept. 7, 2008), http://money.cnn.com/2008/09/07/news/companies/fannie_freddie/.

117 Housing and Economic Recovery Act of 2008, Pub. L. No. 110-289, § 1117, 122 Stat. 2654, 2683.

118 *Id.* § 1101, 122 Stat. at 2661.

119 James B. Lockhart III, Director of FHFA, Statement on Federal Housing Finance Agency, Sept. 7, 2008, at 5, *available at* http://www.fhfa.gov/webfiles/23/FHFAStatement9708final.pdf.

120 Deborah Solomon & Damian Paletta, *US Near Deal on Fannie, Freddie*, WALL ST. J., Sept. 6, 2008, at A1.

121 Ellis, *supra* note 116.

Secretary Henry Paulson said that "a failure would be harmful to economic growth and job creation."[122]

The Housing and Economic Recovery Act established the FHFA as an "independent agency of the Federal government."[123] When the GSEs were placed in conservatorship, the powers previously held by their shareholders and boards were transferred to the FHFA.[124] The agency and its director have general regulatory authority over Fannie Mae, Freddie Mac, the Federal Home Loan Banks, and the Office of Finance.[125] The agency is headed by a director appointed by the president and confirmed by the Senate.[126] The Act requires that the director have requisite knowledge of financial management and markets.[127] The length of the director's term is set at five years with the exception of removal for cause by the president.[128] It is the responsibility of the director of the FHFA to oversee the GSEs and to ensure that they operate in a "safe and sound" manner.[129]

When the Housing and Economic Recovery Act created the FHFA, it dissolved the Office of Federal Housing Enterprise Oversight and the Federal Housing Finance Board, and transferred the powers to the new agency.[130] The Office of Federal Housing Enterprise Oversight had been created by the Housing and Community Development Act of 1992 and was an agency within the Department of Housing and Urban Development.[131] Its purpose was to ensure the financial soundness of Fannie and Freddie.[132] It was headed by a director who was appointed by the president and confirmed by the Senate.[133]

The Federal Housing Finance Board was an independent agency created in the wake of the Savings and Loan Crisis by the Financial Institutions Reform, Recovery, and Enforcement Act of 1989.[134] The board was managed by five directors, consisting of a secretary and four additional directors all of whom were appointed by the president and confirmed by the Senate.[135] It is worth noting that when the Housing and Economic

122 *Id.*

123 Housing and Economic Recovery Act § 1101, 122 Stat. at 2661.

124 Steven Davidoff, *The Subtle Takeover*, NYTIMES.COM (Sept. 8, 2008, 7:40 a.m.), http://dealbook.nytimes.com/2008/09/08/the-subtle-takeover/?scp=3&sq=FHFA&st=nyt.

125 Housing and Economic Recovery Act § 1101, 122 Stat. at 2661.

126 *Id.*

127 *Id.*

128 *Id.*

129 *Id.* § 1102.

130 *See id.* § 1301 (abolishing the Office of Federal Housing Enterprise Oversight), § 1311 (abolishing the Federal Housing Finance Board).

131 Housing and Community Development Act of 1992, 12 U.S.C. § 4511 (2006). The demise of the Office of Federal Housing Enterprise Oversight is described by David Reiss in *Fannie Mae and Freddie Mac and the Future of Federal Housing Finance Policy: A Study of Regulatory Privilege*, 61 ALA. L. REV. 907, 912–22 (2010).

132 Housing and Community Development Act, § 1313, 106 Stat. at 3945.

133 *Id.* §1312, 106 Stat. at 3945.

134 Financial Institutions Reform, Recovery, and Enforcement Act of 1989, Pub. L. No. 101-73, §702(a), 103 Stat. 183, 413.

135 *Id.*

Recovery Act dissolved the Federal Housing Finance Board, it structured its successor, the FHFA, with a single director rather than a multimember board. The legislative history describes the structure of the FHFA, but does not explain why the new agency is headed by a single director.[136]

The Housing and Economic Recovery Act also established the Federal Housing Oversight Board.[137] The board is charged with advising the director of the FHFA regarding policies and strategies related to his duties.[138] The director cannot delegate any of his duties to the board, and the board cannot exert any executive authority.[139] The board is to be composed of four members consisting of the secretary of the treasury, the secretary of housing and urban development, the chair of the SEC, and the director—who serves as chair.[140] The board is required to report to Congress on the overall safety and soundness of the GSEs and to evaluate their operational status.[141]

Although the conservatorship was meant to be a short-term solution to the housing crisis, the FHFA still exercises control over Fannie and Freddie. Both GSEs have continued to experience economic troubles since the government intervention. A year after the conservatorship began Fannie had lost $111 billion dollars, and the efforts to salvage both Fannie and Freddie cost taxpayers $121 billion by the end of 2009.[142] Programs implemented at the request of the Treasury Department to modify mortgages in order to decrease the amount of loan defaults were thought to add to losses sustained by Fannie.[143]

In August 2009 James Lockhart stepped down as director and Edward DeMarco, who had been chief operating officer of FHFA under Lockhart, was named acting director. DeMarco was at odds with the Obama administration when it came to decisions regarding the direction Fannie and Freddie should take in order to revive the mortgage market.[144] The tension arose from DeMarco's conflicting statutory responsibilities: on

---

136 *See* H.R. Rep. No. 110-142 at 88–89.

137 Housing and Economic Recovery Act § 1103, 112 Stat. at 2665 (codified as amended at 12 U.S.C. § 4513a).

138 *Id.*

139 *Id.*

140 *Id.*

141 *Id.*

142 Zachary A. Goldfarb, *Hit by Huge Loss, Fannie Mae Seeks More Federal Aid*, Wash. Post, Nov. 6, 2009, http://www.washingtonpost.com/wp-dyn/content/article/2009/11/05/AR2009110505223.html.

143 *Id.*

144 *See* Statement by Edward J, DeMarco, Acting Director, Federal Housing Finance Agency, on the Use of Principal Forgiveness by Fannie Mae and Freddie Mac, July 31, 2012, *available at* http://www.fhfa.gov/webfiles/24113/PFStatement73112.pdf. DeMarco remarked:

> After extensive analysis of the revised HAMP PRA [(Home Affordable Modification Program's Principal Reduction Alternative)], including the determination by the Treasury Department to begin using Trouble Asset Relief Program (TARP) monies to make incentive payments to Fannie Mae and Freddie Mac, FHFA has concluded that the anticipated benefits do not outweigh the costs and risks. Given our multiple responsibilities to conserve the assets of Fannie Mae and Freddie Mac, maximize assistance to homeowners to avoid foreclosures, and minimize the expense of such assistance to taxpayers, FHFA concluded that HAMP PRA did not clearly improve foreclosure avoidance while reducing costs to taxpayers relative to the approaches in place today. *Id.*

the one hand to see that Fannie and Freddie facilitate affordable housing and an accessible mortgage market, but on the other to ensure that the GSE's are financially sound and not a burden to taxpayers.[145] DeMarco said that his mission was "to conserve Fannie and Freddie's assets and that sometimes means putting his foot down on well-meaning but expensive new initiatives."[146] DeMarco felt bound by the language in the Housing and Economic Recovery Act, which entrusts the director of the FHFA with preserving the financial soundness of the GSEs.[147] In this contemporary example of agency independence, Congress also chimed in, urging the president to dismiss DeMarco.[148] The future of these GSEs is unclear as there have been growing calls to in some way privatize them "so the private sector can take on more of the secondary market as the GSEs depart."[149]

3. THE CONTINUING SAGA OF THE CONSUMER FINANCIAL PROTECTION BUREAU: BIRTH OF THE IDEA

The idea of an agency that would regulate consumer financial products was introduced by Harvard law professor Elizabeth Warren in her 2007 article "Unsafe at Any Rate." In that article, Warren argued that a model based on the Consumer Product Safety Commission, which has protected consumers from purchasing defective or dangerous goods through uniform safety standards and regulation, would be just as useful in the financial products market.[150]

---

145 Brad Plumer & Ezra Klein, *The Most Powerful Man in Housing Policy*, WASH. POST (Aug. 31, 2011, 3:55 p.m.), http://www.washingtonpost.com/blogs/ezra-klein/post/the-most-powerful-man-in-housing-policy/2011/08/25/gIQAouktrJ_blog.html.

146 Nick Timiraos, *An Accidental Housing Chief Embraces the Power of "No,"* WALL ST. J., Aug. 31, 2011, http://online.wsj.com/article/SB10001424053111904199404576538803284685440.html?mod=googlenews_wsj.

147 Housing and Economic Recovery Act § 1102, 122 Stat. at 2663. *See also* Timiraos, *supra* note 146.

148 *See* Christopher Matthews, *Congressmen Accuse Fannie and Freddie Boss of Ideological Bias*, TIME, May 7, 2012, http://business.time.com/2012/05/07/congressmen-accuse-fannie-and-freddie-boss-of-ideological-bias/.

149 PETER J. WALLISON ET AL., TAKING THE GOVERNMENT OUT OF HOUSING FINANCE: PRINCIPLES FOR REFORMING THE HOUSING FINANCE MARKET, AMERICAN ENTERPRISE INSTITUTE POLICY WHITE PAPER 3 (2011), *available at* http://www.aei.org/files/2011/03/23/AEI-White-Paper-FINAL-3-22-11.pdf.

The Obama administration had been unable to replace DeMarco due to the difficulty of getting nominations approved by the Senate. *See* Deborah Solomon, *Ed DeMarco is in Line to Replace Himself*, BLOOMBERG, Aug. 1, 2012, http://www.bloomberg.com/news/2012-08-01/ed-demarco-is-in-line-to-replace-himself.html; David Dayen, *Why Ed DeMarco Won't Be Fired*, FDL NEWSDESK, Aug. 1, 2012, http://news.firedoglake.com/2012/08/01/why-ed-demarco-wont-be-fired/. Following historic changes made to Senate confirmation procedures, in December 2013 Mel Watt, former Democratic congressman of North Carolina, was confirmed as DeMarco's replacement. Ed O'Keefe & Paul Kane, *Senate Confirms Patricia Millett, Mel Watt Using New Majority Rules*, WASH. POST, Dec. 10, 2013, http://www.washingtonpost.com/blogs/post-politics/wp/2013/12/10/senate-proceeding-as-scheduled-tuesday/.

150 Elizabeth Warren, *Unsafe at Any Rate*, DEMOCRACYJOURNAL.ORG, Summer 2007, at 8, *available at* http://www.democracyjournal.org/pdf/5/Warren.pdf.

Warren insisted that a new commission was necessary because traditional mechanisms for regulation had failed.[151] She noted that while agencies such as the Federal Reserve Board have some power to control unfair practices in financial products markets, their "main mission is to protect the financial stability of banks and other financial institutions, not to protect consumers."[152] Warren argued that "[w]hether it is housed in a current agency like the CPSC or stands alone, the point is to concentrate the review of financial products in a single location, with a focus on the safety of the products as consumers use them."[153]

a. Freestanding Independent Agency

After the financial crisis, the Obama administration began looking for ways to regulate the financial industry. In June 2009, the Treasury Department released a report titled "Financial Regulatory Reform: A New Foundation."[154] The report proposed the establishment of a Consumer Financial Protection Agency,[155] an independent entity governed by a multimember board and headed by a director.[156] It promoted the idea of a board representing "a diverse set of viewpoints and experiences,"[157] and suggested that at least one member of the board should be the head of a "prudential regulator."[158] The institutional design of the agency stressed its independence by proposing a funding stream partially stemming from "fees assessed on entities and transactions" across the regulated private sector financial institutions.[159]

In July 2009 Barney Frank, chairman of the House Financial Services Committee, introduced the "Consumer Financial Protection Agency Act of 2009."[160] The Act sought to establish a Consumer Financial Protection Agency similar to the one proposed in the Treasury report. The Act proposed by Frank set up the agency as "an independent agency in the executive branch to regulate the provision of consumer financial products or services."[161] The agency would have been headed by a five-member board appointed by the president, confirmed by Congress, for staggered five-year terms.[162] The bill died in committee.

---

151 *Id.* at 15.

152 *Id.* at 15–16.

153 *Id.* at 18. The politics of the effort to create such an entity from Warren's perspective can be found in Elizabeth Warren, A Fighting Chance, 130–205 (2014).

154 Dep't of the Treasury, Financial Regulatory Reform: A New Foundation (2009), *available at* http://www.treasury.gov/initiatives/Documents/FinalReport_web.pdf.

155 *Id.* at 55.

156 *Id.* at 58.

157 *Id.*

158 *Id.*

159 *Id.*

160 H.R. 3126, 111th Cong. (1st Sess. 2009).

161 *Id.* § 111(a).

162 *Id.* § 112.

In December 2009 Frank tried again when he introduced H.R. 4173. That bill called for an independent multimember agency headed by a commission of five appointees chosen by the president and led by a chair of the commission.[163] The bill also provided for the agency to be funded through the Federal Reserve, with 10 percent of the Fed's budget going to the agency every year.[164]

In the run-up to the Senate version of Dodd-Frank, Senator Christopher Dodd suggested that a consumer protection bureau be created within the Treasury Department. In a memo leaked to various news agencies in February 2010, Dodd proposed a Bureau of Financial Protection inside the Treasury Department that would have a director appointed by the president and a budget stemming from assessments on large banks and nonbank lenders.[165] Many saw this as an attempt to find middle ground with Republicans.[166] After resistance from Republican senator Richard Shelby, Dodd changed his approach and included language slotting the bureau within the Federal Reserve.[167]

In April 2010 Dodd introduced his version of the bill. It differed from the House bill in a number of respects. In the Senate version the agency would be called the Bureau of Consumer Financial Protection and would be headed by a single director appointed by the president with the advice and consent of the Senate.[168] The other significant difference is that the Senate version established the bureau within the Federal Reserve system,[169] and sought to secure the autonomy of the bureau by determining that "the Board of Governors may not intervene in any matter or proceeding before the Director... appoint, direct or remove any officer or employee of the Bureau; or merge or consolidate the Bureau, or any of the functions or responsibilities of the Bureau, with any division or office of the Board of Governors or the Federal reserve banks."[170]

Thus while Dodd did give up on the idea of a stand-alone agency, he retained the notion of an entity that would be independent. During congressional debate over Dodd-Frank, Dodd made a point to highlight the agencies' independence: "It is housed in the Federal Reserve in our bill, which has caused some people to wonder how independent it can be. It is totally independent.... The budget this agency would have is going to be separate from other budgets. It will have its own line of funding to go forward."[171]

---

163 H.R. 4173, 111th Cong. § 4103(b)(d) (2009) (as passed by House, Dec. 11, 2009).

164 *Id.* § 4111(a).

165 Sewell Chan, *Dodd Proposes Financial Protection Agency*, N.Y. TIMES, Feb. 27, 2010, at B6. For the leaked memo from Senator Dodd, see MOTHER JONES, http://motherjones.com/files/Dodd-Consumer-Protection-Plan-MoJo.pdf.

166 Chan, *supra* note 165.

167 Sewell Chan, *Dodd Proposes Giving Fed the Task of Consumer Protection*, N.Y. TIMES, Mar. 2, 2010, at B2.

168 S. 3217, 111th Cong. § 1011(b) (2d Sess. 2010).

169 *Id.* § 1011(a).

170 *Id.* § 1012 (c)(2).

171 156 CONG. REC. S2156 (daily ed. Mar. 26, 2010) (statement of Sen. Christopher Dodd).

The final version of the bill was signed into law by President Barack Obama on July 21, 2010.[172] Under the law, the bureau is an "independent" and autonomous entity within the Federal Reserve.[173] The bureau is headed by a director, appointed by the president, and confirmed by the Senate, for a term of five years.[174] The bureau has identified six areas that it plans to supervise, including consumer reporting, consumer credit and related activities, money transmitting, check cashing and related activities, prepaid cards, and debt relief services.[175] Congress transferred authority to the bureau to assume responsibility for all functions related to consumer financial protection from several other federal agencies.[176]

b. Elizabeth Warren, Czar

In September 2010, President Obama did not appoint Elizabeth Warren as director of the CFPB, as many liberals had hoped, but instead as a special adviser to himself and to the secretary of the treasury, Timothy Geithner.[177] As a so-called czar, Warren had the power only to serve in an advisory capacity, yet was simultaneously tasked with managing the creation of the bureau.[178] Dissent regarding this decision arose immediately, even within the president's own party. While Representative Barney Frank was "very pleased" with the "creative way to put her in charge of the agency" without Senate confirmation,[179] Senator Susan Collins, a Republican, called the move "a disingenuous effort to circumvent the Senate confirmation process.... The last thing we need is another 'czar' that is unaccountable to Congress and the American people. This is certainly not what Congress intended when it created this important position."[180]

---

172 Dodd-Frank Wall Street Reform and Consumer Protection Act, Pub. L. No. 111-203, 124 Stat. 1376 (2010).

173 *Id.* § 1011(a) (codified as amended at 12 U.S.C. § 5491(a)). Independence is discussed at Dodd-Frank Act § 1011(a) and autonomy at § 1012(c).

174 *Id.* § 1011(b)(1)–(2), (c)(1). The director is removable for cause, including "inefficiency, neglect of duty, or malfeasance in office." *Id.* § 1011(c)(3).

175 Deborah Solomon & Maya Jackson-Randall, *Agency Outlines Role*, WALL ST. J., June 24, 2011, http://online.wsj.com/news/articles/SB10001424052702304231204576403984131808742.

176 Dodd-Frank Act § 1061 (codified as amended at 12 U.S.C. § 5581) (transferor agencies include the Board of Governors of the Federal Reserve, the FDIC, the FTC, the NCUA, the Office of the Comptroller of the Currency, and the Department of Housing and Urban Development).

177 Sewell Chan, *Consumer Advocate to Lead New Watchdog Agency as Assistant to Obama*, N.Y. TIMES, Sept. 16, 2010, at B3. The Obama administration's view was that she was unconfirmable as director due to Republican opposition. The back-and-forth is recounted in TIMOTHY GEITHNER, STRESS TEST 435–38 (2014).

178 Chan, *supra* note 177.

179 Brady Dennis, *Capitol Hill divided on Obama plan to bypass approval for Elizabeth Warren*, WASH. POST, Sept. 17, 2010, at A14.

180 Brady Dennis, *Warren Expected to Be Adviser*, WASH. POST, Sept. 16, 2010, at A18; *see also* Dennis, *supra* note 179 (Senator Chris Dodd, the coauthor of the bill creating the organization, was less pleased: "Advisers are advisers. You still have to have a director. You've got to have someone who has earned the respect and the support of the Senate. The confirmation process is very, very important.").

c. Interim Authority of the Treasury

Under Dodd-Frank the CFPB was subject to the interim authority of the Treasury, and was housed there under the guidance of Tim Geithner and Elizabeth Warren until transferred to the Federal Reserve on July 21, 2011.[181] The secretary of the treasury was responsible for implementation of the bureau until a director was appointed and confirmed.[182] Once the bureau was transferred to the Federal Reserve, it was restricted in its regulatory capacity without a director in place but had a limited ability to conduct investigations.[183]

The inspector general of the treasury and inspector general of the Board of Governors of the Federal Reserve System issued a joint response concerning the bureau, following a request for information from Congress in November 2010. The letter was issued in January 2011 and addressed the facets of the Treasury's interim authority both before and after transfer to the Federal Reserve.[184] After the transfer date, the secretary was still able to prescribe rules and guidelines that were previously carried out by the Board of Governors, the Office of the Comptroller of the Currency, the FDIC, the NCUA, and the FTC.[185] The secretary also continued to have the authority to "conduct examinations (for federal consumer financial law purposes) of banks, savings associations, and credit unions with total assets in excess of $10 billion, and any affiliates thereof."[186]

However, without a director in place the secretary of the treasury was unable to carry out some key administrative duties assigned to the bureau by Dodd-Frank, including being unable to prohibit "unfair, deceptive, or abusive acts or practices" or "supervise nondepository institutions."[187]

d. Housed in the Federal Reserve

Although the bureau is housed within the Federal Reserve, the only connection the bureau actually has to the Fed is its funding mechanism.[188] "We view the identification

---

181 Dodd-Frank Act § 1066 (codified as amended at 12 U.S.C. § 5586).

182 *Id.* This interim authority allowed Elizabeth Warren to effectively lead the establishment of the CFPB prior to the appointment of a director. Warren acted as a designate of the treasury secretary, not the White House, for any "executive" acts.

183 Josh Boak, *Bureau Can Open Without Chief*, POLITICO, June 17, 2011, at 4.

184 Letter from Eric M. Thorson, Inspector General, Dep't of the Treasury, and Elizabeth A. Coleman, Inspector General, Bd. of Governors of the Federal Reserve System, to Spencer Bachus, Chairman of the House Comm. on Financial Services, and Judy Biggert, Chairwoman of the Subcomm. on Insurance, Housing, and Community Opportunity (Jan. 10, 2011), *available at* http://www.treasury.gov/about/organizational-structure/ig/Documents/OIG-CA%2011004%20Committee%20of%20Financial%20Services%20Response%20CFPB.pdf.

185 *Id.* at 5.

186 *Id.*

187 *Id.* at 7.

188 Dodd-Frank Act § 1017 (codified as amended at 12 U.S.C. § 5497).

of the Bureau's source of funding as indicative of—indeed, as a sort of guarantee of—the Bureau's financial independence from political sources."[189] The director of the bureau determines the amount needed to finance its activities according to what is "reasonably necessary" to carry out its operations.[190] Although the Federal Reserve has no regulatory authority over the bureau, the funding mechanism does provide for a statutory funding cap not to exceed 12 percent of the total operating expenses of the Federal Reserve budget.[191]

The Board of Governors of the Federal Reserve has virtually no other authority over the bureau. The board may not approve or review any of the regulations set forth by the bureau.[192] "In other words, Congress has provided the Bureau a condominium within the Federal Reserve complex, but the Bureau is not beholden to the Federal Reserve merely because they share walls."[193] The bureau's independence is strengthened by the fact that although it is funded by the Fed, that agency has no directorial or policy influence.

It has been argued that the fact that it is headed by an appointed director instead of a multimember board further insulates it from outside political and oversight influence. "The bureau is an exotic, but not a unique, administrative creature. It is an independent establishment that rests within—yet is not accountable to—another independent establishment."[194] Although the Federal Reserve has no administrative power over the bureau, regulations issued by the bureau are subject to review and veto by the Financial Stability Oversight Council, a council also created out of the Dodd-Frank legislation.[195]

e. A Multimember Board?

Republicans, fearing the strength of a unitary director of the bureau and the general lack of oversight, have recently taken several measures to change the structure of the bureau, attempting to create a commission to lead it. Representative Spencer Bachus called a multimember commission "the proper approach—it's actually Elizabeth Warren's

---

189 Susan Block-Lieb & Edward J. Janger, *Reforming Regulation in the Markets for Home Loans*, 38 Fordham Urb. L.J. 681,700 (2011).

190 Dodd-Frank Act § 1017(a).

191 *Id.*

192 *Id.* § 1012(c).

193 Kent Barnett, *The Consumer Financial Protection Bureau's Appointment with Trouble*, 60 Am. U. L. Rev. 1459, 1476–77 (2011).

194 *Id.* at 1472.

195 Dodd-Frank Act § 111 (codified as amended at 12 U.S.C. § 5321) (voting members of the Financial Stability Oversight Council include the secretary of the treasury, the chair of the Board of Governors of the Federal Reserve System, the comptroller of currency, the director of the CFPB, the chair of the SEC, the chair of the FDIC, the chair of the Commodity Futures Trading Commission, the director of the FHFA, the chair of the NCUA board, and an independent member with insurance expertise that is appointed by the president and confirmed by the Senate for a six-year term). For further discussion of the Financial Stability Oversight Council, see *infra* text accompanying notes 335–45.

proposal."[196] More cynically, the commission model is said to have arisen because the Republicans "lack the power to repeal the bill outright, [to] override a certain Obama veto."[197] As a result, the opponents of a strong CFPB sought to "weaken the CFPB in the name of transparency and accountability."[198]

A number of bills have been proposed to alter the structure of the CFPB. H.R. 1121 proposed a five-person commission, with members serving staggered five-year terms.[199] This suggestion has concerned the bureau's defenders. "It's critical for the CFPB to be led by a single director," says Pamela Banks, senior policy counsel for Consumers Union. "We can't afford to hamstring the CFPB with an unnecessarily complicated bureaucratic structure. Replacing the CFPB's director with a commission would slow down its decision making process and make it more prone to internal discord."[200]

Two weeks later, H.R. 1315 attempted to reduce from two-thirds to a simple majority the votes required by the Financial Stability Oversight Council to overturn a regulation of the CFPB.[201] H.R. 1640 would have shifted the bureau's budget from the Federal Reserve to the regular appropriations process through Congress.[202] These bills addressed Republicans' additional concerns that the decisions made by the director of the CFPB would have virtually unchecked power in decision-making, and that there would be little to no congressional oversight since the bureau is not funded through appropriations.

In addition, Senate Republicans outlined their criticisms of the CFPB as currently enacted in a letter to President Obama in May 2011.[203] They called for three general amendments, very much in keeping with previous concerns: "establish a board of directors" for the bureau, "subject the [CFPB] to the appropriations process," and "establish a safety-and-soundness check for the prudential regulators"—in effect giving regulators more ability to overturn CPFB regulations.[204] The letter criticized the funding mechanism of the bureau, specifically the fact that the director has great discretion in setting the budget, and Congress has no oversight over the how the agency is managing its money.[205]

---

196 Joseph Williams, *Warren Shows Few Signs of Soothing Hill Critics*, POLITICO, May 25, 2011, at 20.

197 *Id.*

198 *Id.*

199 H.R. 1121, 112th Cong. (1st Sess. 2011). *See also* H.R. REP. NO. 112-107 (2011) (noting that "a commission structure promotes predictability in rulemaking by preventing a new CFPB Director from unilaterally and abruptly reversing decisions made by a previous Director").

200 Chris Morran, *Washington Already Considering Ways to Ruin Consumer Financial Protection Bureau*, THE CONSUMERIST (May 3, 2011, 11:45 a.m.), http://consumerist.com/2011/05/washington-already-considering-ways-to-ruin-consumer-financial-protection-bureau.html.

201 H.R. 1315, 112th Cong. (1st Sess. 2011).

202 H.R. 1640, 112th Cong. (1st Sess. 2011).

203 Letter from Sen. Mitch McConnell and Sen. Richard Shelby to President Barack Obama (May 2, 2011) (on file with the authors).

204 *Id.*

205 *Id. See also* David Hirschmann, *The CFPB Needs More Accountability*, POLITICO, Dec. 8, 2011, at 38.

f. A Director Is Nominated

On July 18, 2011, President Obama nominated former Ohio attorney general Richard Cordray to head the CFPB. Cordray faced the same opposition from Republicans without structural changes made to the leadership and authority of the CFPB. The same attitude toward replacing the director with a multimember board remained.[206] Once again Senator Mitch McConnell reiterated on the Senate floor: "We will not support the consideration of any nominee, regardless of party affiliation, to be the CFPB director until the structure of the Consumer Financial Protection Bureau is reformed."[207] President Obama eventually skirted Republican opposition by appointing Richard Cordray on January 4, 2012, using the recess appointment process.[208] The appointment was controversial, because the Senate was actually in session pro forma,[209] and was successfully challenged in court.[210] In July 2013, after a delay of nearly two years, Cordray was confirmed as part of a "package" deal that put off changes in the Senate filibuster rules.[211]

---

206 Binyamin Appelbaum, *Former Ohio Attorney General to Head New Consumer Agency*, N.Y. TIMES, July 18, 2011, at B1 (Senator Richard Shelby of Alabama issued a statement saying "Until President Obama addresses our concerns by supporting a few reasonable structural changes, we will not confirm anyone to lead it.").

207 157 CONG. REC. S4625-01 (daily ed. July 18, 2011). (statement of Kentucky senator Mitch McConnell). *See also* Scott Wong, *Senate GOP Blocks Cordray's CFPB Nomination*, POLITICO, Dec. 9, 2011, at 3.

208 Helene Cooper & Jennifer Steinhauer, *Bucking Senate, Obama Appoints Consumer Chief*, N.Y. TIMES, Jan. 5, 2012, at A1; David Nakamura & Felicia Sonmez, *Obama Defies Senate, Puts Cordray in Consumer Post*, WASH. POST, Jan. 5, 2012, at A1.

209 *See* Jonathan Weisman, *Appointments Challenge Senate Role, Experts Say*, N.Y. TIMES, Jan. 8, 2012, at 19; Michael McConnell, *Democrats and Executive Overreach*, WALL ST. J., Jan. 10, 2012, at A13 (arguing that the president was using "unconstitutional means" to circumvent the advice and consent requirement, and pointing out that substantive work—such as the enactment of a payroll tax holiday extension—was being performed during these pro forma sessions); Bruce Ackerman, *Recess Appointments: Release the Legal Advice*, WALL ST. J., JAN. 11, 2012, at A13; Editorial, *Contempt for the Constitution*, WALL ST. J., Jan. 13, 2012, at A12. For arguments made in defense of the Cordray appointment, see Lawrence Tribe, *Games and Gimmicks in the Senate*, N.Y. TIMES, Jan. 6, 2012, at A25 (arguing that "The Constitution that has guided our Republic for centuries is not blind to the threat of Congress's extending its internal squabbles into a general paralysis of the entire body politic, rendering vital regulatory agencies headless and therefore impotent"); Ezra Klein, *The Reason for Obama's Recess Appointments*, WASH. POST, Jan. 6, 2012, at A2. For the White House's legal justification of the appointment, see *Lawfulness of Recess Appointments During a Recess of the Senate Notwithstanding Periodic Pro Forma Sessions*, OLC Memorandum, Jan. 6, 2012. *See* Charlie Savage, *Justice Dept. Defends Obama Recess Appointments*, N.Y. TIMES, Jan. 13, 2012, at A12.

210 NLRB v. Noel Canning, 134 S. Ct. 2550 (2014); *see also*, Robert Pear, *Senate Republicans Announce Plan to Support Challenge to Recess Appointments*, N.Y. TIMES BLOGS (THE CAUCUS) (April 17, 2012, 6:00 p.m.), http://thecaucus.blogs.nytimes.com/2012/04/17/senate-republicans-announce-plan-to-support-challenge-to-recess-appointments/.

211 Danielle Douglas, *Senate Confirms Cordray to Head Consumer Financial Protection Bureau*, WASH. POST, July 16, 2013, www.washingtonpost.com/business/economy/senate-confirms-consumer-watchdog-nominee-richard-cordray/2013/07/16/965d82c2-ee2b-11e2-a1f9-ea873b7e0424_story.html. The Republicans agreed to vote on Cordray and two other stalled Obama appointments, and Obama agreed to withdraw the two recess appointments to the NLRB that had led to the *Canning* case. *See*

g. Accountability and Independence

Politics aside, the gravamen of the Republican complaint against the CFPB is its lack of democratic accountability.[212] And indeed that may well be the case. But a better way of analyzing the CFPB statute is to recognize it "as an effort to hyperdepoliticize the CFPB. In effect, the enacting Congress may well be signaling to future Congresses that they should adopt the same deferential approach to oversight, and the same relinquishment of budgetary authority."[213] While it seems clear that the text of Dodd-Frank sought to insulate the bureau from politics, this does not mean that the president, Congress, or even the other agencies lack ways of influencing the bureau's regulatory and enforcement activity. The president's influence, of course, comes from his ability to nominate a single director, which makes the president's influence in the policy of the agency, *ex ante* at least, even greater.

And as regards the influence of Congress and other agencies, as Susan Block-Lieb points out,

> the CFPB's jurisdiction is best portrayed as Venn diagrams. A prudential regulator cannot alone veto a regulation issued by the CFPB, but it can comment on it in the public record, lobby for the Council to set it aside, and thwart enforcement efforts. Moreover, although the CFPB is financially independent and headed by a single director, Congress can exert influence on the Bureau through its influence on other administrative agencies. It can reverse CFPB regulation legislatively. It can repeal the legislation that created the Bureau.[214]

---

supra chapter 4, section B. *See also* Michael A. Memoli, *In Obama Win, Senate Reaches Filibuster Deal*, L.A. TIMES, July 17, 2013, http://articles.latimes.com/2013/jul/17/nation/la-na-0717-senate-filibuster-20130717. The "deal" apparently lasted for some months only, and in November 2013 the Senate ultimately voted to weaken the power of the filibuster for executive and judicial nominees (excepting Supreme Court nominees). Susan Davis & Richard Wolf, *U.S. Senate Goes "Nuclear," Changes Filibuster Rules*, USA TODAY (Nov. 21, 2013), http://www.usatoday.com/story/news/policitics/2013/11/21/harry-reid-nuclear-senate/3662445.

212 Kate Davidson, *Republicans Promise to Block Cordray Nomination—Again*, POLITICO, (Feb. 1, 2013) http://www.politico.com/blogs/on-congress/2013/02/republicans-promise-to-block-cordray-nomination-again-155896.html (quoting a letter to Pres. Obama signed by forty-three Republican leaders who had "serious concerns about the lack of congressional oversight of the agency and the lack of normal, democratic checks on its sole director").

213 For the Rubin quote, see Edward Rubin, *Hyperdepoliticization*, 47 WAKE FOREST L. REV. 631, 677 (2012). It is of course, "an empirical question whether such hyperdepoliticization will be effectuated." *Id.* However, the Dodd-Frank Act does include an amendment to the Paperwork Reduction Act adding the CFPB to its list of independent regulatory agencies for paperwork reduction purposes. That list is often used to identify independent agencies generally as with the Executive Order 12,866 exemption of independent agencies from centralized OIRA review. For the Dodd-Frank Amendment, see Pub. L. 96-211 § 1100(D)(a), 124 Stat. at 2111 (codified as amended at 44 U.S.C. § 3502 (5)). And for its use as an identifier of independent agencies see, 44 U.S.C. § 3502 (5). For Exec. Order 12,866, see 58 Fed. Reg. 51735 (1993).

214 Susan Block-Lieb, *Accountability and the Bureau of Consumer Financial Protection*, 7 BROOK. J. CORP. FIN. & COMMERCIAL L. 25, 55 (2012).

E. Successful Closures

1. CIVIL AERONAUTICS BOARD

The Civil Aeronautics Board was in the business of regulating airlines from 1938 to 1985. The history of the board's development is murky. It started life in 1938 as the Civil Aeronautics Authority, with responsibility for economic and safety matters.[215] The 1938 statute also established an administrator for the authority, who was the forerunner of the federal aviation administrator, and a separate Air Safety Board to investigate accidents, which was an institutional precursor to the National Transportation Safety Board.[216] A Presidential Reorganization Plan in 1940 consolidated the functions of the Civil Aeronautics Authority and the Air Safety Board into a new Civil Aeronautics Board and placed it within the Commerce Department.[217] The administrator was placed under the direction of the secretary of commerce.[218] The board's safety functions were shifted to the newly created DOT by the Federal Aviation Act of 1958.[219]

Airline deregulation in the 1970s was part of a shift away from traditional regulation by multimember commission. A 1982 article by Gary Edles observed that a "unique confluence of factors brought about airline deregulation."[220] In fact, the passage of the Airline Deregulation Act "has been compared to launching a rocket—the mission was successful only because scores of separate yet interrelated factors came together in a precise sequence of events."[221] Among the key factors that influenced the Act was an impressive empirical database (including clearly identifiable anecdotal evidence) that conveyed the benefits of unregulated competition, the strong divisions within the regulated sector over the continuing benefits of government intervention, the lack of a well-organized opposition to deregulation, and the commitment of two presidential administrations and the agency (and its staff) itself.[222]

Timing was critical. First, airline deregulation was on the agenda during relatively prosperous and improving economic times for the airline industry.[223] Second, the Civil Aeronautics Board, which had historically been able to retain the loyalty of all segments of the airline industry to some extent, established policies during the Nixon

---

[215] *See* Civil Aeronautics Act of 1938, Pub. L. No. 75-706, ch. 601, 52 Stat. 973, 973-1030.

[216] *See* CUSHMAN, *supra* note 10, at 401–02.

[217] *See* Reorganization Plan No. 4 of 1940, 3 C.F.R. 1302 (1938–1943), *reprinted in* 5 U.S.C. app. at 1444 (1994).

[218] *See id.; see also* CUSHMAN, *supra* note 10, at 415–16.

[219] Pub. L. No. 85-726, 72 Stat. 731 (codified as amended 49 U.S.C. § 40101).

[220] Gary J. Edles, *The Strategy of Regulatory Change*, 49 ICC PRAC. J. 626, 626 (1982).

[221] *Id.*

[222] *See id.* at 626–31; *see generally* DERTHICK & QUIRK, *supra* note 57 (discussing deregulation of the Civil Aeronautics Board, ICC, and FCC).

[223] *See* Edles, *supra* note 220, at 626.

administration that divided the industry's loyalty. As economist George Hilton has explained, agencies receive support from all key sectors of the regulated sector by engaging in "minimal squawk" industry pacification behavior in which no constituent group is disaffected in the longer term.[224] There may also have been a generational component at work. Roy Pulsifer, a career government lawyer actively involved in promoting airline deregulation during his tenure at the Civil Aeronautics Board, asked the essential question: "Why... should the criticisms that academic economists have been making for more than twenty years and government economists since the early 1960s suddenly become popular issues, and why should the Administration be proposing drastic changes in the law?"[225] Pulsifer offers the following explanation:

> The basic reason appears to be that the end of the great post–World War II boom, and the recent recession, compounded by the negative impact on income resulting from petroleum price increases, have made the public sensitive to claims of the adverse impact of economic regulation on consumer prices. Put another way, the impact of governmental regulation on the allocation of resources, on how the pie is sliced, becomes a matter of intensified public concern when the overall economy, the pie, is not expanding. A second factor, although far from understood, is the maturation of the generation born during and in the decade after World War II. This group, by education and upbringing in a time of prosperity, is skeptical of government protectionism, and is likely to call for changes in any government policy which does not maximize opportunity, including regulatory regimes that seem to favor the *status quo* in industrial organization.[226]

Whatever the reason, or reasons, by 1985 Congress had abolished the Civil Aeronautics Board and transferred its surviving functions to the DOT.[227]

2. TRUCKING DEREGULATION: CLOSING THE INTERSTATE COMMERCE COMMISSION

Timing was also critical to trucking deregulation. Congress acted in 1995 as part of the antiregulation agenda that accompanied the Republican takeover of Congress that year.[228] But the ICC's abolition had been in the works for a while, and was ultimately only partial and somewhat symbolic. Although the government regulation of trucking ended, Congress retained railroad regulation and replaced the ICC with the smaller

---

224 *See* George W. Hilton, *The Basic Behavior of Regulatory Commissions*, 62 AMER. ECON. REV. 47, 48 (1972).

225 Roy Pulsifer, *Introduction*, 41 J. AIR L. & COM. 573, 575 (1975).

226 *Id.* at 575–77.

227 *See* Civil Aeronautics Board Sunset Act of 1984, Pub. L. No. 98-443, 98 Stat. 1703.

228 *See, e.g.*, ICC Termination Act of 1995, Pub. L. No. 104-88, 109 Stat. 803.

STB. But this action gave the STB, a new multimember agency, responsibility for overseeing the gradual decrease of government intervention in this area. The new board is now administratively part of the DOT.[229] The railroad industry's support for "an industry-friendly forum for their mergers"—rather than review by the DOJ—and the support from congressional committees "whose clout stood to be greatly diminished by elimination of the ICC" helped ensure that the ICC was "reinvented," not simply abolished.[230]

F. Independent Oversight Agencies

While the "split enforcement model" discussed in section I[231] places decisional authority in the hands of an independent, multimember agency, Congress on occasion uses the multimember agency as an advisory check on the work of the executive branch departments. Although the work of these agencies is entirely or primarily advisory, their multimember structure encourages the assembly of individuals with diverse and complementary professional qualifications, "diffuses" power, and inhibits executive control of a process designed to review the executive.

Examples of this type of agency are the Defense Nuclear Facilities Safety Board,[232] the National Transportation Safety Board,[233] the Chemical Safety and Hazard Investigation Board (CSB),[234] and the Postal Regulatory Commission.[235] The Defense Nuclear Facilities Safety Board reviews the design of defense nuclear facilities run by the DOE, makes recommendations to the DOE regarding the safety of these facilities, and investigates events or practices at these facilities that may affect public health or safety.[236] The National Transportation Safety Board investigates civil aviation accidents and significant accidents in other modes of transportation and, importantly, makes

229 *See* Mary Jacoby, *Foes of Bureaucracy Learn a Tough Lesson*, CHI. TRIB., June 16, 1996, at C1 (reporting that although the ICC's name on the building was removed and its $15 million budget cut in half, three former ICC commissioners and a staff of two hundred were still "at their same desks and mediat[ing] the same railroad rate-charge disputes and mergers, just as before").

230 *Id.* at C12.

231 *See infra* text accompanying notes 280–86.

232 The enabling statute of the Defense Nuclear Facilities Safety Board is the National Defense Authorization Act, Fiscal Year 1989, Pub. L. No. 100-456, § 1441, 102 Stat. 1918, 2076 (1988) (codified as amended at 42 U.S.C. § 2286).

233 The National Transportation Safety Board was created by the Department of Transportation Act, Pub. L. No. 89-670, § 5, 80 Stat. 931, 935 (1966) (codified as amended at 49 U.S.C. § 1101 et seq.).

234 The CSB is established, and its authority defined, by the Clean Air Act Amendments of 1990 under Pub. L. No. 101-549, § 301, 104 Stat. 2399, 2565 (codified as amended at 42 U.S.C. 7412(r)(6)).

235 The Postal Regulatory Commission in its modern form was established and its authority was defined in the Postal Accountability and Enhancement Act, Pub. L. No. 109-435, §§ 601–604, 102 Stat. 3198, 3238–3242 (2006) (codified as amended at 39 U.S.C. §§ 501–505 et seq.).

236 42 U.S.C. § 7412(r)(6) (2009).

recommendations to the Federal Aviation Administration and other bodies.[237] The National Transportation Safety Board, it might be noted, also has regulatory responsibility for the administrative trial and appellate review of Federal Aviation Administration and Coast Guard decisions assessing civil penalties or affecting the certificates of pilots, mariners, or mechanics.[238] But the board is best known for its accident investigation function.

The CSB investigates the probable cause of accidental chemical releases in much the same way as the National Transportation Safety Board investigates transportation accidents.[239] The CSB also conducts research and issues reports concerning the safety of chemical production.[240] The Postal Regulatory Commission is both an adjudicatory and advisory agency that conducts "public on-the-record hearings concerning proposed rate, mail classification or service changes, and [recommends] decisions for action by the postal Governors."[241] Since enactment of the Postal Accountability and Enhancement Act of 2006,[242] it also "develop[s] and maintain[s] regulations for a modern system of rate regulation" and, among other things "consult[s] with the Postal Service on delivery service standards and performance measures."[243]

Congress typically requires that executive departments respond to recommendations in some fashion. For example, the secretary of labor must respond within 180 days to recommendations of the CSB. The Labor Department must indicate whether the secretary will initiate a rulemaking or issue orders to implement the CSB's recommendations. "Any determination by the Secretary not to implement a recommendation or to implement a recommendation only in part... shall be accompanied by a statement from the Secretary setting forth the reasons for such determination."[244] Importantly, none of the multimember agencies has the power to enforce its recommendations. The recommendations, and the department's response, nonetheless remain available as an element of congressional or public oversight.

Skepticism about the executive branch agencies' ability to police themselves undergirds the creation of these advisory boards. They are designed as an independent check

---

237 *See* 49 U.S.C. § 1131 (2009).

238 *See* 49 U.S.C. § 1133 (2009).

239 *See* 42 U.S.C. § 7412(r)(6)(C)(i) (2009).

240 *See* 42 U.S.C. § 7412(r)(6)(C)(ii) (2009). For a discussion of the evolution and role of the CSB, see Mark L. Farley, *Special Report: Investigating Chemical Incidents—The Role of the Chemical Safety and Hazard Investigation Board*, 30 ENV'T REP. CUR. DEV (BNA) 534 (1999).

241 *See* U.S. Postal Regulatory Comm'n, *About PRC*, http://www.prc.gov/prc-pages/about/default.aspx. For a brief discussion of the Postal Regulatory Commission's enhanced powers under the Postal Accountability and Enhancement Act of 2006, see Peter Hettich, *Governance by Mutual Benchmarking in Postal Markets: How State-Owned Enterprises May Induce Private Competitors to Observe Policy Goals*, 32 DAYTON L. REV. 199, 220–21, 229 (2007).

242 Pub. L. No. 109-435, 120 Stat. 3198 (2006).

243 *See* U.S. Postal Regulatory Comm'n, *supra* note 241.

244 42 U.S.C. § 7412(r)(6)(J) (2009).

on the regulatory or operational activities of the executive branch. As the Senate Report observed when setting up the CSB:

> It is unlikely that an agency charged both with rule-making and investigating functions would be quick to acknowledge that existing requirements were insufficient to prevent an accident. In fact, the investigations conducted by agencies with dual responsibilities tend to focus on violations of existing rules as the cause of the accident almost to the exclusion of other contributing factors for which no enforcement or compliance actions can be taken. The purpose of an accident investigation (as authorized here) is to determine the cause or causes of an accident whether or not those causes were in violation of any current and enforceable requirement.... The [multimember advisory agency] is created as an independent source of expertise which may make recommendations for rules and orders.[245]

G. Independent Agencies Squarely in the Executive Branch

From time to time, Congress will recast certain statutes in an effort to accord administrators some additional indicia of autonomy while still retaining the principle of executive supervision. Whether these efforts by Congress are purely rhetorical is as much a question of politics as of doctrine. The restructuring of the Federal Aviation Administration in 1996, for example, provides a useful illustration of an agency head who, despite some statutory changes, remains under the president's plenary control. In the agency's 1996 Reauthorization Act, Congress provided that the administrator shall continue to be appointed by the president with the advice and consent of the Senate, as before, but shall now serve a five-year term. There is a statutory, albeit essentially hortatory, provision that the president "shall consider the fitness of the individual to carry out efficiently the duties and powers of the office," but there is no "for cause" removal provision.[246] Moreover, the administrator continues to report to the secretary of transportation. These statutory provisions create a strong presumption that Congress did not intend to alter the president's historic removal power over the administrator. The five-year term appears simply to be a political compromise designed to encourage continuity of office by according the administrator some added decisional and management freedom.

The legislative history supports this reading of the statute. H.R. 2276, an early version of the reauthorization legislation, would have removed the Federal Aviation Administration from the DOT and replaced the current administrator position with a three-member, presidentially appointed board whose members could only be removed

[245] S. Rep. No. 101-228 (1990), *reprinted in* 1990 U.S.C.C.A.N. 3385, 3613–14.

[246] *See* 49 U.S.C. § 106(b) (2009).

for cause.[247] The Senate approach, which was enacted, simply added a five-year term for the administrator.[248]

Somewhat similarly, the single, ten-year term for the director of the Federal Bureau of Investigation (FBI)[249] indicates a congressional desire to provide some apparent autonomy to the FBI director without genuinely compromising the president's prerogatives. Prior to 1968, the attorney general appointed the FBI director. In that year, Congress provided that future directors would be appointed by the president with senatorial confirmation.[250] In 1976, Congress amended the statute to provide for the ten-year term limit and the prohibition against reappointment.[251] Senator Robert Byrd observed:

> [T]here is no limitation on the constitutional power of the President to remove the FBI Director from office within the 10-year term.... However, the setting of a 10-year term of office by Congress would, as a practical matter, preclude—or at least inhibit—a President from arbitrarily dismissing an FBI Director for political reasons, since a successor would have to be confirmed by the Senate.[252]

As with the administrator of the Federal Aviation Administration, the FBI director's tenure provision does not prevent summary removal by the president before the term expires, and the term limit provision, apart from precluding reappointment, does not reflect any meaningful impairment of the president's prerogatives.[253]

The more challenging question is whether agency heads squarely within the executive branch can be insulated from presidential removal. In *Morrison v. Olson*,[254] the Supreme Court considered whether a statutory provision had impermissibly restrained the

---

247 *See* H.R. Rep. No. 104-475, pt. 1, at 25 (1996).

248 *See* 49 U.S.C. § 106(b); see also S. Rep No. 104-333 (1996).

249 28 U.S.C. § 532 note. *See also* Kenneth Williams, *Gays in the Military: The Legal Issues*, 28 U.S.F. L. Rev. 919, 954 n.286 (1994).

250 *See* Henry B. Hogue, Cong. Research Serv., RS 20963, Nomination and Confirmation of the FBI Director: Process and Recent History 2 (2005).

251 *See id.*

252 *Id.* (quoting 122 Cong. Rec. 23809 (July 26, 1976) (statement of Senator Robert C. Byrd)).

253 In fact, in July 2011, President Obama succeeded in securing a two-year extension for the tenure in office of FBI head Robert Mueller, whose ten-year term was set to expire on Aug. 2, 2011. *See Obama Signs 2-Year Extension to Mueller's FBI Tenure*, CNN Wire, July 26, 2011, http://www.cnn.com/2011/POLITICS/07/26/obama.mueller.term/index.html. This action initially generated opposition in the Senate. *See* Charlie Savage, *Republicans Hold Up Vote on Extension of F.B.I. Term*, N.Y. Times, July 16, 2011, at A13. *See also* Kevin Johnson, *Obama to Pick New FBI Director in Second Term*, USA Today, Nov. 9, 2012, http://www.usatoday.com/story/news/politics/2012/11/08/filling-fbi-chiefs-slot-also-on-list-for-2nd-term/1693277/. The bill in question allowed Obama to nominate Mueller for an additional two years. The Senate unanimously confirmed Mueller for the additional two-year term on July 27, 2011. *See Senate Votes to Confirm Mueller for Two More Years*, Politico, July 27, 2011, http://www.politico.com/blogs/glennthrush/0711/Senate_votes_to_confirm_Mueller_for_2_more_years.html.

254 487 U.S. 654 (1987).

president's power to control the "independent counsel," who was an executive branch criminal enforcement official. The "independent counsel" position, with "for cause" removal protection, was created in 1978 in the wake of the Watergate scandal to investigate alleged corruption by senior administration officials.[255] The majority opinion, by Chief Justice Rehnquist, indicated that the focus is on whether any removal restriction "impermissibly burdens the President's power to control or supervise the [appointee], as an executive official, in the execution of his or her duties under the Act."[256] Phrased differently, does the limitation "interfere impermissibly with [the president's] constitutional obligation to ensure the faithful execution of the laws."[257] In his dissenting opinion, Justice Scalia characterized the Court's approach as "an open invitation for Congress to experiment."[258] What about "a special Assistant Secretary of Defense for Procurement?" he asked.[259] Frankly, no one knows. If the Court's approach was indeed an invitation, Congress has rarely accepted it. Indeed, it even allowed the independent counsel statute to expire in 1998 following criticism of independent counsel Kenneth Starr's investigation of President Clinton.[260]

Multimember agencies emerged in the 1880s as the regulatory vehicle of choice, and flowered during the New Deal.[261] In recent years, that regulatory model has been largely replaced by congressional and presidential interest in agencies with a single head. Twice since *Morrison v. Olson*, Congress passed legislation that attempted to combine the advantages of unified administration and centralized control with the benefits of independence. Congress established as freestanding entities the Office of Special Counsel and the SSA. In both cases Congress removed the entities from their parent organizations, gave the new head of the agency a statutory term, and provided that he or she may be removed by the president only for cause.

Before its creation as a freestanding, independent agency, the Office of Special Counsel was an independent investigative and prosecutorial component of the multimember Merit Systems Protection Board.[262] The Whistleblower Protection Act of 1989 recreated the office as a freestanding, independent agency.[263] The special counsel, who

---

255 Carolyn Bingham Kello, *Drawing the Curtain on Open Government: In Defense of the Federal Advisory Committee Act*, 69 Brook. L. Rev. 345, 356 (1999).

256 487 U.S. at 692.

257 *Id.* at 693.

258 487 U.S. at 726 (Scalia, J., dissenting).

259 *Id.*

260 Kello, *supra* note 255, at 393 n.72.

261 *See generally* Morton Rosenberg, *Congress's Prerogative Over Agencies and Agency Decisionmakers: The Rise and Demise of the Reagan Administration's Theory of the Unitary Executive*, 57 Geo. Wash. L. Rev. 627, 657 (1989); *see also* Sidney A. Shapiro, *A Delegation Theory of the APA*, 10 Admin. L.J. Am. U. 89, 97–98 (1996).

262 *See* Bruce D. Fong, *Whistleblower Protection and the Office of Special Counsel: The Development of Reprisal Law in the 1980s*, 40 Am. U. L. Rev. 1015, 1016 n.2 (1991) (citing 5 U.S.C. § 1026 (1988)). *See also* Civil Service Reform Act of 1978, Pub. L. No. 95-454, 92 Stat. 1111 (1979).

263 Pub. L. No. 101-12, 103 Stat. 16 (1989) (codified as amended at 5 U.S.C. §§ 1211, 1212).

heads the agency, is responsible for enforcing the ban on so-called prohibited personnel practices by federal agencies, especially those involving whistle-blowers, ensuring compliance with provisions of the Hatch Act that deals with political activity, and prosecuting cases involving denial of federal benefits to veterans and reservists.[264] The agency itself is small and employs only about one hundred employees.[265] To ensure the agency's independence, Congress provided that the special counsel be appointed by the President, with the advice and consent of the Senate, serve a five-year term, and may be removed from office only for the classical reasons—"inefficiency, neglect of duty, or malfeasance in office."[266] The special counsel is given explicit statutory power to submit reports and testimony simultaneously to Congress and the president.[267] However, Congress has not given the special counsel the authority to represent himself or herself in court.

The SSA, in contrast, is a large agency that administers what has been described as "the Western world's largest income support program for people unable to engage in substantial gainful activity."[268] Its massive adjudication apparatus handles nearly three million disability claims annually and holds nearly six hundred thousand hearings each year, using over one thousand ALJs.[269] To accord the administrator a measure of independence, Congress removed the SSA from the Department of Health and Human Services in 1994 and provided that the administrator be appointed by the president, with the advice and consent of the Senate, to a six-year term and may be removed only for "neglect of duty or malfeasance in office."[270] The administrator's budget must be submitted to Congress by the president without revision.[271] Like the special counsel, the administrator may not represent himself or herself in court.

The emergence of these two agencies reflects a congressional effort to shift the traditional balance in some, but not all, respects. When Congress enacted the special counsel legislation, President Clinton, based on advice from the DOJ, opined that the removal provision raised a significant constitutional question.[272] Although not all innovative

---

264 *See* Act to Reauthorize Office of Special Counsel, Pub. L. No. 103-424, 108 Stat. 4361 (1994) (codified as amended at 5 U.S.C. §§ 1211(b), 1212); Uniformed Services Employment and Reemployment Rights Act of 1994, Pub. L. No. 103-353, 108 Stat. 3149 (1994) (codified as amended at 38 U.S.C. § 4301). *See generally* Fong, *supra* note 262.

265 *See* U.S. Office of Special Counsel, *Introduction to OSC*, www.osc.gov/intro.htm (last accessed July 18, 2009).

266 5 U.S.C. § 1211(b) (2009).

267 *See* 5 U.S.C. § 1212 (2009) (delineating powers and functions of Office of Special Counsel).

268 Charles H. Koch, Jr., & David A. Koplow, *The Fourth Bite at the Apple: A Study of the Operation and Utility of the Social Security Administration's Appeals Council*, 17 Fla. St. U. L. Rev. 199, 205 (1990).

269 *See* Process Reengineering Program; Disability Reengineering Project Plan, 59 Fed. Reg. 47,887 (1994).

270 42 U.S.C. § 902(a)(3) (2009).

271 *See* 42 U.S.C. § 904(b)(1)(A) (2009).

272 *See President's Statement on Signing the Social Security Independence and Program Improvements Act of 1994*, 1994 Pub. Papers 1471, 1472 (Aug. 15, 1994); Douglas W. Kmiec, *OLC's Opinion Writing Function: The Legal Adhesive for a Unitary Executive*, 15 Cardozo L. Rev. 337, 340 (1993) (citing letter

approaches offend separation-of-powers principles, each must be analyzed from both policy and constitutional perspectives. However, Congress's determination is entitled to some weight. So far, at least, Congress's judgment in these two situations to override the president's ordinary authority over executive branch officials has not been successfully undermined.

However, neither statute may actually be challenged on constitutional grounds. There appears to be little incentive for an aggrieved party to claim that the agency head should not be independent, and we have not found any cases raising the issue. Therefore, it appears likely that this new agency form will join the other accepted structures of government institutions.

During the Clinton administration, the OLC evaluated the president's removal power as part of a wide-ranging reappraisal of separation-of-powers issues. The OLC observed:

> The Supreme Court's removal cases establish a spectrum of potential conclusions about specific removal limitations. At one end of the spectrum, restrictions on the President's power to remove officers with broad policy responsibilities in areas Congress does not or cannot shelter from presidential policy control clearly should be deemed unconstitutional. We think, for example, that a statute that attempts to limit the President's authority to discharge the Secretary of Defense would be plainly unconstitutional and that the courts would so hold.... At the other end of the spectrum, we believe that for cause and fixed term limitations on the power to remove officers with adjudicatory duties affecting the rights of private individuals will continue to meet with consistent judicial approval: the contention that the essential role of the executive branch would be imperiled by giving a measure of independence to such officials is untenable under both precedent and principle.
>
> Between these two extremes, the arguments are less clear.... In situations in which Congress does not enact express removal limitations, we believe that the executive branch should resist any further application of the *Wiener* rationale, under which a court may infer the existence of a for-cause limit on presidential removal, except with respect to officers whose only functions are adjudicatory.[273]

---

from John Harmon, Assistant Attorney General, Office of Legal Counsel, to Senator Abraham Ribicoff, Chairman, Senate Comm. on Governmental Affairs of June 14, 1978, concerning separation-of-powers issue evoked by special counsel's predominantly executive powers).

273 *See* Memorandum of the Office of Legal Counsel, The Constitutional Separation of Powers Between the President and Congress, Memorandum for the General Counsels of the Federal Government, 1996 OLC LEXIS 6 at *147-49 (May 7, 1996).

H. Promoting Executive Branch Autonomy and Accountability to Congress

More recent efforts to reorganize agency structures have focused as much on accountability as on independence. Congress attempted to create a Nuclear Defense Security Agency within the DOE in order to provide that agency with greater access to the secretary.[274] Congress also attempted to make the general counsel of the FEC a Senate-confirmed position. That could have allowed the Senate greater leverage regarding the FEC's docket.[275]

Congress also attempted to expand its authority at the expense of the executive in 2002, when as part of the Department of Justice Appropriations Act, it enacted a provision requiring that the Office of Personnel Management "submit a report to Congress assessing the effectiveness of extended assignment incentive authority as a human resources management tool and mak[e] recommendations for any changes necessary to improve the effectiveness of the incentive authority."[276] President George W. Bush, in his signing statement, indicated his disapproval of the provision, noting that Congress had gone too far in attempting to "require executive branch officials to submit... plans for internal executive branch activities or recommendations relating to legislations" directly to Congress itself.[277] Over the course of his presidency, President Bush objected to well over one hundred similar provisions requiring agency officials to recommend legislation to Congress.[278]

Furthermore, efforts were made in the late 1990s to create a separate agency within the DOT to reduce truck accidents.[279] As seen, the emphasis is no longer on independence per se, but on clarifying lines of authority and accountability. At the same time, Congress has continually tried to inject aspects of autonomy and independence

---

274 *See* 145 CONG. REC. S8937 (daily ed. July 21, 1999) (proposing Agency for Nuclear Stewardship); *see also* Walter Pincus, *Senate Votes for New DOE Nuclear Weapons Agency*, WASH. POST, July 22, 1999, at A6.

275 *See* Bruce T. Rubenstein, *FEC General Counsel's Job Is Threatened by Congress*, CORP. LEGAL TIMES, Nov. 1998, at 4; *see also Senate Acts on FEC Issue, Treasury Funds*, WASH. POST, Sept. 4, 1998, at A7; Sean Scully, *House to Vote on Bill Targeting Election Commission Attorney*, WASH. TIMES, July 14, 1998, at A8.

276 21st Century Department of Justice Appropriations Act, Pub. L. No. 107-273, § 207(d), 116 Stat. 1758, 1780 (2002).

277 Statement on Signing the 21st Century Department of Justice Appropriations Act, 2 PUB. PAPERS 2010, 2011 (Nov. 2, 2002).

278 Curtis Bradley & Eric Posner, *Presidential Signing Statements and Executive Power*, 23 CONST. COMMENT. 307, 322–24 (2006) (noting that although George W. Bush did not utilize signing statements significantly more than his predecessors, he did use the signing statement as a vehicle to attack the constitutionality of congressional enactments more often than Clinton, Regan, or Carter).

279 The bill upgrades the Federal Highway Administration Office of Motor Carrier within the Transportation Department. *See* Motor Carrier Safety Improvement Act of 1999 Pub. L. No. 106-159, § 101, 113 Stat. 1748, 1750 (codified as amended at 49 U.S.C. § 113).

into certain executive agencies, an effort that conflicts with the theory of the unitary executive.

I. Split Enforcement Model

On a handful of occasions, Congress has sought to separate the policy and adversarial functions of agencies by creating independent, multimember boards to adjudicate enforcement proceedings instituted by the executive branch agency instead of dividing those functions within an agency. This so-called split enforcement model gives the cabinet agency the responsibility for promulgating and enforcing regulations and the independent, multimember agency the responsibility for adjudication.[280] The Occupational Safety and Health Act, for example,[281] reflects a congressional fear that the political agendas of executive appointees will inappropriately infiltrate their adjudicatory activities. Labor groups wanted the conventional regime in which all authority would be consolidated in the Department of Labor. Business groups were prepared to allow the department to investigate and prosecute cases but, fearful that the Department of Labor would tend to favor the wishes of employees and unions, wanted separate entities to promulgate health and safety standards and to decide enforcement cases. Specifically, it was the private businesses' fear of Department of Labor pressure that led to the creation of the Occupational Safety and Health Review Commission in the final days of congressional debate. The single agency model sought by the unions and the "troika" approach advocated by the business community led to a compromise amendment proposed by New York senator Jacob Javits. Under the compromise, two agencies were established. Within the Department of Labor, OSHA promulgates standards and prosecutes violations, but the separate Occupational Safety and Health Review Commission decides cases.[282]

---

280 *See*, e.g., 29 U.S.C. § 661 (2009) (establishing Occupational Safety and Health Review Commission to adjudicate cases prosecuted by Occupational Safety and Health Administration of the Department of Labor); 30 U.S.C. §§ 823–825 (2009) (establishing Federal Mine Safety and Health Review Commission to adjudicate cases prosecuted by Mine Safety and Health Administration of the Department of Labor). Certain cases involving the revocation or suspension of licenses issued by the Federal Aviation Administration and some civil penalty cases are prosecuted by the Federal Aviation Administration but adjudicated by the National Transportation Safety Board. Other cases are ultimately decided by the Federal Aviation Administration administrator, although ALJs of the DOT serve as the presiding officers rendering the initial decision in each case. *See generally* Richard H. Fallon, Jr., *Enforcing Aviation Safety Regulations: The Case for a Split-Enforcement Model of Agency Adjudication*, 4 ADMIN. L.J. AM. U. 389 (1991).

281 Occupational Health & Safety Act of 1970, Pub. L. No. 91-596, 84 Stat. 1590 (codified as amended at 29 U.S.C. §§ 651–678).

282 The history is discussed in Benjamin W. Mintz, *Administrative Separation of Functions: OSHA and the NLRB*, 47 CATH. U. L. REV. 877, 885 (1998).

In 1986 the Administrative Conference of the United States, the government's expert advisory body on administrative law and government organization,[283] composed of members from the government and the private sector, examined the split enforcement model. The conference was unable to conclude whether the model achieved greater fairness in adjudication than the traditional model but did recommend that Congress should henceforth make clear which agency is intended to have programmatic responsibility under a split enforcement scheme. The conference also proposed that, as a general rule, the adjudicatory agency should accept the rulemaking agency's interpretation of its own regulations.[284] The Supreme Court came to the same conclusion in *Martin v. OSHRC*,[285] on the way to deciding that "the power to render authoritative interpretations of OSH Act [OSHA] regulations is a 'necessary adjunct' of the Secretary's powers to promulgate and enforce national health and safety standards."[286]

J. Divided Accountability: The Separation of Policy and Adversarial Functions Within Agencies

The drafters of the APA rejected the principle that there must be a total separation of enforcement and adjudicatory functions through the establishment of separate agencies.[287] As the Supreme Court has concluded, the concentration of functions within the same agency, and even in the same person, does not automatically violate recognized principles of due process.[288] The APA requires only that, within an agency, staff employees who are involved in adversarial proceedings be insulated from those with decisional responsibilities.[289] Importantly, that "separation of functions" provision does not apply to the politically responsible head(s) of agencies.[290]

Congressional attempts to deviate from this arrangement have been sporadic and driven by pragmatic or political, and not institutional or doctrinal, considerations. Only a year after the enactment of the APA, Congress rejected the general APA model in the labor–management context. In the Taft-Hartley Act,[291] concerned that the NLRB was "prosecutor, judge, and jury at the same time,"[292] Congress modified the structure of the

---

283 For a description of the Administrative Conference of the United States and its activities, see Gary J. Edles, *The Continuing Need for an Administrative Conference*, 50 ADMIN. L. REV. 101, 110–16 (1998).

284 51 Fed. Reg. 46986 (Dec. 30, 1986).

285 499 U.S. 144 (1991).

286 499 U.S. at 152.

287 5 U.S.C. § 554(d).

288 *See* Withrow v. Larkin, 421 U.S. 35, 58 (1975).

289 *See* 5 U.S.C. § 554(d)(2) (2009).

290 5 U.S.C. § 554(d)(C) (2009).

291 Pub. L. No. 80-101, 61 Stat. 136 (1947) (codified as amended at 29 U.S.C. §§ 151–167 (2009)).

292 93 CONG. REC. 3,471, 3,472 *reprinted in* 1 LEGISLATIVE HISTORY OF THE LABOR MANAGEMENT RELATIONS ACT, 1947, 594 (1948) (statement of Virginia Representative Howard V. Smith).

NLRB to allow the board's general counsel to be appointed by the president with the advice and consent of the Senate and to have independent authority to prosecute unfair labor practice charges.[293] Although remaining within the board's structural umbrella, the general counsel's discretion whether or not to prosecute is not reviewable by the board itself. Congress amended the Taft-Hartley Act to insulate the "charging" function from the board out of fear of prolabor commissioners[294] Further, while individual NLRB members have personal assistants who review the record in particular cases (e.g. law clerks), unlike most agencies, the NLRB "may not employ any attorneys for the purpose of reviewing transcripts of hearings or preparing drafts of opinions."[295]

The attempt to change the structure of the FEC was also driven by pragmatic or political considerations. The commission is responsible for enforcement of the federal campaign financing laws.[296] So, unlike most other independent agencies, its work affects members of Congress personally. In 1998, congressional dislike of the FEC led to an effort to split off that agency's general counsel, making him an advice and consent appointee of the president rather than a civil servant directly accountable to the commission.[297] The effort was not undertaken to protect the independence of the general counsel, who was a career civil servant, but instead reflected congressional displeasure at the incumbent.[298] Congress wanted a chance to vote on his tenure. The effort ultimately failed, but it demonstrated how a desire for political accountability can undermine technical expertise or the type of policy impartiality associated with the civil service.

In 1952, the members of the FCC and the agency's ALJs (then called examiners) were prohibited statutorily from having staff to consult with, as at the NLRB.[299] That

---

293 *See* 29 U.S.C. § 153(d) (2009).

294 *See* Michael Ellement, *Labor Law in 3(d): Reexamining the General Counsel of the NLRB as an Independent Prosecutor of Labor Violations* (29 A.B.A. J. Lab. & Emp. L. 477 (2014)) *See also* Christy Concannon, Comment, *The EAJA and the NLRB: Chilling the General Counsel's Prerogative to Issue Unfair Labor Complaints?*, 36 Cath. U. L. Rev. 175, 176–79 (1986).

295 29 U.S.C. § 154(a) (2009); Ellement, *supra* note 294, at 8–9. *See generally* Mintz, *supra* note 282, at 881–82 (arguing that "Congress in Taft-Hartley established a structure for the NLRB which embodied a form of total separation between investigating and prosecution on one hand, and decision making on the other.").

296 *See* Federal Election Comm'n, www.fec.gov/info/mission.shtml (last accessed on July 11, 2012) (noting its responsibility "to administer and enforce the Federal Campaign Act (FECA)—the statute that governs the financing of federal elections.") *See generally Federal Election Commission Panel Discussion: Problems and Possibilities*, 8 Admin. L.J. Am. U. 223 (1994) (comments of former FEC general counsel Lawrence Noble and Elizabeth Hedlund, director of FEC Watch).

297 *See* H.R. 3748, 105th Cong. (2d Sess. 1998). See amendment discussed in *House Hearings on FEC Authorization Act of 1998*, H.R. Rep. No. 105-606 (1998). For further discussion, see also 144 Cong. Rec. S9,912 (daily ed. Sept. 3, 1998).

298 *See* Rubenstein, *supra* note 275, at 4; *see also* Amy Keller, *FEC Counsel Tries to Prevent His Ouster*, Roll Call, Oct. 1, 1998, *available at* LEXIS, Allnewsplus Library.

299 *See* Daniel J. Gifford, *Federal Administrative Law Judges: The Relevance of Past Choices to Future Directions*, 49 Admin. L. Rev. 1, 11–12 (1997) (discussing the Taft-Hartley Act and the Communications Act of 1952's prohibition against consultation). Specifically, "In amendments to the Communications

prohibition, which lasted less than a decade, was dropped in 1961.[300] The Senate committee explained that such a strict prohibition against access to the agency's expert staff was "wasteful and inefficient."[301] At most agencies, personal assistants or the members themselves work on separate statements.[302] At other agencies, such as the Federal Mine Safety and Health Review Commission, staff assistance is provided, if needed. At the EEOC, by tradition, no dissenting statement is issued even if a commission member disagrees with the majority's determination.[303]

The abolition of the multimember Civil Aeronautics Board in 1985, and the transfer of its remaining functions to the DOT, presented Congress with a classic choice between independence and political accountability. Among the functions transferred to DOT was the board's responsibility for adjudicating competing international route licensing applications. Historically, such licensing cases were heard initially by one of the board's ALJs, although the decisions of ALJs were always reviewed by the board itself in a collegial fashion and then transmitted to the president, who made the final decision.[304] To allay concerns that international licensing cases would henceforth be decided on political grounds, the DOT informed Congress that it would create procedures that "insulated" certain decisions from political pressure. Congress accepted those assurances.[305]

Under the compromise that followed, Congress authorized the DOT to process applications either through the traditional hearing method or through simplified nonhearing procedures.[306] Implementing the legislation, the DOT issued regulations that provided, among other things, that "carrier selection proceedings for international route authority and such other hearing cases as the Secretary deems appropriate" would be adjudicated through a hearing process, and the final decision would be made by the department's "senior career official,"[307] that is, its most senior civil servant. Final decisions by the senior career official are subject to a "petition for reconsideration" filed with the presidentially appointed assistant secretary. But such petition is limited to "questions of national transportation policy," and the assistant secretary's options are limited

Act, enacted in 1952, Congress forbade FCC hearing examiners presiding over proceedings arising under the Communications Act to consult with others about any matter whatsoever. As a result, FCC hearing examiners were more insulated from staff assistance on policy questions or background information than section 554 of the APA required. Moreover, examiners had to operate in ignorance of new policy developments within the FCC." *Id.*

300 "By 1961, the experiment was deemed a failure and Congress repealed the 1952 legislation, restoring Communications Act adjudication to governance by the APA." *Id.*

301 S. Rep. No. 87-576 (1961), *reprinted in* 1961 U.S.C.C.A.N. 2462, 2465.

302 *See infra* appendix A.

303 *See infra* appendix A.

304 *See* Chi. & S. Air Lines, Inc. v. Waterman S.S. Corp., 333 U.S. 103, 114 (1948) (noting that board orders are "not mature" until they are "finalized by Presidential approval").

305 Delta Air Lines, Inc. v. DOT, 51 F.3d 1065, 1070–72 (D.C. Cir. 1995).

306 *See* 49 U.S.C. § 41111 (2009).

307 14 C.F.R. § 302.18 (2009).

to affirming the decision of the senior career official or remanding it for further action pursuant to instructions—options more limited than the normal decisional options available when the politically accountable members of an agency review the underlying decision of a career civil servant.[308]

The compromise reduced political accountability somewhat by departing from the typical pattern of responsibility embedded in the APA that accords the agency itself all the powers when reviewing an initial or recommended decision by a career civil servant that it would have had it made the decision in the first instance.[309] Other hearing cases and nonhearing cases are decided directly by the assistant secretary.[310] Significantly, the department construes its regulations to give the assistant secretary discretion to determine what procedures will be used.

The D.C. Circuit has upheld the regulations against challenges from all quarters. In one case, the court noted that the procedure limiting the assistant secretary's review to affirmance or remand has "an artificial quality" but is not illegal.[311] Subsequently, the court observed in another case that the fact that "this scheme does not minimize the participation of political appointees to the extent desired by [the petitioning airline] does not make it plainly erroneous."[312]

K. Shared Regulatory Space: An Assessment

While the split enforcement model seeks to divide regulation over a single subject matter between multiple agencies, often regulatory overlap occurs when different agencies share the same regulatory space.[313] Such overlap is often criticized by the executive branch, which

---

308 14 C.F.R. § 302.18(b) (2009).

309 *See* 5 U.S.C. § 557(b) (2009) (APA § 7(a), dealing with discretionary review by an agency of decisions by its administrative law judges). An agency may, with some limitations, review the evidence de novo and substitute its judgment on issues of law, policy, discretion and even facts, for that of its presiding officer. *See* Valkering, U.S.A., Inc. v. Dep't of Agric., 48 F.3d 305, 308 (8th Cir. 1995) (holding that agency determination, if reasonable, must be upheld by Court even if different from that of subordinate hearing officer); NLRB v. Brooks Cameras, Inc., 691 F.2d 912, 915 (9th Cir. 1982) (finding court must uphold factual determinations of board).

310 *See* 14 C.F.R. § 302.18 (2009).

311 USAir, Inc. v. DOT, 969 F.2d 1256, 1262 (D.C. Cir. 1992).

312 Delta Air Lines v. DOT, 51 F.3d 1065, 1071 (D.C. Cir. 1995).

313 The literature on this subject is growing exponentially. *See* Eric Biber, *The More the Merrier: Multiple Agencies and the Future of Administrative Law Scholarship*, 125 HARV. L. REV. F. 78 (2012); Eric Biber, *Too Many Things to Do: How to Deal with the Dysfunctions of Multiple-Goal Agencies*, 33 HARV. ENVTL. L. REV. 1 (2009); Keith Bradley, *The Design of Agency Interactions*, 111 COLUM. L. REV. 745 (2011); J.R. DeShazo & Jody Freeman, *Public Agencies as Lobbyists*, 105 COLUM. L. REV. 2217 (2005); Jody Freeman & Jim Rossi, *Agency Coordination in Shared Regulatory Space*, 125 HARV. L. REV. 1131 (2012); Jacob F. Green, *Overlapping and Underlapping Jurisdiction in Administrative Law*, 2006 SUP. CT. REV. 201; Jason Marisam, *Duplicative Delegations*, 63 ADMIN. L. REV. 181 (2011).

may prefer neatness in its bureaucratic divisions. The Obama administration, for instance, in Executive Order 13,563 called on agencies to "promote... coordination, simplification, and harmonization" in order to reduce "redundant, inconsistent, or overlapping" regulatory requirements.[314] Notwithstanding the increased transaction costs for government, the increased compliance costs for regulated parties, and the increased confusion (including inconsistent regulations) for the agencies themselves, regulatory overlap is a reality that affects agency autonomy and accountability.[315] Regulatory space is often shared across the spectrum of federal agencies. Two "pure" executive branch agencies could share an issue, two independent agencies could share an issue, or executive branch agencies could share an issue with an independent agency. Given the nature of the regulatory focus of independent agencies, regulatory space is often shared by *at least* one independent agency.

Statute-based sharing of regulatory space arises if Congress can foresee and chooses to address potential conflicts when designing or redesigning an agency. The FERC, an independent agency, provides examples of various compositions of statute-based shared regulatory space, both vertically and horizontally, across the executive branch.

Vertically, under the Department of Energy Reorganization Act of 1977, the secretary of energy has the authority to "propose rules, regulations, and statements of policy" in areas that fall under the jurisdiction of the FERC, as the FERC was established within the DOE.[316] However, while the FERC must take up the DOE secretary's proposals within the secretary's time limits, the FERC is under no compulsion to adopt such proposals.[317] While providing a degree of external pressure on the FERC, this structure largely permits an autonomous FERC.

---

314 Improving Regulation and Regulatory Review, Exec. Order No. 13,563, 76 Fed. Reg. 3821 (Jan. 18, 2011).

315 Confusion as to jurisdiction occurs most frequently when agency authority is created under a number of different statutes, passed over the course of many years. For instance, there is a substantial overlap between OSHA, which is directed by the Occupational Safety and Health Act of 1970 to promulgate "occupational safety and health standards," and the EPA, which has a much broader mandate but is also authorized to regulate risks in the workplace, such as those arising from exposure to hazardous and toxic substances, for instance, under the Clean Air Act Amendments of 1990, the Toxic Substances Control Act, and the Comprehensive Environmental Response, Compensation, and Liability Act. *See* Todd S. Aagaard, *Regulatory Overlap, Overlapping Legal Fields, and Statutory Discontinuities*, Va. Envtl. L.J. 237, 240–43 (2011). Aagaard outlines a number of case studies of how the two agencies manage these areas of overlap, and finds that the two agencies enjoy a fairly cooperative, positive relationship. *Id. See, e.g.*, Jerry W. Markham, *Merging the SEC and CFTC—A Clash of Cultures*, 78 U. Cin. L. Rev. 537, 569 (2009) (providing a detailed account of the rivalry between the two commissions). Although the Commodity Futures Trading Commission and the SEC settled some of their differences under the Shad-Johnson Accords of 1982, the conflict was renewed following the stock market crash of 1987, and has never been resolved. *Id. See also* Eric J. Pan, *Structural Reform of Financial Regulation in Canada: A Research Study Prepared for the Expert Panel on Securities Regulation* 26 (Cardozo Sch. of Law, Jacob Burns Inst. for Advanced Legal Studies, Paper No. 250, 2009), *available at* http://ssrn.com/abstract=1333385.

316 Department of Energy Reorganization Act of 1977, Pub. L. No. 95-91, § 403, 91 Stat. 565, 585 (codified as amended at 42 U.S.C. § 7173(a)).

317 *Id.* § 7173(b). *See* Barkow, *supra* note 1, at 51 n.199.

Horizontally, before granting hydropower licenses, the Federal Power Act requires the FERC to "give due weight to the recommendations, expertise, and statutory responsibilities" of the National Marine Fisheries Service, the U.S. Fish and Wildlife Service, and the state fish and wildlife agencies in order to "adequately protect, mitigate damages to, and enhance fish and wildlife... affected."[318] Again, by statutory design, FERC rulemaking autonomy is preserved, but overlapping regulatory interests must at least be acknowledged.

While consultation can be statutorily established, consultation is at times a matter of custom or "best practice." The FDA and the FTC provide an example of regulatory and enforcement coordination in overlapping regulatory space.[319] Regulation of food labeling (i.e. nutritional content) is delegated to the FDA,[320] while the regulation of food advertisement (i.e. packaging) falls under the purview of the FTC.[321] This area of shared regulation presented itself following the passage of the Nutrition Labeling and Education Act of 1990,[322] which established a new labeling regime to be enacted by the FDA.[323]

According to the FTC's Enforcement Policy Statement on Food Advertising, issued in response to the passage of the Nutrition Labeling and Education Act,

> [t]he Commission recognizes the importance of consistent treatment of nutrient content and health claims in food advertising and labeling and seeks to harmonize its advertising enforcement program with FDA's food labeling regulations to the fullest extent possible.... The Commission recognizes the scientific expertise of the FDA in this area. The Commission has traditionally accorded great weight to FDA's scientific determinations in matters of nutrition and health and will continue to do so. [A]s a general matter, it is unlikely that the Commission will take action under Sections 5 and 12 of the FTC Act regarding nutrient content and health claims if they comply with FDA's regulations.[324]

The FTC did not yield the regulatory space unreservedly. Following the commission's deferential position above, it asserted the independent agency's unmitigated authority,

---

318 16 U.S.C. § 803(j)(2)(A)-(B). *See* Freeman & Rossi, *supra* note 313, at 1157–58.

319 *See* Thomas B. Leary, *The Ongoing Dialogue Between the Food and Drug Administration and the Federal Trade Commission*, 59 FOOD & DRUG L.J. 209, 210–11 (2004).

320 21 U.S.C. § 343.

321 15 U.S.C. §§ 52, 55.

322 Pub. L. No. 101-535, 104 Stat. 2353 (1990).

323 The Nutrition Labeling and Education Act provided food label regulatory authority to the Department of Health and Human Services; however, the department delegated such authority to the FDA, a component of the department. For the purposes of this discussion of Nutrition Labeling and Education Act authorities, "FDA" will be used rather than "Department of Health and Human Services."

324 59 Fed. Reg. 28388-01 (June 1, 1994).

stating that the FDA's labeling regulatory authority "did not change the FTC's statutory authority to prohibit deceptive acts and practices under Section 5 of the FTC Act."[325] While FTC independence is not statutorily limited in this case, sharing regulatory space with an executive branch agency will surely impact the function of the independent agency.[326]

Similarly, the FTC and the Antitrust Division of the DOJ, which share statutory authority under the Clayton Act to enforce a variety of antitrust laws, have often been in conflict over the review and clearance of merger proposals.[327] The Hart-Scott-Rodino Antitrust Improvements Act of 1976 established a premerger clearance process with a thirty-day waiting period set aside for the review of the merger proposal.[328]

---

325 *Id.* Even this largely voluntary arraignment is not without statutory consultation guidance. Under 21 U.S.C. § 378, the potential conflict is recognized. If the FDA seeks to initiate an action against any food product because it is misbranded because of its advertising or the food's advertising causes the food to be misbranded, it must notify the FTC. 21 U.S.C. § 378(a). Following notice, the FTC has thirty days to respond to the FDA as to its action on the matter. 21 U.S.C. § 378(b). If sixty days pass after the FTC responds to the FDA and no action is taken, the FDA may take action. *Id.* Interestingly, the statute provides that the "Secretary [of Health and Human Services] shall coordinate any action taken because of advertising" by both the FDA for misbranding and the FTC with respect to advertising. *Id.* § 378(d).

326 On occasion, an independent agency can frustrate, if not trump, an executive agency—at least temporarily. A dispute between the NRC and the DOE over the Yucca Mountain, Nevada, nuclear waste repository is an illustration. Opposing the Yucca Mountain facility, newly elected President Obama directed the DOE to seek permission to withdraw an earlier-filed application for a license to construct the permanent disposal site. However, a staff board at the NRC denied the request, and the D.C. Circuit, in July 2011, held that the board's determination was not ripe for judicial review. *In re* Aiken Cnty., 645 F.3d 428 (D.C. Cir. 2011). Following the court's decision, the commission took up the board's decision but divided equally (two to two) on how to proceed, with a fifth member recused and not participating. *In the Matter of U.S. Department of Energy (High Level Waste Repository)*, CLI 11-07, 74 N.R.C. 212 (2011). Although for lack of funding of the project the proceeding was suspended, subsequently the D.C. Circuit concluded that the NRC violated its statute by not completing the proceeding as Congress directed. *In re* Aiken Cnty., 725 F.3d 255 (D.C. Cir. 2013), *rehearing en banc denied* 2013 U.S. App. LEXIS 22033 (D.C. Cir. Oct. 28, 2013). Judge Kavanaugh noted in his 2011 *In re Aiken County* concurrence:

> This case is a mess because the executive agency (the Department of Energy) and the independent agency (the Nuclear Regulatory Commission) have overlapping statutory responsibilities.... In particular, both agencies have critical roles in interpreting the relevant statutes and in exercising discretion under those laws.

In re Aiken Cnty., 645 F.3d at 439. (Kavanaugh, J., concurrence).

327 Clayton Antitrust Act of 1914, Pub. L. No. 63-212, 38 Stat. 730 (codified as amended at 15 U.S.C. §§ 12–27, 29 U.S.C. §§ 52–53). The DOJ and FTC share the authority to enforce Sections 2, 3, 7, and 8 of the Clayton Act, which prohibits a number of anticompetitive business practices that harm consumers, such as price fixing, exclusive dealing, and mergers or acquisitions that undermine competition. U.S. Dep't of Justice, Antitrust Division Manual, ch. VII (2009), *available at* http://www.justice.gov/atr/public/divisionmanual/. Section 7 of the Clayton Act authorizes both the FTC and the DOJ to prevent the formation of monopolies. *See* 15 U.S.C. § 18 (2006).

328 The relevant portion of the Hart-Scott-Rodino Antitrust Improvements Act is codified in 15 U.S.C. § 18 (§ 7A of the Clayton Act). The purpose of the Act was to push the FTC and DOJ to prevent the formation of anticompetitive mergers, due to the difficulty and collateral damage associated with actual breakups.

While the statute did establish a clearance period for consultation between the DOJ and FTC, it did not define a procedure for such consultations.[329] Although the statute can be viewed as an effort to compel the DOJ and FTC to cooperate,[330] the interagency disputes continued to consume much of the clearance period, leaving little time for actual review of the proposed merger in question.[331] On March 5, 2002, the FTC and the DOJ Antitrust Division established a division of labor based on agency expertise, and announced a Merger Clearance Accord.[332] The agreement proved to be short-lived, however, as the two agencies were successfully pressured into abandoning the agreement due to the persistent and vitriolic resistance of Senator Ernest Hollings,[333] who threatened to cut the funding for both agencies.[334] The relationship between independent and executive branch agencies sharing the same regulatory space raises perpetual issues for the notion of independence as well as the notion of the unitary executive.

In whatever form agency coordination takes, such efforts likely impact agency independence to some degree. The Financial Stability Oversight Council was established as part of Dodd-Frank to seek coordination amongst agencies regulating the financial markets including independent agencies such as the Board of Governors of the Federal

---

329 15 U.S.C. § 18a(b)(1).

330 By imposing a statutory framework, the § 18a of the Hart-Scott-Rodino Antitrust Improvements Act compelled the DOJ and FTC to promptly resolve any disputes in order to avoid "missing the only window of opportunity for thwarting the merger before it occurred." Lauren Kearney Peay, *The Cautionary Tale of the Failed 2002 FTC/DOJ Merger Clearance Accord*, 60 VAND. L. REV. 1307, 1316 (2007).

331 Kris Dekeyser et al., *Coordination Among National Antitrust Agencies*, 10 SEDONA CONF. J. 43, 51 (2009); Federal Trade Comm'n, *Clearance Delays* (2002), *available at* http://www.ftc.gov/opa/2002/02/clearance/cleardelaystats.htm.

332 Although the FTC and DOJ issued joint merger guidelines in 1993 and 1995, neither agreement succeeded in expediting the merger clearance process. According to an FTC report, the average delay in a clearance dispute in FY 2000 and 2001 was seventeen and a half days (of the thirty days available for clearance). Federal Trade Comm'n, *Clearance Delays, supra* note 331.

333 *See* Timothy J. Muris, *Comments on the FTC-DOJ Clearance Process Before the Antitrust Modernization Commission*, 17 (2005), *available at* http://www.appliedantitrust.com/07_mergersI_guidelines/clearance/muris_statement_amc11_3_2005.pdf.

334 *See* Amanda L. Wait, *Surviving the Shipwreck: A Proposal to Revive the Failing Division Defense*, 45 WM. & MARY L. REV. 429, 467 (2003); Brent Shearer, *Merger Clearance Accord Turns Nasty*, MERGERS & ACQUISITIONS: DEALMAKERS J., June 1, 2002, at 4 ("The highlights of the dispute... included a threat by Hollings to cut the salaries of Muris and other senior regulators. Speaking to a reporter in a Capitol Hill hallway, Hollings said he was going to 'eliminate' Muris."). *See also* Peay, *supra* note 330, at 1334. Even in the absence of outside pressure, executive and independent agencies are sometimes simply unable to resolve their differences. For instance, The FEC and the DOJ abandoned efforts to update a "decades-old" memorandum of understanding to reflect changes wrought by the 2002 Bipartisan Campaign Reform Act, which "enhanced... [the] DOJ's ability to prosecute [campaign finance] crimes." Although the FEC still had the authority to initiate civil enforcement actions, only the Justice Department had the authority to bring criminal cases. *See FEC, DOJ Gave Up Effort to Improve Coordination on Campaign Finance Law*, LEGAL NEWS, Vol. 80, No. 18 at 645 (11-51-11).

Reserve System, SEC, FDIC, Commodity Futures Trading Commission, FHFA, and NCUA.[335] Under Dodd-Frank, this body seeks to coordinate independent agency financial regulatory policy with that of the White House.[336] The Financial Stability Oversight Council replaces the President's Working Group on Financial Markets, an informal interagency panel that served to informally solve jurisdictional disputes between the various financial regulators.[337]

The Financial Stability Oversight Council was designed both to coordinate policy more formally and to resolve jurisdictional conflicts. The council is composed of ten voting members—nine government officials (including independent agency chairs) plus one presidential appointee confirmed by the Senate—and five nonvoting members.[338] The secretary of the treasury serves as the council chair.[339] The council has been vested with several meaningful authorities, but one of its more controversial and important powers is to assert "authority to require supervision and regulation [by the Federal Reserve Board] of [systemically important] nonbank financial institutions."[340] The council may make such a determination only with the assent of "2/3 of the voting members then serving, including an affirmative vote of the Chairperson."[341] Such construction clearly provides the chair, the secretary of the treasury, with a predominate influence over council voting. Notwithstanding the fact that independent agencies make up the vast majority of the council, Eugene A. Ludwig persuasively argues that the Financial Stability Oversight Council will likely be "a creature of the Treasury."[342] According to Ludwig, "it

---

335 Pub. L. No. 111-203, § 111, 124 Stat. 1376, 1392 (2010) (codified as amended at 12 U.S.C. § 5321).

336 *Id.* § 112. The purpose of the Financial Stability Oversight Council is (A) "to identify risks to the financial system of the U.S. that could arise from the material financial distress or failure... of large, interconnected bank holding companies or nonbank financial companies..."; (B) "to promote market discipline, by eliminating expectations... that the Government will shield them from losses in the event of failure" (i.e., to eliminate "too big to fail"); and (C) "to respond to emerging threats to the stability of the United States financial system." U.S. 12 U.S.C. § 5322(a)(1)(A)–(C) (2010). *See* Jacob E. Gersen, *Administrative Law Goes to Wall Street: The New Administrative Process*, 65 ADMIN. L. REV. 689, 693–702 (2013).

337 The Working Group was composed of the chairs of the Federal Reserve, SEC, and Commodity Futures Trading Commission and headed by the secretary of the treasury. Exec. Order No. 12,631, 3 C.F.R § 559 (1988). *See also* Earnest Patrikis, *A Better System for Systemic Risk,* AMER. BANKER (Aug. 14, 2009); Bressman & Thompson, *supra* note 1, at 642–43.

338 12 U.S.C. § 5321.

339 12 U.S.C. § 5321(b)(1). *See* Bressman & Thompson, *supra* note 1, at 627–28. The nonvoting members are noted at 12 USC §5321 (b)(2).

340 12 U.S.C. § 5323.

341 12 C.F.R. § 1310.10; 12 U.S.C. § 5323(a)–(b). *See also* Eugene A. Ludwig, *Assessment of Dodd-Frank Financial Regulatory Reform: Strengths, Challenges, and Opportunities for a Stronger Regulatory System*, 29 YALE J. ON REG. 181, 186, 195 (2013); Charles K. Whitehead, *Regulating for the Next Financial Crisis*, 24 PAC. MCGEORGE GLOBAL BUS. & DEV. L.J. 3, 10–11 (2011).

342 Ludwig, *supra* note 341, at 186. This, despite the fact that it was created to monitor the treasury secretary's administration of the TARP fund.

is oftentimes easier not to act than to gain consensus of a body, such as the FSOC, that has a variety of constituencies, each with its own agenda."[343]

In addition, federal regulators and state supervisors may lose power at the expense of the Federal Reserve if the council begins to make findings that large financial companies are systemically important, and may attempt to prevent such a finding.[344] The ramifications of the Financial Stability Oversight Council's influence is largely still unknown, but the effect of such coordination efforts place statutory and political limits on the functional independence of independent regulatory agencies. There can be no doubt that the need for extensive coordination can slow down the regulatory process (at times, one wonders whether it is intended to do so). Freeman and Rossi take this view, arguing that overlapping authority in the same subject matter can "produce redundancy, inefficiency, and gaps" if not "profound coordination challenges."[345]

The recent "sign-off" by agencies of the so-called Volcker Rule,[346] some three years after passage of the Dodd-Frank Act, serves as an example.[347] The rule was heavily

---

The fact is that the treasury secretary has generally been able to do what he thinks is necessary, especially in the context of an economic crisis. *See, e.g.*, Brent J. Horton, *The Tarp Bailout of GM: A Legal, Historical, and Literary Critique*, 14 TEX. REV. L. & POL. 217 (2010); Jonathan G. Katz, *Who Benefited from the Bailout?*, 95 MINN. L. REV. 1568 (2011); J.W. Verret, *Treasury Inc.: How the Bailout Reshapes Corporate Theory and Practice*, 27 YALE J. ON REG. 283 (2010); Claire Hill & Richard Painter, *Compromised Fiduciaries: Conflicts of Interest in Government and Business*, 95 MINN. L. REV. 1637 (2011). A fascinating example of how the independent and executive agencies interacted is in the Federal Open Market Committee meetings with bailing out AIG. *See* ANDREW ROSS SORKIN, TOO BIG TO FAIL, 394–97 (2009).

343 Ludwig, *supra* note 341, at 186.

344 *Id.*

345 Freeman & Rossi, *supra* note 313, at 1135.

346 The "Volcker Rule" is a section of the Dodd-Frank Act proposed by Paul Volcker, former chair of the Federal Reserve Board. *See* Pub. L. No. 111-203, §619, 124 Stat. 1376, 1620 (codified as amended at 12 U.S.C. §1851). The Rule would "prohibit deposit-taking banks from trading for their own accounts. Proprietary trading—wherein banks make bets in pursuit of profit, putting depositors and taxpayers at risk—shouldn't be that hard to define." Peter Loy, *The Volcker Rule Is Tough. It's Complicated. Will It Be Effective?*, BLOOMBERG BUSINESSWEEK (Dec. 12, 2013), http://www.businessweek.com/articles/2013-12-11/the-volcker-rule. *See also* John C. Coffee, Jr., *The Political Economy of Dodd-Frank: Why Financial Reform Tends to be Frustrated and Systemic Risk Perpetuated*, 97 CORNELL L. REV. 1019, 1073–74 (2012). The legislative politics leading to inclusion of the Volcker Rule in the Dodd-Frank Act is well described in Alison K. Gary, *Creating a Future Economic Crisis: Political Failure and the Loopholes of the Volcker Rule*, 90 OREGON L. REV. 1339, 134–45 (2012). For the politics from Volcker's perspective, see WILLIAM L. SILBUR, VOLCKER: THE TRIUMPH OF PERSISTENCE 273-296 (2012). The literature on the Volcker Rule is voluminous, starting from the rule itself in 964 pages, including an 893-page preamble. *See* Onning H. Dombalagian, *The Expressive Synergies of the Volcker Rule*, 64 B.C. L. REV. 169 (2013) *passim*.

347 The rule was to be promulgated July 21, 2012, but was in fact only approved in December 2013. Joint Agency Press Release, Federal Reserve Board, CFTC, FDIC, OCC, SEC, agencies issue Final Rules Implementing the Volcker Rule (Dec. 10, 2013), http://www.occ.treas.gov/news-issuances/news-releases/2013/nr-ia-2013-186.html. To approve the new rule the following multiple agency actions were necessary:

> Votes by the federal Deposit Insurance Corp. and the Federal Reserve Board unanimously approved the measure, while the Securities and Exchange Commission approved it by a vote of

lobbied by the financial industry,[348] and some commentators believe that given the need for multiple sign-offs, the "five agencies responsible for promulgating the implementing regulations had difficulty reaching a consensus,"[349] and this may have led to some dilution of the rule.[350] Looking forward, the regulatory community fears a "legal minefield" with confusing and contradicting oversight of the Volcker Rule by the five agencies involved.[351]

L. Inspectors General

Inspectors general, and the more recent additions of special inspectors general for Iraq reconstruction, Afghanistan reconstruction, and TARP provide further examples of congressional efforts to increase inspector general autonomy in the executive branch.[352] The original Inspector General Act of 1978 created several inspector general offices housed within, but independent of, various federal agencies. The inspectors general, who have

---

> 3-2. The Commodity Futures Trading Commission voted 3-1 to approve it. At the Office of the Comptroller of the Currency, Comptroller Thomas Curry, the organization's sole voting member, was the final regulator to sign off.

Scott Patterson et al., *U.S. Starts New Era in Bank Regulation,* WALL ST. J. (European ed.), Dec. 11, 2013, at A1.

348 The extensive lobbying campaign is discussed in THOMAS O. MCGARITY, FREEDOM TO HARM: THE LASTING LEGACY OF THE LAISSEZ-FAIRE REVIVAL, 243–46 (2013). *See also* Kimberly D. Krawiec, *Don't "Screw Joe the Plummer": The Sausage-Making of Financial Reform*, 55 ARIZ. L. REV. 53, 71–78 (2013) (analyzing some eight thousand public comment letters received by the Financial Stability Oversight Council regarding Volcker Rule implementation).

349 MCGARITY, *supra* note 348, at 243.

350 *See* Jesse Eisinger, *The Volcker Rule, Made Bloated and Weak*, N.Y. TIMES DEALBOOK (Feb. 22, 2012, 12:04 p.m.), http://dealbook.nytimes.com/2012/02/22/the-volcker-rule-made-bloated-and-weak/; *see also* Evan Weinberger, *Wall Street Reform Group Warns Against Volcker Changes*, LAW360 (Jan. 21, 2014, 5:55 p.m.), http://www.law360.com/articles/502769/wall-street-reform-group-warns-against-volcker-changes.

351 Jenna Greene, *Five Cooks in Volcker Kitchen*, NAT'L L.J., Feb. 10, 2014, at 1–4. Congressional critics of the Volcker Rule implementation are troubled by the overlapping agency jurisdiction and lack of guidance for coordination under the Rule, expressing serious doubts about the effectiveness of a working group as a remedy. *See The Impact of the Volcker Rule on Job Creators, Part II: Hearing Before the House Committee on Financial Services*, 103d Cong. (2014) (statements of California Rep. Ed Royce).

352 Not all congressional action related to the inspectors general insulated them from executive control, however. For instance, the Justice Department inspector general, unlike other inspectors general, has not been provided with statutory authority to investigate all claims of wrongdoing inside his agency. Rather, within the DOJ, the Office of Professional Responsibility internally investigates certain wrongdoings. This caused controversy in 2010 when lawmakers called for Glenn Fine, the DOJ inspector general, to investigate complaints of the DOJ's "unfounded dismissal" of voter intimidation charges against the New Black Panther Party. Fine responded that he lacked jurisdiction to investigate the complaints, and the investigation could only be carried out by the Office of Professional Responsibility—which he doubted was "capable of conducting an unbiased and independent review" of the claim. *See* Jerry Seper, *Justice IG Can't Probe Panther Case Dismissal,* WASH. TIMES, Feb. 4, 2010, at A1.

been described as "unusual creatures in the federal bureaucracy,"[353] audit and investigate the agency in which they are situated.[354] Currently there are nearly sixty federal inspectors general,[355] including the three abovementioned special inspectors general, whose appointment, removal, and supervision highlight their peculiar role within the executive.

The original Inspector General Act provides for appointment of inspectors general by the president, with the advice and consent of the Senate, which is also required for the appointment of principal officers of the United States; however, Congress modified this traditional method of appointment for certain special inspectors general.[356] The president does not have direct power to appoint the special inspector general for Iraq reconstruction, though the president may have indirect authority, as this special inspector general is appointed by the secretary of defense and the secretary of state, cabinet level members of the executive branch.[357] Interestingly, the special inspector general for Afghanistan reconstruction is appointed by the president alone, and advice and consent of the Senate is not required.[358] Though this appears to give the president greater control over the special inspector general for Afghanistan reconstruction, the divergence of this provision from other congressional efforts to increase independence may be explained by further provisions providing that the president may appoint the special inspector general for Iraq reconstruction to also serve as the special inspector general for Afghanistan, though this has not been the case.[359] All inspectors general are appointed based on their expertise and ability, and appointment is not to be based on the inspector general's political affiliation.

Though the original Inspector General Act allowed the president to freely remove inspectors general without cause, the 2008 amendments require the president to report the reasons for removal to Congress thirty days prior to firing or transferring an inspector general.[360] In 2009, President Obama's removal of an inspector general sparked controversy and speculation that the removal was for inappropriate political reasons.

---

353 Stephen Barr, *Administration Opposes Bill on Inspectors General*, WASH. POST, Oct. 2, 2007, at D4.

354 5 U.S.C. App. § 2. The inspectors general are "to conduct and supervise audits and investigations" of the agencies' programs and "to provide a means for keeping the head of the establishment and the Congress fully and currently informed about the problems and deficiencies." *Id.*

355 Barr, *supra* note 353, at D4.

356 5 US.C. App. § 3(a). Appointment under the original Inspector General Act was solely to be based on "integrity and demonstrated ability in accounting, auditing, financial analysis, law, management analysis, public administration, or investigations" without regard for political affiliation. *Id.*

357 Emergency Supplemental Appropriations Act for Defense and for the Reconstruction of Iraq and Afghanistan, Pub. L. No. 108-106, § 3001, 117 Stat. 1209 1234 (2003).

358 National Defense Authorization Act for Fiscal Year 2008, Pub. L. No. 110-181, § 1229(c)(1), 122 Stat. 3, 379.

359 *Id.*

360 5 U.S.C. App. § 3(b). The George W. Bush administration protested against an earlier version of the amendments that would have required specific reasons, rather than just congressional notification. Office of Mgm't & Budget, Statement of Administration Policy: H.R. 928—To Amend the Inspector General Act Of 1978 to Enhance Independence of Inspectors General, to Create a Council of the Inspectors General on Integrity and Efficiency and for Other Purposes (Oct. 1, 2007), *available at* http://www.whitehouse.gov/sites/default/files/omb/legislative/sap/110-1/hr928sap-r.pdf.

President Obama fired Gerald Walpin, inspector general for the Corporation for National and Community Service, claiming a loss of his "fullest confidence" in Walpin's abilities.[361] It was widely noted, however, that Walpin's removal came on the heels of his investigation of misuse of federal grants by a nonprofit group led by Kevin Johnson, a prominent supporter of President Obama's campaign,[362] leading both the press and members of Congress to question the firing and whether President Obama had satisfied the requirements of the Inspector General Act.[363]

Reporting requirements further insulate the special inspectors general from the executive branch. Though inspectors general under the original Act reported to and were under the supervision of the agency heads,[364] the new special inspectors general report directly to Congress, bypassing the head of the agency they inspect.[365] In 2007, a controversial attempt to allow inspectors general to submit budget requests directly to Congress was dropped due to White House veto threats.[366] Nonetheless, the amendments as finally enacted provided inspectors general with their own legal counsel and required a separate line item in each agency's proposed budget request for the costs of operating the Office of the Inspector General.[367] President George W. Bush also objected to proposals that would have required cause for the removal of inspectors general as "an intrusion on the President's removal authority."[368] The for cause removal proposal was dropped from the legislation, though a provision remained requiring the president of agency heads to inform Congress at least thirty days in advance of a decision to remove an inspector general.[369] When President Bush signed the reform bill in October 2008, he also issued a signing statement noting his continuing concerns that the reforms governing budget line items and general counsels for the inspectors general infringed on executive agency and White House authority.[370]

---

361 Editorial, *Walpin-Gate: Obama Fires an IG*, WASH. TIMES, June 15, 2009, at A20.

362 *Id.*

363 *Id.* The legislative history of the Inspector General Act explains that "[t]he requirement to notify Congress in advance of the reasons for the removal should serve to ensure that Inspectors General are not removed for political reasons...." S. REP. NO. 110-262, at 8 (2008).

364 5 U.S.C. App. § 3(a) ("Each Inspector General shall report to and be under the general supervision of the head of the establishment involved.").

365 *Compare* Emergency Supplemental Appropriations Act for Defense and the Reconstruction of Iraq and Afghanistan § 3001(i)(1–3) (2004) (providing that the special inspectors general will transmit reports directly to Congress, and then to the secretary of state and the secretary of defense) *with* 5 U.S.C. § 5(b) (requiring inspectors general to transmit reports to the head of the agency they inspect first, and then requiring the agency head to submit the report and comments to Congress within thirty days of receipt).

366 *House Votes Overwhelmingly in Favor of Bill to Enhance IG Independence, Accountability*, 76 LEGAL NEWS 13, 2208 (Oct. 9, 2007).

367 *Bush Issues Signing Statement on Measure to Reform System of Inspector General*, 77 LEGAL NEWS 15, 2240 (Oct. 21, 2008).

368 Barr, *supra* note 353, at D4.

369 *Bush Issues Signing Statement on Measure to Reform System of Inspector General*, 77 LEGAL NEWS 15, 2240 (Oct. 21, 2008).

370 *Id.*

M. Observations

Over the years, independent entities have come, gone, and transformed as the political branches respond to changing circumstances. Three factors seem to be significant in producing change.

First, generational receptivity can serve as an important foundation for change. Pulsifer expressly makes this point with regard to the deregulation of air transportation. The Depression era population, he argues, that saw government as the solution to problems was slowly replaced by a generation that experienced relative affluence and was receptive to innovation and experimentation.[371]

Second, academic or popular (or populist) analysis of problems appears to be at least a useful, if not necessarily essential, underpinning of change. As noted in chapter 2, the intellectual impetus for government oversight of the railroad industry, including to some extent the form that it should take, was the brainchild of Charles Francis Adams, Jr. In the 1860s and 1870s, he wrote several influential articles about the economics of railroad operation that influenced the creation and structure of the ICC, the first independent regulatory agency. Recently, the idea of an agency that would regulate consumer financial products was espoused by Elizabeth Warren in her 2007 article "Unsafe at Any Rate."[372] Her argument that a new entity based on the independent agency model would be useful in protecting consumers in the financial products market was influential in the creation of the most recent regulatory agency, the CFPB.[373] A transformation from the original proposal for a multimember consumer financial protection board to its emergence as an entity headed by a single director with funding independent of annual congressional appropriations has been detailed in this chapter. But the political clash has not ended. The appointment of the CFPB's first director through the highly controversial use of the president's recess appointment power in the face of efforts to reform its structure reflect the disagreements between and within the political branches of government.

But third, and undoubtedly most important, crisis begets change; it is the primary catalyst. If some form of change seems required, institutional design frequently reflects a pragmatic compromise that accommodates the political tension between autonomy and accountability. The perception of agency bias or lack of accountability may lead Congress to design a structure that separates power. For example, Congress created the split enforcement model for occupational health and safety regulation, and

371 *See supra* text accompanying notes 225–26. *See also* Paul S. Dempsey, *The Rise and Fall of the Interstate Commerce Commission The Tortuous Path from Regulation to Deregulation of America's Infrastructure*, 95 MARQ. L. REV. 1151, 1175 (2012) (arguing that "[t]he generation of Americans who grew up during the Great Depression and World War II saw government as an essential companion..." while "the generation...who grew up in the 1960s and 1970s emerged cynical....").

372 *See supra* section D(3).

373 *Id.*

mining regulation, with some responsibility resting with an independent multimember board, because the business community resisted placing all regulatory authority in the Department of Labor. The independent oversight agencies discussed above in section F reflect a desire for some form of scrutiny by an independent entity without divesting the relevant executive branch agency of its ultimate power. The use of "superagencies" like the Financial Stability Oversight Council can be seen both as a way of securing "buy-in" by a multiplicity of agencies whose subject matter jurisdictions overlap.[374] The mix of both executive and independent agencies in such superagencies can on occasion be a way of reintroducing presidential influence into independent agency decision-making as with the designation of the secretary of the treasury to chair the Financial Stability Oversight Council.[375]

At the same time we cannot ignore the politics between the executive and Congress. It is obvious that even liberal presidential staff today accept the constitutionality of centralized executive control of independent agencies. Yet the desire to avoid political confrontation has led presidents of both parties to decline to exercise what most academic observers believe is their authority to oversee the rulemaking process at independent agencies.[376]

Efforts to alter the structure or design of independent bodies may fail entirely, notwithstanding the presence of the factors noted above. This is due principally to division among relevant interest groups, including, at times, competing congressional committees, or executive branch opposition where Congress attempts to confer additional elements of independence for any new independent entities.

---

374 The term "super agencies" is drawn from Gersen, *supra* note 336, at 692–93.

375 Gersen, *supra* note 336, at 699. One cannot but think of the 1935 statute to remove the secretary of the treasury from the Federal Reserve Board. *See* chapter 2, text at notes 225–33. *Autre temps, autre mores.*

376 *See supra* chapter 6, section D.

8

Further Along on the Continuum

GOVERNMENT FUNCTIONS AND PRIVATE ENTERPRISE

NOTWITHSTANDING THE INCREASED focus on issues of agency accountability since the Great Society, recent years have seen a seeming efflorescence of entities created to meet the challenges of the modern administrative state—all with varying levels of government control. Two such regimes are public corporations and GSEs. Public corporations, also called federal government corporations (FGCs), are generally statutorily created governmental entities structured like corporations that are owned or controlled by the U.S. government.[1] A GSE is further removed from government control and more closely resembles a private enterprise. Beyond FGCs and GSEs, private parties have increasingly taken over a variety of public functions through privatization,[2] which includes "contracting out."[3] Regulatory functions have been privatized by contracting them to

---

[1] The Government Corporation Control Act defines government corporations as either mixed-ownership corporations or wholly owned government corporations. While the Act lists twenty-eight entities as government corporations, several of those listed are now obsolete. 5 U.S.C. § 103 (2006); 31 U.S.C. § 9101–9110; *see* KEVIN KOSAR, CONG. RESEARCH SERV., RL30365, FEDERAL GOVERNMENT CORPORATIONS: AN OVERVIEW 2–4, 13 (2011) (stating that the Government Corporation Control Act fails to provide a standard definition or the characteristics of what makes a government corporation and that entities, such as the now defunct Pennsylvania Avenue Development Corporation, remain untouched within the contents of the Act). The definition utilized by the Congressional Research Service concludes that a government corporation "is an agency of the federal government, established by congress to perform a public purpose." *Id.* at 2. Using that definition, the Congressional Research Service considers seventeen entities to be government corporations. For a list of these entities, see *infra* note 14.

[2] *See* Marianne Lavelle, *Public Works Go Private*, NAT'L L.J., Sept. 25, 1995, at 13. *See infra* chapter 8, section E.

[3] Daniel Guttman, *Public Purpose and Private Service: The Twentieth Century Culture of Contracting Out and the Evolving Law of Diffused Sovereignty*, 52 ADMIN. L. REV. 859, 923–26 (2000). *See generally* DAVID

private industry, as have enforcement functions through the use of industry self-audits and third-party audits.[4] Jody Freeman has incisively referred to regimes of "mixed administration" where the government and private actors share regulatory roles.[5] Some of these more flexible arrangements might be described as part of the burgeoning "new governance" approach to regulation, which seeks out public-private partnership approaches to regulation.[6]

A. Public Corporations

1. HISTORICAL FOUNDATIONS

When Congress chooses to employ a public corporation to undertake the nation's business, it does so because it believes that public corporations[7] can more easily utilize the expertise of the private sector to combat significant problems that it is believed require a government response.[8] As the conference committee creating the TVA noted, "[w]e intend that the corporation shall have much of the essential freedom and elasticity of a private business corporation."[9] Examples of public corporations include the Legal Services Corporation,[10] the Corporation for Public Broadcasting,[11] the National

Osborne & Ted Gaebler, Reinventing Government: How the Entrepreneurial Spirit Is Transforming the Public Sector (1992).

4 Jody Freeman, *The Private Role in Public Governance*, 75 N.Y.U. L. Rev. 543, 597 (2000). *See infra* section E, subsection 4.

5 Jody Freeman, *Private Parties, Public Functions and the New Administrative Law*, 52 Admin. L. Rev. 813, 816 (2000).

6 "New governance" refers to "innovative modes of public governance," which reject "command-style, fixed rule regulation by administrative fiat" for alternative flexible modes of regulation. Bradley C. Karkkainen, *"New Governance" in Legal Thought and in the World: Some Splitting as Antidote to Overzealous Lumping*, 89 Minn. L. Rev. 471, 472–73 (2004); *see* Lester M. Salamon, *The New Governance and the Tools of Public Action: An Introduction*, 28 Fordham Urb. L.J. 1611 (2001). *See generally* Law and New Governance in the EU and the US (Grainne de Burca & Joanne Scott eds., 2006); Jason M. Solomon, *Law and Government in the 21st Century Regulatory State*, 86 Tex. L. Rev. 819 (2008) (reviewing Law and New Governance in the EU and the US).

7 We interchangeably use the synonymous terms "public corporation" and "federal government corporation" (FGC).

8 *See* Harold J. Krent, *The Private Performing the Public: Delimiting Delegations to Private Parties*, 65 U. Miami L. Rev. 507, 521 (2011). Such approaches have been collectively termed "new governance." *See supra* note 6.

9 *Operation of Muscle Shoals Properties*, H.R. Rep. No. 73-130, 19 (1933).

10 42 U.S.C. § 2996b (2006). *See* Earl Johnson, Jr., Justice and Reform: the Formative Years of the American Legal Services Program x–xxiii (1978); Scott Cummings, *The Politics of Pro Bono*, 52 UCLA L. Rev. 1, 21–23 (2004) (discussing a brief history of the Legal Services Corporation).

11 47 U.S.C. § 396 (2006); *see also* A History of Public Broadcasting (Steve Behrens ed., 2000); Michele Hilmes, Only Connect: A Cultural History of Broadcasting in the United States 231–33 (2002).

Railroad Passenger Corporation (Amtrak),[12] and the Pension Benefit Guaranty Corporation.[13] While some FGCs serve nonprofit objectives in a corporate structure, others resemble private corporations both in structure and marketplace competitiveness. In 2011, the Congressional Research Service identified seventeen government corporations that "provide market-oriented public service and... produce revenues that meet or approximate its expenditures."[14] The cornerstone of these entities is their independence, which they possess because of their location outside of the political realm. While they share similar characteristics with the independent agencies—such as expertise, independence, and reduced accountability—their corporate structure is the feature that sets them apart.[15] As pointed out by Ronald Moe, "[c]orporations could be, it was believed, 'depoliticized' and run on a professional basis."[16] And such "[p]rofessional managers," Moe continues, "would be insulated to a degree from overt politics."[17]

Public corporations became integrated into our government system during the Progressive and New Deal eras. Although the existence of public corporations in America dates at least as far back as the creation of the First Bank of the United States in the early nineteenth century, and possibly as far back as the colonial period and entities like the Massachusetts Bay Company.[18] Indeed, whether Congress had the power to charter corporations, such as the Bank of the United States, was "one of the most controversial of the

---

12 49 U.S.C. § 24301(a) (establishing that Amtrak "shall be operated and managed as a for-profit corporation").

13 29 U.S.C. § 1302 (2006); *see* John J. Topoleski, Cong. Research Serv., Pension Benefit Guaranty Corporation (PBGC): A Fact Sheet (2012).

14 Kosar, *supra* note 1, at 2, 15 (applying a market-oriented and revenue producing definition of FGC, the following entities are included: Commodity Credit Corporation, Export-Import Bank, Federal Crop Insurance Corporation, Federal Deposit Insurance Corporation, Federal Financing Bank, Federal Prison Industries (UNICOR), Financing Corporation, Government National Mortgage Corporation, National Railroad Passenger Corporation (Amtrak), Overseas Private Investment Corporation, Pension Benefit Guaranty Corporation, Presidio Trust of San Francisco, Resolution Funding Corporation, St. Lawrence Seaway Development Corporation, TVA, U.S. Postal Service, and Valles Caldera Trust.). Kosar notes that while new government corporations are occasionally established, existing corporations are also frequently dissolved. *Id.* at 2.

15 Interestingly, the U.S. Postal Service is statutorily identified as an "independent establishment of the executive branch" and not a government corporation. 39 U.S.C. § 201 (2006). However, its enabling statute includes provisions normally found in those of government corporations such as the right to "sue or be sued." 39 U.S.C. § 401 (2006). Regardless of the statutory language, the Postal Service functions much like, and at times is considered, a government corporation. *See, e.g.*, Gerald Cullinan, The United States Postal Service 231–32 (1973); Kosar, *supra* note 1, at 4.

16 *See* Ronald Moe, Cong. Research Serv., S. Prt. 104-18, Managing the Public's Business: Federal Government Corporations 2–3 (1995) [hereinafter Moe Report].

17 *Id.*

18 *See* Harold Archer Van Dorn, Government Owned Corporations 227–28 (1926). *See also* James Beermann, *Privatization and Political Accountability*, 28 Fordham Urb. L.J. 1507, 1550 (2001); Oliver Peter Field, *Government Corporations: A Proposal*, 48 Harv. L. Rev. 775, 775 (1935).

many issues that arose in the early years of the Republic,"[19] and is, of course, the gravamen of the Supreme Court's ruling in *McCulloch v. Maryland*.[20]

Chartered in 1791, the First Bank of the United States is one of the earliest examples of a shared ownership structure between the federal government and private corporate enterprise.[21] Operating pursuant to a mixed-ownership structure, the government reserved the right to purchase 20 percent of the First Bank's shares.[22] However, as the First Bank's charter specifically provided that government shares had no voting power, the government had no power to elect the First Bank's board of directors.[23] Speaking of the leadership of the First Bank, Alexander Hamilton wrote:

> What nation was ever blessed with a constant succession of upright and wise administrators? The keen, steady, and, as it were, magnetic sense of their own interest, as proprietors, in the directors of the bank, is the only security that can always be relied upon for a careful and prudent administration. It is, therefore, the only basis on which an enlightened, unqualified, and permanent confidence can be expected to be erected and maintained.[24]

However, despite the confidence of Hamilton, as discussed below, the Second Bank of the United States and most modern public corporation models provide for government control over some, if not all, board appointments.[25]

The first outright acquisition of a corporation by the federal government occurred in 1904 with the purchase of the Panama Railroad Company.[26] With the authority

---

19 Mark Killenbeck, M'Culloch v. Maryland: Securing a Nation 13–14 (2006).

20 McCulloch v. Maryland, 17 U.S. 316 (1819) (determining that the necessary and proper clause contained within Art. I, § 8, cl. 18 of the Constitution permitted Congress to establish corporations) *see also* A. Michael Froomkin, *Reinventing the Government Corporation*, 1995 U. Ill. L. Rev. 543, 551–53 (1995).

21 Prior to the First Bank of the United States, Alexander Hamilton and Robert Morris, the superintendent of finance, presented a plan to Congress for the Bank of North America. The act incorporating the Bank of North America was passed by the Congress of the Confederation on December 31, 1781. 21 J.C.C. 1186 (Dec. 31, 1871). The government was the majority shareholder of the Bank of North America, whereas with the First Bank of the United States, the government was the largest albeit not the majority shareholder. *See* Van Dorn, *supra* note 18, at 227–31. *See generally* Lawrence Lewis, Jr., A History of the Bank of North America (1882).

22 See, An Act to Incorporate the Subscribers to the Bank of the United States, ch. 10, 1 Stat. 191, 191–96 (1791) (the current version of the National Bank Act is 12 U.S.C. § 38 (2006)). *See* Kosar, *supra* note 1, at 3.

23 An Act to Incorporate the Subscribers to the Bank of the United States, ch. 10, 1 Stat. 191, 191–96 (1791) (the current version of The National Bank Act is 12 U.S.C. § 38 (2006)). *See also* Edwin J. Perkins, American Public Finance and Financial Services 1700–1815, 235–36 (1994).

24 James O. Wettereau, *New Light on the First Bank of the United States*, 61 Pa. Magazine of History & Biography 263, 273 (1937) (quoting Alexander Hamilton, *American State Papers: Finance I*, 67–76).

25 Perkins, *supra* note 23, at 235–36.

26 *See* Marshall Dimock, Government-Operated Enterprises in the Panama Canal Zone 55–59 (1934); Van Dorn, *supra* note 18, at 235 (indicating that the assets of the Panama Railroad Company, including its shares, were turned over to the New Panama Canal Company, which was formed in 1894).

provided by the Spooner Act of 1902, President Theodore Roosevelt purchased the "rights, privileges, franchises, concessions, grants of land, right of way . . . and other property, real, personal, and mixed" of the company, with its shares and stock, for roughly 40 million dollars.[27] Following the acquisition, the president promptly arranged for the election of a board of directors to assure that the policy of the board was "completely harmonized" with that of the U.S. government.[28]

The number of FGCs established during both world war eras further demonstrates the heightened significance of the relationship between the government, private corporations, and the fluctuating needs of the American public. The FGC structure was particularly appreciated by Progressives, who espoused theories of scientific management and valued the potential for efficiency and freedom from partisan politics.[29] Following the mobilization efforts during World War I, President Wilson stressed the need to bring business principles to the government and successfully compelled Congress to establish several public corporations during his term.[30] During 1917 and 1918, the following wartime corporations were chartered: the U.S. Shipping Board Emergency Fleet Corporation, Food Administration Grain Corporation, War Finance Corporation, U.S. Housing Corporation, and Sugar Equalization Board.[31] President Franklin D. Roosevelt increased the total number of public corporations in response to the Great Depression, a

---

27 Panama Canal (Spooner) Act of 1902, 32 Stat. 481 (superseded by the Panama Canal Act of 1979 codified as 22 U.S.C. § 3601 (2006)). *See* VAN DORN, *supra* note 18, at 237. The United States purchased the French company named the New Panama Canal Company or Compagnie Nouvelle du Canal de Panama, which was originally held by the United States as the Panama Canal Railroad Company. The name was changed by statute to the Panama Canal Company in 1950. Act of September 26, 1950, 64 Stat. 1038 (1950).

28 VAN DORN, *supra* note 18, at 237.

29 *See* MOE REPORT, *supra* note 16, at 2. For more on the role of the Progressive movement in the promotion of scientific management in government, *see* chapter 2, *supra* at notes 124–30 and accompanying text.

30 KOSAR, *supra* note 1, at 3–4 (noting that spurts in the prevalence of government corporations tend to follow national emergencies and that after the passing of such emergencies many of the government corporations chartered to respond are "abolished or absorbed into the permanent executive branch agencies.") *See also* Field, *supra* note 18, at 776 ("[w]hen the War came, and later when the depression of 1929 came, government participation in corporations and use of the corporate form of organization again came to the fore. The need for cutting 'red tape' and delay and for escaping the traditionalism of bureaucratic administration [was] emphasized.").

31 JOHN MCDIARMID, GOVERNMENT CORPORATIONS AND FEDERAL FUNDS, 24–30 (1938). These FGCs were chartered through a variety of methods—U.S. Shipping Board Emergency Fleet Corporation, Shipping Act of 1916, 39 Stat. 728 (Sept. 7, 1916); Food Administration Grain Corporation, *Authority to Organize Food Administration Grain Corporation*, Exec. Order No. 2681 (Aug. 14, 1917); War Financing Corporation, War Finance Corporation Act, 40 Stat. 506 (Apr. 5, 1918); U.S. Housing Corporation, Emergency Appropriation Act of June 4, 1918, 40 Stat. 595 (Jun. 4, 1918) (allowing the creation of the U.S. Housing Corporation by the secretary of labor on July 8, 1918, pursuant to Exec. Order No. 2889 (June 18, 1918)); Sugar Equalization Board, established within the Food Administration by Executive action on July 11, 1918. Two additional FGCs, the Spruce Production Corporation and the Russian Bureau, Inc., were created in 1918, but became inactive shortly after their chartering due to the end of the World War I. *See* MCDIARMID, *supra* note 31, at 29–30.

trend that continued throughout the New Deal.[32] For example, the Commodity Credit Corporation, Federal Housing Administration, and TVA were all created in 1933.[33]

President Roosevelt valued the public corporation because its structure lent itself to experimentation as a mechanism for confronting the large-scale problems that plagued the American population.[34] For example, the TVA employed scientists and engineers for their expertise to control the spread of the malaria epidemic in the South.[35] Such public corporations were also valued for their greater emphasis on "managerial values," which steered government policy further from "partisan political values."[36] In a case study of the TVA, sociologist Philip Selznick described its managerial autonomy as "[a] revolt against the conception of government as a necessary evil and government officials as inherently tainted."[37] The public corporation structure was even applauded by the Brownlow Committee, which largely disapproved of the concept of the independent agency.[38]

During World War II, the government continued to establish new corporations to aid the war effort.[39] Problems arose when Congress authorized the Reconstruction Finance

32 *See* JERRY MITCHELL, THE AMERICAN EXPERIMENT WITH GOVERNMENT CORPORATIONS 25 (1999). *See also* U.S. GOV'T ACCOUNTABILITY OFFICE, GAO-10-97, FEDERALLY CREATED ENTITIES: AN OVERVIEW OF KEY ATTRIBUTES 13 (2009) [hereinafter GAO, FEDERALLY CREATED ENTITIES] (stating that government corporations are entities created by federal charters addressing a public purpose while assuming a corporate form).

33 MOE REPORT, *supra* note 16, at 30. *See, e.g.*, MARGUERITE OWEN, THE TENNESSEE VALLEY AUTHORITY 177–79 (1973); WAYNE D. RASMUSSEN AND GLADYS L. BAKER, THE DEPARTMENT OF AGRICULTURE 53, 237 (1972).

34 MOE REPORT, *supra* note 16, at 4.

35 Polly J. Price, *Federalization of the Mosquito: Structural Innovation in the New Deal Administrative State*, 60 EMORY L.J. 325, 347 (2010).

36 MOE REPORT, *supra* note 16, at 2–3.

37 PHILIP SELZNICK, TVA AND THE GRASS ROOTS: A STUDY IN THE SOCIOLOGY OF FORMAL ORGANIZATION 29 (1949); *See id.* at 29–37 (claiming the characteristics ensuring the TVA's managerial autonomy were (1) freedom from control by the Civil Service Commission; (2) freedom from the control of the GAO; and (3) freedom to apply revenues to current operational expenses). This autonomy matured throughout the history of the TVA. The TVA was subject to GAO oversight at its inception in 1933, but this administrative check on the TVA was removed statutorily by 1935. John McDiarmid, *The Financial Powers of Government as Defined in Acts of Congress*, 15 TEX. L. REV. 437, 450–52 (1937). Such autonomy does vary as, for example, the Federal Prison Industries, Inc. does function under the oversight of the GAO. *Id.* at 451–52. We note that in a 1940 case, the Sixth Circuit Court of Appeals upheld the removal of a TVA director by the president. Morgan v. TVA, 115 F.2d 990 (6th Cir. 1940) *cert. denied*, 312 U.S. 701 (1941). The court found that the TVA exercised "predominately an executive or administrative function," *id.* at 993, and was at that time classified as "predominately an administrative arm of the executive department." *Id.* at 994. Today the TVA describes itself as "a corporation owned by the U.S. government." Tennessee Valley Authority, *About TVA*, http://www.tva.com/abouttva/index.htm (last visited Aug. 31, 2012).

38 PRESIDENT'S COMMITTEE ON ADMINISTRATIVE MANAGEMENT, ADMINISTRATIVE MANAGEMENT IN THE GOVERNMENT OF THE UNITED STATES (1937).

39 *See* KOSAR, *supra* note 1, at 5.

Corporation to create corporations without specific congressional authorization.[40] This corporation, originally established to deal with Depression-related issues, took advantage of this new authority and began incorporating its own corporations.[41] In response, Congress passed the Government Corporation Control Act to establish standards for FGC budgets, audits, debt management, and depository practices.[42] The statute also stated that FGCs were, in effect, government agencies and subject to the same rules and regulations as any other federal agency.[43] It also prohibited the creation of new FGCs without specific authorization from Congress.[44]

The Government Corporation Control Act also mandated that corporations that had been created without specific grants from Congress be dissolved.[45] Therefore, after World War II ended, many of the corporations created during the war ceased to exist.[46] The trend toward the expansion of FGCs fizzled out, at least until the 1960s.[47]

2. ORGANIZATION OF THE PUBLIC CORPORATION

Aside from some aspect of governmental control, no two FGCs are exactly alike.[48] The goal of an FGC is to "combine the superior features of each sector" in a manner that separates politics and administration while still possessing an indirect obligation of public accountability.[49] The private expertise within public corporations also provides an important benefit to the American public. Public corporations are generally designed to be self-sustaining and profit-making entities—thus a degree removed from the political fray.[50]

---

40 *See* Paul E. Lund, *Federally Chartered Corporations and Federal Jurisdiction*, 36 FLA. ST. U. L. REV. 317, 320–26 (2009) (discussing the history of the creation of FGCs during the twentieth century); *see also* Lebron v. National R.R. Passenger Corp., 513 U.S. 374, 388–89 (1995).

41 *See* Lund, *supra* note 40, at 323. These corporations included, *inter alia*, Defense Plant Corporation, the Defense Supplies Corporation, the Metals Reserve Company (which itself created several subsidiaries), the Petroleum Reserves Corporation, the Rubber Development Corporation, and the War Damage Corporation. *Id.; see also Lebron*, 513 U.S. at 389.

42 *See* Government Corporation Control Act, Pub. L. No. 79-248, 59 Stat. 597 (1945) (codified as amended at 31 U.S.C. §§ 9101–10 (2006)); KOSAR, *supra* note 1, at 5; *see also* Benjamin A. Kemplin, *The Public Trust in Private Hands: Social Security and the Politics of Government*, 96 KY. L.J. 369, 385 (2008) (discussing the passage of the Government Corporation Control Act). The Government Corporation Control Act is further discussed in section B, subsection 2, *infra*.

43 *See* Government Corporation Control Act, Pub. L. No. 79-248, 59 Stat. 597 (1945).

44 *See id.; see also Lebron*, 513 U.S. at 389.

45 *See* Government Corporation Control Act, Pub. L. No. 79-248, 59 Stat. 597 (1945); *see also Lebron*, 513 U.S. at 389.

46 *See Lebron*, 513 U.S. at 389.

47 *See* Lund, *supra* note 40, at 324.

48 KOSAR, *supra* note 1, at 5.

49 MITCHELL, *supra* note 32, at 11 (while this is the general intention behind government corporations, the structure and characteristics of individual government corporations vary greatly).

50 They do not, of course, always make the hoped for profit. *See, e.g.*, Deb Richmann, *Pension Agency Faces Huge Shortfall: $33 Billion Deficit Could Force Bailout*, PITTSBURGH POST-GAZETTE, May 20, 2009, at

Congress typically defines FGCs as either wholly owned or mixed ownership corporations.[51] Wholly owned public corporations such as the Pension Benefit Guaranty Corporation, TVA, and Commodity Credit Corporation are treated like agencies located within the executive branch and subject to executive control.[52] However, mixed ownership public corporations, such as the FDIC,[53] are considered more akin to private entities, and presidential control over them is tenuous. Thus it has been argued that when the federal government owns more than half of the shares of a mixed-ownership FGC, the corporation should be constitutionally recognized as a state actor.[54]

Public corporations are frequently utilized because of their unique organizational structure. They are managed by a board of directors or governors that may be only partially composed of members who are appointed by the president (with the advice and consent of the Senate), while the remaining members are appointed by shareholder election.[55] The FGC board of directors is intended to function just like the board of

---

A6 ("[t]he beleaguered agency is being saddled with the underfunded pension plans of companies going bankrupt in the worst economic slump since the Great Depression.... [a] midyear financial update... shows the $11.1 billion deficit that the agency posted at the end of its fiscal year... has swelled by $22.5 billion").

[51] "Government corporation" is defined in the United States Code as "a mixed-ownership Government corporation and a wholly owned Government Corporation." "wholly owned government corporations," "mixed-ownership government corporations." 31 U.S.C. § 9101(1). The Code defines "mixed-ownership Government Corporation" by listing the following FGCs: the Central Bank for Cooperatives, the FDIC, the Federal Home Loan Banks, the Federal Intermediate Credit Banks, the Federal Land Banks, the NCUA Central Liquidity Facility, the Regional Banks for Cooperatives, the Rural Telephone Bank (as defined in (2)(H)), the Finance Corporation, the Resolution Trust Corporation, and the Resolution Funding Corporation. 31 U.S.C. § 9101 (2). The Code defines "wholly owned Government Corporations" by listing the following FGCs: the Commodity Credit Corporation, the Community Development Financial Institutions Fund, the Export-Import Bank of the United States, the Federal Crop Insurance Corporation, Federal Prison Industries, Inc., the Corporation for National and Community Service, the Government National Mortgage Association, the Overseas Private Investment Corporation, the Pennsylvania Avenue Development Corporation, the Pension Benefit Guaranty Corporation, the Rural Telephone Bank (as defined by (3)(K)), the Saint Lawrence Seaway Development Corporation, the secretary of housing and urban development when carrying out duties and power related to the Federal Housing Administration Fund, the TVA, the Panama Canal Commission, the Millennium Challenge Corporation, and the International Clean Energy Foundation. 31 U.S.C. § 9101(3). *See* Froomkin, *supra* note 20, at 608.

[52] *See* U.S. Gov't Accountability Office, GAO-08-1162T, Pension Benefit Guaranty Corporation: Improvements Needed to Address Financial and Management Challenges 1 (2008) (statement of Barbara D. Bovbjerg, director, Education, Workforce and Income Security); W. V. Howard, Authority in TVA Land (1948); Owen, *supra* note 33, at 177–79; Froomkin, *supra* note 20, at 554–55 (in wholly owned federal corporations, the government holds 100 percent of the equity in addition to exercising 100 percent of the voting power of the governing body whereas the government may own a portion or none of the equity in mixed ownership corporations).

[53] 12 U.S.C. § 1811 (2006) (establishing the FDIC)*; see also* 12 U.S.C. § 1819 (2006) (describing the corporate powers of the FDIC)*; see, e.g.*, Lewis Seidman, Full faith and Credit: The Great S & L Debacle and Other Washington Sagas 65–68 (2000).

[54] Froomkin, *supra* note 20, at 572.

[55] *Id.* at 555, 573–75. The presence of board members appointed by the president does not automatically translate to the corporation being a state actor; therefore the private legal character of a public corporation is not undermined.

a large public corporation, where members are presumably qualified to recognize and address issues specific to the industry in which the corporations are engaged.[56]

The United States Postal Service, for example, is an independent establishment within the executive branch that is overseen by an eleven-member Board of Governors, only nine of whom are appointed by the president with the advice and consent of the Senate.[57] The chair is elected by the Board of Governors.[58] Much like traditional multimember independent agencies, the governors serve staggered fixed terms with "for cause" removal protection and with the nine presidentially appointed governors reflecting a mandated partisan balance.[59] However, like a private corporation, the structure of the United States Postal Service includes committees with the task of overseeing particular areas, such as the audit and finance committee.[60]

The FDIC has five board members, of whom three are presidential appointees.[61] Similarly, prior to its privatization, the Communications Satellite Corporation was composed of fifteen board members, of whom three were appointed by the president with the advice and consent of the Senate.[62] In contrast, all eleven board members of the Legal Services Corporation and all nine for Corporation for Public Broadcasting are presidential appointees.[63] In 1998, Amtrak's original board of directors was replaced by a "Reform

---

[56] Disagreements nevertheless persist regarding the usefulness, necessity, and role boards of directors play in government corporations. KOSAR, *supra* note 1, at 9; *Answering the Administration's Call for Postal Reform—Parts I, II, and III: Hearings Before the Special Panel on Postal Reform and Oversight of the H. Comm. of Government Reform*, 108th Cong. 334 (2004) (statement of David Fineman, Chairman, United States Postal Service Board of Governors).

[57] 39 U.S.C. §§ 201–202 (2006).

[58] 39 U.S.C. § 202 (2006). It is important to note that no more than five appointees are permitted to be adherents of the same political party. Under the former U.S. Post Office Department, which was eradicated in 1971, the postmaster general was a member of the president's cabinet. The reorganization of the postal service was intended to remove politics and politicians from the management of the organization. *See* CULLINAN, *supra* note 15, at 231–32.

[59] 39 U.S.C. § 202(a)(1)–(b)(1).

[60] *See* 39 U.S.C. § 402. *See also Answering the Administration's Call for Postal Reform—Parts I, II, and III: Hearings Before the Special Panel on Postal Reform and Oversight of the H. Comm. of Government Reform*, 108th Cong. 324 (2004) (written testimony of William L. Davis, chairman, president and CEO of RR Donnelley).

[61] 12 U.S.C. §§ 1811, 1812 (2006). The remaining two board positions are *ex officio* members, the comptroller of the currency and the director of the CFPB. *Id.*

[62] Communications Satellite Act of 1962, Pub. L. No. 87-624, § 303(a), 76 Stat. 419. In 2000, the Communications Satellite Corporation was acquired by Lockheed Martin after roughly two years of clearing statutory and regulatory hurdles inhibiting the privatization of the public corporation. *Lockheed Martin Gets Approval to Complete Acquisition of Comsat*, WALL ST. J., Aug. 1, 2000, at B2. *See* Open Market Reorganization for the Betterment of International Telecommunications Act, Pub. L. No. 106-180, 114 Stat. 48 (2000) (allowing for the private industry acquisition of Communications Satellite Corporation, amending key provisions of the Communications Satellite Act of 1962, Pub. L. No. 87-624, 76 Stat. 419).

[63] 47 U.S.C. § 396(c) (2006); 42 U.S.C. § 2996 (2006). Government corporations such as these, however, do not perform commercial functions, nor do they rely solely on annual congressional appropriations. KOSAR, *supra* note 1, at 5.

Board" with seven members—all of whom are appointed by the president with the advice and consent of the Senate.[64] Since these boards are separate from the traditional three branches of the federal government, they operate outside the constitutional systems of checks and balances and are exempt from many federal statutes.

3. RECENT DEVELOPMENT OF PUBLIC CORPORATIONS

Recently established FGCs include the Millennium Challenge Corporation[65] and the International Clean Energy Foundation, both of which require that specific cabinet level officers sit on the board of directors.[66] The Millennium Challenge Corporation was established in 2004 to provide assistance in global development with the purpose of promoting economic growth, eliminating extreme poverty, and encouraging good governance abroad.[67] Much like a traditional corporation, and unlike a government agency, the International Clean Energy Foundation (responsible for both energy security and reducing greenhouse gas emissions worldwide)[68] has a chief executive officer who is appointed by the board, but with the advice and consent of the Senate, and is under the direct authority of the board.[69]

Some observers have advocated the public corporation model as a means to address issues of administrative flexibility and efficiency. In a 2005 report, the National Academy of Public Administration proposed the transition of the United States Patent and Trademark Office to a wholly owned government corporation in order to "enable the agency to respond more forcefully and effectively to fluctuations in workload volume and changes in technology."[70] The proposal, however, does not appear to have gained any legislative traction.

---

64 49 U.S.C. § 24302 (2006). There are three board members for Amtrak and each is appointed by the president with the advice and consent of the Senate. 16 U.S.C. § 831a (2006).

65 22 U.S.C. § 7703 (2012) (the board of the Millennium Challenge Corporation must include the secretary of state, secretary of the treasury, and administrator of the Agency for International Development).

66 42 U.S.C.§ 17352 (2012) (the International Clean Energy Foundation's board must also include the secretary of state, as well as the secretary of energy).

67 22 U.S.C. § 7701 (2012); GAO, FEDERALLY CREATED ENTITIES, *supra* note 32, at 14.

68 42 U.S.C. § 17352(a)(3) (2012).

69 42 U.S.C. § 17352(b)(2) (2012).

70 NATIONAL ACADEMY OF PUBLIC ADMINISTRATION, U.S. PATENT AND TRADEMARK OFFICE: TRANSFORMING TO MEET THE CHALLENGES OF THE 21ST CENTURY 166 (2005). *See* U.S. CHAMBER OF COMMERCE, RECOMMENDATION FOR CONSIDERATION BY THE INCOMING ADMINISTRATION REGARDING THE U.S. PATENT AND TRADEMARK OFFICE 15–16 (2008); *see also* Jeffery M. Samuels and Linda B. Samuels, *The Trademark Office as a Government Corporation*, 7 FORDHAM INTELL. PROP. MEDIA & ENT. L.J. 137 (1996).

B. Government Constraints and Constitutional Obligations on Public Corporations

1. GENERAL OBLIGATIONS

Federal government corporations are subject to varying degrees of government control, consequently raising concerns over their legitimacy as well as governmental accountability. Overall, government corporations have greater independence than independent agencies and executive departments and entities because they generally do not depend on annual government appropriations.[71] Generally silent on the operations of public administration, the Constitution does not prohibit the creation of government corporations and the authority of the public officials who create them.[72] Those that are wholly owned or controlled by the government are often subject to regulatory statutes such as the APA or F.O.I.A. and are treated more like agencies, while those that have a more tenuous connection to the government possess greater autonomy.[73]

Like independent agencies, government corporations have been created in an ad hoc manner and can be structurally ambiguous.[74] Each is uniquely tailored to address an aspect of national policy that needs specialized attention. Politicians highlight their supervision and control over corporations when their programs are effective and advantageous to the politician; but they can also distance themselves from public corporations when problems materialize.[75] As the nature of the corporation moves closer to the private ownership end of the spectrum, the amount of control that the government wields over the corporation's activities wanes. For example, the Communications Satellite Corporation was created specifically with the objective of being categorized as a private corporation, not an FGC.[76] By not having it fall within the admittedly ambiguous

---

71 *See, e.g.*, GAO, FEDERALLY CREATED ENTITIES, *supra* note 32, at 14 (noting that as a consequence of such independence, Congress typically grants government corporations greater operational flexibility).

72 MITCHELL, *supra* note 32, at 18.

73 *Compare* Irwin Mem'l Blood Bank v. American Nat'l Red Cross, 640 F.2d 1051, 1057 (9th Cir. 1981) (explaining that the Red Cross is "a close ally" of the United States but not an "agency" subject to the FOIA), *with* Rocap v. Indiek, 539 F.2d 174, 181 (D.C. Cir. 1976) (holding that "federal characteristics" of the Federal Home Loan Mortgage Corporation make it a government corporation subject to the FOIA); *see also* Lee Constr. Co. v. Fed. Reserve Bank of Richmond, 558 F. Supp. 165, 178–80 (D. Md. 1982) (holding that the Federal Reserve Bank is subject to the APA, specifically noting that although not all members of the bank's board of directors are presidentially appointed and the Bank is federally chartered and subject to close governmental control).

74 The size and variation of functions of government corporations are demonstrated by the broad scope they cover. *See, e.g.*, MITCHELL, *supra* note 32, at 47, 89 (stating that they have been created because of entrepreneurial activity, pressure, willingness expressed by public officials and social benefit).

75 *See id.* at 95 (listing inconsistencies in practices associated with board governance).

76 MOE REPORT, *supra* note 16, at 11 (the Communications Satellite Corporation was established as a private, for-profit corporation as opposed to a government corporation).

definition of an FGC, the federal government was able to play a role in "shaping" the corporation within the private sector while, at the same time, bestowing on the corporation some governmental advantages.[77]

In contrast, despite calls to privatize the U.S. Postal Service, the 2002–2003 President's Commission on the United States Postal Service rejected privatization alternatives in favor of more modest reforms, retaining the U.S. Postal Service's statutory model as an "independent establishment within the executive branch."[78] The Postal Accountability and Enhancement Act, passed in 2006, increased governmental controls over the Postal Service.[79] For example, the legislation replaced the Postal Rate Commission with a stronger oversight body, the Postal Regulatory Commission, with greater authorities to monitor and regulate the Postal Service than its predecessor.[80]

2. STATUTORY OBLIGATIONS

Chartered directly by an act of Congress or persons acting pursuant to congressional authority, FGCs are considered separate legal entities.[81] The vast majority of public corporations are subject to the APA.[82] Those that are not bound by the APA include:, the National Coalition on Health Care, the Corporation for Public Broadcasting, the Legal Services Corporation, and the National Park Foundation.[83] Similarly, while most public corporations are subject to the FOIA,[84] several are exempt, including the Corporation for Public Broadcasting and the National Park Foundation.[85]

---

77 The success of the Communications Satellite Corporation encouraged the federal government to explore other types of government entity organizational structures. *Id.*

78 Nye Stevens, Postal Reform, Cong. Research Serv., IB10104, 7 (Jun. 23, 2005). For eight months a nine-member bipartisan presidential commission held public meetings in addition to meeting with stakeholders to assess the needs and concerns afflicting the Postal Service. President's Commission on the United States Postal Service, Exec. Order No. 13,278 (Dec. 11, 2002), 67 Fed. Reg. 76671 (Dec. 13, 2002).

79 Postal Accountability and Enhancement Act, Pub. L. No. 109-435, 120 Stat. 3198 (Dec. 20, 2006).

80 Kevin R. Kosar, The Postal Accountability and Enhancement Act: Overview and Issues for Congress, Cong. Research Serv., R40983, 3 (Dec. 14, 2009).

81 Froomkin, *supra* note 20, at 552 (statutes creating such corporations may provide for either a federal charter or may specify for incorporation in the District of Columbia).

82 The APA defines the agencies to which the Act applies broadly, including "each authority of the Government of the United States, whether or not it is within or subject to review by another agency." 5 U.S.C. § 551 (2006).

83 A detailed examination of the APA and government corporations can be found in Jack M. Beermann, *The Reach of Administrative Law in the United States, in* The Province of Administrative Law 171, 173–75 (Michael Taggart ed., 1997).

84 The FOIA relies on the APA's definition of agency, but further specifies those agencies that are governed by the FOIA as including "any executive department, military department, government corporation, government controlled corporation, or any other establishment in the executive branch." "FOIA" refers to the short title of the statute. The statute formally covers the administrative procedure of public information. 5 U.S.C. § 552 (2006).

85 *See* Craig D. Feiser, *Privatization and the Freedom of Information Act: An Analysis of Public Access to Private Entities under Federal Law*, 52 Fed. Comm. L.J. 21 (1999).

The Government Corporation Control Act of 1945 establishes a common framework of internal controls and financial reporting mechanisms for government corporations.[86] The Act was implemented in response to the growth of public corporations following the Great Depression and both World Wars. While the Act identifies the government corporations to which it applies, it does not provide a specific definition as to what constitutes an FGC. Although the enactment of the Government Corporation Control Act standardized budget, auditing, depository, and management practices, government corporations generally remain subject to all federal laws governing agencies.[87] Those subject to the Government Corporation Control Act include: the Commodity Credit Corporation, Federal Crop Insurance Corporation, Federal Savings and Loan Insurance Corporation, Overseas Private Investment Corporation, Pension Benefit Guaranty Corporation, TVA, and Amtrak.[88] The Act should not be mischaracterized as a general incorporation act; rather, the enabling legislation by Congress for each individual government corporation acts as the charter equivalent to that of traditional corporations in the states.[89]

Indeed, public corporations such as the Federal Financing Bank, Neighborhood Reinvestment Corporation, Corporation for Public Broadcasting, Legal Services Corporation, and National Park Foundation are not subject to the Government Corporation Control Act.[90] Those public corporations that enjoy exemption from these government controls are located closer to the private ownership end of the spectrum.

3. STATE ACTION DOCTRINE

A further question is the extent to which public corporations are state actors such that constitutional constraints like the First Amendment and the due process clause are applicable. State action is present when the constitutional implications of a challenged action cannot be completely privatized "because of the function it represents" or the challenged action is performed by an entity that is not privatized enough "to remove the action from the Constitution's purview."[91] Although courts have formerly held that

---

86 Government Corporation Control Act, 31 U.S.C. §§ 9101–9110 (2006). *See, e.g.*, MITCHELL, *supra* note 32, at 142 (in 1992, amendments to the Act created additional controls on government corporations in areas such as financial reporting); KOSAR, *supra* note 1, at 4 (explaining that the Government Corporation Control Act does not function as a general incorporation Act as such Acts operate at the state level).

87 *See* KOSAR, *supra* note 1, at 4 (except where provisions of general management laws provide exemptions).

88 *See id.*

89 *See id.*

90 *See* FRANCES J. LEAZES, JR., ACCOUNTABILITY AND THE BUSINESS STATE: THE STRUCTURE OF FEDERAL CORPORATIONS 63 (1987).

91 GILLIAN E. METZGER, *Private Delegations, Due Process, and the Duty to Supervise*, *in* GOVERNMENT BY CONTRACT 291–92 (Jody Freeman & Martha Minow eds., 2009) (further arguing that the private delegation doctrine focuses on whether the delegation of specific powers to private actors are prohibited by the Constitution).

public corporations are state actors for constitutional purposes,[92] there is no bright-line rule dictating this outcome, and indeed, courts have been reluctant to do so.[93] Federal incorporation alone does not equate to state actor status of a government corporation.[94]

Confronted with the question of whether Amtrak was a governmental agency, the Supreme Court in *Lebron v. National Railroad Passenger Corporation* held that Amtrak was a state actor for First Amendment purposes.[95] The Court noted that, although Amtrak's authorizing statute declared it "will not be an agency or establishment of the United State Government," presidential appointment of a majority of the corporation's directors gave the government sufficient control over Amtrak to find that it was a state actor.[96] Thus, corporations created for public purposes subject to the government's permanent control are generally considered federal actors.[97] Subsequent lower court cases have distinguished the *Lebron* decision from cases where the government corporation, unlike Amtrak, is led by a majority of board members who are not subject to presidential appointment.[98] However, as Justice Scalia importantly noted in *Lebron*, the federal

---

92 *See* Lebron v. Nat'l R.R. Passenger Corp., 513 U.S. 374, 397 (1995) ("It surely cannot be that government, state or federal, is able to evade the most solemn obligations imposed in the Constitution by simply resorting to the corporate form.").

93 Donna Nagy, *Playing Peekaboo with Constitutional Law: The PCAOB and Its Public/Private Status*, 80 NOTRE DAME L. REV. 975, 1030–31 (2005) ("The Supreme Court... has yet to come to grips with the more pragmatic analysis of public/private power [that is reflected in government trends of privatization]. Instead, modern constitutional law continues a longstanding allegiance to two related notions: that the categories of public and private are distinct, and that only public or 'state' actors can be subject to constitutional restraints."). *See also* Jackson v. Metropolitan Edison Co., 419 U.S. 345 (1974); MITCHELL, *supra* note 32, at 88; PAUL VERKUIL, OUTSOURCING SOVEREIGNTY: WHY PRIVATIZATION OF GOVERNMENT FUNCTIONS THREATENS DEMOCRACY AND WHAT WE CAN DO ABOUT IT 86–87 (2007). In the specific context of privatization there have been few instances where private entities where found to be state actors. *See* chapter 8, section E, subsection 1.

94 *See* Froomkin, *supra* note 20, at 564.

95 Lebron, 513 U.S. at 400. The D.C. Circuit in 2013 found Amtrak to be a private entity for purposes, at least, of the the non-delegation doctrines. See, *infra* text at notes 186–201.

96 *Id.* at 392 ("If Amtrak is, by its very nature, what the Constitution regards as the Government, congressional pronouncement that it is not such can no more relieve it of its First Amendment restrictions than a similar pronouncement could exempt the Federal Bureau of Investigation from the Fourth Amendment.").

97 *See* Froomkin, *supra* note 20, at 561.

98 *See* Am. Bankers Mortg. Corp. v. Fed. Home Loan Mortg. Corp., 75 F.3d 1401, 1409 (9th Cir. 1996) (holding that Freddie Mac is not subject to due process constraints on state action because appointment of a minority of directors by the president is insufficient to provide federal government control of the corporation); Olelo: The Corp. for Cmty. Television v. Office of Info. Practices, 173 P.3d 484, 488 (Haw. 2007) (holding that a corporation was not an agency subject to the Uniform Information Practices Act due in part to the nine-person commission appointed by a state director); Varicon Int'l v. Office of Personnel Mgmt., 934 F. Supp. 440, 447 (D.D.C. 1996) (emphasizing the absence of governmental control and the inability of the government to appoint the board of directors of private companies when government agencies decide to privatize functions). The *Varicon* case involved an attempt by the Office of Personnel Management to privatize its investigation functions. *Varicon Int'l*, 934 F. Supp. at 448. The private company that took over these functions, USIS, was not under government control. *Id.* Employees of USIS were likewise not

government should not be allowed to "evade the most solemn obligations imposed in the Constitution by simply resorting to the corporate form."[99]

Government control is not the only factor under consideration when determining whether a public corporation is a state actor. Scholars have suggested, and courts have recognized, that in evaluating state actor status, no one factor is absolute.[100] Factors considered aside from political appointment of board members include whether the corporation was created to fulfill "important governmental objectives" and the extent to which the corporation's activities are funded by federal appropriations for assistance and benefits.[101] Even clearly private associations can be deemed to be state actors when there is "pervasive entwinement of public institutions and public officials in [a private organization's] composition and workings."[102] This has, however, proved a high hurdle.[103] Thus, again in the constitutional context, it seems that the application of government obligations to public corporations turns, unsurprisingly, on consideration of where on the public-private spectrum the public corporations in question reside.

A subsequent question is whether the protections, as opposed to obligations, of being a government actor apply to public corporations. Specifically, do public corporations enjoy sovereign immunity? This question is easily answered where Congress has provided

under government control, and were therefore not government employees in any capacity, and the Office of Personnel Management had no influence in the composition of the Board of Directors of the company. *Id.* Therefore, despite the fact that these employees were performing Office of Personnel Management functions, the court held that USIS was not created to "act as an agency," and therefore found no state action. *Id.*

99 *Lebron*, 513 U.S. at 397. *See* Anne Joseph O'Connell, *Bureaucracy at the Boundary*, 162 U. Pa. L.Rev. 841, 909 (2014) ("The courts, not Congress, determine a boundary organization's status for constitutional obligations.").

100 *See* Ronald Krotozynski, *Back to the Briarpatch: An Argument in Favor of Constitutional Meta-Analysis in State Action Determinations*, 94 Mich. L. Rev. 302, 314 (1995)*; see also* Wilkinson v. Legal Servs. Corp., 27 F. Supp. 2d 37, 45 (D.D.C. 1998).

101 *See Wilkinson*, 27 F. Supp. 2d at 45–46 (holding that the Legal Services Corporation was a state actor because all of its board members were political appointees, almost all of its funding was derived from federal appropriations, and its formation was for the important governmental purpose of providing legal services to impoverished populations. The court noted that "from the reasoning and holding of *Lebron*, there is no question that LSC is a state actor for purposes of the Fifth Amendment's Due Process Clause… LSC may be sued for violating Due Process.")*; see also* Froomkin, *supra* note 20, at 563–64.

102 Brentwood Acad. v. Tennessee Secondary Sch. Athletic Ass'n, 531 U.S. 288, 289 (2001) (holding private voluntary athletic organizations were state actors).

103 *See, e.g.*, Rendell-Baker v. Kohn, 457 U.S. 830, 838–43 (1982) (holding that the receipt of public funds does not make the personnel decisions of a private school state action); *see also* Blum v. Yaretsky, 457 U.S. 991, 995, 1004 (1982) (holding that the fact of government regulation does not indicate state action, and that the test is rather whether the regulation emerged as a result of a significant nexus between the state and the challenged action); Nat'l Collegiate Athletics Assoc. v. Tarkanian, 488 U.S. 179 (1988) (holding that a public university's suspension of an employee in response to the National Collegiate Athletics Association's threatened sanctions did not mean that it was a state actor, and therefore there was no violation of the employee's Fourteenth Amendment rights).

that the entity may "sue or be sued" in the corporation's organic statute.[104] And, indeed, this is the approach Congress has almost always taken with public corporations.[105]

The more interesting inquiry is whether, in the face of congressional silence, public corporations may claim sovereign immunity. As discussed by Froomkin, "[t]he greater an FGC's entitlement to sovereign immunity, the more it enjoys an advantage over private competitors."[106] In *Galvan v. Federal Prison Industries*, the D.C. Circuit determined that immunity could be claimed by Federal Prison Industries,[107] a wholly owned government corporation, at least in response to a suit under the Federal False Claims Act.[108] Federal Prison Industries was formed to further the Federal Bureau of Prisons' goal of providing meaningful work opportunities to inmates. As neither Federal Prison Industries' organic statute nor the False Claims Act waive the sovereign immunity of governmental entities, the D.C. Circuit reasoned that the "typical presumption in favor of sovereign immunity" applied to Federal Prison Industries because "federal agencies or instrumentalities performing federal functions always fall on the 'sovereign' side of the fault line."[109]

The court further noted that a suit is considered to be against a sovereign whenever "the judgment sought would expend itself on the public treasury or domain, or interfere with the public administration."[110] Because Federal Prison Industries was wholly owned by the government and all money under the corporation's control was held by the U.S. Treasury, any judgment against Federal Prison Industries would have required payment out of the public treasury.[111] So at least in some cases, public corporations do enjoy sovereign protection.

C. Government Sponsored Enterprises

Government sponsored enterprises are even further removed from governmental control than public corporations. Unlike FGCs, where the government retains full ownership,

---

[104] *See* Keifer & Keifer v. Reconstruction Fin. Corp., 306 U.S. 381, 390–91 (1939) (finding that insertion of a sue-and-be-sued clause in a government corporation or agency's organic statute is an indication of congressional intent to waive sovereign immunity).

[105] *See* Chris Flack, *Recent Decision of the United States Court of Appeals for the District of Columbia Circuit: Federal Sovereign Immunity*, 69 Geo. Wash. L. Rev. 656, 663 (2001).

[106] Froomkin, *supra* note 20, at 591. An entirely private corporation does not have sovereign immunity unless it is granted by Congress.

[107] 18 U.S.C. § 4121 (2006).

[108] Galvan v. Fed. Prison Indus., Inc., 199 F.3d 461, 463 (D.C. Cir. 1999).

[109] *Id.* at 463 (quoting Auction Co. of Am. v. FDIC, 132 F.3d 746, 752 (D.C. Cir. 1997)), 467.

[110] *Id.* at 463 (quoting Dugan v. Rank, 372 U.S. 609, 620 (1963)).

[111] *Id.* at 463 ("[A]ll money under FPI's control is held by the U.S. Treasury to the credit of FPI. Thus, any judgment in [plaintiff's] favor would require FPI to pay damages directly from the public treasury." (citations omitted)).

or at least a substantial degree of control, GSEs are both publicly and privately owned.[112] While the degree of private ownership varies, GSEs are generally characterized as mixed-ownership government corporations with the limited function of lending to particular constituency groups or lending for specific purposes.[113]

Congress's primary objective in creating GSEs has been to increase the availability of credit to disadvantaged sectors of the economy, particularly those hampered by the credit markets.[114] Proponents of GSEs argue that objectives such as these cannot be satisfied absent GSEs' existence.[115] These entities create secondary markets in which primary lenders' interests in obtaining funds are integrated with the capital markets' supply of money.[116]

The five GSEs that exist today are Fannie Mae,[117] Freddie Mac,[118] the Federal Agricultural Mortgage Corporation (Farmer Mac),[119] the Federal Home Bank Loan System,[120] and the Farm Credit System.[121] Fannie Mae, Freddie Mac, and Farmer Mac were designed to be investor owned; while the Federal Home Loan Bank System and the Farm Credit System are jointly owned by their borrowers.[122]

Like the FGC, there is no standard definition or list of criteria defining what constitutes a GSE. Despite their differences, GSEs tend to share four attributes that represent a combination of both public and private organization: "private ownership; implicit federal guarantee of obligations; activities limited by congressional charter; and limited

---

112 *See, e.g.*, Benjamin A. Templin, *The Government Shareholder: Regulating Public Ownership of Private Enterprise*, 62 ADMIN. L. REV. 1127, 1183 (2010).

113 *See* Froomkin, *supra* note 20, at 555–57 (noting examples of targeted constituencies include: farmers, students and homeowners; while targeted purposes for example include recapitalizing on insolvent savings and loans).

114 KEVIN KOSAR, CONG. RESEARCH SERV., THE QUASI GOVERNMENT: HYBRID ORGANIZATIONS WITH BOTH GOVERNMENT AND PRIVATE SECTOR LEGAL CHARACTERISTICS 8 (2011).

115 *Id.*

116 *See* Carrie Stradley Lavargna, *Government-Sponsored Enterprises Are "Too Big to Fail": Balancing Public and Private Interests*, 44 HASTINGS L.J. 991, 997–98 (1993) (describing creation of secondary markets that facilitate flow of credit to lenders).

117 12 U.S.C. § 1716 (2006). Initially formed in 1938, Fannie Mae responded to the institutional failures left in the wake of the Great Depression. In 1954, following significant growth, Congress established Fannie Mae as a mixed-ownership government corporation with the ultimate goal of entirely private ownership of Fannie Mae stock. Then in 1968, Fannie Mae was deemed a GSE with a limited scope of activities provided by Congress. A majority of the Board of Directors were elected by the private shareholders. *Id.*

118 12 U.S.C. § 1452 (2006).

119 12 U.S.C. § 2279aa–1 (2006).

120 12 U.S.C. § 1421 (2006).

121 12 U.S.C. § 2001 (2006). The Student Loan Marketing Association (Sallie Mae) was previously considered a GSE and is now wholly private. 20 U.S.C. § 1087-2 (2006). In addition, the Financing Corporation and the Resolution Funding Corporation were given GSE status in order to bypass the federal borrower label for federal budget purposes. *See* KOSAR, *supra* note 114, at 8.

122 *Id.* at 8–9.

competition."[123] The GSEs are under private ownership, but operate under government supervision and exist to serve the public interests mandated by Congress. The often conflicting private and public interests have resulted in harsh criticism of the GSEs and calls for institutional reform.[124]

Another characteristic that makes GSEs susceptible to criticism is their governance by federal charter absent direct government management rather than articles of incorporation. The structure causes issues contrary to common law rules of corporate governance because GSEs are granted certain benefits and privileges that are unavailable to fully private corporations.[125] The GSEs are not subject to the FOIA or SEC registration requirements, are exempt from the bankruptcy code, are immune from provisions under the Federal Tort Claims Act, and are exempt from state and local income taxes.[126] In addition, due to the technically incorrect, but widely held, assumption that the GSEs are backed by the full faith and credit of the United States, they are able to borrow at lower rates than private corporations.[127] As government instrumentalities, GSEs maintain a unique position among government entities. Moe and Stanton argue:

> The federal government's control over an institution differs significantly depending on whether that institution is an agency or instrumentality. The government manages an agency directly through the federal management hierarchy. As a general rule, an agency is subject to... federal procurement laws, and to the federal budget and other direct federal management controls. By contrast, an instrumentality is a privately owned institution that is supervised but not directly managed by the government.[128]

That said, the GSE resembles the independent agency in several respects. For example, Congress uses the GSE structure to insulate programs from the executive branch, which has ultimately allowed Congress greater control over the entities.[129] Although

---

123 *Id.* at 7–8 (GSEs as a whole provide a variety of financial services that include guaranteeing mortgage-backed securities, issuing capital stock, funding activities, and collecting fees for guarantees and other services).

124 *See* Viral V. Acharya, Matthew Richardson, Stijn Van Nieuwerburgh & Lawrence J. White, Guaranteed to Fail 186 (2011) (noting that as of August 2010 the estimated total cumulative losses neared $150 billion with the potential to multiply if the housing market further deteriorated). It must be noted that in terms of satisfying the initial congressional objective behind GSEs (liquefying mortgage credit markets on a national basis), the GSEs have been effectual in that respect despite their failures. *See also* Kosar, *supra* note 114, at 9; Templin, *supra* note 112, at 1183.

125 In return for certain benefits and privileges that are beyond the scope of this discussion, the government has the ability to limit the activities of GSEs in order to keep them aligned with public policy goals. *See* Kosar, *supra* note 114, at 8.

126 *See, e.g.*, Gretchen Morgenson & Joshua Rosner, Reckless Endangerment 66–68 (2011).

127 *Id.* at 16.

128 Ronald C. Moe & Thomas H. Stanton, *Government-Sponsored Enterprises as Federal Instrumentalities: Reconciling Private Management with Public Accountability*, 49 Pub. Admin. Rev. 321, 323 (1989).

129 *See, e.g.*, Froomkin, *supra* note 20, at 558.

the president retains the power to appoint and remove the directors authorized by statute,[130] he does not have the ability to remove directors that he has not appointed without specific statutory authorization.[131] Therefore, public directors sit alongside the shareholder-elected private directors.[132]

The fact that GSEs are privately held with public purposes has caused intense debate as to whether they are making the most of the governmental benefits that they receive.[133] The GSEs receive an indirect governmental subsidy since they are able to avoid many of the expenses incurred by commercial lenders. As previously stated, GSEs do not have to expend funds to comply with the SEC registration requirements, they are exempt from local and state taxation, and they receive favorable interest rates.[134] Although GSEs were originally established to address problems in specific sections of the capital market, many are currently seeking ways to infiltrate the primary market. David Reiss argues: "Fannie and Freddie have relied upon their hybrid public/private structure to obtain and protect economic rents at the expense of homeowners as well as Fannie and Freddie's competitors."[135]

The 2007–2009 financial crisis pressed the GSEs to an even greater extent by adding to the already prevalent criticisms. Undoubtedly, the lack of oversight and accountability combined with inadequate regulation created the ultimate recipe for the failures of Fannie Mae and Freddie Mac that resulted in their being placed in conservatorship in 2008 under control of the FHFA.[136] Many argue that Fannie Mae and Freddie Mac take

---

130 *See id.* at 613 (explaining that president's removal power derives primarily from appointment power).

131 *See id.*

132 *See id.* at 573.

133 *See generally* Julia Patterson Forrester, *Fannie Mae/Freddie Mac Uniform Mortgage Instruments: The Forgotten Benefit to Homeowners*, 72 Missouri L. Rev. 1077, 1106–08 (2007).

134 *See, e.g.*, Gretchen & Rosner, *supra* note 126, at 66–68.

135 David Reiss, *Fannie Mae and Freddie Mac and the Future of Federal Housing Finance Policy: A Study of Regulatory Privilege*, 61 Ala. L. Rev. 907, 911 (2010). Reiss further explains: "Because of the federal government's implied guarantee of their debt securities, Fannie and Freddie have been able to profit greatly from [their purchase of residential mortgages and related securities]. This is because they can make money on the spread between their low cost of funds and what they must pay for the mortgage-related investments in their portfolios." *Id.* at 913. Reiss concludes: "Fannie and Freddie reflect what is worst in GSE design. After fulfilling their purpose of creating a national mortgage market, they have taken on monstrously large lives of their own. In the midst of their bailout, Congress should take the opportunity to convert them to fully private status." *Id.* at 955.

136 In 2008, the FHFA assumed control of Fannie Mae and Freddie Mac as a conservator. The transfer of control included the sale of $1 billion of senior preferred stock to the U.S. Treasury on behalf of each GSE individually. N. Eric Weiss, Cong. Research Serv., R 40800, Options to Restructure Fannie Mae and Freddie Mac 1 (2009). Both were given a line of credit up to $100 billion amid the deterioration of credit markets and government findings that the GSEs overstated their capital. *See, e.g.*, Acharya et al., *supra* note 124, at 151–52, 186; Steven M. Davidoff & David Zaring, *Regulation by Deal: The Government's Response to the Financial Crisis*, 61 Admin. L. Rev. 463, 486–87 (2009); Templin, *supra* note 112, at 1183. Anne Joseph O'Connell notes that FHFA control over Fannie Mae and Freddie

advantage of the inherent government guarantee on their bonds to increase their risk to unmanageable levels.[137] Waving the banner of home ownership for all, Fannie and Freddie fought off stricter government regulation while they "dumbed down" mortgage lending so as to increase profits.[138] The resultant collapse of "subprime borrowing" cost taxpayers $150 billion.[139] As the housing market has improved, Fannie and Freddie have turned profitable.[140] Still, there has been much discussion of reforming[141] and even terminating them.[142] President Obama recently supported[143] Senate legislation that would wind down the GSEs and form a government corporation modeled after the FDIC in that the corporation would "collect insurance premiums and maintain a deposit fund on all outstanding obligations."[144] At printing, Fannie Mae and Freddie Mac continue to operate under FHFA conservatorship.[145]

Mac functions to move these GSEs from the "public-private border" toward more direct federal control. O'Connell, *supra* note 99, at 873.

137 *See supra* text accompanying note 127.

138 *See, e.g.*, ACHARYA ET AL., *supra* note 124, at 148–52; GRETCHEN & ROSNER, *supra* note 126, at 16–18.

139 *See* GRETCHEN & ROSNER, *supra* note 126, at 16–18.

140 On Aug. 8, 2013, Fannie announced that its profits for the quarter amounted to $10.1 billion, and that it planned on returning $10.2 billion to the Treasury. Joe Nocera, *Don't Kill Fannie Mae*, N.Y. TIMES, Aug. 13, 2013, at A19. This would mean that it would pay more money back to the Treasury than it had borrowed in the first place. *Id.* The billions recouped from annuity agent fraud companies for mortgage immunity will go to the Treasury and not the shareholders. *See* Danielle Douglas, *Fannie, Freddie Recoup Losses but Money Goes to Treasury*, WASH. POST, Oct. 23, 2013, at A13.

141 While most recent legislation has focused on terminating Fannie and Freddie, critics in the media have voiced their desire to reform Fannie and Freddie rather than demolish them. *See, e.g.*, Joe Nocera, *Don't Kill Fannie Mae*, N.Y. TIMES, Aug. 13, 2013, at A23; Jason Gold, *The Foolish Push to Scrap Fannie Mae and Freddie Mac*, U.S. NEWS (Aug. 21, 2013), http://www.usnews.com/opinion/blogs/economic-intelligence/2013/08/21/fannie-mae-and-freddie-mac-need-to-be-reformed-not-scrapped.

142 A House Bill to terminate Fannie and Freddie completely has also recently cleared the House Financial Services Committee. *See* Protecting American Taxpayer and Homeowners Act of 2013, H.R. 2767, 113th Cong. (2013). *See also* GRETCHEN & ROSNER, *supra* note 126, at 16–18.

143 *See* President Barack Obama, Remarks by the President on Responsible Home Ownership (Aug. 6, 2013) (transcript *available at* http://www.whitehouse.gov/the-press-office/2013/08/06/remarks-president-responsible-homeownership).

144 *See* Press Release, Senator Corker, Summary of Legislation: Housing Finance Reform and Taxpayer Protection Act (June 25, 2013), *available at* http://www.corker.senate.gov/public/_cache/files/f6951d82-1a9c-40d2-9291-dcdd5c153cbe/06-25-13%20GSE%20reform%20Summary.pdf; *see also* Housing Finance Reform and Taxpayer Protection Act of 2013, S. 1217, 113th Cong. (2013). This is a bipartisan bill introduced by Senators Warner and Corker. *Id.*

145 On June 13, 2014, the FHFA's annual report to Congress affirmed the agency's ongoing role as "regulator and conservator" of Fannie Mae and Freddie Mac. FED. HOUSING FIN. AGENCY, REPORT TO CONGRESS 2013 i (2014), *available at* http://www.fhfa.gov/AboutUs/Reports/ReportDocuments/FHFA_2013_Report_to_Congress.pdf. The report notes that as Fannie Mae and Freddie Mac continue in conservatorship the FHFA is "preparing the Enterprises for any transition policymakers set forth." *Id.* at 1.

D. Private Action by Federal Agencies

On occasion, Congress may authorize independent agencies to undertake nonagency tasks, vesting authorities that blur the private–public distinction. For example, government may take on the role of a "market actor" akin to any private sector actor. When government takes on the market actor role, it acts

> much as private actors do in particular markets. They employ the same means toward their ends. They do so, however for *public* rather than *private* ends, thereby defying, in limited ways, such venerable but misleading dichotomies as the "public/private" divide. They do so, moreover, with greater influence than private parties are typically able—or permitted—to bring to bear. And we permit our governments this form of market power, in turn, precisely because it is public rather than private power—power wielded on behalf of and in the name of us all.[146]

On such occasions, one can ask whether the agency is acting as part of the federal government constrained by applicable federal law or as a private party.

As one example, the NCUA is given authority to act as a "liquidator."[147] It has characterized this power to liquidate insolvent credit unions as succeeding "to all rights, titles, power and privileges of the credit union" and asserting that the agency may "operate the credit union with the powers of the members or shareholders, the directors, and the officers of the credit union."[148] The FDIC is given similar bank liquidation powers.[149]

The NCUA's position was that when acting as a "liquidating agent" it was not acting as a federal agency,[150] "engaged in... ongoing litigation with banks that sold toxic mortgage-backed securities to failed credit unions."[151] On this basis, the NCUA claimed authority to use attorneys on a contingent fee basis,[152] notwithstanding

---

[146] Robert C. Hockett & Saule T. Omarova, *"Private" Means to "Public" Ends: Governments as Market Actors*, 3–4 (Cornell Law School Research Paper No. 13-84, 2013), *available at* http://ssrn.com/abstract=2222444.

[147] 12 U.S.C. § 1787(b)(2)(A)(i) (2010) (authorizing the agency to act as a liquidating agent).

[148] NCUA Board as Liquidating Agent, 12 C.F.R. § 709.2 (1991).

[149] *See* 12 U.S.C. § 1813 (2010).

[150] The NCUA claims it is exempt from that Executive Order when it is acting as a "liquidating authority." *See* 12 U.S.C. § 1821(d)(2)(A)(i). The NCUA functions as both an independent agency and under a claimed statutory power that gives the agency all powers a state gives to a liquidating authority. *See* James V. Grimaldi & Alicia Mundy, *Nice Payday for "Toxic" Work*, WALL ST. J., Oct. 25, 2012, at C1.

[151] Letter from Chairman Issa, Oversight and Government Reform Committee to the Inspector General of the National Credit Union Administration, Regarding Use of Contingency Fees, Apr. 5, 2012, on file with the author.

[152] 12 C.F.R. § 709.2; *see* NATIONAL CREDIT UNION ADMINISTRATION, OFFICE OF THE INSPECTOR GENERAL, REPORT TO CHAIRMAN ISSA REGARDING USE OF CONTINGENCY FEE ARRANGEMENTS (Feb. 6, 2013) *available at* http://www.ncua.gov/about/Leadership/CO/OIG/Documents/OIG20130206IssaResponse.pdf.

presidential Executive Order 13,433 banning federal agencies from the use of contingent fee arrangements.[153] In response to an inquiry by the chair of the Oversight and Government Reform Committee,[154] the NCUA's inspector general "concluded that E.O. 13433 does not prohibit the NCUA from entering into contingency fee arrangements" because the agency "'steps into the shoes' of the credit union and is no longer functioning as a government agency."[155]

Similarly, the FDIC has been characterized as an entity that acts both an agency of the United States and as a private receiver.[156] Both agencies base their claims on virtually identical statutory authorities,[157] and both claim to assume the identity of private entities for the purposes of liquidation.[158] *O'Melveny & Myers v. Federal Deposit Insurance Corporation* brought this issue to the forefront. The Supreme Court characterized the FDIC, when acting as a receiver of a failed bank,[159] as a private party for the purpose of its receivership, even while acknowledging that it was an agency of the United States.[160] Subsequent courts have been reluctant to adopt the rationale of *O'Melveny*, narrowly distinguishing *O'Melveny* from certain types of receiverships or under state

---

153 *Protecting American Taxpayers from Payment of Contingency Fees*, Exec. Order No. 13,433, *reprinted at* 72 Fed. Reg. 28441 (May 16, 2007) ("To help ensure the integrity and effective supervision of the legal and expert witness services provided to or on behalf of the United States, it is the policy of the United States that organizations or individuals that provide such services to or on behalf of the United States shall be compensated in amounts that are reasonable, not contingent upon the outcome of litigation or other proceedings, and established according to criteria set in advance of performance of the services, except when otherwise required by law").

154 *See* Letter from Chairman Issa, Oversight and Government Reform Committee to the Inspector General of the National Credit Union Administration, Regarding Use of Contingency Fees, Apr. 5, 2012, on file with the author; *see also* Letter from Chairman Issa, Oversight and Government Reform Committee to the Inspector General of the National Credit Union Administration, Regarding Use of Contingency Fees, Oct. 16, 2012, *available at* http://oversight.house.gov/wp-content/uploads/2012/10/2012-10-16-DEI-to-DeSarno-NCUA-IG-contingency-fees.pdf.pdf.pdf.

155 Letter from William A. Sarno, NCUA Inspector General, to Chairman Issa, Oversight and Government Reform Committee, Feb. 6, 2013, *available at* http://www.ncua.gov/about/Leadership/CO/OIG/Documents/OIG20130206IssaResponse.pdf.

156 Adam Shajnfeld, *An Identity in Disarray: The Federal Deposit Insurance Corporation's Government-Agency Status* 128 Banking L.J. 36 (2011).

157 *Compare* 12 U.S.C. § 1821(d)(2)(A)(i) (2010) *with* 12 U.S.C. § 1787(b)(2)(A)(i) (2010).

158 *See* United States v. Beszborn, 21 F.3d 62 (5th Cir. 1994) (relating to the NCUA). *Compare* O'Melveny & Myers v. FDIC, 512 U.S. 79, 90 (1994).

159 O'Melveny & Myers v. FDIC, 512 U.S. 79, 88 (1994) ("The rules of decision at issue here do not govern the primary conduct of the United States or any of its agents or contractors, but affect only the FDIC's rights and liabilities, as receiver, with respect to primary conduct on the part of private actors that has already occurred. Uniformity of law might facilitate the FDIC's nationwide litigation of these suits, eliminating state-by-state research and reducing uncertainty—but if the avoidance of those ordinary consequences qualified as an identifiable federal interest, we would be awash in 'federal common-law' rules.").

160 *Id.* The Seventh Circuit had reasoned that FDIC officials, even when acting as receivers, were still part of the United States, and therefore were bound by all applicable law. FDIC v. Hartford Ins. Co. of Ill., 877 F.2d 590, 592 (7th Cir. 1989).

law.[161] One commentator has argued that the FDIC acts as a private party when it stands in a position that would be occupied by a bank or private party absent federal banking legislation.[162]

E. Privatization

An abundance of scholarly work has been devoted to privatization, its appropriate scope,[163] its social costs and benefits,[164] and its legal implications.[165] Regardless of one's views on privatization, it is an ever-present trend[166]—one that significantly affects the administrative state.[167] Privatization differs from state action in that it accepts the status of private actors; however, questions exist regarding the constitutionality of the scope of responsibilities delegated to such actors.[168] Sometimes privatization is used as

---

[161] *See, e.g.*, Delta Sav. Bank v. United States, 265 F.3d 1017, 1023 (9th Cir. 2001) ("The Court specifically held that because California state law imputes the knowledge of corporate officers to their corporation, the FDIC is treated no differently when it 'steps into the shoes' of a failing bank; the knowledge possessed by the former bank directors is imputed to the FDIC. *Id.* The strongest proposition that can be drawn from this holding is that the FDIC cannot escape the limitations that a state imposes on other corporations just because the language of FIRREA is expansive. In fact, in *O'Melveny*, the Court explicitly noted that there might be exceptions to the absolute rule it put forth"); Ferguson v. FDIC, 164 F.3d 894, 897 (5th Cir. 1999) ("Although *O'Melveny* disclaimed again the existence of a general federal common law and required the application of state law to claims made by or against the FDIC in its capacity as a receiver, it did not purport to overrule case law holding that the Government is not bound by the actions of agents acting outside the scope of their authority."); Motorcity of Jacksonville, Ltd. v. Se. Bank, N.A., 83 F.3d 1317, 1329 (11th Cir. 1996) *cert. granted, judgment vacated sub nom.* Hess v. FDIC, 519 U.S. 1087 (1997) ("The Supreme Court rejected the lower courts' use of state law and instead created a federal common law rule by drawing an analogy to provisions of the Federal Reserve Act...."); Grant Thornton, LLP v. FDIC, 535 F. Supp. 2d 676, 703 (S.D. W. Va. 2007) *rev'd sub nom.* Ellis v. Grant Thornton LLP, 530 F.3d 280 (4th Cir. 2008) ("In an action brought by the FDIC as receiver, state law governs the imputation of knowledge of the failed institution's management to the receiver"). *See generally* Shajnfeld, *supra* note 156, at 40–41.

[162] Shajnfeld, *supra* note 156, at 44.

[163] *See* Jody Freeman, *The Contracting State*, 28 FLA. ST. L. REV. 155 (2000); Dru Stevenson, *Privatization of Welfare Services: Delegation by Commercial Contract*, 45 ARIZONA L. REV. 83 (2003).

[164] *See* Sidney A. Shapiro, *Outsourcing Government Regulation*, 53 DUKE L.J. 389 (2003); Oliver Williamson, *Public and Private Bureaucracies: A Transaction Cost Economics Perspective*, 15 J.L. ECON. & ORG. 306 (1998).

[165] *See* Gillian Metzger, *Privatization as Delegation*, 103 COLUM. L. REV. 1367, 1371 (2003) (addressing the constitutional implications of privatization and the expansion of privatization as a phenomenon).

[166] Freeman notes: "in the United States, federal, state, and local governments now routinely employ contracts with private providers to furnish services, deliver benefits, and perform significant (sometimes traditionally 'public') functions." Freeman, *supra* note 163, at 155.

[167] *See id.* at 158 (suggesting that privatization through contracting with private third parties often allows government agencies to indirectly accomplish policy goals, which for political or legal reasons the agency may be unable to accomplish on its own). Many federal agencies rely on contracts with private entities to implement their missions. *See also* Guttman, *supra* note 3, at 872–78 (discussing such arrangements at the EPA, the DOE, and NASA).

[168] *See infra* notes 179–210 and accompanying text.

it is more efficient. Other times, it can offer a "workaround" in that "contracting out" provides

> the outsourcing agency with the means of achieving distinct public policy goals that—but for the pretext of technocratic outsourcing—would be impossible or much more difficult to attain in the ordinary course of nonprivatized public administration. In short, workarounds enable the executive to exercise greater unilateral discretion—at the expense of the legislature, the judiciary, the people, and successor administrations.[169]

The proper role for privatization is no doubt a highly relevant issue in the continuing debate on the provision of government services for the public. It is difficult, however, to distinguish when private parties are acting on behalf of the federal government as compared to when such parties are merely providing services to the federal government.[170]

Between 2000 and 2005 the fastest growing portion of Congress's discretionary budget went to federal contracts for goods and services—government spending in this area grew at two times the rate of other discretionary government spending.[171] Where traditional government services or functions are contracted out to private parties there are serious questions of public participation, accountability, and transparency.[172] The sharing of authority between the private and public sectors blurs the line as to who exerts control over and accepts responsibility for government programs.[173] As Jody Freeman notes, "[m]any people have a viscerally negative reaction to the idea that some government functions—those they view as symbolically important or inherently government—might be contracted out to private parties."[174]

1. THE CHALLENGE OF DELEGATING GOVERNMENT FUNCTIONS TO PRIVATE PARTIES

Privatization of traditionally governmental functions has long existed in certain sectors.[175] Customary examples of such private involvement include social services, as

---

169 Jon D. Michaels, *Privatization's Pretensions*, 77 U. CHI. L. REV. 717, 719 (2010).

170 Metzger, *supra* note 165, at 1371.

171 Martha Minow, *Outsourcing Power: Privatizing Military Efforts and the Risks to Accountability, Professionalism, and Democracy*, *in* GOVERNMENT BY CONTRACT 110 (Jody Freeman & Martha Minow eds., 2009).

172 JOHN DONAHUE, THE PRIVATIZATION DECISION (1989); Freeman, *supra* note 163, at 174–76.

173 Metzger, *supra* note 165, at 1370.

174 Freeman, *supra* note 4, at 631 n.367.

175 "As early as the late nineteenth century, local governments were contracting with private entities to provide social services, in some cases for the bulk of their poverty-relief efforts." Nestor M. Davidson, *Relational Contracts in the Privatization of Social Welfare: The Case of Housing*, 24 YALE L. & POL'Y REV. 263, 268 (2006). State and local governments have also followed the trend of privatization of government

well as education.[176] However, an increasing array of government functions has experienced at least some degree of privatization.[177]

Other than during the early days of the New Deal,[178] "the private exercise of public powers rarely has been litigated."[179] To some extent, the debate has focused on what government functions can be delegated to private parties. Rhetorically, the Supreme Court is clear:

> [W]ould it be seriously contended that Congress could delegate its legislative authority to trade or industrial associations or groups so as to empower them to enact the laws they deem to be wise and beneficent for the rehabilitation and expansion of their trade or industries?... The answer is obvious. Such a delegation of legislative power is unknown to our law and is utterly inconsistent with the constitutional prerogatives and duties of Congress.[180]

---

functions, which include "administering welfare and public benefits programs, processing parking tickets, providing private security services, collecting government debts, fighting fires, and overseeing foster care and child placement programs." *See* Richard Frankel, *Regulating Privatized Government Through § 1983*, 76 U. CHI. L. REV. 1449, 1451–52 (2009).

176 *See* Metzger, *supra* note 165, at 1388 (the privatization of public education has grown in recent years, largely due to the expansion of charter schools, voucher programs, and the private management of public schools on behalf of educational management organizations).

177 *See* Alison Stanger, *Foreign Policy, Privatized*, N.Y. TIMES, Oct. 5, 2007, at A25; Miriam Seifter, Comment, *Rent-a-Regulator: Design and Innovation in Privatized Governmental Decisionmaking*, 33 ECOLOGY L.Q. 1091 (2006) (discussing privatization in the environmental sector).

178 *See, e.g.*, Carter v. Carter Coal Co., 298 U.S. 238, 311 (1936) (calling delegation to private actors "legislative delegation in its most noxious form."). Codes of Competition drafted for the kosher poultry industry by a private poultry industry committee under the National Industrial Recovery Act were found unconstitutional notwithstanding that the Codes were subject to presidential sign-off. *See* ALA Schecter Poultry v. United States, 295 U.S. 495, 521–53, 521 n.4 (1935) (the so-called sick chicken case). In an earlier case, Panama Refining v. Ryan, 293 U.S. 388 (1935) (this is the so-called Hot Oil case), the Court struck down a different provision of the NIRA (§ 9(c)) related to the criteria for presidential control of interstate petroleum shipment on grounds that Congress had set no criteria to govern the president's course. *See Panama Refining*, 293 U.S. at 415. The development of the nondelegation doctrine during the New Deal is reviewed in Andrew J. Ziaja, *Hot Oil and Hot Air: The Development of the Nondelegation Doctrine Through the New Deal, A History*, 35 HASTINGS CONST. L. Q 921 (2008). *But see* Sunshine Anthracite Coal v. Adkins, 310 U.S. 381 (1940) (finding that Congress had not "delegated its legislative authority to the industry" when it created a tax on coal producers but exempted members of the private industry). According to the Court in Adkins,

> The members of the code function subordinately to the Commission. It, not the code authorities, determines the prices. And it has authority and surveillance over the activities of these authorities. Since law-making is not entrusted to the industry, this statutory scheme is unquestionably valid.

Adkins, 310 U.S. at 399.

179 Krent, *supra* note 8, at 509.

180 *Schecter Poultry*, 295 U.S. at 537.

But in practice, this has been an elusive rule to implement. And the courts have "been quite permissive about delegations to private parties."[181] Indeed, a recent article in the *Yale Law and Policy Review* noted that "it is becoming increasingly challenging to identify core government functions that cannot be performed by private parties."[182]

As example, in *Gentiva Healthcare Corporation v. Sebelius*,[183] the Department of Health and Human Services was granted authority to subdelegate to Medicare contractors the determination of the standard for calculating overpayment of Medicare claims.[184]

In accord, Harold Krent has suggested that the core government function doctrine does not

> limit the power of the President or Congress to utilize private parties to enforce federal law or implement federal programs. Rather, it holds that, when Congress or the President chooses to use private parties, then such private parties must be bound by certain core constitutional restraints. The core government functions test has not been used to prevent delegation ab initio.[185]

In a recent case, *AARP v. Department of Transportation*,[186] Judge Janice Brown resurrected the private delegation doctrine relying on broad principles from *Free Enterprise*.[187] The case covered Section 207 of the Passenger Rail Investment and Improvement Act of 2008, which authorizes Amtrak and the Federal Railroad Administration to cultivate joint performance measures "to enhance enforcement of the statutory priority Amtrak's passenger rail service has over other trains."[188]

The *AARP* court found that Congress had gone a bridge too far. The Supreme Court, it has been suggested, has never approved a regulatory scheme that so drastically empowers a private entity in the way Section 207 empowers Amtrak.[189] The D.C. Circuit found that arrangement unconstitutional as it allowed a private entity to "jointly exercise regulatory power on equal footing with an administrative agency."[190] However, the reach of the decision is unclear. While the Court takes note of, it does not analyze whether the

---

181 Stephen G. Breyer, Richard B. Stewart, Cass. R Sunstein & Adrian Vermeule, Administrative Law and Regulatory Policy: Problems, Text, and Cases 49 (7th ed. 2011).

182 Davidson, *supra* note 175, at 267.

183 Gentiva Healthcare Corporation v. Sebelius, 723 F.3d 292 (D.C. Cir. 2013).

184 *See id.* at 296 ("we cannot find that Congress unambiguously barred the Secretary from delegating that task to an outside contractor").

185 Krent, *supra* note 8, at 540.

186 AARP v. Dept. of Transportation, 721 F.3d 666 (D.C. Cir. 2013); *cert.* granted 62 USLW 3533 (June 23, 2014).

187 *See* Free Enterprise Fund v. Public Co. Accounting Oversight Board, 130 S.Ct. 3138 (2010).

188 *AARP*, 721 F.3d at 668.

189 *See* Panama Refining v. Ryan, 293 U.S. 388, 415 (1935).

190 *Id.*

facts violate, the due process clause rather than the delegation doctrine.[191] Further, its claim that congressional delegations of regulatory authority to public bodies are evaluated by the "intelligible framework" test while private delegations are "per se illegitimate" is likely incorrect.[192] It is more likely that "[t]he nondelegation doctrine is indifferent to the identity of individual exercising the power—if legislative standards exist, the individual's private status does not come into play."[193] Indeed as a well-known commentator suggests, "[t]he nondelegation doctrine might be strictly about the question of what Congress can give away, not who the constitutionally permissible recipients are."[194]

There are other arguments against private delegation. As intimated above, the "doctrine forbidding delegation of public power to private groups is, in fact, rooted in a prohibition against self-interested regulation that sounds more in the Due Process Clause than in the separation of powers."[195] Further, as attention to this area of our law grows, the discussion refocuses thought on one of the rationales against excessive delegation: the harm done thereby to principles of political accountability. Such harm is doubled in degree in the context of a transfer of authority from Congress to an agency and then from the agency to private individuals. The strength of challenges to the former type of transfer is suspect, but to the latter, unquestionable.[196] Privately run prisons provide one example of the privatization of a function traditionally administered by the government. Due to fiscal constraints on state governments, private prison administration has become a growth industry.[197] The "public status" of private prisons remains unsettled. *Richardson v. McKnight* makes clear that private prison guards lack qualified immunity, but did not decide whether the guards were state actors.[198] The present view seems to be that "confinement of wrongdoers—though sometimes delegated to private entities—is a fundamentally governmental function."[199] Likewise, private security firms or prisons

[191] *See* Alexander Volokh, *A New Private Regulation Doctrine?*, Reason Foundation (Aug. 1, 2013), http://reason.org/news/show/private-delegation-doctrine-amtrak; *see also* Alexander Volokh, *The New Private-Regulation Skepticism: Nondelegation, Due Process, and Antitrust Challenges*, 37 Harv. J.L. & Pub. Pol'y 931, 970–73 (2014).

[192] Alexander Volokh, *A New Private Regulation Doctrine?*, Reason Foundation (Aug. 1, 2013), http://reason.org/news/show/private-delegation-doctrine-amtrak.

[193] Krent, *supra* note 8, at 511.

[194] Breyer et al., *supra* note 182, at 49.

[195] A. Michael Froomkin, *Wrong Turn in Cyberspace: Using ICANN To Route Around the APA and the Constitution*, 50 Duke L.J. 17, 153 (2000).

[196] Nat'l Ass'n of Regulatory Util. Comm'rs v. FCC, 737 F.2d 1095, 1143, n.41 (D.C. Cir. 1984).

[197] *See* Terry Carter, *Prison Break: Budget Crises Drive Reform, but Private Jails Press On*, 2012 A.B.A. J. 44–51 (2012) (describing the pressure on states to privatize prisons, or even sell state prisons, to private incarceration companies given current state budget shortfalls); *see, e.g.*, Corrections Corporation of America, A Guide to Our Code of Ethics and Business Conduct 3 (2005) (providing the mission statement: "In partnership with government, we will provide a meaningful public service by operating the highest quality adult corrections company in the United States.").

[198] Richardson v. McKnight, 521 U.S. 399, 402 (1997).

[199] Rosborough v. Mgmt. & Training Corp., 350 F. 3d 459, 461 (5th Cir. 2003) (*per curiam); see* Peoples v. CCA Detention Ctr., 422 F. 3d 1090 (10th Cir. 2005), *vacated en banc*, 449 F.3d 1097 (10th Cir. 2006).

under control of the federal government have raised significant concerns.[200] This issue remains largely unsettled.[201]

A recurring debate arises as to where the line should be drawn in limiting the extent to which government can delegate functions to the private sector. When the president and Congress assign portions of their authority or responsibilities to private individuals, a multitude of governmental responsibilities are exercised by private actors.[202] The unitary executive theory asserts that the Constitution vests exclusive power in the president to execute the laws of the United States. As discussed in chapters 4 and 5, both the appointment and removal of public officials act as "a device to keep officials exercising federal authority somewhat politically accountable."[203] As a result, the appointment and removal clauses present a significant challenge when it comes to the delegation of authority to private individuals.[204]

Under some textual interpretations of the appointments clause, privatization and outsourcing may constitute substantial constitutional violations.[205] Likewise, when traditional government responsibilities are delegated to private individuals, separation-of-powers concerns are often implicated.[206]

When private parties are given the authority to participate in governance, the accountability and traceability of exercised authority becomes a serious concern.[207]

---

200 *See* Gnatt v. Sec., USA, Inc., 356 F.3d 547 (4th Cir. 2004).

201 Recent Supreme Court opinions regarding governmental immunity applying to private actors demonstrate the highly factual character of such determinations. *Compare* Richardson v. McKnight, 521 U.S. 399 (1997) (holding that a private prison guard performing a public function is not automatically protected by governmental immunity) *with* Filarsky v. Delia, 132 S. Ct. 1657, 1667 (U.S. Apr. 17, 2012) (holding a private investigator entitled to qualified immunity, although not a public employee, when conducting an official investigation).

202 *See* Krent, *supra* note 8, at 523; MITCHELL, *supra* note 32, at 11. Notably, in 2012, the Supreme Court refused to extend the availability of *Bivens* actors to federal prisoners held in a facility run by a private company. Minneci v. Pollard, 132 S.Ct. 617 (2012) (finding that Pollard could have sued under state law, thus producing an alternative to *Bivens*); *see also* Bivens v. Six Unknown Named Agents of Federal Bureau of Narcotics, 403 U.S. 388 (1971) (allowing federal prisoners to sue federal agents for damages under the Fourteenth Amendment).

203 Kelsey Elizabeth Stapler, *The Auditor for the Auditors' Auditor: Accounting for the Unitary Executive in Free Enterprise Fund v. Public Company Accounting Oversight Board*, 38 PEPP. L. REV. 709, 711 (2011).

204 *See* Beermann, *supra* note 18, at 1510–11. *See also* Landry v. FDIC, 204 F.3d 1125, 1130–34 (D.C. Cir. 2000) (holding that not all federal government employees, such as ALJs in this case, must be appointed pursuant to the appointments clause).

205 *See, e.g.*, VERKUIL, *supra* note 93, at 107; Beermann, *supra* note 18, at 1513; Jack M. Beermann, *Public Oversight of Public/Private Partnerships*, 28 FORDHAM URB. L.J. 1357, 1360 (2001).

206 *See* VERKUIL, *supra* note 93, at 113 (stating that a sharing of powers is implicated by the presence of the advice and consent functions). *See also* Stapler, *supra* note 203, at 716–18 (arguing that the modern debate over the unitary executive is shaped by arguments relating to accountability and separation of powers); Beermann, *supra* note 18, at 1513 ("any attempt to shield completely officers of the United States from removal initiated by political officials within the executive branch would probably violate accountability-preserving separation of powers principles.").

207 Krent, *supra* note 8, at 531–32.

Those delegated such authority become "unimpeachable," resulting in what Paul Verkuil defines as a loss of a "[c]onstitutionally designed accountability mechanism."[208] Interestingly, while privatized functions may lack Article II control, corporations that take on public functions may face judicial review with attendant liability.[209] So the sharp break between those structures subject to the "unitariness," and those that are not reflect a theoretical break not normally evident in real life.

2. DEPARTMENT OF DEFENSE PRIVATIZATION

Within the federal government, the DOD operates the largest privatization effort.[210] This department contracts out not only support services such as provision of equipment or food services but also, quite controversially, military and intelligence functions.[211] In recent engagements in Iraq and Afghanistan, privatization of military and intelligence functions attracted significant attention, and criticism focused on alleged criminal and human rights violations by the private military and security contractors, such as Blackwater Worldwide (Blackwater).[212]

---

208 VERKUIL, *supra* note 93, at 113; *see also* Krent, *supra* note 8, at 523 (asserting that private self-serving interests become more attainable as a further consequence of weakened accountability absent the reality of impeachment).

209 *See* Samuel D. Walker & N. Christopher Hardee, *Perils of Privatization*, NAT'L. L.J., Oct. 2, 2000, at C1 (discussing § 1983 liability). For instance, airport security is one area commonly prone to private delegation. *See* Paul R. Verkuil, *Public Law Limitations on Privatization of Government Functions*, 84 N.C. L. REV. 397, 441 (2006). The government also frequently contracts with security and military support services, such as the former security firm Blackwater, to assist the U.S. Armed Forces. *See* Richard Frankel, *Regulating Privatized Government Through § 1983*, 76 U. CHI. L. REV. 1449, 1450–52 (2009). While private employees of federal privatization can be subject to *Bivens* actions, private employees contracted by state or local governments are subject to actions brought under 42 U.S.C. § 1983. *See* Charles W. Thomas, *Resolving the Problem of Qualified Immunity for Private Defendants in Section 1983 and Bivens Damage Suits*, 53 LA. L. REV. 449, 450 (1992).

210 *See* Verkuil, *supra* note 93, at 441.

211 *See id.*; Mark Calagus, *Military Privatization: Efficiency or Anarchy?*, 6 CHI.-KENT J. INT'L & COMP. L. 58, 59–60 (2006). *See also* Mark Mazzetti, *Outsiders Hired as C.I.A. Planned to Kill Jihadists*, N.Y. TIMES, Aug. 20, 2009, at A1.

212 In 2009, following a number of highly publicized negative incidents, Blackwater Worldwide was renamed Xe. *US Security Firm Mired in Iraq Controversy Changes Its Name*, GUARDIAN (Feb. 12, 2009), *available at* http://www.guardian.co.uk/world/2009/feb/13/blackwater-changes-name-xe. In 2011, the former Blackwater was again renamed. The security firm is now called Academi. Matthew Barakat, *Another Name Change for Former Blackwater Firm*, BUSINESSWEEK.COM (Dec. 12, 2011, 3:16 p.m.), *available at* http://www.businessweek.com/ap/financialnews/D9RJ62780.htm. Blackwater has certainly not been the only private military contractor to have caused controversy, within Iraq or otherwise. An earlier example of such controversy involved the investigation of several DynCorp contractors for involvement in sex trafficking in Bosnia during the 1990s. *See* E. L. Gatson, *Mercenarism 2.0? The Rise of the Modern Private Security Industry and Its Implications for International Humanitarian Law Enforcement*, 49 HARV. INT'L L.J. 221, 229 (2008). Other government contractors were also the source of controversy related to prisoner treatment in the Abu Ghraib prison. *See* Steven L. Schooner, *Contractor Atrocities at*

Blackwater came under powerful criticism for killing seventeen Iraqi civilians in 2007 and for their involvement in repeated incidents resulting in Iraqi civilian casualties and widespread property damage.[213] Such controversies involving Blackwater are concerning for several reasons. When government contractors engage in such human rights violations, there are of course questions of accountability that run two ways. From one standpoint, there is the issue of whether and how government contactors can be held responsible for their acts. As Martha Minow notes, "difficult issues about what source of law even applies to private contractors have rendered ambiguous the relevant standards of conduct and relevant enforcement mechanisms, potentially jeopardizing the success of military missions."[214] From another standpoint, privatization in this context may be seen as a means for the government to avoid direct accountability. As one commentator has observed, "contractors can facilitate foreign policy by proxy, allowing the government to change events on the ground, but at a distance that allows for plausible deniability."[215] In short, in addition to saving money, contracting out military functions might also serve to avoid statutory and regulatory restrictions on the American military, including the laws of war.[216]

However, in addressing such accountability problems, Laura Dickinson has sought to apply lessons learned in domestic privatization efforts to defense related contexts.[217] For example, Dickinson explains that, domestically, some privatized state prison

---

Abu Ghraib: Compromised Accountability in a Streamline, Outsourced Government, 16 STAN. L. & POL'Y REV. 549 (2005).

213 E. L. Gatson, *supra* note 212, at 229–30. In January 2012, Blackwater settled civil lawsuits filed by victims of the 2007 shootings. The final settlements were not disclosed. Jamie Reese, *Blackwater Settles Last Lawsuit in 2007 Baghdad Shooting Incident*, JURIST (Jan. 9, 2012, 1:04 p.m.), http://jurist.org/paperchase/2012/01/blackwater-settles-last-lawsuit-in-2007-baghdad-shooting-incident.php. Criminal prosecutions of the Blackwater security guards involved in the Nisour Square incident have been plagued by evidentiary challenges and accusations of DOJ mismanagement. Matt Apuzzo, *Trying to Salvage Remains of Blackwater Case*, N.Y. TIMES, May 12, 2014, at A1. In 2008, one guard pled guilty to voluntary manslaughter; however, four guards have pled not guilty—three facing manslaughter charges and one facing first degree murder charges. *Id.* These charges were brought under the Military Extraterritorial Jurisdiction Act of 2000, Pub. L. No. 106-523, 114 Stat. 2488, allowing for criminal punishment of persons "employed by or accompanying the Armed Forces outside the United States." 18 U.S.C. § 3261(a)(1).

214 Minow, *supra* note 171, at 118.

215 Deborah Avant, *Think Again: Mercenaries*, FOREIGN POLICY, July 1, 2004, *available at* http://www.foreignpolicy.com/story/cms.php?story_id=2577&print=1; *see also Privatized War, and Its Price*, N.Y. TIMES, Jan. 11, 2010, at A16 ("[t]here are many reasons to oppose the privatization of war. Reliance on contractors allows the government to work under the radar of public scrutiny. And freewheeling can be at cross purposes with the armed forces.").

216 Further, this kind of "contracting out" can be specifically utilized to limit political accountability for purposes of deniability. The CIA, for example, created In-Q-Tel, a private venture capital fund, to "incubate intelligence technologies." Jan D. Michaels, *The (Willingly) Fettered Executive: Presidential Spinoffs in National Security Domains and Beyond*, 97 VA. L. REV. 801 (2011).

217 LAURA A. DICKINSON, OUTSOURCING WAR AND PEACE: PRESERVING PUBLIC VALUES IN A WORLD OF PRIVATIZED FOREIGN AFFAIRS 69–101 (2011).

administrators are contractually bound to abide by basic constitutional, federal, and state legal protections applied to government actors when working with prisoners.[218] These contractual terms impose financial liability as an incentive for the contractor to act according to standards. Even in the defense contracting arena, Dickinson believes contractually obligating contractors to abide by international standards designed for state actors, such as the Torture Convention or the Geneva Conventions, would provide enhanced control over a contractor at limited cost.[219]

3. PRIVATE STANDARD SETTING ORGANIZATIONS

Increasingly, both state legislatures and Congress have privatized legislative authority by relying on private SSOs for technical (if not policy) expertise.[220] One scholar has dubbed the approach—where the government actually licenses private actors to regulate and certify regulatory compliance—the "rent-a-regulator" approach to privatization.[221] One study of the Code of Federal Regulations has found that it contains at least 9,475 incorporations by reference of private sector standards.[222] The American Society for Testing and Materials, National Fire Protection Association, and American Society of Mechanical Engineers are examples of organizations whose standards have been incorporated into diverse government regulations.[223] The Nationally Recognized Testing Laboratory Program of OSHA[224] recognizes private organizations, such as Underwriters Laboratories, that are qualified to determine if products meet OSHA standards, thus delegating public legislative and enforcement functions to the private sector.[225] The National Technology Transfer and Advancement Act[226] and OMB Circular A-119, last

---

218 *Id.* at 75.

219 *Id.* at 75–76.

220 *See generally* Verkuil, *supra* note 93, at 433–37. *See* Peter L. Strauss, *Private Standards Organizations and Public Law* 5 (Columbia Public Law Working Paper No. 13-334) (Dec. 27, 2012), *available at* http://papers.ssrn.com/sol3/papers.cfm?abstract_id=2194210 (last revised July 24, 2013).

We wish to especially thank Ms. Emily Bremer (ACUS) for her acute observations and emendations to this and the following section.

221 Miriam Seifter, *Rent-a-Regulator: Design and Innovation in Environmental Decision Making, in* GOVERNMENT BY CONTRACT 93 (Jody Freeman & Martha Minow eds., 2009).

222 *See* Emily S. Bremer, *Incorporation by Reference in an Open-Government Age*, 36 HARV. J.L. & PUB. POL'Y 131, 150 (2013).

223 *Id.*

224 *See* Nationally Recognized Testing Laboratories; Clarification of the Types of Procedures, 60 Fed. Reg. 12980–12985 (Mar. 9, 1995); *see also* U.S. Dep't of Labor, Nationally Recognized Testing Laboratories, http://www.osha.gov/dts/otpca/nrtl/ (last visited Mar. 7, 2013).

225 A list of currently recognized organizations is available at http://www.osha.gov/dts/otpca/nrtl/#nrtls (last visited Mar. 7, 2013).

226 National Technology Transfer and Advancement Act of 1995, Pub. L. No. 104-113, § 12(d), 110 Stat. 775, 783 (1996) (codified at 15 U.S.C. 272 note). Congress expressed their finding that "[t]he Federal Government can help the United States business to speed the development of new products and processes by entering

revised in 1998, directs agencies to rely, whenever possible, on private industry in generating codes rather than on what the circular called "government-unique standards."[227]

Although the use of SSOs has been widely accepted, some commentators question how the public interest is preserved when Congress (or a state legislature for that matter) relies on such private organizations.[228] Although the OMB does require that SSOs observe "due process standards," as Paul Verkuil observes, "[w]hat due process means in this context is not explained, but it presumably includes requirements of openness and transparency of membership in the SSO and its deliberations."[229] Verkuil suggests that "[t]he public interest is only preserved in these private delegations though procedural means."[230] In reality, it is difficult to know if privatization of this sort really preserves some level of public interest—especially as many SSOs are statutorily immune from antitrust damages for their legislative actions.[231]

---

into cooperative research and development agreements which make available the assistance of Federal laboratories to the private sector. . . . " § 2, 110 Stat. at 775.

227 *See* OMB Circular No. A-119, Federal Participation in the Development and Use of Voluntary Consensus Standards and in Conformity Assessment Activities, 63 Fed. Reg. 8546, 8549 (Feb. 19, 1998). The OMB is presently considering revisions to the circular. *See* Request for Comments on a Proposed Revision of OMB Circular No. A-119, "Federal Participation in the Development and Use of Voluntary Consensus Standards and in Conformity Assessment Activities," 79 Fed. Reg. 8207 (Feb. 11, 2014). *See also* Nina A. Mendelson, *Private Control over Access to the Law: The Perplexing Federal Regulatory Use of Private Standards*, 112 Mich. L. Rev. 737, 745 & n.40. An additional problem is that, when private standards are incorporated by reference, the text of the standards need not be reprinted in the *Federal Register*, although the text must be "reasonably available to the class of persons affected thereby." 5 U.S.C. § 552(a)(1). This has led to the seemingly bizarre situation where private parties must pay SSOs to secure copies of private standards that they are required by law to follow. *See* Mendelson, *supra*, at 743–44. This anomalous situation has begun to be amended. The American National Standards Institute recently launched a portal that provides free and read-only access to incorporated standards (http://ibr.ansi.org). ASTM International (formerly the American Society for Testing and Materials) has created a similar online "reading room" that provides free access to all of their incorporated standards (http://www.astm.org/readinglibrary/index.html).

228 As discussed by Peter L. Strauss: "Effectively outsourcing rulemaking not only suggests a level of trust in the disinterestedness of the standard-setter that not all persons affected by its standards might find warranted, but it also has the potential of defeating many of the procedural safeguards of federal notice-and-comment rulemaking, hiding from the public (and agency) view that data, formative private inputs and even reasoning." Strauss, *supra* note 220, at 53.

229 Verkuil, *supra* note 93, at 434. Strauss highlights that in many cases SSO standards incorporated by reference into governmental regulations are often not made accessible for free by the public as the SSO retains copyright protections. Strauss, *supra* note 220, at 9.

OMB Circular A-119 defines "due process" for standards development and lays out the basic due process requirements for "voluntary consensus standards." OMB Circular, Par 4(a)(b), http://www.whitehouse.gov/omb/circularA119. The American National Standards Institute further develops these requirements in ANSI, ANSI Essential Requirements: Due Process Requirements for American National Standards, http://publicaa.ansi.org/sites/apdl/Documents/Standards%20Activities/American%20National%20Standards/Procedures,%20Guides,%20and%20Forms/2014_ANSI_Essential_Requirements.pdf.

230 Verkuil, *supra* note 93, at 434.

231 Standards Development Organization Advancement Act of 2004, Pub. L. No. 108-237, 118 Stat. 661, 664 (2004); *see also* Tyler R. T. Wolf, *Existing in a Legal Limbo: The Precarious Legal Position of*

4. SELF-AUDITS AND THIRD PARTY AUDIT REGIMES

Privatization does not only come in the form of contracting out. More and more agencies have contracted out their respective regulatory functions through self-audit and third-party audit regimes.

Self-audit regimes incentivize, through "safe-harbor" type provisions, industry self-inspection and voluntary reporting. Agencies that have made significant use of self-audit approaches include the EPA,[232] OSHA,[233] the Federal Aviation Administration,[234]

Standards-Development Organizations, 65 WASH. & LEE L. REV. 807, 818–27 (2008) (addressing concern that standard setting organizations might "ignore the public interest in favor of industry interests when setting standards.").

We should note that the Administrative Conference of the United States has been particularly active and influential in this area. *See* Administrative Conference of the United States, Recommendation 78-4, *Federal Agency Interaction with Private Standard-Setting Organizations in Health and Safety Regulation*, 44 Fed. Reg. 1357 (Jan. 5, 1979); Recommendation 2011-5, *Incorporation by Reference*, 77 Fed. Reg. 2257, 2257 (Jan. 17, 2012).

232 In the case of the EPA, self-policing is included such final policy as "Incentives for Self-Policing: Discovery, Disclosure, Correction and Prevention of Violations," 65 Fed. Reg. 19618–27 (Apr. 11, 2000). *See EPA's Audit Policy*, http://www.epa.gov/compliance/incentives/auditing/auditpolicy.html (last visited Mar. 30, 2013). While EPA self-audit policy still relies on the 2000 self-policing regulation, the agency has sought to development the policy, *see, e.g.*, Interim Approach to Applying the Audit Policy to New Owners, 73 Fed. Reg. 44911–5006 (Aug. 1, 2008) (Notice; request for comment). *See also* Peter P. Knight, *Encouraging Regulated Entities to Comply with Federal Environmental Mandates: The Need for a Federal Environmental Audit Protection Statute*, 3 N.Y.U. J. LEGIS. & PUB. POL'Y 125 (1999–2000); Thomas R. Carey, *Assessing Environmental Compliance for Business, in* THE IMPACT OF ENVIRONMENTAL ISSUES ON BUSINESS TRANSACTIONS: LEADING LAWYERS ON MANAGING ENVIRONMENTAL REGULATION AND ENFORCEMENT FOR BUSINESS (INSIDE THE MINDS) 39–56 (Aspatore 2012), *available at* 2013 WL 3112 (Jan. 2013); Bradley C. Karkkainen, *Information-Forcing Regulation and Environmental Governance, in* LAW AND NEW GOVERNANCE IN THE EU AND THE US 293–321 (Grainne de Burca & Joanne Scott eds., 2006).

233 Like the EPA, OSHA functions under a policy of self-audits that limits the liability of employers who identify violations while conducting self-audits as described in the Notice of Final Policy, Final Policy Concerning the Occupational Safety and Health Administration Voluntary Employer Safety and Health Self Audits, 65 Fed. Reg. 46498–503 (Jul. 28, 2000). In addition, OSHA administers the Voluntary Protection Program, which serves as OSHA's "premier recognition program" allowing industry to apply for OSHA recognition for safety over a period of time, and once recognized, to enjoy exemption from OSHA programmed inspections. Revisions to the Voluntary Protection Programs to Provide Safe and Healthful Working Conditions, 74 Fed. Reg. 927 (Jan. 9, 2009) (revising the original Voluntary Protection Program adopted by OSHA in 1982, 47 Fed. Reg. 29025 (Jul. 2, 1982)). *See* OSHA GUIDE FOR HEALTH CARE FACILITIES NEWSLETTER, OSHA DEFENDS APPROACH TO VPP AT HEARING (Aug. 2012) (stating that as of May 31, 2012, there were "2,374 total active sites in VPP [Voluntary Protection Program] covering more than 911,000 workers"); *see generally* Orly Lobel, *Governing Occupational Safety in the United States, in* LAW AND NEW GOVERNANCE IN THE EU AND THE US 269–92 (Grainne de Burca & Joanne Scott eds., 2006).

234 The Federal Aviation Administration has overseen a self-reporting program allowing airlines and airline employees to report safety problems under the protection of a guaranteed waiver of sanction. RUSSELL W. MILLS, THE PROMISE OF COLLABORATIVE VOLUNTARY PARTNERSHIPS: LESSONS FROM THE

and the Department of Health and Human Services.[235] There can be little doubt that the use of self-audits by the federal government is growing, even if only driven by budget restraints. These self-audit programs with concomitant compliance incentives have become a growing part of the regulatory map.

At the same time, some federal agencies allow for third-party audit regimes as a means to increase compliance. Such third-party regimes contract out the inspection function of regulatory agencies to agency-approved private entities. Under such a regulatory regime, the regulated private company must retain and pay for an approved third-party auditor to provide a "compliance determination," which can then be relayed back to the regulating agency.[236] For example, the Food Safety Modernization Act of 2011 requires the FDA to accredit third-party auditors to certify food quality standards established by the act.[237] This arrangement allows the regulatory agency to meet its oversight responsibilities while shifting the bulk of actual inspection costs to the private sector. Discussing the increased use of such regimes, Lesley McAllister highlights that the approach "seem appropriate for an era of growing regulatory demands and diminishing governmental resources."[238]

5. SUPERVISED SELF-REGULATION OF THE SECURITIES INDUSTRY

The federal government makes extensive use of private sector SROs in the enforcement of securities laws. These SROs include the Financial Industry Regulatory Authority and the Municipal Security Rulemaking Board, as well as various of the market exchanges themselves.[239] They engage in rulemaking, market surveillance, enforcement, adjudication, and discipline of their members. While the SROs originated as private membership

---

FEDERAL AVIATION ADMINISTRATION 14–16 (2010); *see* Dorit Rubinstein Reiss, *The Benefits of Capture*, 47 WAKE FOREST L. REV. 569, 573–75 (2012).

[235] The Department of Health and Human Services has proposed a self-auditing regime to attempt to prevent Medicare billing abuses. Medicare Program; Reporting and Returning of Overpayments, Proposed Rules, 77 Fed. Reg. 9179–87 (Feb. 16, 2012). *See* J. Michael Grubbs, *Self-Audits Now Required to Avoid Medicare Billing Errors Being Punished as False Claims*, MARTINDALE.COM LEGAL LIBRARY (Feb. 22, 2012), http://www.martindale.com/health-care-law/article_Barnes-Thornburg-LLP_1452002.htm (last visited Jan. 21, 2013).

[236] Lesley K. McAllister, *Regulation by Third-Party Verification*, 53 B.C. L. REV. 1, 2–3 (2012). *See also* Miriam Seifter, *Rent-a-Regulator: Design and Innovation in Environmental Decision Making*, *in* GOVERNMENT BY CONTRACT 104-07 (Jody Freeman & Martha Minow eds., 2009) (noting that these arrangements may present problems with both monitoring and discipline).

[237] FDA Food Safety Administration Act, Pub. Law No. 111-353, 124 Stat. 3885 (Jan. 4, 2011). For a full discussion of the third party regulatory regime implemented by the Act, *see* McAllister, *supra* note 237, at 8–9.

[238] McAllister, *supra* note 237, at 2.

[239] A full list of the various SROS can be found at Self-Regulatory Organization Rulemaking, http://www.sec.gov/rules/sro.shtm/ (last visited July 14, 2014.). The SEC, of course, continues to have enforcement authority over markets and broker-dealers although the exact allocation of such authority is unclear. *See* David A. Lipton, *The SEC or the Exchanges: Who, Shall Do What and When? A Proposal to Allocate Regulatory Responsibility for Securities Markets*, 16 U. C. DAVIS L. REV. 527, 528–31 (1983); David

organizations that standardized the conduct of securities industry professionals,[240] over the course of the last seventy-five years, and most recently in response to the financial crisis, SROs have "become integrated into the scheme of federal statutory regulation."[241]

The self-regulation of stocks and bonds has a two-century history in the United States. Two dozen brokers established the first set of rules for the trading of shares under the iconic Buttonwood Agreement of May 17, 1792.[242] That first agreement led to the creation of the New York Stock and Exchange Board in 1817, which has survived as the New York Stock Exchange into the twenty-first century.[243] In 1934, Congress was not inclined to abolish this nearly 150-year-old voluntary regulatory framework. Indeed, it expanded it to establish a broader coordinated system of federal regulation and industry self-regulation.

The 1934 statute continued the self-regulatory responsibilities of the stock exchanges but placed them under the supervision of the SEC. In 1938, Congress enacted the Maloney Act, which authorized industry self-regulation of brokers and dealers in the securities industry through the creation of registered national securities associations.[244] As one Court of Appeals has explained:

> The intent was to establish a "cooperative regulation" where such associations would regulate themselves under the supervision of the SEC.... Under the Maloney Act, which amended the Exchange Act, registered securities associations are authorized

A. Lipton, *Governance of Our Security Markets, and the Failure to Allocate Regulatory Responsibility*, 34 CATH. U. L. REV. 397, 404–08 (1985). As Justice William O. Douglas has suggested, "Government [should] keep the shotgun, so to speak, behind the door, loaded, well oiled, ready for use but with the hope it would never have to be used." WILLIAM O. DOUGLAS, DEMOCRACY AND FINANCE 82 (1940). It has been suggested that the SROs have gone further than Douglas would have wished.

The Securities Investor Protection Corporation is an additional broker-dealer membership organization created by statute. See generally, Thomas W. Joo, *Who Watches the Watchers? The Securities Investor Protection Act, Investor Confidence and the Subsidization of Failure*, 72 S. CAL. L. REV. 1071 (1999).

One should note the PCAOB, which serves similar functions as an SRO although it describes itself as a "nonprofit agency established by Congress." Pub. Co. Accounting Oversight Bd., About the PCAOB, http://pcaobus.org/about/pages/default.aspx (last visited July 9, 2014). While it is not registered with the SEC as an SRO, "for all practical purposes" it functions as one. See PATRICK S. COLLINS, REGULATION OF SECURITIES, MARKETS AND TRANSACTIONS: A GUIDE TO THE NEW ENVIRONMENT 184 (2011).

240 Roberta S. Karmel, *Should Securities Industry Self-Regulatory Organizations Be Considered Government Agencies?*, 14 STAN. J.L. BUS. & FIN. 151, 159 (2008).

241 *Id.* at 151.

242 *See* New York Stock Exchange, www.nyx.com/en/who-we-ware/history/new-york (last visited Aug. 18, 2012).

243 *Id.*

244 The Maloney Act of 1938, Pub. L. No. 75-719, 52 Stat. 1070 (1978) (codified as amended at 15 U.S.C. § 78o–3). Up to the present, there is only one such association. *See* Jonathan Macey & Caroline Novogrod, *Enforcing Self-Regulatory Organization's Penalties and the Nature of Self-Regulation*, 40 HOFSTRA L. REV. 963, 968 (2012); *see also* Merrill, Lynch, Pierce, Fenner & Smith, Inc. v. Nat'l Ass'n of Sec. Dealers, Inc., 616 F.2d 1363, 1367 (5th Cir. 1980).

> to adopt rules which the SEC must, with limited exceptions, approve prior to their implementation and which the SEC may abrogate or amend as it deems in the public interest, consistent with the requirements of the Exchange Act. See *15 U.S.C. § 78s*.[245]

As a practical matter, SEC supervision of the SROs was somewhat limited until 1975. The Securities Acts Amendments of 1975 gave the commission power to approve all SRO rules and disciplinary and enforcement actions and if necessary add their own rules.[246] Facing continuous stock market scandals, the SEC strengthened its regulation of SROs.[247]

The Financial Industry Regulatory Authority provides the prime example of such cooperative regulation. Formerly called the National Association of Securities Dealers, which seemingly reflected its status as a private sector industry organization, the entity in 2007 became the Financial Industry Regulatory Authority—reflecting its significant regulatory responsibilities—following the expansion of its authority to regulate New York Stock Exchange broker-dealers.[248]

As the Fifth Circuit has observed:

> The concept of self-regulation... pervades the provisions of the Securities Exchange Act of 1934 and its subsequent amendments.... By the Act Congress granted cooperative organizations of investment bankers, dealers and brokers self-regulatory authority over their own members in order to attain and preserve the highest standards of legal and ethical behavior in the nation's securities markets. *15 U.S.C. § 78o*-3; S.Rep. No. 1455, 75th Cong., 3d Sess. 4 (1938). Self-regulation was believed to have many significant benefits, including "the expertise and intimate familiarity with complex securities operations which members of the industry can bring to bear on regulatory problems, and the informality and flexibility of self-regulatory procedures." Report of the Subcommittee on Securities of the Senate Committee on Banking, Housing and Urban Affairs, Securities Industry Study, S.Doc. No. 93-13, 93d Cong., 1st Sess. 149 (1973). Congress... recently reaffirmed its commitment to self-regulation in its 1975 amendments to the Exchange Act. The Senate report on those amendments states: "The self-regulatory roles of the exchanges and the NASD [National Association of Securities Dealers] have been major elements of the regulatory scheme of the Exchange Act since 1934 and 1938, respectively. Although self-regulation has not always performed up to expectations, on the whole it has worked well, and the Committee believes it should be preserved and

245 Jones v. SEC, 115 F.3d 1173, 1179 (4th Cir. 1997), *cert. denied*, 523 U.S. 1072 (1998).

246 Securities Acts Amendments of 1975, Pub. L. No. 94-29, 89 Stat 97. See discussion in Karmel, *supra* note 240 at 157–60.

247 *See id.* at 160–70.

248 Karsner v. Lothian, 532 F.3d 876, 879 n.1 (D.C. Cir. 2008).

strengthened." S.Rep. No. 94-75, 94th Cong., 1st Sess. 23 (1975), U.S. Code Cong. & Admin. News, pp. 179, 201.[249]

While the Financial Industry Regulatory Authority is a private corporation, it possesses the authority that is typical of many federal agencies. It has broad power to enforce—through discipline, not civil or criminal action—the legal requirements laid down in the Securities Exchange Act.[250] It also licenses the admission of individuals or companies into the securities industry. As agent for the SEC, the authority writes regulations governing the conduct of industry members, examines securities firms, ensures truthful advertising by industry members, and adjudicates violations of its regulations through administrative proceedings.[251] By statute, virtually anyone conducting a securities related business must be a member.[252] And the authority can refuse membership to individuals who fail to meet its standards for admission,[253] and can censure, fine, suspend, or expel individuals or firms from membership,[254] for violations of the Securities Exchange Act or association rules as well as "ethical standards going beyond those requirements."[255] Yet it is a private corporation. It operates as it does because, in light of history and tradition, in the 1930s, Congress elected not to abandon the existing regime of industry self-regulation but rather to leverage the regulatory powers of the newly created SEC by utilizing private self-regulatory bodies. The SEC must approve the authority's rules of operation, including its disciplinary rules, and any party aggrieved by the authority's disciplinary decision may appeal first to the SEC and, in due course, to the federal courts.[256]

The operation of SROs in the securities industry raises "state actor" issues akin to those discussed earlier.[257] The extent to which the Financial Industry Regulatory Authority is seen as a state actor is a murky question, depending on "conflicting intuitions concerning

---

[249] Merrill Lynch, Pierce, Fenner & Smith, Inc., 616 F.2d at 1366–67.

[250] *Id.* at 1367.

[251] Financial Industry Regulatory Authority, Get to know us, *available at* www.finra.org/web/groups/corporate/@corp@about/documents/corporate/p118667.pdf (last visited Apr. 2, 2013); *see also* M. Todd Henderson, *Self-Regulation for the Mortgage Industry* 31 (Coase-Sandor Institute for Law and Economics, Working Paper No. 638, 2013) (explaining that "FINRA does nearly everything that the SAFE Act and Mortgage Act require of a variety of state and federal regulators, plus much more."), available at, http://papers.ssrn.com/2013/papers/cfm?abstractidz2241799.

[252] 15 U.S.C. § 78o(a)(1), (b)(8), § 78o–3(g)(3)(B); *see also In re* Series 7 Broker Qualifications Exam Scoring Litig. v. NASD, Inc., 548 F.3d 110, 112 (D.C. Cir. 2008).

[253] *In re* Series 7 Broker Qualifications Exam Scoring Litig. et al v. NASD, Inc., 548 F.3d, at 112.

[254] See 15 U.S.C. § 78o-3(b)(7); see also Swirsky v. NASD, 124 F.3d 59 (1st Cir. 1997).

[255] Merrill, Lynch, Pierce, Fenner & Smith, Inc., 616 F.2d at 1367 (citing S. Rep. No. 94-75, 94th Cong., 1st Sess. 23 (1975)).

[256] *Id.* An overview of the regulatory framework governing the National Association of Securities Dealers (now the Financial Industry Regulatory Authority) disciplinary proceedings can be found in Austin Municipal Securities, Inc. v. National Association of Securities Dealers, Inc., 757 F.2d 676, 679–81 (5th Cir. 1985).

[257] *See* section B(3), *supra*.

what is public, or somehow of the State, and what is private, or not of the State."[258] Courts have come down in different directions, some finding that the authority is a state actor, with others finding that it is not.[259] Some have avoided the specific question altogether.[260] In an unpublished 2011 opinion, the Eleventh Circuit acknowledged the circuit split, noting "[w]e have not yet determined whether FINRA is a government actor," and proceeded to avoid the question in deciding the case.[261] Far more important, in 2011, the Second Circuit (the leading circuit court on securities issues) reaffirmed the doctrine of absolute immunity for those activities of SROs that are "incident to … [the] … regulatory functions" of the SRO.[262]

While the legal trend (as noted above) has been to increase the legal protections of SROs, the recent financial crisis has refocused attention on their effectiveness.[263] Some, like former SEC chair Harvey Pitt, have even questioned its future utility.[264] This said, it is clear that self-regulation will continue to play a critical role in the oversight of the financial industry far into the future. "Indeed, legislation has been introduced in the House to shift investment-advisor oversight to an SRO-based regulation model.[265] The trend toward self-regulation has not abated.

---

258 Christian Turner, *State Action Problems*, 65 FLA. L. REV. 281, 284 (2013).

259 The classic case, *United States v. Solomon,* found the New York Stock Exchange was not a state actor for the purposes of the Fifth Amendment. 509 F.2d 863, 867–70 (2d Cir. 1975).The court did not decide, however, "whether stock exchanges may be subject to some due process requirements for [disciplinary] action." *Id.* at 871. *See* D'Alessio v. SEC, 380 F.3d 112, 120 n.12 (2d Cir. 2004) (determines the NYSE to be a "private entity"); Desiderio v. Nat'l Ass'n of Sec. Dealers, Inc.,", 191 F.3d 198, 206 (2d Cir. 1999) ("The NASD is a private actor, not a state actor. It is a private corporation that receives no federal or state funding. Its creation was not mandated by statute, nor does the government appoint its members or serve on any NASD board or committee. [T]he fact that a business entity is subject to 'extensive and detailed' state regulation does not convert that organization's actions into those of the state.").

260 *See* Rooms v. SEC, 444 F.3d 1208, 1213–14 (10th Cir. 2006).

261 *See* Busacca v. SEC, 449 F. App'x 886 (11th Cir. 2011). *Busacca* is critiqued in Jerrod M. Lukacs, Note, *Much Ado About Nothing: How the Securities SRO State Action Circuit Split Has Been Misinterpreted and What It Means for Due Process at FINRA*, 47 GA. L. REV. 923, 939–48 (2013), which discusses the split between the circuits on this issue. *See also* Nicholas J. Wagoner, *Are Private Regulators Above the Constitution?*, CIRCUIT SPLITS (Jan. 11, 2012, 6:00 a.m.), http://www.circuitsplits.com/securities-and-exchange-commission/.

262 Standard Inv. Chartered v. National Ass'n of Securities Dealers, Inc., 637 F.3d 112, 116 (2d Cir. 2011) *cert. den.* 132 S.Ct. 1093 (2012).

263 *See* U.S. Gov't Accountability Office, GAO, Securities Regulation: Opportunities Exist To Improve SEC's Oversight of the Financial Industry Regulatory Authority 3 (2012). *See also* Macey & Novogrod, supra note 244, at 975–76. (noting various criticisms of recent Financial Industry Regulatory Authority practices).

264 *See* Former SEC Chair Harvey Pitt pointing out that "the SRO [self-regulatory organization] function was once crucial but in terms of exchanges it no longer is," in Andrew Ackerman, Scott Patterson & Jacob Bunge, *Policing of Exchanges Questioned*, WALL ST. J., Oct. 2, 2013.

265 *See* Investment Adviser Oversight Act of 2012, H.R. 4624, 112th Cong. (2012). This bill, cosponsored by Representatives Spencer Bachus and Carolyn McCarthy, proposed delegating registration and disciplinary authority over investment advisors to "registered national investment advisor association[s]."

F. Observations

If the traditional, multimember independent agencies are designed to be somewhat removed from direct presidential control, government corporations, GSEs, and private entities utilized by government are expressly designed by structure to fall even further outside the realm of direct presidential or congressional control. As we have attempted to show in earlier chapters, traditional independent agencies have evolved differently among themselves in the precise level of executive or legislative branch oversight and control to which they are subject as a legal or practical matter. The same is true of those entities further along the continuum of government control. Both seek to incorporate a private sector structure believed to be better suited to the task at hand. A variety of what Moe and Stanton call "federal management controls" apply to a far lesser extent to government corporations and GSEs. However, each entity has also been created in a somewhat ad hoc manner designed to address some unique element of national policy that needs specialized attention. At the far end of the spectrum, private sector entities such as private SSOs or SROs are at times enlisted as a "fifth branch" of government,[266] to assist federal agencies in their regulatory responsibilities. Here, too, historic or pragmatic considerations dictate this result.

The clear growth in "privatization" (however defined) underscores that the challenges of the "administrative state" force both Congress and the executive to seek to develop structures and modalities that are in some tension with the demands of the "unitary executive." The vagaries of efforts to marry government functions with private enterprise is but one example of the struggle to find creative solutions for the role of the state in the twenty-first century. At least under present understandings of the role of the state in contemporary society, less government may mean fewer government structures but does not appear to result in fewer government functions—those functions still take place, albeit under a different guise.

For a critique of this legislation see Letter from Angela Canterbury, Dir. of Pub. Policy, & Michael Smallberg, Investigator, Project on Government Oversight, to Rep. Spencer Bachus, Chair of House Comm. on Fin. Services (May 29, 2012) available at, http://pogoarchives.org/m/fo/sro-letter-20120529.pdf.

266 M. Todd Henderson & William A. Birdthistle, *Becoming a Fifth Branch*, 99 CORNELL L. REV. 1, 5 (2013).

9

Internal Agency Operations

IN ORDER TO understand the contextual nature of how agencies occupy a position of "independence," it is instructive to review their internal operations. Although only rarely examined, internal agency operations affect the position of the agency within the broader governmental structure. Nonetheless, most have been developed and shaped by custom, tradition, or agreement or acquiescence among the members, at times embodied in regulations or internal agency minutes, but only rarely changed, or even questioned, by newly arriving members. Obviously, internal procedures must not be inconsistent with explicit statutory requirements. Occasionally agency practice will influence court decisions, thus translating into law. This practical evolution bears significantly on the ability of the elected branches to influence independent agency decisions.

A. Role of the Chair

There is no doubt that the chair of a multimember agency is its most dominant figure. Agency chairs are appointed to their positions by the president and are generally members of his political party. Often, although not always, they are genuine experts in the field. That is true irrespective of administration. As Cindy Szkrzycki points out in her enlightening book on government regulation, *The Regulators: Anonymous Power Brokers in American Politics*,[1] both President Clinton's appointment of Robert Pitofsky and President George W. Bush's selection of Timothy Muris brought to the FTC recognized academic experts with prior senior level commission experience, albeit with different regulatory philosophies.

---

[1] CINDY SZKRZYCKI, THE REGULATORS: ANONYMOUS POWER BROKERS IN AMERICAN POLITICS 63 (2003).

Writing in 1997, Professor William Kovacic, himself an academic expert with both senior staff experience and service as an FTC member before his selection as chair by President George W. Bush, also points to the Pitofsky selection as a strong one. Kovacic likewise points to President Reagan's choice of economist James Miller as an illustration of a well-credentialed FTC chair.[2]

Agency chairs frequently come to an agency to advance the president's agenda. For example, the promotion of A. Daniel O'Neal from a member to chair of the ICC at the beginning of President Carter's administration began the Administration's shift toward transportation regulatory reform.[3] O'Neil's replacement by Darius Gaskins, who had served at the Civil Aeronautics Board during the deregulatory initiatives of chair Alfred Kahn, shifted the movement toward deregulation.[4] President Carter clearly supported transportation deregulation and ultimately signed both the Airline Deregulation Act of 1978 and the Motor Carrier Act of 1980.[5]

In somewhat similar fashion, William Gould, who had served on the legal staff of a labor union and had a distinguished career as a law professor and arbitrator before his appointment by President Clinton as the NLRB chair, brought to the job a strong belief in market intervention not inconsistent with Clinton administration objectives.[6] He was recruited for the job by the president of the Amalgamated Clothing Workers Union, who spoke directly to President Clinton about Gould's suitability as NLRB chair.[7] Gould was presumably expected to reflect the Clinton administration's perspectives on labor relations matters but did not receive any direct instructions during his tenure. Gould has indicated that he had received "valuable assistance and counsel" from members of the administration before his confirmation;[8] he had no direct or indirect contact with the Clinton administration thereafter.[9] Gould observes, by reference to the NLRB during the Eisenhower administration, that "there was no presidential attempt to devise plans, discuss policy, exchange views, or play on team loyalties. [NLRB chair Guy Farmer] was strictly on his own."[10]

---

[2] William A. Kovacic, *The Quality of Appointments and the Capability of the Federal Trade Commission*, 49 ADMIN. L. REV. 915, 938 & n.87 (1997).

[3] DOROTHY ROBYN, BRAKING THE SPECIAL INTERESTS, TRUCKING DEREGULATION AND THE POLITICS OF POLICY REFORM 27, 32–33, 40, 186 (1987).

[4] *Id.* at 39–41, 182.

[5] Pub. L. No. 95-504 92 Stat. 1705 (1978); Pub. L. No. 96-296, 94 Stat. 793 (1980).

[6] WILLIAM B. GOULD, IV, LABORED RELATIONS: LAW, POLITICS AND THE NLRB—A MEMOIR, Preface, 2 (2000).

[7] *Id.* at 13–16.

[8] He mentions Abner Mikva, counsel to the president, Bob Nash, presidential director of personnel, and Richard Socariides, White House liaison to the Department of Labor. GOULD, *supra* note 6, Preface, at xiv.

[9] GOULD, *supra* note 6, at 124.

[10] *Id.* at 124 (quoting Terry M. Moe, *Interests, Institution and Political Theory: The Politics of the NLRB, in* STUDIES IN AMERICAN POLITICAL DEVELOPMENT 237 (1990)).

Now and then an agency chair will come to the job with a personal agenda somewhat inconsistent with that of the administration. Former ICC chair Reese Taylor told one of the authors that, before his confirmation, he had not spoken to any of President Reagan's transportation policy advisors. Taylor had been a law partner of former Nevada senator Paul Laxalt and chair of the Nevada Public Service Commission and got his job through Senator Laxalt's direct intervention with President Reagan. Taylor's views on restoring the commission's former (prederegulation) authority were entirely his own and largely inconsistent with Reagan administration deregulation objectives.

Commissioner Dan H. Fenn of the former U.S. Tariff Commission, reflecting on the chairs when he was a member, observed:

> The Chairman when I was appointed believed that the Commission should be quiet and unobtrusive. He liked to refer to [the agency] as a fire department, with its staff wrapping hoses and keeping the equipment in good repair against the day when the alarm would ring, when someone would knock on the door with a case to be considered. He might, some of us thought, have added that the first effort in such an event would be to persuade the petitioner to try some other firehouse down the street.[11]

The political difficulty of obtaining confirmation for an NLRB chair in the final two years of the Clinton administration led the president to coax a highly respected career NLRB lawyer, John Truesdale, out of retirement to serve as chair as a recess appointee. At a time when the board had a seven-hundred-case backlog, Truesdale is quoted as saying: "I come in with no preconceived notions of policy but to reduce the amount of time it takes to issue decisions."[12]

Agency chairs frequently resign when a new president is elected, even though their replacement as chair does not affect their entitlement to remain as members.[13] A major exception is the Federal Reserve Board. The board conducts the nation's monetary policy and supervises and regulates banking institutions. Importantly, it has a significant responsibility for maintaining the stability of the financial system. This responsibility requires that markets and the public in general have confidence in the consistency, continuity, and reliability of board policies. Congress recognized this by giving board members statutory fourteen-year terms—the longest of any independent agency,[14]

---

[11] 1 SENATE COMM. ON GOV'T OPERATIONS, STUDY ON FEDERAL REGULATION, S. DOC. NO. 95-25, at 17 (1977) (citation omitted) (alternation in original).

[12] SZKRZYCKI, *supra* note 1, at 64.

[13] Daniel E. Ho, *Measuring Agency Preferences: Experts, Voting, and the Power of Chairs*, 59 DEPAUL L. REV. 333, 338 (2010).

[14] 12 U.S.C. § 242.

although, as Peter Conti-Brown has cogently pointed out, board members rarely serve a full fourteen-year term.[15] Congress has provided, in addition, that the board's chair and two vice chairs serve four-year terms, although they lack explicit statutory "good cause" removal protections regarding those positions.[16] More significant, the need for continuity in board policies has brought about a tradition of bipartisan appointment of board chairs. In fact, since the 1950s, nearly all board chairs have been reappointed by presidents of the other party. Chairman William McChesney Martin, for example, who was the longest serving board chair, served under five presidents from 1951 to 1970, while chairman Alan Greenspan served from 1987 to 2006.[17] In short, the board's substantive mission bears heavily on both the statutory requirements of appointment and tenure and the tradition that has built upon them.

Two agencies—the FEC and the National Mediation Board—select their own chairs. The FEC decides uniquely partisan issues as part of its supervisory role over the election process and its participants. To help ensure that neither major political party can seize management control of the commission for a sustained period, Congress has provided that the chairmanship rotates annually among the members, that a commissioner may serve as chair only once during his or her term, and that the commission's chair and vice chair may not come from the same political party.[18] The National Mediation Board chair is also chosen annually, but there are no other statutory limitations.[19]

Typically, the president chooses one member of the agency to serve as chair, often at the same time he or she is nominated as a member. The typical statute gives the president plenary power to remove the individual as chairman, although not as a member. At the Consumer Product Safety Commission and the Federal Reserve Board, the chair must be confirmed in that post by the Senate. At the Consumer Product Safety Commission, it seems clear that the chair may nevertheless be removed as chair summarily. The original Consumer Product Safety Act provided that one of the commission's members "shall be designated by the President as Chairman. The Chairman, when so designated shall act as Chairman until the expiration of his term of office as Commissioner" (Pub. L. No. 92-573, § 4(a), 86 Stat. 1207, 1210 [1972]). When Congress changed the statute to require Senate confirmation for a new chair, it deleted the statutory provision regarding the end of the chair's term as chair, providing only that "[t]he Chairman shall be appointed by the President, by and with the advice and consent of the Senate, from among the Members of the Commission. An individual may be appointed as a member of the Commission

15 Peter Conti-Brown, *The Structure of Federal Reserve Independence*, 35-36 (Rock Ctr. for Corporate Governance, Working Paper Series No. 139, Jan. 2, 2014 version), *available at* http://www.law.stanford.edu/sites/default/files/publications/431459/doc/slspublic/SSRN-id2275759.pdf.

16 12 U.S.C. § 242. *See also*, Conti-Brown, *supra* note 15, at 36.

17 *See* Bd. of Governors of the Fed. Reserve Sys., www.federalreserve.gov/aboutthefed/bios/board/boardmembership.htm (accessed May 19, 2014).

18 *See* 2 U.S.C. § 437c(a)(5) (1994).

19 45 U.S.C. § 154 (Second).

and as chair at the same time" (Pub. L. No. 95-631, § 2[a], 92 Stat. 3742 [1978]). The OLC reasonably reached the conclusion that the statutory change essentially removed the provision that had tied the term of the chairmanship to his or her term as a commissioner.[20]

The chair and two vice chairs of the Federal Reserve Board likewise must be confirmed by the Senate to those positions. The statute explicitly provides that, from among the board's membership, "1 shall be designated by the President, by and with the advice and consent of the Senate, to serve as Chairman of the Board for a term of 4 years, and 2 shall be designated by the President, by and with the advice and consent of the Senate, to serve as Vice Chairmen of the Board, each for a term of 4 years."[21] Given the lack of any explicit statutory removal protection for these positions, the question of whether this statute permits plenary removal of a chair from that post has been described as "murky."[22] Two leading academic observers have concluded that the chair has secure tenure as chair.[23] Presumably the same would be true of the vice chairs. We agree with the judgment of Peter Conti-Brown that any statutory protection that might be held by the chair and vice chairs is an "open question,"[24] and that a chair's removal is likely constrained more by practical than legal considerations.[25]

The legal relationship between an agency chair and his or her colleagues is statutorily established but nonetheless highly ambiguous and malleable.[26] When Congress removed the ICC from the Interior Department in 1889, it gave the commission as an institution substantive and organizational powers, including the power to appoint officers and employees,[27] establish procedures "as will best conduce to the proper dispatch of business and to the ends of justice,"[28] and lease offices and purchase supplies.[29] However, there was no provision outlining any particular powers of the chair. Indeed, the chair was referred to only once in the organic statute: expenses were to be paid upon the presentation of

---

20 President's Authority to Remove the Chairman of the Consumer Product Safety Commission, 2001 OLC LEXIS 9 (July 31, 2001).

21 12 U.S.C. § 242.

22 A. Michael Froomkin, *In Defense of Administrative Agency Autonomy*, 96 YALE L.J. 787, 809 n.146 (1987).

23 Peter L. Strauss, *The Place of Agencies in Government: Separation of Powers and the Fourth Branch*, 84 COLUM. L. REV. 573, 590, n.66 (1984) ("The Federal Reserve Board, at least, operates in which public confidence has long been thought paramount...."); Paul Verkuil, *The Status of Independent Agencies After* Bowsher v. Synar, 1986 DUKE L.J. 779, 799–800 & n.110.

24 Conti-Brown, *supra* note 15, at 36.

25 *Id. See also* Christopher S. Yoo, Stephen G. Calabresi & Anthony J. Colangelo, *The Unitary Executive in the Modern Era*, 1945–2004, 90 IOWA L. REV. 601, 644 (2005) (noting that President Kennedy received the resignations of all chairs of federal regulatory agencies except for the chair of the Federal Reserve Board).

26 See, by way of example, Division of Power and Responsibilities Between the Chairperson of the Chemical Safety and Hazard Investigation Board and the Board as a Whole, 2000 OLC LEXIS 23 (June 26, 2000), discussing the relationship between the chair of the Chemical Safety Board and his colleagues [hereinafter OLC 2000 Opinion]. This relationship is discussed in greater detail, *infra*.

27 *See* Act of Mar. 2, 1889, ch. 382, § 7, 25 Stat. 855, 861–62.

28 *Id.* § 6, 25 Stat. 861.

29 *See id.* § 7, 25 Stat. 862.

itemized vouchers approved by the chairman.[30] For much of its history, the commission itself selected its own chair from among the members. From 1910 until 1937, the chairmanship simply rotated among the members based on seniority.[31] Other multimember agencies were modeled on the structure of the ICC. In the period up to World War II, agency chairs were as often chosen by their colleagues as by the president.[32] Over time, however, as discussed in subsection 2 below, both presidents and Congress came to recognize that the day-to-day administration of an agency cannot be exercised collectively.

1. SALARY AND STATUS

There is considerable variation in the rate of pay of members of independent agencies that appears to reflect both a rough congressional hierarchy of importance and idiosyncratic considerations. Generally speaking, though, chairs of multimember agencies are paid more than their colleagues.

Presidential appointees are paid at one of five levels, with Level I being the highest. Cabinet secretaries, for example, are paid at Executive Level I. In 2000, Congress raised the level of the chairs of the Federal Reserve Board from Executive Level II to Executive Level I,[33] and she is the only multimember agency chair paid at Executive Level I.[34] The head of the SSA is also paid at Executive Level I.[35] That salary level, as of January 2011, was $199,700 per year.[36] The chairs of the NRC and members of the Federal Reserve Board (other than the chair) are paid at Executive Level II.[37] As of January 2011, officials at Executive Level II were paid $179,700.[38] Executive Level II is also the rate of pay for deputy cabinet secretaries and the administrator of the EPA.[39]

Many regulatory commission chairs—such as the chairs of the FCC, the Federal Maritime Commission, and the FERC—are paid at Executive Level III, as are nonchairman members of the NRC and the Defense Nuclear Facilities Safety Board.[40] The rate of pay for Executive Level III is $165,300.[41] The chairs of the Federal Labor Relations Authority and the Board of Veterans' Appeals, and the nonchairman members of

---

30 *See id.* § 7, 25 Stat. 862.

31 Reorganization Plan No. 1 of 1969, 3 C.F.R. 1066 (1966–1970), *reprinted in* 5 U.S.C. app. at 1547 (1994), authorized the president to select the ICC chair, and transferred administrative responsibility to the chair.

32 *See* Robert E. Cushman, The Independent Regulatory Commissions 683, 747–48 (1941). As noted above, chairs at two agencies are still selected by their colleagues (FEC, National Mediation Board).

33 Pub. L. No. 06-569, § 1002(b), 114 Stat. 3028.

34 5 U.S.C. § 5312.

35 *Id.* § 5312.

36 *Id.* § 5331 note.

37 *Id.* § 5313.

38 *Id.* § 5313 note.

39 *Id.* § 5313.

40 *Id.* § 5314.

41 *Id.* § 5314 note.

most multimember commissions, are paid at Executive Level IV.[42] The rate of pay for Executive Level IV is $155,500.[43] Although Congress typically fixes the pay level of agency members, the statute governing the CSB gave the president the power to establish pay categories for all members.[44] President George H. W. Bush placed all of the board members—including the chair—in Executive Level IV.[45]

2. THE NEED FOR CENTRALIZED ADMINISTRATION

Multimember institutions need some centralized administration. In 1949, the Commission on Organization of the Executive Branch of the Government (Hoover Commission) recommended that all administrative responsibility at multimember agencies be vested in the chairman of the agency. In the commission's view, "[a]dministration by a plural executive is universally regarded as inefficient.... [T]hose cases where administration has been distinctly superior are cases where the administrative as distinguished from the regulatory duties have been vested in the chairman."[46] During the 1950s and 1960s, Presidents Truman and Kennedy, responding to that recommendation, presented several reorganization plans to Congress designed to transfer the power of day-to-day agency administration from the independent agency itself to its chairman.[47] Since then, even nonchairman members of multimember agencies have come to accept the necessity of some centralized administration.[48]

The distribution of power between the chairman and his or her colleagues is an occasional source of interest to members at virtually every multimember agency, particularly those who are new to the job, although most appear to accept without challenge what they perceive to be the agency's modus operandi.

Although the respective powers of a chair and the agency as an institution differ from agency to agency, most chairs are essentially their agency's chief executive and

---

42 *Id.* § 5315.

43 *Id.* § 5316.

44 *Id.* § 5317 (1994).

45 *See* Exec. Order No. 12,814, 57 Fed. Reg. 42483 (Sept. 14, 1992).

46 *See* COMMISSION ON ORGANIZATION OF THE EXECUTIVE BRANCH OF THE GOVERNMENT, THE INDEPENDENT REGULATORY COMMISSIONS 5–6 (1949) [hereinafter HOOVER COMMISSION REPORT] (Recommendation 1).

47 For example, see the reorganization plan of the Federal Power Commission. *See* Reorganization Plan No. 9 of 1950, 3 C.F.R. 1005–06 (1949–1953), *reprinted in* 5 U.S.C. app. at 1470–71 (1994).

48 *See* DAVID M. WELBORN, GOVERNANCE OF FEDERAL REGULATORY AGENCIES 36–38 (1977). The Welborn book is a revision of a study of seven multimember agencies prepared under the auspices of the Administrative Conference of the United States. Although it examines only agencies with regulatory functions, it has relevance, in our view, to all multimember agencies. It attempts to analyze the "inner life" of multimember agencies and addresses the relationship between institutional characteristics and substantive results. Chapter 4 addresses some aspects of the relationship between the chair and his or her colleagues in the management of the agency.

administrative officer. They appoint and supervise the staff, distribute business among the agency's personnel and administrative units, and ordinarily control the preparation (and sometimes actual administration) of the agency's budget and the expenditure of funds.[49] They ordinarily exercise a leadership role in the agency's substantive mission, although the power of an agency chairman in this regard is highly idiosyncratic. For example, former FCC chair Reed Hundt has noted that, by tradition, the FCC chair worked with the staff to make tentative decisions that were then presented to his colleagues for approval. The chair's success was measured by whether he could get a majority of the commission to support his decision.[50] Former NLRB chair William Gould was less sanguine about the power he had as chair. In part that resulted from the statutory organization of the NLRB. The NLRB chair's position is more problematic because the president, subject to Senate confirmation, not the agency chair, appoints its general counsel. The general counsel has important powers over the appointment of personnel, including authority over all the board's lawyers except for ALJs and personal assistants to the members, and sole discretion whether or not to undertake unfair labor practice cases.[51] Gould observed:

> The powers of the chairmanship are only nebulously defined. During most of my term, Congress (whether Democratic or Republican), the bar, the academic community, and the press were far more likely than my fellow Board members and the general counsel to accord me stature and to defer to my leadership.... In the final analysis, the chairmanship—given the authority of the general counsel to appoint regional staff and recommended regional directors to the entire Board (not just the Chairman)—is more like a bully pulpit than a position of leadership.[52]

Even at agencies with strong traditions of leadership by the chair, other agency members can play some role in the agency's management or administration. David Welborn points out:

> One of the major difficulties is finding that delicate balance point at which the members generally are engaged in the large questions in a positive way, but without constricting the chairman in caring for his essential functions. There are no magic formulas for locating the balance. The evidence suggests, however, that the [agencies] almost never give systematic and focused attention to questions of balance, roles, and the quality of the working relationship between members and chairmen.

---

49 *See* appendix *infra*.

50 *See* REED E. HUNDT, YOU SAY YOU WANT A REVOLUTION: A STORY OF INFORMATION AGE POLITICS 13, 146–47 (2000).

51 29 U.S.C. § 153(d).

52 GOULD, *supra* note 6, at 52.

> In most of the agencies, the formal delineations of authority are imprecise. Even when definition has been attempted, substantial gray areas have been left.[53]

We have surveyed over thirty multimember agencies. All of the reorganization statutes and their progeny fundamentally assign substantive authority to the agency as a whole and administrative or executive authority to the chair. Frequently, Congress simply copies from one statute to another, or amalgamates portions of more than one statute into the new statute. But each statute uses its own form of words that can create slightly different demarcations of responsibility. Statutory language is often ambiguous, and even relatively detailed statutes rarely fill in all of the fine points of the agency's organization and operation.

The typical reorganization plan of the 1950s and 1960s contained the following language:

> There are hereby transferred from the ... Commission ... to the Chairman of the Commission ... the *executive* and *administrative* functions of the Commission, including functions of the Commission with respect to (1) the appointment and supervision of personnel employed under the Commission, (2) the distribution of business among such personnel and among administrative units of the Commission, and (3) the use and expenditures of funds.[54]

Use of the term "including" before the specific enumeration of the trilogy of conventional executive or administrative functions suggests that appointment and supervision of staff, the distribution of the agency's work, and the use and expenditure of funds were generally regarded as key executive or administrative functions belonging to the chair. But the full range of executive or administrative powers, and the precise relationship between administration and substance, were undefined. The Hoover Commission could do no better than observe that "[p]urely executive duties [are] those that can be performed far better by a single administrative official."[55]

Importantly, the chair's administrative and executive powers were rarely unfettered. The typical reorganization plan limited the chairman's executive and administrative powers in four key respects:

> 1. In carrying out any of his functions under the provisions of this section the Chairman shall be governed by general policies of the Commission and by such

[53] WELBORN, *supra* note 48, at 150.

[54] *See, e.g.*, Reorganization Plan No. 8 of 1950, 3 C.F.R. 1005 (1949–1953), *reprinted in* 5 U.S.C. app. at 1470 (1994) (emphasis added) (FTC).

[55] HOOVER COMMISSION REPORT, *supra* note 46, at 3.

regulatory decisions, findings, and determinations as the Commission may by law be authorized to make.

2. The appointment by the Chairman of the heads of major administrative units under the Commission shall be subject to the approval of the Commission.
3. Personnel employed regularly and full time in the immediate offices of members of the Commission other than the Chairman shall not be affected by the provisions of this reorganization plan.
4. There are hereby reserved to the Commission its functions with respect to revising budget estimates and with respect to determining upon the distribution of appropriated funds according to major programs and purposes.[56]

In short, Congress sought to centralize day-to-day direction and internal administration of the agency in the chair's hands in order to prevent what one observer has described as "splintered management."[57] However, as noted, Congress did not accord agency chairs absolute authority even as to administrative and executive activity. Not surprisingly, Congress plainly left to each member the selection and supervision of staff in his or her own office. Moreover, Congress required that, in exercising administrative powers, a chairman did so in accordance with the agency's overall policy direction—whatever that meant. And Congress gave the agency as a whole a role to play with respect to certain core responsibilities—such as approval of key staff appointments and the budget—that were likely to affect the agency's substantive functions or mission.

Welborn observed in his study of multimember agencies:

> Although some differences are specified in the prerogatives of chairmen and the membership, ultimate formal responsibility for regulatory policy development and implementation is vested in ... [the agency] to be exercised in a collegial, shared manner.[58]

Where Congress wants to deviate from the normal statutory division of responsibility, it knows how to do so expressly. For example, the statute governing the EEOC confers on its chair express power to "appoint and fix the compensation of [officers and employees] as *he* deems necessary."[59] With such broad powers, the EEOC chair may even effect a

---

56 Decision of the Comptroller General to the Equal Employment Opportunity Commission, No. B-167015, 1974 U.S. Comp. Gen. LEXIS 2550, at *1-2 (Jan. 9, 1975) [hereinafter 1975 Decision of the Comptroller General] (quoting Reorganization Plan No. 8 of 1950, 5 U.S.C. app at 1470).

57 *See* WELBORN, *supra* note 48, at 10 & n.18 (quoting MARVER H. BERNSTEIN, REGULATING BUSINESS BY INDEPENDENT COMMISSION 173 (1955)).

58 WELBORN, *supra* note 48, at 5.

59 42 U.S.C. 2000--4(a). *See also* 1975 Decision of the Comptroller General, *supra* note 56 (emphasis added) (citing Equal Employment Opportunity Act of 1972, Pub. L. No. 92-261, § 8(d), 86 Stat. 103, 109–110).

total reorganization of the agency without the concurrence of colleagues.[60] Similarly, the Federal Maritime Commission chair can make appointments "after consultation with other Commissioners."[61]

Two significant analyses examine the respective responsibilities of the chair of a multimember agency and the agency as a whole. The first is a 1974 opinion of the comptroller general,[62] and an amendment to it issued four months later,[63] dealing with the EEOC. Under a relatively typical organizational statute, the EEOC chair was responsible for the agency's administrative operations. In a dispute over contracting authority, three members of the commission challenged the chair's assertion that his administrative power included authority to execute contracts without submitting them first to the full commission for approval. The three commissioners sought out the comptroller general's advice on the ground that the issue involved the expenditure of appropriated funds; the three commissioners also asked, more generally, that the comptroller general address the respective roles and responsibilities of the chair vis-à-vis the commission as a body.[64] The EEOC statute provided generally that "the Chairman shall be responsible on behalf of the Commission for the administrative operations of the Commission."[65]

Interpreting the statutory provision, the EEOC general counsel drew a broad distinction between the establishment of agency policy, which rested with the commission as a whole, and the implementation of agency policy, which was within the purview of the chair. He concluded that the execution of contracts designed to implement commission policy decisions rested with the chair, although "the award of certain contracts ... may peculiarly fall within the realm of policy determinations and should therefore properly be approved by the Commission as a whole."[66]

The comptroller general opinion supports the historical evidence that Congress ordinarily intends to leave day-to-day agency administration to the chairman while retaining for the agency as a whole a role to play in those administrative or management matters that may affect the agency's substantive functions or mission. Although the words of individual statutes may have differed somewhat, the comptroller general observed that

60 1975 Decision of the Comptroller General, *supra* note 56.

61 *See* Section 104(a) of Reorganization Plan No. 7 of 1961, 26 Fed. Reg. 7315, 75 Stat. 840, incorporating Reorganization Plan. No. 6 of 1949, 14 Fed. Reg. 5228, 63 Stat. 1069, *reprinted in* 5 U.S.C.A. app. at 258 (1996).

62 Decision of the Comptroller General to the Equal Employment Opportunity Commission, B-167015, 1974 U.S. Comp. Gen. LEXIS 1627 (Sept. 19, 1974) [hereinafter 1974 Decision of the Comptroller General].

63 1975 Decision of the Comptroller General, *supra* note 56.

64 *See* 1974 Decision of the Comptroller General, *supra* note 62, at *1-11, and 1975 Decision of the Comptroller General, *supra* note 56, at *1.

65 1974 Decision of the Comptroller General, *supra* note 62, at *2 (quoting 42 U.S.C. § 2000A-4(a)).

66 *Id.* at *10.

the EEOC's statute was analogous to provisions generally vesting administrative responsibilities in the heads of other independent regulatory agencies.[67]

The comptroller general stated, however, that these provisions were "not intended to supersede or diminish in any way the substantive authorities and responsibilities of the Commission[s] as a whole."[68] Based in part on this understanding, the comptroller general approved the full commission's involvement in certain administrative activities:

> [A] number of Commission activities, while in part administrative, also involve substantive determinations of legitimate concern to the full Commission [and]... the Commission as a body has authority to establish reasonable standards to delimit and govern the substantive aspects of such activities.[69]

Drawing on the president's views, the comptroller general attempted to construct the following general line between the functions of the chairman and those of the agency as a whole:

> In regard to the regulatory agencies, the [reorganization] plans distinguish between two groups of functions necessary to the conduct of these agencies. One group includes the substantive aspect of regulation—that is, the determination of policies, the formulation and issuance of rules, and the adjudication of cases. All these functions are left in the board or commission as a whole. The other group of functions comprises the day-to-day direction and internal administration of the complex staff organizations which the commissions require. These responsibilities are transferred to the chairman of the agencies, to be discharged in accordance with policies which the commissions may establish.[70]

There are nonetheless some administrative functions with which the agency as a whole may not interfere. Importantly, however, the comptroller general indicated that "where disputes arise as to what matters are procedural or administrative and what are substantive, the full commission should have the final say."[71]

---

[67] *See id.* at *13–*15 (comparing the EEOC statute with procedures governing the FTC, FPC, and SEC). As noted above, the statute deviated from the classic model by conferring on the EEOC chair express power to "appoint and fix the compensation of [officers and employees] as *he* deems necessary." 1975 Decision of the Comptroller General, *supra* note 56, at *4 (emphasis added) (internal quotation marks omitted).

[68] 1974 Decision of the Comptroller General, *supra* note 62, at *17

[69] 1975 Decision of the Comptroller General, *supra* note 56, at *1. *Compare* Division of Powers and Responsibilities Between the Chairperson of the Chemical Safety and Hazard Investigation Board and the Board as a Whole, 24 Op. O.L.C. 102, 2000 OLC Lexis 27 (2000) at *3–4 (stating that while the chair of the CSB has the authority to superintend and carry out the daily activities necessary to implement the board's substantive decisions, he does not have the authority to make those decisions alone).

[70] 1974 Decision of the Comptroller General, *supra* note 62, at *18.

[71] *See id.* at *19–*20 (citing 96 CONG. REC. 7163–64 (1950)).

A more recent, executive branch opinion is consistent with the comptroller general's approach.[72] An opinion of the DOJ's OLC broadly endorsed the comptroller general's approach.[73] Relying on the dictionary definition of "execute" to mean "put into effect" and "carry out fully," and the definition of "administer" to mean "manage the affairs of," the OLC concluded that the chair "superintends and carries out the day-to-day activities necessary to effectuate the [agency's] ... substantive decisions. He does not, absent some form of [agency] ... approval ..., make those decisions by himself."[74] Significantly, the OLC agreed that, in the event of a disagreement between the agency chair and the agency itself, the agency's decision controls if it is not unreasonable.[75]

Agency statutes are different, and each is, to some extent, sui generis. Statutory deviation from the model of the reorganization plans ordinarily occurs when specific institutional issues are brought to Congress's attention, or are for some reason a matter of congressional (or, more likely, congressional staff) interest or concern. For example, the statute governing the FCC unambiguously assigns key administrative responsibilities to the agency as a whole. The statute provides that the commission:

> may make such expenditures (including expenditures for rent and personal services at the seat of government and elsewhere ...), as may be necessary for the execution of the functions vested in the Commission[;][76]
>
> ... may perform any and all acts, make such rules and regulations, and issue such orders, not inconsistent with this chapter, as may be necessary in the execution of its functions[;][77]
>
> ... may conduct its proceedings in such manner as will best conduce to the proper dispatch of business and to the ends of justice[;][78]
>
> ... shall have authority ... to appoint such officers, engineers, accountants, attorneys, inspectors, examiners, and other employees as are necessary in the exercise of its functions.[79]

---

72 Division of Powers and Responsibilities Between the Chairperson of the Chemical Safety and Hazard Investigation Board and the Board as a Whole, 24 Op. O.L.C. 102, OLC 2000 Opinion, *supra* note 26.

73 OLC 2000 Opinion, *supra* note 26.

74 *Id.* at 104.

75 *Id.* at 103.

76 47 U.S.C. § 154 (g) (1).

77 *Id.* § 154(i).

78 *Id.* § 154(j).

79 *Id.* § 154(f)(1). At first blush, the appointment power in section 154(f)(1) would appear to include the power to appoint a managing director. Nevertheless, Congress goes on to provide expressly that the commission "shall have a Managing Director who shall be appointed by the Chairman subject to the approval of the Commission." *Id.* § 155(e). Presumably, this surplusage is intended to make clear both that the commission must have a managing director and that the commission as a whole must approve the chair's selection.

It further expressly provides:

> From time to time as the Commission may find necessary, the Commission shall organize its staff into (1) integrated bureaus, to function on the basis of the Commission's principal workload operations, and (2) such other divisional organizations as the Commission may deem necessary.[80]

The statute also has an explicit statutory provision requiring meetings:

> [To] be held at regular intervals, not less frequently than once each calendar month, at which times the functioning of the Commission and the handling of its work load shall be reviewed and such orders shall be entered and other action taken as may be necessary or appropriate to expedite the prompt and orderly conduct of the business of the Commission with the objective of rendering a final decision (1) within three months from the date of filing in all original application, renewal, and transfer cases in which it will not be necessary to hold a hearing, and (2) within six months from the final date of the hearing in all hearing cases.[81]

The statute then sets out the chair's powers with some specificity. He or she has the duty to:

> [P]reside at all meetings[;]
>
> [R]epresent the Commission in all matters relating to legislation . . . except that any [individual] commissioner may present his own or minority views or supplemental reports[;]
>
> [Maintain contacts] with other governmental . . . agencies, and . . . coordinate and organize the work of the Commission in such manner as to promote prompt and efficient disposition of all matters within the jurisdiction of the Commission.[82]

Each of the chairman's explicit powers seems to come easily within the ordinary concept of administrative and executive authority. Taken together with those provisions that appear to accord the agency as a whole express and considerable administrative authority, the inclusion of these specific provisions leads to the presumption that Congress intended to leave no doubt as to the distinct responsibilities of the agency and the chair.[83]

---

80 47 U.S.C. § 155(b) (1994).

81 *Id.* § 155(d).

82 *Id.* § 155(a).

83 Former FCC chair Reed Hundt was constantly concerned about the lack of a "reliable majority." *See* HUNDT, *supra* note 50, at 157.

Many statutes are far less detailed regarding the relationship between the chair and the agency as a whole. They simply give the chair undefined administrative and executive powers. For example, the statute governing the Federal Reserve Board provides that "[t]he Chairman of the Board, subject to its supervision, shall be its active executive officer."[84] The NLRB's statute provides simply that the president shall designate one member to serve as chair, but it otherwise has no provisions relating to the chair's duties.[85] As a practical matter, key decisions at both agencies are made collegially,[86] but there seems little doubt that the chair of the Federal Reserve Board is highly influential.

A chair's clearest area of responsibility is the day-to-day administration of the agency. The prototype statute expressly gives the chairman the right to distribute business among agency personnel and administrative units within the agency.[87] No other approach is genuinely workable. This power includes the direction of the work of the staff on behalf of the agency, and may also include the ability to initiate departures from routine or established approaches, either with or without notification of colleagues. The comptroller general has observed, for example, that a reorganization plan that required a chairman to act in accordance with agency directives would not give the agency the power to mandate that, in their day-to-day business, an agency's bureaus or officers must report to someone other than the chairman.[88]

Most agency statutes give the chairman the important right to appoint the staff. During his four years in office, for example, FCC chairman Reed Hundt hired two hundred new people—about 10 percent of the total workforce and 50 percent of the policy ranks.[89] But such hiring authority is frequently subject to some form of agency approval. For example, the Reorganization Plan governing the NRC provides that the chairman may "initiate" the appointment of expressly designated senior staff members (such as the executive director for operations and the general counsel) but such appointments are "subject to the approval of the Commission."[90] As the NRC's official spokesman, however, the NRC chairman nonetheless has exclusive authority to appoint and remove the directors of the Office of Public Affairs and the Office of Congressional Relations.[91] The Reorganization Plan governing the SEC similarly provides that "[t]he appointment by

---

84 12 U.S.C.§ 242 (1994).

85 *See* 29 U.S.C. §§ 153, 154 (1994).

86 *See* appendix A, *infra*.

87 *See,* Reorganization Plan No. 9 of 1950, § 1(a), 3 C.F.R. 1005 (1949–1953), *reprinted in* 5 U.S.C. app. at 1470–71 (1994) (Federal Power Commission), now contained at 42 U.S.C. § 7171(c) (FERC).

88 Letter to George M. Stafford, Interstate Commerce Commission, No. B-181536, 1974 U.S. Comp. Gen. LEXIS 1817, at *3–*6 (July 25, 1974).

89 *See* HUNDT, *supra* note 50, at 69.

90 *See* Reorganization Plan No. 1 of 1980, § 1(b)(1), 45 F.R. 40561, 94 Stat. 3585, *reprinted in* 5 U.S.C.A. *app*. at 521 (1996).

91 *See* Reorganization Plan No. 1 of 1980, § 2(a), 45 F.R. 40561, 94 Stat. 3585, *reprinted in* 5 U.S.C.A. app. at 522 (1996).

the Chairman of the heads of major administrative units under the Commission shall be subject to the approval of the Commission."[92] What constitutes a "major administrative unit" within an agency is left to the agency's determination.[93] However, even those statutes that merely require that the chairman's executive or administrative actions be governed by the "general policies and decisions" of the agency[94] would appear to give the agency as a whole some role, albeit undefined, in agency administration—if it elects to exercise it.

One administrative area where agency members frequently have been involved is budgeting. Many statutes affirmatively accord the agency as a whole the right to revise or approve the annual budget.[95] Even where such authority is not explicitly conferred, the comptroller general has recognized that "budget submissions involve policy determinations."[96] But the chairman also controls the agency's workload and expenditure of funds and is the agency's collegial spokesman with outside groups, including Congress. Although the location of these roles with the chairman does not prevent other agency members from offering their separate, independent views in an appropriate fashion, it accords the chairman the most powerful role in the agency for setting agendas, establishing budget priorities, developing consensus on substantive decisions, and handling external relationships.[97] It nonetheless seems clear, as the comptroller general's opinion at least implies, that the chairman's unitary authority often does not extend beyond the preparation or drafting of budget documents, which is considered an administrative or executive responsibility.[98] This is the system used at many, if not most, agencies with which we are familiar.

According to the OLC, silence in a statute on issues such as an agency's internal organization, practices, and procedures clearly implies that these issues are to be decided by the members of the agency.[99] As a practical matter, virtually every multimember agency inevitably must fill in at least some statutory gaps and arrive at a modus vivendi for

---

92 *See, e.g.*, Reorganization Plan No. 10 of 1950, § 1(b)(2), 15 F.R. 3175, 64 Stat. 1265, *reprinted in* 5 U.S.C.A. *app.* at 131 (1996). *See also* Reorganization Plan No. 1 of 1980, Section 1(b)(1), 45 F.R. 40561, 94 Stat. 3585, reprinted in 5 U.S.C.A. at 521.

93 *See* WELBORN, *supra* note 48, at 51.

94 *See, e.g.*, 49 U.S.C. § 1111(e) (1994) (National Transportation Safety Board).

95 *See, e.g.*, Reorganization Plan No. 10 of 1950, § 1(b)(4), 15 F.R. 3175, 64 Stat. 1265, reprinted in 5 U.S.C.A. app. at 131 (1996) (SEC).

96 1974 Decision of the Comptroller General, *supra* note 62 at *22. At the EEOC, the commissioners do not approve the chair's budget prior to submission. See appendix A.

97 *See* WELBORN, *supra* note 48, at 20, 22–23 (noting the centralized decisionmaking within agencies and discussing the powers of chairs in different agencies).

98 *See* 1974 Decision of the Comptroller General, *supra* note 62, at *22–*23 (indicating that while the chair has significant responsibility for budget preparation, the full commission has authority to approve budget submissions to the OMB and the Congress).

99 *See* National Commission on Neighborhoods (Pub. L. No. 95-24)—Powers—Appropriations, 2 Op. Off. Legal Counsel, 366, 367 n.5 (1977).

its operation. Fortunately, agencies have broad authority to fill in the gaps and resolve ambiguities.

For example, some statutes make no explicit provision for a vice chairman or some other person or persons to temporarily run the agency in the event of the absence or disability of the chairman. While the OLC has concluded that silence in a statute on issues such as an agency's internal organization leaves the agency power to resolve such institutional issues,[100] it has consistently held that statutory silence prevents an agency from explicitly designating an individual as "acting chair" when the chair's position is vacant.[101]

The OLC's view is more symbolic than practical. Even the OLC acknowledges that, in the absence of a chair, an agency may delegate executive and administrative authority to one or more of its members.[102] In fact, even those agencies with limited statutory authority should have ample power to designate one of their members to perform functions that are essential to the continued operation of the agency. That view is consistent with case law. The Supreme Court, after all, has traditionally allowed agencies considerable procedural discretion, observing that agencies "should be free to fashion their own rules of procedure and to pursue methods of inquiry capable of permitting them to discharge their multitudinous duties."[103] Internal operations, in particular, are rarely disturbed by the courts.[104]

Looking at multimember agencies where the chairman has general administrative responsibility, the comptroller general has concluded that, in the absence of a chair, the remaining commissioners retain a "residual power" to perform administrative functions.[105] The OLC, more protective of the president's prerogatives, advised the Federal Reserve Board that its vice chair could not simply assume the duties of the chair when a vacancy occurred because the vice chair had express statutory power only to "preside" at board meetings in the absence of the chair. The OLC acknowledged that a contrary

---

100 *See id.*

101 Authority of the Chemical Safety and Hazard Investigation Board to Delegate Power, 2002 OLC LEXIS 5 (Apr. 19, 2002), citing other opinions.

102 *Id.* at 3–6.

103 Vermont Yankee Nuclear Power Corp. v. NRDC, 435 U.S. 519, 543 (1978) (internal quotation marks omitted) (quoting FCC v. Schreiber, 381 U.S. 279, 290 (1965)).

104 *See* FCC v. Pottsville Broad. Co., 309 U.S. 134 (1940); T.S.C. Motor Freight Lines, Inc. v. United States, 186 F. Supp. 777 (S.D. Tex. 1960), *aff'd per curiam sub nom.* Herrin Transp. Co. v. United States, 366 U.S. 419 (1961). But see KFC National Management Corp. v. NLRB, 497 F.2d 298, 303 (2d Cir. 1974), where the court decided that the NLRB's organic statute precluded it from delegating decisional authority entirely to its staff members. The NLRB thereafter changed its procedures to ensure that board members participated personally in all final agency decisions. KFC National Management Company and Bartenders, Hotel, Motel, Cafeteria and Restaurant Employees Union, Local 116, AFL-CIO, 214 N.L.R.B. 232, n.3 (1974).

105 Occupational Safety and Health Review Commission—Authority of Commissioners, 60 Comp. Gen. 627, 628 (1981).

argument could be made and noted that the Federal Reserve Board had, in the past, actually elected one of its members to serve as chairman pro tempore. Nonetheless, the OLC asserted that, absent an express statutorily prescribed mechanism for filling vacancies, only the president may designate one of the board members to serve as acting chair.[106] More recently, when the CSB was without a chair, it designated one member to conduct certain executive and administrative functions. That individual was designated the "Board Member Delegated Interim Executive and Administrative Authority" but not acting chair.[107]

Most agency internal procedures and allocations of responsibility evolve over time.[108] Institutional determinations regarding these matters receive respect in the courts.[109] In the absence of agency policy on a particular subject, the chair necessarily possesses substantial discretion to act on his or her own. The OLC's general observations on the respective roles of the chair and the agency as a whole are worth setting out in some detail:

> [U]nder the Act and general principles governing the operations of boards, the day-to-day administration of Board matters and execution of Board policies are the responsibilities of the chairperson, subject to Board oversight, while substantive policymaking and regulatory authority is vested in the Board as a whole. In disputes over the allocation of authority in specific instances, the Board's decision controls, as long as it is not arbitrary or unreasonable....
>
> [T]he Act provides that the chairperson "shall be the Chief Executive Officer of the Board and shall exercise the executive and administrative functions of the Board."... [T]he terms ["Chief Executive Officer" and "executive and administrative functions"]... provide some general guidance on the proper division of authority between the chairperson and the Board as a whole.... The chairperson, in other words, superintends and carries out the day-to-day activities necessary to effectuate the Board's substantive decisions. He does not, absent some form of Board approval... make those decisions by himself.

---

106 Federal Reserve Board—Vacancy with the Office of the Chairman—Status of the Vice Chairman, 2 Op. Off. Legal Counsel 394 (1978).

107 *See* Appendix, citing Board Order –3 (May 9, 2002, as amended).

108 *See* Idaho v. ICC, 939 F.2d 784, 788 (9th Cir. 1991) (explaining and upholding the traditional use of the ICC's notation voting procedures), *aff'g* Union Pac. R.R.—Abandonment in Fremont and Teton Counties, Idaho, 6 I.C.C.2d 641 (1990).

109 *See* Falcon Trading Group, Ltd. v. SEC, 102 F.3d 579, 582 (D.C. Cir. 1996) (upholding the SEC's creation of innovative quorum requirements); T.S.C. Motor Freight Lines, Inc. v. United States, 186 F. Supp. 777 (S.D. Tex. 1960), *aff'd per curiam sub nom.* Herrin Transp. Co. v. United States, 366 U.S. 419 (1961) (internal transfer of a case for decision from one of the ICC's divisions to the entire commission, although not the usual practice, was upheld as consistent with the agency's regulations).

> The Act also empowers the Board to "establish such procedural and administrative rules as are necessary to the exercise of its functions and duties...." These could include rules bearing on matters of internal Board governance...as well as rules governing the conduct of Board business with the public....To the extent the Board establishes such rules, the chairperson, as the Board's administrative and executive officer, must put them into practice....
>
> [T]his does not mean that the Board, exercising its oversight authority and its powers to make substantive decisions...may or should attempt to address itself to the plethora of minute administrative problems bound up with the operation of a complex organization. Some degree of managerial discretion is inherent in the concept of an executive or administrative office, and the statutory assignment of the Board's executive and administrative functions to the chairperson necessarily vests the chairperson with a degree of managerial autonomy on which the Board, in the proper exercise of its powers, cannot trench....At the same time...any number of Board activities or day-to-day aspects of Board business, while at least in part administrative and even seemingly mundane, may involve or affect the board's duties and functions in ways that are of legitimate concern to the board as a whole. Where that is the case, it is the prerogative of the Board to pass upon such issues in ways appropriate to its function as a policymaking and rule-setting body.[110]

It must be noted that an agency's statute alone rarely tells the complete story of agency operation. Because most statutes are incomplete or ambiguous and there is no official forum (such as a court) for regular resolution of intraagency management questions, agency chairs may, and at certain times do, assert administrative prerogatives. Former FTC chair Miles Kirkpatrick observed:

> I should make it clear that in the management of the Commission's day-to-day affairs, there are no collegial decisions. Management of the Commission, save for the appointment of the top policy making positions and policy decisions having to do with the allocation of major resources, is placed squarely in the Chairman. In my experience, matters having to do with the management of the Commission's staff are not the subject of debate among the Commissioners.[111]

Welborn indicates generally that "[o]perating arrangements in which the role of Chairman is primary and that of the Commission as a whole is secondary are considered to be entirely appropriate, or legitimate."[112] Even at the FCC, where the chair's

---

110 OLC 2000 Opinion, *supra* note 26, at 2–4 (internal citations omitted).

111 Miles W. Kirkpatrick, *Nineteenth Annual Antitrust Spring Dinner Address*, 40 ANTITRUST L.J. 328, 332 (1971).

112 WELBORN, *supra note* 48, at 36.

powers are somewhat circumscribed by statute, former FCC member Glen Robinson has noted: "From personal experience I can report that the FCC's Chairman and a handful of staff—usually selected by the chair—can and usually do exercise nearly total control over that agency's basic policy agenda."[113] However, the OLC makes it clear that the retention of significant authority in a chair "is a matter of the development, through collegial practice and over time, of the [agency's] own internal policies concerning delegation of authority to the ... chairperson, the [agency's] acquiescence in the chairperson's assertion of authority over certain substantive areas, and the general evolution of the [agency's] current allocation of responsibilities."[114] Responding to a claim by the chair of the CSB that since his agency's statute was modeled on that of the National Transportation Safety Board, he should have the same power as the National Transportation Safety Board chair, the OLC pointed out that, absent an express statutory provision (there was none), the accretion of power by a chair over an agency's affairs is a "matter of the [agency's] grace and does not deprive the [agency] ... of its stated authorities and responsibilities."[115] Although the growth of the National Transportation Safety Board chair's authority may have occurred over the years, it was not automatically replicated at the CSB.

Welborn also suggests that chairs have a relatively greater influence than their colleagues do on substantive matters. He found that agency chairs dissent with far less frequency than their colleagues in substantive, collegial decisions.[116] As a result, decision-making even at multimember agencies is "relatively centralized," and "independent action at lower levels on critical matters is limited."[117] A more recent study by Derthick and Quirk of three multimember agencies (the Civil Aeronautics Board, ICC, and FCC) during the deregulatory period 1975–1980 reached much the same conclusions.[118] They observe:

> Commission members tended in general to defer to the chairman. The formal executive powers that all of the chairmen possessed gave them a great advantage

[113] Glen O. Robinson, *Independent Agencies: Form and Substance in Executive Prerogative*, 1988 DUKE L.J. 238, 245 n.24.

[114] OLC 2000 Opinion, *supra* note 26, at 107.

[115] *Id.* at 107.

[116] *See* WELBORN, *supra* note 48, at 109 (stating that based on a survey of reported decisions since 1961, "[w]ith only a few exceptions, the number of times chairmen dissent during their tenure can be counted on the fingers of one hand.").

[117] WELBORN, *supra* note 48, at 20. This is not to minimize the volume or importance of action taken by the staff. However, such action is typically based on reasonably well-accepted agency precedent or the staff's view of current agency policy. The Welborn study offers a comprehensive examination of the powers of seven independent agency chairs and the relationship of agency chairs to other agency members. *See id.* at 20–27.

[118] *See* MARTHA DERTHICK & PAUL J. QUIRK, THE POLITICS OF DEREGULATION (1985).

> over commission members.... In truth, commission members had very little to do and few resources with which to do it....
>
> Being the president's choice also helped the chairmen.... This created some presumption that the chairman was pursuing policies that were also the president's policies and that he was therefore entitled to support from those commission members who were of the same political party as the president and the chairman.[119]

As a practical matter, the combination of political prestige or support and managerial authority accord some agency chairs the power to dominate and control their agencies' agendas. Such control is obtained more easily at agencies that have a tradition of leadership by the chair.[120] Alfred Kahn was heir to such a tradition when he became chair of the Civil Aeronautics Board in the mid-1970s. More important, his personal association with President Carter and the White House staff allowed him an effective veto over the nomination or reappointment of other board members.[121] This ensured that he worked with a sympathetic set of colleagues.[122] In contrast, former NLRB chair William Gould has complained that he was totally unsuccessful in advancing those he believed to be qualified candidates for board vacancies.[123]

Kahn's political influence at the White House—and, to some degree at least, his overall reputation and personality—also ensured his colleagues' acquiescence on staff appointments and the board's agenda. Although the board had statutory authority to approve the appointment of heads of major administrative units,[124] a board majority gave Kahn carte blanche. Kahn reorganized the board, created a new Office of Economic Analysis, and appointed a number of committed deregulators to critical positions.[125] After key staff members were appointed, the *Washington Post* quoted Kahn as saying: "[a]ll the

---

[119] *Id.* at 86–87.

[120] *See id.* at 77–78 (noting the tradition of chair leadership at the Civil Aeronautics Board and FCC and the lack of it at the ICC). It was not until 1969 that administrative authority was transferred from the ICC collegially to the chair. *See* Reorganization Plan No. 1 of 1969, 3 C.F.R. 1066–67 (1966–1970), *reprinted in* 5 U.S.C. app. at 1547 (1994). The commission's first permanent chair, George Stafford, rarely used it. Derthick & Quirk, *supra* note 118, at 159.

[121] *See* Thomas K. McCraw, Prophets of Regulation 15, 288–89 (1984) (stating that Kahn proposed names for President Carter's consideration and that all appointments to the board itself met with Kahn's approval). Former FCC chair Reed Hundt has noted that during his tenure in the Clinton administration, the Senate Republicans exercised a veto power over Republican seats on the commission. *See* Hundt, *supra* note 50, at 159.

[122] *Compare* Robinson, *supra* note 113, at 245 (noting that "[r]espectful regard for signs of presidential preferences on policy issues is ensured not so much out of gratitude for the favor of the appointment (though this may be a factor) as by the possibility of future rewards for faithful service (including other high appointments in the government)").

[123] Gould, *supra* note 6, at 89.

[124] *See* Reorganization Plan No. 3 of 1961, 3 C.F.R. 873 (1959–1963), *reprinted in* 5 U.S.C. app. at 1508 (1994).

[125] *See* McCraw, *supra* note 121, at 274–75; Derthick & Quirk, *supra* note 118, at 78–79.

bomb throwers are here and in place. You have to judge this agency starting from this point forward; now there are no excuses."[126]

Kahn also used the chair's control of the board's calendar to advance his substantive agenda. He moved two applications from new entrants to the head of the queue for evaluation.[127] One of the authors served as Civil Aeronautics Board deputy general counsel during the Kahn administration. He participated in a meeting at which Kahn's executive director indicated that Kahn wanted the application of Midway Airlines, a new entrant, to be considered by the board within a year. The only way to meet Kahn's deadline was to eliminate the preparation of an initial decision by the presiding ALJ and have the board decide the case itself, as an agency is authorized to do in initial licensing cases under 5 U.S.C. § 557(b)(1) of the APA. So the staff developed a schedule that had the ALJ preside at the hearing but simply certify the record to the board for decision. The general counsel's office worked closely with Kahn and his colleagues in reviewing the evidence and drafting an opinion, and the board issued its decision (technically a "tentative decision") within a year as Kahn had directed.[128]

While heading the SEC, William Casey in 1972 separated the Enforcement Division from the Division of Market Regulation. In the opinion of one former commissioner, this reorganization, coupled with key appointments to the commission and its senior staff, made the Enforcement Division staff the dominant player in setting the commission's agenda. The dynamic changed to some extent when Harold Williams, chair from 1977 to 1981, gave the Office of General Counsel a role to play in analyzing Enforcement Division recommendations.[129]

Chairmanic leadership can take an agency in the opposite direction just as easily. Mark Budnitz observes that the approval process for many FTC rules in the pipeline but not promulgated became "stalled" when James Miller became FTC chair. Miller was generally opposed to use of rulemaking at the FTC.[130] Budnitz notes that Chair Miller did not seek to terminate any rulemaking proceedings, thus leaving open the possibility that a new chair might have resumed them. But, as of 1997, that had not happened.[131] In fact, the FTC's adjudicatory caseload decreased during the Miller administration.[132]

---

[126] McCraw, *supra* note 121, at 275 (quoting Carole Shifrin, *CAB Geared Up to Cut Regulation*, Wash. Post, Jan. 12, 1978, at D9).

[127] *Id.* at 280–82.

[128] Chicago-Midway Low-Fare Route Proceeding, 78 C.A.B. 454 (1978).

[129] *See* Roberta S. Karmel, *Creating Law at the Securities and Exchange Commission: The Lawyer as Prosecutor*, 61 Law & Contemp. Probs. 33, 40–41 (1998).

[130] *See generally* Mark E. Budnitz, *The FTC's Consumer Protection Program During the Miller Years: Lessons for Administrative Agency Structure and Operation*, 46 Cath. U.L. Rev. 371, 413–14, 421–24 (1997). Some rules nonetheless went forward. The FTC unanimously enacted a credit practices rule and promulgated a funeral industry practices regulation over Miller's objection. *Id.*

[131] *See id.* at 436–37.

[132] *See id.* at 391.

In rare instances, a chair's assertion of power can be impeded, or even thwarted, by colleagues.[133] Two episodes illustrate an unusual power struggle between an agency chair and all of his colleagues that led, in both cases, to the chair's loss of influence within the agency and diminished support from the political branches, causing his resignation. Both episodes seemingly had their origins in substantive disputes but played out in a clash over the chair's management style. They demonstrate the inadequacy of law and the ascendancy of political will even in the resolution of internal agency conflicts.

The first involved the 1999 turf battle between the chair of the CSB and his three fellow board members. The CSB's statute and legislative history, not uncharacteristically, fail to delineate precisely the respective roles of the chairman, as the agency's chief administrative officer, and his colleagues, in directing the agency's overall operation. At long-established agencies, this relationship has been worked out over time. It is typically simply accepted as the agency's modus vivendi by newly appointed members. But the CSB was brand new, with four newly appointed members. The chair had a substantive agenda that he believed he had authority to pursue largely unencumbered.

None of the four board members were lawyers. Three of them were distressed that the chair and a newly appointed chief operating officer simply ran the agency without consultation. Among other things, the chair unilaterally decided that the board would not undertake any new investigations—a significant policy determination for an agency whose principal mission was investigation.[134] The other three asked the agency general counsel to provide guidance as to the respective responsibilities of the chair and the board as a whole.

The general counsel opined that the chair was in day-to-day administrative control of the agency, with authority, for example, to assign work to and supervise the staff, but that the board had statutory power to play some admittedly undefined role in the overall administration of the agency, such as approval of senior staff appointments and the agency's annual budget.[135] However, with no express statutory guidance on any division of particular responsibilities, the general counsel proposed that the board members simply agree jointly on a modus vivendi. The three members supported the general counsel's recommendation.[136] The chair, however, declined and, instead, continued to assert total

---

[133] See, for example, Mark E. Budnitz, *supra* note 130, at 385–91, discussing FTC chair James Miller's efforts to reorganize the FTC, the resistance of two of Miller's colleagues to his effort to close most of commission's regional offices, and resultant congressional intervention.

[134] *See* Guy Gugliotta, *Chemical Hazards Board and Chief a Volatile Mix*, WASH. POST, Nov. 24, 1999, at A21.

[135] *Id.* The general counsel's thirty-one-page memorandum was released to the public and made available at the board's website at www.chemsafety.gov/board/1999/docs/boardgovmemo.pdf. Edles served as a consultant to the Office of General Counsel during this period. All material discussed here is from publicly available sources.

[136] *See* Gugliotta, *supra* note 134.

authority to run the agency.[137] Matters came to a head when the chair submitted his own budget request to Congress, effectively establishing the agency's priorities without consulting his colleagues.[138]

There is no official forum for the resolution of such intramural disagreements. The OLC in the DOJ is permitted to offer "informal opinions" or "legal advice" on issues affecting independent agencies pursuant to 28 C.F.R. § 0.25(a) (1999), but will not do so unless the agency agrees to follow its advice. Independent agencies solicit such opinions or advice from time to time, although not very often in our experience. Agencies will seek advice when to do otherwise might expose them to subsequent legal risk or embarrassment. The NLRB did so when it was implementing a novel quorum requirement that it knew would certainly be challenged in court; the NLRB agreed to be bound by the OLC's analysis.[139] But seeking advice—particularly on internal agency operations—may mean that the agency will get an answer it does not like and will then be constrained to follow the advice received.

An administration more typically plays a role by informal intervention, and so too can key members of Congress. In the CSB case, Senator Frank Lautenberg—described as "the board's biggest congressional booster"—endorsed the board majority's power-sharing approach.[140] Given the CSB's tenuous position with Congress,[141] his views were significant. The chair backed down, tendered his resignation as chair (he elected to remain temporarily on the board as a member), and all members signed a "concordat" that went forward with a request for an OLC opinion regarding the general counsel's views. While awaiting the opinion, all board members reviewed and commented on communications submitted to Congress, including the agency's appropriation request, and on contracts involving more than $25,000. In addition, the board members concurred in the hiring of

137 *See id.* (quoting the board chair as indicating that "[h]iring personnel and budget development, in my view, are administrative").

138 *See id.; see also* Dean Scott, *Board Acts Without Chairman, Calls for Justice Department to Settle Rift*, 23 Chem. Reg. Rep. (BNA) 1358, 1358 (Nov. 26, 1999) (reporting that three board members voted to direct the chair to rescind his request for a doubling of the board's budget). The agency's chief operating officer described the dissension as "an ideological disagreement." *Id.* at 1359.

139 *See* New Process Steel, L.P. v. NLRB, 130 S. Ct. 2635, 2638 (2010). *See also, e.g.*, Federal Reserve Board Policy on Bank Examiner Borrowing, 6 Op. Off. Legal Counsel 509 (1982), *clarified in* 17 Op. Off. Legal Counsel 168 (1993) (determining whether board bank examiners may borrow from or hold credit cards from banks they are authorized to examine); Authority of the Nuclear Regulatory Commission to Collect Annual Charges from Federal Agencies, 15 Op. Off. Legal Counsel 74 (1991) (determining whether NRC has statutory authority to collect annual charges from federal agencies that hold licenses issued by NRC).

140 Guy Gugliotta, *Hill Quits as CEO of Chemical Investigations Board*, WASH. POST, Dec. 18, 1999, at A15. A chemical workers' union official who had supported the board blamed the chair for the impasse. *See id.*

141 *See* Dean Scott, *Hazard Investigation Board Members Seek Meeting to Discuss Role in Budget, Policy*, 23 Chem. Reg. Rep. (BNA) 1323 (indicating that some members of Congress questioned the need for the agency, the House Appropriations Subcommittee chair was "skeptical" of the agency's annual request for budget increases, and the Senate Appropriations Subcommittee chair had requested a GAO investigation of the agency's operations).

heads of offices within the agency. The members also agreed to schedule monthly public meetings.[142] The OLC's June 26, 2000, opinion forcefully backed the CSB general counsel and the board majority and largely ended the turf battle.[143]

A clash between Gregory Jaczko, the chair of the NRC and former staffer of Senate majority leader Harry Reid of Nevada,[144] and his four colleagues—two Democrats and two Republicans—revealed a rare public display of internecine agency warfare. It produced a letter complaining about the chair's personal conduct from all four of his colleagues to the White House chief of staff, an internal inspector general report, and congressional hearings with key members of Congress lining up on both sides of the controversy.

The quarrel revolved about the NRC's handling of an application by the DOE to build a spent nuclear fuel and high-level radioactive waste depository at Yucca Mountain, Nevada, and is discussed in chapter 7.[145] While the matter was pending, the commission, in its budget justification to Congress for FY 2011, requested $10 million related to "the orderly closure of the agency's Yucca Mountain licensing support activities." Following Congress's passage of the first in a series of continuing resolutions directing agencies in FY 2011 to continue activities at FY 2010 funding levels, senior NRC staff, at the chair's instruction, directed their subordinates to begin the orderly closure of the technical review. The inspector general concluded that the chair's direction was consistent with his executive powers regarding the use and expenditure of the agency's funds and the commission's FY 2011 budget policy determination. A contretemps erupted, however, when it emerged, as explained by the inspector general, "that the Chairman anticipated that proceeding to close-out in this manner could be controversial and viewed as a policy decision for the full Commission consideration. Therefore, prior to directing issuance of the CR [continuing resolution] budget guidance memorandum [to the staff], he strategically provided three of the four other Commissioners with varying amounts of information about his intention to proceed to closure" yet advised the senior staff that "all the Commissioners were informed and supported issuance of the CR budget guidance memorandum." The inspector general also reported that "a number of interviewees conveyed their perception that [the] Chairman ... controls and restricts the information available to his fellow Commissioners and noted concerns about his interpersonal style." The *New York Times* observed that the inspector general "reported ... that some staff members were troubled by Mr. Jaczko's "aggressive management style" as well as the decision to end the staff's review of the Yucca Mountain application.[146] The *Washington*

---

142 *See* Gary Taylor, *USCSB "Truce" Offers Board Review without Approval*, CHEMICAL NEWS & INTELLIGENCE, Dec. 13, 1999, *available in* LEXIS, News Group File.

143 *See* OLC 2000 Opinion, *supra* note 26.

144 *See* Mike Magner, *Whatever Happened to Gregory Jaczko*, NAT'L J. (Jan. 29, 2014), http://www.nationaljournal.com./energy/whatever-happened-to-gregory-jaczko-20140129.

145 *See supra* chapter 7, note 326.

146 Matthew Wald, *Split with Nuclear Regulatory Agency*, N.Y. TIMES, July 21, 2011, at A15.

Post reported, as well, that the chair "was responsible for a tense and unsettled work environment and that women at the NRC felt particularly threatened."[147] To add to the problem, the informal, nonbinding procedures ordinarily, although not always, employed by the commission to reach decisions were not followed.

The commission over its lifetime has frequently had disagreement between those members who were strongly supportive of nuclear power and those who were more cautious or skeptical. In this case, these differences manifested themselves in an unusual public fight that was facilitated by the ambiguous and amorphous rules and practices found at most multimember agencies concerning the respective roles of a chairman and the agency as a whole.

The battle reemerged in the political arena because the term of Kristine Svinicki, a Republican member of the commission who had been part of the four-member insurgency, was due to expire in June 2012. The commission's enabling statute does not provide for holdover positions,[148] and Republican members of Congress were pressing for her reappointment. However, Senator Harry Reid, the Democratic leader in the Senate, opposed the nomination. In the circumstances, the Obama administration was faced with the choice of renewing her term and displeasing Senator Reid or leaving it unfilled and clashing with Senate Republicans. Eventually, the political cost of a fight with Republicans over an NRC nominee in an election year appeared too great. Commissioner Svinicki was renominated. But that spelled the end for an agency head whose political support had seemingly eroded. Chair Jaczko resigned.[149] President Obama promptly nominated Allison Macfarlane, a geologist and professor at George Mason University, to be the NRC's new head.[150] Macfarlane had served on a presidential panel that recommended the evaluation of alternatives to Yucca Mountain.[151] Her nomination was considered at the same time as that of Commissioner Svinicki; both were confirmed easily in July 2012. This "pairing" constituted a political compromise sufficient to bring the controversy to an end—at least temporarily.

B. Institutional Decision-Making

1. COLLEGIAL DECISION-MAKING AND DISSENTING OPINIONS

When NLRB chair William Gould was about to leave his post in the summer of 1998, he complained about the inability of the board to issue key decisions, noting that even

[147] *Obama Plans to Renominate GOP Nuclear Regulator*, WASH. POST, Apr. 30, 2012, at A14.

[148] *See* 42 U.S.C. § 5841

[149] Steven Mufson & Ed O'Keefe, *Gregory Jaczko, chief of Nuclear Regulatory Commission, Resigns*, WASH. POST, May 21, 2012.

[150] *Obama Names Pick to lead Nuclear Regulatory Commission*, CBS NEWS (May 24, 2012, 6:18 p.m.), http://www.cbsnews.com/8301-250_162-57441280/obama-names-pick-to-lead-nuclear-regulatory-commission.

[151] *Id.*

a single member could hold them up.[152] The problem was one of collegiality, custom, or simple inability to muster a majority.[153]

What happens in case of a procedural roadblock to decision-making, that is, when a dissenting member refuses or is unable to issue his or her opinion? Agencies' members are short-timers. They can lack the tradition of institutional collegiality that judges possess that encourages dissents to be written in a timely fashion so decisions can be issued. Where circumstances require, however, a majority of a multimember agency generally can issue a decision without awaiting preparation of any dissenting or other separate statements. The courts use this technique, usually with the consent of the dissenting members,[154] but it can also be done over the objection of a dissenting colleague.[155] Although the technique can compromise collegial decision-making, those agencies that have specifically addressed the matter ordinarily allow a majority to issue an opinion without awaiting the preparation of dissenting or other separate statements.

The NLRB had particularized this general principle by rule in the 1970s. The NLRB had adopted Rule 76-1 that if a dissent or concurrence regarding a draft opinion was not circulated to colleagues within two weeks of board approval of the majority decision, that decision would issue two weeks hence, unless a dissent or concurring opinion circulated within that time frame. The majority then had two weeks to respond, and the dissenting or concurring member a further week to respond to the majority's revisions. However, Rule 76-1 had never been employed and had in fact apparently lapsed. Chair Gould lacked the political or managerial capital to gain the approval of a board majority for its reinstatement.[156] Gould notes that reinstatement of the Rule was voted down by four to one.[157]

In a highly peculiar case, certain private parties sued the three-member Occupational Safety and Health Review Commission to compel its executive secretary to release a decision that had been signed by two members, one of whom had left the agency before the third member (the chair) had completed his dissenting statement. The remaining

---

152 *See* Karen Alexander, *Gould Goes Out Gunning*, LEGAL TIMES, July 13, 1998, at 1.

153 *See generally* Joan Flynn, *"Expertness for What?": The Gould Years at the NLRB and the Irrepressible Myth of the "Independent" Agency*, 52 ADMIN. L. REV. 465, 517–28 (2000) (detailing breakdown of collegiality within the NLRB).

154 *See, e.g.*, SEC v. Chenery Corp., 332 U.S. 194, 209 (1947) (Frankfurter, J. & Jackson, J., dissenting) (stating that while they dissented, "there is not now opportunity for a response adequate to the issues raised," and that "detailed grounds for dissent will be filed in due course"); Drummond v. Fulton Cnty. Dep't of Family & Children's Servs., 547 F.2d 835, 857 (5th Cir. 1977) (Roney, J., dissenting) (regretting that press of court business prevented preparation of dissent in time for distribution with majority opinion). Judge Roney thereafter authored the court's en banc opinion reversing the panel decision. Drummond v. Fulton County Dep't of Family & Children's Servs. 563 F.2d 1200 (5th Cir. 1977), *cert. denied* 437 U.S. 910 (1978).

155 *See In re* Kirk, 376 F.2d 936, 946 (C.C.P.A. 1967) (Smith, J., dissenting) (protesting publication of majority opinion before dissenting opinions had been completed). Judge Smith subsequently issued a dissenting statement, withdrawing the earlier dissent. *In re* Kirk, 376 F.2d at 1154.

156 GOULD, *supra* note 6, at 61–63.

157 *Id.* at 231.

member of the majority joined in the lawsuit. In due course, following completion of the chair's dissenting statement, the agency released the "two to one" decision, and the court dismissed the case as moot.[158]

The D.C. Circuit has been especially strict in attempting to ensure the accountability intended through collegial decision-making. It has struck down agency decisions that failed to adequately take into account the views of dissenting members.[159] Where four of the five members of the NLRB participated in a case—two joined in a plurality opinion, one concurred separately, and one dissented—the D.C. Circuit reversed the decision because it found that the single concurring member had relied on an impermissible construction of the statute. The court found it unnecessary to examine the plurality opinion because the board, as a whole, had failed to articulate a proper basis for resolving the case.[160] Similarly, where the FEC failed for want of a majority to institute a proceeding, the D.C. Circuit required that the decision of those deciding not to act had to be explained so that the their reasons might be assessed on appeal.[161]

2. THE GOVERNMENT IN THE SUNSHINE ACT AND THE DILEMMA OF COLLEGIALITY

Congress's enactment in 1976 of the Government in the Sunshine Act[162] has played a role in the reduction in collegiality at multimember agencies.[163] As a corollary, it has enhanced the power of agency chairs and staff.

The Sunshine Act was the last in a quartet of statutes designed to enhance the transparency of government agency operation. The other three statutes are the Freedom of Information Act, originally enacted in 1966, amended on several occasions and found in its current form at 5 U.S.C. § 552; the Federal Advisory Committee Act, enacted in 1972, and found as Appendix 2 to Title V of the U.S.C.; and the Privacy Act, enacted in 1974 and now found at 5 U.S.C. § 552a.

Generally speaking, the Sunshine Act requires that, subject to certain exceptions, all meetings of "a collegial body composed of two or more individual members, a majority of whom are appointed to such position by the president with the advice and consent of the

---

158 *See* Arcadian Corp., 17 O.Sh. Cas. (BNA) 1345 (Apr. 27, 1995) (Weisberg, chair, dissenting), dismissed as moot, *In re* Arcadian Corp., 17 O.S.H. (BNA) 1406 (D.C. Cir. Oct. 4, 1995).

159 *See, e.g.*, Amer. Gas Ass'n v. FERC, 593 F. 3d 14, 16, 20 (D.C. Cir. 2010); Chamber of Commerce v. SEC, 412 F. 3d 133, 137–38 (D.C. Cir. 2005).

160 Oil, Chem. & Atomic Workers Int'l Union, AFL-CIO v. NLRB, 46 F.3d 82, 88 (D.C. Cir. 1995).

161 FEC v. Nat'l Republican Senatorial Comm., 966 F.2d 1471, 1476 (D.C. Cir. 1992).

162 5 U.S.C. § 552b.

163 The material in this section is adapted in part from Richard K. Berg, Stephen H. Klitzman & Gary J. Edles, An Interpretive Guide to the Government in the Sunshine Act (Section of Administrative Law and Regulatory Practice, American Bar Association, 2d ed., 2005) [hereinafter 2005

Senate," must be open to public observation.[164] There are more than sixty federal entities subject to the Sunshine Act. Many of them are independent, multimember agencies.[165]

The Sunshine Act's procedures, in the more than three decades since its enactment, have been routinely employed by multimember agencies. A serious criticism of the Act, however, is that its requirement of public deliberation has compromised the collegiality that is supposed to be the cornerstone of the decisional process at multimember agencies.

The issue arises because a "meeting" is defined by the statute as "the deliberations of at least the number of individual agency members required to take action on behalf of the agency where such deliberations determine or result in the joint conduct or disposition of official agency business."[166] The leading text on the Act, *An Interpretive Guide to the Government in the Sunshine Act*, originally published by the Administrative Conference of the United States in 1978 and now in its second edition, concluded that, "at a minimum, a 'meeting' includes any gathering of the requisite number of members where a serious exchange of views achieves a consensus on a matter of official agency business."[167] So, for the typical five-member agency, three members cannot, even over a cup of coffee, attempt to resolve issues pending before the agency. For a three-member agency, the problem is worse because no two members may ever discuss matters that might lead, even informally, to some accord on any substantive issue.

The Supreme Court has moderated the more severe aspects of the problem the definition causes for agency administration in the only Sunshine Act case to reach the high court.[168] Importantly, the Court construed the legislative history of the Act to reveal a congressional intent to exclude from its coverage informal background discussions that merely clarify or expose the views of agency members. Only when a quorum of the agency actually conducts or disposes of agency business does the statute apply.[169] The Court relied in part on the first edition of *the Interpretive Guide to the Government in the Sunshine Act*,[170] which had concluded that the definition of "meeting" should not cover "tentative" or "exploratory" discussions. The first edition of the *Guide* sought to devise an operational distinction between such discussions and those discussions that

---

INTERPRETIVE GUIDE]) with the kind permission of the Section of Administrative Law and Regulatory Practice of the American Bar Association.

164 5 U.S.C. § 552b(a)(1).

165 Others, like the Rural Telephone Bank, do not come within the coverage of the Sunshine Act because their members are not subject to Senate confirmation but are nevertheless subject to the Sunshine Act by virtue of requirements contained in organic statutes. *See, e.g.*, 7 U.S.C. § 945(j). Some federal entities, like the U.S. Civil Rights Commission, whose meetings are also not covered because its members are not subject to Senate confirmation, comply voluntarily. *See* 2005 INTERPRETIVE GUIDE, *supra* note 163, at 263.

166 5 U.S.C. § 552b(a)(2).

167 2005 INTERPRETIVE GUIDE, *supra* note 163, at 10.

168 *FCC v. ITT World Communications*, 466 U.S. 463 (1984), *rev'g* ITT World Commc'ns, Inc. v. FCC, 699 F. 2d 1219 (D.C. Cir. 1983).

169 *ITT World Commc'ns*, 466 U.S. at 470.

170 RICHARD K. BERG & STEPHEN H. KLITZMAN, AN INTERPRETIVE GUIDE TO THE GOVERNMENT IN THE SUNSHINE ACT (Administrative Conference of the United States 1978).

are so immediately related to the process of determining agency action as to fall on the openness side of the line. Accordingly, the *1978 Sunshine Act Guide* concluded that the proper test is the nature of the discussion and not whether it achieves a specific extent of agreement.[171] In light of the Supreme Court's decision, the second edition of the *Interpretive Guide,* revised in 2005, continued to focus on the concept of "deliberations, *i.e.* what the American Bar Association described as 'a discussion and consideration . . . of the reasons for and against a measure.'"[172]

Despite the *Guide*'s position and the Court's effort to ameliorate the most rigid application of the Sunshine Act, the statute has plainly compromised the consensus-building that is supposed to be a cornerstone of the decisional process at multimember agencies. That is because agency general counsels understandably caution against discussion among members that may tilt toward deliberation. And at least some agency members are reluctant to test out preliminary ideas or reveal any lack of information or understanding in public sessions.

It is also clear that the Sunshine Act can compromise the quality of agency deliberations.[173] To avoid Sunshine Act strictures, some agencies engage in so-called round robin meetings among agency members so that a quorum of the full membership is never present at the same time.[174] Studies of multimember agency collegiality in light of the Sunshine Act have also revealed that, since the statute's enactment, there has been an increasing use of so-called notation voting, that is, the disposition of agency business via the seriatim circulation in writing to agency members of proposed actions or draft decisions. The use of the notation process is strongly rooted in the legislative history of the Sunshine Act,[175] and was approved by the courts in the face of Sunshine Act challenges shortly after the statute's enactment.[176] It has been endorsed ever since.[177] As Judge Richard Eaton has pointed out:

> Sequential notational voting is a procedure employed by large multi-member governmental agencies, such as the ITC which conforms with the open

[171] *But see* Department of Justice Letter to Covered Agencies, Apr. 19, 1977, *reprinted as* 2005 INTERPRETIVE GUIDE, *supra* note 163, at appendix E (espousing a broader interpretation of "meeting").

[172] 2005 INTERPRETIVE GUIDE, *supra* note 163, at 25.

[173] See comments of former FERC commissioner Charles Stalon in *Conference: Harvard Electricity Policy Group: Regulatory Decisionmaking Reform,* 8 ADMIN. L.J. AM. U. 789, 798 (1995). He notes the "iron-clad" rule that "the staff shall not embarrass a Commissioner in public," whereas staff can and do correct or help shape a commissioner's positions on issues in private meetings.

[174] *Id.* at 796–97.

[175] 2005 INTERPRETIVE GUIDE, *supra* note 163, at 31–32, citing the House-Senate Conference Report, H. REP. NO. 94-1441 and S. REP. NO. 94-1178, 94th Cong., 2d Sess. 11 (1976), that the prohibition against joint disposition of business at an open meeting "does not prevent agency members from considering individually business that is circulated to them sequentially in writing."

[176] *See, e.g.,* Communications Systems, Inc. v. FCC, 595 F.2d 797, 800–01 (D.C. Cir. 1978).

[177] *See, e.g.,* Republic Airlines v. CAB, 756 F.2d 1304, 1319 (8th Cir. 1985); Amrep Corp. v. FTC, 768 F.2d 1171, 1178 (10th Cir. 1985), *cert. denied* 475 U.S. 1034 (1986); Elkem Metals Co. v. United States, 126 F. Supp. 2d 567, 575 n.4 (C.I.T. 2000).

> meeting requirement of the Sunshine Act... An Action Jacket [used by the ITC] is a form of sequential notational voting. The use of Action Jackets allows the ITC Commissioners to act on agency matters individually, instead of deliberating and voting as a group during an open agency session. This manner of voting is consistent with the Sunshine Act, even though no formal agency meeting is held."[178]

The authors of the *Interpretive Guide to the Government in the Sunshine Act* describe the increased used of notation voting as "one of the unintended consequences or 'costs' of the Sunshine Act."[179] Indeed, one observer who has noted the negative effects of the Sunshine Act expressed concerns that "neither openness nor collegiality values are being served by the present operation of the Act and... many of the open meetings under the Act are *pro forma* or overly rehearsed and scripted sessions that provide the public with less information than it deserves."[180] Agency staffs appear to share this concern. Finally, meetings of agency member staff assistants, operating either under instructions from their principals, or developing consensus on their own, are commonplace at Sunshine Act agencies.

The impact of open meeting laws on collegial decision-making has caused some to rethink Justice Louis Brandeis's oft-quoted declaration at the height of the Progressive Era in 1914 that "[p]ublicity is justly commended as a remedy for social and industrial disease. Sunlight is said to be the best disinfectant and electric light the most efficient policeman."[181] Arthur Bonfield, former chairman of the Section of Administrative Law and Regulatory Practice of the American Bar Association, noted in 1988 that while "mould does not grow where there is light... too much sunshine causes sunburn."[182] A 2004 article written by Nicholas Johnson, a former commissioner of the FCC (1966–1973), called for a reexamination of open meeting laws.[183] He argues that the legal requirement for open meetings, especially as implemented in practice, is actually inconsistent with the goals of rational decision-making and enhanced public accessibility and confidence. Discussing the Iowa open meeting law, Johnson asserts that the purposes of sunshine

---

178 Elkem Metals Co. v. United States, 126 F. Supp. 2d 5672, 575 n.4 (C.I.T. 2000).

179 2005 INTERPRETIVE GUIDE, *supra* note 163, at 33 (citing numerous sources).

180 Letter from Jeffrey S. Lubbers, former Research Director, Administrative Conference of the United States to Carl Rupert, Raleigh Research Director, Clean Water Fund of North Carolina (Nov. 21, 2001) (on file with the authors).

181 *See* LOUIS D. BRANDEIS, OTHER PEOPLE'S MONEY AND HOW THE BANKS USE IT 92 (1914). *Compare* Public Citizen v. National Economic Commission, 703 F. Supp. 113, 125 (D.D.C. 1989) ("Congress, in enacting the Sunshine Act, believed that increased openness would enhance citizen confidence in government, encourage higher quality work by government officials, stimulate well-informed public debate about government programs and policies, and promote cooperation between citizens and government.") (quoting *Common Cause v. NRC*, 674 F.2d 921, 928 (D.C. Cir. 1982)).

182 *See* Arthur Bonfield, *Chairman's Message*, 40 ADMIN. L. REV. iii–iv (1988), quoted in Nicholas Johnson, *Open Meetings and Closed Minds: Another Road to the Mountaintop*, 53 DRAKE L. REV. 11 (Fall 2004).

183 Johnson, *supra* note 182, at 11.

laws "are, in some contexts, often better served by less rather than more openness. The objectives of these laws can still be served—indeed, better served in those instances—by affording agency members the freedom to engage in closed discussions that alone can produce the quality of creativity and analysis the laws seek to promote."[184]

Former SEC commissioner Bevis Longstreth also explains that "[t]he Act tends to shift power in a multi-headed agency from the collegial body to its chairman.... [T]he Chairman typically meets with staff or outsiders alone, formulating policy without the benefit of timely and meaningful comment from other members of the collegial body.... In particular, the chairman's meetings with the staff have a powerful tendency to shape the staff's responses and recommendations, which might well be different if it were possible for the other members to be present."[185]

Citing a study of the Sunshine Act for the Administrative Conference of the United States, Justice Breyer and the professors Stewart, Sunstein, Vermeule, and Herz observe that:

> Open-meeting law had changed the behavior of those subject to it. A survey of several hundred relevant individuals led the authors to conclude that "public access to information has been enlarged." On the other hand, commissioners tended to make up their minds about issues before meetings, they were reluctant to engage in meaningful negotiation and debate at meetings, and they hesitated to discuss sensitive issues in public. The result is that "the focus of decisionmaking activity has shifted toward the offices of individual members and to the staff level."[186]

The Sunshine Act, of course, is not entirely responsible for any compromise in collegiality. Agency statutes and traditions, and the personalities of agency members, especially the chair, are dominant factors that also help determine the level of collegiality at a particular agency.

A 1986 Report prepared by the Congressional Research Service for Senator Lawton Chiles attempting to rebut the findings of the 1984 study claimed that there was "no clear evidence to indicate that the quality of collegial decision making has deteriorated." The Report stated that "it might be argued that because members are better prepared the quality of collegial decision making has improved."[187] Nonetheless, the evidence is

---

[184] Johnson, *supra* note 182, at 14.

[185] 2005 Interpretive Guide, *supra* note 163, at 222 n.18.

[186] Stephen G. Breyer, Richard B. Stewart, Cass R. Sunstein, Adrian Vermeule & Michael E. Herz, Administrative Law and Regulatory Policy: Problems, Text and Cases 885 (7th ed. 2011).

[187] *See* Report of Rogelio Garcia, Analyst in American National Government, Congressional Research Service, to Honorable Lawton Chiles (May 8, 1986), at 11, *cited in* 2005 Interpretive Guide, *supra* note 163, at 222 n.18.

reasonably persuasive that while the Sunshine Act has reduced collegiality, it has, as a corollary, served to enhance the influence of agency chairs and staff.[188]

A more specific and colorful critique comes from the pen of Richard Pierce:

> Open decision-making is a concept that is attractive to those who seek to reform the administrative process. But it is not an unqualified virtue. The perverse effect of the concept upon the process of collegial decision-making is indicative of a more general problem. Notions of fairness (implicit in the openness principle) have the potential to trammel upon equally important principles of political accountability. At this time, the Sunshine Act has earned only two cheers.[189]

> [The Government in the Sunshine Act, or GSA], renders collegiality impossible in a collegial body that heads an agency.... Because of GSA, meetings among members of multi-member agencies are infrequent; such agencies often make important decisions through notational voting with *no* prior deliberation; and communications at open meetings are grossly distorted by the presence of the public. Commissioners are reluctant to express their true views for fear that they will expose their ignorance or uncertainty with respect to issues of fact, policy, and law. They attempt to disguise their uncertainties with stilted and contrived discussions that greatly impede the kind of frank exchange of views that is essential to high quality decisionmaking by a collegial body.

> It is peculiar that multi-member agencies are singled out for a type of public exposure that inevitably impairs their ability to act in effective and informed ways. There can be no doubt that GSA has this effect. It is highly unlikely, for instance, that the Supreme Court would have issued its unanimous, bold decision in *Brown v. Board of Education,* 347 U.S. 483 (1954), if the Justices had been required to conduct the decade-long debate that preceded *Brown* only in public meetings. It is tempting to indulge the cynical assumption that Congress enacted GSA for the purpose of crippling multi-member agencies. Whatever may have been Congress's intent, GSA certainly has that effect.[190]

---

188 *See generally* PETER STRAUSS, ADMINISTRATIVE JUSTICE IN THE UNITED STATES, 286–87 (2d ed. 2002) (citing the 1984 study for the Administrative Conference by Welborn, Lyons, and Thomas and the 1997 Administrative Conference study by the Special Committee to Review the Government in the Sunshine Act).

189 RICHARD J. PIERCE, ADMINISTRATIVE LAW TREATISE (5th ed. 2010), at 479.

Richard Merrill notes, in the context of the Consumer Product Safety Commission, that the Sunshine Act has impeded the interaction between commission members and the agency's technical staff. Richard A. Merrill, *CPSC Regulation of Cancer Risks in Consumer Products: 1972–1981*, 67 VA. L. REV. 1261, 1267–68 (1981).

190 PIERCE, *supra* note 189, at 294, 296. For more favorable views of open meeting laws and the Sunshine Act, see Larry W. Thomas, *The Courts and the Implementation of the Government in the Sunshine Act*, 37 ADMIN.

When coupled with a chair's management of the agency's docket, the Sunshine Act plainly has the effect of further centralizing control of the agency's decisional course in the hands of the chair or staff.

Both the Administrative Conference of the United States and the American Bar Association have made recommendations concerning the definition of "meeting" and methods of improving collegiality while attempting to retain a degree of openness.[191] A special committee of the Administrative Conference in 1995 took testimony from current and former agency officials and members of the private bar seeking to address the question of collegiality. Although there was no opportunity for the usual Administrative Conference consideration by a full plenary session, the committee published its recommendations.[192] The committee was concerned that "the public is neither receiving the enhanced access to the governmental decisionmaking process that the Act envisioned, nor... is it receiving the benefit of better agency decisions through collegial decisionmaking."[193] The committee's central proposal was a five- to seven-year pilot program that would allow Sunshine Act agency members to meet in private as long as such meetings were memorialized and a "detailed summary" of the meeting was made public five days later "that would indicate the date, time, participants, subject matters discussed, and a review of the nature of the discussion," but without identifying positions of individual commissioners. In exchange for such relaxation of Sunshine Act requirements, a

L. REV. 259–60 (1985) (arguing that "democracy is dependent upon a well informed citizenry, which in turn necessitates a firsthand view of the governmental decision-making process"); David A. Barrett, Note, *Facilitating Government Decision Making: Distinguishing Between Meetings and Nonmeetings Under the Federal Sunshine Act*, 66 TEX. L. REV. 1195–96 (1988) (discussing the benefits of open government to the democratic system); Maurice Baskin, Note, *The Federal "Government in the Sunshine Act": A Public Access Compromise*, 29 U. FLA. L. REV. 881–83, n.13 (1977) (citing historical sources for the idea that open government is an essential part of the democratic process); and Susan T. Stephenson, Comment, *Government in the Sunshine Act: Opening Federal Agency Meetings*, 26 AM. U. L. REV. 154, 156–57 (1976) (reviewing the positive effects openness has on the democratic system)." *See also* 133 CONG. REC. 5177 (1987) (statement of Senator Lawton Chiles, author of the Sunshine legislation, on tenth anniversary of the Sunshine Act, that "there is no common sense reason why citizens shouldn't be able to watch how Government spends their money and reaches decisions affecting their businesses, their communities and their future. Citizens cannot hold Government officials accountable if they don't know what those officials are doing.") *See also* Jessica M. Natale, *Exploring Virtual Legal Presence*, 1 J. HIGH TECH. L. 157–58 (2002) (stating that the primary purpose of open meetings laws "is to maintain or restore confidence in the political process through disclosure").

191 *See* 2005 INTERPRETIVE GUIDE, *supra* note 163, Appendix F, for the American Bar Association's February 1987 *Report and Recommendation* about Sunshine Act reform. See 2005 INTERPRETIVE GUIDE, *supra* note 163, Appendix G, for the Administrative Conference's 1984 Report and Recommendation 84-3, Improvements in the Administration of the Government in the Sunshine Act.

192 *See* Randolph May, *Reforming the Sunshine Act*, 49 ADMIN. L. REV. 415 (1997).

193 *Id.* at 424. (The Administrative Conference of the United States Special Committee noted, for example, that "true collective decisionmaking does not occur at agency public meetings," that instead the Act "promotes inefficient practices" like seriatim, notation voting of agency items, which erodes collegial decisionmaking and the ultimate quality of agency decisions.) *See* 2005 INTERPRETIVE GUIDE, *supra* note 163, at Appendix I.

participating agency would have to agree to hold periodic open meetings at which members could address issues discussed in private sessions or items disposed of by notation voting and refrain, to the extent practicable, from using notation voting procedures for such matters. However, agencies would not be relieved of the Act's requirements to conduct votes and take other official actions on important substantive matters in public meetings (absent an applicable exemption).

The American Bar Association's recommendations were issued following the Supreme Court's *ITT World Communications* decision and a later effort by the NRC to amend its definition of "meeting" in its regulations on an "interim" basis to incorporate the test set forth in the Court's opinion.[194] A committee of the American Bar Association's Administrative Law Section presented a report that reviewed in some detail the Supreme Court decision and attempted to provide a gloss on the statutory definition in the light of the Court's opinion. On the basis of this report, as forwarded by the Administrative Law Section, the House of Delegates of the American Bar Association in February 1987 approved the following recommendation:

> *Be it Resolved,* That the American Bar Association offers the following guidelines to Federal agencies and courts with respect to the interpretation of the term "meeting" as used in the Government in the Sunshine Act:
>
> 1. So long as discussions are not sufficiently focused on discrete proposals or issues as to cause or be likely to cause the individual participating [agency] members to form reasonably firm positions regarding matters pending or likely to arise before the agency, the definition of "meeting" does not include: (a) spontaneous casual discussions among agency members of a subject of common interest; (b) briefings of agency members by staff or outsiders; a key element would be that the agency members be primarily receptors of information or views and only incidentally exchange views with one another; (c) general discussions of subjects which are relevant to an agency's responsibilities but which do not pose specific problems for agency resolution; and (d) exploratory discussions, so long as they are preliminary in nature, there are no pending proposals for agency action, and the merits of any proposed agency action would be open to full consideration at a later time.
>
> 2. If agencies intend to hold discussions described in subsections (b), (c), and (d), appropriate mechanisms, such as monitoring by general counsel or other agency representatives, should be undertaken to ensure that such discussions do not proceed to the point of becoming "meetings." In addition, agencies should memorialize such discussions through notes, minutes or recordings as assurance to the public of compliance with the Act.

---

[194] See 2005 INTERPRETIVE GUIDE, *supra* note 163, Appendix F, for the American Bar Association February 1987 Report and Recommendation

The new Administrative Conference of the United States has reexamined the Sunshine Act. It proposed a series of "best practices" to enhance transparency while minimizing compliance burdens. This represents an acknowledgment that significant changes in the statute that might affect the collegiality problems are unlikely to receive congressional support at present.[195]

3. QUORUM AND VOTING REQUIREMENTS

Just as the Government in the Sunshine Act has had the unanticipated effect of concentrating power in the hands of agency chairs at the expense of collegiality, so quorum and voting requirements—along with legal rules and agency practice regarding disqualification or recusal from individual proceedings—have likewise diffused collegial decision-making, but through an alternate trend. When agencies are at less than full strength, which they frequently are, that has had the effect of shifting power to the hands of individual agency members, although not necessarily the chairman, with a potential reduction in the collegial accountability envisioned by Congress.

Agency quorum and voting requirements are established by statute or, in the absence of a statutory provision, by agency regulation or tradition. The Communications Act contains an example of a traditional statutory provision. It provides simply that the commission shall be composed of five members and three members constitute a quorum.[196]

Congress also often includes separate statutory provisions intended to allow an agency to operate where a full complement of authorized members may otherwise be unavailable. The original Act to Regulate Commerce, for example, provided that vacancies on the ICC did not impair the right of the remaining members to act. A similar provision has been incorporated into many subsequent statutes.[197] And the courts have ordinarily endorsed the continued operation of agencies at below full strength. *Assure Competition Transportation, Inc. v. United States* is typical.[198] The ICC at the time had a statutory authorization of eleven members, no more than a majority of whom might be from the same political party, and its statute provided that "[a] majority of the ... Commission ... is a quorum for the transaction of business." The statute also provided that "[a] vacancy in the membership of the Commission does not impair the right of the remaining members to exercise all of the power of the Commission." Although only four and five of the six commissioners then in office participated in two of the commission's decisions, the court concluded that a majority of the commissioners actually in office—not a majority of the statutory eleven—constituted a quorum. When the commission's membership dropped to four, with three Republicans and only one Democrat, the Sixth Circuit reached the

---

195 *See* Recommendation 2014-2, Government in the Sunshine Act, 79 Fed. Reg. 35988 (June 25, 2014).

196 *See* 47 U.S.C. § 154(a), (h).

197 *See, e.g.*, 29 U.S.C. § 153(a) (NLRB); U.S.C. § 41 (FTC).

198 629 F.2d 467, 472–74 (7th Cir. 1980), *cert. denied*, 449 U.S. 1124 (1981).

same conclusion even though the commission, as then constituted, had more than a majority from one party.[199]

Agency quorum and voting requirements do vary, however, and agencies obviously must follow such explicit statutory requirements. At the Federal Reserve Board, for example, a simple majority of the seven board members constitutes a quorum for the purposes of taking board action, except in two instances. First, board action with respect to the waiver of reserve ratio limits in extraordinary circumstances, and the imposition of supplemental reserves under section 19(b) of the Federal Reserve Act, require the affirmative vote of five members.[200] Second, board action with respect to advances, 12 U.S.C. § 347a, discounts, and rediscounts under sections 10A, 11(b), and 13, respectively, of the Federal Reserve Act, requires the affirmative vote of five members.

Two multimember agencies, the FEC and ITC, have an even number of members and a requirement of bipartisanship. Congress has designed different, and opposite, quorum and voting requirements for them. The statute creating the FEC, which administers and enforces the federal statutes governing the financing of federal elections, provides that no more than three of its six members may be affiliated with the same political party and explicitly requires four affirmative votes out of six commissioners—that is, guaranteed bipartisanship—before the FEC may act on certain items; so a vote of three to two, with one abstention, for example, is insufficient.[201] The statute governing the six-member ITC, whose responsibilities include investigation and recommendation, as well as making decisions in certain international trade matters, also provides that no more than three of its six members may be affiliated with the same political party. Yet Congress has provided that certain investigations should go forward where the commission is equally divided[202] and that decisions by an equally divided commission in certain cases shall be considered to be an affirmative vote of the commission.[203] The constitutionality of this provision under the due process clause was upheld in *Border Brokerage Co. v. United States*.[204]

Absent a statutory provision, multimember federal agencies generally follow the common law "majority of the quorum" rule, which means that a quorum is needed before the agency may act, but only a majority of the quorum is needed for action once a quorum is constituted. Thus, if an agency's enabling legislation provides that it has five members and that three members shall constitute a quorum, the agency may take action by a two-to-one vote. Such arrangements are akin to the statute governing the United States courts of appeals. Two of three judges (a majority) of a three-member court of appeals

---

199 Michigan Dep't of Transp. v. ICC, 698 F.2d 277, 279 (6th Cir. 1983).

200 12 U.S.C. § 461(b)(3), (4)(A).

201 *See* 2 U.S.C. § 437c(c) (1994).

202 *See, e.g.*, 19 U.S.C. § 1330(d).

203 19 U.S.C. § 1677(11).

204 646 F.2d 539, 545 (C.C.P.A. 1981).

panel constitute a quorum, and those two judges may ordinarily issue a decision.[205] It is legally immaterial that only a minority of the agency's total membership participates or that any statutorily intended political balance is disrupted. This is made clear by *FTC v. Flotill Products, Inc.*, where the Supreme Court approved the FTC's adoption of the "majority of the quorum" rule in the absence of a statutory quorum rule.[206] Indeed, at one point the ICC, which had statutory authority to delegate decisional authority to a three-member division, had a practice of having the third member participate only if the other two were in disagreement.[207]

To be counted as part of an agency quorum, individual members need not offer their views on the merits of a proceeding.[208] As the New Jersey Supreme Court observed in connection with a multimember state agency:

> Insofar as the presence of a legal quorum is in issue, all that matters is whether the physically present commissioners participated in agency deliberations and took purposeful action by joining, concurring in, dissenting from, or even abstaining from the final decision.[209]

Decisions by numerous courts and agencies establish that agency members who did not participate at the agency's oral argument may nonetheless familiarize themselves with the record and participate in the decision.[210]

The "majority of the quorum" rule is not mandatory. Absent statutory requirements, a multimember agency may, within reason, use its other statutory powers to determine how its quorum requirements will be satisfied.

The failure of the president to appoint, or the Senate to confirm, a full complement of members at some agencies, coupled with individual attitudes toward disqualification or recusal, have caused some agencies to modify their historic rules regarding quorums. This tends to do two things. First, it allows the agency to function despite a smaller than

---

205 Nguyen v. United States, 539 U.S. 69, 82–83 (2003). *See also* Englehard Corp. v. NLRB, 437 F.3d 374 (3d Cir. 2006) (citing 28 U.S.C. § 46(d), two judges decided the case following Justice Alito's elevation to the Supreme Court).

206 389 U.S. 179, 183–84 (1967).

207 *See* Nicholson v. Mo. Pac. R.R., 366 I.C.C. 69 (1982). The D.C. Circuit was apparently not troubled by the practice. *See* Nicholson v. ICC, 711 F.2d 364, 367 (D.C. Cir. 1983), *cert. denied* 464 U.S. 1056 (1984).

208 Morris v. CFTC, 980 F.2d 1289, 1293–94 (9th Cir. 1992) (stating that agency member who merely concurred in the result held to have participated in the decision for quorum purposes).

209 King v. New Jersey Racing Comm'n., 511 A.2d 615, 618–19 (N.J. 1886).

210 *See, e.g.*, Porter & Dietsch, Inc. v. FTC, 605 F.2d 294, 298–99 (7th Cir. 1979), *cert. denied* 445 U.S. 950 (1980) (discussing the principle and possible exceptions, citing Gearhart & Otis, Inc. v. SEC, 348 F.2d 798, 802 (D.C. Cir. 1965)).

authorized complement of members. Second, it can effectively place decisional responsibility in the hands of a minority of agency members.

The enabling statutes for the SEC and the FTC, along with some other agencies, do not have explicit quorum requirements. Those statutes nonetheless authorize the agency to "make such rules and regulations as may be necessary or appropriate to implement the provisions of this chapter for which they are responsible or for the execution of the functions vested in them by this chapter."[211] In 1995, the SEC adopted a regulation that provided that three of its five statutory members constitute a quorum unless the number of members in office is fewer than three, in which case the quorum consists of the number of members actually in office. The regulation further provided that if on any matter of business, the number of members in office minus the number of members who are disqualified to consider the matter is two, then those two members constitute a quorum for purposes of that specific matter (60 Fed. Reg. 17201 (April 5, 1995), codified at 17 C.F.R. 200.41). The D.C. Circuit upheld the validity of the SEC's quorum provision.[212]

In 2005 the FTC followed a similar approach in order to ameliorate the quorum problem associated with recusals. Under a revised quorum rule,

> A majority of the members of the Commission in office and not recused from participating in a matter (by virtue of 18 U.S.C. § 208 or otherwise) constitutes a quorum for the transaction of business in that matter.[213]

The CSB revised its quorum rule in 2003 to the same effect at 40 C.F.R. 1600.5. It states:

> A quorum of the Board for the transaction of business shall consist of three Members; provided, however, that if the number of Board Members in office is fewer than three, a quorum shall consist of the number of Members in Office; and provided further that on any matter of business as to which the number of Members in office, minus the number of Members who have disqualified themselves from consideration of such matter is two, two Members shall constitute a quorum for purposes of such matter. Once a quorum is constituted, a simple majority of voting Members is required to approve an item of the Board's business. A tie vote results in no action.

---

211 15 U.S.C. § 78w(a)(1) (1994) (outlining the SEC's power to promulgate rules and regulations).

212 *See* Falcon Trading Group, Ltd. v. SEC, 102 F.3d 579, 582 (D.C. Cir. 1996) (holding that the SEC was within its authority to promulgate the rule). *See also* SEC v. Feminella & Granston, 947 F. Supp. 722 (S.D.N.Y. 1995) (given the SEC's statutory authority to delegate its functions to an individual commissioner, the vacancies in the positions of three members of the five-member commission did not render the individual commissioner's action invalid).

213 Quorums, Final Rule, 70 Fed. Reg. 53296 (Sept. 8, 2005).

Where an agency has authority to delegate decisional responsibility to an individual or unit smaller than a quorum of the agency itself, there may be limited circumstances where a multimember agency can operate even without an actual quorum. In *Railroad Yardmasters of America v. Harris*, the court decided whether the three-member National Mediation Board had violated its quorum requirement by conferring all powers on a single member.[214] The National Mediation Board has statutory authority "to assign, or refer, any portion of its work, business, or functions ... to an individual member of the Board."[215] In *Harris*, one seat on the board was vacant and another seat was soon to be vacated.[216] On the eve of the resignation of the second board member, the two members delegated decisional authority to the soon to be remaining member who, thereafter, acted for the agency pursuant to the delegation. The D.C. Circuit held the arrangement came within the statutory language and was valid.[217] The NRC relied on Reorganization Plan No. 1 of 1980 to delegate all authority to its chairman in similar circumstances.[218]

Less than a quorum of the agency may ordinarily grant discretionary review of an ALJ's decision. The rule is akin to the "Rule of Four" applied by the Supreme Court to requests for certiorari.[219] Congress placed such a provision in the statute governing the five-member Federal Mine Safety and Health Review Commission, which requires only two votes to take review.[220] By regulation, the five-member SEC grants review on request of only one of its members.[221]

The statute that controls the operations of the Occupational Safety and Health Review Commission allows an ALJ's decision to go into effect "unless any Commission member has directed that such [decision] shall be reviewed by the Commission."[222] Thus, an ALJ's decision can go into effect if no member directs review, even if the commission has no members. At least one Circuit Court of Appeals has permitted judicial review of an Occupational Safety and Health Review Commission "decision"

---

214 *See* R.R. Yardmasters of Am. v. Harris, 721 F.2d 1332, 1333 (D.C. Cir. 1983).

215 *See* 45 U.S.C. § 154 (Fourth) (1994).

216 *See Harris*, 721 F.2d at 1333–35 (explaining one member had retired and a second was about to resign).

217 *See id.* at 1341–42.

218 Delegation, 60 Fed. Reg. 34561 (July 3, 1995).

219 The Supreme Court follows the practice of granting certiorari and hearing a case on the merits if four of the justices (less than a majority) are in favor. ROBERT L. STERN, EUGENE GROSSMAN, STEPHEN M. SHAPIRO & KENNETH S. GELLER, SUPREME COURT PRACTICE § 5.4 (Bureau of National Affairs, 8th ed. 2002). *See also* Ohio *ex rel.* Eaton v. Price, 360 U.S. 246, 247 (1959) (separate statement of Justice Brennan).

220 30 U.S.C. § 823(d)(2)(A)(iii). *See also* 29 C.F.R. § 2704.308(b) (1999) (explaining that novel questions of law or policy only require two votes).

221 *See* 17 C.F.R. § 201.411(c) (providing rules governing review of commission decisions).

222 McLaughlin v. Union Oil Co. of Cal., 869 F.2d 1039, 1041 (7th Cir. 1989).

where no members were available to review an ALJ's decision. The Seventh Circuit observed:

> It might be a scandal for the President or the Senate to prevent an important federal commission from operating by failing to fill vacancies in it . . . , but it would not follow that decisions by the commission's staff were unappealable.[223]

But such approach has been questioned on grounds of basic fairness.[224]

It is clear that an agency's implementation of its quorum requirements is clearly confined to its statutory authority. The Supreme Court has recently addressed the issue of the NLRB's implementation of the quorum and voting requirements in its organic statute in the absence of a full, statutorily authorized quorum in *New Process Steel, L.P. v. National Labor Relations Board*, 130 S. Ct. 2635 (2010). The NLRB was originally created in the 1930s as a three-member board with a statutory quorum of two. In 1947, Congress enlarged the board to five members, with a statutory quorum of three. Unlike most agency statutes, the board's statute indicates that "three members of the Board shall, *at all times*, constitute a quorum of the Board,"[225] but allows the board to delegate responsibility to a three-member panel, where two members constitute a quorum. The delegation provision, not typically included in most independent agency statutes, was intended to permit the board to carry out its adjudicatory responsibilities more efficiently.

With a vacancy on the five-member board, and anticipating the expiration of the terms of two of the remaining four members, the four members delegated to a three-member panel all of the board's powers, notwithstanding that the term of one of the three members would shortly expire, leaving only two members available to decide future cases.[226] In reaching this decision, the board relied heavily on an opinion by the OLC construing the board's statute.[227] The board went down to two members, one Democrat, Member Liebman, and one Republican, Member Schaumber, effective January 1, 2008. Between then and the appointment of two recess appointees in 2010, the two-member panel decided almost six hundred cases.[228]

---

223 *Id.* at 1042.

224 *See* Ed Taylor Constr. Co. v. OSHRC, 938 F.2d 1265, 1269 (11th Cir. 1991) (observing that there may be circumstances in which absence of commissioners available to review ALJ's decision can constitute denial of individual's procedural rights, in which case decision may be returned for review by the commission).

225 29 U.S.C. § 153(b) (italics added).

226 *See* New Process Steel, L.P. v. NLRB, 130 S. Ct. 2635, 2638-39 (2010) (citing Minute of Board Action (Dec. 20, 2007), App. to Brief for Petitioner 5a).

227 Quorum Requirements, Memorandum Opinion for the Solicitor, National Labor Relations Board, 2003 OLC LEXIS 20 (March 4, 2003).

228 *New Process Steel, L.P.*, 130 S. Ct. at 2639.

The board's statute was amenable to at least two constructions. On the one hand, the statute could be interpreted to require only that the board itself have three members at the time of the delegation and that the panel likewise have three members at that time. In such circumstances, the delegation would remain in operation so long as a quorum of the panel remained. On the other hand, the statute could be read to require that either the board or the panel at all times maintain its three members in order that the delegation remain valid. In an appeal presented to the D.C. Circuit, the court determined that the requirement regarding the quorum requirement for the board itself must be satisfied "at all times." The court observed:

> [The Board's construction] ignores the fact that the Board and delegee group quorum requirements are not mutually exclusive. The delegee group quorum provision's language does not eliminate the requirement that a quorum of the *Board* is three members. Rather, it states only that the quorum of any three-member *delegee group* shall be two.... The use of the word "except" is therefore present in the statute only to indicate that the delegee group's ability to act is measured by a different numerical value.... The Board quorum requirement therefore must still be satisfied, regardless of whether the Board's authority is delegated to a group of its members. Reading the two quorum provisions harmoniously, the result is clear: a three-member Board may delegate its powers to a three-member group, and this delegee group may act with two members so long as the Board quorum requirement is, "at all times," satisfied.... But the Board cannot by delegating its authority circumvent the statutory Board quorum requirement, because this requirement must always be satisfied.[229]

The Supreme Court, in a five-to-four decision, also struck down the board's delegation. But the majority rejected the D.C. Circuit's approach and, instead, construed the statutory language to require that the panel retain three members. Although the Court plainly took the board's membership requirements into account when construing the various provisions of the statute, the membership provision of the statute was not determinative. Indeed, the Court left in place the delegations to the board's general counsel and regional directors.[230]

In reaching its conclusion, it described "the Board's longstanding practice"[231] as one factor "driving our decision."[232] The Court indicated that the board historically permitted two members of a three-member group to issue decisions when one member became

[229] Laurel Baye Healthcare of Lake Lanier, Inc. v. NLRB, 564 F.3d 469, 472–73 (D.C. Cir. 2009), *cert. denied* 130 S. Ct. 3498 (2010).

[230] *New Process Steel, L.P.*, 130 S. Ct. at 2643.

[231] *Id.* at 2640.

[232] *Id.* at 2641.

disqualified. But it had not, until recently, authorized decisions by two members of the board itself, or a two-member panel, for an indefinite period.[233] In effect, the Court took into account as reinforcing its statutory construction the board's historic practice while rejecting the current, although presumably well-considered, OLC statutory interpretation adopted by the Board. The dissent concluded that "[n]othing in the statute suggests that a delegation to a three-member group expires when one member's seat becomes vacant,"[234] and found that the board's historic practice of reconstituting panels when a member was no longer available for an extended period should not bar it from exercising a different approach when confronted with a largely unanticipated situation.[235]

That the Court's concern was over institutional elements and practices in light of congressional expectations is revealed not only by the majority's decision itself, but by Justice Stevens's observations at oral argument. Justice Stevens wrote the majority decision, joining four of the Court's conservative members. At oral argument he questioned only the Government's lawyer.

> JUSTICE SCALIA: So knowing when it gave it to this three member panel that it would shortly become a two-member panel, and that thereby the board would be able to act with only two members instead of with three, which is what the quorum requirement for the board is.
>
> I must say that seems to be a very strange procedure when you have a statute that says the board has to—has to have three for a quorum. When the board sees, oh, God, we are about to lose our third member, let's set up a three-member panel with this guy who's about to go off. It will immediately become a two-member panel and then we can act with only two members. That's wonderful.
>
> It doesn't seem to you like an evasion of the whole purpose of the—of the quorum requirement?
>
> MR. KATYAL: I don't think so. I think it's precisely what was—what the text allows, because it's not, Justice Scalia, simply a three-member [*25] quorum requirement. It's a three-member quorum requirement, "except that."
>
> JUSTICE STEVENS: Except—may I just interrupt a bit, just on the "except" clause at the very bottom. When you are talking about individual cases it's easy. Sure, one member dies; the other two can finish. *But you are talking about long-run governance of the board* [emphasis added]. The two members—two members shall constitute a quorum of any group designated pursuant to the first sentence. Now, 2 years later, after—what is the group designated pursuant to the first sentence at the time of the decision 2 years later?

233 *Id.* at 2641.

234 *Id.* at 2646.

235 *Id.* at 2649–50.

MR. KATYAL: It is the same group of people that were—

JUSTICE STEVENS: But there is no such group exists at the time that that power is being exercised.

MR. KATYAL: Well, Justice Stevens, the language is written in the past tense. It's "any"—the language in this is found in the government's brief at 10a.

JUSTICE STEVENS: No, it's not the past tense. "Two members shall constitute a quorum."

MR. KATYAL: "Of any group designated pursuant to" the first sentence.

JUSTICE STEVENS: But there is no group around at the time they're—that this case is being decided, that was designated before.

MR. KATYAL: That group was designated on December 20, 2007, and that met the requirements of—

JUSTICE STEVENS: But your—your inquiry is focusing on what happens 2 years later.

MR. KATYAL: And—and with respect to 2 years later, I submit to you that that penultimate sentence in 153(b) is met. That is a designated group pursuant to the first sentence.[236]

Had the Court adopted the D.C. Circuit's rationale, its decision would have limited impact because the NLRB's statutory "at all times" language is novel. However, the majority was obviously more concerned that Congress had not anticipated that two members would, as a practical matter, constitute the board for an extended period. This concern has potential applicability across government. In effect, the Court rejected a practical plan by which four NLRB members had unanimously approved the delegation, the two remaining members were a bipartisan pair that could only act by agreement, and the board's decision allowed national labor policy to be pursued under unanticipated circumstances. Significantly, the Court looked to the board's historic practice as a partial underpinning of the Court's own statutory construction rather than the board's (and the OLC's) construction of the statute.

Shortly after the *New Process Steel* decision, President Obama made two recess appointments to the board—both Democrats and considered to be prounion—and the newly constituted board, with three Democrats and a lone Republican, began essentially to reexamine and ratify decisions made when the board had only two members.[237] In fact, the board continued with its historic practice of permitting two members of a panel to decide a case where a third member was disqualified.[238] Peter Schaumber, the former Republican member of the "two-member" board, noted that he and his Democratic

---

236 2010 U.S. Trans. LEXIS 25 (Mar. 23, 2010, at 24–26).

237 See, for example, NLRB v. Diversified Enterprises, Inc., 2011 U.S. App. LEXIS 14356 (4th Cir. 2011); NLRB v. Northeastern Land Services, Ltd., 645 F.3d 1475 (1st Cir. 2011).

238 Correctional Medical Services, Inc. et al., 2010 NLRB LEXIS 494 (2010).

counterpart had been able to agree on 90 percent of cases that came before them and later complained about the partisan nature of board decisions under its newly constituted membership.[239]

Whether a tie vote constitutes agency action depends on the agency's statute and regulations, which vary among agencies. Agency and court interpretations reflect an experiential linkage between procedure and substance. Generally speaking, where affirmative agency action is required, a tie vote does not represent agency action because a majority of the agency has failed to agree on a decision.[240] Following this approach, the rules of the SEC expressly provide that an initial decision of one of the agency's ALJs has no effect if a majority of the commission cannot agree to a disposition on the merits of a decision that is under its review.[241] In contrast, when the Federal Mine Safety and Health Review Commission divides equally, two for affirmance and two for reversal, the ALJ's decision is affirmed.[242]

The difference in approach may be explained by the differing substantive roles of particular agencies and their effect on the importance of efficiency compared to accountability. The Federal Mine Safety and Health Review Commission's primary responsibility is dispute resolution. In the circumstances, it is not unreasonable to construe action by an equally divided commission as an affirmance of an ALJ's decision in the interest of bringing the adjudication to a close and permitting prompt judicial review. The SEC on the other hand uses its adjudicatory role as part of its broader policy-making responsibilities. So a majority is sensibly required before the agency may be considered to have acted. The difference in functions between the National Mediation Board and the NLRB was mentioned by the Court of Appeals in *Laurel Baye Healthcare of Lake Lanier, Inc. v. NLRB*, 564 F.3d 469, 472–73 (D.C. Cir. 2009) as a factor in permitting the National Mediation Board to take action without a statutory quorum while suggesting that it would not have allowed the NLRB to do so. In an earlier opinion, the court's majority observed:

> Unlike the National Labor Relations Board, the National Mediation Board is not principally engaged in substantive adjudications; in particular, the... [board] does not adjudicate unfair labor practices or seek to enforce individual rights under the

---

239 Statement of Peter C. Schaumber, Former Chair, National Labor Relations Board, before the Committee on Education and the Workforce, U.S. House of Representatives (July 7, 2011), edworkforce.house.gov/UploadedFiles/07.07.11_schaumber.pdf (last accessed Aug. 1, 2011).

240 *See* Farmers Export Co. v. United States, 758 F.2d 733, 736–37 (D.C. Cir. 1985) (explaining that "there can be no final decision when there is no majority agreement on the merits of a position").

241 *See* 17 C.F.R. § 201.411(f) (1999) (stating that when there is a failure to obtain a majority, an order shall be accordingly issued).

242 *See* Secretary of Labor, Mine Safety and Health Administration and United Mine Workers of America Jim Walter Resources, Inc., 2006 FMSHRC LEXIS 144 [*66] (2006) (citing Secretary of Labor v. Pennsylvania Elec. Co., 12 F.M.S.H.R.C. 1562, 1563–65 (1990), *aff'd on other grounds*, Pennsylvania Elec. Co. v. FMSHRC, 969 F.2d 1501 (3d Cir. 1992)).

> Act. Rather, the Board's main functions involve invocations of *procedures* of the Railway Labor Act.... The nature of the [board's] role is perhaps best illustrated by its critical duty—which it discharged several times in the present case during the period when only one member was in office—of notifying the President that a labor dispute threatens "substantially to interrupt interstate commerce to a degree such as to deprive any section of the country of essential transportation service..." Upon such notification the Board's role ceases.[243]

Despite the generally applicable rule that a majority of a quorum must act in order for an agency decision to be effective, most agencies, either by regulation or practice, provide that a divided vote on *reconsideration* brings an agency action to an end by leaving the original decision in place. This practical construction of agency statutes has received the endorsement of the courts.[244]

How the courts treat decisions that depart from conventional quorum and voting requirements or practice may likewise depend on their view of the proper balance between efficiency and accountability. The Ninth Circuit, for example, upheld a decision by the ICC to allow five members to participate through a written notation vote on a circulating draft decision, although one member had resigned before the last member had voted on the same decision. Although the ICC's regulations did not explicitly cover this eventuality, the court was influenced by the fact that the procedure had been used by the commission for many years and was not invented for the purposes of the instant case.[245] It should be noted that the ICC's approach to finality is not universally followed. The Merit Systems Protection Board, for example, considers its decisions final only when it is signed by the board's clerk. If one board member leaves, and is replaced, the new member may, in his discretion, reconsider the case or allow the previous member's vote to be counted.[246]

The courts disagree on the effect of decisions made by a divided Occupational Safety and Health Review Commission. The three-member commission has solely an adjudicatory function. It provides administrative trial and appellate review of workplace safety and health enforcement complaints brought against employers by OSHA. It is somewhat

---

243 R.R. Yardmasters of Am. v. Harris, 721 F.2d 1332, 1345 (D.C. Cir. 1983).

244 *See* Newark Radio Broad. Ass'n v. FCC, 763 F.2d 450, 453 (D.C. Cir. 1985) (noting that a petition for reconsideration before the agency failed for want of a majority); Ford Motor Co. v. ICC, 714 F.2d 1157, 1163 (D.C. Cir. 1983) (explaining that a three-to-three tie vote by full commission leaves prior panel decision final); Delta Air Lines, Inc. v. CAB, 497 F.2d 608, 615 (D.C. Cir. 1973), *cert. denied*, 417 U.S. 930 (1974) (holding that failure of decision for want of a majority is valid unless the prior determination contained a fundamental defect).

245 *See* Idaho v. ICC, 939 F.2d 784, 788 (9th Cir. 1991), *aff'g* Union Pacific R.R. Co.—Abandonment In Fremont and Tentom Counties, *id.* 6 I.C.C.2d 641, 644 (1990) (explaining the ICC's notation voting procedures).

246 Teria H. Brown v. Dep't of the Treasury, 61 M.S.P.R. 484, 1994 MSPB LEXIS 402, n.1 and dissenting statement of Member Amador (1994).

akin to the Federal Mine Safety and Health Review Commission, discussed above, and has frequently operated with only two members (and occasionally with only one). Some courts have concluded that those decisions by an equally divided agency (one-to-one) purportedly "affirming" an ALJ's decision constitute final, judicially reviewable agency action.[247] Other courts have reached the opposite result.[248] In an effort to resolve a pending case when the commission lacked one member, the remaining two members reviewing the decision of an ALJ disagreed on the substantive merits of the issue before them but nonetheless agreed to affirm the ALJ's decision without according it precedential value. The Ninth Circuit said the commission could not have it both ways: "Either it affirms the hearing officer's decision and the Commission's ruling has the precedential value of a Commission ruling, or the Commission has not officially affirmed the hearing officer's decision."[249]

Under a statutory provision governing the FCC, telephone companies may ask the FCC to refrain or "forebear" from applying certain regulatory requirements regarding broadband services. If the commission does not deny the request within a given time period, the request is deemed by statute to have been granted. When the commission divided two-to-two on a forbearance petition, the "forbearance" was challenged on the ground that the deadlocked vote, in effect, denied the petition. The D.C. Circuit disagreed in *Sprint Nextel Corp. v. FCC*.[250] The court observed:

> The deadlocked vote cannot be considered an order of the Commission nor can it constitute agency action. The votes were actions of the individual Commissioners, not the Commission.... Ties... do not result in Commission action.... The Administrative Procedure Act instructs courts to set aside agency action "found to be arbitrary, capricious, an abuse of discretion, or otherwise not in accordance with law..." We therefore require more than a result: we need the agency's reasoning for that result.... Even when we agree with an agency's ultimate judgment, "[i]n administrative law, we do not sustain a 'right-result, wrong-reason' decision of

247 *See* Curry v. Beatrice Pocahontas Coal Co., 67 F.3d 517, 522 n.8 (4th Cir. 1995) (stating that decision by equally divided agency, like similar court decision, is "affirmance-by-necessity"); Marshall v. Sun Petroleum Prods. Co., 622 F.2d 1176, 1179–80 (3d Cir. 1980) (construing statute to mean that ALJ decision is final agency order unless two of three commissioners vote to the contrary); Pa. Steel Foundry & Mach. Co. v. Secretary of Labor, 831 F.2d 1211, 1214 (3d Cir. 1987) (decision by three-member agency where two members disagreed on the substantive issue and a third member declined to address it constitutes agency action).

248 *See* Cox Bros., Inc. v. Secretary of Labor, 574 F.2d 465, 467 (9th Cir. 1978) (stating that an "affirmance" by an equally divided board was not official because it was supported by one member instead of statutorily required vote of two members); Shaw Constr., Inc. v. OSHRC, 534 F.2d 1183, 1186 (5th Cir. 1976) (deciding that no reviewable order exists in a tie vote of commission).

249 Willamette Iron & Steel Co. v. Secretary of Labor, 604 F.2d 1177 (9th Cir. 1979), *cert. denied,* 445 U.S. 942 (1980).

250 508 F.3d 1129 (D.C. Cir. 2007).

an agency. We send the case back to the agency so that it may fix its reasoning or change its result."[251]

A practical question that arises from time to time is whether members who are disqualified or have recused themselves voluntarily from participation in a matter may, nonetheless, constitute part of a quorum. Members who are disqualified from participation because of some genuine conflict of interest probably cannot be included in the quorum.

There appears to be no direct precedent involving the federal multimember agencies. However, the Third Circuit confronted the issue in a case involving a local draft board.[252] The court determined that participation by a disqualified member, even to constitute a quorum, would conflict with the duty to act impartially.[253] Acknowledging that there is a split of opinion on the issue, the court relied on cases involving corporate boards of directors, and suggested that a strict rule was required when governmental agencies acted in order to protect the due process rights of individuals.[254] The New Jersey Supreme Court reached the same result in a case involving a state administrative agency.[255] The court observed:

> We are thus entirely satisfied that for purposes of determining whether a legal quorum is present, it is not relevant whether a member is physically absent, is disqualified because of interest, bias, or prejudice, or other good cause, or voluntarily recuses himself or herself. A member who is disqualified from participating in a particular matter may not be counted in determining the presence of a legal quorum.[256]

Nevertheless, agencies have been advised by courts to attempt to reach a final decision whenever possible.[257] Where the recusal or disqualification of individuals would prevent the body from acting, and there is no legally available substitute decision-maker, courts have approved the participation of individuals who may be "biased" as a matter of law under a form of the "rule of necessity." Such cases include *United States v. Will*,[258] where the Supreme Court decided an issue involving pay raises for all federal judges even though

---

[251] 508 F.3d at 1131–33.

[252] *See In re* Shapiro, 392 F.2d 397, 399–400 (3d Cir. 1968) (holding that local draft board member who was disqualified due to conflict of interest could not be counted as part of quorum).

[253] *See id.* at 399–400.

[254] *See id.*

[255] *See* King v. New Jersey Racing Comm'n, 511 A.2d 615, 618–19 (N.J. 1986).

[256] *Id.* at 618.

[257] *See, e.g.*, Greater Boston Television Corp. v. FCC, 444 F.2d 841, 861 (D.C. Cir. 1970) (stating agency member's vote, cast simply to avoid an impasse, is "a perfectly sound reason for his vote"); United Air Lines, Inc. v. CAB, 281 F.2d 53, 56 (D.C. Cir. 1960) (finding no abuse of discretion when agency member read briefs and participated in case despite not hearing oral argument).

[258] 449 U.S. 200, 216–17 (1980) (holding that public interest in attaining competent and independent judiciary was more important than the disqualification of judges).

the case affected their salaries, and *FTC v. Cement Institute*,[259] where disqualification of the entire administrative agency would have left no forum available for decision.[260]

The participation rights of a member who voluntarily recuses himself or herself likely depends on the circumstances and terms of the recusal. Some agency decisions reflect an agency's effort to avoid incapacity to act as a result of recusals. During the course of their Senate confirmation hearings, two prospective members of the NRC agreed to limit their participation in a particular license proceeding then pending before the agency, but had differing understandings with the Senate committee regarding the extent of possible participation. In *Public Service Co. of New Hampshire*,[261] with one vacancy on the five-member NRC, the commission denied a motion to reopen the case. This denial indicated that two commissioners voted in favor of the result, one commissioner did not participate, and the fourth abstained.[262] Under established NRC procedure, the quorum count included the abstaining commissioner but not the nonparticipant. Therefore, the agency was able to act with only a two-to-zero vote of the three participating members. In *Consolidated Edison Co. of New York*,[263] there were two vacancies on the five-member NRC. The chairman, who had voluntarily recused himself from consideration of the merits of a particular license proceeding, participated to form a quorum for the sole purpose of preserving the agency's ability to defer the issue until such time as a proper quorum to consider the merits was available.[264] Finally, in *Kellogg Co.*,[265] the FTC decided that a commissioner's voluntary recusal from one phase of a proceeding did not necessarily require his recusal from another, unrelated phase of the proceeding.

Where members of an agency who have disabling conflicts of interest do not participate in the decision, the agency may act if a quorum is nonetheless available. The Court of Appeals for the Second Circuit has observed that, where two members of the SEC did, in fact, recuse themselves, "[d]ue process required no more.... In general, courts have been reluctant to impute a conflict of interest on the part of an individual tribunal member to the entire tribunal."[266] Of course, recusal must come early enough so that the member's activity did not compromise the neutrality of the remaining agency members.[267]

---

259 333 U.S. 683 (1948).

260 *See id.* at 700–01 (holding that commission's expression of views in other official contexts cannot serve to disqualify all commissioners because Congress has not provided for any alternative tribunal). The SEC relied on the *Cement Industries* case when concluding that the entire commission could not be disqualified for bias where no other agency was available to hear the case. In the Matter of Jean-Paul Bolduc et al., 54 S.E.C. 1195 (2001).

261 32 N.R.C. 218, 223 (1990).

262 *See id.* at 223.

263 5 N.R.C. 1330 (1977).

264 *See id.* at 1331.

265 *See* Kellogg Co., 97 F.T.C. 159, 161–62 (1981).

266 MFS Securities Corp. v. SEC, 380 F.3d 611, 618 (2d Cir. 2004).

267 *See* D'Alessio v. SEC, 380 F.3d 112, 123 (2d Cir. 2004) (noting the problem without resolving the issue).

Some multimember agencies permit proxy voting. This typically occurs in one of two ways. First, an agency member may request that a colleague cast a vote on his or her behalf. Second, a member may have an authorized subordinate affix his or her signature to a vote sheet. The courts rarely embroil themselves in the details of how such votes are cast.[268]

4. DISQUALIFICATION, BIAS AND RECUSAL

The right to an impartial, that is, unbiased, decision-maker is a fundamental element of due process.[269] The APA requires that formal proceedings be conducted "in an impartial manner."[270] It further provides that a presiding or participating employee may at any time disqualify himself.[271] But the APA does not contain a substantive definition of bias, nor does the disqualification provision expressly apply to the agency members themselves, except in those rare instances where the agency itself includes them in the definition of "presiding or participating employee," as the Federal Maritime Commission does, or an agency member serves as presiding officer.[272] The law on the subject, which applies to all agencies, whether multimember or not, has been developed in court decisions that rely on basic principles of due process.[273]

The definitions of bias are now reasonably well established and attempt to take into account two critical distinctions between agencies and courts.[274] First, agencies undertake

---

268 *See, e.g.*, Braniff Airways, Inc. v. CAB, 379 F.2d 453, 461–62 (D.C. Cir. 1967) ("the use of assistants in the administrative process is indispensible to the orderly and efficient expedition of great volumes of work and the reconciliation of divergent responsibilities. The courts have consistently approved the administrator's utilization of a staff member he deemed qualified in the performance of his official functions.").

269 Goldberg v. Kelly, 397 U.S. 254, 271 (1970); *In re* Murchison, 349 U.S. 133 (1955).

270 5 U.S.C.A. 556(b) (1996).

271 If disqualification is requested by a party to an agency adjudication, "the agency shall determine the matter as a part of the record and decision in the case." Administrative Procedure Act § 7(a), 5 U.S.C. § 556(b) (1994). The term "presiding or participating employee" refers to those individuals who preside at the reception of evidence, such as ALJs.

272 The provision on disqualification was contained in original section 7 of the APA, which deals with the hearing process. *See* § 7(a), 5 U.S.C. § 556(b); *see also* UNITED STATES DEP'T OF JUSTICE, ATTORNEY GENERAL'S MANUAL ON THE ADMINISTRATIVE PROCEDURE ACT 71–74 (1947). The original APA provided that any presiding or participating employee "may at any time withdraw if he deems himself disqualified" § 7(a), 5 U.S.C. § 556(b); *see also* United Corp., 32 S.E.C. 633, 634 n.3, 635 (1951) (rejecting motion requesting disqualification of SEC commissioners). The Federal Maritime Commission, by regulation, defines "presiding officer" to include members of the commission itself. *See* 46 C.F.R. § 502.25.

273 *See, e.g.*, Goldberg v. Kelly, 397 U.S. 254, 271 (1970) (holding an impartial decision maker is an essential due process requirement in administrative proceedings).

274 *See, e.g.*, Berkshire Employees Ass'n of Berkshire Knitting Mills v. NLRB, 121 F.2d 235, 238–39 (3d Cir. 1941) (reiterating that administrative bodies operate in a different fashion from courts, although

legislative, executive, and quasi-judicial functions simultaneously. If an administrative system is to function without a duplication of personnel or a cloning of politically accountable officials, the mere performance of all three functions by agency members should not, and does not, standing alone, violate due process. The leading Supreme Court case is *Withrow v. Larkin*,[275] deciding that the combination of prosecuting and decisional powers in the same agency does not constitute denial of due process. As the Third Circuit has pointed out:

> It is perfectly clear that the exercise of its duties by an administrative body must necessarily proceed in a different fashion from the orthodox method of administering justice in courts. This administrative body must at times be successively or simultaneously investigator, complainant, prosecutor, trier of facts, declarer of law and administrator, all in the same matter.[276]

Second, agencies are program-oriented institutions that possess substantial discretion in the administration of their duties. They have a responsibility for deciding individual cases within a broad statutory and policy context. Agency members frequently seek agency positions (or are selected for them) precisely because they are experts in the field or hold views on how the agency's statutory responsibilities should be administered. The Supreme Court has recognized that an administrative officer may have an underlying philosophy in approaching a case that does not rise to the level of bias.[277] Applying that concept, the Supreme Court, in a leading case, concluded that the views expressed by members of the FTC on the general illegality of a pricing system did not disqualify them from sitting in judgment on a particular use of that system in a specific industry.[278]

The public benefits when a decision-maker's views are known rather than concealed. So an underlying philosophy of regulation, even publicly articulated, does not ordinarily rise to a level of bias that would violate due process principles. Indeed, in an oft-quoted phrase, the Seventh Circuit has observed that a total absence of preconceptions "would

---

administrative procedures may not involve "too violent a departure" from principles of fair play). *But see* Faulkner Radio Inc. v. FCC, 557 F.2d 866, 872 (D.C. Cir. 1977) (analogizing the bias requirements applicable to federal judges to those applicable to administrative decision-makers in administrative proceedings "of... importance and vast potential consequences."

275 421 U.S. 35, 58 (1975).

276 *Berkshire Employees Ass'n*, 121 F.2d at 238.

277 United States v. Morgan, 313 U.S. 409, 421 (1941). *See also* Kessel Food Markets, Inc. v. NLRB, 868 F.2d 881, 888 (6th Cir. 1989) (commenting that an agency may find reasonable cause for seeking injunction against respondent and subsequently adjudicating merits of case).

278 FTC v. Cement Industries, 333 U.S. 683, 700 (1948). *See also* Skelly Oil Co. v. FPC, 375 F.2d 6, 18 (10th Cir. 1967) (finding no basis for disqualification where member of administrative agency entered proceeding with "advance views on important economic matters in issue"), *modified on other grounds sub nom.* Permian Basin Area Rate Cases, 390 U.S. 747 (1968).

be evidence of a lack of qualification[s] not lack of bias."[279] Gellhorn and Levin have pithily stated: "[T]he law has generally demonstrated a keen awareness that an agency decisionmaker should be open minded, but not empty headed."[280]

Bias can be characterized as either structural or personal. Structural bias arises when there is an appearance of unfairness arising from the circumstances affecting a decision-maker even if he or she is not, in fact, biased. Personal bias arises from a decision-maker's individual prejudices or preferences.

The most common form of structural bias is a financial stake in the outcome of a proceeding. In such circumstances, disqualification is not merely required in the interest of fairness.[281] The federal criminal statutes impose sanctions on any federal officer or employee, including members of independent agencies, who "participates personally and substantially" in a proceeding or matter in which he or she (or certain members of his or her family) "has a financial interest."[282] Agency members, as well as their staffs, are also prohibited from participating in certain cases by the government-wide provisions of the Ethics in Government Act of 1978,[283] and related statutes, including those sections dealing with conflicts of interest and impartiality. Many agency organic statutes also contain additional conflict-of-interest provisions that prohibit both agency members and staff from participating in proceedings in which their impartiality may be suspect.

However, cases in which an agency official actually participates in a proceeding in which he or she has a financial interest or had a prior involvement are now infrequent. The rigorous screening conducted by the White House counsel's office, the Office of Government Ethics, and the agency's ethics officer, during the appointment process go a long way toward ensuring that any agency official who is nominated by the president will not derive personal gain from the position.

Prior personal involvement in a proceeding in an adversary capacity can also result in the appearance of bias sufficient to justify disqualification. Five federal agency cases involving multimember agencies reveal an interesting spectrum of prior involvements deemed sufficient to warrant disqualification in an adjudication. In *Amos Treat & Co. v. SEC*,[284] an SEC commissioner was prohibited from deciding a case involving the revocation of a company's registration where he had actively participated in launching the investigation while a member of the commission's staff. In *Berkshire Employees Ass'n*

---

279 Mattes v. United States, 721 F.2d 1125, 1132 (7th Cir. 1983) (quoting Laird v. Tatum, 409 U.S. 824, 835 (1972) (Rehnquist, J.) (memorandum denying motion to disqualify)).

280 Ernest Gellhorn & Ronald M. Levin, Administrative Law and Process in A Nutshell 277 (4th ed. 1997).

281 *See, e.g.*, Gibson v. Berryhill, 411 U.S. 564, 577 (1973) (involving state licensing board that was deemed to be biased and therefore unable to fairly adjudicate issues before it).

282 18 U.S.C.§ 208.

283 Pub. L. No. 95-521, 92 Stat. 1824 (codified as amended in 5 U.S.C. app. at 1400 (1994)).

284 306 F.2d 260 (D.C. Cir. 1962).

v. NLRB,[285] an NLRB member was disqualified because he had apparently supported the union's position before an unfair labor practice case had actually begun. The court characterized the individual's actions as "comparable to the situation of a lawyer who has represented a client in an endeavor to get a settlement of a claim and, before the claim is settled, is appointed to the bench and sits in the very case as judge."[286] In *American General Insurance Co. v. FTC*,[287] an FTC member was prevented from participating because he had previously participated as the agency's general counsel in related court proceedings involving the same parties. In *Trans World Airlines v. CAB*,[288] a Civil Aeronautics Board member was prohibited from participating in a decision involving mail pay where he had earlier signed a brief in the case as solicitor for the Post Office Department, even though he had never, in fact, reviewed the brief. Finally, in *American Cyanamid Co. v. FTC*,[289] the Sixth Circuit found that an FTC chair who had previously been chief counsel to a congressional committee was barred from participating in a subsequent FTC proceeding because he had played what the court described as "an active role" supervising the congressional committee's investigation of the same parties and same issues involved in the FTC proceeding, including examining witnesses, and had clearly reached conclusions on issues now before the FTC. The *American Cyanamid* decision was subsequently distinguished by the Ninth Circuit in a case involving the same FTC chairman.[290] While the facts of the two cases have numerous parallels, the Ninth Circuit appears to have believed that the chair played a somewhat less active role in the latter case.

As suggested in the cases above, the prior involvement with a proceeding must ordinarily be personal in order to rise to the level of bias. The courts have allowed an agency member to participate in a decisional capacity in a case handled by the staff component in which the member had been an employee where he had no personal connection with the case.[291]

When bias results from personal preferences or prejudices, the courts have adapted concepts of judicial bias to the administrative arena. When an agency is engaged in formal adjudication, most closely resembling dispute resolution as practiced by judges, the courts have created a definition of bias closely resembling that applicable to judges. Allegations of personal bias in adjudicatory proceedings principally arise because agency members are, like judges, supposed to determine the case from the facts presented in the proceeding. As a general matter, a federal judge must disqualify himself "in any proceeding in which his impartiality might reasonably be questioned," where he has a "personal

---

285 121 F.2d 235 at 238–39.

286 *Id.* at 239.

287 589 F.2d 462 (9th Cir. 1979).

288 254 F.2d 90 (D.C. Cir. 1958).

289 363 F.2d 757 (6th Cir. 1966).

290 Safeway Stores, Inc. v. FTC, 366 F.2d 795, 801–02 (9th Cir. 1966), *cert. denied*, 386 U.S. 932 (1967).

291 R. A. Holman & Co. v. SEC, 366 F.2d 446 (2d Cir. 1966), *cert. denied*, 389 U.S. 991 (1967); Au Yi Lau v. Immigration and Naturalization Service, 555 F.2d 1036 (D.C. Cir. 1977).

bias or prejudice concerning a party, or personal knowledge of disputed facts" or has an interest "that could be substantially affected by the outcome of the proceeding."[292] Typically, an agency member is alleged to reveal his or her bias when he or she speaks out forcefully on issues or matters pending before the agency, especially when he or she refers to a particular pending proceeding. The classic disqualification standard applicable in formal administrative adjudications was set forth in *Cinderella Career and Finishing Schools, Inc. v. FTC*: "[t]he test for disqualification [is] whether 'a disinterested observer may concluded that [a decision-maker] has in some measure adjudged the facts as well as the law of a particular case in advance of hearing it.'"[293] In *Cinderella*, in a speech to the National Congress of Petroleum Retailers, FTC Chairman Paul Rand Dixon used one of Cinderella's advertising claims to illustrate a case of possible fraud. The court ruled that Chairman Dixon was disqualified because he had prejudged, or at least appeared to have prejudged, specific facts at issue in an adjudication still pending before him. That test has been frequently applied.[294] But one court refused to find an agency member biased simply because he had disparaged one of the parties in an unrelated proceeding.[295]

The mere exposure to facts as part of an agency member's official duties, apart from adjudication, will not require disqualification.[296] Similarly, having a preconceived position concerning legal or policy issues, which an agency member has acquired while carrying out other duties, will not ordinarily result in disqualification.[297] And providing information to Congress or the public regarding the activities or policies of an agency in general, without making reference to a particular case or a group of potential targets of investigation, most likely does not rise to the level of bias.[298]

The courts have been unwilling to impose the strict *Cinderella* standard when agencies are engaged in informal rulemaking proceedings of a policy nature.[299] For example, in *Association of National Advertisers v. FTC*,[300] FTC Chair Pertschuk spoke out strongly and often about the evils of certain children's advertising, and even committed

---

292 28 U.S.C. § 455(a), (b).

293 425 F.2d 583, 591 (D.C. Cir. 1970) (quoting Gilligan, Will & Co. v. SEC, 267 F.2d 461, 469 (2d Cir. 1959)).

294 *See, e.g.*, Nuclear Information and Resource Service et al. v. NRC, 509 F.3d 562, 571 (D.C. Cir. 2007), Antoniu v. SEC, 877 F.2d 721, 726 (8th Cir. 1989), *cert. denied*, 494 U.S. 1004 (1990).

295 Nuclear Info. & Resource Serv. v. NRC, 509 F.3d 562, 571 (D.C. Cir. 2007).

296 *See* Hortonville Joint Sch. Dist. No. 1 v. Hortonville Educ. Ass'n, 426 U.S. 482, 497 (1976) (holding that the board's familiarity with the case was not sufficient to "overcome the [board's] presumption of honesty and integrity").

297 *See Cement Inst.*, 333 U.S. 683, at 701 (stating that information acquired through an ex parte investigation did not automatically result in bias).

298 American Medical Ass'n v. FTC, 638 F.2d 443 (2d Cir. 1980).

299 *See* Association of Nat'l Advertisers, 627 F.2d at 1168–69 ("The *Cinderella* view of a natural and detached adjudicator is simply an inapposite role model for an administrator who must translate broad statutory commands into concrete social policies.") The *Cinderella* test was not applied to the FTC's hybrid rulemaking. Harry & Bryan & Co. v. FTC, 726 F. 2d 983, 998–99 (4th Cir. 1984).

300 627 F.2d 1151 (D.C. Cir. 1979), *cert. denied*, 447 U.S. 921 (1980).

to ending the practice, but was not disqualified. A court will only disqualify an agency decision-maker when there has been a clear and convincing showing that the agency member has an unalterably closed mind on matters critical to the disposition of the proceeding.[301] Judge MacKinnon has argued that the unalterably closed mind assumption would be "practically impossible to prove,"[302] and he appears to have been correct.[303]

In a thorough discussion of the tension between responsibility for agency action by politically accountable officials, and impermissible bias, Richard Pierce argues that agency decision-makers should never be disqualified from participating in rulemaking proceedings simply because they express strong views on the policy issues to be resolved.[304] Indeed, Pierce contends that the articulation of an agency official's views, even with regard to matters at issue in adjudications, has a salutary effect. It helps the regulated sector understand the agency's policies so that they can shape their conduct accordingly.[305] However, Pierce perceives little harm in the *Cinderella* approach because, as a practical matter, agency officials are careful to use methods of expressing their policy views other than citing to pending adjudications.[306]

Courts do not ordinarily impute bias by an individual agency member to the agency as a whole provided the biased individual does not participate in the decision. In a case in which successive chairs of the SEC recused themselves from participating because of their prior involvement with one of the parties, the court decided that the remaining commissioners could decide the case impartially despite the potential embarrassment to their recused colleagues from their decision.[307] However, in *Antoniu v. SEC*,[308]

---

301 *See* Association of Nat'l Advertisers, 627 F.2d at 1154 (holding the *Cinderella* standard inapplicable).

302 *Id.* at 1181 (MacKinnon, J., concurring and dissenting).

303 *See* 3 Kenneth Culp Davis, Administrative Law Treatise 374–75 (2d ed. 1980) (agreeing that the closed mind standard is impossible to prove). *But see* Northwestern Bell Tel. Co. v. Stofferhahn, 461 N.W.2d 129, 134–35 (S.D. 1990) (applying the "unalterably closed mind test" to disqualify a state regulatory commissioner who opposed deregulation from participating in any proceeding involving issues of "deregulation, classification, or competitive status determination of telecommunication services" where U.S. West Communications was a party). Davis also suggests that the proper distinction lies in the nature of the fact alleged to have been prejudged, not in the nature of the proceeding. He calls the *Cinderella* case "[a]n outstanding example of disqualification for prejudgment of adjudicative facts." Davis, *supra*, at 382. He notes that the leading case of *FTC v. Cement Institute*, 333 U.S. 683 (1948), where the FTC issued cease-and-desist orders against seventy-four companies, involved so-called legislative facts, not adjudicative facts, such that "the question whether the Commission's proceeding was adjudication or rulemaking was of no consequence." Davis, *supra*, at 414.

304 *See* Richard J. Pierce, Jr., *Political Control Versus Impermissible Bias in Agency Decisionmaking: Lessons from* Chevron *and* Mistretta, 57 U. Chi. L. Rev. 481, 488–89 (1990).

305 *See id.* at 489–90.

306 *See id.* at 494–95; *see also* Recommendation 80-4 of the Administrative Conference of the United States, Decisional Officials' Participation in Rulemaking Proceedings, 45 Fed. Reg. 46,777 (1980) (reporting that disqualification for prejudgment in rulemaking should be limited to prejudgments of material "adjudicative" or "specific" facts where the agency's factual determination is based on an evidentiary record).

307 MFS Securities Corp. v. SEC, 380 F.3d 611, 618 (2d Cir. 2004).

308 877 F.2d 721, 726 (8th Cir. 1989), *cert. denied*, 494 U.S. 1004 (1990).

a commissioner gave a speech that made reference to a particular proceeding pending before the agency that the court believed had prejudged the issues in the pending proceeding. Even though he later recused himself from participation in the proceeding, the court struck down all decisions made by the SEC prior to his recusal.

5. THEORY OF POLITICAL CONTACTS AND INDEPENDENCE

Efforts to influence members of independent agencies can often come from members of Congress or administration officials, including the president, who may attempt to sway the agency's decision, either through the public submission of views or via some type of off-the-record contact. Up to a point, efforts to influence or superintend agency activity is a recognized part of the oversight process by elected officials. As the District of Columbia Circuit commented in *Sierra Club v. Costle*:

> Americans rightly expect their elected representatives to voice their grievances and preferences concerning the administration of our laws. We believe it entirely proper for Congressional representatives to represent the interests of their constituents before administrative agencies engaged in informal, general policy rulemaking, so long as individual Congressmen do not frustrate the intent of Congress as a whole as expressed in statute, nor undermine applicable rules of procedure. Where Congressmen keep their comments focused on the substance of the proposed rule... administrative agencies are expected to balance Congressional pressure with the pressures emanating from all other sources. To hold otherwise would deprive the agencies of legitimate sources of information and call into question the validity of nearly every controversial rulemaking.[309]

Public pronouncements, including speeches in Congress or the public filing of documents with the agency, have not posed legal problems. Communications implicate considerations of fairness in two circumstances. First, if political involvement is off the record, that is, it involves communications with the agency not known to the participants in the proceeding or subject to effective rebuttal, it plainly endangers the transparency of the agency's proceeding. The Ninth Circuit struck down an agency decision in a formal proceeding where decision-makers had received ex parte communications from members of the president's staff.[310] Second, political involvement can encourage the agency to decide a matter based on factors not included in a statute as relevant to the agency's consideration. A reliance on impermissible factors renders an agency decision arbitrary.[311] Nonetheless, the courts have taken a highly practical view

---

[309] 657 F.2d 298, 409–10 (D.C. Cir. 1981).

[310] Portland Audubon Society v. Endangered Species Comm., 984 F.2d 1534 (9th Cir. 1993).

[311] *See* Motor Vehicle Mfrs. Ass'n v. State Farm Mut. Aut. Ins. Co., 463 U.S. 29, 46 (1983).

of the relationship between agencies and their political overseers. Outside the context of formal proceedings, at least, the courts now require not merely that congressional committees or members have made statements potentially affecting particular administrative proceedings but that such statements have actually affected the decisional process. That standard is difficult, but not impossible, to prove. In *D.C. Federation of Civic Associations v. Volpe*,[312] the court struck down a decision by the secretary of transportation to approve construction of a bridge where it appeared that the secretary's decision might have rested, at least in part, on threats by members of Congress to cut off funding to particular projects if the bridge was not approved. More typical are *Radio Ass'n on Defending Airwave Rights, Inc. v. U.S. Department of Transportation*, where the court asserted that a congressional committee had "merely expressed its displeasure that the agency had not taken action in the eighteen months since [a notice of proposed rulemaking]... was issued";[313] *Gulf Oil Corp. v. Federal Power Comm'n*,[314] where the court characterized the congressional interest as directed more toward the agency's processes (the case had taken too long to decide) and legal rather than factual matters, and that any "incidental intrusions" did not actually affect the agency's substantive decision; and *Sierra Club v. Costle*,[315] where the court indicated that a rulemaking proceeding would not be set aside as long as influential members of Congress "keep their comments focused on the substance of the proposed rule."

The APA has explicit prohibitions against ex parte contacts that affect all agencies and complement the law of bias. Such provisions prohibit "[an] interested person outside the agency" from communicating off the record with any agency official, whether a member of the staff or a political appointee, "who is or may reasonably be expected to be involved in the decisional process of the proceeding."[316] They also prohibit any decisional official within the agency from making an ex parte communication to "any interested person outside the agency."[317] Because they are included in Section 557, they are applicable only to formal proceedings, and the courts have recognized the distinction between the agency's activity as adjudicator and rulemaker. The Fifth Circuit's decision in the leading case of *Pillsbury Company v. FTC*[318] established the proposition that the courts can set aside an agency's decision in a formal adjudication where it appears that agency members were

---

312 459 F.2d 1231 (D.C. Cir. 1971).

313 47 F.3d 794, 807 (6th Cir. 1995).

314 563 F.2d 588, 611 (3d Cir. 1977).

315 657 F.2d 298, 409–10 (D.C. Cir. 1981).

316 Administrative Procedure Act § 6(a), 5 U.S.C. § 557(d)(1)(A)

317 *Id.* § 5(c), § 557(d)(1)(B); *see also* Professional Air Traffic Controllers Org. v. FLRA, 685 F.2d 547, 562 (D.C. Cir. 1982) (defining "interested person" broadly to include "any individual or other person with an interest in the agency proceeding that is greater than the general interest the public as a whole may have"). It would seem that anyone with sufficient concern to contact the agency on the merits of a case would qualify as an "interested person."

318 354 F.2d 952 (5th Cir. 1966).

unduly influenced by a congressional investigation of a case pending before the agency.[319] Since the high-water mark of the *Pillsbury* case, however, courts have been exceedingly reluctant to condemn members of Congress when they openly express their views to agencies. Courts appreciate that members of Congress and the administration cannot be prevented from attempting to influence agency decisions. The Seventh Circuit referred to the *Pillsbury* decision as "an extreme case" of congressional interference.[320]

The prohibitions on congressional and executive branch intervention in formal adjudicatory proceedings, as outlined in *Pillsbury*, do not extend to less formal agency adjudicatory activity. Examining an agency's prehearing informal activities, the Fifth Circuit observed that the test (at least in such circumstances) should be whether the congressional contacts urged the agency to rely on factors that are not relevant under the statute[321]—a standard with which an agency's skilled professional writing staff should easily be able to deal.

Ex parte contacts in a rulemaking proceeding are not prohibited by the APA. Nonetheless, in *Home Box Office, Inc. v. FCC*,[322] the D.C. Circuit appeared to change the law by concluding that ex parte contacts impermissibly compromised the court's obligation to review an agency's decision based on the body of material contained in the paper record.[323] Shortly thereafter, in *Action for Children's Television v. FCC*,[324] the D.C. Circuit confined its *Home Box Office* ruling to ex parte prohibitions in rulemaking proceedings that involved competing private claims to a valuable privilege, that is, when they resembled adjudicatory proceedings.[325] That limitation is now clearly established.[326]

As a practical matter, most agencies maintain some form of public "ex parte file" for the receipt of "off-the-record" comments, including those from officials of the legislative and executive branches. Such file is not part of the record for decisional purposes.[327] However, the availability of such a file gives members of Congress a useful vehicle for

---

319 *See id.* at 964 (stating that Congress is intervening in agency's judicial function when investigation focuses on mental processes of commission).

320 Monieson v. CFTC, 996 F.2d 852, 865 (7th Cir. 1993).

321 *See DCP Farms*, 957 F.2d at 1187–88 (stating aim of congressional communication was not to influence decision-making body).

322 567 F.2d 9 (D.C. Cir. 1977).

323 *See id.* at 58 (stating that the commission should hold all evidentiary material so that a hearing examiner can determine the nature and source of the ex parte pleas).

324 564 F.2d 458 (D.C. Cir.1977).

325 *See id.* at 477 (holding that the communications were not of the kind susceptible to ex parte influence).

326 *See, e.g.*, Sierra Club v. Costle, 657 F.2d 298, 400, 401 (D.C. Cir. 1981); United Steelworkers of Am. v. Marshall, 647 F.2d 1189, 1215 (D.C. Cir. 1980) (stating that the proceedings in this case are distinguished from those that resolve "'conflicting private claims to a valuable privilege'" or are "'quasi-adjudicatory'" proceedings) (internal citations omitted).

327 *See, e.g.*, 16 C.F.R. 4.7(c) (3) (stating ex parte regulations of the FTC). *See generally* JEFFREY S. LUBBERS, A GUIDE TO FEDERAL AGENCY RULEMAKING 231–33 (3d ed. 1998) (explaining that independent regulatory agencies appear to have the most restrictive rules regarding ex parte contacts in rulemaking proceedings).

transmitting constituent views or even their own opinions. The file also accords agencies a respectful way to acknowledge off-the-record submissions by noting that they have been placed in a public file, without compromising the integrity of the agency's proceedings.[328]

Agencies cannot prevent outsiders from initiating an ex parte communication. That being so, courts sensibly demand simply that agencies follow their own rules on ex parte contacts and attempt (as best they can) to resist off-the-record pressure, even in an adjudication. *ATX, Inc. v. Department of Transportation*[329] is a good illustration of an agency's response to congressional pressure that received strong judicial endorsement. In *ATX*, the former chief executive of Eastern Air Lines during a period of tumultuous labor–management relations, filed an application with the DOT to establish a new airline. At the urging of labor unions, over sixty members of Congress, including key committee chairs, wrote strong letters to the secretary of transportation requesting that he deny the application. Two members of Congress introduced legislation to prevent the individual from reentering the business. The secretary ordered that the application be set for public hearing before an agency ALJ and that the final decision be made by the department's senior career official. The secretary also responded to the congressional communications with a form letter indicating that "it would be inappropriate for me to discuss the merits of the case with you," that the congressional correspondence would be placed in the "ex parte file," and noting that the application would be thoroughly reviewed. Following the hearing, at which one congressman actually testified, the decisional official, the deputy assistant secretary, a career civil servant serving temporarily as acting assistant secretary, rendered a seventy-five-page opinion based entirely on the public record.[330] That was about all the agency could do considering the circumstances, and the court upheld its decision even though the agency had denied the application, which was what the members of Congress had requested. It was probably helpful to the agency's position in court that the agency had affirmed its ALJ's decision. However, as long as the agency had taken proper account of the presiding officer's decision, and had reached a reasonable result supported by the evidence, the agency was entitled to make its own independent assessment of the facts and substitute its judgment for that of the ALJ.[331] It represents a utilitarian accommodation between agencies and their congressional overseers.

---

328 *See* 15 Op. Off. Legal Counsel 5 (1991) (discussing ex parte communications between White House officials and FCC commissioners during FCC rulemaking).

329 41 F.3d 1522 (D.C. Cir. 1994).

330 41 F.3d at 1523–32.

331 *Compare* Universal Camera Corp. v. NLRB, 340 U.S. 474 (1951) (the agency must evaluate, but need not agree with, an ALJ's decision) *and* Valkering, U.S.A., Inc. v. Dep't of Agriculture, 48 F.3d 305, 308–09 (8th Cir. 1995) (holding that secretary of agriculture, reviewing the decision of an ALJ, is authorized to substitute his judgment for that of the ALJ).

a. Agency Supervision of Its Members

It is not entirely clear if multimember agencies have a collegial obligation to evaluate one of their own members to determine if he or she should be disqualified from a proceeding. The legislative history of the APA suggests that the agency's power to disqualify is limited to its presiding officers.[332] But permitting a "biased" agency member to participate in a case can clearly call the agency's substantive decision into question. For example, in *Berkshire Employees Association v. NLRB*,[333] the court determined that the litigants were entitled to an unbiased tribunal, but recognized that it was impossible to determine if one member influenced his or her colleagues. In these circumstances, the agency was required to "determine for itself" whether one of its members should be disqualified from participation.[334] On remand, the agency vacated its original decision and reexamined the issues anew. By that time, however, the allegedly biased member had left the agency, and two new members had been appointed. So the agency never determined whether the member should have been disqualified. The court was satisfied that it was no longer required to do so.[335]

Only a handful of agencies have regulations that explicitly address whether the agency may independently determine whether one of its members should be disqualified from participation in a particular case. Agencies that have considered the matter have taken different positions. Most agencies, such as the SEC, provide that the decision to disqualify a member from a proceeding "rests with that individual member."[336] Despite its general rule, in at least one case the SEC collectively investigated allegations of bias after the two commissioners against whom the allegations were brought voluntarily agreed to have their colleagues assess their culpability.[337] The FTC's regulations, however, allow the commission to examine the issue itself in the event that the commissioner in question declines to recuse himself or herself from the proceeding,[338] The FTC has exercised this authority.[339] However, whether it will exercise its authority depends on the type of proceeding involved. See *In the Matter of Intel Corp.*,[340] noting that the commission's

---

332 *See* S. Doc. No. 79-248, at 206–07, 268–69 (1946).

333 121 F.2d 235 (3d Cir. 1941).

334 *See id.* at 239.

335 Berkshire Knitting Mills v. NLRB, 139 F.2d 134, 136–37 (3d Cir. 1943). But see, more recently, *Overnite Transportation Company*, 329 N.L.R.B. 990 n.1 (1999), where the NLRB as an agency ruled on a motion to disqualify.

336 17 C.F.R. § 200.60.

337 *See* United Corp., 32 S.E.C. 633, 634 n.3 (1951).

338 *See*, 16 C.F.R. § 4.17(b)(3)(ii)

339 *See, e.g., In re* Intel Corp., 2010 FTC LEXIS 8 (2010), considering, but rejecting, a motion to disqualify one of the commissioners, and *see, e.g.*, In the Matter of Jim Walter Corp., 88 F.T.C. 765 (1976), exercising its authority but declining to order disqualification. *Compare* Lone Star Airways, 97 C.A.B. 642, 642 (1982) (considering—and rejecting—an allegation of bias lodged against member of former Civil Aeronautics Board).

340 2010 FTC LEXIS 8 (Jan. 19, 2010).

rules require its consideration of the motion to disqualify only with respect to an adjudication, not with respect to the issue of whether a complaint should be filed; recusal in the latter context is left to the individual commissioner.

Allowing individual agency members to make their own recusal or disqualification decisions is a sensible result. Whether made by the agency or the individual agency member, the decision is reviewable by the courts in the normal course of judicial review. So an affected party gets full judicial scrutiny. There is, of course, the risk that leaving the decision in the hands of the individual member may lead to delay if a court ultimately reverses the agency's substantive decision. But requiring the agency itself to make the decision necessarily pits one agency member against his or her colleagues at a personal level, seriously disrupting collegiality. It may also unnecessarily embroil the agency staff—especially the general counsel—in an internecine battle. And it will encourage an agency member on the short end of a contentious policy issue to ask for staff or agency examination simply as a delaying tactic.

b. Recusal

Neither the APA nor case law indicates whether, and in what circumstances, an agency official who is not legally disqualified from a matter should nevertheless exercise his or her discretion not to participate in the interest of avoiding an appearance of conflict of interest. The principal court decision that evaluates an agency member's discretionary decision not to recuse is *Center for Auto Safety v. FTC*.[341] Judge Harold Greene reviewed the recusal policies of several high-level government officials and determined that the then chair of the FTC did not abuse his discretion in declining to recuse himself from a proceeding involving a former client.[342] Judge Greene indicated that "[a]bsent an abuse of discretion, the decision with regard to recusal is that of the official who is directly involved."[343] The D.C. Circuit has confirmed this "abuse of discretion" standard.[344]

Agency members plainly have different philosophies regarding recusal. Former FTC commissioner Everette MacIntyre's decision in the *National Biscuit Co.* case[345] manifested a determination not to let his participation delay the resolution of a case. In like

---

[341] 586 F. Supp. 1245 (D.D.C. 1984).

[342] *See id.* at 1251 (holding that FTC chair's favorable references and relationship with automobile manufacturer and related testimony given before Congress was not improper participation).

[343] *Id.* at 1250.

[344] Air Line Pilots Ass'n Int'l v. Dep't of Transportation, 899 F.2d 1230, 1232 (D.C. Cir. 1990). *See also* Metro. Council of NAACP Branches v. FCC, 46 F.3d 1154, 1164 (D.C. Cir. 1995) (applying a "deferential, abuse of discretion" standard) (citing Air Line Pilots Ass'n Int'l v. DOT, 899 F.2d 1230, 1231–32 (D.C. Cir. 1990) (finding cabinet secretary's participation in decision declining to investigate client of prospective employer not an abuse of discretion where prospective employer did not represent the client in the proceeding before the cabinet secretary).

[345] National Biscuit Co., 79 F.T.C. 264 (1971).

fashion, the decision of the National Transportation Safety Board chair, John Reed, not to participate in a particular proceeding revealed an intention to avoid even "a scintilla of doubt in the minds of some that my impartiality is in question ... and to assure that not even the slightest question can be raised regarding the objectivity of any Board decision."[346] In contrast, former NRC chair Nunzio Palladino refused to step down in the *Long Island Lighting Co.* proceeding[347] because he feared that if he did so, he would "[appear] to give credence to an accusation that aims baseless charges of impropriety not just at me" but at other NRC officials as well.[348] A student note suggests that agency members tend to recuse themselves from proceedings out of an abundance of caution—even when they need not. The note observes, with particular reference to the FTC: "At the root of the problem is the lack of any uniform statutory standard for administrative recusal, leaving members of the FTC and other executive agencies to formulate their own unarticulated and fluctuating standards. This lack of uniform standard has resulted in recent years in over-recusal among FTC Commissioners, causing many cases to be decided by fewer than the traditional quorum and skewing the careful political balance on the Commission."[349]

C. Observations

Little attention has been paid to the "law" of internal procedures among the various independent agencies. But it should be obvious that questions of the control of internal procedures will impact considerably not only on agency management and efficiency, but on agency independence.

In particular, the power to select the chair and the ability of the chair to control the agency agenda are factors of great significance. And as this chapter makes clear, in the post–World War II era, various executive reorganization plans gave the chair increased power over an agency's agenda and its internal operations.[350]

Direct contacts between the political branches and agency officials, especially in individual cases, can be viewed as violations of agency independence. The broad notion of independence is that the president chooses the agency members, particularly the chair, because of a consonance between their views and the president's views on issues dealt with by the agency, and the Senate approves those selections. However, as explained in chapter 4, other factors, including the influence of members of Congress, now bear heavily on presidential appointments. Importantly, once new members "sail off" in the

346 Air East, Inc., 2 N.T.S.B. 929 (1974).

347 20 N.R.C. 1061 (1984).

348 *Id.* at 1062–63.

349 Kelly M. Falls, Note, *A Quorum of One: Redefining Recusal Standards in the Federal Trade Commission*, 19 Geo. J. Legal Ethics 705, 706 (2006).

350 *See supra* notes 46–54 and accompanying text.

general direction urged upon them by the president or their congressional or other sponsors, they ordinarily maintain radio silence. The consequence of this silence is that they lack the kind of reinforcement or midcourse correction provided to an executive branch official.

Agency chairs have structural tools that give them some advantages in advancing a particular agenda. They ordinarily select and control the staff and the agency's agenda, and Sunshine Act requirements can inhibit, although not prevent, other members from uniting against a chair. But as much can depend on the personality of the relevant players and an agency's tradition regarding chairmanic leadership. And insurgent groups do, in any event, arise from time to time. Equally important, informal institutional agreements typically guide various aspects of the day-to-day workings of agencies, particularly multimember agencies, sometimes resulting in a diffusion of authority. Most internal procedures reflect pragmatic agreement or acquiescence among the members over time, with such arrangements only rarely altered, or even examined, by newly arriving members. The lack of explicit statutory provisions governing most internal agency operations accords agencies a degree of freedom to adopt innovative arrangements regarding quorums to permit decision-making when agencies are not at full strength, with only the rare judicial intervention. These arrangements, and the idiosyncratic understandings regarding disqualification and recusal, can alter the collegial or political balance and independence anticipated by Congress. To be sure, both Congress and the president retain certain oversight tools. And agency chairs remain key directors of policy at many agencies. But, in given cases, or categories of cases, the practicalities of day-to-day administration, and the discretion accorded agencies to fashion their internal procedures, can place effective decisional power in the hands of one or at most a minority of agency members, who can, if they wish, act largely independently of any external political will.

Another subject that requires some mention is the effect of a collegial operation on a board's or commission's decision-making. The experience of the Sunshine Act has underscored how public meetings can at times reduce the possibilities of moderation and result in more extreme positions (at least for public consumption). This insight runs counter to the generally held notion that multimember organizations are a mechanism for moderating agency behavior because the multiplicity of members reduces the swings that would ordinarily occur between different political administrations.

Our study has underscored the value of the comparative analysis of independent agency internal procedures. Our emphasis has been on the comparison of agency regulations and procedures. But more work is needed, much of it empirical, to better understand how independent agencies operate.

10

The Independent Agency as an Institutional Art Form

COMPARATIVE EXAMPLES

A. Introduction

Administrative law scholarship in the United States understandably focuses on domestic rather than comparative elements.[1] Much American work in the field, at least, proceeds from the view that our unique constitutional framework bears heavily on questions of the metes and bounds of agency independence. And it does. Still it is worth considering the extent to which centralization and its attendant mode—bureaucratization—may or may not be the future of regulation in governments globally, and even multinationally or supranationally.

A quick glance through the recent publication *Government Agencies: Practices and Lessons from 30 Countries*,[2] put out by the European Cooperation in Science and Technology, a multinational group for the coordination of nationally funded research, makes abundantly clear that bodies possessing at least some degree of autonomy can be found in countries around the world. However, the concept of an "independent agency" differs from country to country—there is clearly no "one size fits all" independent or

---

[1] *But see generally* BERNARD SCHWARTZ & H. W. R. WADE, LEGAL CONTROL OF GOVERNMENT: ADMINISTRATIVE LAW IN BRITAIN AND THE UNITED STATES (1972); BERNARD SCHWARTZ, FRENCH ADMINISTRATIVE LAW AND THE COMMON-LAW WORLD (1954) (comparing French, English, and American administrative law); MARTIN SHAPIRO, INDEPENDENT AGENCIES: US AND EU (Jean Monnet Chair Papers No. 34, The Robert Schuman Centre, European Univ. Inst., 1996).

[2] GOVERNMENT AGENCIES: PRACTICES AND LESSONS FROM 30 COUNTRIES (Koen Verhoest, Sandra Van Thiel, Geert Bouckaert & Per Lægreid, eds. 2012) [hereinafter GOVERNMENT AGENCIES].

semiautonomous agency model.[3] In many cases, countries appear to hold their independent agencies to greater political (ministerial) accountability. Independent agencies around the world, although clearly not identical, nonetheless have, as a central characteristic, the fact that they "operate at arm's length of the government to carry out public tasks, implement policies, regulate markets and policy sectors, or deliver public services,"[4] but are often not totally independent because "in many cases political executives have ultimate political responsibility for their activities."[5]

Such agencies have evolved with different characteristics. They have greater or lesser decisional independence.[6] The authors point out that "in the majority of the countries studied, the creation of agencies happens in a *ad hoc* way, following a case-by-case approach, rather than a systematic approach based on clear criteria and checklists,"[7] despite a scholarly desire for "a more systematic policy towards agency creation."[8] Although the countries studied may accord their independent entities somewhat less autonomy than that given to American independent agencies, they implicate in some measure the same key issue found in the United States, that is, the tension between autonomy and expertise and political accountability.[9]

There is emerging at the same time a group of institutions with jurisdiction or influence that extends beyond the realm or control of individual nation-states. For example, the transnational or supranational European Union (EU) has as one of its key political components the multifaceted European Commission, possessing significant elements of independence. The European Commission is, in large measure, the administrative and executive arm of the EU, implementing policy in a fashion not unlike American agencies. It is, for example, responsible for the enforcement of European competition law, the imposition of fines, and the control of state aid and subsidies. However, it is also a political initiator, having a significant legislative role, with considerable resemblance to a branch of government.

The EU has also developed a set of separate independent agencies that are part of the EU but not tied directly to the European Commission. Finally, there is an emerging group of specialized bodies engaged in what is described as "transgovernmental regulation and administration" in light of "globalized interdependence" that are now being studied under the rubric of "global administrative law." See the article by Benedict Kingsbury, Nico Krisch, and Richard B. Stewart, "The Emergence of Global Administrative Law"

---

3 Sandra Van Thiel, Koen Verhoest, Geert Bouckaert & Per Laegreid, *Lessons and Recommendations for the Practice of Agencification, in* GOVERNMENT AGENCIES, *supra* note 2, at 414–15.

4 GOVERNMENT AGENCIES, *supra* note 2, at 3.

5 *Id.*

6 *Id.* at 7–8.

7 Van Thiel et al., in Government Agencies, *supra* note 3, at 416.

8 *Id.* at 417.

9 GOVERNMENT AGENCIES, *supra* note 2, at 4, 7–9; Van Thiel et al., *supra* note 3, at 420, 422, 428–29.

(2005). We look briefly at illustrations of all these entities solely to suggest that the independent agency model is by no means uniquely American.

B. National Independent Entities: The United Kingdom

A review of the British system demonstrates the apparent need for independence in a major common law administrative state. There are upward of eleven hundred "semiautonomous public bodies" in the United Kingdom.[10]

The departments of the national or central government, known as departments of state, are the most political entities, and resemble U.S. cabinet departments in many respects.[11] Each department is headed by a politically accountable member of the government, usually a secretary of state, but relies on a large staff of civil servants. British secretaries of state are also members of the legislative branch.

In 1968, the Fulton Committee on the Civil Service recommended the "hiving off" of certain responsibilities from government departments to autonomous or semiautonomous institutions.[12] These "children of departments"[13] are not subject to direct political control. They are, however, subject to certain financial, policy, and performance arrangements that are formulated by the minister, the permanent secretary, and the agency head and embodied in a framework document.[14] For example, the Civil Aviation Authority was created from the Department of Trade and Industry.[15] Originally, the Civil Aviation Authority operated under the general guidance of the minister but that authority was abolished in 1980.[16] Nonetheless, there remains a right of appeal to the minister from Civil Aviation Authority decisions, although not every participant in proceedings before it may appeal.[17] The performance of these agencies is reviewed every three years.[18]

The bodies are unofficially referred to as "nondepartmental public bodies" (NDPBs) or quasi-nongovernmental organizations ("quangos"),[19] and include various regulatory boards and commissions and grant-giving agencies such as the Commission for Racial Equality and the Arts Council.[20] Former U.S. ambassador to Britain Raymond Seitz

---

[10] Oliver James, Alice Moseley, Nicolai Petrovsky & George Boyne, *United Kingdom*, *in* GOVERNMENT AGENCIES, *supra* note 2, at 57.

[11] *See* PATRICK BIRKINSHAW, GRIEVANCES, REMEDIES AND THE STATE 29–34 (2d ed. 1994).

[12] A. W. BRADLEY & K. D. EWING, CONSTITUTIONAL AND ADMINISTRATIVE LAW 303 (12th ed. 1997).

[13] BIRKINSHAW, *supra* note 11, at 26.

[14] *Id.* at 26.

[15] *See* P. P. CRAIG, ADMINISTRATIVE LAW 81–82 (3d ed. 1994).

[16] *See* BIRKINSHAW, *supra* note 11, at 165.

[17] *See id.*

[18] *See id.* at 27 (stating that they are reviewed for completion of objectives, quality of service, financial performance, and levels of efficiency).

[19] *See* BRADLEY & EWING, *supra* note 12, at 327.

[20] *See id.* at 302–03.

observes that the term "quango" is a word of American origin that never caught on in the United States, "perhaps because it sounds too much like a marsupial."[21] Numerous public corporations, such as the BBC and the British Airports Authority, were also created in an effort to remove ministers from day-to-day control of certain administrative or oversight functions.[22]

The broadest initiative to transfer power away from British government departments to independent agencies was the creation of the "Next Step" agencies. An outgrowth of the government's "Next Steps" Report in 1988,[23] these agencies reflected devolution of power to nondepartmental agencies, largely in the areas of service delivery.[24] As of 1992, there were ninety-two Next Step agencies, including the Social Security Benefits Agency, Employment Service, Passport Office, and Driver and Vehicle Licensing Agency.[25] Each has an appointed chief executive, and these agencies have been described as having "managerial autonomy" without "legal independence."[26] In other words, they operate to specified targets with ultimate accountability to ministers.[27]

British statutory tribunals (at times called authorities, commissions, committees, or tribunals) are primarily adjudicatory bodies, designed to apply an established body of rules to particular facts.[28] There are about two thousand such tribunals deciding 250,000 cases a year.[29] These tribunals have antecedents in entities going back to the seventeenth century. The Commissioners of Customs and Excise were given statutory judicial power in 1660.[30] Tribunals decide disputes involving specialty subject areas such as employer–employee relations, social security, taxes, or immigration.[31] Only a few tribunals, such as the transport licensing agencies, decide cases that involve policy issues[32] and resemble, in this respect, the U.S. multimember independent regulatory boards and commissions. Although they adjudicate private rights, they do so within a broader context of the public interest.[33]

Independent tribunals are typically headed by a president, who is responsible for the tribunal's administration.[34] He or she decides, among other things, how many individual

---

21 Raymond Seitz, Over Here 273 n.2 (1998).

22 *See* Bradley & Ewing, *supra* note 12, at 328–29.

23 *See Report to the Prime Minister from the Efficiency Unit, Improving Management in Government, the Next Steps* (HMSO 1988).

24 *See* Craig, *supra* note 15, at 83 (noting reasons for creating departmental agencies).

25 *See id.* at 84.

26 Sandra Van Thiel, *Comparing Agencies Across Countries, in* Government Agencies, *supra* note 2, at 20.

27 James et al., *supra* note 10, at 57.

28 *See* Sir William Wade & Christopher Forsyth, Administrative Law 909 (7th ed. 1994).

29 *See* Birkinshaw, *supra* note 11, at 47.

30 *See* Wade & Forsyth, *supra* note 28, at 905.

31 *See id.* at 904, 908.

32 *See id.* at 910.

33 *See* Birkinshaw, *supra* note 11, at 56.

34 *See* Craig, *supra* note 15, at 147.

tribunals should be established throughout the country.[35] Each individual tribunal is ordinarily headed by a lawyer, with laypersons as panelists.[36] The courts retain a statutory right of review from adverse tribunal decisions on "questions of law."[37] An issue in many cases is what constitutes an "issue of law." Some scholars and court decisions divide matters into legal issues and factual issues. The latter includes inferences from so-called primary facts.[38] Wade and Forsyth view the evolution of tribunals in pragmatic terms. As they see it, "[t]ribunals are subject to a law of evolution." Each is devised for the purposes of some particular statute and is, therefore, so to speak, tailor-made.[39]

Independent tribunals are justified on much the same basis as independent federal agencies. Their processes are cheaper, faster, and less formal than the generalist courts. They also possess greater subject matter expertise and may be more sympathetic to the protection of substantive interests.[40]

The British also have a highly developed system of ombudsmen. The principal ombudsman, known as the parliamentary commissioner for administration, is responsible for investigating complaints concerning administrative functions of the departments and agencies of the central government.[41] There are two principal restrictions on the ombudsman's authority. He may only entertain a complaint referred to him by a member of Parliament and may not examine the merits of an agency's discretionary decisions. He is charged, in other words, with investigating "maladministration."[42] The parliamentary commissioner for administration also serves as the ombudsman for the Health Services. However, in exercising these powers, he may entertain complaints directly from the public.[43] Finally, there are commissions that serve as ombudsmen over local government authorities and a separate ombudsman for Northern Ireland.[44]

Another "independent" structure for review of government action is the statutory inquiry.[45] The British employ the statutory inquiry as a governmental instrument that melds impartiality with political accountability. The statutory inquiry process emerged

---

35 *See id.*

36 *See id.* Membership depends on the nature of the tribunal's business. *See* WADE & FORSYTH, *supra* note 28, at 913. The so-called balanced tribunal includes a legally trained chair, appointed by the lord chancellor, and two members representing opposing interests or perspectives, such as management and labor. *See id.* On such tribunals the chair is ordinarily paid while the others serve without compensation. *See id.* Where greater expertise is required, full-time paid members may be asked to serve on the tribunal. *See id.* at 913–14.

37 *See* CRAIG, *supra* note 15, at 157.

38 *See id.*

39 WADE & FORSYTH, *supra* note 28, at 908.

40 *See* WADE & FORSYTH, *supra* note 28, at 906–07; *see also* BIRKINSHAW, *supra* note 11, at 46–50.

41 *See* CRAIG, *supra* note 15, at 127.

42 *Id.* at 129.

43 *See id.* at 134–35.

44 *See id.* at 138.

45 *See id.* at 160.

in Britain in the latter part of the nineteenth century as a means of resolving primarily local disputes between individuals and public authorities, or between authorities and the national government. Inquiries are most common in the areas of planning and development and serve as either an appeal mechanism or a vehicle for the public presentation of views before government action is taken.[46] For example, a local authority may refuse planning permission for a requested project and the losing applicant can appeal.[47] Alternatively, the public may be asked to offer its views before some form of application or request is granted.[48] Generally, an independent person (or persons) is appointed to gather the facts and report to the relevant minister. However, the minister, or one of his or her immediate associates, makes the final decision.[49]

The British agencies that most closely parallel the American independent agencies are the numerous bodies created during the Thatcher administration to supervise an increasingly privatized industrial sector. Regulatory bodies now supervise, for example, the British telecommunications and television industries (à la the American FCC), the rail industry (somewhat like the STB), and the gas and electric industries (akin to the FERC).[50] Britain has its Office of Fair Trading and a Competition Commission that conduct oversight functions not unlike those performed by the FTC.

The agencies have slightly different institutional structures. By and large, regulatory agencies are simply nondepartmental government entities.[51] Their staffs are composed of civil servants, and in some cases they have authority to assess license fees to support their operations.[52] But some are public corporations, while Britain has also created private companies with public responsibilities.[53]

Generally speaking, British regulatory officials are appointed by, and may be removed from office for good cause by, a cabinet minister accountable to Parliament. Members of the Gas and Electricity Markets Authority (Ofgem), for example, can be removed for "incapacity or misbehaviour."[54] Agencies can be abolished, and some have been over the years.[55] Agency officials can be summoned to appear before select committees of Parliament in a fashion similar to that in the United States.[56]

---

46 *See id.*

47 *See id.*

48 *Id.* at 160.

49 *See id.* at 160–61.

50 *See* Tony Prosser, *Regulation and Legitimacy, in* The Changing Constitution 315 (Jeffrey Jowell & Dawn Oliver eds., 7th ed. 2011).

51 Tony Prosser, The Regulatory Enterprise: Government, Regulation and Legitimacy 179 (2010).

52 *Id.*

53 *Id.*

54 *Id.*

55 James et al., *supra* note 10, at 63–64.

56 W. H. R. Wade & C. F. Forsyth, Administrative Law 156 (9th ed. 2004).

Tony Prosser notes two important trends regarding British agencies. First, there is "no new single paradigm" of the government regulator.[57] Some have traditional economic regulatory responsibilities with a high degree of independence while others operate with less independence where they provide services rather than regulate a private market.[58] Second, Prosser notes the gradual shift away from agencies headed by a single individual in the early years following their creation to the use of collegial bodies.[59] He observes:

> The commission model for regulation has now convincingly won in comparison to the older model of giving powers to an individual director-general. More recently, all the utility regulators have adopted a private-sector model of a board including executive and non-executive members; for example, the board of... [the Gas and Electricity Markets Authority] consists of a chairman and four executive members, together with seven non-executive members.[60]

Several broad theories have been offered to justify creation of independent entities outside the scope of the traditional British government ministries. Douglas Hague observes:

> First, there is the "buffer" theory which sees them as a way of protecting certain activities from political interference. Second, there is the "escape" theory which sees them as escaping known weaknesses of traditional government departments. Third, the "Corson" theory, following Mr. John Corson sees them as used to "put the activity where the talent was," which might be outside government departments. Fourth, there is the participation or "pluralistic" theory which thinks it desirable to spread power. Fifth, there is the "back double" theory. This is based on the analogy with a taxi-driver who finds the main streets too busy and therefore uses back streets—what is known to taxi drivers as "back doubles." The back double theory is that if governments, local authorities or other bodies find that they cannot do the things they want within the existing structure, they set up new organisations which make it possible to do them. Sixth, the "too many bureaucrats" view, mainly an American one, suggests that if the public thinks a country has too many civil servants it can set up quasi-non-governmental organisations whose employees are not classified as civil servants.[61]

---

57 Prosser, *supra* note 51, at 3.

58 *Id.*

59 *Id.* at 315–16.

60 *Id.* at 316.

61 Wade & Forsyth, *supra* note 56, at 362 (quoting Public Policy and Private Interests: The Institutions of Compromise 362 (Douglas C. Hague et al. eds., 1975)).

Patrick Birkinshaw argues that "[t]he method of regulation adopted by government over particular bodies or activities will often reflect the degree of trust with which a body or institution is held by government."[62]

The trend toward the creation of independent entities crosses party lines in Britain. When the Labour government took control in 1997, one of its hallmark policy changes was to separate the central bank from the Treasury Department and create a fully independent Bank of England, not unlike the U.S. Federal Reserve Board.[63] Following the 2010 election, the Conservative–Liberal Democrat coalition government immediately established a new Office for Budget Responsibility to provide independent growth and borrowing forecasts to replace those figures historically provided by the Treasury Department.[64] Not surprisingly, the former Labour Party chancellor criticized the suggestion that Labour had in some manner adjusted the figures to support its budgets. "The suggestion that Treasury civil servants colluded with us in publishing anything other than accurate figures is just wrong," he claimed.[65] But creation of a new independent body carried the day.

C. Supranational Agencies: European Integration and the Place of Independence

The calamity of two massive European wars in the twentieth century produced a belief in some quarters that only cooperation could stave off further conflagration. There is some suggestion that the modern scheme of European integration, and the reasons for it, date to a 1944 Draft Declaration among wartime resistance movements looking toward the reconstruction of postwar Europe. As described by Doreen Collins:

> [T]he experience of the physical destruction and moral division which Europe had brought upon itself proved the stimulus towards the creation of new forms of political organization which it was hoped would provide a more adequate setting for economic development and for the maintenance of a political order than the nation state had hitherto achieved.... [The Draft Declaration] followed a long-standing argument which links the creation of a peaceful world with the pursuit of social progress within a national community by calling for social justice

62 BIRKINSHAW, *supra* note 11, at 163.

63 *See generally* John McEldowney, *Public Expenditure and the Control of Public Finance, in* THE CHANGING CONSTITUTION (Jeffrey Jowell & Dawn Oliver eds., 7th ed. 2011).

64 Suzy Jagger & Roland Watson, *Labour's Parting Shot to New Treasury Team*, TIMES, May 18, 2010, at 1.

65 *Id.*

> and the utilization of economic wealth for the general good as well as for a federal organization of Europe.[66]

As the European Union itself acknowledges:

> The historical roots of the European Union lie in the Second World War.... Soon after the war, Europe is split into East and West as the 40-year-long Cold War begins. West European nations created the Council of Europe in 1949. It is a first step towards cooperation between them, but six countries [Germany, France, Italy, the Netherlands, Belgium and Luxembourg] want to go further.[67]

What seems remarkable about the emergence and evolution of a multinational (or, perhaps, supranational) European entity, now known as the EU, with twenty-eight members, is that it was not, at its inception, composed of nascent political entities but full-fledged nation-states, most of which had been in existence for generations, if not for centuries or even a millennium. France, for example, traces its history as a distinct nation back to the tenth century and Portugal to the twelfth century, while Sweden was formally created in 1523.[68]

The grand philosophical postwar debate pitted advocates of increased economic cooperation among the nations of Europe with those who wanted to replace or seriously transform the existing political arrangement of nation-states into a new federal union somewhat akin to the United States. In due course, a pragmatically based gradualism was the method of either choice or necessity. In this there is a resemblance to the rise of independent government entities in the United States.

1. THE COUNCIL OF EUROPE

The earliest effort at any form of European cooperation occurred with the passage of the Treaty of London in 1949, which created the Council of Europe. The treaty was signed by ten members—Belgium, France, Italy, the Netherlands, and Luxembourg—which would, a year later, join with West Germany to help found those institutions that were the forerunners of the EU, plus three Scandinavian countries, Denmark, Norway, and Sweden, and the United Kingdom. The Council of Europe was composed of two

---

[66] Doreen Collins, The European Communities: The Social Policy of the First Phase, Vol. 1, The European Coal and Steel Community 1951–70 3 (Martin Robertson 1975). Collins, now retired, was senior lecturer, Department of Social Policy and Administration, University of Leeds.

[67] Europa, The History of the European Union, http://europa.eu/abc/history/1945-1959/index_en.htm (official website of the European Union, last accessed Jan. 30, 2010). At the time, Germany was simply West Germany.

[68] DK Atlas 218, 301, 329 (3rd ed. DK Publishing 2007).

entities—the Council of Ministers and the Consultative Assembly.[69] The council was—and remains—essentially a customary international forum for discussion and cooperation among its members. As noted by Derek Urwin:

> In many ways the Council of Europe was little more than a continuation of the traditional format of cooperation transcribed to a bigger stage, and could not itself move forward to a supranational or federalist future.[70]

Significantly, the council did not represent any diminution in the national power and sovereignty of the individual member nations. On significant items, each member had a veto over action, although certain matters, such as the entry of new members, could be decided by a two-thirds majority.[71] The Council of Ministers had express authority to act on behalf of the Council of Europe.[72] In contrast, the Consultative Assembly, composed of members elected by, or appointed from, the national parliaments,[73] was created as the Council of Europe's "deliberative organ," authorized to "debate matters within its competence...and present its conclusions, in the form of recommendations, to the Committee of Ministers."[74]

The Council of Europe has now grown to forty-seven member states.[75] From its inception until the Treaty of Lisbon came into force in 2009, the Council of Europe operated outside the express framework of the EU. Although the Council of Europe has produced numerous treaties during its existence, many academics, and even the Council of Europe itself, appear to consider the enactment of the European Convention for the Protection of Human Rights and Fundamental Freedoms, with the creation of the European Court of Human Rights, as a major achievement.[76]

2. EUROPEAN COAL AND STEEL COMMUNITY

Creation of the European Coal and Steel Community (ECSC) in 1950 was Europe's first genuine step toward the replacement, or at least supplementation, of wholly sovereign national control with at least a modicum of independent, supranational authority.

---

69 Treaty of London, Article 10, European Treaty Series Nos. 1/6/7/8/11, found in its current form at conventions.coe.irt/treaty/en/Treaties/word/001.doc (last accessed Apr. 23, 2010) [hereinafter Treaty of London].

70 Derek W. Urwin, The Community of Europe, A History of European Integration Since 1945 36 (Longman, 2d ed. 1995). At the time of writing the book, Urwin was professor of politics and international relations at the University of Aberdeen.

71 Treaty of London, *supra* note 69. Article 20. *See also* Urwin, *supra* note 70, at 36.

72 Treaty of London, *supra* note 69. Article 13.

73 *Id.* Article 25.

74 *Id.* Articles 22, 23.

75 *See* Council of Europe in Brief, Who We Are, at www.coe.int/about COE/index.asp (last accessed May 14, 2014).

76 D. A. C. Freestone & J. S. Davidson, The Institutional Framework of the European Communities 3–4 (Routledge 1988); Urwin, *supra* note 70, at 38.

The ECSC affected two key industries and introduced a degree of institutional independence from national governments while nonetheless maintaining broad oversight by sovereign states. Under a scheme devised largely by two Frenchmen, Jean Monnet and French foreign minister Robert Schuman, six European countries initially agreed to a multinational accord for joint operation of their coal and steel industries. Monnet is given credit for having "invented the concept of a supranational body."[77] The effort resulted in the Treaty of Paris, signed in 1951 and coming into force in 1952.[78] The decision to create a somewhat independent body to regulate two key industries was not accidental. As the official EU website notes: "[U]nder a common management…none can on its own make the weapons of war to turn against the other, as in the past."[79]

What is significant for comparative purposes is the rather pragmatic creation of a semiautonomous institution "with the capacity to take international decisions yet which did not go too far for current national prejudices."[80]

From the outset, the governing European institutions reflected a tension between technocratic expertise and independence on the one hand and national accountability on the other. Although independence in an American context obviously does not exist in a multinational context, the conceptual and practical tensions are much the same.

Critical to its creation—and important for our purposes—was the early effort at partial separation of ECSC institutions from those of the individual countries and national governments. As Weatherill and Beaumont observe:

> The character of the ECSC was very different from the traditional model of an international organization. It was not merely a forum for joint discussion or intergovernmental decision-making. The Paris Treaty established new institutions, independent of the six member states, with power to supervise the development of the coal and steel industries of the states party to the treaty.[81]

The Treaty of Paris set up four primary institutions. A Council of Ministers, composed of senior government ministers, clearly represented the views of the member nations. Different ministers represented their governments depending on the topic under consideration.[82] The treaty also created Europe's first parliamentary assembly, ultimately

---

77 Martin J. Dedman, The Origins and Development of the European Union 1945–95: A History of European Integration 61 (Routledge 1996).

78 Treaty Establishing the European Coal and Steel Community (1951), 261 U.N.T.S. 140 [hereinafter Treaty of Paris].

79 The History of the European Union, at Europa, official website of the European Union, http://europa.eu/abc/history/1945-1959/index_en.htm (last accessed Jan. 30, 2010).

80 Collins, *supra* note 66, at 7.

81 Stephen Weatherill & Paul Beaumont, EC Law: The Essential Guide to the Legal Workings of the European Communities 2–3 (2d ed. 1995).

82 Collins, *supra* note 66, at 8.

renamed the European Parliament, "composed of representatives of the peoples of the member States... [to] exercise the supervisory powers which are granted to it by the present Treaty,"[83] with delegates appointed, and subsequently elected, from member countries based on population.[84] At its inception, it was not a legislative body in the strict sense. The assembly had no legislative responsibility. Rather, its principal power was its ability by two-thirds majority to require the en masse resignation of the members of the High Authority.[85] The assembly "was added to the initial design at the eleventh hour" to provide a level of political accountability to the technocratic model.[86]

The Treaty created a Court of Justice with nonpolicy responsibilities for resolving disputes, "to ensure the rule of law in the interpretation and application of the present Treaty and of its implementing regulations."[87]

The most innovative structural aspect of the ECSC was the establishment of the so-called High Authority, composed of nine individuals, serving six-year, staggered terms, with one-third of the members selected every two years, and with no more than two coming from any single member country.[88] Note the parallels, in a transnational context, with certain structural elements intended to render American agencies independent. Eight members were chosen by the governments of the six member states, with these eight then selecting a ninth member.[89] In this respect, the High Authority appointment mechanism has parallels with the manner of selection of members of the Board of Governors of the U.S. Postal Service, where the president nominates and the Senate confirms nine governors,[90] those nine then select the postmaster general, who becomes the tenth board member,[91] and the ten members choose the deputy postmaster general, who also becomes a member of the board.[92] However, as Martin Dedman points out, as a practical matter the High Authority members represented the consensus selectees of the six governments, not simply candidates of individual countries.[93] By tacit agreement, two members would come from the three largest countries, with one each from the remaining three smaller states.[94]

---

83 Treaty of Paris, *supra* note 78, Article 20.

84 Germany, Italy, and France had eighteen delegates each, Belgium and the Netherlands had ten, and Luxembourg had four. *See* Treaty of Paris, *supra* note 78. Article 21.

85 Treaty of Paris, *supra* note 78, Article 24. *See also* COLLINS, *supra* note 66, at 9.

86 LIESBET HOOGHE, THE EUROPEAN COMMISSION AND THE INTEGRATION OF EUROPE 145 (2001). Professor Hooghe, a Belgian, teaches at the University of North Carolina at Chapel Hill.

87 Treaty of Paris, *supra* note 78. Article 31.

88 *Id.* Articles 9, 10.

89 *Id.* Article 9.

90 39 U.S.C. § 202(a)(1).

91 39 U.S.C. § 202(c).

92 39 U.S.C. § 202(d).

93 DEDMAN, *supra* note 77, at 67.

94 URWIN, *supra* note 70, at 49.

As in the American context, practical considerations dictated the selection of individual members. Doreen Collins points out that "[t]he members had . . . to be acceptable to governments and . . . it was agreed that at least one member would enjoy the confidence of the trade unions."[95] The High Authority operated by majority vote, with authority to fix its own quorum rules except that at least a majority of the members had to constitute a quorum.[96]

The Treaty included an express provision regarding independence. It stated:

> The members of the High Authority shall exercise their functions in complete independence, in the general interest of the Community. In the fulfillment of their duties, they shall neither solicit nor accept instructions from any government or from any organization. . . . Each member State agrees to respect this supranational character and to make no effort to influence the members of the High Authority in the execution of their duties.[97]

Members had a form of protection against removal from office. Article 12 provided that:

> Members who no longer fulfill the conditions necessary to the exercise of their functions or who have committed a gross fault may be removed from office by the Court on petition by the High Authority or the Council.

However, as noted earlier, the Assembly, by two-thirds majority, could order the removal of the entire membership of the High Authority.[98]

The president of the High Authority occupied a central position somewhat akin to that of the chairs of American multimember agencies. Article 16 of the Treaty of Paris provided:

> Within the framework of general organizational regulations established by the High Authority, the President . . . shall be responsible for the administration of its services, and shall insure the execution of the acts of the High Authority.

This provision, of course, establishes a division of responsibility similar to the administrative arrangements at most U.S. independent agencies. Jean Monnet, a strong supporter of European integration, was the High Authority's first and highly influential president.[99] His disagreement with France's President Pierre Mendès-France led him to resign in 1955 in order to press for increased European integration.[100]

---

95 COLLINS, *supra* note 66, at 7.

96 *Treaty of Paris*, *supra* note 78, Article 13.

97 *Id.* Article 9.

98 *Id.* Article 24.

99 URWIN, *supra* note 70, at 49.

100 DEDMAN, *supra* note 77, at 99.

Overall, the High Authority was not an independent entity in quite the modern American sense. Rather, it had "decision-making and executive powers... under a system of controls operated by the Council of Ministers," which represented the individual governments.[101] The Council of Ministers was established largely at the behest of the smaller countries concerned that a fully independent High Authority might come to be dominated by the two largest countries, France and Germany.[102]

Article 26, for example, gave the Council primary treaty responsibility for "harmonizing the action of the High Authority and that of the governments, which are responsible for the general economic policy of their countries."[103] The High Authority was authorized to undertake research activities, establish production quotas where demand was low, take action to prevent unfair competitive practices, or fix maximum prices.[104] Council approval was necessary for certain actions, and the Council could veto action by the High Authority in certain circumstances. The High Authority, for example, could issue or guarantee loans to individual companies only with the unanimous concurrence of the Council.[105] It had authority to enact quotas to limit supply, or to "establish consumption priorities and determine the allocation of the coal and steel resources of the Community" in the face of shortages. However, if it declined, upon request, to take such action, a member state could seek relief from the Council, which could, by unanimous agreement, direct the High Authority to act.[106] On one occasion the High Authority's effort to establish production quotas was vetoed by the Council because governments preferred unilateral action to protect their own national companies.[107] The High Authority was authorized to fund itself in part through imposition of a Europe-wide tax, that is, "levies on the production of coal and steel."[108] But it could not assess any levies of more than 1 percent on coal or steel products unless authorized by a two-thirds majority of the Council.[109]

The Council also had the power to create a multimember Consultative Committee of "producers, workers and consumers and dealers in equal numbers,"[110] and numerous treaty provisions required consultation by the High Authority with the Consultative Committee. Although the High Authority did so regularly,[111] it has been suggested that this committee in practice acted "only in an advisory capacity" and that "[t]echnically the... [High

---

[101] Collins, *supra* note 66, at 7.

[102] Youri Devuyst, *The European Union's Institutional Balance after the Treaty of Lisbon: "Community Method" and "Democratic Deficit" Reassessed*, 39 Geo. J. Int'l L. 247, 277 (2008).

[103] Treaty of Paris, *supra* note 78, Article 26.

[104] *Id.* Articles 55 (research), 58 (quotas), 60 (unfair competitive practices), 61 (establishment of maximum prices).

[105] *Id.* Article 54.

[106] *Id.* Article 58 (quotas), 59 (shortages).

[107] Dedman, *supra* note 77, at 68.

[108] Treaty of Paris, *supra* note 78, Article 49.

[109] *Id.* Article 50(2).

[110] *Id.* Article 18.

[111] Collins, *supra* note 66, at 9–10.

Authority] did not need to take notice of the opinions of the committee even when bound to ask for them."[112] Martin Dedman has referred to the committee as "ineffectual."[113]

In sum, as explained by Collins:

> Whilst far-reaching powers were transferred to an international institution, their exercise was qualified by the procedures laid down in the treaty which attempted to give due regard to national interests, to the views and requirements of the coal and steel industries and of the community at large.[114]

The Treaty of Paris was intended to last for only fifty years,[115] which it did, and the ECSC formally went out of business in 2002. By then it had been eclipsed by the EU.[116]

3. THE TRANSITION TO A EUROPEAN UNION

Within only a few years of establishing the ECSC, the six ECSC countries signed two treaties, sometimes collectively referred to as the Treaty of Rome,[117] to create the European Atomic Energy Community (Euratom) and, more important for current purposes, the European Economic Community, under structural arrangements both similar to, yet different from, those of the ECSC. The treaty had 248 separate articles, plus numerous annexes and protocols, that broadly created an economic common market,[118] focused on "eliminating custom duties and import and export restrictions... [and] abolition... of obstacles to freedom of movement for persons, services, and capital."[119]

The Treaty of Rome followed the ECSC model by retaining four key institutions. The Assembly had members designated by the national parliaments, with voting weighted by population.[120] The Council consisted of representatives of the member governments, with a president chosen on a six-month, rotating basis.[121] There was a Court of Justice and an independent European Commission.

The commission had nine members, selected by agreement of the member states and jointly by the member governments to serve four-year renewable terms.[122] Members were candidates "chosen on the grounds of their General competence and whose independence

---

[112] *Id.* at 10.

[113] DEDMAN, *supra* note 77, at 68.

[114] COLLINS, *supra note* 66, at 12.

[115] Treaty of Paris, *supra* note 78, Article 97.

[116] *See* Rafael Leal-Arcas, *EU Legal Personality in Foreign Policy*, 24 B.U. INT'L L.J. 165, 212 (2006).

[117] Treaty Establishing the European Economic Community, 298 U.N.T.S. 11 (1957) [hereinafter Treaty of Rome].

[118] *Id.* Article 2. *See also* DEDMAN, *supra* note 77, at 61.

[119] Treaty of Rome, *supra* note 117, Article 3.

[120] *Id.* Article 138(1)(2).

[121] *Id.* Article 146.

[122] *Id.* Article 158

is beyond doubt" and could neither "seek nor take instruction from any Government or from any other body."[123] As a practical matter, the Commission president is now chosen by the parties representing a majority in the European Parliament. Members were protected from arbitrary removal by provisions that allowed only the Court of Justice to remove a member, upon application of the Commission or the Council, if the commissioner "no longer fulfills the conditions required for the performance of his duties or if he has been guilty of serious misconduct." Alternatively, the Commission could be removed en masse by a two-thirds vote of the European Parliament.

Importantly, the experience of the original six members with the actual operation of the ECSC influenced the distribution of power within the European Economic Community. Certain elements were critical. First, as a practical matter, commissioners were, in fact, nominated by their respective governments.[124] Moreover, Commission proposals had to be approved by the Council of Ministers.[125]

The new power-sharing arrangements are described by Martin Dedman:

> The Commission of the EEC [European Economic Community] was the central concept behind the integrated organisation of the EEC.... The Commission had a multifunctional purpose and role, it acted as the EEC's executive civil service and espoused the communities' interest (commissioners took an oath to pursue community and not national interests). The Commission's main role was to initiate policy ("the Commission proposes but the Council disposes").... The nine-man Commission...was different from the ECSC's High Authority in a number of respects....
>
> The six states wanted to retain as much power as possible in their own hands and take all major decisions on proposals originating from the Commission.... The six member states transferred decisions concerning the Common Market and atomic energy to a supranational Council of Ministers drawn from the six states whose decisions were binding on all and had to be followed.
>
> Unlike the ECSC's High Authority the six countries reserved the right to name their own Commissioners...so they were national nominees. The Commission also was wholly dependent on financial contributions from member states (until 1970) ... [and] exercised less power than Monnet's High Authority....[126]

[123] *Id.* Article 157(1)(2).

[124] D. A. C. FREESTONE & J. S. DAVIDSON, THE INSTITUTIONAL FRAMEWORK OF THE EUROPEAN COMMUNITIES 58 (Routledge 1988).

[125] DEDMAN, *supra* note 77, at 84.

[126] *Id.* at 95. *See also* COLLINS, *supra* note 66, at 1 ("[T]he Treaty of Paris which created the ECSC gave greater powers of action to its executive, and the enlarged freedom which comes from an independent income, than was achieved by the Treaty of Rome in the case of the EEC.").

Similarly, as summarized by Youri Devuyst:

> [D]ecision-making was left in the hands of Member State representatives, within the framework of the Council of Ministers. The Council's decision-making powers were counterbalanced, however, by the European Commission's excusive right of legislative initiative and its duty to act as the guardian of the Treaties.

Significantly, the Commission was not given independent funding powers. Instead, the treaty provided for an annual budget to be paid for on a proportional basis by the six member countries. Germany, France, and Italy each contributed 28 percent of each year's budget, while Luxembourg was required to contribute on 0.2 percent.[127]

A Merger Treaty in 1967 coordinated the management of the three "communities," with a common Assembly, a common Court of Justice, a common Council of Ministers, and the ECSC's High Authority structurally amalgamated with the Euratom and European Economic Community commissions to create a single commission composed of the same individuals. Weatherill and Beaumont indicate: "[T]here were still formally three separate treaties and three separate European Communities, but for all practical purposes they were administered on a day-to-day basis as one."[128]

The Treaty allowed for the addition of new member states, and the First Accession Treaty of 1972 brought the United Kingdom, Ireland, and Denmark into the fold. Over time the European Economic Community has transformed into the EU, which has grown to twenty-eight members. But the four key institutions—the Council of Ministers, the Assembly (now the European Parliament), the Court of Justice, and the European Commission—have remained.

Article 10 of the Merger Treaty of 1965 continued to provide that commissioners would be candidates "chosen on the grounds of their general competence and whose independence is beyond doubt" and that they "shall neither seek nor take instructions from any Government or from any other body."[129] The draconian method required to compel the resignation of the entire Commission, a censure motion that must command a two-thirds vote in the European Parliament, and the difficulty in removing individual commissioners—the Council or Commission can ask the Court of Justice to remove a commissioner for misconduct—gave the Commission a high degree of autonomy through the 1980s and into the 1990s. Through the 1980s, four attempts to remove the Commission as a whole failed, and no individual commissioner was removed.[130] So the Commission's autonomy in that respect was maintained. But their substantive powers

---

[127] Treaty of Rome, *supra* note 117, Article 200.

[128] WEATHERILL & BEAUMONT, *supra* note 81, at 4.

[129] Treaty Establishing a Single Council and a Single Commission of the European Communities, found in SWEET & MAXWELL'S EUROPEAN COMMUNITY TREATIES 221 (K. R. Simmonds, advisory ed., 1972).

[130] FREESTONE & DAVIDSON, *supra* note 124, at 59.

were clearly reduced. Even as early as 1957, according to Dedman, "[the] High Authority was considered too powerful by France and Belgium."[131]

The Commission's independent position did not insulate it from governmental scrutiny and control in the face of scandal. Concerns over mismanagement, nepotism, and possible fraud, during the chairmanship of Jacques Santer, the former prime minister of Luxembourg, were actively debated by the European Parliament. Rather than exercise its authority to dismiss the entire Commission in 1999, the European Parliament instead ordered an investigation of the Commission's activities.[132] But the die was cast. The investigation by an independent so-called Committee of the Wise[133] produced a report that highlighted numerous Commission failures. Chief among them was the failure adequately to police the work of contractors, possibly the result of a shortage of staff, although no fraud was actually uncovered.[134] The Report led to the resignation of the entire Commission and its replacement by a new Commission with a new president.[135]

The Commission's resignation is described by Liesbet Hooghe as "the climax of a six-month tug of war between Europe's executive and the European Parliament."[136] In its wake, a new Commission was appointed, under a new president, Romano Prodi, former prime minister of Italy, with a new commissioner for administration, Neil Kinnock, the former British Labour Party leader. This new group undertook major reforms of the Commission's administrative and financial structures to increase its transparency and accountability.[137]

A range of internal reforms, including adoption of a Code of Conduct for commissioners, followed the appointment of the new Prodi Commission.[138] Perhaps more significant were the changes in the procedures for selecting commissioners brought about by the Amsterdam Treaty in 1997. It provides that the member states continue to agree on the Commission's president, whose name is transmitted to the European Parliament for approval. Once approved, the new president and the member states participate jointly in the selection of the remaining commissioners. The president can, in effect, veto a member state's selection, thus according the president significant enhanced powers.[139]

---

131 DEDMAN, *supra* note 77, at 95.

132 Vaughne Miller & Richard Ware, The Resignation of the European Commission, Research Paper 99/32 (House of Commons Library, 12–13, 16 Mar. 1999).

133 *Id.* at 13.

134 *Id.* at 98–99.

135 Paul Craig, *The Fall and Renewal of the Commission: Accountability, Contract and Administration Organisation*, 6 EUROPEAN L.J. 98, 99 (2000).

136 HOOGHE, *supra* note 86, at 142.

137 *See id.* at 142–44; MARTIN J. DEDMAN, THE ORIGINS AND DEVELOPMENT OF THE EUROPEAN UNION, 1945–2008: A HISTORY OF EUROPEAN INTEGRATION 183 (2d ed. Routledge 2010).

138 Craig, *supra* note 135, at 98, 109.

139 *See generally* Vaughne Miller & Richard Ware, The Resignation of the European Commission, Research Paper 99/32 (House of Commons Library, 12–13, 16 Mar. 1999).

One of the results of the Prodi/Kinnock reforms was the emergence of a new set of public subunits—essentially executive agencies—charged with responsibility for specialized administration. They are discussed below. As explained in a 2006 analytical report, these new agencies "are still linked to the European Commission and ... headed by a Commission official [but] ... have a separate legal personality and receive an annual grant from the Commission for [their] ... administrative expenditure."[140]

4. THE EUROPEAN COMMISSION TODAY

The tension continues in the current incarnation of the European Commission. The Commission remains structured to be subject to political oversight but largely free of domination by individual member states. The Commission president continues to be chosen by unanimous agreement of the member states, acting as the European Council. The Lisbon Treaty of 2009, however, provided that the Council, in selecting a Commission president, take into account the results of parliamentary elections.[141] So there is an electoral as well as national dimension to the selection of a president. Although the Lisbon Treaty provided for a reduced number of commissioners, the Council restored the "one state–one commissioner" requirement, as the Treaty authorized it to do.[142] Each of the member states then chooses an individual commissioner, but the Council, now in cooperation with the president, makes the formal nominations, which must be approved by the European Parliament. Commissioners serve five-year terms but may be removed by the European Parliament.[143] The Commission president has the important new power to assign each commissioner his or her subject area of responsibility. In this respect, the president has, over time, obtained heightened powers much as the chairs of U.S. independent agencies gained increased administrative powers as Congress approved presidential reorganization plans.

The Commission issues regulations to implement statutes for essentially the same reasons that U.S. agencies issue them. As the European Community executive, the Commission initially asserted the right to issue regulations on its own.[144] But the member countries were reluctant to abdicate entirely their role in the important task of implementing legislation—in somewhat the same way that Congress attempted, through the legislative veto, to retain residual power over agency rulemaking. Early on, the European

[140] Emanuelle Schön-Quinlivan, Administrative Reform in the European Commission: From Rhetoric to Re-Legitimisation, Project No. 513416, EU Consent, at 20–21 (Oct. 18, 2006).

[141] *See* Europa, Summaries of EU Legislation, *Institutional Affairs*, europa.eu/legislation_summaries/institutional_affairs/treaties/Lisbon_treaty/ai0006_en.htm.

[142] *See* European Council, The European Council Decides on the Number of Members of the European Commission, EUCO 119/13, Presse 210 (May 22, 2013) (last accessed Aug. 13, 2013).

[143] *See generally* Europa, official website of the European Union, http://europe.eu/about-eu/institutions-bodies/european-commission.

[144] Paul Craig, EU Administrative Law 111–13, 136–37 (2012).

Community designed a mechanism—called comitology—as the compromise means of according national government officials some political control over the crafting of implementing regulations. It basically requires the Commission, before issuing regulations, to engage actively with committees made up of subject matter experts designated by the member states. Comitology is the procedural response to the tension between a largely independent Commission and its politically accountable member nations not entirely unlike that which affects the relationship between independent agencies and the political branches in the United States.

Although lacking in a direct parallel to American administration, the comitology regime combines elements similar to negotiated rulemaking, the use of advisory committees, OIRA review, and the legislative veto. As explained by the Commission:

> The term "comitology" is shorthand for the way the Commission exercises the implementing powers conferred on it by the EU legislator, with the assistance of committees of representatives from the EU Member States. The Commission departments submit draft implementing acts [that is, proposed rules in an American context] to the "comitology committees" in order to obtain their opinion.... "Comitology committees" assist the Commission in executing its implementing powers by giving an opinion on draft implementing measures before they are adopted. They include representatives from all EU Member States and are chaired by a Commission official.[145]

The precise details of the comitology regime have changed over the years and can differ depending on the subject matter of a particular regulation. In some cases, the comitology committee views must be evaluated but are entirely advisory. In some cases, a committee can actually block a regulation's implementation. The comitology process recognizes that, like the rulemaking process in the United States, Commission activity involves the exercise of discretion as well as mere technical implementation of legislation. In the circumstances, as Paul Craig describes things, the member states "were unwilling to give the Commission a blank cheque to provide answers to the issues of practical and normative choice left outstanding by the primary... [legislation] because they did not wish to invest the Commission with that degree of power and because they disagreed amongst themselves as to the desirable answers."[146]

Apart from its role as the European executive, responsible for enforcing EU law, the Commission has sole responsibility for the initiation of new legislation. As described by Patrick Birkinshaw, it is "the law enforcer, law preparer, policy initiator, adviser, a law maker and general guardian and overseer of the Community's interests."[147]

---

[145] European Commission, Comitology Register, Frequently Asked Questions, eu.europa/transparency/regcomitology/index.cfm?do=FAQ.FAQ#1 (last accessed Oct. 7, 2012).

[146] Craig, *supra* note 144, at 137.

[147] Patrick Birkinshaw, European Public Law 42 (2003).

The Commission produces an annual budget for approval by the European Parliament and the Council. The Lisbon Treaty authorizes review by the Court of Justice of Commission decisions having legal effect on third parties. In its overall organization and operation, the Commission itself, and its individual members, reflect elements of independence not entirely unlike those of American independent agencies.

5. EUROPEAN INDEPENDENT AGENCIES

Also coming on the scene, starting in 1975, but with a greater push in the 1990s, were a new group of entities—probably about thirty-five separate institutions at present, of which the European Environment Agency is a prototype—intended to be at least somewhat independent not simply of member states, but of the European Commission as well.[148] Each is established under a so-called founding act,[149] which serves, in effect, as the equivalent of an agency's enabling statute in the U.S. context. Agencies are typically headed by a multimember board, with representation from the member states and the Commission. The agency's chief executive is chosen with the input of both the board and the Commission.[150]

It was unclear whether European treaties allowed the creation of subordinate or coordinate multinational European administrative entities alongside the Commission,[151] and the precise place of these European Community institutions remains ambiguous. Renaud Dehousse suggests that their institutional position is something of a compromise. "Agencies owe their existence to a kind of paradox. On the one hand, increased uniformity is certainly needed; on the other hand greater centralization is politically inconceivable, and probably not desirable."[152] Craig points out that, apart from the usual reason for creating independent entities—technical apolitical expertise[153]—they emerged in response to concerns regarding the management of entities set up to assist the Commission, and the structure of these new agencies was intended to address those concerns.[154] These agencies have been created with specific managerial, technical, or

148 *See* Craig, *supra* note 144, at 145–47; Martin Shapiro, Independent Agencies: US and EU 20 (Jean Monnet Chair Papers No. 34, The Robert Schuman Centre, European Univ. Inst., 1996). *See also* Miroslava Scholten, *Independent, Hence Unaccountable? The Need for a Broader Debate on Accountability of the Executive*, 4 Rev. European Admin. L. 5 (2011).

149 *See* Decentralised Agencies, www.europa.eu/agencies/reguatory_agencies_bodies/index_en.htm.

150 Craig, *supra* note 144, at 163.

151 Europa, official website of the European Union, Europa.edu/agencies/documents/2012-12-18_roadmap_on_the_follow_up_+to the_common_approach_on_eu_decentralised_agencies (last accessed Mar. 19, 2013).

152 Renaud Dehousse, Regulation by Networks in the European Community: The Role of European Agencies 20 (Robert Schuman Centre, European Univ. Inst. 1997).

153 Craig, *supra* note 144, at 16–17.

154 Paul Craig, Legal Control of Regulatory Bodies: Principle, Policy and Teleology, 93, 97 (Birkinshaw & Varney eds., 2010).

information gathering and analysis responsibilities, but not ordinarily with independent regulatory power.[155] The European Environment Agency is typical. It describes its mission as being "to provide sound, independent information on the environment" to the European Commission, Parliament, the Council, and the member states, among others.[156]

Koen Verhoest and colleagues refer to these agencies' creation as "agencification."[157] As with their American counterparts, European agencies are rendered "independent," according to Miroslava Scholten, who has studied them, through a mixture of institutional separation from government ministries; some degree of personnel independence, although individual appointees may typically be removed by their appointing states; financial autonomy, although most European agencies are dependent on the European Commission, Council, and Parliament for their budgets; and functional elements.[158] But Martin Shapiro observes that they are not genuinely free of "intergovernmental politics."[159]

As to function, most European agencies lack decisional power. The European Agency for the Evaluation of Medicinal Products and the European Environment Agency, for example, are not regulatory bodies and only have the power to make recommendations to the Commission.[160] To that extent, they have some of the flavor of the historic "Sunshine Commissions" of nineteenth-century America or advisory committees today. Many agencies essentially collect and analyze information.[161] Nonetheless, there are a handful of agencies that can make decisions affecting the public.[162] They ordinarily do so by consensus that does not compromise the prerogatives of individual national administrations.[163] Agency action is reviewable by the Commission, with review of the Commission's determination by the Court of Justice,[164] and all European agencies have some reporting responsibility to the European Commission, Parliament, or Council.[165] Scholten concludes, overall, that EU agencies have far less authority than their American

155 *See* Scholten, *supra* note 148, at 22–23.

156 European Environment Agency, www.eea.europa.eu/about-us (last accessed Oct. 6, 2012).

157 Government Agencies, *supra* note 2, at 4–7.

158 Scholten, *supra* note 148, at 6, 10, 12, 17–20, 33–34.

159 Shapiro, *supra* note 148, at 20.

160 *See* Giandomenico Majone, The New European Agencies: Regulation by Information 2 (Robert Schuman Centre, European Univ. Inst. 1997); Karl-Heinz Ladeur, The New European Agencies: The European Environment Agency and Prospects for a European Network or Environmental Administrations 1–3 (European Union Institute Working Paper No. 96/50, 1996) (on file with Robert Schuman Centre, European Univ. Inst., Florence).

161 Craig, *supra* note 144, at 151–53.

162 *Id.* at 150.

163 *See* Dehousse, *supra* note 152, at 5.

164 Craig, *supra* note 154, at 93, 98. Craig examines the numerous legal questions raised by this review procedure and subsequent judicial review. *Id.* at 98–99.

165 Scholten, *supra* note 148, at 32.

counterparts,[166] and Craig argues that "[t]he EU does not yet possess regulatory agencies as that term is commonly used in national parlance,"[167] although he points out that "[t]he 'gap' between real regulatory agencies and those in the EU has narrowed over time, given that the degree of rulemaking and decisional power granted to some EU Agencies has increased."[168]

6. OTHER INTERNATIONAL ADMINISTRATION

A catchword for international activity in the twenty-first century seems to be "globalization." We take that as shorthand for the recognition that the political, economic, and social problems traditionally dealt with by individual nations has been superseded in an interconnected world by a recognition that multinational or transnational problems exist and can only be dealt with globally. And an international administrative law is emerging to deal with it.[169] The metes and bounds of both problems and responses to globalization are well beyond the purview of this book and are being studied elsewhere.[170] But two things seem clear. First, international independent entities of some form are likely to play a role. Second, these entities are evolving through both formal and informal means that raise issues of accountability.[171] Richard Stewart, who is the director of the Hauser Global Law School Program at New York University Law School, which is studying these issues, observes:

> Underlying the emergence of global administrative law is the vast increase in the reach and form of trans-governmental regulation and administration designed to address the consequences of globalized interdependence in such fields as security, the conditions on development and financial assistance to developing countries, environmental protection, banking and financial regulation, law enforcement, telecommunications, trade in products and services, intellectual property, labor standards, and cross-border movements of populations, including refugees. Increasingly, these consequences cannot be addressed effectively by isolated national regulatory and administrative measures. As a result, various transnational systems of regulation or regulatory cooperation have been established through international treaties and more informal intergovernmental networks of cooperation,

---

166 *Id.*

167 CRAIG, *supra* note 144, at 153.

168 *Id.* at 172.

169 *See, e.g.*, Benedict Kingsbury, Nico Krisch & Richard B. Stewart, *The Emergence of Global Administrative Law*, 68 LAW & CONTEMP. PROB. 15 (2005).

170 *See, e.g.*, Richard B. Stewart, *Courts, Institutions and Access to Justice: Legitimacy and Accountability in Global Regulatory Governance Global Administrative Law and Developing Countries*, 1 JINDAL GLOBAL L. REV. 41 (2009).

171 *See, e.g.*, Kingsbury et al., *supra* note 169, at 15 (2005).

> shifting many regulatory decisions from the national to the global level. Further, much of the detail and implementation of such regulation is determined by transnational administrative bodies—including international organizations and informal groups of officials—that perform administrative functions but are not directly subject to control by national governments or domestic legal systems or, in the case of treaty-based regimes, the states party to the treaty. These regulatory decisions may be implemented directly against private parties by the global regime or, more commonly, through implementing measures at the national level. Also increasingly important are regulation by private international standard-setting bodies and by hybrid public-private organizations that may include, variously, representative of businesses, NGOs, national governments, and intergovernmental organizations.[172]

In these respects it seems likely that the globalized administrative structure will include some of the same problems and elements that bear on the history and evolution of independent agencies in the United States.

D. Observations

Whatever the rationale, it is clear that other nations have seen fit, on occasion, to create administrative structures with diffused lines of authority and accountability similar to, but not necessarily identical to, the independent agencies in the United States. This may be a reflection of a drive toward subsidarity or a recognition of the limits of centralized authority in technologically driven society.

As in America, there has been a tension between the need for political accountability and a desire for independent, expert decision-making that gave rise to governmental, and even supragovernmental, bodies through pragmatic evolution. In the era leading up to and following World War II, there were those who thought that bureaucracy was associated with concepts such as tyranny and centralized authority. The classic text is Franz Neuman, *Behemoth*.[173] Liberals prophesied that a knowledge-based elite, be they scientists or engineers, were taking over. Several scholars have written material that supports this prophecy.[174] Conservatives bewailed the advent of "the Technological

---

172 *Id.* at 15, 16.

173 Franz Neuman, Behemoth (1942) (discussing the history and philosophy of National Socialism as a paradigm example of the centralized state). See also Hannah Arendt, The Origins of Totalitarianism (2d prtg. 1959) for additional material on totalitarianism.

174 *See, e.g.*, John K. Galbraith, The New Industrial State 282–95 (1967) (discussing the educational and scientific establishment); Daniel Bell, *Notes on the Post-Industrial Society (I)*, Pub. Interest, Winter 1967, at 27–28; Zbigniew Brzezinski, *America in the Technetronic Age*, Encounter, January 1968, at 16.

Society."[175] Many accepted the inevitability of continued bureaucratic centralization, as evidenced by the title of a 1994 law review article: "The Rise and Rise of the Administrative State."[176]

But there may be limits to this centrifugal pull in both this country and abroad. Rather than centralization, it is possible that the principles of subsidiarity and accountability, whether diffused or dispersed, may work to undercut centralized "unitary" regulatory authority in other countries that, like the United States, are deeply committed to the administrative state. In the United States, the reasons advanced by Madison and others to support a theory of a unitary executive have modern adherents. Nonetheless, there is another structural tension between bureaucracy and centralization and subsidiarity and local flexibility that affects regulatory efforts within and outside the United States. There can be little doubt that, despite a strong tradition of ministerial responsibility in parliamentary systems, centrifugal pressures toward diffused bureaucratic accountability or what some have called "diffused sovereignty"[177] exist outside the United States.

The rich variety of pragmatic and eclectic organizational structures and differing elements of political control that characterize American administrative management appear in European public administration as well. Departments or ministries under the control of a minister who is a member of the legislative branch and publicly accountable remain the most prominent organizational units in European governments.[178] Nonetheless, both individual European governments and the EU also deploy a diverse

---

[175] *See* Jacques Ellul, The Technological Society x (John Wilkinson trans., 1964) (1954) (stating that the phrase "technological society" describes "the way in which an autonomous technology is in process of taking over the traditional values of every society without exception, subverting and suppressing these values to produce at last a monolithic world culture in which all nontechnological difference and variety is mere appearance.").

[176] Marx's notion of the "Asiatic mode of production" is developed in Karl Wittfogel, Oriental Despotism (1957), which argues that the need for large-scale infrastructure projects led to centralization in precapitalist India and China. Wittfogel (and Marx) is critiqued in Brendan O'Leary, The Asiatic Mode of Production: Oriental Despotism, Historical Materialism and Indian History (1989). *See* Gary Lawson, *The Rise and Rise of the Administrative State*, 107 Harv. L. Rev. 1231, 1231 (1994) (asserting that the post–New Deal administrative state contravenes the Constitution's design). Ironically, modern (before the fall of the Berlin Wall) Marxist scholars as well recognized the dangers inherent in what some termed the *bureaucratisation du monde*. *See* Bruno Rizzo, The Bureaucratization of the World 2 (Adam Westoby trans., 1985) (stating bureaucratization leads to formation of a new "class").

[177] Daniel Guttman, *Public Purpose and Private Service: The Twentieth Century Culture of Contracting Out and the Evolving Law of Diffused Sovereignty*, 52 Admin. L. Rev. 859, 881–82 (2000).

[178] Yvés Mény, Government and Politics in Western Europe: Britain, France, Italy, Germany 283 (Janet Lloyd trans., 2d ed. 1993) (comparing structure of European ministries); *see also* Renate Mayntz & Fritz W. Scharpf, Policy-Making in the German Federal Bureaucracy 63–64 (1975) (discussing structure of German bureaucracy); L. Neville Brown & John S. Bell, French Administrative Law 2–3 (1998).

range of ad hoc institutions that undertake specialized functions. Many of these are not entirely accountable to parliamentary authority. Indeed, the term "public agencies" in France is defined as those that engage in any activity that the government believes should be performed by a public authority in the public interest.[179] In recent years France has seen what Brown and Bell describe as:

> [T]he creation of independent and autonomous agencies to regulate or supervise particular policies or policy areas: the *Commission Nationale de l'Informatique et des Libertés*, which regulates the use of computers and databases; the *Conseil de la Concurrence*, which monitors monopolies, take-overs and restrictive practices; the *Commission des Sondages*, which investigates complaints about opinion polls; the *Commission de la Consommation*, which advises on consumer affairs; the *Commission des Opérations de Bourse*, which regulates the financial markets; and the *Commission Nationale de contrôle des campagnes électorales*, which makes recommendations and monitors the conduct of national electoral campaigns. In the areas of deregulated markets and privatized industries, such agencies have a major role in supervising the operation of the market. Thus the *Conseil Supérieur de l'Audiovisuel* supervises broadcasting, and the *Autorité de régulation des télécommunications* deals with the telecommunications sector. Control by officials is seen in many cases as a way of resolving problems which divide politicians.[180]

So there is a full range of "[p]ublic administrative or industrial and commercial establishments, ... mixed-economy companies, ... agencies, commissions, and offices, not to mention the thousands of organizations funded with public money and camouflaged by their anodyne appearance as associations set up under the law of 1901."[181]

At the same time, even the supranational EU has a growing number of institutional entities less closely linked to politically accountable national governments. And, as Richard Stewart and others have pointed out, the emergence of an interdependent world has produced not simply multinational organizations but "private and hybrid public-private bodies ... to deal with the consequences of globalization. ... [T]hese new centers of power and decisional authority are remote from and barely subject to

---

[179] *See* John Bell, *The Concept of Public Service under Threat from Europe? An Illustration from Energy Law*, 5 EUR. PUB. L. 189, 191–92 (1999). "Public bodies" may be organs of the government or public enterprises of an administrative or commercial kind. *See id.* at 192. For example, the French railroad is a publicly owned commercial enterprise while the French airline, Air France, was created under private law, with the government holding a majority interest.

[180] BROWN & BELL, *supra* note 178, at 26–27.

[181] MÉNY, *supra* note 178, at 300. The Law of 1 July 1901 deals with the right of association. *See* BROWN & BELL, *supra* note 178, at 17.

traditional domestic and international mechanisms of legal and political control and accountability."[182]

The American commentator George Will asks: "Will there be a Europe of states or a state of Europe?"[183] Clearly the place and role of the European Commission reflects an ambiguity over ultimate objectives. The Commission's power appears to ebb and flow in a pragmatic fashion depending on which side of the argument is temporarily in control. Moreover, the role of the Commission, the enhanced power of its chair, and the emergence of numerous European agencies, reflect political ambivalence between the need for democratic accountability and the desirability of impartial technocratic expertise. These traits seem to be endemic in any democratic administration.

182 Richard B. Stewart, *Legitimacy and Accountability in Global Regulatory Governance: Global Administrative Law and Developing Countries*, 1 JINDAL GLOBAL L. REV. 41, 42 (2009).

183 George Will, *European Union: A Coalition of Irresponsibility*, WASH. POST, May 16, 2010, at A17.

11

Conclusion

THE FUTURE OF THE INDEPENDENT AGENCY

A. The Changing Face of Independent Agencies

Independent agencies in their modern form have been around for well over a century since the creation of the ICC in 1887. Despite this long history, or more likely because of it, the precise place of independent agencies in the governmental organization is unclear. The indicia, characteristics, and implications of independence, and whether independent agencies are, or should be treated as, less political than their nonindependent agency counterparts, has not been definitively resolved. There is not even an all-purpose statutory or judicial definition of "independent agency." And, owing to both law and tradition, the political branches exercise different levels of control over different agencies.

Into the 1930s independent agencies as a class were seen to some extent as apolitical government experts. In its leading decision in 1935, the Supreme Court unanimously characterized them as follows:

> The [Federal Trade C]ommission is to be non-partisan; and it must, from the very nature of its duties, act with entire impartiality. It is charged with the enforcement of no policy except the policy of the law. Its duties are neither political nor executive, but predominantly quasi-judicial and quasi-legislative. Like the Interstate Commerce Commission, its members are called upon to exercise the trained judgment of a body of experts "appointed by law and informed by experience."[1]

[1] Humphrey's Ex'r v. United States, 295 U.S. 602, 624 (1935).

Such a simple explanation is no longer viable. They are no longer simply impartial government referees. Most observers now recognize that independent agencies undertake significant regulatory and administrative roles within a broader tug and tussle of interbranch tension. The president's appointment and removal power, as reflected in the Supreme Court's *Myers* decision, has been repelled to some degree by congressional incursion. Clearly others, such as senators from the president's own party or the opposing party, or elements of the regulated sector, often play an important role in the appointment process. The president's plenary removal power was essentially ended as a constitutional issue with the Court's decision in *Humphrey's Executor*. But the president retains influence, bolstered by custom, in prodding independent agency members from office. That is especially true of agency chairs when they lose their positions as chairs, although not legally required to step down as members. However, day-to-day influence over independent agencies has been compromised. Indeed, Congress, perhaps more than the president, is now a primary influence on most independent agencies.

Unlike 1935, the precise place of independent agencies in the governmental structure now divides Supreme Court justices. *Federal Communications Commission v. Fox Television Stations, Inc.* illustrates the point.[2] The case involved a change in the FCC's policy as to whether "fleeting expletives," that is, the nonrepetitive use of references to sexual or excretory functions in both their literal and nonliteral sense, constituted indecent language prohibited by statute. The FCC had originally concluded that fleeting expletives were not actionable but, thirty years later, changed its mind. A majority of the Court concluded that the FCC had adequately explained its change in policy. It found, in separate plurality (four justices) and concurring opinions (by Justice Kennedy), that the agency had fulfilled its obligation in the circumstances of the case simply by recognizing that it was changing policy and setting out a reasonable justification for its new policy. It need not expressly explain why its new policy was better than its old one. The dissenters believed that the agency had not adequately explained its change of course because it had failed to specify why it had rejected its earlier policy in favor of its new one.

The FCC statute does not expressly accord agency members statutory protection from summary removal by the president. Yet the justices' perception of the FCC's status as an independent agency may have had some bearing on their differing conclusions.

Justice Stevens, concurring on his own, argued that independent agencies are somehow different. He acknowledged that such agencies were now subject more to congressional than presidential control. However, he harked back to an earlier era by quoting from the legislative history of the Radio Act of 1927, which he claimed demonstrated that "broadcast regulation 'should be as free from political influence or arbitrary control

---

[2] FCC v. Fox Television Stations, Inc., 556 U.S. 502, 523 (2009) (addressing the majority's disagreement with the dissent on this point).

as possible.'"[3] In his view, "Congress established the FCC with the same measure of independence from the Executive that it had provided the FTC."[4] He referred explicitly to the Court's 1935 decision in *Humphrey's Executor.*[5]

Justice Breyer, speaking in dissent for four members of the Court, indicated that an independent agency's "comparative freedom from ballot-box control makes it all the more important that courts review its decision-making to assure compliance with applicable provisions of the law—including law requiring that major policy decisions be based upon articulable reasons."[6] He did not expressly contrast independent agencies with other executive agencies. And many principles he set out, for example, that an agency must act consistently or explain its reasons for changing policy, apply to all agencies. But the dissent certainly raised the question whether the place of independent agencies in the government is somehow different from executive agencies whose heads are directly subject to presidential oversight and removal. Justice Breyer observed:

> [The] law grants those in charge of independent administrative agencies broad authority to determine relevant policy. But it does not permit them to make policy choices for purely political reasons nor to rest them primarily upon unexplained policy preferences. Federal Communications Commissioners have fixed terms of office; they are not directly responsible to the voters; and they enjoy an independence expressly designed to insulate them, to a degree, from "the exercise of political oversight" [citing Justice Scalia's concurring opinion in *Freytag v. Commissioner,* 501 U.S., 868, 916 (1991) that referred to cabinet or "cabinet-like" executive agencies]. That insulation helps to secure important governmental objectives, such as the constitutionally related objective of maintaining broadcast regulation that does not bend too readily before the political winds.[7]

It should be noted that, in *Fed. Mar. Comm'n v. S. Carolina State Ports Auth.,* Justice Breyer observed that, for constitutional purposes, the Federal Maritime Commission was "appropriately considered to be part of the executive branch " and exercises "powers that the Executive Branch of Government must possess if it is to enforce modern law through administration."[8] By bringing the independent agencies full bore into the executive branch, the justices may have responded to the "logic" of "presidentialism" and

---

[3] *Id.* at 540.

[4] *Id.* at 540.

[5] *Id.* at 540.

[6] *Id.* at 547.

[7] *Id.* at 547.

[8] Fed. Mar. Comm'n v. S.C. State Ports Auth., 535 U.S. 743, 773,774 (2002) (Breyer, J. dissenting). *See also* Freytag v. Comm'r, 501 U.S. 868, 910 (1991) (Scalia, J. concurring in part and concurring in judgment).

the unitary executive theory, although it is certainly not clear that the anomalies in such a classification for our understanding of the executive branch have been fully resolved.[9]

Justice Scalia's plurality opinion in *FCC v. Fox* adhered to his long-held position that, as a matter of constitutional doctrine, independent agencies exercise executive power under a unitary executive.[10] The APA makes no distinction between independent and nonindependent agencies. So the standard for judicial review is the same whether independent or nonindependent agencies are involved.[11]

Nonetheless, Justice Scalia was not prepared to concede that independent agencies are apolitical. Recognizing the reality of congressional oversight, he argued that "[t]he independent agencies are sheltered not from politics but from the President, and it has often been observed that their freedom from presidential oversight (and protection) has simply been replaced by increased subservience to congressional direction."[12] In fact, he pointed out that the FCC's change in policy had received a substantial prod from the pressure exerted during congressional oversight hearings.[13] Indeed, the standard of review adopted by the plurality at least suggested that an independent agency might even be permitted to change policy simply because its current members now had a different view of the costs and benefits of a particular program, as long as the agency did not ignore statutory standards. In *State Farm*, then Justice Rehnquist, on behalf of four members of the Court, had likewise suggested that executive branch agencies, at least (in that case, the DOT) might well be permitted to change policy in light of the perspectives of a new administration.[14]

Justice Kennedy seemed to sum up the dilemma succinctly in his concurring opinion in *Fox Television*. He did not explicitly distinguish between independent and nonindependent agencies when reviewing the FCC's order. Nonetheless, he observed—correctly, in our view—that "the amorphous character of the administrative agency in the constitutional system escapes simple explanation."[15]

We would argue that experience and tradition (let alone politics) has stayed the hand of doctrine. In fact, whatever the doctrinal logic and our evolving understanding of the character of independent agencies since 1935, the Supreme Court has shown no inclination to overturn the independent agency model. And while some academic commentators find

---

9 We should remember Justice Jackson's admonition that the notion of the independent agencies as a "veritable fourth branch" of government has "deranged our three branch legal theories." Fed. Trade Comm'n v. Rubberoid Co., 343 U.S. 470, 487 (1952) (Jackson, J. dissenting).

10 FCC v. Fox Television Stations, Inc., 556 U.S. 502, 524 (2009) (noting that "a scheme giving the power to enforce laws to agents of Congress" would be unconstitutional).

11 *Id. at* 525.

12 *Id.* at 523.

13 *Id.* at 523 & n.4.

14 Motor Vehicle Mfg. Ass'n of the United States, Inc. v. State Farm Mutual Auto. Ins. Co., 463 U.S. 29, 59 (1983).

15 Fox, 556 U.S. at 536.

various "independent" agencies to have alleged constitutional or statutory infirmities,[16] the courts have, by and large, not joined in. That in itself should tell us something.

B. Centralization Theory and the Pushback Against It

In the past few decades we have seen a resurgence of efforts by various administrations to centralize the administrative state. In part this reflects resurgent visions of presidential power exemplified by the theory of the unitary executive. It is reflected, as well, in theories of the president's "completion power"[17] and of presidential "directive authority."[18] And it is reflected in the view of some commentators toward the administrative agency form. In the 1950s (let alone earlier) it was believed that "only through nomination for appointment—and the power to remove commissioners for malfeasance—is the president granted any control over the ICC and independent agencies."[19] That is to say, other than appointment and removal, the independent agencies are free from presidential influence. In sharp contrast, more recently commentators were discussing whether the "good cause" exception includes a refusal to follow presidential orders.[20] This reflects the contemporary shift toward "presidentialism" in constitutional theory and "formalism" in constitutional interpretation.[21]

Notwithstanding the constitutional rationale of some theory of a centralized executive,[22] there are structural tensions in the modern administrative state that—aside

---

[16] *See, e.g.*, Neomi Rao, *A Modest Proposal: Abolishing Agency Independence in* Free Enterprise Fund v. PCAOB, 79 FORDHAM L. REV. 2541, 2560 (2011) (arguing that the Court's emphasis on the importance of presidential control and accountability calls into question the constitutionality of agency independence generally); Note, *The SEC Is Not an Independent Agency*, 126 HARV. L. REV. 781, 786 n.46 (2013) (observing that the statute that created the SEC lacks a provision conferring removal protection and it is a long-standing rule of construction that the President has the power to remove officers he appoints unless Congress explicitly provides otherwise).

[17] *See* Jack Goldsmith & John Manning, *The President's Completion Power*, 115 YALE L.J. 2280, 2282 (2006). See further discussion in *supra* chapter 3, notes 8–11 and accompanying text. *See also* Robert V. Percival, *Who's in Charge? Does the President Have Directive Authority over Agency Regulatory Decisions?*, 79 FORDHAM L. REV. 2511 (2011).

[18] *See* Percival, *supra* note 17, at 2511. *See also* Elena Kagan, *Presidential Administration*, 114 HARV. L. REV. 2245, 2250 (2001). *See also* chapter 3, section E.

[19] Anthony F. Arpaia, *The Independent Agency—A Necessary Instrument of Democratic Government*, 69 HARV. L. REV. 483, 487 (1956).

[20] *See, e.g.*, Peter L. Strauss, *On the Difficulties of Generalization: PCAOB in the Footsteps of Myers, Humphrey's Executor, Morrison, and Freytag*, 32 CARDOZO L. REV. 2255, 2264 (2011) (suggesting that refusal to provide an "opinion in writing" or consider the president's views before taking action might constitute "good cause").

[21] *See supra* chapter 3, notes 21–23 and accompanying text.

[22] *See* Lawrence Lessig & Cass R. Sunstein, *The President and the Administration*, 94 COLUM. L. REV. 1, 110 (1994); *see also* Presidential Review of Agency Rulemaking, 1 C.F.R. § 305.88–9 (1989) (Administrative Conference recommendation endorsing in principle presidential review of rulemaking initiatives of independent multimember agencies).

from executive centralization—keep the independent mode alive. No matter how "strict" the hierarchical requirements of the "theory of the unitary executive" from a constitutional perspective, modern management theory holds clearly that lockstep centralization can inhibit flexibility and credibility in the private sector.[23] Further, the administrative state is too large to be policed efficiently by the president, and Congress is too balkanized to effectively control the agencies closely through oversight and legislation. Indeed, as Congressman Edward Markey has cogently noted:

> In reality, Congress can oversee, in a vigorous fashion, relatively few of the day-to-day activities of the administrative agencies within its oversight boundaries. Congress is a stimulus-response body, and we need a lot of stimulus before taking action to reign in an agency.[24]

On occasion, in fact, Congress and the president have consciously found it necessary to forgo some accountability in order to advance important agendas. An example is the Defense Base Closure and Realignment Act of 1990, which limits the presidential and congressional roles to an up-or-down vote on proposals consisting of a group of proposed closings made by an independent commission.[25] That Act was enacted to remedy the structural inefficiencies that had hindered Congress's previous efforts to close military bases, that is, "potential vote-trading."[26] After 2005, the Congress appeared skittish in giving away its power.[27] In 2013, the Readiness Subcommittee of the House Armed

23 The father of management theory, Peter Drucker, praised decentralization of management in his books such as *The Concept of the Corporation* 122 (1946). His view has been applied to government institutions as well.

24 *See* Edward J. Markey, *Congress to Administrative Agencies: Creator, Overseer, and Partner*, 1990 DUKE L.J. 967, 969.

25 *See* 10 U.S.C. § 2687 (1994 & Supp. IV 1999). Judicial review is not available for closure decisions made by the Base Realignment and Closure Commissions. *See* Dalton v. Specter, 511 U.S. 462 (1994).

26 *See* H.R. REP. NO. 101-923, at 705 (1990); H.R. REP. NO. 101-665, at 384 (1990). "Vote trading" occurred when members who represented districts with military bases would trade their votes with other members, each protecting the bases in their own district. DAVID E. LOCKWOOD & GEORGE SIEHL, MILITARY BASE CLOSURES: A HISTORICAL REVIEW FROM 1988 TO 1995 2 (2004). For a discussion of the political maneuvering and policy developments in base closure, see DAVID S. SORENSON, SHUTTING DOWN THE COLD WAR: THE POLITICS OF MILITARY BASE CLOSURE 41–85 (1998).

27 Interestingly, the Obama administration's proposed 2014 military budget included a provision to close military installations through a renewed fiscal year 2014 Base Realignment and Closure Commission. Office of Management and Budget, Fiscal Year 2014 Budget of the U.S. Government, 72 (2013). As one commentator notes, "[c]losing a base or even a facility is a political hot potato—so much so that Congress not only turned down the last two requests to start the BRAC [Base Realignment and Closure Commissions] process, in 2012 and 2013, but also barred the Pentagon from even planning for one." Walter Pincus, *For Pentagon, It's Always a Tough Battle To Get Congress To Close Military Bases*, WASH. POST, Mar. 17, 2014, http://www.washingtonpost.com/world/national-security/for-pentagon-its-always-a-tough-battle-to-get-congress-to-close-military-bases-facilities/2014/03/17/a7eda064-a887-11e3-8599-ce7295b6851c_story.html.

Services Committee approved a budget amendment that would "prohibit the department from proposing, planning or initiating another round of Base Realignment and Closure."[28] However, this language did not make it into the final version of the bill that was signed into law.[29] Efforts to obtain congressional authorization of a renewed Base Realignment and Closure Commissions process have continued despite this resistance.[30]

At the same time, we have seen efforts by Congress, and even the executive branch, to stake out some elements of independence or perhaps more precisely, autonomy, for the executive branch agencies. Sometimes this reflects semantic desire—as when the EPA is called a "strong independent agency,"[31] sometimes this semantic desire reflects political will,[32] and sometimes it reflects an effort to assert some sense of autonomy in the activities of executive branch agencies.

Importantly, individual independent agencies vary with tradition and political context. The NLRB, as an example, is often thought of as a politicized agency.[33] In contrast, the Federal Reserve Board is viewed (at least in recent years) as relatively free of presidential control. Consider this colloquy with Akhil Reed Amar in a question-and-answer

---

28 Charles S. Clark, *Congress Revs Up Resistance to a New BRAC Round,* GOV'T EXECUTIVE (May 29, 2013), http://www.govexec.com/oversight/2013/05/congress-revs-resistance-new-brac-round/63797/. A week later, the Senate Armed Services readiness subcommittee similarly "approved legislation rejecting the DOD's request to shutter installations and facilities in the United States that are no longer needed as the military branches cut the number of troops in uniform." Richard Lardner & Donna Cassata, *Panel Rejects Request for Military Base Closings,* MILITARY.COM (June 12, 2013), http://www.military.com/daily-news/2013/06/12/panel-rejects-request-for-military-base-closings.html.

29 National Defense Authorization Act for Fiscal Year 2014, Pub. L. No. 113-66, 127 Stat 672 (2013).

30 In February 2014, Defense Secretary Chuck Hagel indicated the DOD's plans to ask for a 2017 Base Realignment and Closure Commissions round to cut billions from infrastructure costs despite being "mindful that Congress has not agreed to [our] BRAC [Base Realignment and Closure Commissions] requests of the last two years." Dep't of Defense Secretary Chuck Hagel, Fiscal Year 2015 Budget Preview Delivered in Pentagon Press Briefing Room (Feb. 24, 2014). Legislators such as Representative Steny Hoyer have voiced their opposition to another Base Realignment and Closure Commissions round: "[n]ot at this point in time. I don't think it's necessary." Andy Medici, *Lawmakers Divided on Possible 2017 BRAC Round,* ARMY TIMES (Mar. 3. 2014), http://www.armytimes.com/article/20140303/NEWS05/303030021/Lawmakers-divided-possible-2017-BRAC-round. However, opposition to a new Base Realignment and Closure Commissions process does not appear to be as strident as it was in the past. Representative Gerry Connolly noted "[i]t's probably inevitable that there will be another round of Base Realignment and Closure Commissions closures because frankly the defense budget is going to have to make some serious adjustments given the fiscal realities." *Id.*

31 *See* Special Message from the President to the Congress About Reorganization Plans to Establish the Environmental Protection Agency and the National Oceanic and Atmospheric Administration, Reorganization Plan No. 3 of 1970 (July 9, 1970). "Because environmental protection cuts across so many jurisdictions, and because arresting environmental deterioration is of great importance to the quality of life in our country and the world, I believe that in this case a strong, independent agency is needed." Interestingly, the term "independent" is not found in the document creating the EPA. *See* Reorganization Plan No. 3 of 1970, 84 Stat. 2086 (1970).

32 *See supra* chapter 3, section D.

33 *See supra* chapter 2, section D, *and* chapter 4, notes 54–56 and accompanying text.

period following a speech he gave, "The President, the Cabinet, and Independent Agencies."

PROFESSOR ROBERT DELAHUNTY: Let me just ask a question about independent agencies, if I may. The Federal Reserve Board, which you mentioned, Professor Amar, is certainly well-entrenched, but it also, as we know, plays a very powerful policy role. Some people who believe in the unconstitutionality of independent agencies, including that one, would argue that—

PROFESSOR AMAR: Which one?

PROFESSOR DELAHUNTY: The Federal Reserve Board. Yes. [*sic*] Would argue that its power is so extensive that it could really thwart the president in a material way from carrying out the policies that he's announced to the nation and was elected to execute. I mean, if we have a president who wants a stimulus plan, but a Federal Reserve Board that is intent on controlling inflation and keeping interest rates high, it frustrates the executive will and probably also the legislative will. Is that an obstacle to the constitutionality of an independent agency like the Federal Reserve Board or not, do you think?

PROFESSOR AMAR: I think that's an outstanding question and so if I were just looking at the text and structure in a vacuum, that might have been my inclination. Now, here's in the end why that's not what I said: Because it's not our practice and it hasn't been our practice for at least seventy-five years, as to the [F]ed itself, because I know of no president, Republican or Democrat, liberal or conservative, who's made the argument that you just made in opposition to the Fed and so it does move me, but many academics have, and I'm not unsympathetic to the theoretical argument, but no president—and if I'm wrong on that fact, then I would need to rethink my theory—

PROFESSOR DELAHUNTY: We thought about it in Bush I, but it came to nothing.[34]

Devotees of the unitary executive continue to fulminate against the notion of independent agencies, focusing not only on the "sins" of principal officers who are not required to bend the knee, but on "inferior officers" who carry with them significant discretionary, yet executive, authority.[35] But, as noted earlier, courts have shifted away from that notion. In *Humphrey's Executor*, for example, the Supreme Court in the mid-1930s observed that the FTC "cannot in any proper sense be characterized as an arm or an eye

[34] Akhil Reed Amar, *The President, The Cabinet, and Independent Agencies*, 5 U. St. Thomas J.L. & Pub. Pol'y 36, 57 (Fall 2010).

[35] *See, e.g.*, Christopher S. Yoo et al., *The Unitary Executive in the Modern Era, 1945–2004*, 90 Iowa L. Rev. 601, 643–45 (2005). *See also* Fed. Mar. Comm'n v. S. C. State Ports Auth., 535 U.S. 743, 776 (2002) (Breyer, J. dissenting) (explaining that "upshot is that this case involves a typical Executive branch agency exercising typical Executive Branch Power seeking to determine whether a particular person has violated federal law").

of the executive.... Its duties are performed without executive leave and, in the contemplation of the statute, must be free from executive control... the commission acts in part quasi-legislatively and in part quasi-judicially.... *To the extent that it exercises any executive function, as distinguished from executive power in the* constitutional sense, it does so in the discharge and effectuation of its quasi-legislative or quasi-judicial powers, or as an agency of the legislative or judicial departments of the government."[36] By the mid-1980s, however, the Court accepted that independent entities may constitutionally exercise executive functions.[37] And the Court, or individual justices, appear to have accepted the independence of both the SEC and FCC despite the statutory language that was central to the *Humphrey's Executor* decision.

While the courts do not appear to have pressed the logic of separation of powers to an ineluctable conclusion (although one circuit court judge has intimated that *Humphrey's Executor* should be a disfavored precedent),[38] "originalist" academics and adherents of a maximal "theory of the unitary executive" have pressed hard on the appointments clause, deploying it to claim that a wide swath of government officials were appointed by flawed constitutional means. In that regard some have argued for a limiting definition of the Constitutional term "head of department."[39] Others have raised questions concerning the definition of inferior officer as with bankruptcy judges,[40] most ALJs,[41] and

---

36 FTC v. Am. Nat. Cellular, Inc., 810 F.2d 1511, 1515 (9th Cir. 1987) (citing Humphrey's Ex'r v. United States, 295 U.S. 602, 628 (1935). *See also* FTC v. Ruberoid Co., 343 U.S. 470, 487–88 (1952) ("Administrative agencies have been called quasi-legislative, quasi-executive or quasi-judicial, as the occasion required, in order to validate their functions within the separation-of-powers scheme of the Constitution. The mere retreat to the qualifying 'quasi' is implicit with confession that all recognized classifications have broken down, and 'quasi' is a smooth cover which we draw over our confusion as we might use a counterpane to conceal a disordered bed").

37 Morrison v. Olson, 487 U.S. 654 (1988).

38 *In re* Aiken Cnty, 645 F. 3d 428, 441–42 (D.C. Cir. 2011) (Kavanaugh, J. concurring).

39 U.S. Const. art. II, § 2, cl. 2. For example, James Pfander argues that the constitutional authorization for Congress to vest the appointment of an inferior officer in the "courts of law" would make the tradition of the chief justice appointing Article III judges to specialty courts unconstitutional. *The Chief Justice, the Appointment of Inferior Officers and the "Court of Law" Requirement*, 107 Nw. U. L. Rev. 1125 (2013)). Such courts include Judicial Panel on Multidistrict Litigation. (See 28 U.S.C. § 1407(d) (2006) and the Alien Terrorist Removal Center (*see* 8 U.S.C. § 1532(a) (2006) ("The Chief Justice... shall publically designate 5 district court judges from 5 of the United States judicial circuits...."), as well as the two courts identified in the Foreign Intelligence Surveillance Act: the Foreign Intelligence Surveillance Court and the Foreign Intelligence Surveillance Court of Review (50 U.S.C. § 1803(a)–(b)(2006)).

40 *See* Tuan Samahon, *Are Bankruptcy Judges Unconstitutional? An Appointments Clause Challenge*, 60 Hastings L.J. 233, 284 (2008) (highlighting the concern "that the appointment of bankruptcy judges by other judges means the political check of the President's nomination and the Senate's confirmation will not apply to powerful officers... appointment by the circuit courts—essentially appointment by committee—may diminish democratic accountability for poor appointments, particularly where the process lacks transparency.").

41 Kent Barnett, *Resolving the ALJ Quandary*, 66 Vand. L. Rev. 797, 802 (2013) (contending that "[p]ermitting a 'Court[] of Law' to appoint ALJs, who are at most 'inferior Officers' within the executive branch, comports with the text of the Appointments Clause and Supreme Court case law"). *See also* Jerome Nelson,

patent judges.[42] Some have focused on the delegation of government power to private or international actors such as UN chemical weapons inspectors,[43] or the need for Senate confirmation of officers of the United States as with the so-called pay czar,[44] and members of the Copyright Royalty Board.[45] Still others have warned of the unconstitutional expansion of an office beyond the contours of the original appointment.[46] This has led to critiques of the constitutionality of offices such as the deputy director of the CFPB.[47]

How this multilayered approach plays out for independent agencies is unclear. Certainly, *Free Enterprise Fund* rejected the idea of "double for cause" when it overturned SEC appointment of PCAOB commissioners for a term of years.[48] At the same time it expanded the notion of "head of department" to encompass appointments voted on by all the commissioners, not just the chair.[49] And most dispiriting to conservatives,[50]

Administrative Law Judges' Removal "Only for Cause": Is That Administrative Procedure Act Protection Now Unconstitutional?, 63 ADMIN. L. REV. 401 (2011) (arguing that ALJs are clearly "officers" because they possess "significan[t] ... duties and discretion," *id.* at 405, but may properly retain removal protection to ensure "adjudicatory independence," *id.* at 416).

42 John F. Duffy, *Are Administrative Patent Judges Unconstitutional?*, 77 GEO. WASH. L. REV. 904 (2009). An earlier version of this essay was published in 2007 and gave rise to a legislative "fix." *See* John F. Duffy, *Are Administrative Patent Judges Unconstitutional?*, 2007 PATENTLY-O PATENT L.J. 21 (July 23, 2007), http://patentlyo.com/media/docs/2007/07/Duffy.BPAI.pdf.

43 John Yoo, *The New Sovereignty and the Old Constitution: The Chemical Weapons Conventions and the Appointment Clause*, 15 CONST. COMMENT. 87 (1998) (noting that "[v]esting authority to conduct searches in an international organization may evade this fundamental political check on domestic law enforcement.").

44 Michael W. McConnell, *The Pay Czar Is Unconstitutional*, WALL ST. J., Oct 30, 2009, at A25. For a review of the issue of White House czars generally, see *supra* chapter 3, section B.

45 The current form of the Copyright Royalty Board was established in 2004 by statute. Copyright Royalty and Distribution Reform Act of 2004, Pub. L. No. 108–419, 118 Stat. 2341 (codified at 17 U.S.C. § 801 et seq.) The board is composed of three copyright royalty judges, who are appointed to staggered six-year terms by the librarian of Congress, tasked with creating schedules and rates for the payment of copyright royalties. *See* Intercollegiate Broad. Sys., Inc. v. Copyright Royalty Bd., 684 F.3d 1332, 1334 (D.C. Cir. 2012), *cert. denied*, 133 S. Ct. 2735, 186 L. Ed. 2d 192 (2013) (remedying the appointments clause violation posed by the Copyright Royalty Board judges' significant ratemaking authority "by invalidating and severing the restrictions on the Librarian of Congress's ability to remove the CRJs").

46 The example used is senior federal judges. *See* David R. Aras & Ryan W. Scott, *Are Senior Judges Unconstitutional?*, 92 CORNELL L. REV. 453 (2007).

47 Kent Barnett, *The Consumer Financial Protection Bureau's Appointment with Trouble*, 60 AM. U. L. REV. 1459 (2011). Barnett argues that "[t]he Appointments Clause permits 'Heads of Departments' to appoint inferior officers like the Deputy Director. But it is unclear if the Bureau is a 'department' and thus if the Director is a department head who can appoint the Deputy Director. Although I argue that the Bureau should be deemed a department, I explain why the Supreme Court's recent decision in *Free Enterprise Fund v. Public Co. Accounting Oversight Board* and prior Appointments Clause jurisprudence suggest otherwise." *Id.* at 1460.

48 Free Enter. Fund v. Pub. Co. Accounting Oversight Bd., 130 S. Ct. 3138, 3151 (2010).

49 *Id.* at 3162–64. Conservatives have not fully accepted this expansive view of "head of department."

50 As but one example, see Hans Bader, *Free Enterprise Fund v. PCAOB: Narrow Separation-of-Powers Ruling Illustrates That the Supreme Court is Not "Pro-Business,"* CATO SUPREME CT. REV. 269–99 (2009–2010).

the Court chose not to invalidate the entire SEC statute but to engage in the more modest step of invalidating the "double for cause" appointments and substituting "at will" appointment by the commission for the PCAOB members.[51] As of now, the Court has not pressed the logic of its appointments clause analysis to its ineluctable conclusion, but the future course of this clause, and its impact on independent agencies is a chapter yet to be written.

Adrian Vermeule has noted that recent law scholarship suggests that there is a

> [d]isconnect between the received wisdom about which agencies are properly viewed as independent... and the formal legal position... because the received wisdom does not seem to be derived from, or responsive to, the language and context of the relevant statutes and the default legal rules. Rather... the identity of the independent agencies is a function of other factors such as political will and public opinion.[52]

Thus it should be no surprise that the independent agency form has undergone various structural changes in recent decades, and will probably experience even more changes now that administrative agencies are charged with a "new paradigm" where "the goals of regulation have become the promotion of competition and maximization of consumer choice."[53] The tensions that create a spur to decentralization of authority and accountability will no doubt continue. Of particular note in this process has been the development of multimember commissions, multimember supervisory agencies, single member independent agencies, and the development of their processes and their place in the administrative state. All these efforts reflect historic (and indeed structural) efforts by Congress to both provide some autonomy from the president for the swath of administrative activities and, in some cases, to keep for themselves some place at the table, no matter how modest.

The last decades make clear the difficulties of hewing to a strict ideological paradigm regarding the ever-evolving administrative state. As Jacob Gersen suggests: "[W]e are in the midst of something of an agency design renaissance—a time period of fundamental change with respect to the federal bureaucracy."[54] New social and economic realities throw up a kaleidoscope of administrative formats to be tested against "core"

---

[51] Free Enter. Fund, 130 S. Ct. at 3161–63.

[52] Adrian Vermeule, *Conventions of Agency Independence*, 113 COLUM. L. REV. 1163, 1179 (2013).

[53] Joseph D. Kearney & Thomas W. Merrill, *The Great Transformation of Regulated Industries Law*, 98 COLUM. L. REV. 1323, 1323, 1364–83 (1998) (discussing institutional roles change from the "original paradigm" where agencies were charged with general regulatory oversight of particular industries).

[54] Jacob E. Gersen, *Administrative Law Goes to Wall Street: The New Administrative Process*, 65 ADMIN. L. REV. 689, 690 (2013). Gersen suggests that this renaissance is driven mainly, although not exclusively, from the emergence of new administrative forms of financial regulation. *Id.*

constitutional values. Our discussion in chapter 8 of the changing role of public and private sector institutions underscores this point. It is our considered view that in the rest of this century, the function filled by the independent agency will also be filled, from time to time, by public corporations, GSEs, and what the British quaintly call quangos, as Congress continues to experiment with institutional arrangements.[55] Further, we expect a significant increase in the "contracting out" and privatization of various (indeed, at times core) government functions. This blurring of public and private regulatory roles is reflective of a general shift toward a more nuanced understanding of the characteristics of the public–private distinction in American jurisprudence. Similarly, our discussion in chapter 6 makes clear that the drive for independence from the executive is a constant counter-theme present in the centralizing trend of the administrative state.[56] And as indicated in chapter 10, the trend toward independence as a separate value is present as well in the international arena. The working out of these developments and their meaning for traditional public law values suggests, we believe, the next frontier in administrative law.

One further point remains.

As we have suggested, the growth of the administrative state has led to an ever-expanding variety of efforts by Congress and the president to manage administrative complexity within constitutional contexts. We have suggested that this development looks to continue as the growth of government "bends the arc" toward ever-evolving and innovative institutional arrangements. We must recognize one caveat however. Whether correct in their analysis or not, a substantial body of the Republican Party is determined to reduce the role and scope of government in the American economy. During the "Gingrich revolution" in the 1990s the Republicans promised to close numerous government agencies as part of their party's "Contract With America,"[57] yet they only

---

55 *See supra* chapter 8, section A.

56 *See supra* chapter 6, section D.

57 During an address to the American people at the end of the first one hundred days of the 104th Congress, Gingrich stated:

> We must restore freedom by ending bureaucratic micromanagement here in Washington. As any good business leader will tell you, decisions should be made as closely as possible to the source of the problem. This country is too big and too diverse for Washington to have the knowledge to make the right decisions on local matters. We've got to return power back to you, to your families, your neighborhoods, your local and state governments. We need to promote economic growth by reducing regulation, reducing taxation and reducing frivolous lawsuits.

Newt Gingrich, *April 7 1995 Address to the Nation*, 104 CONG. REC. (1995).

A 1995 House Budget Committee resolution recommended "[e]liminating the Departments of Education, Commerce, and Energy. These proposals are consistent with plans being drafted by House Republican freshmen to discard needless and unwieldy bureaucratic structures. This budget also terminates or privatizes 284 programs, 13 agencies, and 69 commissions." H.R. REP. NO. 104-120, at 5–6 (1st Sess. 1995) (to accompany H.R. Con. Res. 67, 104th Cong. (1995)). The Senate Budget Committee report was equally aggressive—its "recommendations assume the termination of more than 100 federal programs,

succeeded in shutting down (at least temporarily) three: the Administrative Conference of the United States,[58] the Advisory Commission on Intergovernmental Relations,[59] and a congressional agency, the Office of Technology Assessment.[60] Efforts were made as well to rein in (if not "gut") agency rulemaking, with limited success.[61] Whether the

---

agencies, and commissions" including "the Department of Commerce and the Office of Personnel Management." S. REP. NO. 104-82 (1st Sess. 1995), at 3.

However, one scholar comments, "[e]fforts to eliminate entire Cabinet-level departments of the government also have proved difficult. Conservatives have long sought to pursue a policy of 'rollback' in dealing with proliferating government departments. The prime candidates on the list of government departments conservatives seek to eliminate are the Departments of Commerce, Education, Energy, and Housing and Urban Development." Jeffery B. Gayner, *The Contract with America: Implementing New Ideas in the U.S.*, Heritage Foundation Report (Oct. 12, 1995), http://www.heritage.org/research/lecture/the-contract-with-america-implementing-new-ideas-in-the-us. In 1995, "only the Commerce Department seem[ed] vulnerable.... The combination of disenchantment with the size of the central government and growing budgetary constraints in Congress has created real momentum to seriously reduce the size and scope of central government activities in America." *Id.*

58 *See supra* chapter 1, note 9.

59 Bruce D. McDowell, *Advisory Commission on Intergovernmental Relations in 1996: The End of an Era*, 27 PUBLIUS 111, 121–22 (1997).

60 The Office of Technology Assessment was created during "the Nixon Administration to give Congress technical expertise equal to that available to the executive branch through its many departments and agencies." Warren E. Leary, *Congress's Science Agency Prepares to Close Its Doors,* N.Y. TIMES, Sept. 24, 1995, at A14. The Office of Technology Assessment was defunded in 1995 by the Legislative Branch Appropriations Act of 1996, Pub. L. No. 104-53, 109 Stat. 468 (1995). According to one scholar, the Office of Technology Assessment was "[t]he first federal agency to actually fall at the hand of the 104th Congress" and argues that "[i]ts termination is an example of symbolic budget cutting or 'trophy hunting' as the activity is sometimes called on Capitol Hill." Bruce Bimber, *The Death of An Agency: Office of Technology Assessment and Budget Politics in the 104th Congress* (Feb. 22, 1996), *available at* http://oldsite.english.ucsb.edu/faculty/ayliu/research/bimber.html#House1995a.

61 The 1995 Comprehensive Regulatory Reform Act (which never passed) heightened the standard of judicial review for rulemaking requiring (in its original version) that the agency used "reasoned decision-making in determining that the [agency's] interpretation... is one that maximizes net benefits to society." S. 343, 104th Cong., 1st Sess. § 624 (as introduced Feb. 2, 1995).

The Congressional Accountability Act of 1996 created a mechanism by which Congress could review all "major rules" before they can take effect. For many at the time, the goal of such regulatory reform was "clogging the wheels of the federal bureaucracy," considering that its purpose was to "add more red tape and judicial oversight." Robert W. Hahn, *Regulatory Reform—The Whole Story,* WALL ST. J., Feb. 27, 1995, at A12. At the time, Congressman David McIntosh went on to suggest: "many Americans think paralyzing the federal government would be a good thing." *Hearings on the Regulatory Transaction Act of 1995, H.R. 450 Before the Subcomm. on National Economic Growth, Natural Resources and Regulatory Affairs, Comm. on Government Reform & Oversight*, 104th Cong., 1st Sess. (Jan. 19, 1995), at 122. For a good summary of the Gingrich era rulemaking reform efforts see Robert L. Glicksman & Stephen B. Chapman, *Regulatory Reform and (Breach of) The Contract with America: Improving Environmental Policy or Destroying Environmental Protection?*, 5 KAN. J.L. & PUB. POL'Y 9, 37 n.141 (1996).

More recently, legislation has been proposed that requires the equivalent of formal trial-type rulemakings for "high impact" regulations. *See* Regulatory Availability Act, H.R. 2122 113th Cong. § 553(e) (introductory paragraph) and § 553(b) (2013). For a critique, see H. Rep. 113-23 at 5–6 (2013) (testimony of Ronald L. Levin before U.S. House of Reps. Committee on the Judiciary Hearing on H.R. 2122).

"Tea Party"[62] will succeed in these efforts at this time is far from clear (and indeed as of printing, the pendulum may have begun to swing back),[63] but should they succeed, the impact on the independent agency forum will be significant.

C. Final Thoughts

When Attorney General Tom C. Clark gave his endorsement to the draft legislation that was to become the APA, he concluded that the bill "appears to offer a hopeful prospect of achieving reasonable uniformity and fairness in administrative procedures without at the same time interfering unduly with the efficient and economical operation of the Government."[64] But this prospect for the administrative state is more aspirational than descriptive of reality. The emergence of the independent administrative agencies reflects somewhat the same considerations.

Tom Paine, the great English essayist, who was among the most influential advocates of American independence, in 1776 wrote of the importance of timing. Addressing the circumstances of colonial America, he observed:

> Youth is the seed time of good habits, as well in nations as in individuals. It might be difficult, if not impossible, to form the [American] Continent into one government half a century hence. The vast variety of interests, occasioned by an increase of trade and population, would create confusion. Colony would be against colony. Each being able might scorn each other's assistance: and while the proud and foolish

62 The Tea Party movement emerged in 2009, founded upon frustrations of Americans who had become increasingly disenchanted with "the perceived size and intrusiveness of the federal government." Jared A. Goldstein, *The Tea Party Movement and the Perils of Popular Originalism*, 53 Ariz. L. Rev. 827, 832 (2011). Their foundational principles, suggests Emily Price Foley, include "(1) limited government, (2) unapologetic U.S. sovereignty, and (3) constitutional originalism." Elizabeth Price Foley, The Tea Party: Three Principles xiv (2012). An insightful study concluding that "the impact of the Tea Party will remain evident in American politics for years to come" is Theda Skocpol & Vanessa Williamson, The Tea Party and the Remaking of American Conservatism 217 (2012).

63 During a press conference preceding a December 2013 House vote on a two-year budget deal, Speaker of the House John Boehner sharply criticized the Tea Party members: "[f]rankly, I think they're misleading their followers. I think they're pushing our members into places where they don't want to be. And frankly, I just think that they've lost all credibility." Paul Kane & Ed O'Keefe, *Boehner Attacks Tea Party Groups as House Approves Budget Deal,* Wash. Post (Dec. 12, 2013), http://www.washingtonpost.com/politics/boehner-escalates-feud-with-conservative-groups-as-vote-on-budget-bill-looms/2013/12/12/3986871c-634f-11e3-91b3-f2bb96304e34_story.html. *See also* Stephanie McCrummen, *Feeling Besieged, Tea Party Groups Steel for Battle,* Wash. Post, Dec. 18, 2013, at A1 (quoting Tea Party leader Linda Weeks: "[t]o hear what Boehner said was very upsetting. But from what I hear more and more conservatives are coming out of the woodwork. Instead of pushing back, he has just unleashed us.").

64 United States Dep't of Justice, Attorney General's Manual on the Administrative Procedure Act 6 (1947) (providing detailed analysis of each section of the Act).

> gloried in their little distinctions, the wise would lament that the union had not been formed before.[65]

Without question, timing is critical to the creation or alteration of independent agencies. Circumstances must be propitious if agency change is to be achieved. Derthick and Quirk reasonably argue that a sense of urgency and a consensus of "elite opinion" are essential to reform.[66] But most important, "crisis begets change." Creation of many, if not most, of the independent agencies arose to address some actual or perceived need. That will likely continue into the future.

The administrative process owes more to history and experience than to doctrine. Glen Robinson has observed that "[t]he history of important institutions and government programs is often more one of eclectic confusion than of single-minded purpose."[67] In the constitutional realm, established practice is important, although not determinative,[68] because it reflects an accommodation among affected interests of the way business can be conducted without unduly infringing on the prerogatives of others. That is especially true of the internal operations of agencies, where there is often little more than ambiguous and incomplete legislation to govern or guide agency practice. A structure or practice that begins as a means of simply solving a problem, or asserting power, or experimentally addressing a political dilemma, can either become accepted, or challenged and rejected. But if accepted, the approach becomes a tradition; that tradition, over time, can take on the trappings of precedent and eventually obtain the sanction of law. This pragmatic adaptation will, at times, be thwarted by the Supreme Court's occasional reliance on a formalist approach, as represented by cases like *Free Enterprise Fund, Bowsher*, and *Chadha*.[69] But there is no reason to believe that the Court will follow the "broader implications of *Free Enterprise Fund* to their logical conclusion."[70]

In 1835, during debates over the power of the president to remove the secretary of the treasury summarily, Daniel Webster was of the view that, as an original proposition,

---

[65] Thomas Paine, Common Sense 107–08 (1776) (Isaac Kramnick ed., Penguin Books 1982).

[66] *See* Martha Derthick & Paul J. Quirk, The Politics of Deregulation 238–39 (1985).

[67] Glen O. Robinson, American Bureaucracy: Public Choice and Public Law 12 (1991) (tracing evolution of bureaucracy). Peter Schuck agrees, arguing that the administrative state "shaped by liberal democratic values and by a notoriously messy, unpredictable, pluralistic, institutionally competitive political process." Peter H. Schuck, *Professor Rabin and the Administrative State*, 61 DePaul L. Rev. 595, 614 (2012).

[68] *See, e.g.*, INS v. Chadha, 462 U.S. 919, 967 (1983) (White, J., dissenting) (questioning the Court's decision that struck down the legislative veto placed in nearly two hundred statutes over five decades).

[69] *See* Free Enter. Fund v. Pub. Co. Accounting Oversight Bd., 130 S. Ct. 3138, 3155 (2010); Bowsher v. Synar, 478 U.S. 714, 736 (1986); INS v. Chadha, 462 U.S. 919, 956–57 (1983).

[70] Ronald J. Krotoszynski, Jr., *Cooperative Federalism, the New Formalism, and the Separation of Powers Revisited: Free Enterprise Fund and the Problem of Presidential Oversight of State-Government Officers Enforcing Federal Law*, 61 Duke L.J. 1599, 1658 (2012).

he would not have accorded the president that power.[71] Nevertheless, based on the first forty-five years of the country's history, he conceded that the president had such power. The Decision of 1789, in his view, "has been established by practice, and recognized by subsequent laws, as the settled construction of the Constitution."[72] The role, place, and operation of independent agencies have a comparable pedigree.

[71] *See* Myers v. United States, 272 U.S. 52, 148–49 (1926) (*quoting* 1 PRIVATE CORRESPONDENCE OF DANIEL WEBSTER 486 (national ed., Little Brown 1903)).

[72] *Id.* at 151.

APPENDIX A

Some Characteristics of Independent Agencies

MULTIMEMBER BOARDS AND COMMISSIONS

BOARD OF VETERANS' APPEALS

Lafayette Building
811 Vermont Avenue NW
Washington, DC 20420
(202) 461-8000 General Inquiries
(202) 461-4995 Office of the General Counsel
Website: www.bva.va.gov

Mission and General Statutory Reference: The BVA is in the Department of Veterans Affairs and reviews benefit claims appeals and renders decisions regarding those appeals. 38 U.S.C. §§ 7101–7109.

Agency Statutory History: Initially created by Executive Order No. 6230, pt. 2 (July 28, 1933). Established as a statutory body by Pub. L. 85-857, 72 Stat. 1240 (Sept. 2, 1958), with a chairman "directly responsible to the Administrator," a vice chairman, and "such number (not more than fifty)... associate members as may be found necessary." Section 208 of the Veterans' Compensation and Program Improvements Amendments of 1984, Pub. L. 98-223, 98 Stat. 43 (Mar. 2, 1984), increased the number of associate members to sixty-five. Section 201(b) of Pub. L. 100-687, 102 Stat. 4109 (Nov. 18, 1988), provided that the chairman shall be appointed by the president to a six-year term with the advice and consent of the Senate and other members to be appointed by the veterans' administrator with the approval of the president. Pub. L. 103-271, 108 Stat. 740 (July 1, 1994), removes the numerical limit on the number of associate members. Section 201(c) of Pub. L. 103-446, 108 Stat. 4657 (Nov. 11, 1998), requires the chairman to establish a panel to review the performance of board members. The board is now "under the administrative control and supervision of a chairman directly responsible to the Secretary [of Veterans Affairs]." 38 U.S.C. 7101(a).

Membership: The board consists of a chairman, a vice chairman, and an unlimited number of board members. 38 U.S.C. § 7101(a). The chairman is appointed by the president with the advice and consent of the Senate and serves for a term of six years. The chairman serves at the assistant secretary level and may be appointed to more than one term. He may be removed only for "misconduct, inefficiency, neglect of duty, or engaging in the practice of law or for physical or mental disability which in the opinion of the president prevents the proper execution of the Chairman's duties." 38 U.S.C. § 7101(b)(a). At the close of fiscal year 2011, there were sixty-four members of the board. The secretary designates one member as vice chairman. The vice chairman performs functions specified by the chairman and serves "at the pleasure of the Secretary." 38 U.S.C. § 7101(b)(4). The vice chairman is compensated as a member of the Senior Executive Service. Other members of the board are appointed by the secretary, with approval of the president, based upon the recommendations of the chairman. 38 U.S.C. § 7101A(a). Board members are the only federal employees at this level who require presidential approval for appointment. Board members (other than the chairman) have no limits on their terms, but must be "recertified" at least once every three years under performance standards developed by the chairman with the approval of the Secretary. Board members (other than the chairman and the vice chairman) are paid at rates equivalent to the rates payable under 5 U.S.C. § 5372 (i.e., comparable to that of administrative law judges).

Quorum and Voting Requirements: A proceeding instituted before the board may be assigned to an individual member of the board or to a panel of not fewer than three members of the board. 38 U.S.C. § 7102(a). When a proceeding is assigned to a panel of board members, the decision is by the majority vote of panel members. *See* 38 C.F.R. § 19.7(c) (1999). Proceedings before the board are nonadversarial in nature and less formal than court proceedings. Nevertheless, certain statutory and regulatory prerequisites must be fulfilled before an appeal is properly before the board. However, formal procedures apply for the docketing of appeals and hearings, as well as for the conduct of hearings, motions practice, and other procedures.

Disqualification and Recusal Procedure: Any board member must recuse himself or herself if he or she has participated in the matter or where there are other circumstances that might give the impression of bias. The board chairman, on his or her own motion, may disqualify a member from acting on a particular case. *See* 38 C.F.R. § 19.12(c).

Chairman's Powers: A chairman, who is "directly responsible to the Secretary" of Veterans Affairs, directs the board's activities. *See* 38 U.S.C. § 7101(a). The chairman alone has the authority to select key staff officials, who include board members and administrative personnel, without obtaining the prior approval of the members. Pursuant to 38 U.S.C. § 7101A, the secretary of veterans affairs, with approval of the president of the United States, based upon recommendation of the chairman, appoints members of the board, including the vice chairman. 38 U.S.C. § 7101A(a). In practice, the chairman often seeks the advice of board members when recommending the appointment of new board members. But that decision is purely discretionary.

OMB Bypass Provisions: The board's budget is a component of the department's overall budget, submitted by the secretary to Congress. The chairman is responsible for forwarding budget recommendations to the secretary. The board's budget and legislative submissions are processed through the Department of Veterans Affairs.

Litigation Authority: The board has no authority to litigate appeals of its decisions. The general counsel of the Department of Veterans Affairs represents the secretary before the U.S. Court of Appeals for Veterans Claims.

Selective Bibliography

Books

Board of Veterans' Appeals, Board of Veteran Appeals, 1933–1984 (1984).

Board of Veterans' Appeals, Board of Veteran Appeals 50th Anniversary, 1933–83 (1983).

Board of Veterans' Appeals, The BVA Story . . . : The First 40 Years (1974).

William F. Fox, The United States Board of Veterans' Appeals: the Unfinished Struggle to Reconcile Speed and Justice During the Intra-agency Review (2000).

Articles

Charles L. Cragin, *A Time of Transition at the Board of Veterans' Appeals*, 38 Fed. B. News & J. 485 (1991).

Charles L. Cragin, *The Impact of Judicial Review of the Department of Veterans Affairs' Claims Adjudication Process: The Changing Role of the Board of Veterans' Appeals*, 46 Me. L. Rev. 23 (1994).

Frank Q. Nebeker, *Jurisdiction of the United States Court of Veterans Appeals: Search Out the Limits*, 46 Me. L. Rev. 5 (1994).

Barton F. Sitchman, *The Veterans' Judicial Review Act of 1988*, 38 Fed. B. News & J. 486 (1991).

Donald N. Zillman, *Veterans Law Symposium: Introduction*, 46 Me. L. Rev. 1 (1994).

CHEMICAL SAFETY AND HAZARD INVESTIGATION BOARD

2175 K Street NW
Washington, DC 20037
(202) 261-7600 General Inquiries
(202) 261-7600 Office of the General Counsel
Website: www.csb.gov

Mission and General Statutory Reference: The Chemical Safety Board (CSB) is an independent agency that investigates the cause or probable cause of any accidental chemical release resulting in a fatality, serious injury, or substantial property damage, establishes mandatory rules for reporting accidental chemical releases, and conducts research and issues reports concerning the safety of chemical production. 42 U.S.C. § 7412(r)(6).

Agency Statutory History: The board was created by Section 301(r)(6) of the Clean Air Act Amendments of 1990, Pub. L. 101-549, 104 Stat. 2565 (Nov. 15, 1990). Congress declined to provide an appropriation for the Board until 1997. Its first appropriation of $4 million came in Title III of the Department of Veterans Affairs and Housing and Urban Development and

Independent Agency Appropriations Act of 1998, Pub. L. 105-65, 111 Stat. 1345, 1368 (Oct. 27, 1997). The board began operations in January 1998.

Membership: Five members appointed by the president, with the advice and consent of the Senate, for a five-year term, on the basis of "technical qualification, professional standing, and demonstrated knowledge in the fields of accident reconstruction, safety engineering, human factors, toxicology, or air pollution regulation." 42 U.S.C. § 7412(r)(6)(B). Members may be removed from office for inefficiency, neglect of duty, or malfeasance in office.

Other Presidential Appointees: inspector general. Individual appointed to the position of inspector general of the Environmental Protection Agency holds the position of inspector general of the board. Established annually in appropriations statute. *See, e.g.,* Pub. L. 112-74, 125 Stat. 1031 (2011).

Quorum and Voting Requirements: A quorum of the board for the transaction of business shall consist of three members; provided, however, that if the number of board members in office is fewer than three, a quorum shall consist of the number of members in office; and provided further that on any matter of business as to which the number of members in office, minus the number of members who have disqualified themselves from consideration of such matter is two, two members shall constitute a quorum for purposes of such matter. Once a quorum is constituted, a simple majority of voting members is required to approve an item of the board's business. A tie vote results in no action. 40 C.F.R. § 1600.5.

Disqualification and Recusal Procedure: No special procedures.

Chairman's Powers: The chairman is the board's chief executive officer and exercises the Board's executive and administrative functions, subject to the board's overall direction. When the board was without a chairperson, it designated one member to conduct certain executive and administrative functions. That individual is designated as the "Board Member Delegated Interim Executive and Administrative Authority" but not as acting chairman. Delegation lasts for 180 days or until a new chairperson is selected or the board rescinds the delegation. The delegation may be extended. *See* Board Order 003 (May 9, 2002, as amended).

OMB Bypass Provisions: Board budget and legislative proposals, testimony or comments, and recommendations or studies submitted to the administration, must be submitted concurrently to Congress. No board budget estimate, legislative recommendation or testimony, or other recommendation or study is subject to review by any federal agency, and no government official may require prior approval of budget requests or estimates, legislative recommendations, prepared testimony, comments, or recommendations or reports. 42 U.S.C. § 7412(r)(6)(R).

Litigation Authority: The DOJ represents the board in the federal courts. *See* also 42 U.S.C. 112(r)(6)(H). No part of the conclusions, findings, or recommendations of the board relating to any accidental release or the investigation thereof shall be admitted as evidence or used in any action or suit for damages arising out of any matter mentioned in such report.

Selective Bibliography

Articles

Gary J. Edles, *The Almost Accidental Start of a New Federal Agency*, 47 FED. LAW. 32 (2000).

COMMODITY FUTURES TRADING COMMISSION

Three Lafayette Center
1155 Twenty-first Street NW
Washington, DC 20581
(202) 418-5000 General Inquiries
(202) 418-5120 Office of the General Counsel
Website: www.cftc.gov

Mission and General Statutory Reference: The Commodity Futures Trading Commission (CFTC) is an "independent agency of the United States Government" that regulates derivatives that are subject to the Commodity Exchange Act (futures, commodity options, and swaps) to protect market users, consumers, and the public at large from fraud, manipulation, and other abusive trading practices, and systemic risk, and to foster open, transparent, competitive, and financially sound markets. 7 U.S.C. §§ 2, 5. *See generally* 7 U.S.C. §§ 1–25.

Agency Statutory History: Commission created by Section 101 of the Commodity Futures Trading Commission Act of 1974, Pub. L. 93-463, 88 Stat. 1389 (Oct. 23, 1974). The commission replaced the Commodity Exchange Commission, composed of the secretaries of agriculture and commerce and the attorney general, that had been created by the Commodity Exchange Act of 1936, Pub. L. 74-675, 49 Stat. 1492 (June 15, 1936), which, in turn, had replaced the Grains Futures Commission, also composed of the secretaries of agriculture and commerce and the attorney general, that had been created by Section 6 of the Grains Futures Act, Pub. L. 67-331, 42 Stat. 1001 (Sept. 21, 1922).

Membership: Five members, appointed by the president with the advice and consent of the Senate, serve staggered five-year terms. The president "shall select persons who shall each have demonstrated knowledge in futures trading or its regulation, or the production, merchandising, processing or distribution of one or more of the commodities or other goods and articles, services, rights and interests" covered by the statute, with appropriate balance among the knowledge of the commissioners with respect to such areas. 7 U.S.C. § 2(a)(2)(A)(i)–(ii). No more than three commissioners may belong to the same political party. A commissioner may continue to serve until his successor is appointed and qualified but only up to the expiration of the next session of Congress subsequent to the expiration of his term. There are no express statutory provisions governing removal of commissioners from office.

Significant Case: *Commodity Futures Trading Commission v. Schor*, 478 U.S. 833 (1986) (Commodity Exchange Act constitutionally permits the CFTC to adjudicate state law counterclaims in reparations proceedings).

Quorum and Voting Requirements: Statute contains no explicit quorum provision except that a vacancy in the commission "shall not impair the right of the remaining Commissioners to exercise all the powers of the Commission." 7 U.S.C. § 2(a)(3). Commission regulations define a quorum simply as "at least the minimum number of Commissioners required to take action on behalf of the Commission," i.e., three commissioners if there are no vacancies. 17 C.F.R. § 147.2(f). A majority of the quorum of the commission is required for purposes of taking commission action. However, when it is not feasible to convene a quorum, the senior commissioner available may take emergency action in certain circumstances, subject to review by the full commission. 17 C.F.R. § 140.11(a). In case of a tie, no action is taken, but in the case of review of adjudicatory matters, the decision below is affirmed.

Disqualification and Recusal Procedure: No specific procedures. However, in one case the commission did rule on a request that it disqualify two of its members. *See* James A. Carr, CFTC Docket No. 77-6, 1977 CFTC LEXIS 76, at *7 n.8 (denying the motion to disqualify the chairman and vice chairman).

Chairman's Powers: The chairman is the chief administrative officer. The president may at any time appoint a different member as chairman, with the advice and consent of the Senate. 7 U.S.C. § 74a (2)(a)(2)(B). The commission appoints the general counsel and an executive director, both of whom report directly to the commission and serve at the pleasure of the commission. 7 U.S.C. § 2(a)(4)–(5). Executive and administrative functions are generally exercised solely by the chairman, governed by general policies, plans, priorities, and budgets approved by the commission. The chairman's appointment of heads of major administrative units is subject to approval of the commission. 7 U.S.C. § 2(a)(6). There is no specific statutory provision governing their removal.

OMB Bypass Provisions: Bypass of prior OMB review on both budgetary and legislative matters is secured by means of a concurrent transmittal requirement under 7 U.S.C. § 2(a)(10). In addition, the commission is exempt from prior review or approval of testimony, legislative recommendations, or comments on legislation by any officer of the United States. 7 U.S.C. § 2(a)(10)(B).

Litigation Authority: Commission attorneys are authorized to represent the commission "in courts of law whenever appropriate [and] assist the Department of Justice in handling litigation concerning the Commission in courts of law." 7 U.S.C. § 2(a)(4). The Commodity Exchange Act also provides the commission with authority to bring enforcement actions in the federal district courts. 7 U.S.C. § 13a-1. The commission historically has deferred to the DOJ in certain types of litigation.

Selective Bibliography

Books

JASON H. BURNS, THE COMMODITY FUTURES TRADING COMMISSION (2008).

COMMODITY FUTURES TRADING COMMISSION—THE FIRST TEN YEARS (1985).

READ P. DUNN, THE FUNCTION OF THE COMMODITY FUTURES TRADING COMMISSION (1976).

Articles

Philip F. Johnson, *The Commodity Futures Trading Commission Reauthorization Process: A View from the Trenches*, 1979 DET. C.L. REV. 1 (1979).

Michael S. Sackheim, *Judicial Equitable Enforcement of the Federal Commodities Laws*, 32 AM. U. L. REV. 945 (1983).

Howard Schneider & Fred M. Santo, *Commodity Futures Trading Commission: A Review of the 1978 Legislation*, 34 BUS. LAW. 1755 (1979).

Donald L. Tendick & John G. Gaine, *Introducing the Regulator: the Commodity Futures Trading Commission*, 35 BUS. LAW. 751 (1980).

Note, *Role of the Commodity Futures Trading Commission Under the Commodity Futures Trading Commission Act of 1974*, 73 MICH. L. REV. 710 (1975).

CONSUMER PRODUCT SAFETY COMMISSION

4330 East-West Highway
Bethesda, MD 20814
(301) 504-7923 General Inquiries
(301) 504-0403 Office of the General Counsel
Website: www.cpsc.gov

Mission and General Statutory Reference: The Consumer Product Safety Commission (CPSC) is "an independent regulatory commission" that issues and enforces standards to protect the public against unreasonable risk of injury or death associated with consumer products, develops voluntary industry standards, and, as necessary, bans products, obtains the recall of products, or arranges for their repair. 15 U.S.C. §§ 2051–2084.

Agency Statutory History: The commission was created by the Consumer Product Safety Act of 1972, Pub. L. 92-573, 86 Stat. 1210 (1972). *See generally* S. REP. NO. 92-835 and H.R. REP. NO. 92-1593 (Conf. Rep.), reprinted in 1972 U.S. CODE CONG. & ADMIN. NEWS p. 4573. *See also* Postal Accountability and Enhancement Act of 2006, Pub. L. 109-435, 120 Stat. 3238 (Dec. 20, 2006).

Membership: Five members, appointed by the president with the advice and consent of the Senate, serve staggered seven-year terms. Since fiscal year 1987, however, Congress has funded only three commissioner positions in the commission's annual appropriations act. In making appointments, the statute directs the president to consider "individuals who [are qualified] by reason of their background and expertise in areas related to consumer products and protection of risks to safety." 15 U.S.C. § 2053(a). Not more than three of the commissioners may be affiliated with the same political party. Commissioners may continue to serve after the expiration of their term until a successor takes office, but for no more than one year. A commissioner may be removed from office by the president for "neglect of duty or malfeasance in office but for no other cause." 15 U.S.C. § 2053(a). The commission annually elects a vice chairman to act in the chairman's absence, disability, or vacancy of the office.

Quorum and Voting Requirements: Three commissioners constitute a quorum. However, two commissioners may constitute a quorum if there are only three members serving. If, due to vacancies, only two members of the commission are serving, those two constitute a quorum for six months. 15 U.S.C. § 2053(d). Generally, the commission issues a press release a few hours after a Commission decision meeting or one day after a ballot vote. commissioners may issue separate statements to be provided when the press release is issued. However, announcement of the commission's decision is not delayed for a commissioner's separate statement. Commissioners have their own staffs who assist in the preparation of their statements. The commission has no provision for proxy voting. Many administrative functions are delegated to the staff. The commission maintains a Directive System that contains delegations of authority. See 16 C.F.R.

1000.13. A complete set of delegations is available in the commission's reading room. However, the authority to issue subpoenas cannot be delegated.

Disqualification and Recusal Procedure: No specific procedures.

Chairman's Powers: The chairman is appointed by the president with the advice and consent of the Senate. The chairman serves as the principal executive officer with authority that includes the expenditure and use of funds and the appointment and supervision of personnel. 15 U.S.C. § 2053(f)(1) and (g)(1)(A). However, budget requests and appointments of senior staff (e.g., the executive director, the general counsel, and various associate executive directors) require commission approval. Section 2053(g)(1)(B)(i) further states that no individual may be appointed to such a position on an acting basis for a period longer than ninety days unless such appointment is approved by the commission. No appointment of any officer or employee may be subject to review or prior approval of anyone within the Executive Office of the President.

OMB Bypass Provisions: Bypass of OMB review on budgetary and legislative matters is secured by means of a requirement for concurrent transmittal and a prohibition on prior executive review of the commission's legislative communications. 15 U.S.C. § 2076(k)(1)–(2).

Litigation Authority: The commission has limited authority to represent itself in United States district courts. *See* 15 U.S.C. §§ 2061(e), 2071(a), 2076(b)(7) (1994).

Selective Bibliography

Books

Bureau of National Affairs, The Consumer Product Safety Act: Text, Analysis, Legislative History (1973).

Articles

Rachel E. Barkow, *Insulating Agencies: Avoiding Capture Through Institutional Design*, 89 Tex. L. Rev. 15 (2010).

DEFENSE NUCLEAR FACILITIES SAFETY BOARD

625 Indiana Avenue NW, Suite 700
Washington, DC 20004
(202) 694-7088 General Inquiries
(202) 694-7000 Office of the General Counsel
Website: www.dnfsb.gov

Mission and General Statutory Reference: The Defense Nuclear Facilities Safety Board is an "independent establishment in the executive branch" that provides technical safety oversight of the DOE's defense nuclear facilities. It makes recommendations with respect to these facilities, reviews designs of them, investigates any event or practice that may adversely affect public health and safety, and recommends to the secretary of energy any necessary modifications to ensure adequate protection of the public health and safety. 42 U.S.C. 2286–2286i.

Agency Statutory History: The board was created by Section 1441 of the National Defense Authorization Act, Fiscal Year 1989, Pub. L. 100-456, 102 Stat. 2076 (Sept. 29, 1988).

Significant Case: Energy Research Found. v. Def. Nuclear Facilities Safety Bd., 917 F.2d 581 (D.C. Cir. 1990) (As an "independent establishment in the executive branch," the board is an "agency" for the purposes of the Freedom of Information and Sunshine Act provisions of the Administrative Procedure Act).

Membership: Five members are appointed by the president with the advice and the consent of the Senate and serve staggered five-year terms. No more than three members of the board may be affiliated with the same political party. In making appointments, the statute directs the president to consider "United States citizens who are respected experts in the field of nuclear safety with a demonstrated competence and knowledge relevant to the independent investigative and oversight functions of the Board." 42 U.S.C. § 2286(b)(1) (1994). The president designates a chairman and vice chairman of the board from among the board's members. Board members may be reappointed. However, any member appointed to fill a vacancy occurring prior to the end of the term of office for which such member's predecessor was appointed shall only be appointed for the remaining portion of such term. A member may continue to serve after the expiration of his or her term until a successor has taken office.

Quorum and Voting Requirements: Three members of the board constitute a quorum. However, a lesser number of board members may hold hearings. The board has no provision for proxy voting. With one exception, every vote of the board has been unanimous since the agency's creation.

Disqualification and Recusal Procedure: No special procedures.

Chairman's Powers: The chairman serves as the chief executive officer of the board. Subject to the board's overall direction the chairman has authority that includes the use and expenditure of funds, the appointment and supervision of employees of the board, and the organization of any administrative units established by the board. 42 U.S.C. § 2286(c)(2). The board tends to defer to the chairman on administrative matters, but he keeps them advised and works cooperatively. In accordance with 42 U.S.C. § 2286(c)(3), the chairman may delegate any of his functions to any other member or to any appropriate officer of the board. The vice chairman acts as chairman in the event of the absence of the chairman or in the case of a vacancy in the office of the chairman.

OMB Bypass Provisions: "Whenever the Board submits or transmits to the President or the Director of Management and Budget any legislative recommendation, or any statement or information in preparation of a report to be submitted to the Congress ... the Board shall submit at the same time a copy thereof to the Congress." 42 U.S.C. § 2286h–1. Its annual request for appropriations is sent to the OMB for approval and inclusion in the president's budget.

Litigation Authority: The DOJ represents the Board in the federal courts.

Selective Bibliography

Articles

Anne Kornhauser, *Nuclear Watchdog Agency Off to a Bumpy Start*, 12 Legal Times 6 (Feb. 12, 1990).

EQUAL EMPLOYMENT OPPORTUNITY COMMISSION

131 M Street NE
Washington, DC 20507
(202) 663-4900 General Inquiries
(202) 694-7000 Office of Legal Counsel
Website: www.eeoc.gov

Mission and General Statutory Reference: The Equal Employment Opportunity Commission (EEOC) promotes equal opportunity in employment through administrative and judicial enforcement of the federal civil rights laws, and education and technical assistance. 42 U.S.C. §§ 2000e-4–2000e-6.

Agency Statutory History: Created by Section 705 of the Civil Rights Act of 1964, Pub. L. 88-352, 78 Stat. 258 (July 2, 1964). Superseded the President's Committee on Equal Employment Opportunity, created by executive order by President Kennedy and composed of the vice president, several cabinet officers and agency heads, and "other members as the President may from time to time appoint." Exec. Order No. 10,925 (Mar. 6, 1961), 3 C.F.R. 448 (1959–1963 comp.). Numerous equal employment bodies had been created by executive orders of earlier presidents. *See, e.g.,* President's Committee on Government Employment Policy, created by executive order by President Eisenhower. Exec. Order No. 10,590 (Jan. 18, 1955), 3 C.F.R. 237 (1954–1958 comp.).

Membership: Five members, appointed by the president with the advice and consent of the Senate, serve staggered five-year terms. No more than three of the commissioners can be members of the same political party. Any individual chosen to fill a vacancy shall be appointed only for the unexpired term of the member whom he shall succeed, and all members of the commission shall continue to serve until their successors are appointed and qualified, except that no such member of the commission shall continue to serve (1) for more than sixty days when the Congress is in session unless a nomination to fill such vacancy shall have been submitted to the Senate, or (2) after the adjournment *sine die* of the session of the Senate in which such nomination was submitted. The president designates one member to serve as chairman of the commission, and one member to serve as vice chairman. 42 U.S.C. § 2000e-4(a).

Other Presidential Appointees: General counsel. The general counsel of the commission is appointed by the president with the advice and consent of the Senate for a term of four years. 42 U.S.C. § 2000e-4(b).

Quorum and Voting Requirements: Three members of the commission constitute a quorum. 42 U.S.C. § 2000e-4(c). In case of a tie vote, a proposal fails and no action is taken. The commission does not employ the use of dissenting opinions. If a commissioner disapproves a decision, but is in the minority, the decision is ordinarily issued without a dissenting opinion. The commission does not employ proxy voting. Any person claiming to be aggrieved can file a charge of discrimination or an individual commissioner can file a charge based on his or her belief that individual or systematic discrimination is occurring. *See* 29 C.F.R. § 1601.6(a) (2000). Charges may be dismissed or investigated or sent to mediation. If, upon completion of an investigation, the commission finds cause to believe that discrimination has occurred, it attempts to resolve the matter informally. If attempts at conciliation fail, the commission may bring a civil action.

Disqualification and Recusal Procedure: No special procedures. However, because individual commissioners have statutory authority to initiate investigations, the commission's rules provide that, where a member of the commission has filed a commissioner charge, he or she shall abstain from participation in the commission determination upon completion of the investigation. 42 U.S.C. §§ 1601.19(b), 1601.21(c). Such cases are known as "commissioner charges."

Chairman's Powers: The chairman is responsible for the administrative operations of the commission, and except as provided in 42 U.S.C. § 2000e-4(b), shall appoint such officers, agents, attorneys, hearing examiners, and employees as he deems necessary to assist the commission in the performance of its functions and duties. The chairman does not usually request the opinions of other commission members. The chairman must fix personnel compensation in accordance with the provisions of chapter 51 and subchapter III of chapter 53 of Title V, United States Code, relating to classification and General Schedule pay rates, provided that assignment, removal, and compensation of hearing examiners be in accordance with Sections 3105, 3344, 5362, and 7521 of Title V, U.S.C. The chair is responsible for the preparation and submission of the agency's budget.

OMB Bypass Provisions: The commission complies with all OMB directives applicable to the executive branch.

Litigation Authority: The general counsel is responsible for conducting enforcement litigation on behalf of the commission under the Americans with Disabilities Act of 1991, *see* 42 U.S.C. § 1331(d)(1) (Supp. IV 1998), Title VII, Civil Rights Act of 1964, *see* 42 U.S.C. § 2000e-5(f)(2) (1994), the Age Discrimination in Employment Act of 1967, *see* 42 § 2000e-4 (1994), and the Equal Pay Act of 1963, *see* 42 U.S.C. § 2000e-4 (1994). The general counsel has such other duties as the commission may prescribe or as may be provided by law and shall concur with the chairman of the commission on the appointment and supervision of regional attorneys. Attorneys appointed under 42 U.S.C. § 2000e-4 may, at the direction of the commission, represent the commission in any court, provided, however, that the attorney general conducts all litigation in the Supreme Court to which the commission is a party.

Selective Bibliography

Books

U.S. Equal Employment Opportunity Commission, The Story of the United States Equal Employment Opportunity Commission: Ensuring the Promise of Opportunity for 35 Years, 1965–2000 (2000).

Clinton L. Doggett & Lois T. Doggett, The Equal Opportunity Commission (Know Your Government) (1990).

Articles

Gilbert F. Casellas, *The Equal Employment Opportunity Commission: Challenges For The Twenty-First Century*, 1 U. Pa. J. Lab. & Emp. L. 1 (1998).

Naomi C. Earp, *Forty-Three and Counting: EEOC's Challenges and Successes and Emerging Trends in the Employment Arena*, 25 Hofstra Lab. & Emp. L.J. 133 (2007).

Julia S. Gibbons, *CLE Symposium: Fortieth Anniversary of Title VII*, 36 U. Mem. L. Rev. 19 (2005).

Maurice E. R. Munroe, *The EEOC: Pattern and Practice Imperfect*, 13 Yale L. & Pol'y Rev. 219 (1995).

Anne Noel Occhialino & Daniel Vail, *Why The EEOC (Still) Matters*, 22 Hofstra Lab. & Emp. L.J. 674 (2005).

Cornelius J. Peck, *Equal Employment Opportunity Commission: Developments in the Administrative Process 1965–75*, 51 Wash. L. Rev. 831 (1976).

FARM CREDIT ADMINISTRATION

1501 Farm Credit Drive
McLean, VA 22102
(703) 883-4056 General Inquiries
(703) 883-4021 Office of Legal Counsel
Website: www.fca.gov

Mission and General Statutory Reference: The Farm Credit Administration (FCA) is "an independent agency in the executive branch" that is responsible for regulating and examining the banks, associations, and related entities that constitute the Farm Credit System. The FCA board may use its enforcement power to obtain corrective action if an institution violates statutes or regulations or operates in an unsafe or unsound manner. *See* 12 U.S.C. §§ 2241–2274.

Agency Statutory History: FCA, managed by a three-member FCA board, statutorily created by Section 201 of the Farm Credit Amendments Act of 1985, Pub. L. 99-205, 99 Stat. 1688 (Dec. 23, 1985). The new board replaced the Farm Credit Board, composed of the secretary of agriculture and twelve others appointed by the president with the advice and consent of the Senate, created by Sections 5.7 and 5.8 of the Farm Credit Act of 1971, Pub. L. 92-181, 85 Stat. 617 (Dec. 10, 1971). Original Federal Farm Loan Board, composed of the secretary of the treasury and four other members, was created by Section 3 of the Federal Farm Loan Act of 1916, Pub. L. 64-158, 39 Stat. 360 (July 17, 1916). Exec. Order No. 6084 (Mar. 27, 1933) abolished the Farm Credit Board and established the FCA headed by a single individual. The chairman of the Federal Farm Board was redesignated as the governor of the FCA, pursuant to emergency powers conferred on President Roosevelt by Sections 401–403 of the Legislative Branch Appropriation Act, fiscal year 1933, Pub. L. 72-212, 47 Stat. 413 (June 30, 1932), as amended.

Membership: Policy-making is vested in a full-time, three-member board appointed by the president with the advice and consent of the Senate. Board members serve staggered, six-year terms, and may not be reappointed after serving a full term or more than three years of a previous member's term. The president designates one of the members as chairman. There is no statutory "for cause" removal provision.

Quorum and Voting Requirements: The board may transact business only when a quorum, i.e., two members, is present. 12 U.S.C. § 2242(c). A majority of the board may act even if the minority delays in completing any dissenting statements. There is no provision in the Farm Credit Act for the board members to vote by proxy.

Disqualification and Recusal Procedure: No special procedures.

Chairman's Powers: The chairman is designated by the president to serve as chairman for the duration of his or her terms as a member. 12 U.S.C. 2242(a). The chairman serves as the agency's chief executive officer and may appoint the agency's staff, fix pay levels, and direct the staff. 12 U.S.C. § 2245(c)(2)(A). The appointment of the heads of major administrative units is subject to the board's approval. 12 U.S.C. § 2245(b). In accordance with 12 U.S.C. § 2245, the powers of the chairman as CEO that are necessary for day-to-day management may be exercised and performed by the chairman through such other officers and employees of the administration as the chairman shall designate. The chairman, however, may not delegate powers specifically reserved to the chairman by the Farm Credit Act without the approval of the FCA board.

OMB Bypass Provisions: All legislative information, such as testimony and reports, go directly to Congress without OMB clearance. 12 U.S.C. § 2252(a)(3). The FCA sends its appropriation request to the OMB for inclusion in the president's budget request, but not for approval. The FCA is funded by assessments paid by regulated institutions.

Litigation Authority: The DOJ represents the FCA in the federal courts. Nonetheless, FCA attorneys assist with the preparation of pleadings and presentation of the case and ordinarily prepare legal memoranda and litigation reports. Referrals to the DOJ are handled informally or by letter. There are no agency regulations regarding such referrals. 12 U.S.C. § 2244(c) also provides that "[a]ttorneys designated by the Chairman may represent the Farm Credit Administration in any other civil proceeding or civil action when so authorized by the Attorney General under provisions of title 28." The Farm Credit Act also provides that, except with regard to litigation before the Supreme Court, attorneys designated by the chairman shall represent the FCA in any civil proceeding or civil action brought in connection with the administration of conservatorships and receiverships. 12 U.S.C. § 2244(c).

Selective Bibliography

Books

VALENTINE A. SKULZACEK, THE FARM CREDIT ADMINISTRATION: A STUDY OF THE LEGISLATIVE HISTORY AND THE ORGANIZATIONAL STRUCTURE OF THE NATIONAL GOVERNMENT AGENCY FOR FARM CREDIT, 1943 Dissertation: Thesis (M.A.—Politics), Catholic University of America (1943) (only available in CUA libraries).

HOMER G. SMITH, A CHALLENGE TO U.S. AGRICULTURE: BUILDING THE COOPERATIVE PRODUCTION CREDIT SYSTEM (1987).

U.S. FARM CREDIT ADMINISTRATION, THE FEDERAL LAND BANK SYSTEM, HOW IT OPERATES (1951).

Articles

H. Emmerich, *Distinguishing Administrative Aspects of the Farm Credit Administration*, 30 AM. POL. SCI. REV. 1117 (1936).

A. S. Goss, *Farm Credit Administration*, 14 TITLE NEWS 22 (1935).

James T. Massey, *Farmers Home Administration and Farm Credit System Update*, 73 NEB. L. REV. 187 (1994).

FEDERAL COMMUNICATIONS COMMISSION

445 12th Street SW
Washington, DC 20554
(202) 418-0200 General Inquiries
(202) 418-1700 Office of General Counsel
Website: www.fcc.gov

Mission and General Statutory Reference: The Federal Communications Commisssion (FCC) regulates interstate and international communications by radio, television, wire, satellite, and cable. 47 U.S.C. §§ 151–159.

Agency Statutory History: Created by Communications Act of 1934, Pub. L. 73-416, 48 Stat. 1064 (June 19, 1934). The seven-member FCC replaced the five-member Federal Radio Commission created by the Radio Act of 1927, Pub. L. 69-632, 44 Stat. 1162 (Feb. 23, 1927). Radio was first brought under federal control by the Radio Act of 1912, Pub. L. 62-264, 37 Stat. 302 (Aug. 14, 1912), administered by the secretary of commerce and labor. The 1927 statute provided that the president would designate the first chairman but, thereafter, the commission would select its own chairman. 44 Stat. 1163. The 1934 statute gave the president the authority to appoint the chairman. 48 Stat. 1066. Congress reduced the size of the FCC from seven to five in 1986. Pub. L. 99-334, 100 Stat. 513 (1986).

Membership: Five members, appointed by the president with the advice and consent of the Senate, serve staggered five-year terms. The maximum number of commissioners from any party is a number equal to the least number that would constitute a majority. A member may serve until his successor takes the oath of office but not past expiration of the next session of Congress subsequent to the end of the fixed term. There is no statutory provision concerning removal of commissioners from office.

Significant Case: Federal Communications Comm'n v. Fox Television Stations, Inc., 556 U.S. 502 (2009) (whether FCC's status as an independent agency affects judicial review of its change of policy in a rulemaking proceeding).

Quorum and Voting Requirements: Three commissioners constitute a quorum for purposes of taking commission action. 47 U.S.C. § 154(h). As a general matter, so long as a quorum is present, commission action may be taken by a majority of the members present. In case of a tie, no commission action is taken. If a tie occurs with respect to an application for review of action taken by delegated authority, 47 U.S.C. § 155(c)(4)–(6), or a petition for reconsideration of prior commission action, 47 U.S.C. § 405 the previous decision stands. 47 U.S.C. § 155(c)(3); *see also* Newark Radio Broad. Ass'n v. FCC, 763 F.2d 450 (D.C. Cir. 1985). The commission permits proxy voting.

Disqualification and Recusal Procedure: The commission exercises the right to disqualify one of its members. *See, e.g.*, WXIA-TV, 7 F.C.C.R. 925 (1992).

Chairman's Powers: The chairman serves as the chief executive officer. A managing director, appointed by the chairman with the commission's approval, is vested with whatever administrative and executive authority the chairman may designate. There is no provision for a vice chairman. In case of vacancy, absence, or disability, the commission may temporarily designate one of its members as acting chairman. 47 U.S.C. § 155. The commission's budget and the appointment and removal of senior staff must be approved by the commission.

OMB Bypass Provisions: The commission is required by 47 U.S.C. § 154(k) to submit an annual report to Congress that includes specific legislative recommendations. This is to include, as well, all legislative proposals submitted for approval to the OMB. While this provision does not appear to confer a legislative bypass on the commission, the commission asserts informal (non-statutory) bypass authority and does not ordinarily submit legislation or reports or testimony on legislation to the OMB for clearance.

Litigation Authority: The DOJ is responsible for the conduct of district court litigation to which the commission is a party. This includes Freedom of Information Act and Sunshine Act lawsuits, employment discrimination actions, and actions brought to enforce commission orders. The U.S. attorneys offices also bring criminal prosecutions for violations of the Communications Act; in those cases the commission is technically not a party. *See* 47 U.S.C. § 401(c) (granting duty to prosecute to attorney general); *see also* 28 U.S.C. §§ 516, 519. In the above cases, the U.S. attorneys represent the commission in court, while commission attorneys ordinarily prepare pleadings, legal memoranda, and litigation reports. Commission attorneys may also appear in court to assist with the presentation of the case. Referrals to the DOJ are handled informally or by letter. There are no agency regulations regarding such referrals.

Appeals of district court cases are handled by the DOJ with the assistance of commission attorneys; however, the commission does exclusively handle appeals under section 402(b) of the Communications Act relating to radio and television licensing and Bell Operating Company (BOC) entry into the long-distance market. *See also* 47 U.S.C. § 154(f)(1). Appeals under Section 402(a) of the Communications Act, involving review of commission final actions unrelated to radio and television licensing or entry of Bell Operating Companies into the long-distance market, are governed by the Judicial Review Act. 28 U.S.C. §§ 2341–2353 (1994 & Supp. IV 1998). While 28 U.S.C. § 2348 generally provides that the attorney general is responsible for and has control of the interests of the government in all court proceedings, the commission, as the agency in interest, appears as a respondent represented by its own attorneys. Commission counsel, maintaining a close liaison with the DOJ, prepare briefs and present oral arguments in these cases.

Section 402(j) of the Communications Act and section 2350(a) of the Judicial Review Act give the commission the right to file petitions for writ of certiorari. Under current practice, the commission coordinates its petitions with the solicitor general.

Selective Bibliography

Books

Federal Communications Commission, Federal Communications Commission Log, 50th Anniversary, 1934–1984: A Chronological History (1984).

Carl J. Friedrich, Congress and the control of radiobroadcasting (history of broadcasting: radio to television) (1971).

Robert Sears McMahon, Federal Regulation of the Radio and Television Broadcast Industry in the United States, 1927–1959: With Special Reference to the Establishment and Operation of Workable Administrative Standards (1979).

Bernard Schwartz, The Economic Regulation of Business and Industry: A Legislative History of U.S. Regulatory Agencies (1973).
Kimberly Zarkin & Michael J. Zarkin, The Federal Communications Commission: The Front Line in the Culture and Regulation Wars (2006).

Articles

Larry King, *The FCC Plus Sixty*, 47 Fed. Comm. L.J. 291 (1994).
Michael I. Meyerson, *Ideas of the Marketplace: A Guide to the 1996 Telecommunications Act*, 49 Fed. Comm. L.J. 251 (1994).
Abner J. Mikva, *Up with the FCC: An Essay of Esteem for the Commission on Its Sixtieth Birthday*, 47 Fed. Comm. L.J. 295 (1994).
Susan Ness, *Reflections on the Sixtieth Anniversary of the Communications Act*, 47 Fed. Comm. L.J. 311 (1994).
Joel Rosenbloom, *On the Sixtieth Anniversary of the Communications Act of 1934*, 47 Fed. Comm. L.J. 365 (1994).

FEDERAL ELECTION COMMISSION

999 E Street NW
Washington, DC 20463
(800) 424-9530 General Inquiries
(202) 694-1650 Office of the General Counsel
Website: www.fec.gov

Mission and General Statutory Reference: The Federal Election Commission (FEC) administers and enforces the federal statutes governing the financing of federal elections. 2 U.S.C. §§ 437c–437d; *see also* Presidential Election Campaign Fund Act, 26 U.S.C. §§ 9001–9013; Presidential Primary Matching Payment Account Act, 26 U.S.C. §§ 9031–9042.

Agency Statutory History: The FEC was originally created by the Federal Election Campaign Act Amendments of 1974, Pub. L. 93-443, 88 Stat. 1280–1282 (Oct. 15, 1974), composed of six voting members, two appointed by the president with the approval of a majority of both houses of Congress and four appointed by Congress, plus the Secretary of the Senate and the clerk of the House of Representatives as ex officio members. Supreme Court held in Buckley v. Valeo, 424 U.S. 1 (1976), that the limit placed on the president's power to appoint the voting members rendered the commission's composition unconstitutional under the appointments clause. The commission was reconstituted by the Federal Election Campaign Act Amendments of 1976, Pub. L. 94-283, 90 Stat. 475 (May 11, 1976), to replace the congressional appointees with six members appointed by the president with the advice and consent of the Senate but retained the Secretary of the Senate and the clerk of the House of Representatives as ex officio members. The U.S. Court of Appeals for the District of Columbia Circuit has held that the inclusion of the ex officio members violates separation of powers principles, *see* Federal Election Comm'n v. NRA Political Victory Fund, 6 F.3d 821 (D.C. Cir. 1993), cert. dismissed 513 U.S. 88 (1994), and these members no longer serve on the FEC.

Membership: Six members appointed by the president serve staggered six-year terms. 2 U.S.C. § 437c(a)(1). No more than three commissioners may be of the same political party. Members serve a single six-year term but may continue to serve following the expiration of their terms until a new member is confirmed. There is no statutory provision governing removal, but a D.C. Circuit opinion has suggested that the statute may confer "for cause" protection on commission members. Fed. Election Comm'n v. NRA Political Victory Fund, 6 F.3d 821, 826 (D.C. Cir. 1993), cert. dismissed 513 U.S. 88 (1994).

Significant Case: Fed. Election Comm'n v. NRA Political Victory Fund, 6 F.3d 821, 826 (D.C. Cir. 1993), cert. dismissed 513 U.S. 88 (1994) (suggesting that the statute may confer "for cause" removal protection despite statutory silence on the issue).

Quorum and Voting Requirements: Four of the commission's six members must vote in the affirmative for the commission to take action. Proxy voting is prohibited by statute. 2 U.S.C. § 437c(c). If the commission splits three-to-three, the matter is dismissed or otherwise fails to go forward. All decisions of the commission must be made by a majority vote, except that the affirmative vote of four members of the commission is required to (1) participate in litigation; (2) render advisory opinions; (3) develop forms and prescribe rules; (4) conduct investigations and hearings, encourage voluntary compliance through the civil enforcement process, and report apparent violations to the appropriate law enforcement authorities; and (5) take action to administer and enforce the public financing statutes. A commissioner may not delegate his or her vote or decisionmaking authority.

Disqualification and Recusal Procedure: Each commissioner determines requests for disqualification or recusal.

Chairman's Powers: The commissioners elect a chairman from among their members, who serves for one year as chairman. A commissioner may serve as chairman only once during his or her term. The chairman and the vice chairman must be affiliated with different political parties. The vice chairman acts as chairman in the absence or disability of the chairman or when there is a vacancy in the office of the chairman. The commissioners jointly select the staff director and general counsel, and the chairman plays no special role in the selection process. Choice of a staff director and general counsel requires the affirmative vote of the commissioners.

OMB Bypass Provisions: Whenever the commission submits any budget estimate or request to the president or the OMB, it must concurrently transmit a copy to Congress. 2 U.S.C. § 437d(d)(1). The commission is required to submit an annual report to the president and each House of Congress that contains any legislative recommendations the commission considers appropriate. Under 2 U.S.C. § 437d(d)(2), concurrent submission is also required whenever the commission submits any other legislative recommendation, testimony, or comments on legislation requested by Congress, the president, or the OMB. Section 437d(d)(2) also provides that no agency or officer of the United States may require the commission to submit its legislative recommendation, testimony, or comments for approval prior to its submission of such material to Congress.

Litigation Authority: The commission has authority to initiate, defend, or appeal any civil action to enforce the provisions of the Federal Election Campaign Act and chapters 95 and 96 of the Internal Revenue Code through its general counsel. 2 U.S.C. 437d(a)(6). The general counsel represents the commission in litigation at the District Court and Circuit Court levels, including FOIA litigation. He also represents the commission before the Supreme Court in cases arising under the Title 26 provisions, but Supreme Court litigation arising under Title II is handled by the solicitor general. 2 U.S.C. § 437c(f)(4); 26 U.S.C. §§ 9010(a), 9040(a). But *see* Federal Election Commission v. NRA Political Victory Fund, 513 U.S. 88 (1994) (FEC cannot independently file a petition for certiorari in the U.S. Supreme Court under 2 U.S.C. § 437d(a)(6)). The DOJ represents the commission in certain proceedings such as tort litigation.

Selective Bibliography

Books

The Federal Election Commission, The First 10 Years, 1975–1985 (1985).

John Leo Moore, Elections A to Z (2003).

Federal Election Commission, Legal History of the Presidential Election Campaign Fund Act (1991).

Maurice C. Sheppard, The Federal Election Commission: Policy, Politics, and Administration (2007).

Articles

Joan D. Aikens, *The Federal Election Commission and Enforcement*, 34 Fed. B. News & J. 59 (1987).

Herbert E. Alexander, *The Impact of the Federal Election Campaign Act on the 1976 Presidential Campaign: The Complexities of Compliance*, 29 Emory L.J. 315 (1980).

Jan W. Baran, *Federal Election Commission: A Guide for Corporate Counsel*, 22. Ariz. L.Rev. 519 (1980).

Michael T. Bierman, Note, *Federal Election Reform: An Examination of the Constitutionality of the Federal Election Commission*, 51 Rev. Notre Dame Law. 451 (1976).

William T. Mayton, *Politics, Money, Coercion and the Problem with Corporate PACS*, 29 Emory L.J. 375 (1980).

Timothy S. Perry, *Campaigns on Credit: Financing by National Banks in Federal Election Campaigns*, 29 Emory L.J. 417 (1980).

Jamin Raskin, Federal Election Commission: *"A Complicated and Indirect Encroachment": Is The Federal Election Commission Unconstitutionally Composed*, 52 Admin. L. Rev. 609 (2000).

Daniel J. Swillinger, *Federal Regulation o the Campaign Finance Activity of Trade Associations—An Overview*, 29 Emory L.J. 395 (1980).

Symposium on the Federal Election Commission, 10 J.L. & Pol. 369 (1994).

Scott E. Thomas & Jeffrey H. Bowen, *Obstacles to Effective Enforcement of the Federal Election Campaign Act*, 52 Admin. L. Rev. 575(2000).

Melvin I. Urofsky, *Campaign Finance Reform Before 1971*, 1 Alb. Gov't L. Rev. 1 (2008).

Biz Van Gelder, *Precedential Debates: A Case Study of the Federal Election Commission's Regulation of Candidate Appearances*, 29 Emory L.J. 339 (1980).

Burton D. Wechsler, *Constitutional Implications or Campaign Reform*, 8 Admin. L.J. Am. U. 161(1994).

Note, *The Federal Election Commission, the First Amendment, and Due Process*, 89 Yale L.J. 1199(1980).

FEDERAL ENERGY REGULATION COMMISSION

888 First Street NE
Washington, DC 20426
(866) 208-3372 General Inquiries
(202) 502-6000 Office of the General Counsel
Website: www.ferc.gov

Mission and General Statutory Reference: The Federal Energy Regulatory Commission (FERC) is an "independent regulatory commission" administratively within the DOE. It regulates interstate aspects of the electric power, natural gas, oil pipeline, and hydroelectric industries. 42 U.S.C. §§ 7171–7178.

Agency Statutory History: The FERC was created by Section 401 of the Department of Energy Organization Act, Pub. L. 95-91, 96 Stat. 582 (1977), "within the Department [of Energy]" as an "independent regulatory commission," 42 U.S.C. § 7171(a). The statute provides that FERC officials "are not responsible to or subject to the supervision or direction of any officer, employee or agent of any part of the Department." 42 U.S.C. § 7171(d). Members were originally appointed to four-year terms. The Federal Energy Regulatory Commission Member Term Act of 1990, Pub. L. 101-271, 104 Stat. 135 (1990), extended the terms of new members to five years. A predecessor agency, the Federal Power Commission (FPC), was created by the Federal Water Power Act, Pub. L. 66-280, 41 Stat. 1063 (1920). It was composed of the secretaries of war, interior, and agriculture, whose departments had responsibility for various aspects of water power generation on federal land. The FPC was designed essentially to encourage coordination of responsibility into a single, national plan. It was replaced in 1930 by a new Federal Power Commission composed of five members, appointed to the commission by the president with the advice and consent of the Senate. Pub. L. 71-412, 46 Stat. 797 (1930). The 1930 Federal Power Commission members lacked statutory protection against removal except for cause but that was changed with creation of the FERC. The hydroelectric-focused authority was subsequently expanded to include electric power authority, 16 U.S.C. §§ 824-825r, natural gas authority, 15 U.S.C. §§ 717–717w, and oil pipeline authority, 49 App. U.S.C., §§ 1 et seq.

Membership: Five members, appointed by the president with the advice and consent of the Senate, serve staggered five-year terms. No more than three members may belong to the same political party. Terms expire on June 30. However, a commissioner may serve up to the end of the Congress in which his or her term expires, unless he or she is replaced before the end of the session. Commissioners may be removed by the president only for inefficiency, neglect of duty, or malfeasance in office.

Significant Case: New York v. FERC, 535 U.S. 1 (2002) (reviewing the history of regulation of the electric power industry and upholding FERC jurisdiction over transmission of electric energy).

Quorum and Voting Requirements: Three members constitute a quorum, and a majority of the quorum is required to take commission action. The commission's enabling statute provides that "[a]ctions of the Commission shall be determined by a majority vote of the members present." 42 U.S.C. § 7171(e). The commission cannot undertake any official business when no quorum is present or the membership is equally divided. However, a tie vote on rehearing serves to leave the original action in place. The commission automatically takes review of all aspects of an ALJ's initial decision as to which timely exceptions and briefs are filed. In the absence of exceptions, the commission has ten days in which to decide whether to initiate review. Review may be initiated by majority vote. The commission has no express rule as to whether the majority may issue a decision if the minority delays in completing any separate statements. In practice, members are afforded a reasonable time to complete a dissenting statement. If a compelling reason exists to issue a decision without further delay, the majority can issue it with a statement that a dissent will be issued at a later time. Typically, commissioners complete dissents without assistance from staff other than their own personal staffs. On the infrequent occasions when a dissenting commissioner requests assistance from the commission's advisory staff, such assistance is provided. The commission has no provisions for proxy voting, and it is not employed.

Disqualification and Recusal Procedure: No special provisions. Regulations require only that written notification of any recusal decision be provided to the commission's ethics officer. 5 C.F.R. § 3401.103 (2000). Apart from regulations issued by the Office of Government Ethics applicable to all agencies, the FERC has supplemental ethics regulation at 5 C.F.R. pt. 3401. They specify financial interests that FERC personnel are prohibited from owning or acquiring, 5 C.F.R. pt. 3401.102, and recusal procedures for employees other than commissioners, 5 C.F.R. pt. 3401.103.

Chairman's Powers: One member is designated by the president as chairman. The chairman is "responsible on behalf of the Commission for the executive and administrative operation of the Commission." 42 U.S.C. § 7171(c). The chairman is empowered to designate (in advance) any other member as acting chairman to act during the chairman's absence. The chairman is responsible for administrative and executive functions, the appointment of personnel, including hearing examiners and an executive director, as he deems necessary. The chairman has authority to distribute business among personnel and administrative units. 18 C.F.R. § 376.105(4). The chairman also maintains the authority to approve the Commission's budget. Department of Energy Organization Act, § 401(c), Pub. L. No. 95-91. In addition, the commission (not the Chairman acting alone) has delegated authority to its advisory staff to act in individual proceedings, such as by authorizing commission advisory staff to undertake certain actions in connection with the proceeding. *See, e.g.,* 18 C.F.R. §§ 375.301–375.315.

OMB Bypass Provisions: Bypass of prior OMB review on legislative matters is secured by means of a statutory concurrent transmittal provision. 42 U.S.C. § 7171(j) (1994). The commission sends its annual appropriation request to the OMB for approval and inclusion in the president's budget. Although the FERC receives annual appropriations from congress, its funding effectively comes from fees and annual charges that the FERC assesses to entities that initiate proceedings at the FERC and to regulated industries. These fees and charges are calculated for each fiscal year to equal the costs incurred by the FERC in that fiscal year. 42 U.S.C. § 7178(1). The collected monies are paid into the Treasury. The effect is to fund the FERC through fees and charges while leaving the FERC subject to the annual appropriation cycle.

Litigation Authority: Unless otherwise provided by 28 U.S.C. § 518, which relates to litigation before the Supreme Court, attorneys designated by the chairman may represent the commission in civil actions brought by or against the commission. 42 U.S.C. § 7171(i). In general, the FERC appears on its own behalf to defend its order. The FERC has also represented itself in other matters, such as bankruptcy cases in which the FERC had a claim. However, pursuant to its authority under 28 U.S.C. § 516, the DOJ conducts litigation on behalf of the commission in civil suits that are not based on commission orders, such as tort claims, and suits under the employment discrimination laws and the FOIA.

Selective Bibliography

Books

James H. McGrew, ferc: Federal Energy Regulatory Commission (2003).

David W. Miller, The Courts' View of Regulation at the Federal Energy Regulatory Commission (1988).

Articles

J. Evans Atwell, *Drawbacks of Federal Natural Gas Regulation*, 13 Tulsa L.J. 751 (1978).

Conference—Harvard Electricity Policy Group: Regulatory Decisionmaking Reform, 8 Admin. L. J. Am. U. 789 (1995).

T. G. Johnson, *FERC and the Courts: Evolution of the Commission's "Discretion,"* 42 Inst. On Oil and Gas L. & Tax'n 3.1 (1991).

Elizabeth Moler, David Ward, Robert C. Platt, Sherman Poland & David Benkin, *A Salute: 75 Years for the FPC and FERC*, 16 Energy L.J. 293 (1995).

Richard G. Morgan & Charles W. Garrison, *Enforcement Policies and Procedures of the Federal Regulatory Energy Commission*, 15 Tulsa L.J. 501 (1980).

FEDERAL LABOR RELATIONS AUTHORITY

1400 K Street NW
Washington, DC 20424
(202) 218-7740 General Inquiries
(202) 218-7999 Office of the Solicitor
Website: www.flra.gov

Mission and General Statutory Reference: The Federal Labor Relations Authority (FLRA) establishes policies and guidance relating to matters under the Federal Service Labor-Management Relations statute, 5 U.S.C. § 7101 et seq. The agency also adjudicates appeals concerning unfair labor practices and representation petitions, disputes concerning the negotiability of collective bargaining agreement proposals, and exceptions to grievance arbitration awards relating to federal-sector labor-management relations. 5 U.S.C. §§ 7104–7105. The general counsel is the FLRA's independent investigative and prosecutorial component akin to the general counsel of the National Labor Relations Board. 5 U.S.C. § 7104(f)(2)(A)–(B). The Federal Service Impasses Panel (FSIP) is "an entity within the Authority, the function of which is to provide assistance in resolving negotiating impasses between agencies and exclusive representatives," 5 U.S.C. § 7119(c)(1), including those arising under the Federal Employees Flexible and Compressed Work Schedules Act, Pub. L. 97-221, 96 Stat. 227, 232 (July 23, 1982), 5 U.S.C. 6131(c).

Agency Statutory History: Created by Section 7104 of the Civil Service Reform Act of 1978, Pub. L. 95-454, 92 Stat. 1196 (Oct. 13, 1978). The Civil Service Miscellaneous Amendments Act of 1983, Pub. L. 98-224, 98 Stat. 47 (Mar. 2, 1984), established that the chairman is the "chief executive and administrative officer of the Authority."

Membership: The FLRA's authority component is composed of three full-time members appointed by the president for five-year terms, with the advice and consent of the Senate. Not more than two of the members may be of the same political party. A member may serve until the member's successor takes office or until the expiration of the next session of congress subsequent to the end of the member's fixed term, whichever comes earlier. 5 U.S.C. § 7104(c)(1)–(2). A member may be removed by the president only upon notice and hearing, and only for inefficiency, neglect of duty, or malfeasance in office. The president appoints one member to serve as chairman. 5 U.S.C. § 7104(b).

The FLRA also supports the Foreign Service Labor Relations Board and the Foreign Service Impasse Disputes Panel. These entities administer the labor-management relations program and resolve impasses for Foreign Service employees in the U.S. Information Agency, the Agency for International Development, and the Departments of State, Agriculture, and Commerce. The Foreign Service Labor Relations Board is composed of the chairman of the FLRA and two members whom the chairman appoints from nominees approved by their respective agencies. 22 U.S.C. § 4106(a). These members may be removed by the FLRA chairman only for "corruption, neglect of duty, malfeasance, or demonstrated incapacity to perform his or her functions, established at a hearing." 22 U.S.C. § 4106(c). The Foreign Service Impasse Disputes Panel is composed of five members appointed by the chairman of the FLRA pursuant to membership composition requirements of 22 U.S.C. § 4110(a). Another "entity within the... [FLRA]" is the FSIP, whose function is "to provide assistance in resolving negotiation impasses between agencies and exclusive representatives." 5 U.S.C. § 7119(c). The president appoints the FSIP Chairman and six other members to five year terms. Members of the FSIP may be removed by the president without statutory limitation. 5 U.S.C. § 7119(c)(2), (3).

Other Presidential Appointees: General counsel. The president, with the advice and consent of the Senate, appoints a general counsel for a term of five years. The general counsel is the FLRA's independent investigative and prosecutorial component. The general counsel investigates alleged unfair labor practices and prosecutes unfair labor practice complaints. 5 U.S.C. § 7104(f)(2)(A)–(B). The statute states that the general counsel "may be removed at any time by the President." 5 U.S.C. § 7104(f)(1). The general counsel has unreviewable discretion to decline to issue unfair labor practice complaints. The general counsel also has direct authority over the FLRA's regional office employees. 5 U.S.C. § 7104(f)(3).

The president appoints the Chairman and six other members to the Federal Service Impasses Panel.

Quorum and Voting Requirements: Two authority members constitute a quorum for purposes of taking FLRA action. A vacancy in the authority membership shall not impair the right of the remaining members to exercise all of the powers of the FLRA. 5 U.S.C. § 7104(d)(1994). In the case of a tie, no FLRA action is taken. When exceptions to the decisions of the ALJs are filed, the decisions may be affirmed, modified or reversed in whole or in part by the authority. If no exceptions are timely filed to an ALJ's decision, the decision is adopted by the authority and, without precedential significance, becomes final and binding. 5 C.F.R. § 2423.41. The FLRA is authorized to delegate to subordinate officers the authority to perform such duties and make such expenditures as the FLRA may deem necessary. 5 U.S.C. § 7105(d)–(e).

Disqualification and Recusal Procedure: No special procedures.

Chairman's Powers: The chairman of the FLRA serves as its chief executive and administrative officer. The chairman is also a member of the National Council on Federal Labor-Management Relations established by Exec. Order No. 13,522, 74 Fed. Reg. 66,203 (2009), to promote labor-management partnerships in the federal service. The chairman also heads the Foreign Service Labor Relations Board and appoints the members of the Foreign Service Impasse Disputes Panel.

OMB Bypass Provisions: The FLRA is required by 5 U.S.C. § 7104(e) to submit an annual report to Congress, which shall include information as to cases heard and decisions rendered. This provision does not confer a legislative bypass on the FLRA. The FLRA submits an annual request for appropriations to the OMB.

Litigation Authority: Except as provided by 28 U.S.C. § 518, relating to Supreme Court litigation, "attorneys designated by the Authority may appear for the Authority and represent the Authority in any civil action brought in connection with any function carried out by the Authority pursuant to this title." 5 U.S.C. § 7105(h). The Office of the Solicitor represents the authority in court proceedings before all U.S. courts of appeals and federal district courts. The FLRA solicitor represents the FLRA in the Supreme Court in appropriate cases, by delegation of the solicitor general and the U.S. attorney general.

Selective Bibliography

Books

PETER BROIDA, A GUIDE TO FEDERAL LABOR RELATIONS AUTHORITY LAW AND PRACTICE (2008).
FEDERAL LABOR RELATIONS AUTHORITY, FLRA: 20 YEARS, 1979–1999 (1999).

FEDERAL MARITIME COMMISSION

800 North Capitol Street NW
Washington, DC 20573
(202) 523-5773 General Inquiries
(202) 523-5738 Office of the General Counsel
Website: www.fmc.gov

Mission and General Statutory Reference: The Federal Maritime Commission (FMC) is an "independent establishment of the United States Government." 46 U.S.C. § 301. It is responsible for the regulation of ocean-borne transportation in the foreign commerce of the United States. The passage of the Shipping Act of 1984, Pub. L. 98-237, 98 Stat. 67 (1984), brought about significant changes in the regime applicable to shipping companies operating in the U.S. foreign commerce, including changes to the procedure for permitting agreements filed with the

Commission to become final. The subsequent passage of the Ocean Shipping Reform Act, Pub. L. 105-258, 112 Stat. 1902 (1998), signaled a further and significant shift in shipping regulation by allowing common carriers and shippers to negotiate individual shipping contracts.

Agency Statutory History: The FMC was established as an independent regulatory agency "not part of an executive department or under the authority of the head of any executive department" by Reorganization Plan No. 7 of 1961, 3 C.F.R. pt. 875 (1959–1963 comp.) (Aug. 12, 1961). Prior to that time, the Federal Maritime Board was responsible for both the regulation of ocean commerce and the promotion of the U.S. Merchant Marine. Under the reorganization plan, the shipping laws were separated into two categories—regulatory and promotional—with the newly created FMC charged with the administration of the regulatory provisions of the shipping laws. The responsibilities associated with the promotion of an adequate and efficient U.S. Merchant Marine were assigned to the Maritime Administration, now located within the Department of Transportation. The original five-member U.S. Shipping Board was created by Section 3 of the Shipping Act of 1916, Pub. L. 64-260, 39 Stat. 729 (Sept. 7, 1916). The Shipping Board was abolished by Exec. Order No. 6166 (Jan. 10, 1933) and its functions transferred to the Department of Commerce. Section 201 of the Merchant Marine Act, Pub. L. 74-835, 49 Stat. 1985 (June 29, 1936), established the five-member FMC to replace the earlier abolished U.S. Shipping Board. Reorganization Plan No. 21 of 1950, 3 C.F.R. pt. 1012 (1949–1953 comp.) (May 24, 1950), replaced the FMC with the three-member Federal Maritime Board within the Department of Commerce. The board, which existed until replaced by the current FMC, was independent of the Department of Commerce, but Section 106 of Reorganization Plan No. 21 indicated that it should be "guided by the general policies of the Secretary of Commerce."

Membership: Five Commissioners are appointed by the president with the advice and consent of the Senate, for staggered five-year terms. No more than three commissioners may belong to the same political party. The president designates one commissioner to serve as chairman. Commissioners are removable by the president for inefficiency, neglect of duty, or malfeasance in office.

Significant Case: Federal Maritime Commission v. South Carolina State Ports Authority, 535 U.S. 743 (2002) (given the similarities between administrative proceedings and civil litigation, state sovereign immunity under the Eleventh Amendment bars the FMC from adjudicating a private party's complaint against a nonconsenting state).

Quorum and Voting Requirements: "The affirmative vote of a majority of the members of the Commission is required to dispose of any matter before the Commission" and "A vacancy or vacancies in the membership of the . . . Commission do not impair the power of the Commission to executive its functions." 46 U.S.C. § 302. For purposes of holding a formal meeting for the transaction of commission business, the actual presence of two commissioners shall be sufficient. Proxy votes of absent members are permitted. *See* 46 C.F.R. § 501.2. The commission has the authority "to delegate, by published order or rule, any of its functions to a division of the Commission, an individual Commissioner, an administrative law judge, or an employee or employee board, including functions with respect to hearing, determining, ordering, certifying, reporting or otherwise acting as to any work, business or matter." 46 C.F.R. § 501.21. However, the commission shall retain a discretionary right to review any action taken as a result of the commission's delegation of its functions upon its own initiative or petition of a party or intervenor to the action. 46 C.F.R. § 501.21(f). The majority may issue its decision without the dissenting opinion if there is a delay. Federal Maritime Commission Order 87, § 3.10 (Feb. 6, 1981), states that reports accompanied by concurring and/or dissenting opinions, where practicable, shall be served no later than thirty-five workdays following the commission decision. A deviation from this procedure can only be accomplished by majority vote of the commission. *See* Comm. Order No. 87, § 3.11 (Feb. 6, 1981). Any assistance to a dissenting commissioner would be provided by his or her counsel.

Disqualification and Recusal Procedure: Parties may file an affidavit of personal bias or disqualification against any "presiding or participating officer," and the commission determines the matter as part of the record and decision in the case. 46 C.F.R. § 501.149. The term "presiding officer" includes "a member of the Commission or an administrative law judge." 46 C.F.R. § 502.145.

Chairman's Powers: The chairman serves as chief executive and administrative officer of the agency. 46 U.S.C. § 301(c)(2). The chairman appoints the heads of major organizational units, but only after consultation with the other commissioners. 46 U.S.C. § 301(c)(3)(ii). The chairman supervises the expenditure of money for administrative purposes. 46 U.S.C. § 301(c)(3)(iv).

OMB Bypass Provisions: The commission does not enjoy bypass of OMB review on budgetary matters. Although there appears to be no formal provision for bypass on legislative matters, the FMC asserts informal (nonstatutory) bypass authority in practice.

Litigation Authority: The commission has authority to represent itself in actions in the U.S. courts of appeals when its rules, regulations, or final orders are challenged. 28 U.S.C. § 2348. The DOJ is responsible for the conduct of district court litigation to which the commission is a party. 28 U.S.C. § 516. However, the commission may represent itself in district court and appellate court upon notice or approval of the attorney general with regard to seeking injunctions under certain provisions of the Shipping Act of 1984. 46 U.S.C. § 41307(d). The commission may also file a petition for certiorari in the U.S. Supreme Court. 28 U.S.C. § 2350.

Selective Bibliography

Articles

Todd Buchwald, *Federal Maritime Commission Jurisdiction over Terminal Operators*, 12 J. MAR. L. & COM. 209 (1981).

Paul S. Edelman, *The Ocean Shipping Reform Act of 1998*, 9 CURRENTS INT'L TRADE L.J. 65 (2000).

Timothy J. May, *The Status of Federal Maritime Commission Shipping Regulation Under Principles of International Law*, 54 GEO. L.J. 794 (1966).

Ralph C. Walker, *Regulating Ocean Shipping: Powers and Problems of the Federal Maritime Commission*, 51 CAL. L. REV. 986 (1963).

FEDERAL MINE SAFETY AND HEALTH REVIEW COMMISSION

1331 Pennsylvania Avenue, NW
Washington, DC 20004

(202) 434-9900 General Inquiries
(202) 434-9935 Office of the General Counsel
Website: www.fmshrc.gov

Mission and General Statutory Reference: The Federal Mine Safety and Health Review Commission (FMSHRC) is an adjudicatory agency that provides administrative trial and appellate review of mine safety and health enforcement actions brought by the Department of Labor's Mine Safety and Health Administration. Most cases deal with civil penalties assessed against mine operators. In such cases, the commission determines whether health or safety violations occurred and assesses appropriate penalties. 30 U.S.C, § 801 et seq.

Agency Statutory History: Commission established by Section 113 of the Federal Mine Safety and Health Act of 1977, Pub. L. 95-164, 91 Stat. 1290, 1313 (Nov. 9, 1977). 30 U.S.C. § 823. Congress created the Bureau of Mines in the Department of the Interior in 1910, Pub. L. 61-179, 36 Stat. 369 (May 16, 1910), but Section 5 of the statute expressly prohibited the bureau from inspecting or supervising mines or metallurgical plants. The bureau was first authorized to inspect mines by the Coal Mine Health and Safety Act of 1941, Pub. L. 77-49, 55 Stat. 177 (May 7, 1941). The Federal Coal Mine Health and Safety Act, Pub. L. 82-582, 66 Stat. 692, 697 (July 16, 1952), created a three-member Federal Coal Mine Safety Board of Review to review requests for annulment or revision of orders by the Bureau of Mines directing that individuals be withdrawn from, or debarred from, dangerous mines. Federal safety enforcement was extended to noncoal mines by the Federal Metal and Nonmetallic Mine Safety Act ("Metal Act"), Pub. L. No. 89-577, 80 Stat. 772 (1966), which also created the Federal Metal and Nonmetallic Mine Safety Board of Review. The board was abolished in 1975. *See* Pub. L. 94-41, 89 Stat. 226 (1975). The Federal Coal Mine Health and Safety Act of 1969, Pub. L. 91-173, 83 Stat. 742 (Dec. 30, 1969), authorized miners to request federal inspections and provided for fines for violations of the statute.

Membership: Five members are appointed by the president with the advice and consent of the Senate to staggered six-year terms. There is no provision limiting the number of commissioners who can be affiliated with the same political party. A member may be removed by the president for inefficiency, neglect of duty, or malfeasance in office. 30 U.S.C. § 823(b)(11).

Quorum and Voting Requirements: The commission is authorized to delegate to any group of three or more members any or all of the powers of the commission, and two members shall constitute a quorum of any group designated. 30 U.S.C. § 823(c). There is no other quorum requirement. During one period of time when no quorum of three was present, the commission simply waited until such a quorum was available to take official action on case disposition. After a commission ALJ has rendered a decision that constitutes his or her final disposition of the proceedings, the commission, by an affirmative vote of two commissioners, may direct review by either granting a petition for discretionary review within forty days after the issuance of the decision, or by directing review on its own motion within thirty days after the issuance of the decision. If the commission does not grant review, the decision of the ALJ becomes a final decision of the commission forty days after its issuance. 30 U.S.C. § 823(d)(1). After directing review, commission action on exceptions to the ALJ's decision may be taken only by a majority vote, provided a quorum is present. When the commission is equally divided, two in favor of affirming the ALJ's decision and two for vacating or reversing the decision, the decision stands as if affirmed. *See*

Secretary of Labor v. Pennsylvania Elec. Co., 12 F.M.S.H.R.C. 1562, 1563–1565 (1990), *aff'd on other grounds*, Pennsylvania Elec. Co. v. Federal Mine Safety and Health Review Commission, 969 F.2d 1501 (3d Cir. 1992). The commission issues majority and dissenting opinions simultaneously. In one reported case, the majority and dissenting opinions were issued on different dates. *See* Contests of Respirable Dust Sample Alteration Citations, 17 F.M.S.H.R.C. 1819 (Nov. 29, 1995) (majority opinion); Contests of Respirable Dust Sample Alteration Citations, 17 F.M.S.H.R.C. 1883 (Dec. 6, 1995) (dissenting opinion). A dissenting commissioner's opinion is drafted by the commissioner and/or his or her counsel. However, in some circumstances, the commissioner may also receive staff assistance, particularly if the commissioner's view adopts the staff recommendation.

Disqualification and Recusal Procedure: Each commissioner may recuse himself or herself from a proceeding whenever he or she deems such action appropriate. The commission's rules provide that "[a] party may request a Commissioner... to withdraw on grounds of personal bias or other disqualification." 29 C.F.R. § 2700.81(b). If a commissioner declines to withdraw, the ruling and grounds for the ruling are stated in the record. 29 C.F.R. § 2700.81(c).

Chairman's Powers: The president designates one of the members to serve as chairman. The chairman is responsible for the administrative operations of the commission. 30 U.S.C. § 823(b)(2). In the past the chairman has appointed key staff officials without prior approval of other members of the commission. The other members of the commission typically do not approve budget requests before their submission.

OMB Bypass Provisions: The commission does not possess a budgetary bypass of OMB review.

Litigation Authority: As a matter of discretionary policy, the commission has left to the litigating parties who appear before it the task of defending commission decisions in the U.S. courts of appeals, where commission decisions are reviewed or enforced. The commission has an understanding with the DOJ that should the commission wish to file a brief or otherwise defend its decisions, the commission would coordinate its efforts with the DOJ. The commission, however, does file routine procedural motions, through the Office of General Counsel, in the courts of appeals. Under the Mine Act, the Department of Labor has specific litigating authority in the areas of injunctive relief and enforcement of commission orders and decisions. 30 U.S.C. §§ 816(b), 818, & 822. The commission has subpoena enforcement authority in the U.S. district courts. 30 U.S.C. § 823(e). Litigation involving personnel matters has been and would be handled by the Office of the General Counsel. The commission has not had occasion to be involved in FOIA and Sunshine Act lawsuits. In such lawsuits, however, defense would be coordinated between the commission's Office of General Counsel and the DOJ.

Selective Bibliography

Articles

R. Henry Moore, *The Doctrine of Judicial Deference and the Independence of the Federal Mine Safety and Health Review Commission*, 107 W. VA. L. REV. 187(2004).

BOARD OF GOVERNORS OF THE FEDERAL RESERVE SYSTEM

20th Street and Constitution Avenue NW
Washington, DC 20551
(202) 452-3204 General Inquiries
(202) 452-3583 Office of the General Counsel
Website: www.federalreserve.gov

Mission and General Statutory Reference: The Federal Reserve Board is the central bank of the United States. It conducts the nation's monetary policy, supervises and regulates banking institutions, maintains the stability of the financial system, protects the credit rights of consumers, and provides certain financial service for the U.S. government, the public, financial institutions, and foreign official institutions. 12 U.S.C. §§ 241–251.

Agency Statutory History: Board created by Section 10 of the Federal Reserve Act, Pub. L. 63-43, 38 Stat. 260 (Dec. 23, 1913). Board originally composed of seven members, five appointed by the president with Senate confirmation, plus the secretary of the treasury and the comptroller of the currency as ex officio members. Appointed members served ten-year terms, with the first appointees serving staggered terms of two to ten years. Section 203 of the Act to Amend the Federal Reserve Act, Pub. L. 67-230, 42 Stat. 620 (June 3, 1922), increased the board membership to eight members. Section 203 of the Banking Act of 1935, Pub. L. 74-305, 49 Stat. 704 (Aug. 23, 1935), changed the name of the agency to the Board of Governors of the Federal Reserve System, changed the names of the governor and vice governor to chairman and vice chairman, and reduced the membership to seven by eliminating the ex officio positions of the secretary of the treasury and the comptroller of the currency, effective Feb. 1, 1936. Section 203(b) establishes the fourteen-year term of office. 38 Stat. 704. The Federal Reserve Reform Act of 1977, Pub. L. 95-188, 91 Stat.1387, 1388 (1977), established a four-year renewable term for the members chosen as chairman and vice chairman and required separate Senate confirmation for those terms. The Dodd-Frank Wall Street Reform and Consumer Protection Act, Pub. L. 111-203, 124 Stat. 2126 (2010) added the position of vice chairman for supervision.

Membership: The board consists of seven members appointed by the president with the advice and consent of the Senate. 12 U.S.C. § 241. No more than one member may be appointed from any one Federal Reserve District. The full term of a board member is fourteen years, and the seven terms are staggered so that one expires in every even-numbered year. A member may not be appointed after having served a full term. The president may remove members for cause.

Quorum and Voting Requirements: A majority of the board members constitutes a quorum for the purposes of taking board action. This is not true, however, in the following two contexts. First, board action with respect to the waiver of reserve ratio limits in extraordinary circumstances and the imposition of supplemental reserves under section 19(b) of the Federal Reserve Act requires the affirmative vote of five members. 12 U.S.C. § 461(b)(3)–(4)(A). Second, board action with respect to advances, 12 U.S.C. § 347a, discounts, and rediscounts under sections 10A, 11(b), and 13, respectively, of the Federal Reserve Act requires the affirmative vote of five members. The board has the power to delegate any of its authority, except with regard to rulemaking and monetary policy decisions. 12 U.S.C. § 248(k).

Disqualification and Recusal Procedure: No special procedures.

Chairman's Powers: The chairman, subject to board supervision, serves as its "active executive officer." 12 U.S.C. § 242. The chairman and two vice chairmen are designated for four-year terms by the president from among the board members, subject to Senate confirmation, and may be redesignated as long as their terms as board members have not expired. One vice chairman serves in the absence of the chairman. The other vice chairman is designated as the vice chairman for supervision, with responsibility for developing policy recommendations for the board regarding the supervision and regulation of depository institutions and other firms supervised by the board, and supervising these firms. The full board, rather than the chairman, has the authority to appoint members of the board's staff. The board also approves the agency's budget.

OMB Bypass Provisions: The board does not submit legislation or testimony on legislation to the OMB for clearance. Under 12 U.S.C. § 250, no federal officer or agency can require the board to submit legislative recommendations, testimony, or comments for approval or review prior to their submission to Congress, provided that such communication to Congress include a statement that views expressed therein do not necessarily reflect the views of the president. Under the provisions of the Federal Reserve Act, the board obtains its funds through semiannual fees imposed on member banks. 12 U.S.C. 243.

Litigation Authority: The board has independent litigation authority with regard to enforcement, supervision, and regulation of financial institutions, and the administration of board operations. 12 U.S.C. § 248(p). The board's own lawyers handle FOIA cases filed in the U.S. District Court for the District of Columbia (and occasionally in other districts as well), but ordinarily appear along with the U.S. Attorney's Office in other districts.

Selective Bibliography

Books

Board of Governors of the Federal Reserve System, The Federal Reserve System, Purposes and Functions (9th ed. 2005).

J. Lawrence Broz, The International Origins of the Federal Reserve System (1986).

Edward G. Griffin, The Creature from Jekyll Island: A Second Look at the Federal Reserve (2002).

Elgin Earl Groseclose, America's Money Machine: The Story of the Federal Reserve (1980).

Robert F. Himmelberg, Growth of the Regulatory State, 1900–1917: State and Federal Regulation of Railroads and Other Enterprises (1994).

Roger T. Johnson, Historical Beginnings: The Federal Reserve (1990).

Clyde Johnson King & J. H. Willits, The Federal Reserve System, Its Purpose and Work (1922).

James Livingston, Origins of the Federal Reserve System: Money, Class and Corporate Capitalism 1890–1913 (1986).

Allen H. Meltzer, A History of the Federal Reserve (2003).

Jeffrey A. Miron, The Founding of the Fed and the Destabilization of the Post-1914 Economy (1988).

Carl H. Moore, The Federal Reserve System: A History of the First 75 Years (1990).

Pauline H. Smale, Board of Governors of the Federal Reserve System History, Membership, and Current Issues (1995).

Donald R. Wells, The Federal Reserve System: A History (2004).

Articles

Arthur Selwyn Miller, *Observations on the Constitutional Position of the Federal Reserve Board*, 40 N.D. L. Rev. 231 (1964).

FEDERAL TRADE COMMISSION

600 Pennsylvania Avenue NW
Washington, DC 20580
(202) 434-9900 General Inquiries
(202) 434-9935 Office of the General Counsel
Website: www.ftc.gov

Mission and General Statutory Reference: The Federal Trade Commission (FTC) enforces more than seventy federal antitrust and consumer protection statutes. The FTC's organic statute is set out at 15 U.S.C. §§ 41–58.

Agency Statutory History: The FTC was established by Section 1 of the Federal Trade Commission Act, Pub. L. 63-203, 38 Stat. 717 (Sept. 26, 1914). In 1903, Congress established within the Department of Commerce a Bureau of Corporations, headed by a commissioner of corporations appointed by the president but without Senate confirmation. The commissioner had authority to investigate the practices of corporations and report to the president. The bureau's investigatory powers were modeled on those held by the ICC. *See* Section 6 of Pub. L. 57-87, 32 Stat. 827–828 (Feb. 14, 1903). The bureau's responsibilities were transferred to the FTC upon its creation in 1914. The Wheeler-Lee Act of 1938 added "unfair or deceptive acts or practices" to the "unfair methods of competition" proscribed by the FTC Act. Section 3 of Reorganization Plan No. 8 of 1950, 3 C.F.R. pt. 1005 (1949–1953 comp.), transferred from the commission to the president the power to appoint the commission chairman, and Section 1 transferred executive and administrative functions, including the distribution of business among personnel and administrative units, and the use and expenditure of funds, from the commission to the chairman. Reorganization Plan No. 4 of 1961, 3 C.F.R. pt. 874 (1961 comp.), authorized the commission to delegate functions by published rule or order.

Membership: Five members serve staggered seven-year terms and are appointed by the president with the advice and consent of the Senate. Commissioners may serve until a successor is appointed and qualified. No more than three commissioners may be from one political party. Commissioners may be removed by the president for inefficiency, neglect of duty, or malfeasance in office. 15 U.S.C. § 41.

Other Presidential Appointees: None.

Significant Cases: Humphrey's Executor, 295 U.S. 602 (1935) (statute limiting president's removal power over FTC commissioners to "inefficiency, neglect of duty, or malfeasance in office" is constitutional).

Quorum and Voting Requirements: There is no statutory quorum requirement. However, under commission rules, a quorum is a majority of the members "in office and not recused from participating in a matter." 16 C.F.R. § 4.14(b) (2000). A motion fails for lack of a majority or lack of a quorum when a vote is cast and one month passes without another vote being cast. Commission Rule 4.14(c) provides that "No Commissioner may delegate the authority to determine his or her vote in any matter requiring Commission action," but Rule 4.14(c) permits commissioners to direct members of their staffs to report their votes. Review of an ALJ decision is required where a party has filed a timely notice of appeal. Commission rules permit the commission to place an ALJ decision on its own docket for review. The commission may delegate, by published order or rule, certain of its functions to a division of the commission, an individual commissioner, an ALJ, or an employee or employee board, and retains a discretionary right to review such delegated action upon its own initiative or upon petition of a party to or an intervenor in such action. 16 C.F.R. § 0.7.

Disqualification and Recusal Procedure: Disqualification or recusal rests in the first instance with each individual commissioner. If the commissioner declines to recuse him or herself, "the Commission shall determine the [disqualification motion] without that Commissioner's participation." 16 C.F.R. § 4.17(b)(3).

Chairman's Powers: The president designates a chairman from among the membership. The executive and administrative functions of the commission are vested in the chairman subject to the general policies established by the commission. Appointment of heads of major administrative units is subject to approval of the commission. The commission has authorization to revise budget estimates and to determine the distribution of appropriated funds. The commission may delegate functions to divisions of the commission, hearing examiners, and other employees and retains a discretionary review authority that may be triggered by a vote of the majority less one. The chairman has the authority to designate which personnel, including commissioners, are to perform these delegated functions.

OMB Bypass Provisions: The commission has no statutory legislative bypass provision. However, it asserts informal (nonstatutory) bypass authority and ordinarily does not submit legislation, reports on legislation, or testimony to the OMB for clearance. The commission submits its annual request for appropriations to the OMB for approval and inclusion in the president's budget.

Litigation Authority: Section 56 of the Federal Trade Commission Act (the Act), 15 U.S.C. § 56 (1994), specifically authorizes the commission to represent itself by its own attorneys in four categories of cases; (1) suits for injunctive relief under Section 53 of the Act, 15 U.S.C. § 56(a)(2)(A); (2) suits for consumer redress under Section 57(b) of the Act, 15 U.S.C. § 56(a)(2)(B); (3) petitions for judicial review of commission rules or orders, 15 U.S.C. § 56(a)(2)(C); (4) suits to enforce compulsory process under Sections 46 and 49 of the Act, and (5) seeking orders against the notification of investigation targets, by the recipients of compulsory process demands, in certain circumstances. 15 U.S.C. § 46(a)(2)(D). Section 56 also provides that with respect to "any civil action involving this subchapter (including an action to collect a civil penalty)," the commission may represent itself if the attorney general does not agree to do so after forty-five days notice. 15 U.S.C. § 56(a)(1)(A)–(B). This catchall provision enables the commission to prosecute and defend by its own attorneys a wide variety of cases that the DOJ declines to litigate (particularly civil penalty actions under Sections 5(l) and 5(m) of the Act). The commission is authorized to represent itself in suits to enforce civil investigative demands. 15 U.S.C. § 57b-1(e). In addition, the DOJ may appoint commission attorneys as special U.S. attorneys to represent the United States in litigation conducted by the DOJ. The commission also participates as amicus curiae in cases raising important issues under antitrust and consumer protection laws. The Justice Department ordinarily represents the commission in cases of common concern to all agencies, such as FOIA, tort or personnel litigation.

Separate provisions govern representation before the Supreme Court. Section 56(a)(3), defines certain circumstances under which the commission may appear in the Supreme Court "in any civil action in which the Commission represented itself [in the courts below] pursuant to [Sections 56(a)(1) or (2)]." Specifically, the commission may represent itself if it requests authority to do so from the solicitor general within ten days of the lower court judgment and the solicitor general, within sixty days after entry of the judgment, either authorizes the commission's appearance, declines to represent the commission, or fails to respond to the request.

Selective Bibliography

Books

KENNETH W. CLARKSON & TIMOTHY J. MURIS, THE FTC SINCE 1970: ECONOMIC REGULATION AND BUREAUCRATIC BEHAVIOR (2008).

FEDERAL TRADE COMMISSION, FULFILLING THE ORIGINAL VISION: THE FTC AT 90 (2004).

GERARD CARL HENDERSON, THE FEDERAL TRADE COMMISSION: A STUDY IN ADMINISTRATIVE LAW AND PROCEDURE (1924).

ROBERT V. LABAREE, THE FEDERAL TRADE COMMISSION: A GUIDE TO SOURCES (2000).

Articles

Roger E. Schechter, A Retrospective of the Reagan FTC: Musings on the Role of an Administrative Agency, 42 ADMIN. L. REV. 489 (1990).

Federal Trade Commission 75th Anniversary Symposium, 58 ANTITRUST L.J. 795 (1989).

Hilary Greene, Agency Character and the Character of Agency Guidelines: An Historical and Institutional Perspective, 72 ANTITRUST L.J. 1039 (2005).

Caswell O. Hobbs, III, Swings of the Pendulum—The FTC's First Seventy-Five Years, 58 ANTITRUST L.J. 9 (1989).

Tim Muris & Bob Pitofsky, More Than Law Enforcement: the FTC's Many Tools—A Conversation with Tim Muris and Bob Pitofsky, 72 ANTITRUST L.J. 773 (2005).

F. M. Sherer, Sunlight and Sunset at the Federal Trade Commission, 42 ADMIN. L. REV. 461 (1990).

Marc Winerman, The FTC at Ninety: History Through Headlines, 72 ANTITRUST L.J. 9 (2005).

Marc Winerman, The Origins of the FTC: Concentration, Cooperation, Control, and Competition, 71 ANTITRUST L.J. 1 (2003).

INDEPENDENT PAYMENT ADVISORY BOARD

Mission and General Statutory Reference: The Independent Payment Advisory Board (IPAB) is an "independent board" charged with studying the costs of the Medicare program and developing recommendations to Congress designed to "reduce the per capita rate of growth in Medicare expenditures." Its recommendations become law unless Congress enacts contrary legislation. The board begins submitting reports after January 15, 2014. 42 U.S.C. § 1395kkk. The statute provides a legislative mechanism for Congress to abolish the Board in 2018. 42 U.S.C. § 1395kkk (f)(3)(B)(C).

Agency Statutory History: The Medicare Payment Advisory Commission was established as a congressional advisory body by the Balanced Budget Act of 1997, Pub. L. 105-33, 111 Stat. 350 (Aug. 5, 1997), to make recommendations to Congress on payment policy regarding Medicare providers. The comptroller general appointed its fifteen members, with its chairman and vice chairman also designated by the comptroller general. 111 Stat. 352. The commission was transformed into "an independent board" by Section 3403 of the Patient Protection and Affordable Care Act, Pub. L. 111-148, 124 Stat. 489, 502–503 (Mar. 23, 2010) and its name changed to the Independent Payment Advisory Board by Section 10320(b) of the same Act, 124 Stat. 952.

Membership: The board is composed of fifteen members appointed by the president with the advice and consent of the Senate to six-year terms and may only be removed by the president "for neglect of duty or malfeasance in office, but for no other cause." Twelve of the fifteen members are selected by the president after consultation with leaders of both parties in congress. 42 U.S.C. § 1395kkk(g)(1)(E). In addition, the secretary of health and human services, the administrator of the Health Resources and Services Administration, and the administrator of the Center for Medicare and Medicaid Services serve as nonvoting ex officio members of the Board.

The appointed membership of the board shall include (but not be limited to) physicians and other health professionals, experts in the area of pharmaco-economics or prescription drug benefit programs, employers, third-party payers, individuals skilled in the conduct and interpretation of biomedical, health services, and health economics research and expertise in outcomes and effectiveness research and technology assessment. Such membership shall also include representatives of consumers and the elderly. Individuals who are directly involved in the provision or management of the delivery of items and services covered under this subchapter shall not constitute a majority of the appointed membership of the board.

Quorum and Voting Requirements: A majority of the board constitutes a quorum. 42 U.S.C. § 1395kkk (h)(2).

Chairman's Powers: The chairperson, appointed to that position by the president with the advice and consent of the Senate, is the "principal executive officer of the Board" with power to appoint and supervise the staff, distribute business among staff, and use and expend funds, except that the appointment of an executive director and the submission of any appropriations request must be approved by the board. 42 U.S.C. § 1395kkk (g)(3)(A). The board annually selects its own vice chairperson who acts if the chairperson is unavailable.

OMB Bypass Provisions: Level and method of funding expressly provided for by statute. 42 U.S.C. § 1395kkk (m).

N.B.: As of this printing President Obama has not nominated any members of the board. At the same time, the board need not make any reports until 2015. *See* Patient Protection and Affordable Care Act § 3202 (a) codified at 42 U.S.C. 1395kkk(o)(1), although Secretary Kathleen Sebelius has suggested that no "recommendation would be targeted until 2019." Numerous unsuccessful efforts have been made to repeal the Board. *See,* for example, these 2013 efforts:

- H.R. 351 (introduced in January 2013):
  - Press Release: http://roe.house.gov/news/documentsingle.aspx?DocumentID=317471
  - Bill: www.gpa.gov/fdsys/pkg/BILLS-113hr351ih/pdf/BILLS-113hr351ih.pdf
- H.R. 37 (introduced January 2013):
  - Bill: www.gpo.gov/fdsys/pkg/BILLS-113hr37ih/pdf/BILLS-113hr37ih.pdf
- S. 1316 (Introduced July 2013):
  - www.gpo.gov/fdsys/pkg/BILLS-113hr37ih/pdf/BILLS-113hr37ih.pdf

Further, if the IPAB is not in operation by the time it is required to issue recommendations its powers will devolve to the secretary of health and human services.

Selective Bibliography

Books

David Newman & Christopher M. Davis, Cong. Research Serv., RL 41511, The Independent Payment Advisory Board (2010).

Articles

Michael H. Cook, *Independent Payment Advisory Board: Part of the Solution for Bending the Cost Curve*, 4 J. Health & Life Sc. L. 102 (2010).

Jacqueline Fox, *Death Panels: A Defense of the Independent Payment Advisory Board*, 66 Admin. L. Rev. 131 (2014).

Timothy Stoltzfus Jost, *Focus on Health Care Reform: The Medicare Advisory Board*, 11 Yale J. Health Pol'y L. & Ethics 21 (2011).

Eleanor D. Kinney, *The Affordable Care Act and the Medicare Program: The Engines of True Health Reform*, 13 Yale J. Health Pol'y L. & Ethics 253 (2013).

Ann Marie Marciarille & J. Bradford DeLong, *Bending the Health Care Curve: The Promise and Peril of the Independent Payment Advisory Board*, 12 Health Matrix 75 (2012).

UNITED STATES INTERNATIONAL TRADE COMMISSION

500 E Street SW
Washington, DC 20436
(202) 205-1819 General Inquiries
(202) 205-3061 Office of the General Counsel
Website: www.itc.gov

Mission and General Statutory Reference: The United States International Trade Commission (ITC) determines the impact of imports on U.S. industries and directs actions against certain unfair trade practices, such as patent, trademark, and copyright infringement. 19 U.S.C. §§ 1330–1341. It investigates and publishes reports on U.S. industries and publishes and updates the Harmonized Tariff Schedule of the United States. 19 U.S.C. §§ 1202, 1330, 1337, 1484, 1671–1677n, 2241, & 3005.

Agency Statutory History: The original United States Tariff Commission was established by Section 700 of the Revenue Act of 1916, Pub. L. 64-271, 39 Stat. 795 (Sept. 8, 1916), and the commission was renamed by Section 171 of the Trade Act of 1974, Pub. L. 93-618, 88 Stat. 2009 (Jan. 3, 1975).

Membership: Six commissioners serve staggered nine-year terms and are appointed by the president with the advice and consent of the Senate. No more than three of the commissioners may belong to the same political party. Members of a different political party are to be appointed "alternately as nearly as may be practicable." A person who has served for more than five years may not be reappointed. A member may continue to serve until his successor is appointed and qualified. 19 U.S.C. § 1330(a)(b).

Quorum and Voting Requirements: A majority of the commissioners in office constitutes a quorum, and the commission may function notwithstanding vacancies. Unless otherwise provided for by statute, a tie vote is the same as a no vote; the motion or other attempted action fails for lack of majority. However, by statute, one-half the number of commissioners voting can authorize the institution of an investigation, and in the case of an equally divided commission, under sections 201 and 406 of the Trade Act of 1974, the president may consider the determination of either group of commissioners to be the determination of the commission. In antidumping and countervailing duty cases, by statute, an evenly divided commission vote shall be treated as an affirmative determination. By published commission rule, a vote in favor of review by only one commissioner is all that is necessary to require review by the full commission of all or part of an initial determination of an ALJ in matters under section 337 of the Tariff Act of 1930. The commission majority may issue its determination even if the minority delays in completing any dissenting statements. A dissenting commissioner can obtain staff assistance in preparing any dissenting views. There is no statutory provision for voting by proxy. The commission's organic statute contains no specific provision for the commission to delegate its functions; the commission delegates responsibilities generally through the use of directives and other internal rules.

Disqualification and Recusal Procedure: No special procedures.

Chairman's Powers: The president designates a chairman and vice chairman for two-year terms. He may not designate for chairman (1) a commissioner who has less than one year of continuous service as a commissioner as of the date the designation is being made, or (2) a commissioner who is a member of the same political party as chairman for the immediately preceding term. He may not name as vice chairman a member of the same political party as the chairman. If the president does not appoint a chairman by the beginning of the term, the commissioner with the longest period of continuous service as a commissioner who is of a different party from the chairman for the immediately preceding term will serve as chairman until a presidentially designated chairman takes office. If a commissioner does not complete a term as chairman or vice chairman due to certain specified causes, the president shall designate a commissioner of the same political party to serve the remainder of the term. The vice chairman acts as chairman in case of the absence or disability of the chairman. During any period in which there is no chairman or vice chairman, the commissioner having the longest period of continuous service as a commissioner shall act as chairman. 19 U.S.C. § 1330.

The chairman of the commission is authorized to "appoint and fix the compensation of such employees of the Commission as he deems necessary." 19 U.S.C. § 1331(a)(1)(A)(i) (1994). However, the chairman's decisions in this regard "shall be subject to disapproval by a majority vote of all the commissioners in office." 19 U.S.C. § 1331(a)(1)(C). The chairman's appointment powers do not extend to the personal staff of each commissioner. The chairman formalizes an annual budget that is subject to the approval of a majority of all the commissioners. 19 U.S.C. § 1331(a)(2)(B).

OMB Bypass Provisions: The commission is specifically excluded from the provisions of the Budget and Accounting Act of 1921 by Section 175 of the Trade Act of 1974, which directs that the commission's estimated expenditures and proposed appropriations be included without revision in the president's budget. 19 U.S.C. § 2232. Moreover, the commission asserts an informal (nonstatutory) legislative bypass and does not, consequently, clear testimony or comments through the OMB. Assertion of a legislative bypass is based on 19 U.S.C. § 2232, which, besides providing the commission with a budgetary bypass, states that the commission shall not be considered to be a department or establishment for purposes of the Budget and Accounting Act.

Litigation Authority: The commission has statutory authority to represent itself in judicial proceedings through its own attorneys. 19 U.S.C. § 1333(g). Alternatively, the commission can request that the attorney general represent it in such proceedings.

Selective Bibliography

Books

John M. Dobson, Two Centuries of Tariffs: The Background and Emergence of the U.S. International Trade Commission (1976).

Articles

Preston Brown, Unfair Competition in Importation: the Expanded Role of the U.S. International Trade Commission Under § 337 of the Tariff Act of 1930, as Amended by the Trade Act of 1974, 31 Bus. Law. 1627 (1976).

Wendy Hansen, The International Trade Commission and the Politics of Trade Protectionism, 84 Am. Pol. Sc. Rev. 21 (1990).

Will E. Leonard & F. David Foster, The Metamorphosis of the U.S. International Trade Commission Under the Tariff Act of 1974, 16 Va. Int'l L. 719 (1976).

Daniel Minchew, The Expanding Role of the United States International Trade Commission, 27 Mercer L. Rev. 429 (1976).

Daniel Minchew & R. Dan Webster, Regulating Unfair Practices in International Trade: The Role of the United States International Trade Commission, 8 Ga. J. Int'l & Comp. L. 27 (1978).

William E. Perry, Administration of Import Trade Laws by the United States Trade Commission, 3 B.U. INT'L L.J. 345 (1985).

Paula Stern, Regulating U.S. Trade and Foreign Investment, 21 U. MIAMI INTER-AM. L. REV. 1 (1989).

James A. Toupin, Siblings Before the Bench: The International Trade Commission and the Department of Commerce before the Court of International Trade. (United States Court of International Trade Eighth Annual Judicial Conference), 25 L. & POL'Y INT. BUS. 147 (1993).

MERIT SYSTEMS PROTECTION BOARD

1615 M Street NW
Washington, DC 20419
(800) 209-8960 General Inquiries
(202) 653-7171 Office of the General Counsel
Website: www.mspb.gov

Mission and General Statutory Reference: The Merit Systems Protection Board (MSPB) adjudicates appeals by federal employees of major personnel actions taken against them, including removals or demotions, decisions by the Office of Personnel Management in retirement matters, certain personnel actions involving discrimination or reprisal for whistle-blowing, and actions brought by the Office of Special Counsel involving alleged prohibited personnel practices or violations of the Hatch Act. The MSPB also reviews certain significant actions by the Office of Personnel Management, such as regulations, and conducts studies of the merit system. 5 U.S.C. §§ 1201–1206.

Agency Statutory History: Created by Section 201 of the Civil Service Reform Act of 1978, Pub. L. 95-454, 92 Stat. 1121–1122 (Oct. 13, 1978).

Membership: The board consists of a chairman, a vice chairman, and a member, with no more than two of its members from the same political party. Board members are appointed by the president, confirmed by the Senate, and serve overlapping nonrenewable seven-year terms. Members whose terms expire may continue to serve until a successor is appointed and qualified, but the extension is limited to one year. Members can be removed only for inefficiency, neglect of duty, or malfeasance in office. The president appoints one member as chairman with the advice and consent of the Senate and designates one member as vice chairman. The vice chairman performs the chairman's functions in the absence of the chairman.

Quorum and Voting Requirements: There are no statutory quorum requirements. By regulation, the board has provided that two of the board's three members constitute a quorum. When, because of a vacancy, recusal, or other reason, the board is unable to decide a matter, the decision, recommendation, or order under review is deemed the final decision of the board. When the matter does not involve a decision, recommendation, or order, the chairman may direct referral of the matter to an ALJ or other official for final disposition. When the board itself is unable to decide a matter, any decisions issued shall not be deemed precedential. The board has no provision for operation with only one member. 5 C.F.R. § 1200.3.

Disqualification and Recusal Procedure: Individual members of the board decide questions of recusal or disqualification.

Chairman's Powers: The chairman serves as chief executive and administrative officer of the board. The chairman has authority to appoint senior staff and prepare the board's budget without the approval of the board. The board may delegate "the performance of any of its functions" to a board employee. 5 U.S.C. § 1204(g).

OMB Bypass Provisions: Legislative recommendations, and budget requests and proposals, are transmitted simultaneously to the president and congress. 5 U.S.C § 1204(k)–(l). The board may transmit information to congress without prior OMB clearance. 5 U.S.C. § 1205.

Litigation Authority: Board attorneys may represent the board except as to matters in the Supreme Court. However, the DOJ handles cases of common concern to all agencies, such as FOIA litigation.

Selective Bibliography

Books

PETER BROIDA, A GUIDE TO MERIT SYSTEMS PROTECTION BOARD LAW AND PRACTICE (2007).

JOHN P. STIMSON, UNSCRAMBLING FEDERAL MERIT PROTECTION (1996).

ROBERT G. VAUGHN, MERIT SYSTEMS PROTECTION BOARD: RIGHTS AND REMEDIES (1998).

Articles

Cathy Drew, *Project on the Merit Systems Protection Board: The Civil Service Reform Act of 1978*, 29 HOW. L.J. 279 (1986).

Dennis S. Hansen, *Federal Agency Practice: Complying with Merit Systems Protection Board Interim Relief Orders*, 1992 ARMY LAW. 3 (October 1992).

Jessica L. Parks, *The Merit Systems Protection Board as a Model Forum*, 4 FED. CIR. B.J. 15 (1994).

Robert G. Vaughn, *The Opinions of the Merit Protection Board: A Study in Administrative Adjudication*, 34 ADMIN. L. REV. 25 (1982).

NATIONAL CREDIT UNION ADMINISTRATION

1775 Duke Street
Alexandria, VA 22314
(703) 518-6300 General Inquiries
(703) 518-6541 Office of the General Counsel
Website: www.ncua.gov

Mission and General Statutory Reference: The National Credit Union Administration (NCUA) supervises, examines, and insures federal credit unions and those state credit unions that apply and qualify for insurance. 12 U.S.C. § 1752a.

Agency Statutory History: The three-member NCUA was established in its current form by Section 501 of the Financial Institutions Regulatory and Interest Rate Control Act of 1978, Pub. L. 95-630, 92 Stat. 3680 (Nov. 10, 1978). However, the Administration marks its creation "as an independent agency" with Pub. L. 91-206, 84 Stat. 49 (Mar. 10, 1970). Section 3 of the

1970 statute established the position of Administrator appointed by the president with the advice and consent of the Senate, serving at the pleasure of the president. The administrator was the administration's chief executive officer, with power to appoint personnel and expend funds. Section 3 of Pub. L. 91-206 also created a board with a chairman appointed by the president with the advice and consent of the Senate, serving at the pleasure of the president, and one board member for each federal credit union region, each serving a six-year term. Section 209 of Pub. L. 91-468, 84 Stat. 994 (1970), thereafter gave the administrator independent litigation authority. The position of administrator was abolished, and the administration was placed under the management of its current three-member board in the 1978 statute. The administration structure created in 1970 succeeded a Bureau of Federal Credit Unions within the Department of Health, Education and Welfare that had been established by the Federal Credit Union Act, Pub. L. 86-354, 73 Stat. 628 (Sept. 22, 1959). The bureau director was appointed by the secretary of health, education and welfare and operated "under the general direction and supervision of the Secretary." Credit unions initially came under federal supervision when Congress enacted the Federal Credit Union Act of 1934, Pub. L. 107-252, 48 Stat. 1216 (June 26, 1934). Section 6 of the 1934 Act placed initial responsibility for supervision of credit unions with the Governor of the Farm Credit Administration. *See* 48 Stat. 1216–1218.

Membership: The NCUA Board is composed of three members who are "broadly representative of the public interest," have "education, training or experience" in financial services, and are appointed by the president to six-year terms with the advice and consent of the Senate. 12 U.S.C. § 1752a(b)(1)–(2)(A). Not more than two members of the board may be members of the same political party. Not more than one member of the board shall have recent experience as a credit union committee member, officer, director, employee, or institution-affiliated party. 12 U.S.C. § 1752a(b)(2)(B). Members may not be appointed to succeed themselves, unless they have not served a full six-year term. Any board member may continue to serve after the expiration of his or her term until a successor is qualified. The president designates a chairman, and the board may designate one of its members as vice chairman.

Significant Case: Swan v. Clinton, 100 F.3d 983 (D.C. Cir. 1996) (assuming, without deciding, that board members have "for cause" removal protection despite lack of statutory language, but protection does not extend to holdover members).

Quorum and Voting Requirements: A majority of the board constitutes a quorum. 12 U.S.C. § 1752a(d). The agreement of two of the three members is required for board action. There is no statutory or regulatory provision that prohibits a majority of the board from issuing its decision if the minority delays completing a dissenting statement. Although a board member who disagrees with a decision may state such disagreement at a meeting, written dissenting statements are not issued. Proxy voting is prohibited.

Disqualification and Recusal Procedure: No special procedures.

Chairman's Powers: The chairman is the spokesman for the board, represents the board and the NCUA in its official relations with other branches of government, determines each member's area of responsibility, and reviews such assignments biannually. The chairman is the presiding officer at meetings and makes procedural rulings, although, upon appeal, a majority decision by the board determines any disputed ruling.

The authority to appoint senior staff, with the exception of each board member's personal staff, is reserved to the board. However, the chairman does have the authority to select the executive director given the prior agreement by the board. The chairman also maintains the authority for all board human resource decisions in the event of an emergency. Any such actions taken by the chairman will remain effective for thirty days or until the next closed board meeting. Budget approval authority is reserved to the board. The executive director, reporting to the chairman, may approve the reprogramming of up to $150,000 of budget amounts per quarter under powers delegated by the board, given that all necessary circumstances are met.

OMB Bypass Provisions: Bypass of OMB review on legislative matters is secured by means of a prohibition on prior executive review provided that the NCUA include a statement that its views do not necessarily represent those of the president. 12 U.S.C. § 250. The NCUA is funded through assessments leveled on credit unions and does not receive appropriated funds.

Litigation Authority: The NCUA engages in litigation without the DOJ only when it acts as liquidating agent or conservator for a credit union. Otherwise, the DOJ is responsible for the conduct of federal court litigation brought by or against the NCUA in its capacity as a federal agency.

Selective Bibliography

Books

Wendell V. Fountain, THE CREDIT UNION WORLD: THEORY, PROCESS, PRACTICE—CASES AND APPLICATION (2007).

Articles

Michael F. Crotty, *Turf Wars: Banks v. Credit Unions*, 30 CREIGHTON L. REV. 657 (1997).

Michael P. Malloy, *Balancing Public Confidence and Confidentiality: Adjudication Practices and Procedures of the Federal Bank Regulatory Agencies*, 61 TEMPLE L. REV. 723 (1988).

NATIONAL INDIAN GAMING COMMISSION

90 K Street NE, Suite 200
Washington, DC 20002
(202) 631-7003 General Inquiries
(202) 631-7003 Office of the General Counsel
Website: www.nigc.gov

Mission and General Statutory Reference: The National Indian Gaming Commission (NIGC), established within the Department of the Interior, enforces the mandates of the Indian Gaming Regulatory Act, 25 U.S.C. § 2701 et seq., of promoting tribal economic development, self-sufficiency, and strong tribal governments. Congress established the commission to protect Indian gaming as a means of generating tribal revenue. The commission works in tandem with tribes, states, and federal agencies to provide oversight of Indian gaming. Among other activities, the commission monitors Class II gaming operations, approves all gaming operation management contracts, provides training and technical assistance to tribes, and brings enforcement actions to ensure compliance with the Indian Gaming Regulatory Act, NIGC regulations, and tribal ordinances. 25 U.S.C. §§ 2701–2721.

Agency Statutory History: The NIGC was created by Section 5 of the Indian Gaming Regulatory Act of 1988, Pub. L. 100-497, 102 Stat. 2469 (Oct. 17, 1988).

Significant Case: California v. Cabazon Bd. of Mission Indians, 480 U.S. 202 (1987) (affirmed the authority of tribal governments to operate gaming facilities on Indian lands independent of state regulation provided that the state in question permits gaming. Subsequent to this case, Congress enacted the Indian Gaming Regulatory Act in 1988).

Membership: Three members each serve three-year terms. All members may continue to serve until a successor is appointed. The chair is appointed by the president with the advice and consent of the Senate. The two associate commissioners are appointed by the secretary of the interior. Two members must be enrolled members of an Indian tribe. No more than two members can be of the same political party. The commission selects, from one its own associate members, the vice chair by a majority vote. The vice chair serves as chair during commission meetings in the absence of the chair. Members have "for cause" removal protection.

Quorum and Voting Requirements: Two members, one of whom who must be the chair or the vice chair, are required to constitute a quorum. The effect of a tie vote depends on the particular matter before the commission, although the commission is required to have an affirmative vote of no less than two of its members before it can establish an annual gaming fee rate, issue subpoenas, and make a temporary closure order final. 25 U.S.C. § 2706(a).

Disqualification and Recusal Procedure: No special procedures.

Chairman's Powers: The chair has the authority to: issue orders of temporary closure of gaming activities and operations; levy and collect civil fines for violations of the Indian Gaming Regulatory Act, NIGC regulations, and/or tribal gaming regulations, ordinances, or resolutions; approve tribal gaming ordinances; and approve gaming management contracts. 25 U.S.C. § 2705(a). The chair also has the authority to appoint and supervise commission staff. 25 U.S.C. § 2707.

OMB Bypass Provisions: The commission has a permanent appropriation that is funded by fees collected from certain gaming operations. 25 U.S.C. § 2717a. The commission adopts its fiscal budget on an annual basis. 25 U.S.C. § 2717(a)(3).

Litigation Authority: The DOJ represents the commission in the federal courts.

Selective Bibliography

Articles

Michael D. Cox, *The Indian Gaming Regulatory Act: An Overview*, 7 St. Thomas L. Rev. 769 (1995).

Kevin K. Washburn, *Agency Conflict and Culture: Federal Implementation of the Indian Gaming Regulatory Act by the National Indian Gaming Commission, the Bureau of Indian Affairs, and the Department of Justice*, 42 Ariz. St. L.J. 303 (2010).

NATIONAL LABOR RELATIONS BOARD

1099 14th Street NW
Washington, DC 20570
(202) 273-1991 General Inquiries
(202) 273-1962 Office of the Solicitor
(202) 273-3700 Office of the General Counsel
Website: www.nlrb.gov

Mission and General Statutory Reference: The National Labor Relations Board (NLRB) conducts secret-ballot elections to determine whether employees want union representation and investigates and adjudicates claims of unfair labor practices by employers and unions. 29 U.S.C. §§ 151–169.

Agency Statutory History: Section 3 of the Wagner Act of 1935, Pub. L. 74-198, 49 Stat. 449, 451 (July 5, 1935) created a three-member board. The Labor Management Relations Act of 1947 (Taft-Hartley Act), Pub. L. 80-101, 61 Stat. 136, 139 (June 23, 1947) expanded the board to five members and authorized the board to delegate decisional authority to panels of three members.

Membership: Five members serve staggered five-year terms and are appointed by the president with the advice and consent of the Senate. The statute is silent on party membership, but by tradition two of the five seats on the board have been reserved for individuals who are not members of the president's party. There is no provision for members to serve after their terms expire pending the appointment of a new member, although members are eligible for reappointment. The president may remove a member, upon notice and hearing, for neglect of duty or malfeasance in office, but not for any other cause.

Other Presidential Appointees: General counsel. The president also appoints a general counsel with the advice and consent of the Senate, for a term of four years. The general counsel has final authority to investigate charges and institute complaints involving unfair labor practices. 29 U.S.C. § 153(d) (1994). He also exercises general supervision over all attorneys employed by the Board (other than ALJs and legal assistants to board members) and the officers and employees of the twenty-eight regional offices (the board's regional office consolidation is ongoing). He also has such other duties as may be delegated by the board. Appeals from decisions of regional directors for the failure to institute an unfair labor practice complaint are of right and go to the general counsel or his or her designee. Appeals of a regional director's decision not to proceed on a representation petition (styled "requests for review" in the board's rules) are discretionary and lie with the board.

Significant Case: NLRB v. Jones & Laughlin Steel Corp., 301 U.S. 1 (1937) (upholding the constitutionality of the Wagner Act).

Quorum and Voting Requirements: Three of the five members constitute a quorum for purposes of taking board action. Since 1947, the statute has authorized the board to delegate any or all of its powers to a panel of three of its members, and two members constitute a quorum of three-member panels. 29 U.S.C. § 153(b). Such delegations are made routinely in deciding unfair labor practice and representation (election) cases. Since 1947, in those instances where the board has fallen below three members, it has historically declined to rule on pending contested matters until a third member has been appointed. For about a two-year period starting in 2007, however, in anticipation of losing two of its existing four members, the four -member board delegated all of the board's powers to a three-member panel. When the recess appointment of one of the three members expired, the remaining two members, acting as a two-member quorum, continued to exercise the powers that had been delegated to the three-member group. The Supreme Court concluded that such exercise violated the statute. A panel must ordinarily maintain a membership of three in order to exercise the authority delegated to it by the board. *See* New Process Steel. v. NLRB, 130 S. Ct. 2635 (2010).

Inasmuch as the statute provides for five board members with three constituting a quorum, tie votes generally occur only when there is a vacancy on the board or a member is disqualified from participating. The board members do not vote on whether to take review of a decision by an ALJ because an appeal from such a decision is a matter of right. 29 U.S.C. § 160(c). Since 1976 the board has had a procedure that permits majority decisions to be issued without awaiting a dissenting opinion in the event that the dissenting opinion was not circulated in a timely manner (generally four weeks from approval of the majority draft). However, this procedure has never actually been implemented in any case. The statute provides that each member shall have his or her own staff of attorneys to review cases and prepare drafts of opinions, and members routinely rely on their staffs for assistance in drafting both majority and dissenting opinions. In addition, the board has delegated limited authority to its executive secretary to rule on procedural motions respecting the filing of formal documents, such as requests for extensions of time. Board procedures assure personal participation of the board members in the decision of all other contested issues, and subordinates are not issued general proxies with respect to such matters.

Disqualification and Recusal Procedure: Individual Board members decide questions of recusal or disqualification. *See* Caterpillar Inc., 321 N.L.R.B. 1130, 1132–1134 (1996) (statements of Chairman Gould and Member Browning); Service Employees Int'l Union, Nurses Alliance, Local 121 RN, 355 N.L.R.B. 234, 238 (2010) (statement of Member Becker).

Chairman's and General Counsel's Powers: The president designates one member to serve as chairman. The statute is silent as to the chairman's authority. As a practical matter, all key administrative decisions, such as approval of the budget, are made jointly by the chairman and the general counsel, in consultation with the board members. The general counsel investigates alleged unfair labor practices and prosecutes unfair labor practice complaints. 29 U.S.C. § 153(d); *see also* 5 U.S.C. § 7104(f)(2)(A)–(B). The general counsel has unreviewable discretion to decline to issue unfair labor practice complaints. The general counsel also has direct authority over NLRB regional office employees. 5 U.S.C. § 7104(f)(3).

OMB Bypass Provisions: The board does not assert a budgetary or legislative bypass of OMB review.

Litigation Authority: The board enjoys independent litigating authority under its statute. 29 U.S.C. §§ 154(a), 160(e), and 161(1)–(2). The board also handles its own FOIA and Equal Access to Justice Act litigation. The DOJ is involved in Supreme Court litigation and non-program litigation, such as tort claims and other suits for damages.

Selective Bibliography

Books

ABA Section of Labor and Employment Law, The Developing Labor Law: The Board, the Courts and the National Labor Relations Act (6th ed. 2012).

The Developing Labor Law (John E. Higgins, Jr., ed., 5th ed. 2006).

James A. Gross, The Making of the National Labor Relations Board: A Study in Economics, Politics, and the Law, 1933–1937 (1974).

James A. Gross, The Reshaping of the National Labor Relations Board: National Labor Policy in Transition, 1937–1947 (1981).

NLRB, A Guide to basic law and Procedures Under the National Labor Relations Act (1991).

David E. Strecker, labor law: A Basic Guide to the National Labor Relations Act (2011).

Articles

Joan Flynn, *A Quiet Revolution at the Labor Board: The Transformation of the NLRB, 1935–2000*, 61 Ohio St. L.J. 1361 (2000).

Derek C. Bok, *Reflections on the Distinctive Character of American Labor Laws*, 84 Harv. L. Rev. 1394 (1971).

John E. Higgins, Jr., *Labor Czars—Commissars—Keeping Women in the Kitchen—The Purpose and Effects of the Administrative Changes made by Taft-Hartley*, 47 Cath. U. Law. Rev. 941 (1997).

Ida Klaus, *The Taft-Hartley Experiment in Separation of NLRB Functions*, 11 Ind. & Lab. Rel. Rev. 371 (1958).

Kenneth C. McGuiness, *Effect of the Discretionary Power of the General Counsel on the Development of the Law*, 29 Geo. Wash. L. Rev. 385 (1960).

Arnold Ordman, *Fifty Years of the NLRA: An Overview*, 88 W. Va. L. Rev. 15 (1985).

NATIONAL MEDIATION BOARD

1301 K Street NW
Washington, DC 20005
(202) 692-5050 General Inquiries
(202) 692-5040 Office of the General Counsel
Website: www.nmb.gov

Mission and General Statutory Reference: The National Mediation Board (NMB) is an "independent agency in the executive branch" that mediates disputes for the airline and railroad industries. Strikes, lockouts, and other forms of self-help in these industries may occur only after the Board has determined that further mediation would not be successful and after a cooling-off period of thirty days following NMB release from mediation. The Board also certifies employee representatives in the airline and railroad industries. 45 U.S.C. §§ 154–155.

Agency Statutory History: The Board was created by Section 4 of Pub. L. 73-442, 48 Stat. 1193 (June 21, 1934). The three-member board replaced the five-member Board originally created by the Railway Labor Act, Pub. L. 69-257, 44 Stat. 579 (May 20, 1926).

Membership: Three members appointed by the President with advice and consent of the Senate to three-year terms. No more than two members may be of the same political party. Individuals appointed to fill a vacancy may only serve for the unexpired portion of the term. Members may serve after expiration of their term until a successor is qualified. Members may be removed by the President for "inefficiency, neglect of duty, malfeasance in office, or ineligibility, but for no other cause." 45 U.S.C. § 154.

Significant Case: Switchmen's Union of North America v. National Mediation Board, 320 U.S. 297 (1943) (Board decision designating a collective bargaining unit is not subject to judicial review under the Railway Labor Act).

Quorum and Voting Requirements: Two members constitute a quorum.

Disqualification and Recusal Procedure: No specific procedures.

Chairman's Powers: The board annually selects its own chairman. 45 U.S.C. § 154(Second). The board may delegate "any portion of its work, business, or functions" to an individual Board member or staff member. 45 U.S.C. § 154(Fourth).

OMB Bypass Provisions: The NMB sends its annual appropriation request to the OMB for approval and inclusion in the President's budget. The NMB also submits testimony and legislative recommendations to the OMB for clearance.

Litigation Authority: The DOJ represents the Board in the federal courts.

Selective Bibliography

Books

National Mediation Board, The Railway Labor Act and the National Mediation Board (1940).

Charles M. Rehmus, The National Mediation Board at 50: Its Impact on Railroad and Airline Labor Disputes (1984).

Articles

Todd A. Newman, *A Suggested Approach to Applying the National Mediation Board's Railroad Merger Procedures*, 15 Lab. Law. 483 (2000).

Shaunta M. Knibb, *The Jurisdictional Shadowland Between the NLRB and the National Mediation Board: Who's in Charge*, 72 Wash. L. Rev. 241 (1997).

NATIONAL TRANSPORTATION SAFETY BOARD

490 L'Enfant Plaza East SW
Washington, DC 20594

(202) 314-6100 General Inquiries
(202) 314-6080 Office of the General Counsel
Website: www.ntsb.gov

Mission and General Statutory Reference: The National Transportation Safety Board (NTSB) is an "independent establishment of the United States Government" that investigates all civil and most public aircraft accidents and significant accidents in other modes of transportation. 49 U.S.C. § 1111. It also serves as an adjudicatory body providing administrative trial and appellate review of decisions by the Federal Aviation Administration, assessing civil penalties, and reviewing decisions by the Federal Aviation Administration or the U.S. Coast Guard affecting the certificates or licenses of any carrier, airman, mechanic, or mariner. 49 U.S.C. §§ 1101, 1111–1155. In addition, upon request, the NTSB will assist the armed forces or foreign governments with accident investigations.

The Aviation Disaster Family Assistance Act of 1996, as amended, Pub. L. 104-264, Title VII, § 702(a)(1), 110 Stat. 3265 (Oct. 9, 1996), 49 U.S.C. § 1136, requires the NTSB to coordinate the disaster response resources of federal, state, local, and volunteer agencies. The NTSB works closely with these agencies and air carriers, including foreign air carriers, to meet the needs of aviation disaster victims and their families. Similarly, the Rail Safety Improvement Act of 2008, Pub. L. 110-432, Div. A, Title V, §§ 501–503, 122 Stat. 4894 (Oct. 16, 2009), 49 U.S.C. § 1139, requires the NTSB to coordinate the disaster response resources of federal, state, local, and volunteer agencies following a major rail passenger accident involving Amtrak. Also, although there is no legal requirement for the NTSB to offer family assistance services for general aviation accidents, or accidents not involving air carriers, foreign air carriers, or passenger rail, the NTSB works with state agencies to coordinate assistance and information for family members, friends, and survivors.

Agency Statutory History: The Air Commerce Act of 1926 created an Aeronautics Branch within in the U.S. Department of Commerce, and assigned it various powers to ensure civil aviation safety, including investigating aviation accidents and investigating the causes of aircraft accidents. Pub. L. 69-254, 44 Stat. 568 (1926). The Civil Aeronautics Act of 1938, Pub. L. 75-706, 52 Stat. 973 (1938), transferred the federal government's civil aviation role to a new independent agency, the Civil Aeronautics Authority. The 1938 Act also created an Air Safety Board, as an independent entity for the investigation of civil aviation accidents. Later, that responsibility was given to the Civil Aeronautics Board's Bureau of Aviation Safety, when it was created in 1940. In 1967, Congress consolidated transportation activities into a new U.S. DOT and established the NTSB as an independent agency placed within the DOT for administrative purposes pursuant to Section 5 of the Department of Transportation Act, Pub. L. 89-670, 80 Stat. 935 (Oct. 15, 1966). The NTSB was reestablished as a freestanding agency by the Independent Safety Board Act of 1974, Pub. L. 93-633, Title III, 88 Stat. 2167 (Jan. 3, 1975).

Membership: The board is composed of five members, who serve staggered five-year terms and are appointed by the president with the advice and consent of the Senate. No more than three board members may be of the same political party. 49 U.S.C. § 1111(b). At any given time, no fewer than three members of the board must be individuals who have been "appointed on the basis of technical qualification, professional standing, and demonstrated knowledge in accident reconstruction, safety engineering, human factors, transportation safety, or transportation regulation." 49 U.S.C. § 1111(b). Any individual appointed to fill a vacancy occurring on the board prior to the expiration of the term of office for which his predecessor was appointed is appointed for the remainder of that term. Upon the expiration of his term of office, a member shall continue to serve until his successor is appointed and shall have qualified. Any member of the board may be removed by the president for inefficiency, neglect of duty, or malfeasance in office.

Quorum and Voting Requirements: Three members of the board constitute a quorum for the transaction of any function of the board, 49 U.S.C. § 1111(f), and official action can be taken by a majority of a quorum. Although the board permits proxy voting, a proxy may not be used to establish a quorum for a board meeting. Official action can be taken at a board meeting or by notation. Items discussed at a meeting are usually adopted or disapproved by voice vote. However, a member who will be absent from the meeting may request that the chairman hold the record open for his or her later vote, and in such cases adoption or disapproval would not occur at the board meeting. An absent member may vote by proxy. The proxy must include the member's voting intent and the holder of the proxy determines whether any changes to the item at the board meeting have affected the item such that the proxy should not be voted. Any member can change his or her vote, or "recalendar" an item for discussion, within twenty-four hours of the board's vote. When the board is equally divided, no official action can be taken. Where official action is taken, a member can file a dissenting or concurring statement. The member's special assistant or the board's staff are available to assist in its drafting. *See generally* 49 C.F.R. § 800.21–800.28 (explaining delegations of authority from the board and the chairman to office directors). The board has also delegated the investigation of certain aircraft accidents to the Federal Aviation Administration, although the board retains ultimate responsibility for the investigation and makes all "probable cause" determinations.

Disqualification and Recusal Procedure: The board's rules provide that motions seeking to disqualify a member be filed with the board. 49 C.F.R. § 821.15. However, the prevailing practice appears to leave the decision over disqualification or recusal exclusively in the hands of the individual member. *See generally* Air East, Inc., 2 N.T.S.B. 929 (1974) (members separately stating individual bases for not being disqualified). In one somewhat unusual case, the board itself ruled on a motion seeking to disqualify "any Board member" who had any association with certain labor organizations. *See* Administrator v. Taylor, NTSB Order No. EA-4509, at 3 n.4 (Dec. 11, 1996).

Chairman's Powers: The president designates, by and with the advice and consent of the Senate, an individual to serve as the chairman of the board. The president, without Senate confirmation, also designates an individual to serve as vice chairman. The term of chairman and vice chairman is two years. The chairman is the chief executive and administrative officer of the board. When necessary, the vice chairman is authorized to act as chairman. 49 U.S.C. § 1111(d). The chairman of the board selects key staff officials. Such selections are not subject to the approval of the other board members, although in practice, the chairman often consults with senior career employees before making his selections. Although the chairman alone approves the final budget before it is transmitted to the OMB, a draft is sent to the other board members.

OMB Bypass Provisions: Whenever the board submits or transmits any budget information, recommendations, comments, or testimony regarding legislation to the president or the OMB, it is required to concurrently submit a copy of the material to Congress. No officer or agency of the United States has any authority to require the board to submit its budget requests or estimates or its legislative comments or recommendations for approval or review prior to the submission of that material to Congress. 49 U.S.C. § 1113(c).

Litigation Authority: The DOJ is responsible for the conduct of civil litigation to which the board is a party. Federal district court litigation includes cases that the Board brings to enforce its subpoena authority, removal of actions against the agency brought by private litigants in state courts, and tort claims. Court of appeals cases include petitions for review of board orders. Pursuant to Section 2(d)(1) of the Pilot's Bill of Rights, Pub. L. 112-153, 126 Stat. 1159 (Aug. 3, 2012), a person substantially affected by an order of the Board upholding an order or a final decision of the Administrator of the Federal Aviation Administration denying an airman certificate, or imposing a punitive civil action or an emergency order of revocation, may elect to file an appeal in either federal district court or a U.S. circuit court of appeals. By an express delegation of authority on a case-by-case basis from the attorney general through the director of the Civil Division's appellate staff, the Federal Aviation Administration is responsible for the defense of board orders affirming the administration's action in certificate enforcement appeals. Referrals to the DOJ are handled informally or by letter in cases involving district court litigation. Petitions for court of appeals review of board orders are transmitted to the administrator, who is, by statute, a named respondent. 49 U.S.C. § 44709(f).

Selective Bibliography

Books

National Transportation Safety Board, We Are All Safer: NTSB-Inspired Improvements in Transportation Safety (1995).

Articles

Richard H. Fallon, *Enforcing Aviation Safety Regulations: The Case for a Split-Enforcement Model of Agency Adjudication*, 4 Admin. L.J. 389 (1991).

Patricia A. Goldman, *NTSB Procedures*, 9 Air L. 42 (1984).

NUCLEAR REGULATORY COMMISSION

11555 Rockville Pike
Rockville, MD 20852
Mail address: Nuclear Regulatory Commission, Washington, DC 20555
(301) 415-8200 General Inquiries
(301) 415-1743 Office of the General Counsel
Website: www.nrc.gov

Mission and General Statutory Reference: The Nuclear Regulatory Commission (NRC) is an "independent regulatory commission" that regulates commercial nuclear power reactors, non-power research, test and training reactors, fuel cycle facilities, medical, academic, and industrial uses of nuclear materials, and the transport, storage, and disposal of nuclear materials and waste.

The NRC also has jurisdiction over some facilities operated by the DOE. Among other things, the NRC licenses the construction and operation of nuclear reactors and other nuclear facilities, and the possession, use, processing, handling, and export of nuclear material. 42 U.S.C. § 5841.

Agency Statutory History: The commission was created in its current form by Section 201 of the Energy Reorganization Act of 1974, Pub. L. 93-438, 88 Stat. 1242–1244 (Oct. 11, 1974), which also created the DOE. Nuclear materials and power were initially brought under federal regulatory control by the Atomic Energy Act of 1946, Pub. L. 79-585, 60 Stat. 755 (Aug. 1, 1946). Section 2 of the Act created the Atomic Energy Commission, 60 Stat. 756, with authority over both military and commercial use of nuclear power materials and facilities, including the power to "engage in the production of atomic bombs, atomic bomb parts, or other military weapons utilizing fissionable materials." 60 Stat. 763. The Atomic Energy Commission was retained by Section 21 of the Atomic Energy Act of 1954, Pub. L. 83-703, 68 Stat. 924 (Aug. 30, 1954), with the expectation that increased emphasis would be placed on peaceful applications of nuclear power. The Atomic Energy Commission had responsibility for both regulation and promotion of nuclear power under the 1946 and 1954 Acts. The 1974 Act divided these responsibilities, placing regulatory authority with the NRC and promotional responsibilities with the Energy Research and Development Administration, which later was transferred to the newly created DOE.

Membership: Five members are appointed by the president with the advice and consent of the Senate and serve staggered five-year terms. No more than three commissioners may belong to the same political party. 42 U.S.C. § 5841(b)(2). There is no provision for members to sit after their term has expired. The president may remove any member for inefficiency, neglect of duty, or malfeasance in office. The president designates one member as Chairman, who serves at the pleasure of the president.

Other Presidential Appointees: Inspector general. Added to Inspector General Act by Section 102(c) of the Inspector General Act Amendments of 1988, Pub. L. 100-504, 102 Stat. 2515–2516 (1988).

Significant Case: Vermont Yankee Nuclear Power Corp. v. Natural Resources Defense Council, Inc., 435 U.S. 519 (1978) (NRC complied with APA rulemaking requirements, and reviewing courts may not impose additional requirements beyond those required by the APA).

Quorum and Voting Requirements: Three members constitute a quorum. 42 U.S.C. § 5841(a)(1). Action may be taken by a majority of those present.

Disqualification and Recusal Procedure: Individual commissioners decide questions of recusal or disqualification. *See, e.g.*, Yankee Atomic Elec. Co., 43 N.R.C. 53, 56 n.3 (1996) (setting out the general commission practice of having each commissioner decide the issue for himself or herself), and Long Island Lighting Co., 20 N.R.C. 1061 (1984) (NRC chairman declining to recuse himself for fear that it would give credence to accusations of impropriety against him and other NRC officials).

Chairman's Powers: By the Reorganization Plan No. 1 of 1980, 45 Fed. Reg. 40,561, the commission retains all policy-making, rulemaking, and adjudicatory functions of the agency. All other functions are transferred to the chairman, who is the principal executive officer of the commission. The chairman appoints certain heads of major administrative units, subject to the approval of the commission, and the chairman or a member of the commission may initiate an action for removal, subject to the approval of the commission, of a number of heads of major administrative units and panels, including the executive director for operations. Others are named by the chairman, after consultation with the executive director, subject to the approval of the commission. The function of appointing, removing, and supervising the staff of various offices, such as the general counsel, are delegated by the reorganization plan to the respective heads of these offices. In general, the chairman is to delegate all administrative functions to the executive director for operations, who reports to the chairman. All commission functions pertaining to an emergency at a requested facility are specifically vested in the chairman. Development of budget estimates for commission consideration lies with the chairman, but the commission must approve budget proposals for submission to the OMB. 42 U.S.C. § 5841(a)(5).

OMB Bypass Provisions: The NRC submits its authorization and appropriations proposals for OMB clearance. However, it asserts informal (nonstatutory) legislative bypass authority as an independent agency, *see* 42 U.S.C. § 5841(a)(1). It does not acknowledge clearance authority by the OMB in any other matters, including bills, supporting testimony, and legislative reports.

Litigation Authority: The commission has litigation authority to represent itself in the courts of appeals. 28 U.S.C. § 2348. The commission works with the DOJ and the local U.S. Attorney's Office in any case litigated in federal district court.

Books

GEORGE T. MAZUZAN & J. SAMUEL WALKER, CONTROLLING THE ATOM: THE BEGINNINGS OF NUCLEAR REGULATION, 1946–1962 (1984).

J. SAMUEL WALKER, CONTAINING THE ATOM: NUCLEAR REGULATION IN A CHANGING ENVIRONMENT, 1963–1971 (1992).

J. SAMUEL WALKER, THE ROAD TO YUCCA MOUNTAIN: THE DEVELOPMENT OF RADIOACTIVE WASTE POLICY IN THE UNITED STATES (Univ. California Press 2009).

J. SAMUEL WALKER, THREE MILE ISLAND: A NUCLEAR CRISIS IN HISTORICAL PERSPECTIVE (2004).

J. SAMUEL WALKER AND THOMAS R. WELLOCI, A SHORT HISTORY OF NUCLEAR REGULATION, 1946–2009 (NUREG/BR-0175, Rev. 2 Oct. 2010), www.nrc.gov/reading-rm/doc-collections/nuregs/brochures/br0175.pdf.

Articles

Stephen G. Burns, *Looking Backward, Moving Forward: Licensing New Reactors in the United States*, NUCLEAR LAW BULLETIN NO. 81, at 7 (2008), www..oecd-nea.org/law/nlb.

Louise Carol Gross, *Energy Reorganization Act of 1974: More Power to the People?*, 7 LOY. U. CHI. L. J. 410 (1976).

James Quirk & Katsuaki Terasawa, *Nuclear Regulation: An Historical Perspective*, 21 NAT. RESOURCES J. 833 (1981).

Anthony Z. Roisman, Erin Honaker, & Ethan Spaner, *Regulating Nuclear Power in the New Millennium (The Role of the Public)*, 26 PACE ENVTL. L. REV. 317 (2009).

Tyson Smith, *Licensing the Rebirth of Nuclear Power: A Primer*, 35 ECOLOGY L. CURRENTS 3 (2008).

OCCUPATIONAL SAFETY AND HEALTH REVIEW COMMISSION

One Lafayette Center
1120 20th Street NW
Washington, DC 20036
(202) 606-5370 General Inquiries
(202) 606-5410 Office of the General Counsel
Website: www.oshrc.gov

Mission and General Statutory Reference: The Occupational Safety and Health Review Commission (OSHRC) is an adjudicatory agency that provides administrative trial and appellate review of workplace safety and health enforcement complaints brought against employers by OSHA. 29 U.S.C. § 661.

Agency Statutory History: Commission was established by Section 12 of the Occupational Safety and Health Act of 1970, Pub. L. 91-596, 84 Stat. 1590, 1603 (Dec. 29, 1970).

Membership: Three members serve staggered six-year terms and are appointed by the president with the advice and consent of the Senate. Members are chosen from among persons who are qualified by reason of training, education, or experience to carry on the functions of the commission. A vacancy caused by death, resignation, or removal of a member prior to the expiration of the term for which the member was appointed shall be filled only for the remainder of the unexpired term. A member of the commission may be removed by the president for inefficiency, neglect of duty, or malfeasance in office. The president shall designate one of the members as chairman. There is no provision for a vice chairman.

Significant Case: Martin v. Occupational Safety and Health Review Commission, 499 U.S. 144, 154 (1991) (in contrast with traditional unitary agency model, Congress intended to delegate to the OSHRC "the type of nonpolicymaking adjudicatory powers typically exercised by a court in the agency-review context... [so the OSHRC is authorized to review the Secretary of Labor (OSHA's) statutory or regulatory interpretations] only for consistency with the regulatory language and for reasonableness.")

Quorum and Voting Requirements: Two of the commission's three members constitute a quorum. Official action can be taken only on the affirmative vote of at least two members. An ALJ, appointed by the commission, decides proceedings instituted before the commission. The decision of the ALJ becomes the final order of the commission within thirty days, unless any individual commissioner directs, within that period, that the ALJ's decision be reviewed by the full commission. An ALJ's decision goes into effect if a commissioner does not specify review of the ALJ's decision. The commission has no regulations governing proxy voting.

Disqualification and Recusal Procedure: The question of disqualification of a commission member is left to the member concerned. *See, e.g.*, National Mfg. Co., 8 O.S.H. Cas. (BNA) 1435 (May 30, 1980).

Chairman's Powers: The chairman is responsible for the administrative operations of the commission. The chairman appoints ALJs and other employees as she or he deems necessary to assist in the performance of the commission's functions, and fixes their compensation according to law.

OMB Bypass Provisions: The commission does not have a provision for bypass of legislative or budgetary review by the OMB.

Litigation Authority: The DOJ represents the commission in the federal courts.

Books

FRED BLOSSER, PRIMER ON OCCUPATIONAL SAFETY AND HEALTH (1992).

Articles

T. P. Cleary, *Inter-agency Relationships Under OSHA: A Brief Review of OSHRC Decisions*, 29 LAB. L.J. 3 (1978).

Samuel D. Elswick & Richard A. Bales, *No Harm, No Foul: The OSHRC's Authority to Label an OSH Act Violation de Minimis and to Require No Abatement*, 22 N. ILL. U. L. REV. 383 (2002).

Benjamin W. Mintz, *Administrative Separation of Functions: OSHA and the NLRB*, 27 CATH. U. L. REV. 877 (1998).

Mark A. Rothstein, *Judicial Review of Decisions of the Occupational Safety and Health Review Commission—1973–1978: An Empirical Study*, 56 CHI. KENT L. REV. 607 (1980).

POSTAL REGULATORY COMMISSION

901 New York Avenue NW, Suite 200
Washington, DC 20268
(202) 789-6800 General Inquiries
(202) 789-6820 Office of the General Counsel
Website: www.prc.gov

Mission and General Statutory Reference: The Postal Regulatory Commission (PRC) is an "independent establishment of the executive branch of the Government." 39 U.S.C. § 501. It is responsible for establishing and updating a system of rate regulation for market dominant products, 39 U.S.C. § 3621 et seq.; reviewing competitive product rates, 39 U.S.C. § 3631 et seq.; collecting information and issuing reports and compliance determinations, 39 U.S.C. § 3651 et seq.; developing a public record and advisory opinions on changes in the nature of postal services, § 39 U.S.C. § 3661; hearing and resolving complaints, 39 U.S.C. § 3662; establishing modern service standards, 39 U.S.C. § 3691; hearing appeals of decisions to close or consolidate post offices, 39 U.S.C. § 404(d); and regulating nonpostal products, 39 U.S.C. § 404(e).

Agency Statutory History: The Postal Reorganization Act, Pub. L. 91-375, 84 Stat. 719 (Aug. 12, 1970) created the Postal Rate Commission. The statute also created the United States Postal Service. The Postal Accountability and Enhancement Act of 2006, Pub. L. 109-435, 120 Stat. 3198, 3241, changed the name of the agency to the Postal Regulatory Commission. It also gave the commission authority to develop and maintain standards for rate regulation, establish delivery service standards and performance measures, and adjudicate complaints and levy fines in cases of deliberate noncompliance with postal laws.

Membership: Five members are appointed by the president with the advice and consent of the Senate and serve staggered six-year terms. Commissioners are chosen on the basis of professional qualifications and may be removed only for cause. No more than three commissioners may be affiliated with the same political party. 39 U.S.C. § 502(a).

Significant Case: U.S. Postal Service v. Postal Regulatory Comm'n, 599 F.3d 705 (D.C. Cir. 2010) (where Congress delegated to the PRC authority to implement the Postal Accountability and Enhancement Act, the Commission's statutory interpretation is entitled to *Chevron* deference despite a contrary interpretation by the Postal Service).

Quorum and Voting Requirements: A majority constitutes a quorum, and action may be taken by a majority of the quorum. No decisions are delegated to staff offices. The commission, which employs no ALJs or other subordinate hearing officers, sits en banc in cases set for hearing and issues its decisions directly following briefing and oral argument. In addition, the commission has authority to make rules and regulations and to establish procedures, subject to the APA, and take any other action necessary and proper to perform its functions, free of supervision by the Postal Service. 39 U.S.C. § 503. When the membership is equally divided, a positive action may not ensue. Commission decisions are governed by strict statutory time limits, and, by practice, the commission puts primary emphasis on publishing all its decisions within these time frames. In theory, a dissent may issue after a majority decision, but this has not occurred. A dissenting member may get staff assistance in preparing his or her dissent. Proxy voting is permitted but not frequently used.

Disqualification and Recusal Procedure: No special procedures.

Chairman's Powers: The chairman is designated by the president and serves in that position at the pleasure of the president. The commission annually elects a vice chairman from among its members. 39 U.S.C. § 502(e). The chairman is the principal executive officer of the commission. 39 U.S.C. § 504. He is responsible for the appointment of personnel, except heads of major administrative units whose appointments must be approved by a majority the commission, the supervision of personnel, the assignment of work, and the use and expenditure of funds. The chairman may appoint all other employees, generally does not seek the advice of the commission prior to hiring these individuals, and may assign responsibilities to employees within the agency. Each commissioner is consulted during the internal process of developing a draft budget, and the budget is considered and approved at a public meeting.

OMB Bypass Provisions: The commission's annual budget is submitted through, and approved by, the OMB although commission funds are taken from the Postal Service Fund. The commission participates in OMB legislative review as a matter of long-standing practice. The commission supplies reports on legislation as requested by the OMB and submits its draft reports on legislation to the OMB when they are requested by members of Congress.

Litigation Authority: The DOJ represents the commission in any action arising from commission responsibilities. In other situations, the DOJ represents the Postal Service. The commission may intervene as of right and represent itself in cases relating to its authority if it is not otherwise a party. Special arrangements have been made where the commission and the Postal Service were on opposite sides of a controversy. In one such case, the DOJ decided to present the Postal Service position, but attached a memorandum giving the commission's opposite view. In another situation, the DOJ allowed both the commission and the Postal Service to represent themselves. *See generally,* 39 U.S.C. 409(g).

RAILROAD RETIREMENT BOARD

844 North Rush Street
Chicago, IL 60611
(877) 772-5772 General Inquiries
(312) 751-4935 Office of the General Counsel
Website: www.rrb.gov

Mission and General Statutory Reference: The Railroad Retirement Board is an "independent agency in the executive branch" that administers a retirement, unemployment, and sickness benefit program for railroad workers and their families. 45 U.S.C. § 231f. Because the board is made up of representatives of the parties to the disputes determined by the board, it is not an agency within the meaning of the APA. 5 U.S.C. § 551(1)(E). Therefore, it is not subject to statutes such as the Regulatory Flexibility Act or the Federal Advisory Committee Act. However, the board is subject to the Government in the Sunshine Act and the FOIA.

Agency Statutory History: The board was initially established by the Railroad Retirement Act of 1934, 48 stt. 1283, but, following invalidation of that Act, was reestablished by Section 6 of the Railroad Retirement Act of 1935, Pub. L. 74-399, 49 Stat. 970 (Aug. 29, 1935); reconfirmed by Section 10 of the Railroad Retirement Act of 1937, Pub. L. 75-162, 50 Stat. 314 (June 24, 1937) and Section 7 of the Railroad Retirement Act of 1974, Pub. L. 93-445, 88 Stat. 1338 (Oct. 16, 1974).

Membership: Three members are appointed by the president with the advice and consent of the Senate and serve staggered five-year terms. One member is appointed based on the recommendations of railway labor; one member is appointed based on the recommendations of railway management; and one, the chairman, is appointed without recommendation from either railway labor or management. The chairman must not be in the employment of or be financially or otherwise interested in any railroad employer or railroad labor organization. A member serves until a successor has been appointed and confirmed.

Other Presidential Appointees: Inspector General. Added to Inspector General Act by Section 102(c) of the Inspector General Act Amendments of 1988, Pub. L. 100-504, 102 Stat. 2515–2516 (1988). An inspector general was first appointed pursuant to Section 23 of the Railroad Retirement Act of 1974, which was added to the Act by Section 418 of Public Law 98-76.

Significant Case: Railroad Retirement Board v. Alton Railroad Co., 295 U.S. 330 (1935) (invalidating the original Railroad Retirement Act of 1934).

Quorum and Voting Requirements: A quorum of the board consists of a majority of those members in office. 45 U.S.C. § 231f(a). However, all rules, regulations or decisions of the board require the approval of two members. 45 U.S.C. § 231f(b)(5). The majority will generally permit a dissenting member to prepare any dissenting statement before issuing the majority opinion. A board member can obtain staff assistance in drafting any dissent. Authority is delegated to subordinate officials of the board by board order.

Disqualification and Recusal Procedure: No specific provisions.

Chairman's Powers: No statutory provisions. Appointment and removal of senior staff officers is by the board collegially. The chief financial officer prepares a draft budget that is reviewed by a staff panel but must be approved by the board as a whole.

OMB Bypass Provisions: Whenever the board submits any budget estimate, budget request, supplemental budget estimate, or other budget information, legislative recommendation, prepared testimony, or comment on legislation to the president or the OMB, the board sends a concurrent copy of the submission to the Congress. 45 U.S.C. § 231f(f). The board sends its regulations to the OMB for review under Exec. Order No. 12,866.

Litigation Authority: The DOJ has delegated to the board the authority for representing the board in certain cases. Appeals from board decisions are handled by the board's legal staff.

Selective Bibliography

Books

DAVID B. SCHREIBER, THE LEGISLATIVE HISTORY OF THE RAILROAD RETIREMENT AND RAILROAD UNEMPLOYMENT INSURANCE SYSTEMS (RAILROAD RETIREMENT BOARD 1978).

Articles

Rowland L. Young, *Railroads... Retirement*, 67 A.B.A. J. 212 (1981).

SECURITIES AND EXCHANGE COMMISSION

100 F Street NW
Washington, DC 205489
(888) 732-6585 General Inquiries
(202) 551-5100 Office of the General Counsel
Website: www.sec.gov

Mission and General Statutory Reference: The Securities and Exchange Commission administers the federal securities laws, and regulates firms engaged in the purchase or sale of securities, investment companies, and people who provide investment advice. 15 U.S.C. § 78d–78d-2 (1994); *see also* Reorganization Plan No. 10, 3 C.F.R. pt. 1006 (1949–1953 comp.), reprinted in 5 U.S.C. app., at 1471 (1994).

Agency Statutory History: The Securities Act of 1933, Pub. L. 73-22, 48 Stat. 74 (1933), required the filing of registration statements in connection with securities offered to the public. The statute was administered by the FTC. A year later, in the Securities Exchange Act of 1934, Pub. L. 73-291, 48 Stat. 881 (June 6, 1934), Congress extended the disclosure requirement to securities traded on stock exchanges. Section 4 created the SEC to administer the securities laws, including those originally administered by the FTC. *See also* Investment Company Act of 1940, Pub. L. 76-768, 54 Stat. 789 (Aug. 22, 1940); Securities Act Amendments of 1975, Pub. L. 94-29, 89 Stat. 97 (June 4, 1975); Sarbanes-Oxley Act of 2002, Pub. L. 107-204, 116 Stat. 745 (July 30, 2002); Dodd-Frank Wall Street Reform and Consumer Protection Act, Pub. L. 111-203, 124 Stat. 1376 (July 21, 2010).

Membership: Five members are appointed by the president with the advice and consent of the Senate and serve staggered five-year terms. No more than three commissioners can be of the same political party. In making appointments, members of different political parties are to be appointed alternately as nearly as is practicable. A member may serve until his or her successor is appointed and has qualified up to the expiration of the next session of Congress subsequent to the expiration of the term. There is no statutory provision concerning removal from office. However, in Free Enterprise Fund et al. v. Public Company Accounting Oversight Board, 130 S. Ct. 3138 (2010), the Supreme Court assumed, without deciding, that SEC members could only be removed for cause.

Quorum and Voting Requirements: The Exchange Act does not define a quorum of the commission. In 1995, the commission adopted a rule that provides that a quorum consists of three members; provided, however, that if the number in office is less than three, a quorum consists of the number of members in office; and provided further that on any matters of business as to which the number of members in office, minus the number of members who are disqualified to consider such matter, is two, then two members constitute a quorum for purposes of such matter. *See* 17 C.F.R. § 200.41 (1999). Two federal courts have upheld the validity of the new quorum rule. *See* Falcon Trading Group v. SEC, 102 F.3d 579, 582 (D.C. Cir. 1996); SEC v. Feminella, 947 F. Supp. 722, 728 (S.D.N.Y. 1996), The effect of a tie vote depends on the particular matter before the commission. For example, if the commission were voting on whether to promulgate a rule or bring an enforcement action, a tie vote would result in no rule being promulgated and no action being brought. However, if the commission were reviewing a sanction imposed by an ALJ in an administrative proceeding, a tie vote would result in the dismissal of the proceeding.

Disqualification and Recusal Procedure: Each commissioner decides the question for himself or herself. The commission's rules provide that a commissioner "should disqualify himself in the event he obtained knowledge prior to becoming a member of the facts at issue before him in a quasi-judicial proceeding, or in other types of proceeding in any matter involving parties in which he has any interest or relationship directly or indirectly." 17 C.F.R § 200.60.

Chairman's Powers: The commission initially selected its own chairman. However, under section 3 of the Reorganization Plan No. 10 of 1950, 3 C.F.R. pt. 1006 (1949–1953 comp.), the function of the commission with respect to choosing a chairman from among the members was transferred to the president. The Reorganization Plan also transferred to the chairman from the commission the administrative and executive functions of the Commission, including the appointment and supervision of personnel, the distribution of business, and the use and expenditure of funds. Appointment by the chairman of the heads of major administrative units is subject to the approval of the commission. Pursuant to the Inspector General Act of 1978, as amended by Section 989B of the Dodd-Frank Wall Street Reform and Consumer Protection Act, the "head" of the SEC responsible for appointing and exercising "general supervision" over the inspector general is the entire commission. The chairman is to be governed by general policies established by the commission and by regulatory decisions, findings, and determinations as the commission may by law make. The commission retains its functions as to revising budget estimates and determining the distribution of appropriated funds according to major programs and purposes.

The commission may delegate any of its functions, other than general rulemaking or the making of rules pursuant to Exchange Act Section 19(c) regarding self-regulatory organization rules. The commission retains a discretionary right to review any action taken by delegated authority, either upon its own initiative or upon petition of a party to or intervenor in the action. The vote of any one member of the commission is sufficient to bring any delegated matter to the commission for review. In addition, a person or party shall be entitled to review by the commission in certain circumstances. *See* 15 U.S.C. § 78d-1(a)–(b).

OMB Bypass Provisions: Bypass of OMB review on legislative matters is secured by means of a prohibition on prior executive review contained in 12 U.S.C. § 250 provided that the SEC include a statement indicating that its views do not necessarily represent those of the president. The SEC historically submitted its budget requests to the OMB. However, in the Dodd-Frank Wall Street Reform and Consumer Protection Act, Pub. L. 111-203 (2010), Congress provided that it submit its budget request simultaneously to the OMB and Congress. 15 U.S.C. § 78ee(m).

Litigation Authority: The commission has independent litigation authority and handles litigation with its own attorneys at both the trial and court of appeals levels. In the Supreme Court, the commission participates through the Office of the Solicitor General. The commission's litigation authority is contained in a number of statutes. For instance, Section 21(d) of the Securities and Exchange Act of 1934 authorizes the commission to initiate actions in federal court to obtain injunctions. 15 U.S.C. § 78u(d)(1). The commission also defends actions brought against it or its current or former members and employees for acts arising from the performance of their duties. *See* SEC v. Robert Collier & Co., 76 F.2d 939, 940 (2d Cir. 1935) ("commission has complete autonomy in civil prosecutions"). *See also* SEC v. Sloan, 535 F.2d 679, 681 (2nd Cir. 1976) (declining to overrule SEC v. Robert Collier & Co.).

The commission has authority to seek remedies for violations of the Act. The commission is also authorized to seek writs of mandamus and other orders, and to enforce its subpoenas. 15 U.S.C. § 78u(c)–(e). The Securities Enforcement Remedies and Penny Stock Reform Act of 1990, Pub. L. No. 101-429, 104 Stat. 931 (1990) (codified in scattered sections of 15 U.S.C.), authorizes the commission to seek civil money penalties in district court actions and to impose money penalties in administrative proceedings brought against broker dealers. Parallel civil and criminal investigations by the SEC and DOJ are permissible so long as (1) the government does not misrepresent that no criminal investigation exists, and (2) the civil investigation is not being conducted solely for purposes of advancing a criminal case. *See* United States v. Stringer, 535 F.3d 929 (9th Cir. 2008).

Selective Bibliography

Books

John W. Graham, The U.S. Securities and Exchange Commission: A Research and Information Guide (1993).

Thomas Lee Hazen, Treatise on the Law of Securities Regulation (6th ed. 2009).

Gary John Previts & Alfred R. Roberts, Federal Securities Law and Accounting, 1933–1970: Selected Addresses (1986).

Joel Seligman, The Transformation of Wall Street: a History of the Securities and Exchange Commission and Modern Corporate Finance (3rd ed. 2003).

Brian J. Wilder, The Securities and Exchange Commission (SEC): Background, Issues, Selective Bibliography (2004).

United States Securities and Exchange Commission, "Good People, Important Problems and Workable Laws": 50 Years of the U.S. Securities and Exchange Commission (1984).

Articles

Harvey J. Goldschmid, *The SEC at 70: Let's Celebrate Its Reinvigorated Golden Years*, 80 Notre Dame L. Rev. 825 (2005).
Elizabeth Keller and Gregory A. Gehlmann, *A Hisorical Introduction to the Securities Act of 1933 and the Securities Exchange Act of 1934*, 49 Ohio St. L.J. 329 (1988).
Jonathan R. Macey, *Administrative Agency Obsolescence and Interest Group Formation: A Case Study of the SEC at Sixty*, 15 Cardozo L. Rev. 909 (1994).
Martin Nussbaum, *WALL STREET: FROM THE ROBBER BARONS TO REGULATION BY SEC IN 95 YEARS*, 191 N.Y. L.J. 48 (1984).
David L. Ratner, *The SEC at Sixty: A Reply to Professor Macey*, 16 Cardozo L. Rev. 1765 (1995).
Note, *The SEC Is Not an Independent Agency*, 126 Harv. L. Rev. 781 (2013).

SURFACE TRANSPORTATION BOARD

395 E Street SW
Washington, DC 20423
(202) 245-0245 General Inquiries
(202) 245-0260 Office of the General Counsel
Website: www.stb.dot.gov

Mission and General Statutory Reference: The Surface Transportation Board, administratively housed within the DOT, is responsible for the economic regulation of interstate surface transportation, primarily railroads. 49 U.S.C. §§ 701–706, 721–727.

Agency Statutory History: The Surface Transportation Board is the successor agency to the ICC. The Board was created by Section 201 of the ICC Termination Act of 1995, Pub. L. 104-88, 109 Stat. 803, 932 (Dec. 29, 1995), and the ICC was simultaneously abolished by Section 101 of the Act. The ICC, the earliest of the multimember independent regulatory agencies, was created by Section 11 of the Act to Regulate Commerce, Pub. L. 49-104, 24 Stat. 379, 383 (Feb. 4, 1887). The name of the 1887 statute was changed to the Interstate Commerce Act by Section 2 of the Transportation Act of 1920, Pub. L. 66-152, 41 Stat. 457 (Feb. 28, 1920).

Membership: Three members serve staggered five-year terms and are appointed by the president with the advice and consent of the Senate. No more than two board members may belong to the same political party. A member may continue to serve no more than one year after the term of office ends, and no more than two terms. At least two members must have a professional background in transportation, and at least one member shall have professional or business experience in the private sector. The president may remove a member for inefficiency, neglect of duty, or malfeasance in office. 49 U.S.C. § 701(b)(3).

Significant Explanatory Case: Western Coal Traffic League et al. v. Surface Transportation Board and the United States, 216 F.3d 1168 (D.C. Cir. 2000) (two-to-one decision) (Because the STB's statute does not address an unanticipated conflict between the statutory process by which it is to review a proposed merger and the purposes for which the board is to conduct its review, the board, under *Chevron*, reasonably construed its statutory authority to permit it to issue a merger moratorium temporarily prohibiting new applications where doing so is administratively necessary to realize the broader goals of the statute).

Quorum and Voting Requirements: The statute has no express quorum requirement. It does provide that a vacancy in the membership of the board does not impair the right of the remaining members to exercise all of the powers of the board and, on rare occasions, a decision has been issued by a single member. When the membership is equally divided, no action may be taken by the board. A majority agency decision may be issued prior to the release of any dissenting statement. The board does not provide for proxy voting. Authority is delegated within the agency generally by a notice published in the Code of Federal Regulations and/or the Federal Register.

Disqualification and Recusal Procedure: Issues of disqualification or recusal are for each affected member to consider and determine himself or herself.

Chairman's Powers: The president shall designate one member to serve as chairman. The chairman is "head of the Board." 49 U.S.C. § 701(c)(1). The board may designate a member to act as chairman during any period in which there is no chairman designated by the president. 49 U.S.C. § 701(c)(1). The board annually selects a vice chairman, who serves as acting chairman in the absence of the chairman. The chairman appoints and supervises the officers and employees of the board, except that appointment of the heads of major administrative units requires the approval of the board pursuant to 49 U.S.C. § 701(c)(2)(A)–(B). Under 49 U.S.C. § 701(c)(2)(D), the chairman prepares requests for appropriations, but they require prior approval of the board. The chairman supervises the expenditure of such funds. 49 U.S.C. § 701(c)(2)(E). Subject to the general policies, decisions, findings, and determinations of the board, the chairman is responsible for administering the board.

OMB Bypass Provisions: The board is decisionally independent and not subject to executive branch supervision or review. 49 U.S.C. § 703(c). Bypass of prior OMB review on budgetary and legislative matters is secured by means of concurrent transmittal requirement under 49 U.S.C. § 703(g) and 31 U.S.C. § 1108(f). In addition, those provisions establish that no officer of an agency may impair communications between the board and Congress concerning budget estimates or requests. 49 U.S.C. § 703(g).

Litigation Authority: The board has the right to represent itself in any civil action involving any function carried out by the board. Moreover, under the so-called Hobbs Act, the board is authorized to appear as a party in its own right in any proceeding involving the validity of any order or requirement. 28 U.S.C. § 2323. The board also has authority to initiate and litigate enforcement actions in courts independently of the DOJ, pursuant to 49 U.S.C. §§ 11702, 14702, and 15902.

Selective Bibliography

Study

Laurits R. Christensen Assoc., Inc., A Study of Competition in the U.S. Freight Railroad Industry and Analysis of Proposals That Might Enhance Competition (Revised Final Report,

Nov. 2009), prepared for the Surface Transportation Board, available at www.stb.dot.gov/stb/docs/CompetitionStudy/Executive Summary.pdf and related links.

Books

GABRIEL KOLKO, RAILROADS AND REGULATION 1877–1916 (1965).
ISAIAH SHARFMAN, THE INTERSTATE COMMERCE COMMISSION: A STUDY IN ADMINISTRATIVE LAW AND PROCEDURE (1931–1937) (multivolume study).
RICHARD D. STONE, THE INTERSTATE COMMERCE COMMISSION AND THE RAILROAD INDUSTRY: A HISTORY OF REGULATORY POLICY (1995).
SURFACE TRANSPORTATION BOARD, WHO'S WHO AND WHAT DOES IT DO? (2000).
STEPHEN J. THOMPSON, THE INTERSTATE COMMERCE COMMISSION IS REPLACED BY THE SURFACE TRANSPORTATION BOARD: AN OVERVIEW (1996).
STEPHEN J. THOMPSON, THE SURFACE TRANSPORTATION BOARD (STB): AN OVERVIEW AND SOME POLICY CONSIDERATIONS (1997).
FRANK L. WILNER, COMES NOW THE INTERSTATE COMMERCE PRACTITIONER (1993).

Articles

Richard A. Allen, *Rail Access in the Twenty-First Century: A Rail Attorney's Perspective*, 70 TRANSP. L., LOGIST. & POL'Y 192 (2003).
Paul Stephen Dempsey, *Transportation: A Legal History*, 30 TRANSP. L.J. 235 (2003).
Nicholas J. DeMichael, *Rail Access in the Twenty-First Century: A Shipper Attorney's Perspective*, 70 TRANSP. L., LOGIST. & POL'Y 175 (Winter 2003).
Robert M. Hardaway, *Transportation Deregulation (1976–1984): Turning the Tide*, 14 TRANSP. L. J. 101 (1985).

SINGLE ADMINISTRATOR AGENCIES

CONSUMER FINANCIAL PROTECTION BUREAU

1700 G Street NW
Washington, DC 20552
(202) 435-7000 General Inquiries
(855) 729-CFPB (2372) Consumer Help
(202) 435-7770 Office of the General Counsel
Website: www.consumerfinance.gov

Mission and General Statutory Reference: The Consumer Financial Protection Bureau (CFPB) is an "independent bureau" of the Federal Reserve System. The purpose of the bureau is to implement and enforce federal consumer financial laws consistently for the purpose of ensuring that all consumers have access to markets for consumer financial products and services and that such markets are fair, transparent, and competitive. 12 U.S.C. §§ 5491–5511. Under the statute, the Federal Reserve Board may not interfere with the appointment, direction, or removal of bureau officials or employees or any matter or proceeding before the bureau. 12 U.S.C. § 5492(c)(2)(3).

Agency Statutory History: The CFPB was created by the Dodd-Frank Wall Street Reform and Consumer Protection Act of 2010, Pub. L. 113-203, 124 Stat. 1376, 1964 (2010).

Appointment and Removal Provisions: A director is appointed by the president with the advice and consent of the Senate to a five-year term and, upon expiration of his or her term, may serve until a replacement is qualified. 12 U.S.C. § 5491(c)(1)(2). The director may only be removed for "inefficiency, neglect of duty, or malfeasance in office." 12 U.S.C. § 5491(c)(3).

OMB Bypass Provisions: Under 12 U.S.C. § 5492(c) (4), no federal officer or agency can require the bureau to submit legislative recommendations, testimony, or comments on legislation for approval or review prior to their submission to Congress, provided that such communications to Congress include a statement that the views expressed therein do not necessarily represent the views of the president or the board of Governors of the Federal Reserve System. The director establishes the bureau's budget within guidelines created under a statutory funding ceiling linked to the operating expenses of the Federal Reserve Board and free from oversight by the OMB. 12 U.S.C. § 5497(a). The bureau is exempt from OIRA review per 44 U.S.C. § 3502(5) and E.O. 12,866.

Litigation Authority: The bureau has independent litigation authority to bring a civil action or represent itself in court in any civil action. 12 U.S.C. § 5564(b). It may also represent itself in the Supreme Court if the Attorney General declines to do so. 12 U.S.C. § 5564(e).

Selective Bibliography

Articles

Rachel E. Barkow, *Insulating Agencies: Avoiding Capture Through Institutional Design*, 89 TEX. L. REV. 15 (2010).

Leonard J. Kennedy, Patricia A. McCoy & Ethan Bernstein, *The Consumer Financial Protection Bureau: Financial Regulation for the Twenty-First Century*, 97 CORNELL L. REV. 1141 (2012).

Recent Legislation: Dodd-Frank Act Creates the Consumer Financial Protection Bureau, 124 HARV. L. REV. 2123 (2011).

Elizabeth Warren & Oren Bar-Gill, *Making Credit Safer*, 157 U. PA. L. REV. 1 (2008).

Note, Lee A. Duncan, Defending a Wolf Clad As a Wolf: Formalism and Functionalism in Separation of Powers Suits against the Consumer Financial Protection Bureau, 37 Rev. Banking & Fin. Law 543 (2014).

John E. Villafranco & Kristen A. McParland, *What You Need to Know About the Consumer Financial Protection Bureau*, 10-2 ANTITRUST SOURCE 1 (ABA Dec. 2010).

FEDERAL HOUSING FINANCE AGENCY

1700 G Street NW, Fourth Floor
Washington, DC 20552
(202) 414-3800 General Inquiries
(202) 414-3788 Office of the General Counsel
Website: www.fhfa.gov

Mission and General Statutory Reference: The Federal Housing Finance Agency is an "independent agency of the Federal Government" that oversees the various components of the nation's secondary mortgage markets, such as Fannie Mae, Freddie Mac, and the Federal Home Loan Banks. *See* 12 U.S.C. § 4511.

Agency Statutory History: The FHFA was created by Section 1101 of the Housing and Economic Recovery Act of 2008, Pub. L. 110-289, 122 Stat. 2654, 2662 (July 30, 2008) as the successor agency to the Federal Housing Finance Board and the Office of Federal Housing Enterprise Oversight within the Department of Housing and Urban Development. It also took over certain responsibilities from that department with regard to community development and access to affordable housing on a nondiscriminatory basis. The Federal Housing Finance Board, in turn, had replaced the five-member Federal Home Loan Bank Board, created by Section 17 of the Federal Home Loan Bank Act, Pub. L. 72-304, 47 Stat. 736 (July 22, 1932). The Federal Housing Finance Board was abolished by Section 1311, 122 Stat. 2797, which had, in turn, been created by Section 702 of the Financial Institutions Reform, Recovery, and Enforcement Act of 1989, Pub. L. 101-73, 103 Stat. 183, 413 (Aug. 9, 1989). Section 1301 of the 2008 Act abolished the Office of Federal Housing Enterprise Oversight within the Department of Housing and Urban Development, 122 Stat. 2797, which had authority over Freddie Mac and Fannie Mae, with the authority transferred to the new agency. Other department responsibilities were transferred by 122 Stat. 2794.

Appointment and Removal Provisions: The director is appointed by the president with the advice and consent of the Senate to a five-year term. The director must possess "demonstrated understanding of financial management or oversight, and have a demonstrated understanding of capital markets, including the mortgage securities market and housing finance." 12 U.S.C. § 4512(a). The director may only be removed for cause. 12 U.S.C. § 4512(b)(2).

OMB Bypass Provisions: Bypass of OMB review on legislative matters is secured by means of a prohibition on prior executive review contained in 12 U.S.C. § 250, provided that the FHFA includes a statement indicating that its views do not necessarily represent those of the president. The FHFA derives its funds, which are neither government funds nor appropriated monies, from assessments levied on regulated entities and from other sources. 12 U.S.C. § 4516.

Litigation Authority: The FHFA is authorized to act in its own name and through its own attorneys in enforcing the Bank Act or FHFA regulations and in any action, suit, or proceeding in which the FHFA is a party that involves the agency's regulations or supervision of any bank. 12 U.S.C. § 4513(c). The DOJ handles all other litigation.

Office of Special Counsel
1730 M Street NW, Suite 218
Washington, DC 20036
(202) 254-3600 General Inquiries
(202) 254-3608 Associate Special Counsel and Legal Counsel
Website: www.osc.gov

Mission and General Statutory Reference: The Office of Special Counsel (OSC) investigates and prosecutes allegations of prohibited personnel practices, with an emphasis on protecting federal government whistle-blowers. It is authorized to file complaints with the Merit System Protection Board seeking corrective action remedies, such as reinstatement and back pay, and disciplinary action against individuals who commit prohibited personnel practices. It also provides a secure channel through which federal workers may disclose information about workplace improprieties, misuse of funds, fraud and abuse, and substantial dangers to the public health or safety. The OSC also provides advisory opinions on the Hatch Act dealing with political activities by federal employees, and enforces the Hatch Act before the Merit Systems Protection Board. 5 U.S.C §§ 1211–1219.

Agency Statutory History: Created by Section 1204 of the Civil Service Reform Act of 1978, Pub. L. 95-454, 92 Stat. 1122 (Oct. 13, 1978).

Appointment and Removal Provisions: The special counsel is appointed to a five-year term by the president with the advice and consent of the Senate. The special counsel must be "an attorney who, by demonstrated ability, background, training, or experience, is especially qualified to carry out the functions of the position." 5 U.S.C. § 1211(b). The special counsel may be removed by the president only for inefficiency, neglect of duty, or malfeasance in office. 5 U.S.C. § 1211(b).

OMB Bypass Provisions: Freedom from OMB review of matters relating to the functions of the special counsel is secured by a provision for concurrent transmittal of reports and testimony to Congress and the president or other executive branch agencies. 5 U.S.C. § 1217. However, as a matter of practice, the OSC submits both its appropriations request and legislative matters to the OMB.

Litigation Authority: The OSC does not have independent litigation authority.

Selective Bibliography

Books

United States of America, Office of Special Counsel, The Role of the Office of Special Counsel (1992).

Articles

Carolyn M. Abbate, *It's Time to "Hatch" a New Act: How the OSC's Interpretation of the Hatch Act Chills Protected Speech*, 18 Fed. Cir. B.J. 139 (2008).

Scott J. Bloch, *The Judgment of History: Faction, Political Machines, and the Hatch Act*, 7 U. Pa. J. Lab. & Emp. L. 225 (2005).

Thomas M. Devine & Donald G. Aplin, *Abuse of Authority: the Office of the Special Counsel and Whistleblower Protection*, 4 Antioch L.J. 5 (1986).

Bruce D. Fong, *Whistleblower Protection and the Office of Special Counsel: the Development of the Reprisal Law in the 1980s*, 40 Am. U. L. Rev. 1015 (1991).

SOCIAL SECURITY ADMINISTRATION

6401 Security Boulevard
Baltimore, MD 21235
(800) 325-0778 General Inquiries
(410) 965-0600 Office of the General Counsel
Website: www.ssa.gov

Mission and General Statutory Reference: The Social Security Administration (SSA) is an independent agency in the executive branch that administers the Old Age and Survivor Insurance Program, the Disability Insurance Program, and the Supplemental Income Program. 42 U.S.C.

§§ 901–913. It issues Social Security numbers, processes claims and determines eligibility, maintains beneficiary rolls covering nearly 44 million people, and dispenses benefits totaling nearly $29 million monthly.

Agency Statutory History: Removed from the Department of Health and Human Services and established "as an independent agency" headed by a Commissioner of Social Security by Section 101 of the Social Security Independence and Program Improvements Act of 1994, Pub. L. 103-296, 108 Stat. 1464 (Aug. 15, 1994). Originally created as a three-member Social Security Board by the Social Security Act of 1935, Pub. L. 74-271, 49 Stat. 635 (Aug. 14, 1935). The board was placed "under the direction and supervision of the Federal Security Administrator" within the newly created Federal Security Agency by Section 202 of Reorganization Plan No. 1 of 1939, 3 C.F.R. pt. 1288, 1289 (1938–1943 comp.). Section 4 of Reorganization Plan No. 2 of 1946, 3 C.F.R. pt. 1064 (1943–1948 comp.), abolished the board and transferred its functions to the federal security administrator. Section 401 of the Social Security Act Amendments of 1950, Pub. L. 81-734, 64 Stat. 558 (Aug. 28, 1950), created a commissioner for social security "appointed by the [Federal Security] Administrator, who shall perform such functions related to social security as the Administrator shall assign to him." Reorganization Plan No. 1 of 1953, 3 C.F.R. pt. 1022, 1023 (1949–1953 comp.), abolished the Federal Security Agency, created the Department of Health, Education and Welfare, and created, within the department, a commissioner of social security, appointed by the president with the advice and consent of the Senate. Department of Education Organization Act, Pub. L. 96-88, 93 Stat. 668, 695 (Oct. 17, 1979), established a Department of Education, redesignated the Department of Health, Education and Welfare as the Department of Health and Human Services, and retained the commissioner of social security within the Department of Health and Human Services.

Appointment and Removal Provisions: The commissioner is appointed by the president with the advice and consent of the Senate to a six-year term. The commissioner may be removed by the president only for "neglect of duty or malfeasance in office." 42 U.S.C. § 902(a)(3).

Other Presidential Appointees: Inspector general. Established by Section 102 of Pub. L. 103-296, 108 Stat. 1467 (Mar. 31, 1995). A deputy commissioner is also appointed by the president to a six-year term with the advice and consent of the Senate, but there is no provision for removal. There is also a Social Security Advisory Board composed of seven members. Three of the members are appointed by the president with the advice and consent of the Senate, two are appointed by the president pro tempore of the Senate, and two are appointed by the Speaker of the House of Representatives. 42 U.S.C. § 903.

OMB Bypass Provisions: The commissioner's budget must be submitted to Congress by the president without revision together with the president's annual budget for the administration. 42 U.S.C. § 904(b)(1). Legislative matters are subject to OMB clearance and approval.

Litigation Authority: The SSA does not have independent litigation authority.

Selective Bibliography

Books

Edward D. Berkowitz, Mr. Social Security: The Life of Wilbur J. Cohen (1995).

Jerry R. Cates, Insuring Inequality: Administrative Leadership in Social Security, 1935–54 (1983).

SOCIAL SECURITY ADMINISTRATION, A BRIEF HISTORY OF SOCIAL SECURITY: ISSUED ON SOCIAL SECURITY'S 65TH ANNIVERSARY (2000).

Articles

Frank S. Bloch, Jeffrey S. Lubbers & Paul R. Verkuil, *The Social Security Administration's New Disability Adjudication Rules: A Significant and Promising Reform*, 92 CORNELL L. REV. 235 (2007).

Wilbur J. Cohen, *The Early Days of Social Security*, 58 SOC. SEC. BULL. 21 (1985).

John J. Corson, *Social Security—A Recollection*, 48 SOC. SEC. BULL. 23 (1985).

Michael A. Cronin, *Fifty Years of Operations in the Social Security Administration*, 48 SOC. SEC. BULL. 14 (June 1985).

Rita L. DiSimone, *Social Security Administration Created as an Independent Agency: Public Law 103-296*, 58 SOC. SEC. BULL. 57 (Spring 1995).

Jack S. Futterman, *Social Security and Its Founding Staff*, 48 SOC. SEC. BULL. 28 (August 1985).

Colleen E. Medill, *Transforming the Role of the Social Security Administration*, 92 CORNELL L. REV. 322 (2007).

Robert E. Rains, *A Response to Bloch, Lubbers and Verkuil's the Social Security Administration's New Disability Adjudication Rules: A Cause for Optimism... and Concern*, 92 CORNELL L. REV. 249 (2007).

Ethel Zelenske, *The Social Security Administrative Reform Act of 1994*, 28 CLEARINGHOUSE REV. (1994).

APPENDIX B

Comparing Multimember Independent Agencies

Agency	Statutory "for cause" protection	Explicit staggering of terms	Party balance provision
Chemical Safety & Hazard Invest. Board	X		
Commodity Futures Trading Comm.		X	X
Consumer Product Safety Commission	X	X	X
Defense Nuclear Facilities Safety Board		X	X
Equal Employment Opportunity Comm.			X
Farm Credit Administration		X	X
Federal Communications Commission			X
Federal Election Commission		X	X
Federal Energy Regulatory Commission	X	X	X
Federal Labor Relations Authority	X		X
Federal Maritime Commission	X	X	X
Federal Mine Safety & Health Rev. Comm.	X	X	
Federal Reserve Board	X	X	X
Federal Trade Commission		X	
Independent Payment Advisory Board	X		X
Merit Systems Protection Board		X	X
National Credit Union Administration	X	X	X

Agency	Statutory "for cause" protection	Explicit staggering of terms	Party balance provision
National Indian Gaming Commission	X	X	X
National Labor Relations Board	X		X
National Mediation Board	X		X
National Transportation Safety Board	X	X	
Nuclear Regulatory Commission	X	X	X
Occupational Safety & Health Rev. Comm.	X	X	X
Postal Regulatory Commission		X	X
Railroad Retirement Board	X	X	X
Securities & Exchange Commission		X	
Surface Transportation Board	X		
U.S. International Trade Commission			
Board of Veterans' Appeals			

Note: Table adapted from David E. Lewis & Jennifer L. Selin, Sourcebook of the United States Executive Agencies (1st ed. Administrative Conference of the United States December 2012).

Table of Cases

C

D

N

O

P

V

W

Y

Table of Statutes, Bills, and Reorganization Plans

Bibliography

BOOKS

Viral V. Acharya et al., Guaranteed to Fail (2011).

Charles F. Adams, Jr., & Henry Adams, Chapters of Erie, and Other Essays (1871).

Gordon Adams et al., The Iron Triangle: The Politics of Defense Contracting (1981).

Akhil Reed Amar, America's Constitution: A Biography (2005).

American Bar Association, Commission on Law and the Economy, Federal Regulation: Roads to Reform (1979).

James E. Anderson, The Emergence of the Modern Regulatory State (1962).

Carmen R. Apaza, Integrity and Accountability in Government: Homeland Security and the Inspector General (2011).

Hannah Arendt, The Origins of Totalitarianism (2d prtg. 1959).

Steven K. Bailey, Congress in the Seventies (2d ed. 1970).

Lance Banning, The Sacred Fire of Liberty: James Madison and the Founding of the Federal Republic (1995).

John Bell, Comparative Administrative Law: The Oxford Handbook of Comparative Administrative Law (2006).

Michael Les Benedict, The Impeachment and Trial of Andrew Johnson (1973).

Richard K. Berg, Stephen H. Klitzman & Gary J. Edles, An Interpretive Guide to the Government in the Sunshine Act (2d ed. 2005).

George Bermann, Charles H. Koch, Jr., & James T. O'Reilly, Administrative Law of the European Union (2008).

Marver H. Bernstein, Regulating Business by Independent Commission (1955).

Patrick Birkinshaw, European Public Law (2003).

Patrick Birkinshaw, Grievances, Remedies and the State (2d ed. 1994).

Thomas C. Blaisdell, Jr., The Federal Trade Commission: An Experiment in the Control of Business (1932).

A. W. Bradley & K. D Ewing, Constitutional and Administrative Law (12th ed. 1997).

Louis D. Brandeis, Other People's Money and How the Banks Use It (1914).

Stephen G. Breyer, Richard B. Stewart, Cass R. Sunstein, Adrian Vermeule & Michael E. Herz, Administrative Law and Regulatory Policy, Problems, Text, and Cases (7th ed. 2011).

Bringing the States Back In (Peter Evans, Dietrich Rueschemeyer & Theda Skocpol eds. 1985).

L. Neville Brown & John S. Bell, French Administrative Law (1998).

John P. Burke, The Institutional Presidency (2d ed. 2000).

George Bush & Brent Scowcroft, A World Transformed (1998).

Steven G. Calabresi & Christopher S. Yoo, The Unitary Executive: Presidential Power from Washington to Bush (2008).

Daniel Carpenter, The Forging of Bureaucratic Autonomy: Reputation, Networks and Policy Innovation in Executive Agencies, 1862–1928 (2001).

Daniel Carpenter, Reputation and Power: Organizational Image and Pharmaceutical Regulation at the FDA (2010).

Gerhard Casper, Separating Power: Essays on the Founding Period (1997).

The Changing Constitution (Jeffrey Jowell & Dawn Oliver eds., 7th ed. 2011).

Doreen Collins, The European Communities: The Social Policy of the First Phase. Vol. 1. The European Coal and Steel Community 1951–70 (Martin Robertson 1975).

Patrick S. Collins, Regulation of Securities, Markets and Transactions: A Guide to the New Environment (2011).

Comparative Administrative Law (Susan Rose-Ackerman & Peter Lindseth eds. 2010).

Compilation of Messages and Papers of the Presidents (James D. Richardson ed. 1897).

A Compilation of the Messages and Papers of the Presidents: 1789–1897, Vol. 7 (James D. Richardson ed. 1898).

Paul Craig, EU Administrative Law (2d ed. 2012).

P. P. Craig, Administrative Law (3d ed. 1994).

A Crossroads of Freedom: The 1921 Campaign Speeches of Woodrow Wilson (John Wells Davidson ed. 1956).

Gerald Cullinan, The United States Postal Service (1973).

Shelby M. Cullom, Fifty Years of Public Service (2d ed. 1911).

Robert E. Cushman, The Independent Regulatory Commissions (1941).

Robert E. Cushman, The Independent Regulatory Commissions (1972).

Robert Dahl, A Preface to Democratic Theory (1956).

Kenneth Culp Davis, Administrative Law Treatise (2d ed. 1980).

Kenneth Culp Davis & Richard J. Pierce, Jr., Administrative Law Treatise (1994).

Martin J. Dedman, The Origins and Development of the European Union 1945–95: A History of European Integration (Routledge 1996).

Renaud Dehousse, Regulation by Networks in the European Community: The Role of European Agencies (Robert Schuman Centre, European Univ. Inst. 1997).

Edward J. DeMarco, The Conservatorships of Fannie Mae and Freddie Mac (2012).

Martha Derthick & Paul J. Quirk, The Politics of Deregulation (1985).
Laura A. Dickinson, Outsourcing War and Peace: Preserving Public Values in a World of Privatized Foreign Affairs (2011).
Marshall Dimock, Government-Operated Enterprises in the Panama Canal Zone (1934).
John Donahue, The Privatization Decision (1989).
William O. Douglas, Democracy and Finance (1940).
Wilson K. Doyle, Independent Commissions in the Federal Government (1939).
Peter Drucker, The Concept of the Corporation (1946).
Marriner S. Eccles, Beckoning Frontiers: Public and Personal Recollections (1951).
Economic Regulation of Business and Industry: A Legislative History of U.S. Regulatory Agencies (Bernard Schwartz ed. 1973).
Marc Allen Eisner, Regulatory Politics in Transition (1993).
Mark Elliott & Robert Thomas, Public Law (2011).
Jacques Ellul, The Technological Society (John Wilkinson trans. 1964).
The European Legal Order After Lisbon (Birkinshaw & Varney eds. 2010).
The Federalist (Roy P. Fairfield ed., 1st ed. 1981).
Kenneth Finegold, Experts and Politicians: Reform Challenges to Machine Politics in New York, Cleveland, and Chicago (1995).
James O. Freedman, Crisis and Legitimacy: The Administrative Process and American Government (1978).
D. A. C. Freestone & J. S. Davidson, The Institutional Framework of the European Communities (Routledge 1988).
Charles Fried, Order and Law: Arguing the Reagan Revolution (1991).
Barry Friedman, Regulation in the Reagan-Bush Era: The Eruption of Presidential Influence (1995).
Jack Fruchtman, Thomas Paine: Apostle of Freedom (1996).
John K. Galbraith, The New Industrial State (1967).
Omar V. Garrison, The Dictocrats: Our Unelected Rulers (1970).
Timothy Geithner, Stress Test (2014).
Ernest Gellhorn & Ronald M. Levin, Administrative Law and Process in a Nutshell (4th ed. 1997).
Barton Gellman, Angler: The Cheney Vice Presidency (2008).
Erving Goffman, The Presentation of Self in Everyday Life (1959).
Jack Goldsmith, Power and Constraint: The Accountable Presidency After 9/11 (2012).
Jack Goldsmith, The Terror Presidency: Law and Judgment Inside the Bush Administration (2007).
Frank J. Goodnow, Politics and Administration (1900).
Frank J. Goodnow, The Principles of the Administrative Law of the United States (1905).
William B. Gould IV, Labored Relations, Law, Politics and the NLRB—A Memoir (2000).
Government Agencies: Practices and Lessons from 30 Countries (Koen Verhoest, Sandra Van Thiel, Geert Bouckaert & Per Lægreid eds. 2012).
Joanna L. Grisinger, The Unwieldy American State: Administrative Politics Since the New Deal (2012).
James A. Gross, The Reshaping of the National Labor Relations Board: National Labor Policy in Transition 1937–1947 (1981).

A Guide to Our Code of Ethics and Business Conduct (Corrections Corporation of America 2005).

Samuel Haber, Efficiency and Uplift: Scientific Management in the Progressive Era 1890–1920 (1964).

Lewis H. Haney, A Congressional History of Railways in the United States (1910).

Stephen Hess & James P. Pfiffner, Organizing the Presidency (3rd ed. 2002).

Michele Hilmes, Only Connect: A Cultural History of Broadcasting in the United States (2002).

A History of Public Broadcasting (Steve Behrens ed., 2000).

W. Stull Holt, The Federal Trade Commission: Its History, Activities and Organization (1922).

Liesbet Hooghe, The European Commission and the Integration of Europe: Images of Governance (Cambridge U. Press 2001).

Morton J. Horwitz, The Transformation of American Law 1970–1960: The Crisis of Legal Orthodoxy (1992).

Reed E. Hundt, You Say You Want a Revolution: A Story of Information Age Politics (2000).

Sidney Hyman, Marriner Eccles: Private Entrepreneur and Public Servant (1976).

Earl Johnson, Jr., Justice and Reform: The Formative Years of the American Legal Services Program (1978).

Harry Kalvan, Jr., & Hans Zeisel, The American Jury (1996).

Herbert Kaufman, Are Government Agencies Immortal (1976).

Edwin Walter Kemmerer & Donald L. Kemmerer, The ABC of the Federal Reserve System (12th ed. 1950).

Donald F. Kettl, Leadership at the Fed (1986).

Mark Killenbeck, McCulloch v. Maryland: Securing a Nation (2006).

Henry Kissinger, Years of Upheaval (1982).

James T. Klopppenberg, Uncertain Victory: Social Democracy and Progressivism in European and American Thought 1870–1920 (1986).

Gabriel Kolko, Railroads and Regulation 1877–1916 (1965).

Kevin Kosar, Federal Government Corporations: An Overview (2011).

James M. Landis, The Administrative Process (1938).

Magali Sarfatti Larson, The Rise of Professionalism: A Sociological Analysis (1977).

Earl Latham, Group Basis of Politics (1952).

Law and New Governance in the EU and the US (Grainne de Burca & Joanne Scott eds. 2006).

Frances J. Leazes, Jr., Accountability and the Business State: The Structure of Federal Corporations (1987).

David E. Lewis, The Politics of Presidential Appointments (2008).

David E. Lewis & Jennifer L. Selin, ACUS Sourcebook on The Federal Executive Establishment in the United States (2012).

Lawrence Lewis, Jr., A History of the Bank of North America (1882) (2010).

Paul Charles Light, Monitoring Government: Inspectors General and the Search for Accountability (1993).

Theodore J. Lowi, The End of Liberalism: The Second Republic of the United States 309 (1979).

Jeffrey S. Lubbers, A Guide to Federal Agency Rulemaking (3d ed. 1998).

James Madison, Writings (Jack N. Rakove ed. 1999).

Giandomenico Majone, The New European Agencies: Regulation by Information (Robert Schuman Centre, European Univ. Inst. 1997).
Frederick V. Malek, Washington's Hidden Tragedy: The Failure to Make Government Work (1978).
James Mann, The Rise of the Vulcans: The History of Bush's War Cabinet (2004).
Jerry L. Mashaw, Greed, Chaos, and Governance: Using Public Choice to Improve Public Law (1997).
Renate Mayntz & Fritz W. Scharpf, Policy-Making in the German Federal Bureaucracy (1975).
Richard L. McCormick, The Party Period and Public Policy: American Politics from the Age of Jackson to the Progressive Era (1986).
Thomas K. McCraw, Prophets of Regulation (1984).
John McDiarmid, Government Corporations and Federal Funds (1938).
Thomas O. McGarity, Freedom to Harm: The Lasting Legacy of the Laissez-Faire Removal (2013).
Allan H. Meltzer, A History of the Federal Reserve. Vol. 1. 1913–1951 (2003).
Yves Mény, Government and Politics in Western Europe: Britain, France, Italy, Germany (Janet Lloyd trans., Oxford U. Press 2d ed. 1993).
Gillian E. Metzger, Private Delegations, Due Process, and the Duty to Supervise, in Government by Contract (Jody Freeman & Martha Minow eds., 2009).
Ann-Marie Meulendyke, U.S. Monetary Policy and Financial Markets (1998).
Russell W. Mills, The Promise of Collaborative Voluntary Partnerships: Lessons from the Federal Aviation Administration (2010).
Jerry Mitchell, The American Experiment with Government Corporations (1999).
Richard Nathan, The Administrative Presidency (1983).
William E. Nelson, The Roots of American Bureaucracy, 1980–1900 (1982).
Franz Neuman, Behemoth (1942).
Richard E. Neustadt & Harvey V. Fineberg, The Epidemic That Never Was: Policy-Making and the Swine Flu Scare (1st ed. 1983).
William A. Niskanen, Jr., Bureaucracy and Representative Government (1971).
David W. Noble, The Progressive Mind 1890–1917 (rev. ed. 1981).
Mancur Olson, The Logic of Collective Action (1965) (1971).
David Osborne & Ted Gaebler, Reinventing Government: How the Entrepreneurial Spirit Is Transforming the Public Sector (1992).
Thomas Paine, Common Sense (1776) (Isaac Kramnick ed. 1982).
Henry Parris, Government and the Railways in Nineteenth-Century Britain (1965).
Bradley H. Patterson, Jr., The White House Staff: Inside The West Wing and Beyond (2000).
Ron Paul, End the Fed (2009).
Richard J. Pierce, Administrative Law Treatise (5th ed. 2010).
Richard J. Pierce, Jr., Sidney A. Shapiro, & Paul R. Verkuil, Administrative Law and Process (1999).
Eric Posner & Adrien Vermeule, The Executive Unbound: After the Madisonian Republic (2011).
President George W. Bush's Influence over Bureaucracy and Power (Colin Provert & Paul Teske eds., 2009).
Tony Prosser, The Regulatory Enterprise: Government, Regulation and Legitimacy (2010).

Public Policy and Private Interests: The Institutions of Compromise (Douglas C. Hague et al. eds., 1975).

John Quarles, Cleaning Up America: An Insider's View of the Environmental Protection Agency (1976).

Wayne D. Rasmussen & Gladys L. Baker, The Department of Agriculture (1972).

Robert V. Remini, Andrew Jackson and the Course of American Democracy 1843–1845 (1984).

Donald A. Ritchie, James M. Landis: Dean of the Regulators (1938).

Bruno Rizzo, The Bureaucratization of the World (Adam Westoby trans., 1985).

Glen O. Robinson, American Bureaucracy: Public Choice and Public Law (1991).

Dorothy Robyn, Braking the Special Interests: Trucking Deregulation and Politics of Policy Reform (1987).

Leon I. Salomon, The Independent Federal Regulatory Agencies (1959).

Arthur M. Schlesinger, Jr., The Imperial Presidency (1973).

Bernard Schwartz, Administrative Law (3d ed. 1991).

Bernard Schwartz, French Administrative Law and the Common-Law World (1954).

Bernard Schwartz & H. W. R. Wade, Legal Control of Government: Administrative Law in Britain and the United States (1972).

Lewis Seidman, Full Faith and Credit: The Great S & L Debacle and Other Washington Sagas (2000).)

Raymond Seitz, Over Here (1998).

Philip Selznick, TVA and the Grass Roots: A Study in the Sociology of Formal Organization (1949).

Peter M. Shane, Madison's Nightmare: How Executive Power Threatens American Democracy (2009).

I. L. Sharfman, The Interstate Commerce Commission: A Study in Administrative Law and Procedure (1931).

William L. Silbur, Volcker: The Triumph of Persistence (2012).

Theda Skocpol, State and Policy in America's New Deal (1995).

Theda Skocpol, Protecting Soldiers and Mothers: The Political Origin of Social Policy in the United States (1992).

Theda Skocpol & Vanessa Williamson, The Tea Party and the Remaking of American Conservatism (2012).

Stephen Skowronek, Building a New American State: The Expansion of National Administrative Capacities 1977–1920 (1982).

David S. Sorenson, Shutting Down the Cold War: The Politics of Military Base Closure (1998).

David O. Stewart, Impeached: The Trial of President Andrew Johnson and the Fight for Lincoln's Legacy (2009).

Richard J. Stillman II, Creating The American State: The Moral Reformers and the Modern Administrative World They Made (1998).

Richard D. Stone, The Interstate Commerce Commission and the Railroad Industry: A History of Regulatory Policy (1991).

Peter L. Strauss, An Introduction to Administrative Justice in the United States (1989).

Peter L. Strauss, An Introduction to Administrative Justice in the United States (2d ed. 2002).

Cindy Szkrzcki, The Regulators: Anonymous Power Brokers in American Politics (2003).

Laurence H. Tribe, American Constitutional Law (2d ed. 1988).

David Truman, The Governmental Process (1951).
Derek W. Urwin, The Community of Europe: A History of European Integration Since 1945 (2d ed. 1995).
Harold Archer Van Dorn, Government Owned Corporations (1926).
Paul Verkuil, Outsourcing Sovereignty: Why Privatization of Government Functions Threatens Democracy and What We Can Do About It (2007).
W. H. R. Wade & C. F. Forsyth, Administrative Law (9th ed. 2004).
William Wade & Christopher Forsyth, Administrative Law (7th ed. 1994).
Elizabeth Warren, A Fighting Chance (2014).
Stephen Weatherill & Paul Beaumont, EC Law: The Essential Guide to the Legal Workings of the European Communities (2d ed. 1995).
Private Correspondence of Daniel Webster 486 (national ed. 1903).
David M. Welborn, Governance of Federal Regulatory Agencies (1977).
Donald R. Wells, The Federal Reserve System: A History (2004).
Jay Wexler, The Odd Clauses: Understanding the Constitution Through Three of Its Most Curious Provisions (2011).
Leonard D. White, The Jacksonians (1954).
Leonard D. White, The Republican Era: 1969–1901 (1958).
Christine Whitman, It's My Party Too (2007).
Frank N. Wilner, Comes Now the Interstate Commerce Practitioner (1993).
Peter Woll, American Bureaucracy (1977).
World Atlas (3d ed. Dorley Kindersley 2007).

ARTICLES

Luis Aguilar, Creating Reform That Is Sustainable for Investors, 10 J. Int'l Bus. & L. 115 (2011).
Akhil Reed Amar, The President, the Cabinet, and Independent Agencies, 5 U. St. Thomas J. L. & Pub. Pol'y 36 (2010–11).
David R. Aras & Ryan W. Scott, Are Senior Judges Unconstitutional, 92 Cornell L. Rev. 455 (2007).
Anthony F. Arpaia, The Independent Agency—A Necessary Instrument of Democratic Government, 69 Harv. L. Rev. 483 (1956).
Antitrust in the Transportation Industry—Has Deregulation Gone Too Far, Too Fast?, 54 Antitrust L.J. 465 (1985).
Hans Bader, Free Enterprise Fund v. PCAOB: Narrow Separation-of-Powers Ruling Illustrates That the Supreme Court Is Not Pro-Business, 2009–10 Cato Sup. Ct. Rev. 269 (2009-2010).
Nicholas Bagley & Richard L. Revesz, Centralized Oversight of the Regulatory State, 106 Colum. L. Rev. 1260 (2006).
Daphne Barak-Erez, The Administrative Process as a Domain of Conflicting Interests, 6 Theoretical Inquiries L. 193 (2005).
Rachel E. Barkow, Insulating Agencies: Avoiding Capture Through Institutional Design, 89 Tex. L. Rev. 15 (2010).

Kent Barnett, Avoiding Independent Agency Armageddon, 87 Notre Dame L. Rev. 1349 (2012).

Kent Barnett, The Consumer Financial Protection Bureau's Appointment with Trouble, 60 Am. U. L. Rev. 1459 (2011).

Kent Barnett, Resolving the ALJ Quandary, 66 Vand. L. Rev. 797 (2013).

David J. Barron, From Takeover to Merger: Reforming Administrative Law in an Age of Agency Politicization, 76 Geo. Wash. L. Rev. 1095 (2008).

Frank Baumgartner & Bryan D. Jones, Agenda Dynamics and Agency Subsystems, 53 J. of Politics 1044 (1991).

Janice A. Beecher, The Prudent Regulator: Politics, Independence, Ethics, and the Public Interest, 29 Energy L.J. 577 (2008).

Jack M. Beermann, Congressional Administrations, 43 San Diego L. Rev. 61 (2006).

Jack M. Beermann, Essay: An Inductive Understanding of Separation of Powers or Why the PCAOB Decision Doesn't Change Anything Yet, 1 Boston U. Sch. of Law, BU Working Paper, No. 10-24), *available at* http://www.bu.edu/law/faculty/scholarship/workingpapers/2010.html.

Jack M. Beermann, An Inductive Understanding of the Separation of Powers, 63 Admin. L. Rev. 467 (2011).

Jack M. Beermann, Public Oversight of Public/Private Partnerships, 28 Fordham Urb. L.J. 1357 (2001).

Jack M. Beermann, Privatization and Political Accountability, 28 Fordham Urb. L.J. 1507 (2001).

Jack M. Beermann, The Reach of Administrative Law in the United States, in The Province of Administrative Law 171 (Michael Taggart ed., 1997).

Jack M. Beermann, Privatization and Political Accountability, 28 Fordham Urb. L.J. 1507 (2001).

Daniel Bell, Notes on the Post-industrial Society (I), Pub. Int., Winter 1967.

Griffin B. Bell, The Attorney General: The Federal Government's Chief Lawyer and Chief Litigator, or One Among Many?, 46 Fordham. Rev. 1049 (1978).

John Bell, The Concept of Public Service Under Threat from Europe? An Illustration from Energy Law, 5 Eur. Pub. L. 189 (1999).

Leonard Bierman, Judge Posner and the NLRB: Implications for Labor Law Reform, 69 Minn. L. Rev. 881 (1985).

Susan Low Bloch, The Early Role of the Attorney General in Our Constitutional Scheme: in the Beginning There Was Pragmatism, Duke L.J. 561 (1989).

Susan Block-Lieb, Accountability and the Bureau of Consumer Financial Protection, 7 Brook. J. of Corp. Fin. & Com. L. 25 (2012).

Susan Block-Lieb & Edward J. Janger, Reforming Regulation in the Markets for Home Loans, 38 Fordham Urb. L.J. 681 (2011).

Theodore Y. Blumoff, Illusions of Constitutional Decisionmaking: Politics and the Tenure Powers in the Court, 73 Iowa L. Rev. 1079 (1988).

James F. Blumstein, Regulatory Review by the Executive Office of the President: An Overview and Policy Analysis of Current Issues, 51 Duke L.J. 851 (2001).

Helen G. Boutrous, Regulatory Review in the Obama Administration: Cost-Benefit Analysis for Everyone, 62 Admin. L. Rev. 243 (2010).

Keith Bradley, The Design of Agency Interactions, 111 Colum. L. Rev. 745 (2011).

Curtis Bradley & Eric Posner, Presidential Signing Statements and Executive Power, 23 Const. Comment 307 (2006).

Marshall J. Breger, The Administrative Conference of the United States: A Quarter Century Perspective, 53 Pitt. L. Rev. 813 (1992).

Marshall J. Breger, The Quest for Legitimacy in American Administrative Law, 40 Israel L. Rev. 73 (2007).

Marshall J. Breger, Thoughts on Accountability and the Administrative Process, 39 Admin. L. Rev. 399 (1987).

Steven Breker-Cooper, The Appointments Clause and the Removal Power: Theory and Séance, 60 Tenn. L. Rev. 841 (1995).

Emily S. Bremer, Incorporation by Reference in an Open-Government Age, 36 Harv. J.L. & Pub. Pol'y 131 (2013).

Lisa Schultz Bressman & Robert B. Thompson, The Future of Agency Independence, 63 Vand. L. Rev. 599 (2010).

Lisa Schultz Bressman & Michael P. Vandenbergh, Inside the Administrative State: A Critical Look at the Practice of Presidential Control, 105 Mich. L. Rev. 437 (2006).

Christina Orsini Broderick, Note, Qui Tam Provisions and the Public Interest: An Empirical Analysis, 107 Colum. L. Rev. 949 (2007).

Keith S. Brown & Adam Candeub, Independent Agencies and the Unitary Executive Debate: An Empirical Critique 10 (Mich. State Univ. College of Law, Legal Studies Research Paper Series, Research Paper No. 06-04), *available at* http://papers.ssrn.com/sol3/papers.cfm?abstract_id=1100125##.

Keith S. Brown & Adam Candeub, Partisans and Partisan Commissions, 17 Geo. Mason L. Rev. 789 (2010).

Kimberley N. Brown, Government by Contract and the Structural Constitution, 87 Notre Dame L. Rev. 491 (2011).

James J. Brudney, Isolated and Politicized: The NLRB's Uncertain Future, 20 Comp. Lab. L. & J. 221 (2005).

James J. Brudney, The National Labor Relations Board in Comparative Context: Isolated and Politicized: The NLRB's Uncertain Future, 26 Comp. Lab. L. & Pol'y 221 (2005).

Harold H. Bruff, Presidential Management of Agency Rulemaking, 57 Geo. Wash. L. Rev. 353 (1989).

Harold H. Bruff, Presidential Power Meets Bureaucratic Expertise, 12 U. Pa. J. Const. L. 461, 485 (2010).

Beth C. Bryant, Comment, FERC's Dam Decommissioning Authority Under the Federal Power Act, 74 Wash. L. Rev. 95 (1999).

Zbigniew Brzezinski, America in the Technetronic Age, Encounter, January 1968.

Mark E. Budnitz, The FTC's Consumer Protection Program During the Miller Years: Lessons for Administrative Agency Structure and Operation, 46 Cath. U. L. Rev. 371 (1997).

Jason Buhi & Lin Feng, The International Joint Commission's Role in the United States–Canada Transboundary Air Pollution Control Regime: A Century of Experience to Guide the Future, 11 Vt. J. Envtl. L. 107 (2009).

Jay Bybee & Tuan Samahon, William Rehnquist, The Separation of Powers, and the Riddle of the Sphinx, 58 Stan. L. Rev. 1735 (2006).

Shannon Cain, The Case for Judicial Review of President Obama's January 4 Recess Appointments, 64 Admin. L. Rev. 993 (2012).

Steven G. Calabresi, The Vesting Clause as Power Grant, 88 Nw. U. L. Rev. 1377 (1994).

Steven G. Calabresi & Saikrishna Prakash, The President's Power to Execute the Laws, 104 Yale L.J. 578 (1994).

Steven G. Calabresi & Kevin H. Rhodes, The Structural Constitution, Unitary Executive, Plural Judicial, 105 Harv. L. Rev. 1153 (1992).

Steven G. Calabresi & Christopher S. Yoo, The Unitary Executive During the First Half-Century, 47 Case W. L. Rev. 1451 (1997).

Steven G. Calabresi & Christopher S. Yoo, The Unitary Executive During the Second Half of the Century, 26 Harv. J. L. & Pub. Pol'y 667 (2003).

Mark Calagus, Military Privatization: Efficiency or Anarchy? 6 Chi.-Kent J. Int'l & Comp. L. 58 (2006).

Robert L. Calhoun, the Interstate Commerce Commission, 1912-1937, 16 Transp. L.J. 59 (1988).

Evan Caminker, The Constitutionality of Qui Tam Actions, 99 Yale L.J. 341 (1989).

Timothy A. Canova, American Wartime Values in Historical Perspective: Full-Employment Mobilization or Business as Usual, 13 ILSA J. Int'l & Comp. L. 1 (2006).

Timothy A. Canova, Black Swans and Black Elephants in Plain Sight: An Empirical Review of Central Bank Independence, 14 Chap. L. Rev. 237 (2011).

Timothy A. Canova, Democracy's Disappearing Duties: The Washington Consensus and the Limits of Citizen Participation, in Democratic Citizenship and War (Yoav Peled et al. eds., 2011).

Letter from Angela Canterbury, Dir. of Pub. Policy & Michael Smallberg Investigatory Project on Government Oversight, to Rep. Spencer Bachus, Chair of House Comm. on Fin. Services (May 29, 2012) available at, http://pogoarchives.org/m/fo/sro-letter-20120529.pdf.

Thomas R. Carey, Assessing Environmental Compliance for Business, in The Impact of Environmental Issues on Business Transactions: Leading Lawyers on Managing Environmental Regulation and Enforcement for Business (Inside the Minds) (2012).

Michael A. Carrier, Note, When Is the Senate in Recess for the Purposes of the Recess Appointments Clause?, 92 Mich. L. Rev. 2204 (1994).

Terry Carter, *Prison Break: Budget Crises Drive Reform, but Private Jails Press On*, 2012 A.B.A. J. (2012).

Gerhard Casper, An Essay in Separation of Powers: Some Early Versions and Practices, 30 Wm. & Mary L. Rev. 211 (1989).

Josh Chafetz, Executive Branch Contempt of Congress, 76 U. Chi. L. Rev. 1083 (2009).

Jim Chen, Book Review: The Nature of the Public Utility: Infrastructure, the Market, and the Law, 98 Nw. U. L. Rev. 1617, 1638 (2004).

John C. Coffee, Jr., The Political Economy of Dodd-Frank: Why Financial Reform Tends to be Frustrated and Systemic Risk Perpetuated, 97 Corn. L. Rev. 1019 (2012).

Cary Coglianese, Presidential Control of Administrative Agencies: A Debate over Law or Politics?, 12 U. Pa. J. Const. L. 637 (2010).

Daniel Cohen & Peter L. Strauss, Congressional Review of Agency Rulemaking, 49 Admin. L. Rev. 95 (1996).

Wilbur J. Cohen, The Development of the Social Security Act of 1935: Reflections Some Fifty Years Later, 68 Minn. L. Rev. 379 (1983).

Thomas Combs, A Proposal for Regulation of the Government Sponsored Entities, 84 St. John's L. Rev. 759 (2010).

Conference: Harvard Electricity Policy Group: Regulatory Decisionmaking Reform, 8 Admin. L.J. Am. U. 789 (1995).

Peter Conti-Brown, The Structure of Federal Reserve Independence, Working Paper Series No. 139, Rock Ctr. For Corporate Governance (Jan. 2, 2014 version)

Peter Conti-Brown, The Structure of Federal Reserve Independence, Working Paper Series No. 139, Rock Ctr. For Corporate Governance (Jun. 7, 2013 version).

Charles J. Cooper, Robert D. Dinerstein et. al., The Fifth Annual Robert C. Byrd Conference on the Administrative Process: The First Year of Clinton/Gore Reinventing Government or Refining Reagan/Bush Initiatives?, 8 Admin. L.J. Am. U. 23 (1994).

Robert Cooper, The Office of Thrift Supervision, 59 Fordham L Rev. S363 (1991).

Curtis W. Copeland, Economic Analysis and Independent Regulatory Agencies (Apr. 30, 2013), *available at* the website of the Administrative Conference of the United States, http://www.acus.gov/sites/default/files/documents/Indep%20Agency%20BCAs%20Draft%20Rec%20Final%202-15-2013.pdf.

Curtis W. Copeland, The Role of the Office of Information and Regulatory Affairs in Federal Rulemaking, 33 Fordham Urb. L.J. 1257 (2006).

Edwin S. Corwin, The Steel Seizure Cases: A Judicial Brick Without Straw, 53 Colum. L. Rev. 53 (1953).

Paul Craig, The Fall and Renewal of the Commission: Accountability, Contract and Administration Organisation, 6 Eur. L.J. 98 (2000).

Frank B. Cross & Emerson H. Tiller, Understanding Collegiality on the Court, 27 J. L. & Pol. 405 (2012).

Scott Cummings, The Politics of Pro Bono, 52 UCLA L. Rev. 1 (2004).

Bruce Y. Curry, Note, President's Power of Removal—Consent of United States Senate Myers v. United States, 6 Or. L. Rev. 165 (1926–27).

Lloyd N. Cutler, Moderator, Managing the Regulatory Process, 32 Admin L. Rev. 239 (1980).

Kirti Datla & Richard Revesz, *Deconstructing Independent Agencies (and Executive Agencies)*, 98 Cornell L. Rev. 769 (2013).

Steven M. Davidoff & David Zaring, Regulation by Deal: The Government's Response to the Financial Crisis, 61 Admin. L. Rev. 463 (2009).

Nestor M. Davidson, Relational Contracts in the Privatization of Social Welfare: The Case of Housing, 24 Yale L. & Pol'y Rev. 263 (2006).

Paul Stephen Dempsey, Congressional Intent and Agency Discretion—Never the Twain Shall Meet: The Motor Carrier Act of 1980, 58 Chi.-Kent L. Rev. 1 (1981).

Paul Stephen Dempsey, The Rise and Fall of the Interstate Commerce Commission: The Tortuous Path From Regulation to Deregulation of America's Infrastructure, 95 Marquette L. Rev. 1151 (2012).

Paul Stephen Dempsey, Transportation Deregulation—On a Collision Course?, 13 Transp. L.J. 329 (1984).

Christopher C. Demuth & Douglas H. Ginsberg, White House Review of Agency Rulemaking, 99 Harv. L. Rev. 1075 (1986).

Blake Denton, While the Senate Sleeps: Do Contemporary Events Warrant a New Interpretation of the Bd. of Governors of the Fed. Res. Sys. Ann. Rep. Clause?, 58 Cath. U. L. Rev. 751 (2009).

Charles S. Devas, Monopolies and Fair Dealing, 12 Int'l J. Ethics 59 (1901).

Neal Devins, Congress, the FCC, and the Search for the Public Trustee, 56 Law & Contemp. Probs. 145 (1993).

Neal Devins, Political Will and the Unitary Executive: What Makes an Independent Agency Independent?, 15 Cardozo L. Rev. 273 (1993).

Neal Devins, Unitariness and Independence: Solicitor General Control Over Independent Agency Litigation, 82 Cal. l. Rev. 255 (1994).

Neal Devins & Michael Herz, The Battle That Never Was: Congress, the White House, and Agency Litigation Authority, 61 Wtr. Law & Contemp. Probs. 205 (1998).

Neal Devins & Michael Herz, The Consequences of DOJ Control of Litigation on Agencies' Programs, 52 Admin. l. Rev 1435 (2000).

Neal Devins & Michael Herz, The Uneasy Case for Department of Justice Control of Federal Litigation, 5 U. Pa. J. Const. L. 558 (2003).

Neal Devins & David E. Lewis, Not-So Independent Agencies: Party Polarization and the Limits of Institutional Design, 88 B.U. L. Rev. 459 (2008).

Youri Devuyst, The European Union's Institutional Balance after the Treaty of Lisbon: "Community Method" and "Democratic Deficit" Reassessed, 39 Geo. J. Int'l L. 247 (2008).

Rita L. Di Simone, Social Security Administration Created as an Independent Agency: Public Law 103-296, Social Security Bulletin, Vol. 58, No.1, 57 (1995).

Colin S. Diver, Presidential Powers, 36 Am. U. L. Rev. 519 (1987).

Onning H. Dombalagian, The Expressive Synergies of the Volcker Rule, 64 B.C. L. Rev. 169 (2013).

William J. Donovan & Ralstone R. Irvine, The President's Power to Remove Members of Administrative Agencies, 21 Cornell L. Q. 215 (1936).

Yoav Dotan, Should Prosecutorial Discretion Enjoy Special Treatment in Judicial Review: A Comparative Analysis of the Law in England and Israel, Public Law 513 (1997).

Yoav Dotan & Mehachem Hofnung, Interest Groups in the Israeli High Court of Justice: Measuring Success in Litigation and Out-of-Court Settlements, 23 Law & Policy 1 (2001).

John F. Duffy, Are Administrative Patent Judges Unconstitutional?, 77 Geo. Wash. L. Rev. 904 (2009).

Frank H. Easterbrook, Unitary Executive Interpretation: A Comment, 15 Cardozo L. Rev. 313 (1993).

Gary J. Edles, The Revival of the Administrative Conference of the United States, 12 Tex. Tech Admin. L.J. 281 (2011).

Gary J. Edles, The Strategy of Regulatory Change, 49 ICC Prac. J. 626, 626 (1982).

Harry T. Edwards, The Effects of Collegiality on Judicial Decision Making, 151 U. Pa. L. Rev. 1639 (2003).

Harry T. Edwards & Michael A. Livermore, Pitfalls of Empirical Studies that Attempt to Understand the Factors Affecting Appellate Decision Making, 58 Duke L.J. 1895 (2009).

Michael Ellement, Labor Law in 3(d): Reexamining the General Counsel of the NLRB as an Independent Prosecutor of Labor Violations, 29 A.B.A. J. of Lab. & Emp. L. 477 (2014).

Jonathan L. Entin, The Removal Power and the Federal Deficit, 75 Ky. L.J. 699 (1987).

Jonathan L. Entin, Synecdoche and the Presidency: The Removal Power as Symbol, 47 Case W. Res. L. Rev. 1595 (1997).

Daniel R. Ernst, The Politics of Administrative Law: New York's Anti-bureaucracy Clause and the O'Brian-Wagner Campaign of 1938 in the Late New Deal, 27 L. & Hist. Rev., no. 2 (2009).

Fannie Mae, About Fannie Mae—Our Charter, http://www.fanniemae.com/resources/file/aboutus/pdf/fm-amended-charter.pdf (accessed July 20, 2014).

Cynthia R. Farina, False Comfort and Impossible Promises: Uncertainty, Information Overload and the Unitary Executive, 12 U. Pa. J. Const. L. 357 (2010).

Cynthia R. Farina, Undoing the New Deal Through New Presidentialism, 22 Harv. J. L. & Pub. Pol'y 227 (1998).

Mark L. Farley, Special Report: Investigating Chemical Incidents—the Role of the Chemical Safety and Hazard Investigation Board, 30 Env't Rep. Cur. Dev. (BNA) 534 (1999).

Craig D. Feiser, Privatization and the Freedom of Information Act: An Analysis of Public Access to Private Entities Under Federal Law, 52 Fed. Comm. L.J. 21 (1999).

Oliver Peter Field, Government Corporations: A Proposal, 48 Harv. L. Rev. 775 (1935).

Financial Industry Regulatory Authority, Get to Know Us, www.finra.org/web/groups/corporate/@corp@about/documents/corporate/p118667.pdf.

Jill E. Fisch, How Do Corporations Play Politics: The FedEx Story, 58 Vand. L. Rev. 1495 (2005).

Catherine L. Fisk, The Role of the Judiciary When the Agency Confirmation Process Stalls: Thoughts on the Two-Member NLRB and the Questions the Supreme Court Should Have, but Didn't, Address in New Process Steel, L.P. v. NLRB, 5 FIU L. Rev. 593 (2010).

Chris Flack, Recent Decision of the United States Court of Appeals for the District of Columbia Circuit: Federal Sovereign Immunity, 69 Geo. Wash. L. Rev. 656 (2001).

Martin Flaherty, The Most Dangerous Branch, 105 Yale L.J. 1725 (1996).

Martin S. Flaherty, Relearning Founding Lessons: The Removal Power and Joint Accountability, 47 Case W. Res. L. Rev. 1563 (1997).

Martin S. Flaherty, Synecdoche and the Presidency: The Removal Powers as Symbol, 47 Case W. Res. L. Rev. 1585 (1997).

Joan Flynn, "Expertness for What?": The Gould Years at the NLRB and the Irrepressible Myth of the "Independent" Agency, 52 Admin. L. Rev. 465 (2000).

Joan Flynn, A Quiet Revolution at the Labor Board: The Transformation of the NLRB 1935-2000, 61 Ohio S. L.J. 1361 (2000).

Bruce D. Fong, Whistleblower Protection and the Office of Special Counsel: The Development of Reprisal Law in the 1980s, 40 Amer. U. L. Rev. 1015 (1991).

Julia Patterson Forrester, Fannie Mae/Freddie Mac Uniform Mortgage Instruments: The Forgotten Benefit to Homeowners, 72 Missouri L. Rev. 1077 (2007).

Arthur Fraas & Randall Lutter, On the Economic Analysis of Regulations at Independent Regulatory Commissions, 63 Admin. L. Rev. 213 (2011) (special ed.).

George F. Fraley III, Is the Fox Watching the Henhouse? The Administration's Control of FEC Litigation Through the Solicitor General, 9 Admin. L.J. 15 (1996).

Richard Frankel, Regulating Privatized Government Through § 1983, 76 U. Chi. L. Rev. 1449 (2009).

Jody Freeman, The Contracting State, 28 Fla. St. L. Rev. 155 (2000).

Jody Freeman, Private Parties, Public Functions and the New Administrative Law, 52 Admin. L. Rev. 813 (2000).

Jody Freeman, The Private Role in Public Governance, 75 N.Y.U. L. Rev. 543 (2000).

William J. Friedman, The Fourteenth Amendment's Public/Private Distinction Among Securities Regulators in the U.S. Marketplace—Revisited, 23 Ann. Rev. Banking & Fin. L. 727 (2004).

A. Michael Froomkin, In Defense of Administrative Agency Autonomy, 96 Yale L.J. 787 (1987).

A. Michael Froomkin, Reinventing the Government Corporation, 1995 U. Ill. L. Rev. 543 (1995).

Gerald E. Frug, The Ideology of Bureaucracy in American Law, 97 Harv. L. Rev. 1277 (1984).

William Funk, Close Enough for Government Work?—Using Informal Procedures for Imposing Administrative Penalties, 24 Seton Hall L. Rev. 1 (1993).

William F. Funk, The Paperwork Reduction Act: Paperwork Reduction Meets Administrative Laws, 24 Harv. J. on Legis 1 (1987).

Alison K. Gary, Creating a Future Economic Crisis: Political Failure and the Loopholes of the Volcker Rule, 90 Oregon L. Rev. 1339, 134–45 (2012).

E. L. Gatson, Mercenarism 2.0? The Rise of the Modern Private Security Industry and its Implications for International Humanitarian Law Enforcement, 49 Harv. Int'l L.J. 221 (2008).

Jacob E. Gersen, Administrative Law Goes to Wall Street: The New Administrative Process, 65 Admin. L. Rev. 689 (2013).

Jacob Gersen, Designing Agencies, in Research Handbook on Public Choice and Public Law (Daniel Farber & Annie O'Connell eds., 2010).

Charles Gardner Geyh & Emily Field Van Tassel, The Independence of the Judicial Branch in the New Republic, 74 Chi.-Kent L. Rev. 31 (1998).

Daniel J. Gifford, The New Deal Regulatory Model: A History of Criticisms and Refinements, 68 Minn. L. Rev. 299 (1983).

Robert L. Glicksman & Stephen B. Chapman, Regulatory Reform and (Breach of) The Contract With America: Improving Environmental Policy or Destroying Environmental Protection?, 5 Kan. J.L. & Pub. Pol'y 9 (1996).

Jack Goldsmith & John Manning, The President's Completion Power, 115 Yale L.J. 2280 (2006).

Jared A. Goldstein, The Tea Party Movement and the Perils of Popular Originalism, 53 Ariz. L. Rev. 827 (2011).

William B. Gould, IV, The NLRB at Age 70: Some Reflections on the Clinton Board and the Bush II Aftermath, 26 Berkeley J. Emp. & Lab. L. 309 (2005).

Heather J. Gradison, Welcome, The Interstate Commerce Commission Centennial Proceedings, 16 Transp. L.J. 37 (1987).

John D. Graham, Saving Lives Through Administrative Law and Economics, 157 U. Pa. L. Rev. 395 (2008).

John D. Graham et al., Managing the Regulatory State: The Experience of the Bush Administration, 33 Fordham Urb. L.J. 953 (2006).

J. Michael Grubbs, Self-Audits Now Required to Avoid Medicare Billing Errors Being Punished as False Claims, Martindale.com Legal Library, Jan. 21, 2013 (2012), *available at* http://www.martindale.com/health-care-law/article_Barnes-Thornburg-LLP_1452002.htm.

Daniel Guttman, Public Purpose and Private Service: The Twentieth Century Culture of Contracting Out and the Evolving Law of Diffused Sovereignty, 52 Admin. L. Rev. 859 (2000).

Robert W. Hahn & Cass R. Sunstein, A New Executive Order for Improving Federal Regulation? Deeper and Wider Cost-Benefit Analysis, 150 U. Pa. L. Rev. 1489 (2002).

Cynthia M. Hajost, From Oversight to Conservatorship: What Does the Housing and Economic Recovery Act of 2008 Hold for GSE's Fannie Mae and Freddie Mac?, 18 J. Affordable Housing & Community Dev. L. 3 (Fall 2008).

Peter J. Hammer, Antitrust Beyond Competition: Market Failures, Total Welfare, and the Challenge of Intramarket Second-Best Tradeoffs, 98 Mich. L. Rev. 849 (2000).

James R. Harvey III, Loyalty in Government Action Litigation: Department of Justice Representation of Agency Clients, 37 Wm. & Mary L. Rev. 1569 (1996).

Julian Helisk, Essay: The Fault, PCAOB, Lies Not in the Appointments Clause, but in the Removal Power, That You Are Unconstitutional, 77 Geo. Wash. L. Rev. 1063 (2009).

M. Todd Henderson, Self-Regulation for the Mortgage Industry (Coase-Sandor Institute for Law and Economics, Working Paper No. 638, 2013).

M. Todd Henderson & William A. Birdthistle, Becoming a Fifth Branch, 99 Cornell L. Rev. 1 (2013).

Michael Herz, Abandoning Recess Appointments? A Comment on Hartnett (and Others), 26 Cardozo L. Rev. 443 (2005).

Michael Herz, Unites States v. United States: When Can the Federal Government Sue Itself?, 32 Wm. & Mary L. Rev. 893 (1991).

Peter Hettich, Governance by Mutual Benchmarking in Postal Markets: How State-Owned Enterprises May Induce Private Competitors to Observe Policy Goals, 32 Dayton L. Rev. 199 (2007).

Robert L. Hetzel & Ralph F. Leach, The Treasury-Fed Accord: A New Narrative Account, 87 Fed. Res. Bank Richmond Econ. Q. 33 (2001).

Jeffrey M. Hirsch, Law of Termination: Doing More with Less, 68 Md. L. Rev. 89 (2008).

Daniel E. Ho, Measuring Agency Preferences: Experts, Voting, and the Power of Chairs, 59 DePaul L. Rev. 333 (2010).

Henry B. Hogue, The Law: Recess Appointments to Article III Courts, 34 Presidential Stud. Q. 656 (2004).

Ari Hoogenboom, The Pendleton Act and the Civil Service, 64 Am. Hist. Rev. 301 (1959).

Aziz Z. Huq, Removal as a Political Question, 65 Stan. L. Rev. 1 (2013).

Whitney Innes, The Unaccountability of the Accounting Regulators: Analyzing the Constitutionality of the Public Company Accounting Oversight Board, 42 J. Marshall L. Rev. 1019 (2009).

Louis L. Jaffe, The Effective Limits of the Administrative Process: A Reevaluation, 67 Harv. L. Rev. 1105 (1954).

George Robert Johnson, Jr., The Split-Enforcement Model: Some Conclusions from the OSHA and MSHA Experiences, 39 Admin. L. Rev. 315 (1987).

Nicholas Johnson, Open Meetings and Closed Minds: Another Road to the Mountaintop, 53 Drake L. Rev. 11 (2004).

Thomas W. Joo, Who Watches the Watchers? The Securities Investor Protection Act, Investor Confidence and the Subsidization of Failure, 72 S. Cal. L. Rev. 1071 (1999).

Elena Kagan, Presidential Administration, 114 Harv. L. Rev. 2245 (2001).

Bradley C. Karkkainen, Information-Forcing Regulation and Environmental Governance, in Law and New Governance in the EU and the US 293 (Grainne de Burca & Joanne Scott eds., 2006).

Bradley C. Karkkainen, "New Governance" in Legal Thought and in the World: Some Splitting as Antidote to Overzealous Lumping, 89 Minn. L. Rev. 471 (2004).

Roberta S. Karmel, Creating Law at the Securities and Exchange Commission: The Lawyer as Prosecutor, 61 Law & Contemp. Probs. 33 (1998).

Roberta S. Karmel, Should Securities Industry Self-Regulatory Organizations Be Considered Government Agencies? 14 Stan. J. L. Bus. & Fin. 151 (2008).

Elliott Karr, Independent Litigation Authority and Calls for the Views of the Solicitor General, 77 Geo. Wash. L. Rev. 1080 (2009).

Sally Katzen, Can Greater Use of Economic Analysis Improve Regulatory Policy at Independent Regulatory Commissions (Apr. 7, 2011), Resources for the Future, *available at* http://www.rff.org/Documents.Events/Workshops%20and%20Congerences/110407_Regulation_KatzenRemarks.pdf.

Sally Katzen, OIRA at Thirty: Reflections and Recommendations, 63 Admin L. Rev. 103 (2011).

Sally Katzen, A Reality Check on an Empirical Study: Comments on "Inside the Administrative State," 105 Mich. L. Rev. 1497 (2007).

Brent Kavanaugh, Separation of Powers During the Forty-Fourth Presidency and Beyond, 93 Minn. L. Rev. 1454 (2009).

Neal Kaytal, Internal Separation of Powers: Checking Today's Most Dangerous Branch from Within, 115 Yale L.J. 2314 (2006).

Joseph D. Kearney & Thomas W. Merrill, The Great Transformation of Regulated Industries Law, 98 Colum. L. Rev. 1323 (1998).

Kathleen M. Keller, Federalizing Social Welfare in a World of Gender Difference: A History of Women's Work in New Deal Policy, 8 S. Cal. Rev. L. & Women's Stud. 145 (1999).

William K. Kelley, The Constitutional Dilemma of Litigation Under the Independent Counsel System, 83 Minn. L. Rev. 1197 (1999).

Carolyn Bingham Kello, Drawing the Curtain on Open Government: In Defense of the Federal Advisory Committee Act, 69 Brooklyn L. Rev. 345 (1999).

Benjamin A. Kemplin, The Public Trust in Private Hands: Social Security and the Politics of Government, 96 Ky. L.J. 369 (2008).

Joshua Kershner, Political Party Restrictions and the Appointments Clause: The Federal Election Commission's Appointments Process is Constitutional, 32 Cardozo L. Rev. 615 (2010).

Mark F. Kightlinger, Nihilism with a Happy Ending? The Interstate Commerce Commission and the Emergence of the Post-Enlightenment Paradigm, 113 Penn. St. L. Rev. 113 (2008).

Benedict Kingsbury, Nico Krisch & Richard B. Stewart, The Emergence of Global Administrative Law, 68 Law & Contemp. Probs. (2005).

Heidi Kitrosser, The Accountable Executive, 93 Minn. L. Rev. 1741 (2009).

Douglas W. Kmiec, OLC's Opinion Writing Function: The Legal Adhesive for a Unitary Executive, 15 Cardozo L. Rev. 337 (1993).

Peter P. Knight, Encouraging Regulated Entities to Comply with Federal Environmental Mandates: The Need for a Federal Environmental Audit Protection Statute, 3 N.Y.U. J. Legis. & Pub. Pol'y 125 (1999–2000).

Charles H. Koch, Jr., & David A. Koplow, The Fourth Bite at the Apple: A Study of the Operation and Utility of the Social Security Administration's Appeals Council, 17 Fla. St. U. L. Rev. 199 (1990).

Harold Hongju Koh, Setting the World Right, 115 Yale L. J. 2350 (2006).

William A. Kovacic, The Quality of Appointments and the Capability of the Federal Trade Commission, 49 Admin. L. Rev. 915 (1997).

George A. Krause & Brent M. Dupay, Coordinated Action and the Limits of Presidential Control over the Bureaucracy: Lessons from the Bush Presidency, in President George W. Bush's Influence over Bureaucracy and Policy 81 (Colin Provert & Paul Teske eds., 2009).

Kimberly D. Krawiec, Don't "Screw Joe the Plummer": The Sausage-Making of Financial Reform, 55 Ariz. L. Rev. 53 (2013).

Harold J. Krent, From a Unitary to a Unilateral Presidency, 88 B.U. L. Rev. 523 (2008).

Harold J. Krent, The Private Performing the Public: Delimiting Delegations to Private Parties, 65 U. Miami L. Rev. 507 (2011).

Harold J. Krent, The Sometimes Unitary Executive: Presidential Practice Throughout History, 25 Const. Comment. 489 (2009).

Ronald Krotozynski, Jr., Back to the Briarpatch: An Argument in Favor of Constitutional Meta-analysis in State Action Determinations, 94 Mich. L. Rev. 302 (1995).

Ronald J. Krotoszynski, Jr., Cooperative Federalism, the New Formalism, and the Separation of Powers Revisited: Free Enterprise Fund and the Problem of Presidential Oversight of State-Government Officers Enforcing Federal Law, 61 Duke L.J. 1599 (2012).

Charles Kruly, Essay, Self-Funding and Agency Independence, 81 Geo. Wash. L. Rev. 1733 (2013).

Julian Ku, Unitary Executive Theory and Exclusive Presidential Powers, 12 U. Pa. J. Const. L. 615 (2010).

Karl-Heinz Ladeur, The New European Agencies: The European Environment Agency and Prospects for a European Network or Environmental Administrations (European Union Institute Working Paper No. 96/50, 1996).

Amanda S. La Forge, The Toothless Tiger—Structural, Political and Legal Barriers to Effective FEC Enforcement: An Overview and Recommendations, 10 Admin. L. Rev. Am. U. 351 (1996).

Carrie Stradley Lavargna, Government-Sponsored Enterprises Are "Too Big to Fail": Balancing Public and Private Interests, 44 Hastings L.J. 991 (1993).

Gary Lawson, Burying the Constitution Under a TARP, 33 Harv. J. L. & Pub. Pol'y 55 (2010).

Gary Lawson, The Rise and Rise of the Administrative State, 107 Harv. L. Rev. 1231 (1994).

Clarence F. Lea, The Federal Power Commission as an Agency of Congress, 14 Geo. Wash. L. Rev. 1 (1945).

Rafael Leal-Arcas, EU Legal Personality in Foreign Policy?, 24 B.U. Int'l L.J. 165 (2006).

Bruce Ledewitz, The Uncertain Power of the President to Execute the Law, 46 Tenn. L. Rev. 757 (1984).

Frederic P. Lee, The Origins of Judicial Control of Federal Executive Action, 36 Geo. L.J. 287 (1948).

Margaret H. Lemos, The Consequences of Congress's Choice of Delegate: Judicial and Agency Interpretations of Title VII, 63 Vand. L. Rev. 363 (2010).

Margaret H. Lemos, The Other Delegate: Judicially Administered Statutes and the Nondelegation Doctrine, 81 S. Cal. L. Rev. 405 (2008).

Margaret H. Lemos, The Solicitor General as Mediator Between Court and Agency, 2009 Mich. St. L. Rev. 185 (2009).

Lawrence Lessig & Cass R. Sunstein, The President and the Administration, 94 Colum. L. Rev. 1 (1994).

William E. Leuchtenburg, The Case of the Contentious Commissioner: Humphrey's Ex'r v. U.S., in Freedom and Reform: Essays in Honor of Henry Steele Commager 276, 278–312 (Harold M. Hyman & Leonard W. Levy eds., 1967).

Laurie L. Levenson, Live and Learn: Depoliticizing the Interim Appointments of U.S. Attorneys, 31 Seattle U. L. Rev. 297 (2008).

David A. Lipton, Governance of Our Security Markets and the Failure to Allocate Regulatory Responsibility, 34 Cath. U. L. Rev. 397 (1985).

David A. Lipton, The SEC or the Exchanges: Who Shall Do What and When? A Proposal to Allocate Regulatory Responsibility for Security Markets, 16 U.C. Davis L. Rev. 397 (1983).

Orly Lobel, Governing Occupational Safety in the United States, in Law and New Governance in the EU and the US 269 (Grainne de Burca & Joanne Scott eds., 2006).

Todd Lochner, the Relationship between the Office of Solicitor General and the Independent Agencies: A Reevaluation, 79 Va. L. Rev. 549 (1993).

Theodore J. Lowi, President v. Congress: What the Two-Party Duopoly Has Done to the American Separation of Powers, 47 Case W. Res. L. Rev. 1219 (1997).

Jerrod M. Lukacs, Note, Much Ado About Nothing: How the Securities SRO State Action Circuit Court Split Has Been Misinterpreted and What It Means for Due Process at FINRA, 47 Ga. L. Rev. 923 (2013).

Arthur Lupie & Matthew McCabbins, Learning From Oversight: Fire Alarms and Police Patrols Reconstructed, 10 J.L. Econ. & Org. 96 (1994).

William G. Mahoney, The Interstate Commerce Commission/Surface Transportation Board as Regulator of Labor's Rights and Deregulator of Railroads' Obligations: The Contrived Collision of the Interstate Commerce Act with the Railway Labor Act, 24 Transp. L.J. 241 (1997).

Kenneth L. Marcus, The Right Frontier for Civil Rights Reform, 19 Geo. Mason CRLJ 77 (2008).

Edward J. Markey, Congress to Administrative Agencies: Creator, Overseer, and Partner, 1990 Duke L.J. 967 (1990).

Jerry L. Mashaw, Governmental Practice and Presidential Direction: Lessons from the Antebellum Republic, 45 Willamette L. Rev. 659 (2009).

Jerry L. Mashaw, Public Law and Public Choice: Critique and Rapprochement, in Research Handbook on Law and Public Choice and Public Law (Daniel A. Farber & Anne Joseph O'Connell eds., 2010).

Jerry L. Mashaw, Reluctant Nationalists: Federal Administration and Administrative Law in the Republican Era, 1801–1829, 116 Yale L.J. 1636 (2007).

Jerry L. Mashaw, Rethinking Judicial Review of Administrative Action: A Nineteenth Century Perspective, 32 Cardozo L. Rev. 2241 (2011).

Jerry L. Mashaw & Avi Perri, Administrative Statutory Interpretation in the Antebellum Republic, [2009] Mich. St. L. Rev. 7.

Michael Coyn Mateer, Casenote, When the Lights Go Out: The Impact of House Bill 6 on Regional Transmission Organizations and the Reliability of the Power Grid, 12 Geo. Mason L. Rev. 775 (2004).

Randolph May, Reforming the Sunshine Act, 49 Admin. L. Rev. 415 (1997).

Randolph J. May, Defining Deference Down, Again: Independent Agencies, Chevron Deference, and Fox, 62 Admin. L. Rev. 433 (2010).

Lesley K. McAllister, Regulation by Third-Party Verification, 53 B.C. L. Rev. 1 (2012).

Matthew D. McCabbins & Thomas Schwartz, Police Patrols v. Fire Alarms, 28 Am. J. Pol. Sci. 165 (1984).

John McDiarmid, The Financial Powers of Government as Defined in Acts of Congress, 15 Tex. L. Rev. 437 (1937).

Bruce D. McDowell, Advisory Commission on Intergovernmental Relations in 1966: The End of an Era, 27 Publius 111 (1997).

Joseph W. Mead, Interagency Litigation and Article III, 47 Ga. L. Rev. 1217 (2013).

Rick E. Melberth & Gary D. Bass, In Defense of Regulatory Peer Review, 38 Envtl. L. Rep. News & Analysis 10561 (2008).

Nina A. Mendelson, Private Control over Access to Public Law: The Puzzling Regulatory Use of Private Standards, 112 Mich. L. Rev. 737 (2014).

Richard A. Merrill, CPSC Regulation of Cancer Risks in Consumer Products, 1972–1981, 67 Va. L. Rev. 1261 (1981).

Thomas W. Merrill, Article III, Agency Adjudication, and the Origins of the Appellate Review Model of Administrative Law, 111 Colum. L. Rev. 939 (2011).

Thomas W. Merrill, The Constitutional Principle of Separation of Powers, 1991 Sup. Ct. Rev. 225.

Gillian Metzger, Privatization as Delegation, 103 Colum. L. Rev. 1367 (2003).

Jon D. Michaels, Privatization's Pretensions, 77 U. Chi. L. Rev. 717 (2010).

Jon D. Michaels, The (Willingly) Fettered Executive: Presidential Spinoffs in National Security Domains and Beyond, 97 Va. L. Rev. 801 (2011).

Geoffrey P. Miller, Independent Agencies, Sup. Ct. Rev. 41 (1986).

Geoffrey P. Miller, The Unitary Executive in a Unified Theory of Constitutional Law: The Problem of Interpretation, 15 Cardozo L. Rev. 201 (1993).

James C. Miller III, The Early Days of Reagan Regulatory Relief and Suggestions for OIRA's Future, 63 Admin. L. Rev. 93 (2011).

James C. Miller III, Keynote Address to ICC Centennial Celebration, April 3, 1987, 16 Transp. L.J. 40 (1987).

Martha Minow, Outsourcing Power: Privatizing Military Efforts and the Risks to Accountability, Professionalism, and Democracy, in Government by Contract 110 (Jody Freeman & Martha Minow eds., 2009).

Benjamin W. Mintz, Administrative Separation of Functions: OSHA and the NLRB, 47 Cath. U. L. Rev. 877 (1998).

Ronald C. Moe & Thomas H. Stanton, Government-Sponsored Enterprises as Federal Instrumentalities: Reconciling Private Management with Public Accountability, 49 Pub. Admin. Rev. 321 (1989).

Gilbert H. Montague, Antitrust Laws and the Federal Trade Commission, 1914–1927, 27 Colum. L. Rev. 650 (1927).

Angel Manuel Moreno, Presidential Coordination of the Independent Regulatory Process, 8 Admin. L.J. Am. U. 461 (1994).

Charles J. Morris, How the National Labor Relations Act Was Stolen and How It Can Be Recovered: Taft-Hartley Revisionism and the National Labor Relations Board's Appointment Process, 33 Berkeley J. Emp. & Lab. L. 1 (2012).

Alan B. Morrison, OMB Interference with Agency Rulemaking: The Wrong Way to Write a Regulation, 99 Harv. L. Rev. 1059 (1986).

Joan Solanes Mullor, Why Independent Agencies Deserve Chevron Deference, InDret 4/2010 (2010), *available at* http:// www.Indret.com/pdf/762_en.pdf.

Donna Nagy, Is the PCAOB a "Heavily Centralized Compartment" of the SEC? A Essential Question in the Constitutional Controversy, 27 U. Pitt. L. R. 361 (2010).

Donna Nagy, Playing Peekaboo with Constitutional Law: The PCAOB and Its Public/Private Status, 513 Notre Dame L. Rev 374 (2005).

Robert G. Natelson, The Original Meaning of the Constitution's "Executive Vesting Clause": Evidence from Eighteenth Century Drafting Practice, 31 Whittier L. Rev. 1 (2009).

Joseph S. Neely, Justice Frankfurter, Universal Camera and a Jurisprudence of Judicial Review of Administrative Action, 25 Tol. L. Rev. 1 (1994).

Jerome Nelson, Administrative Law Judges' Removal "Only for Cause": Is That Administrative Procedure Act Protection Now Unconstitutional?, 63 Admin. L. Rev. 401 (2011).

Richard E. Neustadt, Presidency and Legislation: The Growth of Central Clearance, 48 Am. Pol. Sci. Rev. 641 (1954).

Note, D.C. Circuit Holds That the SEC Chairman Is Not the "Head" of the SEC—Free Enterprise Fund v. Public Co. Accounting Oversight Board, 122 Harv. L. Rev. 2267 (2009).

Note, Independence, Congressional Weakness, and the Importance of Appointment: The Impact of Combining Budgetary Autonomy with Removal Protection, 125 Harv. L. Rev. 1822 (2012).

Note, The Mysteries of the Congressional Review Act, 122 Harv. L. Rev. 2162 (2009).

Note, The SEC Is Not an Independent Agency, 126 Harv. L. Rev. 781 (2013).

Jennifer Nou, Agency Self-Insulation Under Presidential Review, 126 Harv. L. Rev. 1756 (2013).

Anne Joseph O'Connell, Bureaucracy at the Boundary, 162 U. Pa. L. Rev. 841 (2014).

Thomas J. O'Dowd, Comment, The Hollywood Ceramics–Shopping Kart Merry-Go-Round: Where Will It Stop?, 20 Santa Clara L. Rev. 157 (1980).

Jaron M. Patlis, Riders on the Storm, or Navigating the Crosswinds of Appropriations and Administration of the Endangered Species Act: A Play in Five Acts, 16 Tul. Envtl. L.J. 257 (2003).

Robert V. Percival, Presidential Management of the Administrative State: The Not-So-Unitary Executive, 51 Duke L.J. 963 (2001).

Robert V. Percival, Who's in Charge? Does the President Have Directive Authority over Agency Regulation Decisions?, 79 Fordham L. Rev. 2487 (2011).

Richard J. Pierce, Jr., What Should We Do about Administrative Law Judge Disability Decisionmaking? 26 (George Washington U. Law Sch. Public Law & Legal Theory Paper, Paper No. 573, 2011), *available at* http://ssrn.com/abstract=1890770.

Richard J. Pierce, Jr., Political Control Versus Impermissible Bias in Agency Decisionmaking: Lessons from Chevron and Mistretta, 57 U. Chi. L. Rev. 481 (1990).

Richard J. Pierce, Jr., Saving the Unitary Executive Theory from Those Who Would Distort and Abuse It: A Review of The Unitary Executive by Steven G. Calabresi and Christopher S. Yoo, 12 U. Pa. J. Const. L. 593 (2010).

Richard Pildes, Free Enterprise Fund, Boundary-Enforcing Decisions, and the Unitary Executive Branch Theory of Government Administration, 6 Duke J. Const. L. & Pub. Pol'y 1 (2010).

Richard H. Pildes, Separation of Powers, Independent Agencies, and Financial Regulation: The Case of the Sarbanes-Oxley Act, 5 N.Y.U. J. L. & Bus. 485 (2009).

Richard H. Pildes & Cass R. Sunstein, Reinventing the Regulatory State, 62 U. Chi. L. Rev. 1 (1995).

Jason Pinny, Note, The Federal Energy Regulatory Commission and Environmental Justice: Do the National Environmental Policy Act and the Clean Air Act Offer a Better Way?, 30 B.C. Envtl. Aff. L. Rev. 353 (2003).

Saikrishna Prakash, Removal and Tenure in Office, 92 Va. L. Rev. 1779 (2006).

Saikrishna Bangalore Prakash, Imperial and Imperiled: The Curious State of the Executive, 50 Wm. & Mary L. Rev. 1021 (2008).

Polly J. Price, Federalization of the Mosquito: Structural Innovation in the New Deal Administrative State, 60 Emory L.J. 325 (2010).

Roy Pulsifer, Introduction, 41 J. Air L. & Com. 573, 575 (1975).

Jonathan D. Puvak, Note, Executive Branch Czars, Who Are They? Are They Needed? Can Congress Do Anything about Them?, 19 Wm. & Mary Bill of Rts.J. 1091 (2011).

Steven M. Pyser, Recess Appointments to the Federal Judiciary: An Unconstitutional Transformation of Senate Advice and Consent, 8 U. Pa. Const. L. 61 (2006).

Kevin M. Quinn, The Academic Study of Decision Making on Multimember Courts, 100 Cal. L. Rev. 1493 (2012).

Steven A. Ramirez, Depoliticizing Financial Regulation, 41 Wm. & Mary L. Rev. 503 (2000).

Neomi Rao, A Modest Proposal: Abolishing Agency Independence in Free Enterprise Fund v. PCAOB, 79 Fordham L. Rev. 2541 (2011).

Jamie B. Raskin, "A Complicated and Indirect Encroachment": Is the Federal Election Commission Unconstitutionally Composed?, 52 Admin L. Rev. 609 (2000).

Laura Krugman Ray, From Prerogative to Accountability: The Amenability of the President to Suit, 80 Ky. L.J. 739 (1991–92).

Recent Legislation, Dodd-Frank Act, Pub. L. No. 111-203, 124 Stat. 1376 (2010), 124 Harv. L. Rev. 2123 (2011).

Robert J. Reinstein, The Limits of Executive Power, 59 Am. U. L. Rev. 259 (2009).

David Reiss, Fannie Mae and Freddie Mac and the Future of Federal Housing Finance Policy: A Study of Regulatory Privilege, 61 Ala. L. Rev. 907 (2010).

Doris Rubinstein Reiss, The Benefits of Capture, 47 Wake Forest L. Rev. 569 (2012).

Michael Rich, Prosecutorial Indiscretion: Encouraging the Department of Justice to Rein in Out-of-Control Qui Tam Litigation Under the Civil False Claims Act, 76 U. Cin. L. Rev. 1233 (2008).

David B. Rivkin, Jr., The Unitary Executive and Presidential Control of Executive Branch Rulemaking, 7 Admin. L.J. Am. U. 309 (1993).

Glen O. Robinson, Independent Agencies: Form and Substance in Executive Prerogative, Duke L.J. 238 (1988).

Morton Rosenberg, Congress's Prerogative over Agencies and Agency Decision Makers: The Rise and Demise of the Reagan Administration's Theory of the Unitary Executive, 57 Geo. Wash. L. Rev. 627 (1988–89).

Morton Rosenberg, Presidential Control of Agency Rulemaking, An Analysis of Constitutional Issues That May Be Raised by Executive Order 12,291, 23 Ariz. L. Rev. 1200 (1981).

Victor Rosenblum, in Lloyd N. Cutler, Moderator, Managing the Regulatory Process, 32 Admin L. Rev. 239, 261 (1980).

Steven R. Ross, Raphael A. Prober & Gabriel K. Gilbert, *The Rise and Permanence of Quasi-Legislative Independent Commissions*, 27 J.L. & Pol. 415 (2012).

Jim Rossi, The Electric Deregulation Fiasco: Looking to Regulatory Federalism to Promote a Balance Between Market and the Provision of Public Goods, 100 Mich. L. Rev. 1768 (2002).

Mark J. Rozell & Mitchel A. Sollenberger, Executive Privilege: The Bush Record and Legacy, in Testing the Limits: George W. Bush and the Imperial Presidency 199–218 (Mark J. Rozell & Gleaves Whitney eds., 2009).

Edward Rubin, Hyperdepoliticization, 48 Wake Forest L. Rev. 631 (2012).

J. B. Ruhl & James Salzman, In Defense of Regulatory Peer Review, 84 Wash. U. L. Rev. 1 (2006).

Aaron J. Saiger, Obama's "Czars" for Domestic Policy and the Law of the White House Staff, 79 Fordham L. Rev. 2577 (2011).

Lester M. Salamon, The New Governance and the Tools of Public Action: An Introduction, 28 Fordham Urb. L.J. 1611 (2001).

Tuan Samahon, Are Bankruptcy Judges Unconstitutional? An Appointments Clause Challenge, 60 Hastings L.J. 233 (2008).

Jeffery M. Samuels & Linda B. Samuels, *The Trademark Office as a Government Corporation*, 7 Fordham Intell. Prop. Media & Ent. L.J. 137 (1996).

Thomas O. Sargentich, The Contemporary Debate About Legislative-Executive Separation of Powers, 71 Cornell L. Rev. 430 (1987).

Thomas O. Sargentich, The Emphasis on the Presidency in U.S. Public Law: An Essay Critiquing Presidential Administration, 59 Admin. L. Rev. 1 (2007).

Frederick Schauer, On the Supposed Jury-Dependence of Evidence Law, 155 U. Pa. L. Rev. 165 (2006).

Seymour Scher, The Congressional Committee Members as Independent Agency Overseers, 34 Am. Pol. Sc. Rev. 911 (1960).

Miroslava Scholten, Independent, Hence Unaccountable? The Need for a Broader Debate on Accountability of the Executive, 4 Rev. of Eur. Admin. L. 5 (2011).

Heidi Mandanis Schooner, The Role of Central Banks in Bank Supervision in the United States and the United Kingdom, 28 Brook. J. Int'l L. 435 (2003).

Steven L. Schooner, Contractor Atrocities at Abu Ghraib: Compromised Accountability in a Streamlined, Outsourced Government, 16 Stan. L. & Pol'y Rev. 549 (2005).

Peter H. Schuck, Professor Rabin and the Administrative State, 61 DePaul L. Rev. 595 (2012).

Bernard Schwartz, An Administrative Law "Might Have Been"—Chief Justice Burger's Bowsher v. Synar Draft, 42 Admin. L. Rev. 221 (1990).

Mark Seidenfeld, A Big Picture Approach to Presidential Influence on Agency Policy-Making, 80 Iowa L. Rev. 1 (1994).

Miriam Seifter, Rent-a-Regulator, in Government by Contract (Jody Freeman & Martha Minow eds., 2009).

Miriam Seifter, Comment, Rent-a-Regulator: Design and Innovation in Privatized Governmental Decision-Making, 33 Ecology L. Q. 1091 (2006).

Adam Shajnfeld, An Identity in Disarray: The Federal Deposit Insurance Corporation's Government-Agency Status, 128 Banking L.J. 36 (2011).

Peter M. Shane, Independent Policymaking and Presidential Power: A Constitutional Analysis, 57 Geo. Wash. L. Rev. 596 (1989).

Peter M. Shane, Presidential Regulatory Oversight and the Separation of Power: The Constitutionality of Executive Order No. 12, 291, 23 Ariz. L. Rev. 1235 (1981).

Peter Shane, The Separation of Powers and the Rule of Law: The Virtues of the "Seeing the Trees," 30 Wm. & Mary L. Rev. 375 (1989).

Martin Shapiro, Independent Agencies: US and EU 20 (Jean Monet Chair Papers No. 34, Robert Schuman Centre, European Univ. Inst., 1996).

Sidney A. Shapiro, A Delegation Theory of the APA, 10 Admin. L.J. Am. U. 89 (1996).

Sidney A. Shapiro, Outsourcing Government Regulation, 53 Duke L.J. 389 (2003).

George B. Shepherd, Fierce Compromise: The Administrative Procedure Act Emerges from New Deal Politics, 90 Nw. U. L. Rev. 1557 (1996).

Kevin Sholette, The American Czars, 20 Cornell J. L. & Pub. Pol'y 219 (2010).

J. Gregory Sidak, The Recommendation Clause, 77 Geo. L.J. 2079, 2080 (1989).

Jonathan R. Siegel, Suing the President: Nonstatutory Review Revisited, 97 Colum. L. Rev. 1612 (1997).

Signing Statements and Executive Power, 23 Const. Comment. 307 (2006).

Jason M. Solomon, Law and Government in the 21st Century Regulatory State, 86 Tex. L. Rev. 819 (2008).

David B. Spence & Frank Cross, A Public Choice Case for the Administrative State, 89 Geo. L.J. 97 (2000).

Kevin M. Stack, The Statutory President, 90 Iowa L. Rev. 539 (2005).

Kelsey Elizabeth Stapler, The Auditor for the Auditors' Auditor: Accounting for the Unitary Executive in Free Enterprise Fund v. Public Company Accounting Oversight Board, 38 Pepp. L. Rev. 709 (2011).

Glen Staszewski, Textualism and the Executive Branch, Mich. St. L. Rev. 143 (2009).

Charles N. Steele & Jeffrey H. Bowman, The Constitutionality of Independent Regulatory Agencies Under the Necessary and Proper Clause: The Case of the Federal Election Commission, 4 Yale J. on Reg. 363 (1987).

Michael Ashley Stein, Book Review: Hardball, Politics and the NLRB, 22 Berkeley J. Emp. & Lab. L. 507 (2001).

Rena Steinzor, The Independent Regulatory Analysis Act as Critiqued by Co-sponsor Susan Collins and Me, Center for Progressive Reform Blog (Aug. 1, 2012), *available at* www.progressivereform/CPRBlog.cfm?idBlog=E42958C4-B61A-8FDA-62ACBF689F7D0313.

Dru Stevenson, Privatization of Welfare Services: Delegation by Commercial Contract, 45 Ariz. L. Rev. 83 (2003).

Richard B. Stewart, Courts, Institutions and Access to Justice: Legitimacy and Accountability in Global Regulatory Governance Global Administrative Law and Developing Countries, 1 Jindal Global L. Rev. 41 (2009).

Richard B. Stewart, The Reformation of American Administrative Law, 88 Harv. L. Rev. 1669 (1975).

George J. Stigler, The Theory of Economic Regulation, 2 Bell. J. Econ. & Mgmt. Sci. (1971).

Peter L. Strauss, Formal and Functional Approaches to Separation-of-Powers Questions—A Foolish Inconsistency? 72 Cornell L. Rev. 488 (1987).

Peter L. Strauss, On the Difficulties of Generalization: PCAOB in the Footsteps of Myers, Humphrey's Executor, Morrison, and Freytag, 32 Cardozo L. Rev. 2255 (2011).

Peter L. Strauss, Overseer, or "The Decider?" The President in Administrative Law, 75 Geo. Wash. L. Rev. 696 (2007).

Peter L. Strauss, The Place of Agencies in Government: Separation of Powers and the Fourth Branch, 84 Colum. L. Rev. 573 (1984).

Peter L. Strauss, Private Standards Organizations and Public Law, Columbia Public Law Research Paper, Apr. 2, 2013 (2012), *available at* http://papers.ssrn.com/s013/papers.cfm?abstract_id=2194210.

Peter Strauss, The Purposes and Limits of Independent Agencies, 1988 Duke L.J. 257, 274–75 (1988).

Cass R. Sunstein, Administrative Substance, Duke L.J. 607 (1991).

Cass R. Sunstein, The Office of Information and Regulatory Affairs: Myths and Realities, 126 Harv. L. Rev. 1838 (2013).

Survey, Constitutional Challenges to Independent Agency Enforcement Action, 2 Admin. L.J. 423 (1988).

Symposium, The Independence of Independent Agencies, Duke L.J. 215 (1988).

Alane Tempchin, Fall from Grace: Federal Election Commission v. NRA Political Victory Fund and the Demise of the FEC's Independent Litigating Authority, 10 Admin. L.J. Am. U. 385 (1996).

Benjamin A. Templin, The Government Shareholder: Regulating Public Ownership of Private Enterprise, 62 Admin. L. Rev. 1127 (2010).

Charles W. Thomas, Resolving the Problem of Qualified Immunity for Private Defendants in Section 1983 and Bivens Damage Suits, 53 La. L. Rev. 449 (1992).

Charles Tiefer, The Constitutionality of Independent Officers as Checks on Abuses of Executive Power, 63 B.U. L. Rev. 59 (1983).

Seth Barrett Tillman, Citizens United and the Scope of Professor Teachout's Anti-corruption Principle, 107 Nw. U. L. Rev. 399 (2012).

Seth Barrett Tillman, Why Our Next President May Keep His or Her Senate Seat: A Conjecture on the Constitution's Incompatibility Clause, 4 Duke J. Const. L. & Pub. Pol'y 107 (2009).

Jim Tozzi, OIRA's Formative Years: The Historical Record of Centralizing Regulatory Review Preceding OIRA's Founding, 63 Admin. L. Rev. 37 (2011).

Christian Turner, State Action Problems, 65 Fla. L. Rev. 281 (2013).

Ronald Turner, Ideological Voting on the National Labor Relations Board, 8 U. Pa. J. Lab. & Emp. L. 707 (2006).

Mark Tushnet, Administrative Law in the 1930s: The Supreme Court's Accommodation of Progressive Legal Theory, 60 Duke L.J. 1565 (2011).

William W. Van Alstyne, A Critical Guide to Marbury v. Madison, 1 Duke L.J. 1 (1969).

Jeff Van Dam, The Kill Switch: The New Battle over Presidential Recess Appointments, 107 Nw. U. L. Rev. 361 (2012).

Paul R. Verkuil, Jawboning Administrative Agencies: Ex Parte Contacts by the White House, 80 Colum. L. Rev. 943 (1980).

Paul R. Verkuil, Public Law Limitations on Privatization of Government Functions, 84 N.C. L. Rev. 397 (2006).

Paul R. Verkuil, The Purposes and Limits of Independent Agencies, Duke L.J. 257 (1988).

Paul R. Verkuil, The Status of Independent Agencies After Bowsher v. Synar, Duke L.J. 779 (1986).

Paul R. Verkuil & Jeffrey S. Lubbers, Alternative Approaches to Judicial Review of Social Security Disability Cases, 55 Admin. L. Rev. 730 (2003).

Adrian Vermeule, Conventions of Agency Independence, 113 Colum. L. Rev. 1163 (2013).

Alexander Volokh, The New Private-Regulation Skepticism, 37 Harv. J.L. & Pub. Pol'y 931 (2014).

Patricia M. Wald, Judicial Review in Midpassage: The Uneasy Partnership Between Courts and Agencies Plays On, 32 Tulsa L.J. 221 (1996).

Dennis P. Walsh, Procedural Barriers That Prevent the NLRB from Resolving Major Workers Rights Issues, 15 Emp. Rts. & Emp. Pol'y J. 545 (2011).

Charles Warren, Presidential Declarations of Independence, 10 B.U. L. Rev. 1 (1930).

Elizabeth Warren, Unsafe at Any Rate, DemocracyJournal.Org, Summer 2007, at 8, *available at* http://www.democracyjournal.org/pdf/5/Warren.pdf.

David C. Weiss, The International Boundary Commission, Treaty Interpretation and the President's Removal Power, 41 Loy. U. Chi. L.J. 39 (2009).

David C. Weiss, Nothing Improper? Examining Constitutional Limits, Congressional Action, Partisan Motivation, and Pretextual Justification in the U.S. Attorney Removals, 107 Mich. L. Rev. 317 (2008).

Keith Werhan, Delegalizing Administrative Law, [1996] U. Ill. L. Rev. 423.

Daniel P. Westman, The Significance of Sarbanes-Oxley Whistleblower Provisions, 21 Lab. Law. 141 (2005).

James O. Wettereau, New Light on the First Bank of the United States, 61 Pa. Magazine of History and Biography 263 (1937).

Burton K. Wheeler, The Federal Power Commission as an Agency of Congress, 14 Geo. Wash. L. Rev. 1 (1945).

Leonard D. White, The Origin of Utility Commissions in Massachusetts, 29 J. Pol. Econ. 177 (1921).

Kenneth Williams, Gays in the Military: The Legal Issues, 28 U.S.F. L. Rev. 919 (1994).

Oliver Williamson, Public and Private Bureaucracies: A Transaction Cost Economics Perspective, 15 J. L. Econ. & Org. 306 (1998).

Woodrow Wilson, Democracy and Efficiency, 87 Atl. Monthly 289 (1901).

Woodrow Wilson, The Study of Administration, 2 Pol. Sci. Q. 197 (1887).

Marc Winerman, The Origins of the FTC: Concentration, Cooperation, Control, and Competition, 71 Antitrust L.J. 1 (1922).

Tyler R. T. Wolf, Existing in a Legal Limbo: The Precarious Legal Position of Standards-Development Organizations, 65 Wash. & Lee L. Rev. 807 (2008).

B. Dan Wood & Richard W. Waterman, The Dynamics of Political Control of the Bureaucracy, 85 Amer. Pol. Sci. Rev. 801 (1991).

Ann Woolhandler, Judicial Deference to Administrative Action—A Revisionist History, 43 Admin. L. Rev. 197 (1991).

Christopher S. Yoo, Stephen G. Calabresi & Anthony J. Colangelo, The Unitary Executive in the Modern Era, 1945–2000, 90 Iowa L. Rev. 601 (2005).

Christopher S. Yoo, Steven G. Calabresi & Lawrence D. Nee, The Unitary Executive During the Third Half-Century, 1889–1945, 80 Notre Dame L. Rev. 1 (2004).

MONOGRAPHS AND REPORTS

Ryan Patrick Alford, Not Even Wrong: The Use of British Constitutional History to Defend the Vesting Clause Thesis (Oct. 27, 2012) (unpublished manuscript), *available at* http://papers.ssrn.com/sol13/papers.cfm?abstract_id=2167760.

Bruce Bimber, The Death of an Agency: Office of Technology Assessment & Budget Politics in the 104th Congress (Feb. 22, 1996).

Center for Regulatory Effectiveness, A Blueprint for OMB Review of Independent Regulation, March 2002.

Jeffrey B. Gayner, The Contract With America: Implementing New Ideas in the U.S., Heritage Foundation Report (1995).

Robert C. Hockett & Saule T. Omarova, "Private" Means to "Public" Ends: Governments as Market Actors (Cornell Law School Research Paper No. 13-84, 2013), available at http://ssrn.com/abstract=2222444.

President's Comm'n on the Accident at Three Mile Island Report, The Need for Change: The Legacy of TMI 22 (Oct. 1979), *available at* ThreeMileIsland.org, http://threemileisland.org/downloads//188.pdf.

Alexander Volokh, A New Private Regulation Doctrine?, Reason Foundation (Aug. 1, 2013), *available at* http:reason.org/news/show/private-delegation-doctine-amtrak.

Peter J. Wallison, Alex J. Pollock & Edward J. Pinto, Taking the Government out of Housing Finance: Principles for Reforming the Housing Finance Market, American Enterprise Institute Policy White Paper, Mar. 24, 2011, *available at* http://www.aei.org/files/2011/03/23/AEI-White-Paper-FINAL-3-22-11.pdf.

MEDIA ARTICLES

Bruce Ackerman, Recess Appointments: Release the Legal Advice, Wall Street Journal, Jan. 11, 2012, at A13.

Andrew Ackerman, Scott Patterson & Jacob Bunge, Policing of Exchanges Questioned, Wall St. J., Oct. 2, 2013.

The Administration: Man in the Storm, Time, June 30, 1958, *available at* http://www.time.com/time/magazine/article/0,9171,891889,00.html.

Karen Alexander, Gould Goes Out Gunning, Legal Times, July 13, 1998, at 1.

Allday Tells President April 12 Is His Last Day at FERC, Energy Daily, Mar. 2, 1993, at 4.

Binyamin Appelbaum, Former Ohio Attorney General to Head New Consumer Agency, N.Y. Times, July 18, 2011, at B1.

Matt Apuzzo, Trying to Salvage Remains of Blackwater Case, N.Y. Times, May 12, 2014, at A1.

Army Bill Passes; Vote is 349 to 25—Hay Admits Carson Joker, N.Y. Times, May 21, 1916.

Deborah Avant, Think Again: Mercenaries, Foreign Policy, Jul. 1, 2004, http://www.foreign-policy.com/story/cms.php?story_id=2577&print=1.

Matthew Barakat, Another Name Change for Former Blackwater Firm, Businessweek.com (Dec. 12, 2011), *available at* http: businessweek.com/ap/financialnews/D9RJ62780.htm.

Robert Barnes, Harvard Dean, Chosen as Solicitor General, Goes Before Senators, Wash. Post, Feb. 10, 2009, A4.

Stephen Barr, Administration Opposes Bill on Inspector General, Wash. Post, Oct. 2, 2007, at D4.

William M. Blair, Adams Concedes Calling Agencies; Denies Pressure, N.Y. Times, June 13, 1958.

William M. Blair, Goldfine Case Toppled Adams, N.Y. Times, Sept. 23, 1958, at 19.

William M. Blair, Inquiry Indicates that Goldfine Got Agencies' Favors, N.Y. Times, July 12, 1958.

Josh Boak, Bureau Can Open Without Chief, Politico, June 17, 2011, at 4.

David S. Broder, Rebels Without a Pause, Wash. Post Mag., Dec. 31, 1995, at 13.

John Broder, Obama Administration Abandons Stricter Air Quality Standards, N.Y. Times, Sept. 2, 2011, *available at* http://www.nytimes.com/2011/09/03/science/earth/03air.html?_r=1&.

Brooksley Born, Self-Funding of Regulators Would Help Fiscal Mess, Politico, Mar. 10, 2013.

Merrill Brown, Agencies Reject Pleas for OMB Review, Wash. Post, July 9, 1981, at D9.

Bush Issues Signing Statement on Measure to Reform System of Inspector General, Legal News, Oct. 21, 2008.

Sewell Chan, Consumer Advocate to Lead New Watchdog Agency as Assistant to Obama, N.Y. Times, Sept. 16, 2010, at B3.

Sewell Chan, Dodd Proposes Financial Protection Agency, N.Y. Times, February 27, 2010, at B6.

Changes at the Top for the F.B.I, N.Y. Times, July 21, 1993, at A16.

Gina Chon, Fannie and Freddie Fall Amid Senate Reform Push, Financial Times, Mar. 11, 2014, at 11.

Charles S. Clark, Congress Revs Up Resistance to a New BRAC Round, Government Executive, May 29, 2013.

Helene Cooper & Jennifer Steinhauer, Bucking Senate, Obama Appoints Consumer Chief, N.Y. Times, Jan. 5, 2012, at A1.

Richard Corbett, Ireland Has a Diplomatic Victory but the Real Winner Is Europe, euobserver.com, Dec. 12, 2008, 5:17 p.m., http://euobserver.com/opinion/27296.

Court Weighs Contested Obama Recess Appointments, Wall St. J., Dec. 5, 2012, http://online.wsj.com/article/SB10001424127887324640104578161631830451910.html?mod=googlenews_wsj.

John H. Cushman, Jr., Senate Stops Consumer Nominee, N.Y. Times, Dec. 9, 2011, G1.

Steven Davidoff, The Subtle Takeover, NYTimes.com, Sept. 8, 2008, 7:40 a.m., http://dealbook.nytimes.com/2008/09/08/the-subtle-takeover/?scp=3&sq=FHFA&st=nyt.

Kate Davidson, Republicans Promise to Block Cordray Nomination—Again, Politico (Feb. 1, 2013).

David Dayen, Why Ed DeMarco Won't Be Fired, FDL Newsdesk, Aug. 1, 2012, http://news.firedoglake.com/2012/08/01/why-ed-demarco-wont-be-fired/.

Brady Dennis, Capitol Hill Divided on Obama Plan to Bypass Approval for Elizabeth Warren, Wash. Post, Sept. 17, 2010, at A14.

Brady Dennis, Warren Expected to Be Adviser, Wash. Post, Sept. 16, 2010, at A18.

Stephen Dinan, Czar War Escalates Between Congress, White, Wash. Times, Oct. 23, 2009, at A1, A3.

Stephen Dinan, Senators Join Suits on Recess Appointments, Wash. Times, Feb. 3, 2012, at A4.

DOJ Memo on Jurisdiction over Independent Agencies, Legal Times, July 27, 1981, at 24.

Danielle Douglas, Senate Confirms Cordray to Head Consumer Financial Protection Bureau, Wash. Post (July 16, 2013).

Editorial, Contempt for the Constitution, Wall St. J., Jan. 13, 2012, at A12.

Editorial, The Infinitesimal Recess, N.Y. Times, December 8, 1903, *available at* http://query.nytimes.com/gst/abstract.html?res=F40911FD3E5B11738DDDA10894DA415B838CF1D3.

Editorial, Overreach on Oversight, Wash. Post, Aug. 22, 2011, at A14.

Editorial, Transparently Destructive: The House's Financial Reform Bill Includes an Assault on the Fed's Independence, Wash. Post, Dec. 19, 2009, at A16.

Juliet Eilperin, Obama Halts Tighter Rules on Ozone Emissions, Wash. Post, Sept. 3, 2011, at A1.

Jesse Eisinger, The Volcker Rule, Made Bloated and Weak, N.Y. Times Dealbook (Feb. 22, 2012, 12:04 p.m.), http://dealbook.nytimes.com/2012/02/22/the-volcker-rule-made-bloated-and-weak/.

David Ellis, U.S. Seizes Fannie and Freddie, CNNmoney.com, September 7, 2008

Aaron Epstein, Controversy Seethes as Prosecutor Leaves, Hous. Chronicle, Apr. 3, 1993, at A8.

FERC Restructuring Plan Is Unveiled: Johnston, Dingell Unimpressed, Inside F.E.R.C., Mar. 4, 1991, at 1.

FERC Restructuring Takes Back Seat as Senate Energy Markup Begins, Inside F.E.R.C., Apr. 22, 1991, at 1.

Zachary A. Goldfarb, Hit by Huge Loss, Fannie Mae seeks more federal aid, Wash. Post, Nov. 6, 2009, http://www.washingtonpost.com/wp-dyn/content/article/2009/11/05/AR2009110505223.html.

Mark Gongloff, Senate Delays Vote on Bill That Would Banish Financial Regulation to Cost-Benefit Analysis Hell, Huffington Post, Nov. 14, 2012.

Alberto R. Gonzales, They Lost My Confidence, USA Today, Mar. 7, 2007.

Robert Gordon & Mary Orndorff, Martin to Resign Post on Friday, Birmingham News, June 17, 2009, at 1.

Phil Gramm & Peter Wallison, Worse Than Fannie and Freddie, Wall St. J. , April 17, 2014, at A15.

Jenna Greene, Five Cooks in Volcker Kitchen, Nat'l L. J., Feb. 10, 2014.

James V. Grimaldi & Alicia Mundy, Big Payday for "Toxic" Work—Outside Law Firms for U.S. Regulator to Net Quarter of Credit-Union, Wall St. J., Oct. 25, 2012, at C1.

Guy Gugliotta, Chemical Hazards Board and Chief a Volatile Mix, Wash. Post, Nov. 24, 1999, at A21.

Guy Gugliotta, Hill Quits as CEO of Chemical Investigation Board, Wash. Post, Dec. 18, 1999, at A15.

Ray Gustini, Senate Votes Unanimously to Keep Robert Mueller as FBI Director, National Journal, July 27, 2011.

Robert W. Hahn, Regulatory Reform—The Whole Story, Wall St. J., Feb. 27, 1995, at A12.

Doug Halonen, Ness Closer to Confirmation: FCC Commissioner's Campaign Nears End, Electronic Media, Mar. 27, 2000.

David Hirschmann, The CFPB Needs More Accountability, Politico, Dec. 8, 2011, at 38.

Jessica Holser, House Panel Targets Consumer Bureau, SEC Budgets, Wall St. J., June 23, 2011, http://online.wsj.com/news/articles/SB10001424052702302303339904576404102094921400.

Mary Jacoby, Foes of Bureaucracy Learn a Tough Lesson, Chi. Trib., June 16, 1996, at C1.

Suzy Jagger & Roland Watson, Labour's Parting Shot to New Treasury Team, Times (London), May 18, 2010.

Carrie Johnson, Crisis Poses Big Test for Markets' Regulator, Wash. Post, Sept. 19, 2008, at D1.

Kevin Johnson, Obama to Pick New FBI Director in Second Term, USA Today, Nov. 9, 2012, http://www.usatoday.com/story/news/politics/2012/11/08/filling-fbi-chiefs-slot-also-on-list-for-2nd-term/1693277/.

Robert G. Kaiser, How a Crusade to Protect Consumers Lost Its Steam, Wash. Post, Jan. 31, 2010 at G1.

Paul Kane, Deal at Hand on Nominees, Roll Call, June 20, 2002.

Paul Kane, Reid, Democrats Trigger "Nuclear" Option; Eliminate Most Filibusters on Nominees, Wash. Post, Nov. 22, 1013, at A1.

Paul Kane & Ed O'Keefe, Boehner Attacks Tea Party Groups as House Approved Budget Deal, Wash. Post., Dec. 12, 2013.

Key Players in the CIA Leak Investigation, Wash. Post, July 3, 2007, http://www.washingtonpost.com/wp-srv/politics/special/plame/Plame_KeyPlayers.html.

Ezra Klein, The Reason for Obama's Recess Appointments, Wash. Post, Jan. 6, 2012, at A2.

Charles Krauthammer, The Imperial Presidency Revisited, Washington Post Writers Group, July 5, 2912, 2012 WLNR 20308904.

Marianne Lavelle, Public Works Go Private, National Law Journal, Sept. 25, 1995, at 13.

Neil A. Lewis, Libby Guilty of Lying in C.I.A. Leak Case, N.Y. Times, Mar. 7, 2007.

Eric Licthblau & Scott Shane, Attorney General Held Firm on War Policies, N.Y. Times, Aug. 28, 2008.

Paul Light, Nominate and Wait, N.Y. Times, Mar. 24, 2009, at A27.

Adam Liptak, For Federal Prosecutors, Politics Is Ever-Present, N.Y. Times, Mar. 18 2007, http://www.nytimes.com/2007/03/18/weekinrevier/18liptak.html?_r=0.

Lockheed Martin Gets Approval to Complete Acquisition of Comsat, Wall St. J., Aug. 1, 2000, at B2.

Peter Loy, The Volcker Rule Is Tough. It's Complicated. Will It Be Effective? Bloomberg Business Week (Dec. 12, 2013).

Kim Masters, Legal Support for Strategy on "Independents" Revealed, Legal Times, July 20, 1981, at 1

Christopher Matthews, Congressmen Accuse Fannie and Freddie Boss of Ideological Bias, Time, May 7, 2012, http://business.time.com/2012/05/07/congressmen-accuse-fannie-and-freddie-boss-of-ideological-bias/.

Mark Mazzetti, Outsiders Hired as C.I.A. Planned to Kill Jihadists, N.Y. Times, Aug. 20, 2009, at A1.

Colman McCarthy, Mourning an Agency Mugged by Congress, Wash. Post, Nov.7, 1995, 1995 WLNR 5931474.

Michael McConnell, Democrats and Executive Overreach, Wall St. J., Jan. 10, 2012, at A13.

Stephanie McCrummen, Feeling Besieged, Tea Party Groups Steel for Battle, Wash. Post, Dec. 18, 2013, at A1.

James H. McGrew, Let's Streamline, Not Abolish FERC, Pub. Util. Fortnightly, June 15, 1992, at 12.

Andy Medici, Lawmakers Divided on Possible 2017 BRAC Round, Army Times (March 3, 2014).

Michael A. Memoli, In Obama Win, Senate Reaches Filibuster Deal, L.A. Times, July 17, 2013.

Doug Miller, Blackwater Settles Nisoor Square Lawsuit, Charlotte Observer, Jan. 6, 2012, *available at* http://charlotteobserver.com/2012/01/06/2904465/blackwater-settles-with-families.html#storylink-cpy.

Barbara S. Mishkin, Agency Review Bill Opposed by CFPB, Federal Banking Regulators and Consumer Groups, CFPB Monitor, Nov. 1, 2012, http://www.cfpbmonitor.com/2012/11/01/agency-review-bill-opposed-by-cfpb-federal-banking-regulatory-and-consumer-groups/.

Chris Morran, Washington Already Considering Ways to Ruin Consumer Financial Protection Bureau, Consumerist, May 3, 2011, 11:45 a.m., http://consumerist.com/2011/05/washington-already-considering-ways-to-ruin-consumer-financial-protection-bureau.html.

David Nakamura & Felicia Sonmez, Obama Defies Senate, Puts Cordray in Consumer Post, Wash. Post, Jan. 5, 2012, at A1.

Nathaniel C. Nash, Freddie Mac Clears Stock Sale, N.Y. Times, July 14, 1988, *available at* http://www.nytimes.com/1988/07/14/business/freddie-mac-clears-stock-sale.html.

New York Stock Exchange, Who We Are, http://www.nyx.com/who-we-are/history/new-york.

Joe Nocera, Don't Kill Fannie Mae, N.Y. Times, Aug. 13, 2013, at A23.

Robert D. Novak, Mission to Niger, Wash. Post, July 14, 2003, at A31.

Barack Obama, Toward a 21st-Century Regulatory System, Wall St. J., Jan. 18, 2011, at A17.

Obama Plans to Renominate GOP Nuclear Regulator, Wash. Post, Apr. 30, 2012, at A14.

Obama Regulations Chief Pressed Attacks on Ozone Standards, The Hill, Aug. 8, 2012, http://thehill.com/blogs/e2-wire/e2-wire/242667-obama-regs-chief-pressed-attacks-on-ozone-standards.

Obama Signs 2-Year Extension to Mueller's FBI Tenure, CNN Wire, July 26, 2011, http://www.cnn.com/2011/POLITICS/07/26/obama.mueller.term/index.html.

Ed O'Keefe & Paul Kane, Senate Confirms Patricia Millett, Mel Watt Using New Majority Rules, Wash. Post, Dec. 10, 2013.

Scott Patterson, Shayanti Raice & Katy Burne, U.S. Starts New Era in Bank Regulation, Wall St. J. (Dec. 2013) at A1.

Robert Pear, Senate Republicans Announce Plan to Support Challenge to Recess Appointments, N.Y. Times Blogs (The Caucus), Apr. 17, 2012, http://thecaucus.blogs.nytimes.com/2012/04/17/senate-republicans-announce-plan-to-support-challenge-to-recess-appointments/

Walter Pincus, For Pentagon, It's Always a Tough Battle to Get Congress to Close Military Bases, Wash. Post, Mar. 17, 2014.

Walter Pincus, Senate Votes for New DOE Nuclear Weapons Agency, Wash. Post, July 22, 1999, at A6.

Brad Plumer & Ezra Klein, The Most Powerful Man in Housing Policy, Wash. Post, Aug. 31, 2011, 3:55 p.m., http://www.washingtonpost.com/blogs/ezra-klein/post/the-most-powerful-man-in-housing-policy/2011/08/25/gIQAouktrJ_blog.html.

Privatized War, and Its Price, N. Y. Times, Jan. 11, 2010, at A16.

Manu Raju, Democrats Join Job Czar War, Politico, Sept. 17, 2009.

Jamie Reese, Blackwater Settles Last Lawsuit in 2007-Baghdad Shooting Incident, Jurist (Jan. 9. 2012).

Reese Taylor Moves to Halt Trucking Industry Deregulation, Wall St. J., Aug. 5, 1981, at 50.

Spencer Rich, Independent Agency for Social Security Approved by Senate, Wash. Post, Mar. 3, 1994, at A06, *available at* http://web2.westlaw.com/find/default.wl?rs=WLW11.07&rp=%2ffind%2fdefault.wl&vr=2.0&fn=_top&mt=Westlaw&cite=1994+WLNR+892834&sv=Split.

Deb Richmann, Pension Agency Faces Huge Shortfall: $33 Billion Deficit Could Force Bailout, Pittsburgh Post-Gazette, May 20, 2009, at A6.

David Rogers, GOP Steps Up Efforts to Cut Funding for U.S. Agencies Opposed by Its Allies, Wall St. J., July 13, 1995, at A12.

Charlie Savage, Justice Dept. Defends Obama Recess Appointments, N.Y. Times, Jan. 13, 2012, at A12

Charlie Savage, Republicans Hold Up Vote on Extension of F.B.I. Term, N.Y. Times, July 16, 2011, at A13.

Charlie Savage, Shift on Executive Power Lets Obama Bypass Rivals, N.Y. Times, Apr. 23, 2012, at Al.

A Scandal That Keeps Growing, N.Y. Times, May 6, 2007.

Peter Schroeder, GOP Targets Funding of Consumer Bureau, The Hill, June 15, 2011, http://thehill.com/blogs/on-the-money/appropriations/166531-gop-sets-sights-on-consumer-bureau-in-latest-approps-bill.

Peter Schroeder, Republican Lawmakers Begin Pushback Against Obama Recess Appointments, The Hill (Jan. 30, 2012,), http://thehill.com/blogs/on-the-money/other/104316-republican-lawmakers-begin-pushback-against-obama -recess-appointments.

Dean Scott, Board Acts Without Chairman, Calls for Justice Department to Settle Rift, 23 Chem. Reg. Rep. (BNA) 1358, Nov. 26, 1999.

Dean Scott, Hazard Investigation Board Members Seek Meeting to Discuss Role in Budget Policy, 23 Chem. Reg. Rep. (BNA) 1323 (Nov. 19, 1999).

Sean Scully, House to Vote on Bill Targeting Election Commission Attorney, Wash. Times, July 14, 1998, at A8.

Katherine Q. Seele, Often Isolated, Whitman Quits as EPA Chief, N.Y. Times, May 22, 2003.

Senate Acts on FEC Issue, Treasury Funds, Wash. Post, Sept. 4, 1998, at A7.

Senate Votes to Confirm Mueller for Two More Years, Politico, July 27, 2011, http://www.politico.com/blogs/glennthrush/0711/Senate_votes_to_confirm_Mueller_for_2_more_years.html.

Jerry Seper, Justice IG Can't Probe Panther Case Dismissal, Wash. Times, Feb. 4, 2010, at A1.

Katie Sheppard, House Votes to Block EPA Climate Regs, Mother Jones (Feb. 18, 2011), http://motherjones.com/blue-marble/2011/02/house-votes-block-epa-climate-regs.

Alexis Simendinger & Shane Harris, Please Resign, Bush Tells Political Appointees, National Journal, Dec. 8, 2008.

Deborah Solomon, Ed DeMarco Is in Line to Replace Himself, Bloomberg, Aug. 1, 2012, http://www.bloomberg.com/news/2012-08-01/ed-demarco-is-in-line-to-replace-himself.html.

Deborah Solomon & Maya Jackson-Randall, Agency Outlines Role, Wall St. J., June 24, 2011, http://onlinewsj.com/article/SB10001424052702304231204576403984131808742.htm.

Deborah Solomon & Damian Paletta, US Near Deal on Fannie, Freddie, Wall St. J., Sept. 6, 2008, at A1.

Sons of Fannie Mae, Wall St. J., April 14, 2014, at A18.

Andrew Ross Sorkin, Top Securities Lawyers Call for Self-Funded SEC, N.Y. Times Dealbook, June 11, 2010.

Greg Stohr & Bob Ivry, Fed Will Release Bank Loan Data as Top Court Rejects Appeal, Bloomberg, Mar. 21, 2011.

Gary Stolberg & Robert Pear, Mysterious Fax Adds to Intrigue over Drug Bill, N.Y. Times, Mar. 18, 2004, at A24.

James B. Stewart, As a Watchdog Starves, Wall St. Is Tossed a Bone, N.Y. Times, July 16, 2011, at A1.

Alison Stranger, Foreign Policy, Privatized, N.Y. Times, Oct. 5, 2007, at A25.

Stroke of Clinton's Pen Fells ICC—Oldest Regulatory Agency, L.A. Times, Dec. 31, 1995, at A13.

Margaret Talev, Byrd Challenges Obama on Naming of Policy Czars, Pittsburgh Post-Gazette, Feb. 28, 2009, at A9.

Mark Theodore, Oral Arguments Heard over Validity of Recess Appointments of NLRB Members, JD Supra Law News (Dec. 7, 2012), http://www.jdsupra.com/legalnews/oral-arguments-heard-over-validity-of-re-72105/

Nick Timiraos, An Accidental Housing Chief Embraces the Power of "No," Wall St. J., Aug. 31, 2011, http://online.wsj.com/article/SB10001424053111904199404576538803284685440.html?mod=googlenews_wsj.

Nick Timiraos, Plan for Mortgage Giants Takes Shape, Wall St. J., March 12, 2014, at A1.

Timm Resigns, Hits White House Staff, Aviation Wk. & Space Tech., Dec. 15, 1975, at 28.

Lawrence Tribe, Games and Gimmicks in the Senate, N.Y. Times, Jan. 6, 2012, at A25.

Theresa Tritch, Making Independent Agencies Less Independent, N.Y. Times, Nov. 6, 2012, http://takingnote.blogs.nytimes.com/2012/11/06/making-inmdependent-agencies-less-independent/.

Melanie Trottman, Federal Court Weighs Contested Obama Appointments, Wall St. J., Dec. 5, 2012.

Peter T. Tschanz, NLRB Hears Oral Argument in Noel Canning v. NLRB, Lexology, Dec. 7, 2012, www.lexology.com/library/detail.aspx?g=a590e532-c355-45d8-8c7e-fce2cc20405f.

US Security Firm Mired in Iraq Controversy Changes Its Name, Guardian (Feb. 12, 2009), *available at* http://www.guardian.co.uk/world/2009/feb/13/blackwater-changes-name-xe.

Nicholas J. Wagoner, Are Private Regulators Above the Constitution?, Circuit Splits (Jan. 11, 2012), at www.circuitsplits.com/securities-and-exchange-commission.

Matthew Wald, Split Within Nuclear Regulatory Agency, N.Y. Times, July 21, 2011, at A15.

Walpin-Gate: Obama Fires an IG, Wash. Times, June 15, 2009, at A20.

Evan Weinberger, Wall Street Reform Group Warns Against Volcker Changes, Law360 (Jan. 21, 2014, 5:55 p.m.), http://www.law360.com/articles/502769/wall-street-reform-group-warns-against-volcker-changes.

Jonathan Weisman, Appointments Challenge Senate Role, Experts Say, N.Y. Times, Jan. 8, 2012, at 19.

Jonathan Weisman & Jennifer Steinbauer, Senate Strikes Filibuster Deal, Ends Logjam on Nominees, N.Y. Times, July 17, 2013, at A1, A14.

Jordan Weissmann, Royalty Board's Right to Rule Under Attack, National Law Journal, Sept. 14, 2009, at 17.

George Will, European Union: A Coalition of Irresponsibility, Wash. Post, May 16, 2010, at A17.

Joseph Williams, Warren Shows Few Signs of Soothing Hill Critics, Politico, May 25, 2011, at 20.

Michael Wines, House Backs Independence for Social Security Agency, N.Y. Times, May 18, 1994.

Scott Wong, Senate GOP Blocks Cordray's CFPB Nomination, Politico, Dec. 9, 2011, at 3.

Edward Wyatt & Ben Protess, Foes Revise Plan to Curb New Agency, N.Y. Times, May 5, 2011, at B1.

GOVERNMENT DOCUMENTS

3 C.F.R. § 638.

12 C.F.R. § 709.2 (2006).

16 C.F.R. § 4.17.

17 C.F.R. § 200.60.

17 C.F.R. § 201.411.

29 C.F.R. § 2704.308(b).

45 C.F.R. § 16.5(a).

47 C.F.R. § 0.3(b) (2006).

47 C.F.R. § 0.3.

About the Public Company Accounting Oversight Board (PCAOB), http://pcaobus/about/pages/default.aspx.

About TVA, Tennessee Valley Authority, Aug. 31, 2012, http://www.tva.com/abouttva/index.htm.

ACUS Recommendation 88-9, Presidential Review of Agency Rulemaking, *available at* http://www.acus.gov/acus-recommendations/presidential-review-of-agency-rulemaking.

Administrative Assessment of Civil Penalties Against Federal Agencies under the Clean Air Act, 21 Op. O.L.C. 109 (1997).

Administrative Conference of the United States, Recommendation 78-4, Federal Agency Interaction with Private Standard-Setting Organizations in Health and Safety Regulation, 44 Fed. Reg. 1357 (Jan. 5, 1979).

Chester A. Arthur, Veto Message (July 2, 1884), available at BookRags, www.bookrags.com/ebooks/12754/168.html.

Application of Emoluments Clause to Part-Time Consultant for the Nuclear Regulatory Commission, 10 Op. O.L.C. 96, 98 (1986).

Authority of the Chemical Safety and Hazard Investigation Board to Delegate Power, 2002 OLC LEXIS 5 (2002).

Authority of the Nuclear Regulatory Commission to Collect Annual Charges from Federal Agencies, 15 Op. Off. Legal Counsel 74 (1991).

Authority to Organize Food Administration Grain Corporation, Exec. Order 2681 (1917).

Board of Governors, Fed. Reserve Sys., The Federal Reserve System: Its Purposes and Functions (2d ed. 1947).

Board of Governors of the Fed. Res. Sys., Annual Report 99 (1951).

Board of Governors of the Fed. Res. Sys., Annual Report: Budget Review (2010).

Bureau of Statistics, Interstate Commerce Commission Activities 1887–1937 (1937).

George H. W. Bush, Presidential Statement on Signing the National and Community Service Act of 1990, 2 Pub. Papers 1613 (Nov. 16, 1990), American Presidency Project, *available at* http://www.presidency.ucsb.edu/ws/index.php?pid=19052.

George W. Bush, Grant of Executive Clemency: A Proclamation by the President of the United States of America, July 2, 2007, *available at* http://georgewbush-whitehouse.archives.gov/news/releases/2007/07/20070702-4.html.

Jimmy Carter, Presidential Statement on Signing the U.S. International Trade Commission Appropriations Bill, 2 Pub. Papers 1479 (Aug. 18, 1977), *available at* American Presidency Project, http://www.presidency.ucsb.edu/ws/index.php?pid=7972.

Chicago-Midway Low-Fare Route Proceeding, 78 C.A.B. 454 (1978).

Vivian S. Chu, Cong. Research Serv., RL 33009, Recess Appointments: A Legal Overview (2011).

Commission on Organization of the Executive Branch of the Government, The Independent Regulatory Commissions (1949) (Hoover Commission Report).

Congressional Research Service Memorandum, The Noel Canning Decision and Recess Appointments Made from 1981–2013, February 4, 2013, *available at* http://democrats.edworkforce.house.gov/sites/democrats.edworkforce.house.gov/files/documents/112/pdf/Recess%20Appointments%201981-2013.pdf.

Consolidated Edison Co. of New York, 32 N.R.C. 218 (1990).

The Constitutional Separation of Powers Between the President and Congress, 20 Op. O.L.C. 124, 134 n.33 (1996).

Constitutionality of Nuclear Regulatory Comm'n's Imposition of Civil Penalties on the Air Force, 13 Op. O.L.C. 131 (1989).

Correctional Medical Services, Inc. et al., 2010 NLRB LEXIS 494 (2010).

Council of Europe, The Council of Europe in Brief: Who We Are, www.coe.int/aboutCOE/index.asp?page=quisammesnous&l=en.

Decision of the Comptroller General to the Equal Employment Opportunity Comm'n, No. B-167015, 1974 Com. Gen. LEXIS 2550 (1975).

Dep't of Justice, Investigation into the Removal of Nine U.S. Attorneys in 2006 53 (2008).

Division of Power and Responsibilities Between the Chairperson of the Chemical Safety and Hazard Investigation Board and the Board as a Whole, 2000 OLC LEXIS 23, June 26, 2000.

Jim Dukes, Memorandum from Jim Dukes, Assistant Director for Legislative Reference, Office of Management and Budget, to OMB Policy Officers (Feb. 20, 2001).

Education & Workforce Committee Press Release, Unconstitutional NLRB Appointment Scheme Creates Uncertainty for All Americans, February 13, 2013, *available at* http://edworkforce.house.gov/news/documentsingle.aspx?DocumentID=319892.

Enforcement Jurisdiction of the Special Counsel for Immigration Related Unfair Employment Practices, 16 Op. O.L.C. 121 (1992).

Environmental Protection Agency, National Ambient Air Quality Standards for Ozone, 75 Fed. Reg. 2938 (2010).

EPA, EPA's Audit Policy, http://www.epa.gov/compliance/incentives/auditing/auditpolicy.html.

Europa, Summaries of EU Legislation, Institutional Affairs, europa.eu/legislation_summaries/institutional_affairs/treaties/Lisbon_treaty/ai0006_en.htm.

European Commission, Frequently Asked Questions, Comitology Register, http://ec.europa.eu/transparency/regcomitology/index.cfm?do=FAQ.FAQ (last accessed Oct. 7, 2012).

European Environment Agency, About EEA: Who We Are, www.eea.europa.eu/about-us.

European Union, The History of the European Union, Europa.eu (last visited June 6, 2013), http://europa.eu/abc/history/1945-1959/index_en.htm.

European Union, Official Site, www.europa.eu/agencies/regulatory_agencies_bodies/index_en.htm.

Exec. Order No. 10,939, To Provide a Guide on Ethical Standards to Government Officials, 26 Fed. 3951 (May 5, 1961).

Exec. Order No. 11,821, Inflation Impact Statements, 39 Fed. Reg. 41501 (Nov. 27, 1974).

Exec. Order No. 12,044, Improving Government Regulations, 43 Fed. Reg. 51938 (1978), 3 C.F.R § 152 (Mar. 23, 1978).

Exec. Order No. 12,067, 43 Fed. Reg. 28967 (1978).

Exec. Order No. 12,291, Federal Regulation, 46 Fed. Reg. 13,193 (1981).

Exec. Order No. 12,498, Regulatory Planning Process (Jan. 4, 1985), 50 Fed. Reg. 1036 (1985), 3 C.F.R. § 323 (1986).

Exec. Order No. 12,866, Regulatory Planning and Review, 58 Fed. Reg. 51734 (1993), 3 C.F.R. § 638 (1993), *reprinted in* 5 U.S.C. § 601 (2006).

Exec. Order No. 13,132, Federalism, 64 Fed. Reg. 43,255 (Aug. 4, 1999).

Exec. Order No. 13,422, Further Amendment to Executive Order 12866 on Regulatory Planning and Review, 72 Fed. Reg. 2763 (Jan. 18, 2007).

Exec. Order No. 13,497, Revocation of Certain Executive Orders Concerning Regulatory Planning and Review, 74 Fed. Reg. 6113 (Jan. 30, 2009).

Exec. Order No. 13,563, Improving Regulation and Regulatory Review, 76 Fed. Reg. 3821 (Jan. 21, 2011).

Exec. Order No. 13,579, Regulation and Independent Regulatory Agencies, 76 Fed. Reg. 41587 (July 11, 2011).

Executive Office of the President, Materials on President Reagan's Program of Regulatory Relief 12 (June 12, 1981).

Executive Office of the President, Regulatory Program of the United States Government, Apr. 1, 1990–Mar. 31, 1991, at 5 (1990).

Ex Parte Communications During FCC Rulemaking, 15 Op. O.L.C. 5 (1991).

Fannie Mae and Freddie Mac, Fed. Housing Fin. Agency, Report to Congress 2013 (2014), *available at* http://www.fhfa.gov/AboutUs/Reports/ReportDocuments/FHFA_2013_Report_to_Congress.pdf.

Federally Created Entities: An Overview for Key Attributes, U.S. Gov't Accountability Office, 2009.

Federal Reserve Board Policy on Bank Examiner Borrowing, 6 Op. Off. Legal Counsel 509 (1982), clarified at 17 Op. Off. Legal Counsel 168 (1993).

Federal Reserve Board—Vacancy with the Office of the Chairman—Status of the Vice Chairman, 2 Op. Off. Legal Counsel 394 (1978).

Federal Reserve Board, CFTC, FDIC, OCC, SEC, Joint Agency Press Release, Agencies Issue Final Rules Implementing the Volcker Rule (Dec. 10, 2013).

Fed. Trade Comm'n, Annual Report of the Federal Trade Commission (1916).

Food Administration Exec. Action (July 11, 1918).

General Knit, 239 N.L.R.B. 619 (1978).

Government Accountability Office, Report on the Federal Deposit Insurance Corporation Funds' 2011 and 2012 Financial Statement (February 2013).

Government Accountability Office, SEC Operations, Implications of Alternative Funding Structures, GAO-020864 (2002).

Greenspan Commission, Social Security Online, http://www.ssa.gov/history/reports/gpsan.html (last modified Aug 1, 2011).

Haslerig Trucking Co., Inc. Extension—General Commodities Contract Services, 1985 MCC LEXIS 422 (ICC, May 14, 1985).

Hollywood Ceramics Co., 140 N.L.R.B. 221 (1962).

In re Intel Corp., 2010 FTC LEXIS 8 (2010).

In the Matter of Jean-Paul Bolduc et al., 54 S.E.C. 1195 (2001).

In the Matter of Jim Walter Corp., 88 F.T.C. 765 (1976).

Kellogg Co., 97 F.T.C. 159 (1981).

KFC National Management Co. and Bartenders Hotel, Motel, Cafeteria and Restaurant Employees Union Letter to George M. Stafford, Interstate Commerce Commission, No. B-181536, 1974 Comp. Gen LEXIS 1817 (1974).

Kevin R. Kosar, The Postal Accountability and Enhancement Act: Overview and Issues for Congress, Cong. Research Serv. (2009).

Kevin R. Kosar, The Quasi Government: Hybrid Organizations with Both Government and Private Sector Legal Characteristics, Cong. Research Serv. (2011).

Lawfulness of Recess Appointments During a Recess of the Senate Notwithstanding Periodic Pro Forma Sessions, 36 Op. O.L.C. 2 (2012).

Letter by NLRB Chairman Gould to Republican Members of House Economic and Educational Opportunities Committee April 19, 1995, Daily Labor Report, Apr. 20, 1995.

Letter from Angela Canterbury, Director of Public Policy, & Michael Smallberg, Investigator, Project on Government Oversight, to Rep. Spencer Bachus, Chair of House Comm. on Fin. Services (May 29, 2012) available at, http://pogoarchives.org/m/fo/sro-letter-20120529.pdf.

Letter from William A. Sarno, NCUA Inspector General, to Chairman Issa, Oversight and Government Reform Committee, Feb. 6, 2013, http: www.ncua.gov/about/Leadership/CO/OIG/Documents/OIG20130206IssaResponse.pdf.

Letter from Cass R. Sunstein, Adm'r, OIRA (Sept. 2, 2011) (regarding National Ambient Air Quality Standards for Ozone, 75 Fed. Reg. 2938 (Jan. 19, 2010) (Proposed Rule)), 75 Fed. Reg. 2938 (Jan. 19, 2010).

Letter from Cass R. Sunstein, Adm'r, OIRA, to David Strickland, Adm'r, National Highway Traffic Safety Admin. (Mar. 19, 2010).

Letter from Eric M. Thorson, Inspector General, Dep't of the Treasury, and Elizabeth A. Coleman, Inspector General, Bd. of Governors of the Federal Reserve System, to Spencer Bachus, Chairman of the House Comm. on Financial Services, and Judy Biggert, Chairwoman of the Subcomm. on Insurance, Housing, and Community Opportunity (Jan. 10, 2011) *available at* http://www.treasury.gov/about/organizational-structure/ig/Documents/OIG-CA%20 11004%20Committee%20of%20Financial%20Services%20Response%20CFPB.pdf.

Letter of David A. Clanton, Chairman, Federal Trade Commission to Vice President George Bush, June 25, 1981, *reprinted in* Role of OMB in Regulation: Hearing Before the Subcomm. on Oversight and Investigations of the H. Comm. on Energy and Commerce, 97th Cong. (1981), at 187–91.

Letter Sent to Independent Agencies by George H. W. Bush, Executive Office of the President, Materials on President Reagan's Program of Regulatory Relief 94–95 (June 12, 1981).

Local 116, AFL-CIO, 214 N.L.R.B. 232 (1974).

James B. Lockhart III, Director of FHFA, Statement on Federal Housing Finance Agency, Sept. 7, 2008, at 5, *available at* http://www.fhfa.gov/webfiles/23/FHFAStatement9708final.pdf.

David E. Lockwood & George Siehl, Military Base Closures: A Historical Review from 1988 to 1995, Congressional Research Service Report for Congress (2004).

Lone Star Airways, 97 C.A.B. 642 (1982).

Office of Management and Budget, Fiscal Year 2014 Budget of the U.S.

OMB Circular No. A-119, Federal Participation in the Development and Use of Voluntary Consensus Standards and in Conformity Assessment Activities, 63 Fed. Reg. 8546 (1998).

OMB Circular, Par 4(a)(b), http://www.whitehouse.gov/omb/circularA119.

Mary L. Schapiro, Chairman, Sec. & Exchange Comm'n, Letter to the Honorable Mitch McConnell, Apr. 15, 2010, http://www.sec.gov/news/speech/2010/spch041510mls-mcconnell-letter.pdf.

Mary L. Schapiro, Chairman, Sec. & Exchange Comm'n, Statement Concerning Agency Self-Funding, Apr. 15, 2010, http://www.sec.gov/news/speech/2010/spch041510mls.htm.

Memorandum for the President from James McIntyre, March 1978.

Memorandum for Wayne Granquist from Simon Lazarus (Dec. 9, 1977).

Memorandum for Simon Lazarus, U.S. Dep't of Justice (July 22, 1977).

Memorandum from John D. Graham for the President's Management Council, Sept. 20, 2001, at 5.

Memorandum from John D. Graham to Heads of Selected Independent Agencies: Independent Agency Response to Public Regulatory Reform Nominations (Jan. 22, 2003), Office of Information and Regulatory Affairs, http://www.reginfo.gov/public/prompt/graham_responseregreform.pdf.

Memorandum from George P. Shultz, Dir., Office of Mgmt. & Budget, for the Heads of Departments and Agencies: Agency Regulations, Standards, and Guidelines Pertaining to Environmental Quality, Consumer Protection, and Occupational and Public Health and Safety (Oct. 5, 1971), Center for Regulatory Effectiveness, *available at* http://www.thecre.com/ombpapers/QualityofLife1.htm.

Memorandum from Larry L. Simms, Acting Assistant Attorney Gen., Office of Legal Counsel, to Honorable David Stockman, Dir., Office of Mgmt. & Budget (Feb. 12, 1981).

Memorandum of the Office of Legal Counsel, The Constitutional Separation of Powers Between the President and Congress, Memorandum for the General Counsels of the Federal Government, 1996 OLC LEXIS 6 at *147–49 (May 7, 1996).

Memorandum on Implementing Government Reform, 37 Weekly Comp. Pres. Doc. 1028 (July 11, 2001).

Memorandum on Implementing Management Reform in the Executive Branch, 58 Fed. Reg. 52,393 (Oct. 1, 1993).

Memorandum on Transparency and Open Government, 74 Fed. Reg. 4685 (Jan. 21, 2009).

Memorandum Opinion for the Counsel to the President, Appointment of a Member of the Holocaust Memorial Council, 2003 OLC Lexis 14 (2003).

Memorandum Opinion for the Counsel to the President, Removal of Holdover Officials Serving on the Federal Housing Board and the Railroad Retirement Board, 21 Op. O.L.C. 135 (1997).

Memorandum to the Chairman of the Interstate Commerce Commission, 52 Comp. Gen. 556, 556–58 (1973).

Midland Nat'l Life Ins. Co., 263 N.L.R.B. 127 (1982).

Ronald Moe, Managing the Public's Business: Federal Government Corporations, Cong. Research Serv. (1995).

National Academy of Public Administration, U.S. Patent and Trademark Office: Transforming to Meet the Challenges of the 21st Century 166 (2005).

National Biscuit Co., 79 F.T.C. 264 (1971).

National Commission on Neighborhoods (Pub. L. 95-24)—Powers—Appropriations, 2 Op. Off. Legal Counsel 366 (1977).

National Credit Union Association, Office of the Inspector General, Report to Chairman Issa Regarding Use of Contingency Fee Arrangements (Feb. 6, 2013), *available at* http://www.ncua.gov/about/Leadership?CO/OIG/Documents?OIG20130206IssaResponse.pdf.

Nicholson et al. v. Missouri Pacific RR, 366 I.C.C. 69 (1982).

Notice of Final Policy, Final Policy Concerning the Occupational Safety and Health Notice of Final Policy Concerning the Occupational Safety and Health Administration Voluntary Employer Safety and Health Self Audits, 65 Fed. Reg. 46498–503 (Jul. 28, 2000).

Nye Stevens, Postal Reform, Cong. Research Serv. IB10104 (2005).

Occupational Safety and Health Review Commission—Authority of Commissioners, 60 Comp. Gen. 627 (1981).

Office of the Comptroller of the Currency, About the OCC, *available at* www.occ.gov/about/what-we-do/mission.

Office of Legal Counsel, Authority of the Chemical Safety and Hazard Investigation Board to Delegate Power, 2002 OLC LEXIS 5 (Apr. 19, 2002).

Office of Mgmt. & Budget, Exec. Office of the President, Letter to the Department of Homeland Security on "Secure Flight Proposed Rule" (Dec. 7, 2007), Office of Information and Regulatory Affairs, *available at* http://www.reginfo.gov/public/posteeview/Coldebella.pdf.

Office of Mgmt. & Budget, 2012 Report to Congress on the Benefits and Costs of Federal Regulations and Unfunded Mandates on State, Local, and Tribal Entities, OMB, at 4, *available at* http://www.whitehouse.gov/sites/default/files/omb/inforeg/2012_cb/2012_cost_benefit_report.pdf.

OMB Guidelines for Ensuring and Maximizing the Quality, Objectivity, Utility, and Integrity of Information Disseminated by Federal Agencies (OMB Data Quality Guidelines), 67 Fed. Reg. 369, 376 (Jan. 3, 2002).

Operation of Muscle Shoals Properties (1933).

Opinion of Comptroller General Warren to Director, Administrative Office of the United States Courts, Appointments—Recess Appointments, 28 Comp. Gen. 30 (1948).

OSHA Defends Approach to VPP at Hearing (OSHA Guide for Health Care Facilities Newsletter 2012).

Overnite Transportation Company et al., 329 N.L.R.B. 990 (1999).

Pension Benefit Guaranty Corporation: Improvements Needed to Address Financial and Management Challenges U.S. Gov't Accountability Office, 2008.

Pine Hill-Kingston Bus Corp. Extension—New York and New Jersey Regular Routes etc., 1984 MCC LEXIS 564 (ICC, June 11, 1984).

Plain Language in Government Writing, (President's) Memorandum for the Heads of Executive Departments and Agencies, 63 Fed. Reg. 31,885 (June 1, 1998).

Power of the President to Remove Presidential Appointees from the National Capital Planning Comm'n, 6 Op. O.L.C. 191 (1982).

Presidential Appointees—Resignation Subject to the Appointment and Qualification of a Successor, 3 Op. O.L.C. 152 (1979).

Presidential Authority to Direct Departments and Agencies To Withhold Expenditures From Appropriations Made, 1 Op. Att'y Gen. 624 (1937).

Presidential Review of Agency Rulemaking, 1 C.F.R. § 305.88–305.89 (1989).

President's Authority to Make a Recess Appointment to the National Labor Relations Board, Op. O.L.C. Lexis 27 (2001).

President's Authority to Remove the Chairman of the Consumer Product Safety Comm'n, 2001 OLC Lexis 9 (2001).

President's Committee on Administrative Management, Administrative Management in the Government of the United States (1937).

President's Statement on Signing the Social Security Independence and Program Improvements Act of 1994, 1994 Pub. Papers 1471, 1472 (Aug. 15, 1994).

Process Reengineering Program; Disability Reengineering Project Plan, 59 Fed. Reg. 47,887 (1994).

Proposed Revisions of OMB Circular 4(a)(1), ANSI Essential Requirements: Due Process Requirements for American National Standards, http://publicaa.ansi.org/sites/apdl/Documents/Standards%20Activities/American%20National%20Standards/Procedures,%20Guides,%20and%20Forms/2014_ANSI_Essential_Requirements.pdf.

Proposed Tax Assessment Against the USPS, 1 Op. O.L.C. 79 (1977).

Quality Management Program and Misadministration: NRC Override of OMB Disapproval of NRC Information Collection Request, 57 Fed. Reg. 41376 (Sept. 10, 1992).

Quorum Requirements, Memorandum Opinion for the Solicitor, National Labor Relations Board, 2003 OLC LEXIS 20 (2003).

Recommendation 78-4, Federal Agency Interaction with Private Standard-Setting Organizations in Health and Safety Regulation, 44 Fed. Reg. 1357 (Jan. 5, 1979).

Recommendation 80-4 of the Administrative Conference of the Unites States, Decisional Officials' Participation in Rulemaking Proceedings, 45 Fed. Reg. 46777 (1980).

Recommendation 88-9, Presidential Review of Agency Rulemaking, 54 Fed. Reg. 5207 (1989).

Recommendation 2011-5, Incorporation By Reference, 77 Fed. Reg. 2257 (Jan. 17, 2012).

Recommendation for Consideration by the Incoming Administration regarding the U.S. Patent and Trademark Office, U.S. Chamber of Commerce (2008).

Regulatory Accountability Act of 2011, Hearing Before the Comm. on House Judiciary, 112th Cong. 1 (2011) (testimony of C. Boyden Gray).

Janet Reno, Assertion of Executive Privilege with Respect to Clemency Decision (Sept. 16, 1999), *available at* http://www.justice.gov/olc/falnpotus.htm (last visited Aug. 7, 2012).

Report of the Federal Courts Study Committee (Apr. 2, 1990).

Report to the Prime Minister from the Efficiency Unit, Improving Management in Government, the Next Steps (HMSO 1988).

Request for Comments on a Proposed Revision of OMB Circular No. A-119, Federal Participation in the Development and Use of Voluntary Consensus Standards and in Conformity Assessment Activities, 79 Fed. Reg. 8207 (Feb. 11, 2014).

Morton Rosenberg, Congressional Research Service, Congressional Review of Agency Rulemaking: Update and Assessment of the Congressional Review Act After a Decade 6-7 (May 8, 2008), Federation of American Scientists, *available at* www.fas.org/sgp/crs/misc/RL30116.pdf.

Emanuelle Schőn-Quinlivan, Administrative Reform in the European Commission: From Rhetoric to Re-legitimisation, Project No. 513416, EU Consent, at 20–21 (Oct. 18, 2006).

Secretary of Labor v. Pennsylvania Elec. Co., 12 FMSHRC 1562 (1990).

Securities and Exchange Commission, FY 2010 Performance and Accountability Report, 2011.

Separate Statement of Commissioner Michael Pertschuk, reprinted in Role of OMB in Regulation: Hearing Before the Subcomm. on Oversight and Investigations of the H. Comm. on Energy and Commerce, 97th Cong. (1981).

Shopping Kart Food Market, Inc., 228 N.L.R.B. 1311 (1977).

Small Business Administration, Agency Compliance with Executive Order 13272, A Report to the Office of Management and Budget, September 2003.

Staff Report and Analysis in Response to Chairman Dingell's May 11, 1991 Letter of Chairman Martin Allday, Chairman, FERC 3 (June 14, 1991), *reprinted in* National Energy Strategy (Part 6), Hearing Before the H. Subcomm. on Energy and Power of the Comm. on Energy and Commerce, 102d Cong. (1991).

Statement by Edward J. DeMarco, Acting Director, Federal Housing Finance Agency, on the Use of Principal Forgiveness by Fannie Mae and Freddie Mac, July 31, 2012, *available at* http://www.fhfa.gov/webfiles/24113/PFStatement73112.pdf.

Statement of Cass R. Sunstein, OIRA Administrator, OMB, The Views of the Administration on Regulatory Reform: An Update: Hearing Before the Subcommittee on Oversight and Investigations of the H. Comm. on Energy and Commerce, 112th Cong. 12–50 (June 3, 2011).

Statement of Hon. Elmer B. Staats, Comptroller Gen. of the United States (1966–1981), Establishing the Social Security Administration as an Independent Agency: Before the S. Comm. on Finance, 103rd Cong. 14–15 (1993).

Statement on Signing the 21st Century Department of Justice Appropriations Act, 2 Pub. Papers 2010, 2011 (Nov. 2, 2002).

Status of the United States Postal Service as an "Executive Agency" Under Executive Order No. 12,250, 5 Op. O.L.C. 239 (1981).

Cass Sunstein, Memorandum for the Heads of Executive Departments and Agencies and of Independent Regulatory Agencies (Feb. 2, 2011).

Surface Transportation Board, 1996/1997 Annual Report 1 (1998).

Teria H. Brown v. Dep't of the Treasury, 61 M.S.P.R. 484 (1994).

The Constitutional Separation of Powers Between the President and Congress, 20 Op. O.L.C. 124 (1996).

The Federal Reserve System, Purposes and Functions (9th ed. 2005).

The Jewels of the Princess of Orange, 2 Op. Att'y Gen. 482 (1831).

The President's Comm. on Administrative Management, Report of the Committee with Studies of Administrative Management in the Federal Government (1937).

The United Corp., 32 S.E.C. 633 (1951).

John J. Topoleski, Pension Benefit Guaranty Corporation (PBGC): A Fact Sheet, Cong. Research Serv., 2012.

Types of Presidential Appointments Requiring Senate Approval, available *at* http://www.transitionjobs.us/types-presidential-appointments-requiring-senate-approval (last visited Jan. 15, 2011).

Uncharted Territory: What Are the Consequences of President Obama's Unprecedented "Recess" Appointments?, Hearing before the House Comm. on Oversight & Government Reform, 112th Cong. (2012).

United States Dep't of Justice, Attorney General's Manual on the Administrative Procedure Act (1947).

U.S. Dep't of Labor, Nationally Recognized Testing Laboratories (NRTLs), http://www.osha.gov/dts/otpca/nrtl/.

U.S. Gov't Accountability Office, Federal Reserve System: Opportunities Exit to Strengthen Policies and Processes for Managing Emergency Assistance (2011).

U.S. Gov't Accountability Office, GAO-12-625, Securities Regulation: Opportunities Exist To Improve SEC's Oversight of the Financial Industry Regulatory Authority 3 (2012).

Validating Regulatory Analysis: 2005 Report to Congress on the Costs and Benefits of Federal Regulations and Unfunded Mandates on State, Local, and Tribal Entities, OMB, 2005.

Vaughne Miller and Richard Ware, The Resignation of the European Commission, Research Paper 99/32, House of Commons Library (16 Mar. 1999), *available at* http://www.parliament.uk/documents/commons/lib/research/rp99/rp99-032.pdf.

Walter Resources, Inc., 2006 FMSHRC LEXIS 144 (2006).

LEGISLATIVE DOCUMENTS

17 Cong. Rec. 7292 (1886).

18 Cong. Rec. 171 (1886).

19 Cong. Rec. 5150 (1888).

19 Cong. Rec. 6001 (1888).

19 Cong. Rec. 8576 (1888).

39 Cong. Rec. 3824 (daily ed. Mar. 2, 1905).

51 Cong. Rec. 11092 (1914).

93 Cong. Rec. 3,471, 3,472, reprinted in 1 Legislative History of the Labor Management Relations Act, 1947, 594 (1948) (statement of Virginia Representative Howard V. Smith).

95 Cong. Rec. H6196 (daily ed. June 29, 1978).

144 Cong. Rec. S9,912 (daily ed. Sept. 3, 1998).

146 Cong. Rec. H11960 (daily ed. Dec. 5, 2000).

156 Cong. Rec. S2156 (daily ed. Mar. 26, 2010) (statement of Sen. Christopher Dodd).

157 Cong. Rec. S4625 (daily ed. July 18, 2011).

157 Cong. Rec. S8783 (daily ed. Dec. 17, 2011).

157 Cong. Rec. S8789 (daily ed. Dec. 23, 2011).

158 Cong. Rec. S24 (daily ed. Jan. 23, 2012).

H.R. Con. Res. 133, 94th Cong. (1975).

H.R. Rep. No. 64-695 (1916) (Conf. Rep.).

H.R. Rep. No. 74-742 (1935).

H.R. Rep. No. 85-2711 (1959).

H.R. Rep. No. 95-539 (1977) (Conf. Rep.).

H.R. Rep. No. 95-774 (1977).

H.R. Rep. No. 101-665 (1990).

H.R. Rep. No. 101-923 (1990).

H.R. Rep. No. 104-4120 (1995).

H.R. Res. 1023, 112th Cong. (2011).

S. Doc. No. 41, 22nd Cong. (1832).

S. Rep. No. 49-46 (1886).

S. Rpt. No. 58-4389 (1905).

S. Doc. No. 79-248 (1946).

S. Doc. No. 88, 19th Cong. (1930).

S. Doc. No. 95-91 (1977).

S. Rpt. No. 95-1177 (1978).

S. Doc. No. 103, 21st Cong. (1830).

S. Doc. No. 109, 23rd Cong. (1835).

S. Rpt. No. 104-82 (1995).

S. Rpt. 107-205, 2002 WL 1443523.

Amending Executive Order 12,866: Good Governance or Regulatory Usurpation? Part I and Part II: Hearing Before the House Comm. on Science and Technology, 110 Cong., Feb, 13, 2007 (Statement of David C. Vladek).

Answering the Administration's Call for Postal Reform—Parts I, II, and III: Hearings before the Special Panel on Postal Reform and Oversight of the H. Comm. of Government Reform, 2004.

Executive Overreach: The President's Unprecedented "Recess" Appointments Before the H. Comm. on the Judiciary, 112th Cong. 3–4 (2012) (statement of John P. Elwood).

Hearings on the Regulatory Transaction Act of 1995, H.R. 450, before the Subcommittee on National Economic Growth, Natural Resources and Regulatory Affairs, House Comm. on Government Reform and Oversight, 104th Cong. (1995).

Henry B. Hogue, Nomination and Confirmation of the FBI Director: Process and Recent History, Congressional Research Service Report for Congress, RS20963 (updated Mar. 17, 2005), Congressional Research Service, http://fas.org/sgp/crs/natsec/RS20963.pdg (accessed June 24, 2014).

The Impact of the Volcker Rule on Job Creators, Part II: Hearing Before the House Committee on Financial Services, 103rd Cong. (2014) (statements of California Representative Ed Royce).

Joint Hearings, The Universal Telephone Service Preservation Act of 1983, 98th Cong., 1st Sess. 67 (1983).

Kevin R. Kosar, The Postal Accountability and Enhancement Act: Overview and Issues for Congress, Cong. Research Serv., R40983.

Legislative History of the Occupational Safety & Health Act of 1970 (1970).

Letter from Chairman Issa, Oversight and Government Reform Committee to the Inspector General of the National Credit Union Administration, Regarding Use of Contingency Fees. Oct. 16, 2012, House Comm. on Government Oversight and Reform, *available at* http://oversight-house.gov/wp-content/uploads/2012/10.2012-10-16-DEI-to-DeSarno-NCUA-IG-contingency-fees.pdf.

Letter from Senator Abe Ribicoff et al. to President Carter on Dec. 16, 1977, *reprinted in* 124 Cong. Rec. S4863 (1978).

David E. Lockwood & George Siehl, Military Base Closures: A Historical Review from 1988 to 1995, Congressional Research Service Report for Congress (2004).

Ronald Moe, Cong. Research Serv., S. Prt. 104-18, Managing the Public's Business: Federal Government Corporations 2–3 (1995).

Oversight Hearing on the Mutual Fund Industry: Hearing Before the Senate Subcomm. on Secs. of the Comm. on Banking, House & Urban Affairs, 103 Cong. 62 (1993).

Presidential Appointment Efficiency and Streamlining Act of 2011, S. 679, 112th Cong. (2011).

Public Company Accounting Reform and Investor Protection Act of 2002, 148 Cong. Rec. S6327-06, S6330, 2002 WL 1460831.

Regulatory Accountability Act of 2011, Hearing on H.R. 3010 before the House Comm. on the Judiciary, 112th Cong. (2011).

Report from the Select Comm. on Reducing Executive Patronage, S. Doc. No. 88, 19th Cong., 1st Sess. (1826).

Reviewing the Performance of the Social Security Administration as an Independent Agency, Hearing Before the Subcomm. on Social Security of the House Comm. on Ways and Mean, 104th Cong. 12 (1996).

Senate Comm. on Commerce, 94th Cong., Appointments to the Regulatory Agencies: The Federal Communications Commission and the Federal Trade Commission (1949–1974) 391 (Comm. Print 1976).

Senate Comm. on Gov't Operations, Study on Federal Regulation, S. Doc. No. 95-25, at 129 (1977).

Nye Stevens, Postal Reform, Cong. Research Serv., IB10104, 7 (Jun. 23, 2005).

Study on Federal Regulation, 1 S. Comm. on Gov't Operations, S. Doc. No. 95-25 (1977).

United States Government Policy and Supporting Positions, H. Comm. on Oversight & Gov't Reform, 112th Cong. (Comm. Print 2012).

Index

Note: A complete list of cases is printed separately in the Table of Cases and a complete list of statutes, regulations, etc., is printed separately in the Table of Statutes, Bills, and Reorganization Plans.